ENCYCLOPEDIA OF
AMERICAN STUDIES

Encyclopedia of American Studies

ENCYCLOPEDIA OF
AMERICAN STUDIES

PUBLISHED UNDER THE AUSPICES OF THE
AMERICAN STUDIES ASSOCIATION

Edited by

George T. Kurian
Miles Orvell
Johnnella E. Butler
Jay Mechling

Volume 1

Grolier Educational, a division of Scholastic Incorporated
New York, Danbury

Copyright © 2001 by Grolier Educational, a division of Scholastic Incorporated

Library of Congress Cataloging-in-Publication Data

Encyclopedia of American studies/George T. Kurian, general editor; Miles Orvell,
senior editor; Johnnella E. Butler, editor; Jay Mechling, editor
    p. cm.

    "Published under the sponsorship of the American Studies Association."
    Includes bibliographical references and index.
    ISBN 0-7172-9222-3 (alk. paper)
    1. United States—Civilization—Encyclopedias. 2. United States—Civilization—
Study and teaching—Encyclopedias. I. Kurian, George Thomas. II. Orvell, Miles.
III. Butler, Johnnella E. IV. Mechling, Jay, 1945– V. American Studies Association.

E169.1 .E625 2001
973'.03—dc21   2001023415

Printed and Manufactured in the
United States of America

1 3 5 4 2

Table of Contents

Editorial Staff

Preface

The publication of an encyclopedia in any given field says immediately that the subject has academic recognition; it has maturity; there is even possibly a consensus among scholars as to what the subject is. For a field as contentious as American studies, given to a history of self-searching, and seeming at times to press its cause bravely from the margins of established disciplines, the publication of an encyclopedia accordingly signifies something of a milestone. But if a degree of academic status is gratifyingly implied by such an event, that status might at the same time create a certain nervousness among American studies types, who have traditionally prided themselves on their spirit of invention and on a restless inquiry into American culture that almost defies the codifications and stability implied by an encyclopedia. Perhaps, then, it is not altogether surprising that the idea for this work originated outside American studies, on the part of George T. Kurian, the distinguished editor of more than a dozen reference works and encyclopedias in fields relating to American culture and history.

Genesis of the *Encyclopedia of American Studies*

In October 1996 Mr. Kurian brought a proposal to the American Studies Association (ASA), asking that the association commit its support to the publication of a four-volume work, of about one million words, to be published by Grolier Educational as the first of a new series of academic encyclopedias. With American studies being identified increasingly as part of the curriculum in secondary schools, with American studies programs holding their own at the undergraduate and graduate levels, and with the American Studies Association itself growing in its membership rolls each year, the time seemed ripe for a work that would map out the field, reflecting not only the history of American studies but also its present and (to the extent we could anticipate them) future directions.

The Executive Committee of the ASA at the time warmly endorsed the idea, but when it came up for discussion before the ASA Council, a few skeptical voices were heard from among that broader and more contentious lot. One of those skeptics was, as things often happen, asked to communicate with Mr. Kurian and discuss the details of the proposal, and especially to look into the relationship between the ASA editorial board and the publisher. And that skeptic eventually became, as these things also often happen, appointed by the Council to serve as a member of the editorial board (Miles Orvell), along with another skeptic (Johnnella Butler), both being convinced that the project would meet the requirements of the association in giving the responsibility for the design and intellectual development of the encyclopedia to the academic editors. There was also agreement between Grolier and the editors that the resulting work would serve an audience that was to be defined broadly, from beginning students of American studies seeking access to the field, all the way up to professional colleagues who might be looking for a summary of an unfamiliar (or familiar) area, or for a starting point for new research and thinking about a subject. If there was a need being answered by this encyclopedia, it was the need to respond to the immense curiosity of the reader—the curiosity of the American studies type—about the whole gamut of experience in America; and in doing so we would be building on the inherent and habitual eclecticism of the American studies movement.

Orvell and Butler were soon joined by Robert Gross, who was designated by the ASA Council as the third editor; and there was fairly quick agreement among us about some fundamental assumptions: that the encyclopedia was to be inclusionary rather than the opposite—that it would take, in other words, the broadest possible view of American culture, that it would try somehow to bring it all together. Still, it was not that simple; how large an "all" could be contained within the covers of an encyclopedia of American studies? And, at the most practical level, what could we hope to fit into merely four volumes? These questions and many more were discussed at a two-day planning meeting with Mr. Kurian and the Grolier staff, the first of several, at which the editors attempted to define the scope of the project. Our conceptualization of the structure of the *Encyclopedia of American Studies* (*EAS*) occupied us for well over a year, and after this initial phase Robert Gross had to retire from the project; we were very fortunate to have Jay Mechling join us in his place, bringing his experience of over thirty years in American studies and his continuous thinking about and theorizing the field. This team continued to the end of the project.

What Is American Studies?

The term itself, *American studies*, encompasses potentially a vast range of disciplines, all of which, in one way or another, are trying to describe the cultures of the United States. In recent years American studies has also incorporated comparative studies of Canada and Latin America; and indeed a transnational, global perspective on American culture has become one of the leading currents in the field as we begin the twenty-first century. Where, after all, do the borders of America stop, when its influence has been, through the twentieth century, so pervasive on world cultures?

American studies in the early twenty-first century is, it is evident, quite different from its beginnings in the 1930s, when it grew out of the joined and overlapping interests of a very few history and English departments as they sought to give formal discipline to the culturally nationalistic impulse that began earlier in the century to discover a "usable past" in American history. Following the pioneering work of the first generation of American studies scholars (for example, Perry Miller, F. O. Matthiessen), who tended to focus on the New England tradition, came an effort to define broader national characteristics, which eventuated in the highly influential—though later much qualified—work of the "myth and symbol" critics in the 1950s and 1960s (for example, Henry Nash Smith, Leo Marx, R. W. B. Lewis). Then, beginning in the 1970s, and absorbing the impact of the cultural revolutions of the previous decade, American studies broadened its view even more, encompassing popular culture, mass culture, and folk culture, and including the full range of artistic expression, as well as the social, political, intellectual, and economic forms of American life. In the 1980s and 1990s, attention turned increasingly toward areas that had been relatively neglected previously, embracing issues of gender, race, and ethnicity.

Yet it is generally agreed that there is no firm agreement about what exactly, in any pure sense, represents the discipline of American studies; in fact, most academics think of it as interdisciplinary, a practice that combines the perspectives of more than one traditional discipline. In background and training there are roughly two types of American studies scholars who meet within the broad confines of the American Studies Association—those who have migrated from a traditional discipline toward a more integrated approach to problems, themes, and issues that cut across disciplinary lines; and those who have been trained from the beginning in graduate programs that emphasize interdisciplinary thinking, often through the synthesis of two or more traditional disciplines.

The concept that generally unites the disparate work in American studies is *culture*, taking that term in the broadest sense. From an anthropological perspective, culture encompasses the whole of what takes place in a given social group, from language to artifacts to customs, even though we may identify some elements as high or low, popular or elite. But whether it makes sense to talk about American culture as itself whole or whether we should more properly speak of the "cultures" of America, is a notion that is still being debated. This encyclopedia takes the view that many elements of the culture are, and always have been, distinctively different, according to their origins in different geographical regions or in different social classes, in different races or ethnicities or in differing gender identities. (Against the nativist tendencies of the early twentieth century, America at the end of the century would boast of its inclusiveness, its diversity.) Yet at the same time there are elements within American culture that are universally, or nearly universally, shared, a part of everyone's knowledge—whether as a result of politics, social values, religious values, or mass or popular culture. American identity comprises overlapping elements—some distinctive to a particular subgroup, and others shared in common with many others.

Another point of contention in recent scholarship has been the question of whether the American experience is unique in world history, whether America is in its essential culture "exceptional." This notion of exceptionalism has been contested on the grounds that we are discovering many areas of shared experience with other national or cultural experiences, for example in immigration patterns, in slavery, in family traditions, in vernacular and folk culture, and in popular culture. As a result, many studies of American culture are rightly becoming more comparativist in nature. We take the view here that America is in many ways unique, not the least because its experience has been taken by the rest of the world as a special one: at times the United States has been seen as exemplary, a model of democracy by nations struggling to emerge out of colonial dependency. But some of the erosion of American exceptionalism has resulted from more recent studies that recognize that the United States has, in turn, itself had a rich if unsavory history of colonial exploitation and imperialist ventures, one that has pervaded the culture in ways that we are just beginning to understand. And as much as we can accept the uniqueness of American circumstances and conditions (and, after all, every country's history is unique), we also recognize that in the larger view, there are many overlapping and shared cultural experiences—of race, of modernization, of gender, of aesthetic movements—and that comparative cultural study can be richly rewarding.

The scope of this encyclopedia reflects the breadth of this complex and far from simple view of America, encompassing the range and diversity of its culture from folk and vernacular to elite, from regional and sectarian cultures to mass culture. Although it is impossible to claim that one common civilization unites this country, we have to recognize those unifying elements that have held together (to some extent at least) the culture of the United States—institutions such as libraries and museums, educational standards and practices, and mass media such as film, television, and radio. In short, we are committed to a view of American culture that is deliberately self-contradictory in being at once centrifugal and centripetal: we respect the enormous diversity and contradictions of the United States, contradictions that at times threaten to explode and fragment the whole; and yet, in our view, we must also acknowledge the many national institutions, from the federal government to the Internet, that are at the same time pulling it together.

Planning the Structure and Content

One of the first questions we asked ourselves, as we started to talk about this undertaking, was, What distinguishes an American studies encyclopedia from the many encyclopedias that deal with some more narrowly focused discipline? We did not, after all, simply want to encompass "all things American"; nor did we want to compile a diluted compendium of encyclopedias of history, literature, politics, the arts, ethnicity, gender, and all the other fields, subjects, and disciplines that contribute to American studies. What would be distinctive about this work, as an American studies encyclopedia, was its attempt to consider these disparate elements, as well as unifying elements, from the integrative perspective of American culture as a whole. Thus for any given topic, the task was not simply to provide a discussion of the topic on its own terms, but in relation to the broader, interdisciplinary study of American culture: how does a subject contribute to our larger insights about the culture? How is the topic viewed by students of American studies? The special value of the work would lie in its comprehensive synoptic essays that covered topics from an interdisciplinary perspective and that evinced a methodological self-consciousness and rigor about the very act of uncovering meaning in the cultures of America.

There were, following these principles, several different types of articles that we wanted to include: articles that, first of all, dealt directly with the field of American studies itself and its ways of organizing knowledge—articles that, in our alphabetical arrangement often began with the word *America* (for instance, "America: The Idea of America"; "America: American Culture Abroad"; "America: America Perceived"; "American Character"; "American Studies: Approaches and Concepts"; "Class and Culture"; "Culture and Cultural Studies"; and so on). And in a sense these were the easiest articles to agree on; for when we went beyond these and considered that we must obviously also have articles dealing with distinct areas of knowledge typically of interest to students of American culture, there seemed to be no end to the possibilities.

After generating literally thousands of possible topics, we began to sort them into large areas of knowledge, debating in each case the integrity of the broad area itself as well as its proportion relative to the larger whole. These broad categories were: class culture (that is, the cultures of distinct classes and groups in America); communication and culture; crime and deviance; economics and culture; education; ethnicity, race, and culture (including related topics in the broad areas of African American cultures, Asian American cultures, Hispanic American cultures, Jewish American cultures, European American cultures, Native American cultures); everyday life (for example, clothing, Coca-Cola, soul food); expressive culture (which included the broad subtopics architecture and design, art, film, literature, media, music, performing arts, photography, theater); family and kinship; folk culture; gender and culture; government and politics; land use; law and culture; life course (by which we meant childhood, adolescence, youth culture, and so forth); national identity; nature and the environment; periods and periodization; philosophy; political and military cultures; popular culture; recreation and leisure; regions and regionalism; religious culture; reproducing culture (including libraries and museums); social reform and social movements; science, technology, and medicine; the United States and global culture; violence; volunteerism.

Although we attempted, in these broad subject areas, to cover the whole of American culture, we chose to emphasize certain topics over others, depending on the degree to which they had, over the years, attracted the scholarly and teaching interests of American studies practitioners. In some cases—such as literature or painting, history or philosophy—we were dealing with topics with long established traditions of scholarship; in other areas—such as ethnicity and globalization—significant scholarship had begun to emerge only in the last two decades. Still other large areas represented scholarship on American culture that was not typically part of the American studies curriculum but that we wanted to include in our effort to mirror the cultures of the United States in the broadest terms, for instance, "Arcade Games"; "Coins, Currency, Stamps, and Commemorative Medals"; "Fashion"; "Foodways"; "Gangs"; "Magic and Magicians"; "Space Program." Consequently, many of these topics will be familiar to professional students of American studies; others will be much less familiar, and it is our hope that, browsing through the four volumes, readers will find both fresh perspectives on familiar topics as well as the stimulation of encountering subjects not thought of before.

Arriving at the final table of contents for the encyclopedia, once we developed our containing categories, was still not an easy problem, for we realized that we would need not four volumes but at least forty-four to contain the whole of our ambition. From several thousand possible entries, we had, finally, to arrive at about 660, with varying lengths from five hundred words to five thousand words. Eliminating topics we had wanted very much to have, we consoled ourselves with the idea that we could write descriptions of the remaining articles that defined their scope so as to encompass these excised topics. Even so, we managed to retain a number of very specific topics, objects of study that seem unavoidable in any account of American culture. For example, just to take a run of "B" topics, we have the entries "Baby Boom"; "Banks and Banking"; "Barbie"; "Baseball"; "Beat Writers"; "Beauty Contests"; "Beauty Parlors"; "Bible";

"Brown v. Board of Education." But many hundreds of similarly specific topics had to be subsumed in such larger topics as "Broadway Musicals"; "Chicano Literature"; "Consumerism"; "Dance"; "Decorative Arts"; "Design, Commercial and Industrial"; "Feminism"; "Folk Musical Traditions"; "Gay and Lesbian Literature"; "Literature and the Construction of Identity"; "Material Culture"; "Painting"; "Photography"; and many other such topics that had the responsibility of surveying equally vast subjects from an American studies perspective.

A special problem arose with respect to biographies. Knowing we could not possibly encompass the thousands and thousands of Americans who had figured significantly in our cultural history, we thought perhaps we should have none at all. And indeed most of the individuals we had originally thought of as meriting a separate biographical entry eventually became merely mentioned in some larger treatment of a subject. But we wanted to incorporate some few lives, at least, in the *EAS,* to flesh out the abstractions, so to speak, and to arrive at this list we established three criteria: first, that we would include scholars who were in some way crucial to the history and development of American studies; second, that the list as a whole would represent the full diversity of American cultural history; and third, that the significance of the individual must lie not only in his or her importance to a specific field, discipline, art form, or popular form; in addition, the individual must qualify by virtue of having a significance that went beyond the specifics of achievement to attain a broad cultural meaning, almost a symbolic meaning, in American culture. Our final list, by design and by necessity, is diverse and inconsistent, and anyone will find scores or hundreds of notables who are not on it and should be. In the end, we would argue, any such list will be arbitrary, the product of compromise and subjective judgment. We cannot argue for the exclusion of anyone you might think of; but we can say, simply, that those whom we have finally given space to seem indispensable, given our criteria. Our final list also reflects our effort to include not only the obviously "important" figures but also a few persons, at least, whose importance generally has been neglected previously: Jane Addams, Alvin Ailey, Horatio Alger, Muhammad Ali, Andrew Carnegie, Charles Chaplin, César Chávez, Shirley Chisholm, Samuel Clemens, Crazy Horse, Jean de Crèvecoeur, Walt Disney, Frederick Douglass, W. E. B. Du Bois, Bob Dylan, Thomas Edison, Ralph Waldo Emerson, Henry Ford, Benjamin Franklin, Betty Friedan, George Gershwin, Gordon Hirabayashi, Dolores Huerta, Andrew Jackson, William James, Thomas Jefferson, Martin Luther King, Jr., Abraham Lincoln, Malcolm X, Thurgood Marshall, Leo Marx, Cotton Mather, F. O. Matthiessen, Perry Miller, C. Wright Mills, Lewis Mumford, Frederick Law Olmsted, Thomas Paine, Elvis Presley, Paul Robeson, John D. Rockefeller, Franklin Delano Roosevelt, Theodore Roosevelt, Sacagawea, Henry Nash Smith, Gloria Steinem, Harriet Beecher Stowe, Frederick Winslow Taylor, Alexis de Toqueville, Sojourner Truth, Robert Venturi, Alice Walker, Andy Warhol, George Washington, Booker T. Washington, Woodrow Wilson, Carter G. Woodson, Frank Lloyd Wright.

Acknowledgements

It is a pleasure to thank, however inadequately, the many people who have in one way or another contributed to this project. Our thanks first to Robert Gross, whose fertile participation at the early stages of the project was crucial and who had to step out before we began refining the topics and assigning articles to authors. Our thanks to the Grolier staff, above all, for guiding us from the start through the elaborate and rigorously logical process of mapping out an encyclopedia. Mark Cummings, associate publisher of Grolier Educational, was, if not a walking encyclopedia, at least a walking guide to the construction of one, lucid and ingenious; Phil Friedman, the publisher of Grolier Educational, likewise lent his years of experience in dealing with the indispensable building blocks in the process—prospective authors. And later on, when things were getting in gear, Thomas McCarthy came on as project editor, handling the editors and, more important, handling the hundreds of authors involved in this process, with wit, tact, cajoling good humor, encouragement, and practical wisdom. Cheryl Clark read all of the articles with her meticulous and ever-questioning pencil, improving the clarity of these pieces and helping us to preserve, as much as we could, the individual voices of the authors.

The editors agreed to divide the subject areas of the *EAS* according to the following very broad spheres of interest: Johnnella Butler was in charge of articles relating to gender, race, and ethnicity; Jay Mechling handled the articles dealing with American social, political, and economic history; Miles Orvell managed articles relating to the arts and design, science and technology, and urbanism. But not everything fell into these categories, obviously, and each of us handled many articles that escaped these categories. It was the responsibility of the editors, working with advisers as needed, to choose the authors of articles, and it was our responsibility to review and edit them once they were submitted; all articles were then reviewed by the general editor, George Kurian, and by the editorial staff of Grolier.

Helping us along the way were numerous people, who cannot adequately be thanked—most of all, the hundreds of scholars who agreed to write articles for us. Recognizing the opportunity to define and mark the boundaries of a subject, many from the American studies community were eager and happy to join us and volunteered their services. In addition, we were fortunate to be able to enlist a substantial number of experts, well known to the editors, in their respective fields. For authors of articles in fields the editors were less familiar with, we sought the advice of a team of advisers. To all those who answered the call, our deepest thanks for making the encyclopedia possible. It was not uncommon for a prospective author who was for one reason or another unable to accept an assignment to offer a colleague in his or her place; and for these recommendations—by dozens and dozens of scholars—we are most grateful.

The Advisory Board was indispensable and included: Roman Cybriwsky (Temple University), Inés Hernandez-Ávila (University of California, Davis), Thomas Inge (Randolph Macon), Martin Jaffee (University of Washington), Michael Jarrett (Penn State, York), Jeffrey Meikle (University of Texas, Austin), Gail Nomura (University of Washington), Vicki Ruiz (University of California, Irvine), Paul Swann (Temple University), Priscilla Wald (Duke University), John C. Walter (University of Washington). There were additional others who offered crucial advice along the way and to whom we offer special thanks: Sabine Broeck (University of Bremen), Simon Bronner (Penn State, Harrisburg), Lawrence Buell (Harvard University), Richard Butsch (Rider College), Tim Corrigan (Temple University), Allen Davis (Temple University), Rachel DuPlessis (Temple University), H. Bruce Franklin (Rutgers, Newark), Patricia Hills (Boston University), Elizabeth Johns (University of Pennsylvania), Richard Longstreth (George Washington University), Lucy Maddox (Georgetown University), Carey Mazer (University of Pennsylvania), David Nye (Odense University), Sharon O'Brien (Dickinson College), Mary Panzer (National Portrait Gallery), Barry Shank (University of Kansas), Morris Vogel (Temple University), Gyorgy Voros (Virginia Technical University), Shirley Wajda (Kent State University), Don Wilmeth (Brown University).

Throughout the trials and tribulations that are inevitably a part of producing something as complex as an encyclopedia, we had the unvarying good will and resourceful support of John Stephens, executive director of the American Studies Association, and godfather to this project. The presidents of the ASA, over the years that the project was in process, also gave us their enthusiastic support, their advice, and their trust in us, and we thank them: Patricia Limerick (University of Colorado), Mary Helen Washington (University of Maryland), Janice Radway (Duke University), Mary Kelley (Dartmouth College), Michael Frisch (SUNY Buffalo).

Behind this whole effort lies the tolerance, understanding, and good humor of an additional support team—our families; and to them, for putting up with our collective obsession for more than four years, we offer our heartfelt thanks and appreciation.

Miles Orvell, Temple University • Senior Editor

Johnnella Butler, University of Washington • Editor

Jay Mechling, University of California, Davis • Editor

Alphabetical List of Entries

ALPHABETICAL LIST OF ENTRIES

ALPHABETICAL LIST OF ENTRIES

ENCYCLOPEDIA OF
AMERICAN STUDIES

ABOLITIONISM

The desire to outlaw slavery in the North American colonies and then the United States existed nearly as long as the institution itself. The issue became particularly acute when the colonies sought to unite themselves under democratic ideals. The Constitution required that the census for representation should only count African Americans as one-third of a person, and the trade of slaves, the Constitution instructed, would continue until the issue was revisited in the early 1800s. Abolitionism called attention to the irony of slavery's existence in a nation in which "all men are created equal."

The American Anti-Slavery Society was established in 1833, but abolitionist sentiment antedated the republic. For example, the charter of Georgia prohibited slavery, and many of its settlers fought a losing battle against allowing it in the colony. Before independence Quakers, most black Christians, and other religious groups argued that slavery was immoral and incompatible with Christ's teaching. Moreover, a number of revolutionaries saw the glaring contradiction between demanding freedom for themselves while holding slaves.

On January 1, 1794, delegates from the abolition societies of Connecticut, New York, New Jersey, Pennsylvania, Delaware, and Maryland met in Philadelphia, a stronghold of the antislavery Quaker religion. The group voted to petition Congress to prohibit the slave trade and also to appeal to the legislatures of the various states to abolish slavery. The petitions pointed out the inconsistency of slaveholding in a country that had recently rejected the tyranny of kings. Delegates published an address urging U.S. citizens to consider "the obligations of justice, humanity, and benevolence toward our Africa brethren, whether in bondage or free." The group planned to meet each January until slavery was abolished.

Abolitionist literature began to appear about 1820. Until the Civil War the antislavery press produced a steadily growing stream of newspapers, periodicals, sermons, speeches, children's publications, abolitionist society reports, broadsides, and memoirs of former slaves. Broadsides advertised fairs and bazaars that women's groups organized in order to raise money for the cause. Other publications advertised abolitionist rallies, some of which are pictured in prints from contemporaneous periodicals.

Portrait of William Lloyd Garrison, an uncompromising opponent of slavery.

On July 4, 1829, the abolition movement took an important turn with a speech by William Lloyd Garrison concerning a new kind of abolitionism influenced by an anti-Calvinist emphasis on human perfectibility through repudiation of sin. Garrison and his followers saw social evils as symptoms of a deep-seated societal dysfunction, which had to be eliminated for the good of the nation. Garrison began publishing *The Liberator* in 1831 to draw attention to the abolitionist cause and the immorality of slavery. "I am in earnest," he wrote, "I will not equivocate—AND I WILL BE HEARD." Intolerant of moderate points of view such as colonization, Garrison argued that there should be "no Union with slaveholders" and that their breach of the Constitution perpetuated slavery as "a covenant with death, an agreement with Hell." With sixty-two others, Garrison founded the American Anti-Slavery Society in 1833.

Still, even within abolitionist groups, there remained dissension over how to end slavery. The American Anti-Slavery Society distributed an almanac containing poems, drawings, essays, and other abolitionist material. This issue was compiled by Lydia Maria Child (1802–1880), a popular writer recruited to the abolitionist cause by Garrison. In 1833 Mrs. Child produced *An Appeal in Favor of that Class of Americans Called Africans,* a sensational anti-slavery publication that won converts to the movement. From 1841 to 1849 she edited the New York–based *National Anti-Slavery Standard* newspaper. Fugitive slaves aroused sympathy from Northern audiences and made abolitionism personal. Frederick Douglass, a former slave, earned fame as a speaker and writer (*Narrative of the Life of Frederick Douglass,* 1845) for the abolitionist cause.

Amid the growing discourse over slavery came a widely publicized case, the *Amistad* incident. In February 1839 Portuguese slave hunters abducted a large group of Africans from Sierra Leone and shipped them to Havana, Cuba, a center for the slave trade. This abduction violated all of the treaties then in existence. On July 1, 1839, the Africans, led by Cinque, seized the ship, killed both the captain and the cook, and ordered the planters to sail to Africa.

On August 24, 1839, the *Amistad* was seized off Long Island, New York, by the U.S. brigantine *Washington*. The planters were freed and the Africans were imprisoned in New Haven, Connecticut, on charges of murder. Although the murder charges were dismissed, the Africans continued to be held in confinement as the focus of the case turned to salvage claims and property rights. President Van Buren was in favor of extraditing the Africans to Cuba. However, abolitionists in the North opposed extradition and raised money to defend the Africans. Claims to the Africans by the planters, the government of Spain, and the captain of the brig led the case to trial in the Federal District Court in Connecticut. The court ruled that the case fell within federal jurisdiction and that the claims to the Africans as property were not legitimate because they were illegally held as slaves. The case went to the Supreme Court in January 1841, and former President John Quincy Adams argued the defendants' case. Adams defended the right of the accused to fight to regain their freedom. The Supreme Court decided in favor of the Africans, and thirty-five of them were returned to their homeland. The others died at sea or in prison while awaiting trial. The incident, however, gave the nation a crucial opportunity to discuss the future of slavery.

The abolitionist fight grew more fierce as the nation faced the need to choose whether new western territories would be free or slave. Voices in Congress grew so defiant that a gag rule was passed forbidding discussion on the issue; the Wilmot Proviso of 1846 reintroduced the issue on the heels of the Mexican-American War. "Free Soil or Constitutional Protection?" became the ongoing question regarding western lands. While temporary compromises put the issue at bay politically, abolitionists refused to be silenced. Reaction against the Fugitive Slave Act, which was contained in the Compromise of 1850, grew violent in Massachusetts. In 1852 Harriet Beecher Stowe reacted to the act by publishing *Uncle Tom's Cabin*, which told a sentimentalist story of the inhumanity of slavery, and it became the best-selling book in American history up to that point.

The final dramatic act of the abolitionist movement came by the hand of John Brown. His commitment to the ending of slavery grew so great that he was moved to carrying out violence against those Americans favoring slavery. As fighting erupted between these two factions in the 1859 episode known as Bleeding Kansas, Brown led a raid on Harper's Ferry, Virginia, that proved the catalyst for war. With Abraham Lincoln, a well-spoken proponent of abolition, elected president in 1860, war proved imminent. While there were many causes of the Civil War, the refusal of abolitionists to bow to the economic preferences of the South may have been the most important.

[See also SLAVERY; AFRICAN AMERICANS.*]*

BIBLIOGRAPHY

Friedheim, William, et al., *Freedom's Unfinished Revolution: An Inquiry into the Civil War and Reconstruction* (New Press 1996).

Gates, Henry Louis, Jr., ed., *The Classic Slave Narratives* (New Am. Library 1987).

Mayer, Henry, *All on Fire: William Lloyd Garrison and the Abolition of Slavery* (St. Martin's 1998).

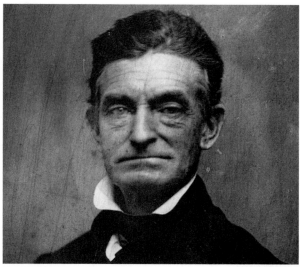

BOSTON ATHENAEUM

John Brown, crusader against slavery, led the raid at Harper's Ferry, Virginia, on October 16, 1859.

Sundquist, Eric J., ed., *Frederick Douglass: New Literary and Historical Essays* (Cambridge 1990).

BRIAN BLACK

ABORTION

Abortion is one of the most controversial issues in American society. Few other topics have so polarized the population; abortion was one of the key components of the "culture wars" of the 1980s and 1990s. The struggle between pro-choice and anti-abortion groups has led to the loss of lives and violence against property. An individual's stance on abortion has also become either a barrier to or gateway for political or judicial office, since the two major political parties in the United States have tacitly adopted "litmus tests" to maintain conformity with a party's position.

For much of American history abortion was not illegal until the later stages of pregnancy. However, the practice was relatively uncommon because of the lack of safe medical procedures. In the 1900s advanced medical techniques made the practice relatively inexpensive and safe for the life of the mother. This led to a backlash among conservatives who opposed abortion on moral or religious grounds. As far back as the mid-1800s, many states passed legislation to outlaw abortion. In 1967 the National Organization for Women (NOW) initiated a nationwide campaign to make abortion legal. However, by the early 1970s most states in the United States banned abortion. These state laws were overturned by the 1973 Supreme Court case *Roe* v. *Wade*.

In *Roe* v. *Wade* the majority opinion of the Supreme Court used the Fourth Amendment right to privacy to make abortion legal. The Court did not define when life begins, and the right to an abortion was held to be absolute only in the first trimester. Thereafter, in the second and third trimesters, states could place limitations on abortions or even outlaw them in the final trimester, with exceptions to preserve the life of the mother. After *Roe*, the Court twice overturned laws requiring women to accept antiabortion counseling.

Although abortion became constitutionally legal, many states passed or attempted to enact antiabortion legislation, which ranged from waiting periods to bans on abortions in the third trimester. Just four years after *Roe*, Congress passed the Hyde Amendment, which denies funding for poor women for abortions. In 1980 the Supreme Court upheld federal and state laws forbidding the use of Medicaid funds to provide abortions for poor women. In addition, some doctors and hospitals were reluctant to engage in the politically sensitive practice. Planned Parenthood endeavored to provide access to abortions and other reproductive services through the establishment of clinics around the nation. Meanwhile, other groups worked to prevent legislative or judicial restrictions on abortion access. The focus of this effort, led by groups such as the National Abortion and Reproductive Rights Action League (NARAL), was to prevent passage of state laws limiting abortion and to act to sponsor *amicus curiae* ("friend of the court") briefs to overturn restrictions.

Conservatives, especially the Religious Right, were outraged over *Roe* and subsequent rulings. A number of antiabortion interest groups emerged that have employed a variety of tactics to overturn or at least limit *Roe* v. *Wade*. Some have endeavored to pass abortion restrictions through state legislatures, a tactic that has met with some success. Others, such as the American Life League, have concentrated on the national level by supporting a constitutional amendment to overturn the 1973 decision. More militant groups, including Operation Rescue, have taken such confrontational steps as blockading clinics that provide abortion services. Operation Rescue staged a series of well-publicized protests by blocking access to clinics. However, some antiabortion extremists have firebombed clinics and used chemicals to damage the facilities. In the 1990s attacks killed or injured several doctors and staffers who performed abortions. The violent tactics may have convinced some doctors and clinics to end abortion services and frightened some women into not seeking abortions, but these actions also alienated the more radical abortion foes from the conservative mainstream religious groups. The escalating violence led to restrictions on antiabortion protests and further eroded dialogue between the opposing sides in the debate. Pro-choice groups initiated programs such as NOW's Project Stand Up for Women, which trains people to serve as clinic escorts and defenders.

In 1994 Congress passed legislation prohibiting protestors from blocking the entrances to clinics. In that same year, in *NOW* v. *Scheidler,* the Supreme Court allowed antiabortion protestors to be prosecuted under federal racketeering laws. This ultimately led to the conviction of Joe Scheidler, one of the leaders of Operation Rescue, on federal racketeering charges for his part in efforts to block access to clinics. In 1997, in *Schenck* v. *ProChoice Network,* the Supreme Court allowed the creation of buffer zones around clinics to prevent interference with those seeking abortions. However, concern over the need to balance abortion rights with First Amendment freedom of speech rights led the Court to refuse to endorse so-called floating buffers, which called for protestors to remain at least fifteen feet (5 m) away from those seeking access to clinics.

President Ronald Reagan was a staunch opponent of abortion, and during his tenure in the 1980s his administration undertook a variety of actions to limit abortion access. Conservative justices were appointed to the federal judiciary, including the Supreme Court, and new rulings placed restrictions on abortion access. President George H. Bush continued this opposition. In 1989 the Supreme Court in *Webster* v. *Reproductive Health Services* upheld a number of restrictions, including a law that states could prohibit publicly supported facilities from performing abortions. Three years later, in *Planned Parenthood* v. *Casey,* the Court upheld even more limitations, including parental notification and a twenty-four-hour waiting period. While abortion remained legal, these rulings were seen by many as evidence of a shift in the Court away from *Roe.*

The election of President Bill Clinton in 1992 seemed to foreshadow the potential for a more "*Roe*-friendly" judiciary, but after Republicans captured both houses of Congress in 1994, many of Clinton's federal judiciary appointments went unconfirmed. This was exacerbated by the president's unwillingness to name adequate new appointees in his second term. In 1997 Clinton vetoed a ban on late-term abortions, but an increasing number of states passed measures outlawing the practice. By a narrow margin, in June 2000 the Supreme Court struck down such bans. In September 2000 the Food and Drug Administration approved the use of RU486, a pill that induces abortion.

[See also ROE V. WADE.*]*

BIBLIOGRAPHY

McDonagh, Eileen, *Breaking the Abortion Deadlock: From Choice to Consent* (Oxford 1996).

Rudy, Kathy, *Beyond Pro-Life and Pro-Choice: Moral Diversity in the Abortion Debate* (Beacon Press 1996).

Solinger, Rickie, ed., *Abortion Wars: A Half Century of Struggle, 1950–2000* (Univ. of Calif. Press 1998).

Tribe, Laurence, *Abortion: The Clash of Absolutes* (Norton 1992).

TOM M. LANSFORD

ADDAMS, JANE

Jane Addams, social reformer, settlement house leader, and peace advocate, was born on September 6, 1860, in Cedarville, Illinois, a little town near

Jane Addams, founder of Hull-House, one of the first American social welfare centers.

the Wisconsin border. A member of the first generation of college women in the United States, she graduated from Rockford [Illinois] Female Seminary (later Rockford College) in 1881. She floundered for the next eight years while she tried to find something useful to do with her life. She resisted attempts to make her a teacher or a missionary, and, like more than fifty percent of the first generation of college women, she never married. Finally in 1889, together with Ellen Gates Starr, a college classmate, she founded Hull-House on the west side of Chicago.

Inspired by Toynbee Hall, which she had visited on one of her European trips, Hull-House quickly became the most famous social settlement in America and a center that promoted many of the most important social reforms of the Progressive Era. Jane Addams attracted talented and powerful men and women to the settlement including Florence Kelley, Julia Lathrop, and Alice Hamilton, but she remained the dominant leader at the settlement. She moved the settlement from a place for reading parties and art exhibits in the early years to a center that led the fight against child labor; for the Americanization of immigrants; for better housing, parks, and playgrounds; and for woman suffrage. Woman suffrage was never her primary concern, but rather it was part of her overall reform plan. She assumed that women, given the vote, would support reform causes. Unlike many suffrage leaders she argued for the vote for the most recent and poorest immigrant women who, she claimed, had a vital concern for municipal housekeeping in order to protect their families. She also tried to ease the burden of Americanization by helping immigrant women preserve their old ways and teach their children the skills and handicrafts of the old country.

Addams was always a compromiser and conciliator. She worked for what she thought was reasonably possible and she often angered those who felt passionately about any issue. She did not entirely escape the prejudice and racism of her day. Hull-House, like most settlements, was segregated in the early years, although Addams was one of the founders of the National Association for the Advancement of Colored People, and she helped to found a settlement in a black section of Chicago.

Addams reached the peak of her popularity and influence in the years before World War I. She lectured widely to women's groups, college students, and social workers in the United States and Europe. She wrote ten books and more than four hundred articles. She told human-interest stories and translated the social research done at the settlement, on housing or prostitution, into a form that reached a wide audience. Her most famous book was her classic autobiography, *Twenty Years at Hull-House* (1910). In 1909 she became the first woman elected president of the National Conference of Charities and Corrections and the first woman awarded an honorary degree by Yale. She was heaped with honors and called "The only Saint that America has produced." Yet her saintly and gentle image hid Addams the tough-minded realist, the expert fundraiser, and the talented business executive who competed with successful men in several fields.

Addams spent the last two decades of her life working for world peace. She became a pacifist not because her father was a Quaker but because she lived in a multicultural and multiethnic neighborhood and she learned that conflict and violence limited reform. Like William James she sought a moral equivalent for war. Addams became active in peace organizations after the Spanish-American War and wrote a series of books and articles, most notably *Newer Ideals of Peace* (1907), in which she argued that women, who were naturally more peace loving than men, had a special responsibility to prevent war.

When war broke out in Europe in 1914 Addams helped to found the Women's Peace Party, and in the spring of 1915 she led the American delegation to the International Congress of Women meeting in The Hague, The Netherlands, where women from both the neutral and the belligerent nations tried to stop the war through mediation. When the United States entered the war in April 1917, Addams stood firm and refused to support the American position. It was perhaps the most difficult decision of her life. Her opposition to American participation in World War I cost her public acclaim. As late as 1926 she was called by one group "the most dangerous woman in America." Awarded the Nobel Prize for Peace in 1931, Addams regained some of her reputation before she died in Chicago on May 21, 1935.

[See also HULL-HOUSE.]

BIBLIOGRAPHY

Addams, Jane, *Twenty Years at Hull-House* (Macmillan 1910) [Jane Addams's classic autobiography].

Bryan, Mary Lynn McCree, and Allen F. Davis, eds., *One Hundred Years at Hull-House* (Ind. Univ. Press 1990) [a collection of letters, documents, articles, and photographs].

Bryan, Mary Lynn McCree, et al., *The Jane Addams Papers: A Comprehensive Guide* (Ind. Univ. Press 1996) [the best starting place for any scholarly study of Jane Addams].

Davis, Allen F., *American Heroine: The Life and Legend of Jane Addams* (Ivan Dee 2000).

Linn, James Weber, *Jane Addams: A Biography* (Appleton 1935) [written by Addams's nephew shortly after her death].

ALLEN F. DAVIS

ADOLESCENCE

Adolescence is the developmental stage between childhood and early adulthood. Generally, adolescence refers to the physical maturation stage between the onset of puberty and physical maturity. In boys adolescence begins at around age fourteen and in girls at about age twelve, although there has been considerable variation over time (puberty beginning earlier) and by race and social class in the United States, evidence of the influence of culture on biology. Puberty brings menstruation in girls and semen production in boys. The hormonal changes bring about the emergence of secondary sex characteristics, such as the appearance of facial, body, and pubic hair as well as the deepening of the voice among boys. Among girls there is the emergence of pubic and body hair, the development of breasts, and the broadening of hips. At this period the sexual drive becomes pronounced.

Granville Stanley Hall (1844–1924) gave overall direction to the growth of psychology in America. He incorporated the ideas of Darwin, Freud, and others into psychology, popularizing and developing them at the same time. Hall was the first person to receive a Ph.D. in psychology in the United States, from Harvard. He also founded *The American Journal of Psychology*. His interest in child and educational psychology led to his work in adolescent psychology. Hall argued that mental and social growth in individuals advanced in evolutionary stages ("recapitulation theory"). In his influential book *Adolescence* (1904), he termed adolescence a period of "storm and stress."

Hall was a strong supporter of psychoanalysis. Clark University, of which he was the founding president, was the only American university to bestow academic recognition on Sigmund Freud. Hall invited Freud and Carl Jung to the university's twentieth anniversary conference in 1909, where Freud presented a series of brilliant lectures, outlining psychoanalytic history and theory (published as *Five Lectures in Psychoanalysis* in 1910).

There have been many attempts to explain the problems that accompany adolescence. One of the frameworks has been that of seeking to explain personality through body type. Ernst Kretschmer (1888–1964) was a German psychiatrist, for example, who sought to follow those who believed that there is a correlation between body build and physical constitution and personality characteristics and mental illness. His most famous and influential book is *Körperbau und Charakter* ("Physique and Character"), 1921, in which he argues that certain mental disorders are more common among people of specific physical types. Kretschmer identifies three main types: tall, thin, and asthenic; more muscular and athletic; and rotund and pyknic. Each type was more likely to develop a particular kind of disorder: the lanky asthenics, and to a lesser degree the athletic types, schizophrenia; the pyknic types, manic-depressive disorders. His work had a great influence among some psychologists and in popular culture, especially among those interested in adolescence and in preventing teenage crime.

Freud, while not discounting physical components of adolescence, was more interested in exploring their psychological correlates. For Freud, adolescence was the period of the "genital" of development, in which the adolescent takes a pleasure, once again, in excretory activity. Additionally, there is frequent engagement in masturbation as the youth explores sexuality. It is also a period of strong single-sex friendship, at least in its early phases. Freud maintained that these friendships are basically homosexual, even if latently so. In later phases, heterosexual interests replace homosexual ones, and ties with the opposite sex are formed. The ego becomes stronger and replaces the superego; that is, one becomes surer of one's identity and is not so prone to follow authority figures blindly, a development that frequently upsets parents and teachers. The adolescent should come to understand that not all rules are equal and that certain flexibility in understanding and following them is necessary for survival.

Erik H. Erikson, however, had far more influence in shaping later concepts of adolescence. Erikson saw the adolescent stage of development as one in which identity is sought. He coined the term *identity crisis* to mark the challenge of this life stage. Influenced by Anna Freud, his mentor, Erikson noted that adolescence is marked by a struggle to develop ego identity, a sense of who one is in the face of change and discontinuity and almost infinite possibilities. In America, at least, the adolescent is obsessed with appearance, how he or she looks. Attraction to important figures promotes hero worship, while the teen is often immersed in one ideology or another. Additionally, this is the stage in which peer identification and, therefore, peer pressure is strongest.

Erikson notes the danger of role confusion at this stage. That confusion is coupled with sexual and occupational identity. It is a period, in sum, of almost infinite possibilities in the modern world, and choice brings danger and uncertainty. The morality of childhood no longer seems to fit the adolescent's reality, and, Erikson notes, the developed ethics of adulthood have not yet been formed. It is a stage of "psychosocial moratorium."

Harry Stack Sullivan disagreed with the Freudian notion of psychosexual development but his ideas were not too far removed from Erikson's. His stages of growth, including those of preadolescence and adolescence, were seen in cultural or interpersonal terms. In sum, the child moves from ties with parents and authority figures to those with peers in these stages. Emotional maturity is linked with the ability to form attachments in increasing circles.

Sullivan remarks that the beginning of preadolescence is marked by the ability to relate to a friend who is outside the family. The friend is able to mirror the preadolescent's identity as a fellow peer. Friendship is a one-on-one relationship. This stage serves to prepare the preadolescent for adult maturity through aiding in the development of empathy, expanding worldview, and linking intimacy with sexual feelings. The friend also provides a means for dialogue, essential in discovering how one's ideas fit into the larger world beyond family. These dialogues provide reality checks for the youth. This period also witnesses the emergence of the peer group, another factor in the separation from the family seen as essential to full development. Sullivan sees the leader of the peer group as an essential role model for development.

Adolescence is a period in which girls must develop a bond with their mothers and boys with their fathers. According to Sullivan, failure to do so will make it difficult to assume adult societal roles. For Sullivan, the family is of primary importance in guiding youth through the hurdles of adolescence. The peer group, however, remains strong, especially in the discussion of sexual urges.

Once the adolescent has found a means for combining intimacy with sexuality, he or she is ready to establish or reestablish an appropriate level of closeness with parents, which should enable the adolescent to form a mature adult sexual relationship and become a member of the community. Additionally the adolescent should feel self-respect, which enables him or her to admire others' accomplishments without feelings of envy or jealousy.

Certainly in popular-culture physiological and psychological theories, there is general agreement that adolescence is a period of rapid and often disturbing changes during which authority is openly or covertly questioned. Popular culture appearing in movies (for example, *Rebel without a Cause*, 1955), music, literature, and melodrama has typically portrayed the adolescent as at best confused and at worst dangerous. The generation gap is perceived as inevitable and bridged only with the onset of age and, perhaps, with the adolescent turmoil of one's own children.

Questions of the inevitability of the storminess of the period have come from anthropologists such as Franz Boas and Margaret Mead, who emphasized that the nature of human development as culture, or nurture, works on the biological makeup common to all human populations. However, the majority of American psychologists and the popular culture they have analyzed continue to view the period as one of almost inevitable storm and stress that is "natural" to this period of development. While not dismissing cultural factors, they tend to downplay them.

[See also YOUTH CULTURE.]

BIBLIOGRAPHY

Erikson, Erik H., *Identity, Youth, and Crisis* (Norton 1968).

Friedman, G., "The Mother-Daughter Bond," *Contemporary Psychoanalysis* 16 (1980):90–97.

Ingram, D., "Poststructural Interpretations of the Psychoanalytic Relationship," *Journal of the American Academy of Psychoanalysis* 2 (1994):175–193.

Kett, Joseph F., *Rites of Passage: Adolescence in America, 1790 to the Present* (Basic Bks. 1977).

Levenson, E., "Follow the Fox: An Inquiry into the Vicissitudes of Psychoanalytic Supervision," *Contemporary Psychoanalysis* 18 (1982):1–15.

Palladino, Grace, *Teenagers: An American History* (Basic Bks. 1996).

Ross, Dorothy, *G. Stanley Hall: The Psychologist as Prophet* (Univ. of Chicago Press 1972).

Sullivan, Harry Stack, *The Interpersonal Theory of Psychiatry,* ed. by Helen Swick Perry and Mary Ladd Gawel (Norton 1953).

FRANK A. SALAMONE

ADVERTISING

Advertising created and shaped many of the institutions of twentieth-century America. David A. Hounshell, a historian of technology, acknowledged that marketing and advertising were the key factors in the success of many American technological innovations. In the 1950s historian David M. Potter pointed out that modern newspapers, slick periodicals, radio, and television all owed their viability to advertising. At the end of the twentieth century, the Internet acquired more social presence hand-in-hand with the growth of advertising on the World Wide Web. Considering its importance it is not surprising that the nature of advertising

© COURTESY, BAYER CORPORATION

"Speedy" Alka Seltzer sought to calm everyone's stomach in the 1950s.

and the manner of its functioning are the subjects of diverse academic inquiry.

Between the 1880s and the 1920s, advertising for nationally distributed brand-named goods increased dramatically. This expansion was linked to the establishment of a national market in the United States and developments in transportation and communication. In this process advertising agents—who had been small-time liaisons (and sometimes charlatans) between newspapers selling and businesses buying advertising space—transformed themselves into professionals in the preparation of advertisements. Daniel Pope, a historian, described this process as part of manufacturers' rationalization and consolidation of the market for goods and services that eroded local autonomy. Another historian, Roland Marchand, suggested that advertising repre-

Think small.

Our little car isn't so much of a novelty any more.
A couple of dozen college kids don't try to squeeze inside it.
The guy at the gas station doesn't ask where the gas goes.
Nobody even stares at our shape.
In fact, some people who drive our little

flivver don't even think that about 27 miles to the gallon is going any great guns.
Or using five pints of oil instead of five quarts.
Or never needing anti-freeze.
Or racking up about 40,000 miles on a set of tires.
That's because once you get used to

some of our economies, you don't even think about them any more.
Except when you squeeze into a small parking spot.
Or renew your small insurance. Or pay a small repair bill. Or trade in your old VW for a new one.
Think it over.

Dealer Name

DDB NEEDHAM WORLDWIDE

Ad slick for the Volkswagen Beetle campaign "Think small."

sented advertisers' attempts to ensure that the demand for goods and services matched production capacities, or at least output. More important, Marchand argued that advertisers in the 1920s shaped the language of modern American life. Advertising in the 1920s both heightened excitement over the new and soothed consumers' anxieties.

Although it is clear that the business of advertising has had a profound impact on American society and culture, the manner in which advertisements themselves affect their audiences is open to numerous interpretations. John Wanamaker, the founder of the Philadelphia department store of the same name, expressed the dilemma of evaluating advertising's effect, stating, "Half the money I spend on advertising is wasted, and the trouble is I don't know which half." At a functional level advertising has two central features: first, advertising categories of products and services; and second, creating loyalty to particular brands of products and services. These two functions can be undertaken concurrently or separately. The nature of these functions is not as clear-cut as this definition. The disjuncture is indicated in the rationalizations advertisers offer for their industry. On the one hand advertising agents proclaim that they merely display things, more or less in the manner of a public service, but on the other hand they emphasize their persuasive powers to clients. Consequently advertisers are wont to defend themselves against the charge of promoting products deemed undesirable by arguing that they do not aim to influence people to consume products but rather to choose particular brands of things they already use.

In his *History of American Advertising*, Stephen Fox delineated the various styles and methods of advertising, as it moved from a descriptive, text-based phenomenon to an industry of imagery. Fox regards advertising as having two grand styles: the Claude Hopkins and Albert Lasker school of reason-why advertising (a style driven by social science and quantification); and the Theodore MacManus and Robert Rubicam school of atmosphere and suggestion (which relies on Freudian tenets and the notion that people reach their important decisions subconsciously). Other developments in advertising, including hard sell, soft sell, the poll methodology of George Gallup, and the creative revolution of the early 1960s, can be seen as parts of the cycle of fashion, which fit or are accommodated to one of these grand styles. Hard sell probably belongs more to the Hopkins-Lasker school and soft sell to the MacManus-Rubicam school, but the divisions are not so firm. For instance Rubicam employed Gallup, a use of polling that would not immediately seem to fit his style.

At the end of the twentieth century, the dangers posed by methods of advertising, which relied on detailed consumer profiles gathered through computer programs that tracked Internet use, were the focus of discussion on the social impact of developing technology. Click-through programs and

Actor Johnny Roventini in bellhop uniform stands on a stack of telephone books to reach the microphone so he can broadcast the famous "call for Philip Morris."

"cookie" technology that allowed Web site owners and advertisers to compile statistics on Web usage and sites visited, and thereby allowed for tailored advertising, were seen as threats to privacy and consumer autonomy. Such developments, though, may have been simply variations on the Hopkins-Lasker model of advertising and a cyclical instance of the hard-sell style. As early as, 2000 advertisers used streaming video clips on the Internet to deliver more atmospheric soft-sell advertisements.

There has been little argument with Fox's schematic of advertising, but the impact and role of advertising has been open to debate. Historians and sociologists have suggested that advertising creates a demand or a desire, which hitherto had not existed, for products and services. Christopher Lasch, in *The Culture of Narcissism*, suggests that advertising creates a perpetually dissatisfied consumer as a means to sell consumption as a "lifestyle." In 1983 T. J. Jackson Lears, and other contributors to *The Culture of Consumption*, saw advertising as promoting a therapeutic release from the ennui brought on by modernization, but simultaneously helping to create a culture that actually reproduced the condition it was meant to solve. Another critic, Stewart Ewen, regarded advertising as a means of defusing potential social unrest brought on by the process of modernization.

Michael Schudson refocused discussions on the impact of advertising in his 1984 work, *Advertising, The Uneasy Persuasion*. The title neatly captured the unease Americans felt about the advertising industry, and the difficulty in ascribing to advertising a cause-and-effect persuasiveness. It also played on the title of Vance Packard's 1957 psychological study, *The Hidden Persuaders*. Schudson disputed the effectiveness of advertising to influence individual consumer purchases. But insofar as it has an effect on stockholders, salespeople, and retailers, whose belief in its impact helps determine what products are available, advertising shapes the market of goods. Moreover, advertising proffered one message: the pleasure of consumption and an easy course of action—buy something. Schudson also tied advertising to anthropological theories of commodities as culture or cultural symbols. If commodi-

11

ties are culture, then advertising is a language with which it is discussed. If commodities are cultural symbols, then advertising is a second-order naming system that is used to reinforce what America's cultural symbols are.

Numerous academics have sought to decode the symbolic referents of advertising and their impact on the sale of goods. Building on the work of Judith Williamson, Matthew McAllister argues that advertisers try to link their products with values and goals of potential consumers through association or referent systems, that is, a person, thing, or situation used to represent a quality, such as "hip" or "cool," and a linkage to the desired quality established through the use of the product. Advertisements often imply a direct linkage between the purchase of the commodity and obtaining the referent system. Advertisers have promoted goods, from tampons to automobiles, as being able to deliver trouble-free, vital lives. In doing so advertising glorifies the consumption of commodities and projects social views that obscure other considerations, such as the condition of production and the cost of consumption.

Lears also analyzes the symbolic modes of advertising. In his important work on advertising, *Fables of Abundance*, Lears recast his earlier views. He found advertising to be not as radical a departure from tradition as is generally thought. He saw the emerging culture of consumption as balancing tensions between release and control of emotion within Protestant traditions. In an echo of the "Other Protestant Ethic," which unleashed the tightly wrapped emotion of Calvinism, the culture of consumption represented a kind of "mystic release" and short-lived gratification followed by renewed longing.

Lears's take on advertising makes it vital to understanding the American psyche. Instead of animating goods with meaning, advertising strips the solidness of materialism from things. Advertising then becomes the language of abundance, but one without substance. Lears holds that in a culture of production things obtain their meaning through an immediacy of use, but in a culture of consumption

that meaning slips away into abstractions (language) in which a symbolic representation has greater meaning than the thing itself. These abstractions are not simply the magic symbolism of the carnivalesque; they also incorporate the Victorian plain-speech tradition. Advertisers helped stabilize market relations around the turn of the twentieth century through remaking commercialism into acts of imagination. In short, advertising stripped language of its pretensions at representing reality and transformed it into an arbitrary code. Advertising, therefore, is a play or performance in which anything goes. Moreover it presents a model of life as performance in which notions of self can constantly be invented or reinvented.

At the end of the twentieth century this vision of advertising and American culture was widely accepted. Whether this was a positive or negative development in American culture is subject to conjecture.

[*See also* CONSUMERISM; COCA-COLA; CREDIT CARD; FASHION; DEPARTMENT STORE; NEWSPAPERS; MAGAZINES; RADIO; TELEVISION.]

BIBLIOGRAPHY

Ewen, Stuart, *Captains of Consciousness: Advertising and the Social Roots of the Consumer Culture* (McGraw-Hill 1976).

Fox, Richard Wrightman, and T. J. Jackson Lears, eds., *The Culture of Consumption: Critical Essays in American History, 1880–1980* (Pantheon Bks. 1983).

Fox, Stephen R., *The Mirror Makers: A History of American Advertising and Its Creators* (Morrow 1984).

Lears, T. J. Jackson, *Fables of Abundance: A Cultural History of Advertising in America* (Basic Bks. 1994).

McAllister, Matthew P. *The Commercialization of American Culture: New Advertising, Control and Democracy* (Sage Pubs. 1996).

Marchand, Roland, *Advertising the American Dream: Making Way for Modernity, 1920–1940* (Univ. of Calif. Press 1985).

Orvell, Miles, *The Real Thing: Imitation and Authenticity in American Culture, 1880–1940* (Univ. of N.C. Press 1989).

Pope, Daniel, *The Making of Modern Advertising* (Basic Bks. 1983).

Schudson, Michael, *Advertising, The Uneasy Persuasion: Its Dubious Impact on American Society* (Basic Bks. 1984).

IAN GORDON

AFFIRMATIVE ACTION

Affirmative action, or positive steps to prevent a recurrence of past discrimination, has been used by policymakers to increase access to jobs, business development opportunities, and schools, and to protect voting rights. Its critics use such terms as *quotas, color-blind theory,* and "reverse discrimination," and its advocates speak of *goals, fair play,* and *special measures,* but beneath the rhetoric of the nation's thirty-five-year affirmative-action debate lie old, deeply rooted divisions over race, liberty, and equality in American political culture. Although affirmative action programs originally sought to end discrimination against African Americans, they soon expanded to include other minorities: women, older Americans, Vietnam-era veterans, and, later, persons with disabilities. Lack of consensus about the legal, moral, and political merits of affirmative action has produced fragmented, often contradictory federal and state policies and erratic standards of judicial review.

The importation of African slaves in 1619, the framers' assent to slavery, and the Supreme Court's *Dred Scott* v. *Sandford* (1857) and *Plessy* v. *Ferguson* (1896) decisions supply benchmarks in the history of racial discrimination that affirmative action was intended to redress. When the Supreme Court reversed *Plessy* by declaring "separate but equal" unconstitutional in *Brown* v. *Board of Education* (1954), it fractured an entrenched system of discrimination born from the failures of Reconstruction. As President Lyndon Johnson told Howard University graduates in 1965, affirmative action seemed essential to fulfilling the promises of *Brown:*

> You do not take a person who for years has been hobbled by chains and liberate him, bring him up to the starting line of a race and then say, "you're free to compete with all the others," and still justly believe that you have been completely fair. . . . We seek not

. . . only equality as a right and a theory, but equality as a fact and equality as a result.

The difference between "equality as a right" and "equality as a result" is at the center of enduring disputes over affirmative action.

The idea that government had a duty to end racial discrimination clearly predates the 1960s, but Johnson's Executive Order 11246 (1965) launched the nation's affirmative action programs and triggered important consequences for federalism. Executive Order 11246 still affects most organizations that work on government contracts, but at the time its target was the construction trades, the same groups eyed by presidents Franklin Roosevelt, Truman, Eisenhower, Kennedy, and Nixon, who collectively shaped the evolution of affirmative-action policy. President Johnson's order directed government agencies and contractors to take "affirmative action to ensure that applicants are employed . . . without regard to their race, creed, color, or national origin."

What distinguished Executive Order 11246 was its affirmative action plan requirement, which applies when any organization with more than fifty employees receives a federally assisted contract in excess of fifty thousand dollars. States and municipalities using federal grants for school construction, urban renewal, and highway projects became obligated to cooperate with the mandate. Nixon's New Federalism, which replaced most Great Society programs with revenue sharing and block grants, increased the amount of federal aid to states and urban areas and the compliance burden. Moreover, Nixon (who later opposed affirmative action rhetorically) amplified Executive Order 11246 by requiring contractors to make "good-faith efforts" to hire minority and women workers and implement affirmative action plans according to "goals and timetables." His 1971 "Philadelphia Plan" forced contractors and trade unions in thirty-five cities to meet minority hiring goals. The transformation of federal-state relations caused by money and mandates transferred the parlance of affirmative action (terms such as *goals, timetables, proportional represen-*

tation, and, ultimately, *quotas*) into states and private industry, often with considerable resistance.

Federal affirmative-action policies had a profound and sometimes explosive impact on schools, colleges, and universities. Despite *Brown,* by 1964 only 2.3 percent of black school-age children nationwide were attending desegregated schools. In 1966 the federal Department of Health, Education, and Welfare (HEW) issued guidelines to implement the Civil Rights Act of 1964 and provide standards for school-desegregation plans required by *Brown.* HEW adopted an affirmative-action strategy, encouraging school authorities to use grade reorganization, school closings, and reassignment of students to achieve racial balance. Two years later the Warren Court followed suit by rejecting a school district's "freedom-of-choice" plan because the schools remained segregated, arguing in *Green* v. *County Board of New Kent County* (1968) that officials had "an affirmative duty to take whatever steps are necessary to convert to a unitary [integrated] system." In *Alexander* v. *Holmes* (1969) and *Swann* v. *Charlotte-Mecklenburg Board of Education* (1971), the Burger Court strengthened judicial policy on affirmative action, leading federal district-court justices to impose busing as a means to comply with *Brown.* States' rights advocates saw federally mandated school desegregation as an invasive attack on federalism. Intense, often violent opposition to busing erupted in such Northern cities as Detroit and Boston, where racially imbalanced schools existed largely because of suburban growth and "white flight," a condition known as "de facto segregation."

Both Congress and the Supreme Court embraced affirmative action to achieve political equality. Under the Voting Rights Act of 1965, Congress banned the South's "Jim Crow" voting laws by making literacy tests illegal, and subjected all voter qualification and related policies in eleven Southern states to review by the U.S. Attorney General. Between 1964 and 1969, the number of registered black voters in the South doubled. The Supreme Court broadly construed the Voting Rights Act to disqualify any changes in state laws that could leave blacks disenfranchised. Thus, proposals to convert elected positions to appointed ones were struck down in several states, along with annexation plans that would have changed the composition of the electorate and caused, in Earl Warren's words, "a dilution of the voting power." When congressional redistricting (reapportionment) practices were challenged in *United Jewish Organizations of Williamsburgh* v. *Carey* (1977), the Supreme Court sanctioned the use of "affirmative racial gerrymandering," echoing Chief Justice Burger's words from *Swann:* "Race must be considered both in determining whether a constitutional violation exists and in determining a remedy."

Just as the Supreme Court unraveled sixty years of "separate but equal" in *Brown,* it also began to unravel affirmative action in *Board of Regents of the University of California* v. *Bakke* (1978). While reasserting precedents established from *Brown* forward, the Court held that the University of California–Davis Medical School had violated the rights of Allen Bakke, a white applicant twice denied admission because of a minority quota system. In one of many 5–4 decisions that signaled a shift in judicial policy (and more conservative Supreme Court appointees), Justice Powell wrote: " . . . the Davis special admissions program involves the use of an explicit racial classification never before countenanced by this Court. The fatal flaw . . . is disregard of individual rights as guaranteed by the Fourteenth Amendment." *Bakke* was only the beginning, for in two later cases, *Fullilove* v. *Klutznick* (1980) and *Wygant* v. *Jackson Board of Education* (1986), the Court's bare-majority decisions were flanked by a flurry of concurring and dissenting opinions.

Affirmative action took hold in an era of centralized federalism. Before *Brown,* the Supreme Court had addressed nondiscrimination by federal authorities, enabling national policymakers to define the endurance of racial inequality as a state and local problem and tailor their remedies accordingly. For nearly two decades Congress, the courts, and the presidency shared remarkable consensus about the legitimacy of affirmative action. By the 1980s, however, the Court's fragmented stance on affirmative action was evident in both the *Bakke* case and a gradual retrenchment from such landmark federal discrimination cases as *Korematsu* v. *United States* (1944) and *Bolling* v. *Sharpe* (1954). A 1995 decision illustrates both the degree of judicial wavering on affirmative action and policy inconsistencies between the Supreme Court and Congress, for in *Adarand Constructors* v. *Peña,* a divided Rehnquist Court struck down mandatory construction set-asides for "disadvantaged business enterprises" (low-income and minority subcontractors) under the national Small Business Act.

[See also AFRICAN AMERICANS; CIVIL RIGHTS AND THE CIVIL RIGHTS MOVEMENT.*]*

BIBLIOGRAPHY

Beckwith, Francis J., and Todd E. Jones, eds., *Affirmative Action: Social Justice or Reverse Discrimination?* (Prometheus Bks. 1997).

Curry, George E., and Cornel West, eds., *Affirmative Action Debate* (Addison-Wesley 1996).

Klinkner, Philip A., and Rogers M. Smith, *The Unsteady March: The Rise and Decline of Racial Equality in America* (Univ. of Chicago Press 1999).

Post, Robert, and Michael Rogin, eds., *Race and Representation: Affirmative Action* (Zone Bks. 1998).

Skrentny, John David, *The Ironies of Affirmative Action: Politics, Culture, and Justice in America* (Univ. of Chicago Press 1996).

Tushnet, Mark V., *Making Constitutional Law: Thurgood Marshall and the Supreme Court, 1961–1991* (Oxford 1997).

JUDITH A. BARRETT

AFRICAN AMERICANS

[The African American heritage in the United States is sufficiently broad as to require treatment in several separate articles in the encyclopedia. Under the present heading, therefore, are grouped nine core articles prepared by eight different scholars. The introductory essay, AN OVERVIEW, *surveys the history and legacy of the African American struggle for freedom and dignity in the continuously evolving nation. The next five articles cover the full range of artistic expression in African American culture and history. These are titled as follows:*

AFRICAN AMERICAN LITERATURE

AFRICAN AMERICAN MUSIC

© BRIAN DOUGLAS/SARAH AND ANNIE ELIZABETH DELANY AND AMY HILL HEARTH

Bessie Delany (*left*) and Sadie Delany, centenarian authors of *Having Our Say* (1993), recounted their lives with humor and wisdom.

AFRICAN AMERICANS IN FILM AND THEATER

AFRICAN AMERICAN DANCE

AFRICAN AMERICAN VISUAL ART

This set of articles is complemented by an entry on AFRICAN AMERICAN FOLKLORE AND HUMOR, *which in turn leads to an entry dealing with* AFRICAN AMERICAN RELIGIONS. *The final article in the group focuses on the topic of* AFRICAN AMERICAN SPEECH AND LANGUAGE. *For related articles in the encyclopedia, see also* AFRO; AFROCENTRISM; HARLEM; SOUL FOOD.*]*

An Overview

The historical forces and events that gave rise to the populations of African-descended Americans constitute one of the most dramatic and complex developments in human history. The contact between Africa and the Americas has resulted in the emergence of a people, particularly in the United States of America, whose legacy has been a history of struggle for human rights, socioeconomic development, and collective survival. It was through the Atlantic slave trade and chattel slavery that the histories of Africa, Europe, and the Americas converged. These inhumane and exploitative economic institutions served as a foundation for the accumulation of capital and the industrial development of western Europe and the United States.

Although the mid-fifteenth-century exchange between western Europe and West Africa began with trade in goods, European greed, lust for power, and drive for global expansion rapidly transformed that exchange into the capture and trade of African bodies. As a result, massive depopulation, social dislocation, and political disruption weakened the African continent and prepared the way for western European imperialism and colonialism during the nineteenth and early twentieth centuries. The turbulent voyage of the "middle passage" from Africa to the Americas, which included the genocide of millions of Africans, resulted in one of the most dramatic and involuntary population transplantations in human history. Africans from numerous nations—from different cultures and language groups—were crammed into slave ships and forced onto American shores. They were Bambara, Malinka, Fon, Dinka, Ewe, Bakongo, Mende, Igbo, Yoruba, Ashanti, Wolof, Serer, Susu, and hundreds more. The colonial-American institution of chattel slavery was the context in which the members of this pan-African assembly fought back, improvised, and refashioned themselves into a new, yet very old, people—African Americans.

The western European rape of Africa was accompanied by much distortion of African and African American history, necessary to rationalize the slavers' barbaric treatment of dark-skinned peoples. Retrieving African history before the intervention of Europe links African-descended Americans to a human, geographical, temporal, and intellectual context beyond the confines of slavery and Western cultural domination in the Americas. African history, then, is part of the collective memory of African-descended Americans, and reclaiming that history has to be one of the vocations of examining the African American experience in slavery and in freedom.

West Africa and Its Significance. An examination of the great ancient and medieval West African empires of Ghana (circa 500–1200), Mali (circa 1000–1400), and Songhai (circa 1000–1595), together with the Hausa-Fulani states (circa 1300–1850), clearly displaces the notion of savage Africans who were incapable of governing themselves before Europeans arrived. Indeed, Ghana, Mali, and Songhai in succession rose and fell while western Europe was experiencing the Dark Ages. From the sixth to the nineteenth century these empires and the Hausa-Fulani states existed in the geographically supportive high grasslands of West Africa—open lands, which allowed for the development of large empires and states. They were sustained economically and culturally by their participation in commerce and the trans-Saharan caravan trade that went as far to the east as Egypt and Arabia.

The spread of Islam across Africa and into Europe after the death of Muhammad resulted in both positive and negative consequences for Ghana, Mali, Songhai, and the Hausa-Fulani states. On the one hand, educational advancement, spiritual development, and commercial trading were enhanced in West Africa because of relationships with Muslim scholars and traders. On the other hand, as the kings of Mali, Songhai, and the Hausa-Fulani states embraced Islam, internal cultural and societal fragmentation, conflict, and eventual decline occurred. Religious wars and other internal contradictions within West African states and nations—from the Old Congo Kingdom in the south to Morocco in the north—served to weaken traditional West African political societies, setting the stage for western European intervention and the consequent slave trade.

Chattel Slavery and Resistance. Perhaps all human societies experienced some kind of slavery. In ancient times, although they were treated harshly and sometimes were refused citizenship, slaves still were considered human beings who could be educated and sometimes hold governmental office. However, the expansion of capitalism and the introduction of mechanical power into military conflict made the transatlantic slave trade and chattel slavery profitable for western Europe, but devastating to African peoples and their American descendants. The illicit trade of African flesh and the institution of chattel slavery set in motion western Europe's Industrial Revolution and served as the foundation for American economic development.

As historian Kenneth Stampp recounted in *The Peculiar Institution: Slavery in the Ante-Bellum South* (1956), slave-owners employed a system of psychological and physical violence as they attempted to create the good, submissive slave. Stampp pointed out five recurring tactics of this system that attempted dehumanization. First, those who managed the slaves had to maintain strict discipline. Second, slave-owners thought that they had to implant in the slave a consciousness of personal inferiority, which they deliberately extended to the slave's past and skin color. Third was to awe the slaves with the sense of the slave-owner's enormous power. It was essential "to make them stand in fear." The fourth tactic was to "persuade the bondsman to take an interest in the master's enterprise and to accept his standards of 'good conduct.'" The final step, according to Stampp, was "to impress Negroes with their helplessness: to create in them a habit of perfect dependence upon their masters."

Here, then, was the system of attempted dehumanization and depersonalization designed and practiced by slave-owners in a desperate attempt to produce perfect slaves. To be sure, all chattel slaves were not submissive, frightened, weak, and dependent. Many were defiant, angry, resentful, and rebellious, as historian John Blassingame demonstrated in his book *The Slave Community: Plantation Life in the Ante-Bellum South* (1972).

Slaves revolted and struggled for freedom throughout the Western Hemisphere. For example, the late-eighteenth-century Haitian Revolution overthrew French slavocracy resulting in the 1803 Louisiana Purchase during Thomas Jefferson's presidency. In an atmosphere of repression and rebellion, many slaves in the American South rose to kill their white oppressors. One example is Nat Turner, who stepped forward on August 22, 1831, to lead a group of avengers in the slaughter of whites in Southampton County, Virginia. Turner later was captured, tried in court, imprisoned, and put to death. Turner's insurrection, however, sent waves of fear throughout the slaveholding South. In reaction, frightened whites indiscriminately massacred hundreds of African Americans.

Often overlooked in American history is the free African American. Even in the worst years of American slavery in the South, free blacks fashioned for themselves a life not unlike that of ordinary whites, except for the constant threat of violence and possible enslavement. A few became wealthy and, in Louisiana in particular, some even owned slaves. In the New England states, after the American Revolution, slavery disappeared by 1820. By this time a significant number of African Americans had lived there for more than two generations as free people, literate, and relatively well-to-do. It was from this group that David Walker came, born legally free in 1785 in Wilmington, North Carolina. Walker traveled throughout the South and witnessed the violent, degrading, and dehumanizing effects of chattel slavery. In 1826, he moved to Boston, Massachusetts, where he joined forces with other African American abolitionists as an organizer, lecturer, and writer. In 1827, *Freedom's Journal,* the first African American newspaper, was published in Boston; Walker became its agent.

In 1829 Walker published a pamphlet, *Appeal,* which set in motion an African American tradition of radical analysis and criticism of white greed and racism, together with an advocacy of black solidarity and liberation, specifically between the free and the enslaved. Clearly energized by Walker's religious zeal and sense of social justice, the *Appeal* combined the two major belief systems in early-nineteenth-century America—Protestant Evangelical Christianity and natural-rights philosophy. Walker linked the struggle for African American freedom to God's justice: the fight for African American liberation was a holy crusade, and resistance to chattel slavery was obedience to God.

African Americans and the Political Economy of Underdevelopment. Chattel slavery, as a form of economic exploitation and racist antiblack oppression, set in motion the character of American political culture. As chattel slavery's legacy, antiblack racism became America's longest hatred. In

A family of sharecroppers picking cotton on Louisiana farmland, circa 1900.

addition, the slave trade and chattel slavery served as the foundation for white America's economic development and black America's economic underdevelopment. Hence, the ideologies of white supremacy and profit maximization, together with the institutional practice of black enslavement, resulted in a culture of domination that uniquely characterized the American nation-state until the mid-twentieth century.

After slavery's abolition the economic and political circumstances of the former bondspeople did not change substantially. Black people had to fight a continuous battle against geographical, socioeconomic, cultural, and political obstacles in order to improve their economic predicament. At the dawn of the twentieth century, most African Americans embarked on a historic journey from rural to urban and from southern to northern regions, seeking better life chances. In the process, they gradually refashioned themselves from mainly rural agricultural peasants to largely urban industrial workers.

Following the nation's transition from agrarian to industrial capitalism, urban skilled factory jobs went to white workers, while African Americans either were excluded or given menial jobs. Hence, white workers were not required to compete with African American workers for employment in the emerging industrial manufacturing sector of the economy. World War I set in motion the African American penetration into America's industrial labor force. In northern cities, African Americans initially entered such industries as steel, meatpacking, and automobile manufacturing as strikebreakers. Even then there were particular jobs, usually the hardest and most dangerous, designed for African American workers. Especially during the Great Depression of the 1930s, white labor unions successfully maintained preferential employment practices for white workers and racially discriminatory and exclusionary practices directed at African American industrial workers.

From World War II to the mid-1960s, African Americans made the transition to a largely urban, working-class population. African American organizational and mass-movement leadership—for example, Marcus Garvey's black nationalist United Negro Improvement Association's movement, the liberal National Association for the Advancement of Colored People (NAACP), and also A. Philip Randolph's socialist Brotherhood of Sleeping Car Porters and Maids labor union—represented in a variety of ways a new stage in the self-conscious, collective struggle of African Americans to confront racially based political and economic oppression in America.

Since the 1960s the African American economic situation has been characterized by both advancement and decline, as trends have indicated a growing economic polarization within the black community. Younger and better-educated African Americans have experienced improved income and occupational status; those with less education but

In an early civil rights demonstration, prominent leaders of the black community march down Fifth Avenue in Harlem, New York City.

with average skills have experienced the ups and downs associated with fluctuating economic conditions; and those at the bottom of the economic ladder have fallen farther behind, even experiencing conditions of semipermanent impoverishment. Hence, the economic situation of African Americans is complicated. On the one hand, and in comparison to whites, there has been a general improvement in individual income, education, white-collar employment, high-visibility occupations (for example, entertainment and professional sports), and professional-managerial positions in private enterprise. On the other hand, conditions for many non-Southern urban African Americans continued to worsen, particularly among teenagers and adult males.

The Politics of Liberation: Contradictions and Dilemmas. The political history of African America can be characterized as the long-standing struggle for human rights, social development, and collective survival. The historic battle has been to dislodge and dismantle the European American systems of cultural domination that have constrained and controlled opportunities of African Americans.

The establishment of the American nation-state was flawed because the American Revolution actually was superficial, leaving the colonial society fundamentally unchanged, and because the founders of the American political system and the U.S. Constitution protected the slave trade and chattel slav-

ery. Moreover, because of fear, economic necessity, and imperialist desires, white Americans developed and used antiblack, racist ideologies to justify the subordination of African Americans. Jacksonian or mass democracy served not to expand African American political participation but to limit it. Federalism and the traditional view of the minimalist role to be played by the federal government enhanced the power of state governments to control and constrain African American political and social development.

The mid-nineteenth century to its close demonstrated white America's ambivalence toward providing authentic freedom to former slaves. When, in 1863 during the Civil War, Republican President Abraham Lincoln issued the Emancipation Proclamation, African Americans began to support the Republican Party. The presidential administration following Lincoln's, that of Andrew Johnson, attempted to reject policies and programs designed to improve the conditions of former slaves. A decade of radical Reconstruction followed, during which time the U.S. Congress ratified the Thirteenth, Fourteenth, and Fifteenth Amendments to the Constitution, freeing former slaves and giving them citizenship and voting rights. African Americans gained a measure of political authority in some Southern state legislatures. However, with the collapse of Reconstruction, the white South reconsolidated its power and, until well into the twentieth century, terrorized and disenfranchised African Americans. While the 1896 Supreme Court ruling in *Plessy* v. *Ferguson* legalized American apartheid in the South, regions outside the South also customarily practiced a racial segregation that severely marginalized and excluded African Americans.

With African Americans' migration to cities in the North and Midwest during the early twentieth century, they gradually shifted political allegiance from the Republican to the Democratic Party. President Franklin D. Roosevelt, who had been elected in 1932, was the major catalyst for this shift. Throughout the 1930s African American leaders, including black-nationalist Marcus Garvey and educator Mary McLeod Bethune, supported the Roosevelt administration, which resulted in growing African American support for the Democrats. African Americans also gained some political strength in big-city politics, but Democratic Party allegiance did not prevent racial discrimination against African American workers and soldiers. In fact, southern Democrats continued to constrain African American political participation.

World War I catalyzed two movements: one, to gain full civil rights through litigation, which declined swiftly after *Plessy* v. *Ferguson,* and the other, a resurgence of litigation and mass public protests during the Harlem Renaissance. But after the war, the "New Negro" movement, allied with the NAACP, began a series of litigations that eventually ended the de jure disenfranchisement in the South in the case of *Terry* v. *Adams* (1953), in graduate schools in *McLaurin* v. *Oklahoma* and *Sweatt* v. *Painter* (1950), and in primary and secondary schools in *Brown* v. *Board of Education* (1954). These triumphs gave impetus to a resurgent moral militance that metamorphosed, in concert with the "Don't buy where you can't work" mass protests begun after World War I, into the modern civil rights movement, beginning with the successful 1955–1956 Montgomery bus boycott.

In the South, hostile white citizens and even law-enforcement personnel terrorized and murdered African American and white civil rights workers, who were engaged in civil-disobedient and nonviolent demonstrations and voter registration campaigns. Lyndon B. Johnson's administration brought out the military to protect civil rights workers. Also, Johnson began to appoint a growing number of African Americans to federal government positions.

However, the South's continued terrorism against nonviolent civil rights activists and organizations, and the 1968 assassination of civil rights leader Martin Luther King, Jr., angered African Americans, many of whom were living in increasingly impoverished urban communities. As the civil rights movement reached its limits in the mid-1960s, African Americans revolted in cities across the nation. Moreover, some black leaders and organizations embraced black-nationalist and revolutionary ideologies, rejecting the liberal integrationist orien-

UPI/BETTMAN

Shirley Chisholm, the first African American woman elected (1968) to Congress.

tation of the civil rights organizations and leaders. Hence, the late 1960s and 1970s represented fierce and radical black resistance to America's dominant white supremacy.

Influenced by the black nationalist ideas of Malcolm X and the revolutionary theories of Frantz Fanon, Che Guevara, Karl Marx, V. I. Lenin, and Mao Tse-tung, the Black Panther Party, founded in 1966 in Oakland, California, by Huey P. Newton and Bobby Seale, gained national and international attention as an organization of defiant young black men and women committed to resisting by any means necessary what Malcolm X had called America's white power structure. Viewing urban black communities as colonies occupied by a system of white, hostile police, the Black Panthers fearlessly contested the power of the state to brutalize black citizens. The Black Panther Party saw itself as a revolutionary vanguard organization within urban black communities.

Although the Black Panthers left a legacy of armed resistance, community service, commitment to the self-determination of all people, and a model of political action for oppressed people, governmental infiltration and repression, together with internal organizational fissures, resulted in the decline and destruction of the party. Emerging in the urban areas of a nation that was largely indifferent to the historic structures and processes of cultural domination, antiblack racism, and economic dispossession, idealistic and resentful members of the Black Panthers represented a serious threat, if only for a short time, to the American social order and its system of governance. The Panthers seized the political space in order to speak audaciously to the people and the powerful about justice, liberation, self-determination, and revolution. The Panthers demanded the radical transformation of power relationships within American society and throughout the world, arguing that in order to destroy the conditions that produced and maintained ignorance and poverty, the dispossessed themselves needed to take hold of the reins of power.

Yet, decades after the Panthers fearlessly championed a system of radical social change, the inequitable socioeconomic conditions against which they struggled continue and, indeed, are worsening for many urban communities. These trends and developments are the result of the winding down of the industrial-capitalist society of money and manufacturing and the winding up of the postindustrial-managerial order of knowledge, science, and high technology. Experiencing growing cynical disillusionment, increasing hopelessness, intensifying meaninglessness, and mounting rage, many urban communities are becoming predatory zones as their residents turn on each other in a desperate and self-destructive attempt to survive in a society that is indifferent to their impoverishment and suffering. This dispiriting and often anarchical situation—much worse than the one from which the Panthers emerged over thirty years ago—cries out for a positive alternative.

African Americans at the beginning of the twenty-first century have not yet achieved uniform equality with the white population. In certain areas of sports, however, they have clearly established a superior record. Given that African Americans do not exceed thirteen percent of the U.S. population,

it is astonishing that they have almost completely dominated track in the Olympics since the 1950s, and basketball and football since the 1960s. Yet, racism still prevails even in those sports, and African American managers and coaches are seldom seen in them.

In popular music, the African American presence seems to be secure. Less so, however, is their presence in movies and the theater. There the black experience has varied with the vagaries of white opinion. Unfortunately for African Americans, the U.S. Supreme Court, from which it had been able to gain a modicum of relief from racial oppression in the civil rights era, has ruled consistently denying relief since the 1980s. Interestingly, it is in the armed forces, especially the U.S. Army, that studies have unanimously shown that African Americans have made the greatest progress. At the start of a new millennium, Americans continue to be haunted by the specter of cultural crosscurrents in a multicultural society.

BIBLIOGRAPHY

Baron, Harold M., "The Demand for Black Labor: Historical Notes on the Political Economy of Racism," in *A Turbulent Voyage: Readings in African American Studies,* 2d ed., ed. by Floyd W. Hayes III (Collegiate Press 1997).

Berry, Mary F., and John W. Blassingame, *Long Memory: The Black Experience in America* (Oxford 1982).

Blassingame, John W., *The Slave Community: Plantation Life in the Ante-Bellum South* (Oxford 1972).

Boahen, Adu, *Topics in West African History,* 2d ed. (Humanities Press 1966).

Davis, Angela, "Reflections on the Black Woman's Role in the Community of Slaves," in *The Angela Y. Davis Reader,* ed. by Joy James (Blackwell 1998).

Hayes, Floyd W., III, "Governmental Retreat, the Dispossessed, and the Politics of African American Self-Reliant Development in the Age of Reaganism," in *African Americans and the New Policy Consensus: Retreat of the Liberal State?,* ed. by Marilyn E. Lashley and Melanie Njeri Jackson (Greenwood Press 1994).

Hayes, Floyd W., III, and Francis A. Kiene III, "All Power to the People: The Political Thought of Huey P. Newton and the Black Panther Party," in *The Black Panther Party Reconsidered,* ed. by Charles E. Jones (Black Classic Press 1998).

James, C. L. R., "The Atlantic Slave Trade and Slavery: Some Interpretations of Their Significance in the Development of the United States and the Western World," in *Amistad: Writings in Black History and Culture*, ed. by Charles F. Harris (Vintage 1970).

Morris, Milton D., *The Politics of Black America* (Harper 1975).

Stampp, Kenneth, *The Peculiar Institution: Slavery in the Ante-Bellum South* (Vintage 1956).

Walker, David, *David Walker's Appeal,* ed. by Charles M. Wiltse (Hill & Wang 1965).

FLOYD W. HAYES III

African American Literature

African American literature from the colonial period to the present provides insight into American race, class, and gender politics and intellectual thought. This literature has been shaped by slavery, Reconstruction, migration, social protest, war abroad, civil rights, integration, and the backlash to affirmative action. This essay focuses on African American literature from the eighteenth century to the present and identifies prevalent genres, themes, and political and social movements reflected in that literature.

African American literary history and production begins with a mass movement on the part of African Americans to challenge racist claims that blacks were intellectually inferior and destined to be subservient to whites. Beginning in the colonial period, African American writers used a variety of genres including oration, epistolary pieces, slave narratives, autobiography, poetry, drama, novels, short stories, and essays. The various genres have allowed black authors creative ways to challenge racist assumptions and foreground major themes including but not limited to the quest theme, self-definition, self-determination, power, resistance, and intersections of race, class, and gender.

Early African American authors reveal the intellectual capabilities of blacks, the contradictions inherent in American political ideology, and the hypocrisy of those who used religious doctrine to justify slavery. These authors also initiated a call for freedom for enslaved African Americans and equality for all, including free blacks. In 1791 Benjamin Banneker challenged Thomas Jefferson's racist claim regarding black inferiority. In a letter to Jefferson, Banneker calls into question the hypocrisy inherent in Jefferson's belief in the equality and rights of all men, because his support and participation in the slave system did not allow blacks the rights outlined in the Declaration of Independence. Providing examples of educated, capable blacks was paramount to discrediting the claim that blacks were intellectually inferior and better suited to be slaves. Banneker stood out because he exemplified black excellence. Not only was Banneker literate and able to engage in intellectual discourse with Thomas Jefferson, but he was also a self-taught scientist.

Through poetry, early African American writers such as Phillis Wheatley and Jupiter Hammon evoke sympathy for those who are enslaved and live under constant threat of violence. Wheatley and Hammon demonstrate their intellectual excellence and expose the evils of slavery and racism. Early black poets focused on the quest theme and the effects of racial violence by showing how blacks suffered literal and psychological deaths as a result of slavery. Wheatley and Hammon are perhaps most well known for their hymns, because they use religious themes and images to speak out against slavery and argue that all humans are created equal in the eyes of God.

Wheatley, Hammon, and George Moses Horton are among the early African American poets who argue that a racial hierarchy exists in the United States. For instance in "Slavery," Horton points out that because of his black skin, whites are adamantly opposed to freeing him. Horton's poem shows how blackness is associated with victimization and oppression, and whiteness is associated with power and freedom. Wheatley addresses the racial hierarchy in "On Being Brought from Africa to America" (1773) when she describes how people of the "sable race" are viewed with contempt, and the color of their skin marks them as targets for victimization. The discussion of race privilege and disadvantage expressed in Horton, Wheatley, and Hammon's poetry is examined throughout African American literature.

Similar to the early poets, African American narrative writers further develop the quest-for-freedom theme in autobiographical narratives. The slave narrative, the most prevalent form of African American autobiography, provides an in-depth view of the heinous nature of slavery from the perspective of those who lived as slaves. The slave narratives introduce gender-based themes found in both African American and American literature. The slave narrative represents another genre used to write blacks into humanity, because it shows real human beings victimized as a result of slavery. These narratives indict the religious, political, and social institutions that condoned slavery. Slave narratives enhance the American literary tradition, because they reflect themes and techniques associated with captivity narratives, sentimental fiction, and regional writing published during the eighteenth and nineteenth centuries.

Slave narratives have common characteristics, yet there are key differences between narratives written by men and those by women. In general the narratives examine the construction and displacement of African American individuals, families, and communities; barriers to literacy; violence directed against blacks; ways in which both blacks and whites suffer as a result of this corrupt system; and the slave's desire for and acquisition of freedom. Male and female narrators emphasize issues that concern their respective genders. Male narrators focus on defining themselves as men and how they acquire status as men in a society that privileges maleness. Female narrators often focus on motherhood and claiming ownership of their own bodies.

In *The Narrative of Frederick Douglass* (1845), Douglass distinguishes between becoming a slave and becoming a man. He describes a physical altercation with the overseer of the plantation, and he dates his freedom and sense of manhood from the point at which he engages in direct physical resistance against his oppressor. Douglass, similar to other slave narrators, distinguishes between psychological and physical freedom.

Harriet Jacobs in *Incidents in the Life of a Slave Girl* (1861) argues that although slavery is terrible for all, black women experience "sufferings and mortifications" specific to their gender. The peculiar sufferings and mortifications Jacobs describes include rape and the slave mother's inability to protect her children from the horrors of slavery. Narratives that record the experiences of African American women expose both the destructive nature of racism and the patriarchal system. Female slave narrators add to the wealth of American women's literature and history that critiques the cult of domesticity and exposes how both black and white women were subjugated by white male authority.

African American writers also produced social and historical essays focused on the displacement and oppression of blacks, strategies for resistance, and African American intellectual thought during the slave period. These essays were often published in African American newspapers such as *Freedom's Journal, Rights of All, Weekly Advocate, National Reformer, The Mirror of Liberty,* and *The North Star.* Frederick Douglass, Martin Delaney, and William Whipper are among the many reformers who served as editors and described strategies for racial uplift in their writing.

African American authors' strategies vary for racial uplift, as illustrated by Whipper, David Walker, and Delaney. Whipper's "An Address on Non-Resistance to Offensive Aggression" argues against violence as a means to gain equality and justice. Delaney was among a group of African Americans who believed black emigration to nonwhite areas of the world was the key to the social, political, and economic development of blacks. While Whipper calls for a nonviolent approach to fighting racism, Walker suggests that acquiescence may work against blacks, and he favors a much more militant approach to fighting racism and violence directed against blacks. Just as Whipper's work is a precursor to Martin Luther King, Jr., the works of Walker and Delaney serve as precursors to Marcus Garvey and Malcolm X.

During Reconstruction, Frances Harper, Pauline Hopkins, Anna Julia Cooper, Ida B. Wells, Paul Laurence Dunbar, Charles Chesnutt, Booker T. Washington, and W. E. B. Du Bois explore identity formation, effects of racial and gender oppression, education as a strategy for racial uplift, and racial violence. Many reconstruction writers challenged the newly developed stereotypes of blacks in mainstream literature and popular culture such as the black brute and the tragic mulatto in their poems, short stories, novels, and essays. Chesnutt, Harper, and Hopkins interrogate African American life in the South, construction of American identity, and the injustices associated with American class and caste systems. These writers explore the symbolic importance of the mixed-race person in American society and the black community. Similar to their predecessors, these authors argue against segregation and reveal race to be more a social construction than a biological fact.

Dunbar and Chesnutt elevate African American oral traditions through their use of dialect. Dunbar illustrates his mastery of black dialect and standard English in his poetry, and Chesnutt does the same in short stories and novels. Dunbar and Chesnutt serve as precursors to such African American writers as Langston Hughes, Zora Neale Hurston, Alice Walker, and Toni Morrison, who use folk idiom and celebrate African American culture, humor, folklore, and language in their writing.

Dunbar's "We Wear the Mask" (1895), "Sympathy" (1899), and "The Poet" (1903), three of his standard English poems, depict what Du Bois describes in *The Souls of Black Folk* (1903) as double consciousness and living behind the veil. In "Sympathy," a caged bird is a metaphor for African Americans who are caged by racism, the black codes, and changes in American society that further displaced all blacks. "We Wear the Mask" focuses on the trope of masking (how blacks veil their true desires and feelings in order to survive) found throughout African American literature. Masking appears in texts including James Weldon Johnson's *The Autobiography of an Ex-Colored Man*, Nella Larsen's *Passing* (1929), or Jessie Fauset's *Plum Bun* (1929) that foreground the passing theme. Masking also appears in such texts as *Uncle Tom's Children* (1938, 1940), Langston Hughes's *The Ways of White Folks* (1934), and Ralph

Ellison's *Invisible Man* (1952), which illustrate the consequences of revealing true feelings or overtly challenging the racist status quo. "The Poet" raises questions, posed later during the Harlem Renaissance and the black arts movement, about the role of the black artist and the conflict between art for art's sake and art as propaganda.

Anna Julia Cooper, Frances Harper, Pauline Hopkins, and Ida B. Wells feature the race problem and gender conflict in their work. African American women writing during Reconstruction were influenced by the proliferation of the African American women's club movement. These women show how the political and social aspects of art and racial uplift are inextricably linked to race, gender, and class concerns. For instance, Cooper critiques the cult of domesticity and racist ideology to argue for justice and equality, and she emphasizes the role of black women in the development of community. Wells's involvement in the suffragist, civil rights, and antilynching movements informed her writing. "Southern Horrors . . . " and "A Red Record . . . " (1895) provide scathing critiques of racial violence directed against blacks as a result of heightened racism, economic and political turmoil, and the racist sexual ideology of Reconstruction.

Booker T. Washington and Du Bois further explore diversity within the black community in terms of strategies for racial uplift and illustrate the instrumental role of blacks in the development of American intellectual thought, culture, and society. Washington's *Up from Slavery* (1901) continues the tradition of autobiography and details his program for improving the condition of African Americans. Washington uses accommodationist rhetoric to appeal to his white reading audience and appease their fears of an increasing black labor force. Du Bois, a prolific writer and dominant voice in intellectual thought, incorporates various genres in his seminal work, *The Souls of Black Folk*. Du Bois identifies and defines the psychological effects of living in a racist country by discussing double consciousness and living behind the veil. Du Bois identifies the problem of the twentieth century as being the problem of the color line, and this theme is addressed in most of the African American litera-

James Weldon Johnson, writer and educator, in a pastel by Winold Reiss, circa 1925.

ture that follows. As a race leader, Du Bois wielded great influence over turn-of-the-century black literature and the literature produced during the Harlem Renaissance. Beginning in 1900, Du Bois, along with others, encouraged young black artists by publishing their work in *Colored Magazine, The Crisis, Messenger,* and *Opportunity.*

Harlem Renaissance writers developed earlier themes including racial consciousness, antiviolence, women's rights, segregation, and integration. Writers including Langston Hughes, Zora Neale Hurston, and James Weldon Johnson celebrated African American culture in their work. Writing of the New Negro movement was informed by the great migration of blacks from the rural South to northern industrial areas, World War I, and the divergent views of race leaders such as Du Bois and Garvey. The patronage system, associated with Carl Van Vechten and Charlotte Osgood Mason, and interaction with white modernist writers also influenced black writers.

Writers of the Harlem Renaissance wrote poetry, novels, plays, short stories, and essays that explore self-determination and the psychological and social consequences of embracing or rejecting African

American cultural identity. Their writing also raises questions about the purpose of black art. The conflict between the aesthetic and propagandistic nature and the role of black art are examined in Alain Le Roy Locke's *The New Negro* and Hughes's "The Negro Artist and the Racial Mountain."

Although poetry was the dominant genre of the Harlem Renaissance, Johnson's *The Autobiography of an Ex-Colored Man* (1912) and Jean Toomer's *Cane* (1923) set the stage for prose. Johnson's work forces readers to consider how historical context and social circumstances inform the protagonist's choice to pass as white. Toomer's *Cane* blends literary genre, celebrates and utilizes folk traditions, explores effects of migration and urbanization, and suggests a return to understanding Southern black roots as a key to understanding history, culture, and individual and communal identity. Johnson and Toomer's influence is seen in the novels *Passing* and *Plum Bun,* the short story "Father and Son" (1933), the play *Colorstruck* (1925), and essays that explore social construction of race and the psychological consequences of racial passing. The antilynching theme in Johnson and Toomer's writing is reinscribed in works including Walter White's *The Fire in the Flint* (1924) and Richard Wright's short stories and novels.

Women of the Harlem Renaissance continued earlier work on the effects of social conventions and definitions of womanhood on black women. Fauset, Larsen, and Hurston examine caste, class formation, the institution of marriage, and power imbalances that are race, class, and gender based. Emphasis on class formation and conflict, employment discrimination, and effects of labor exploitation continues in works from the 1930s to the present by writers including Richard Wright, Anne Petry, Lorraine Hansberry, Gloria Naylor, and many others. Fauset and Larsen are among the writers who examine black life in the North, and they do not portray the North as a promised land.

Following the Harlem Renaissance the literature of the 1930s and the 1940s is primarily known as social protest literature. Wright, Petry, Gwendolyn Brooks, and Walker are among the writers whose

Writer James Baldwin at an outdoor cafe in the artistic community of St. Paul de Vence, France.

works reflect a black and proletariat aesthetic. Wright and Petry explore connections between the environment and self-development. Both of these writers expose causes and effects of poverty and urbanization; however, Wright highlights race, and Petry illustrates intersections of race, class, and gender. Protest writers employ realism to depict social, moral, and economic decay as the end result of racism.

During this period arguments about the purpose of black art were further developed by Richard Wright and later by Baldwin and Ellison. Wright attempts to develop a theoretical frame for black art in "Blue Print for Negro Writing" (1937). James Baldwin in "Everybody's Protest Novel" (1949) rejects the emphasis on protest as described by Wright. Baldwin's writing reflects themes found throughout black literature and emphasizes the role of church and religion in African American culture. Ellison rejects protest and blends realism, myth, and elements of folklore in *Invisible Man*. Ellison's text demonstrates that race marks blacks as both visible yet unseen in American culture.

One can contrast the literature produced in the 1950s with that of the 1960s in terms of shifts in the civil rights movement. Ellison, Baldwin, Brooks,

and Hansberry, to name a few, produced literature within a climate characterized by integration (*Brown* v. *Board of Education*) and a civil rights movement shaped by Martin Luther King, Jr.'s nonviolent resistance strategies, the Southern Christian Leadership Conference (SCLC), and the Congress of Racial Equality (CORE). During the 1960s a shift occurred in the movement owing in part to the development of black intellectual journals, black nationalism, and organizations such as the Black Panther Party, Revolutionary Action Movement (RAM), and the Nation of Islam.

Writers of the 1960s wrote poetry, drama, and social criticism focused on transforming black culture and reclaiming history and ties to the image of Africa. Literature by Amiri Baraka (LeRoi Jones), Sonia Sanchez, Etheridge Knight, Carolyn Rodgers, Nikki Giovanni, Brooks, and others stress the importance of rejecting cultural aspects and ideology associated with whites. Many of these writers describe internal colonization and celebrate the beauty of African American culture in their work. In defining the black aesthetic, these artists emphasize the connections between the artist, art, and the community, similar to such earlier writers as Hughes and Hurston.

As the black arts movement progressed and the second reconstruction (signaled by implementation of affirmative action in the mid-1960s and ending with the second election of Richard Nixon in 1972), there was a move away from depicting blacks as a monolithic group. Contemporary black writers from the 1970s to the present revisit earlier historical conditions, examine sexual identity, and use postmodern literary techniques to interrogate race, class, and gender. The 1970s also marked a resurgence of black women's literature. This proliferation in texts by black women coincides with the development of women's and African American studies programs and departments around the country. Ntozake Shange, Toni Morrison, Alice Walker, Gloria Naylor, Audre Lorde, and Toni Cade Bambara are a few of the women who developed texts focused on construction of black female identity, issues of domestic violence and child abuse within the black community, and the place of black women within the feminist and civil rights movements.

African Americans write in various genres today including poetry, novels, short stories, science fiction, and detective fiction. These authors often pay homage to black writers who came before. Contemporary authors interrogate the slave's experience in texts that build upon the slave-narrative tradition. Shirley Anne Williams's *Dessa Rose* (1986), Toni Morrison's *Beloved* (1987), and Sandra Jackson Opoku's *The River Where Blood Is Born* provide a much more interior view of the psychological effects of slavery and post-slavery than the original eighteenth- and nineteenth-century narratives. Along with revising the slave's narrative, contemporary writers continue to use autobiography to explore poverty, crime, and the benefits and disadvantages of affirmative action.

African American literature explores the complex process of self-definition for African Americans living in a society that essentially negates most of what defines African American culture, history, and diversity. Historically black authors have illustrated the causes and effects of psychic disruption within individuals and the community, and the purpose of the literature has been to effect cultural, social, and political change and raise the moral consciousness of all Americans.

[See also HARLEM RENAISSANCE.*]*

BIBLIOGRAPHY

Baraka, Amiri, *Black Fire: An Anthology of Afro-American Writing,* ed. by LeRoi Jones and Larry Neal (Morrow 1968).

Douglass, Frederick, *Narrative of the Life of Frederick Douglass, An American Slave,* ed. with an intro. by David W. Blight (St. Martin's 1993).

Du Bois, W. E. B., *The Souls of Black Folk* (Modern Library 1996).

Gates, Henry Louis, ed., *The Norton Anthology of African American Literature* (Norton 1996).

Jacobs, Harriet, *Incidents in the Life of a Slave Girl: Written by Herself,* ed. by L. Maria Child and Jean Fagan Yellin (Harvard Univ. Press 1987).

Lewis, David Levering, ed., *The Portable Harlem Renaissance Reader* (Viking 1994).

Morrison, Toni, *Beloved* (Thorndike Press 1987).

DEIRDRE RAYNOR

African American Music

Music has played notable and constitutive roles in African American life. As a means of generating cultural integrity in the face of hostility and oppression it continues to function in the social integration of black Americans. Additionally, African American musical conceptions have been crucial to the worldwide acceptance and influence of American popular music. These distinct but overlapping roles also form the broad outlines of African American musical history.

Initial Developments. Music was one of the few forms of coherent collective experience left to the newly arrived slaves, who typically lost their languages, families, religions, and social norms. Although drums were forbidden (as a potential form of secret communication), singing individually and collectively was tolerated. By the turn of the nineteenth century, African Americans were increasingly encouraged to become Christians. Congregational singing strengthened the development of English as a common language for the former Africans and of a newly integrated, genuinely African American musical culture. When even literacy was forbidden to the slaves, the churches furnished a forum to organize social and expressive values, especially through music. African American adaptations of neo-European psalm and hymn customs quickly saw distinctive variations emerge, such as the ring shout. Southern Protestant practices such as "lining out"—speaking the lines to illiterate congregants immediately before singing them—proved congruent with the "call-and-response" musical patterns familiar to many African cultures.

Plantation (and later sharecropping) experience allowed for the perpetuation of some African musical customs, such as rhythmically organized work through singing. Individualized forms of such neo-African expression as the field holler contributed directly to the eventually emergent musical aesthetics. Later codified in formal musical styles such as the blues, these secular expressions interchanged and exchanged with church practice, gradually shaping a broader but distinctive African American idiom.

While the overwhelming majority of African Americans remained rural and Southern, a free Northern urban population increased gradually but steadily. As Eileen Southern has documented, many of these African Americans found some part of a professional living from music making. The mid-nineteenth-century black-face minstrel show, initially a white mockery of black music and behavior, became a source of theatrical employment for black musicians in the decades after the Civil War and helped to lay the groundwork for a profession. With the concert presentation of spirituals by the Fisk Jubilee Singers, starting in the 1870s, African American music began an inexorable rise to autonomous attention. The culmination of these trends toward professionalization was the rise of ragtime, a predominantly urban, written idiom. Composers such as Scott Joplin saw their music's achievements as a sign of the intellectual and social status of black Americans. Joplin created an opera, *Treemonisha*, soon after the turn of the century, and many later African American composers devoted some or all of their efforts to the musics of European concert tradition. The turn-of-the century popularity of concert and dance bands embraced the success of black band leaders, especially James Reese Europe.

The economic integration of the rural South increased substantially after 1890. In the first decades of the new century, mass-produced, inexpensive musical instruments became available for purchase, especially guitars. Gramophones and radios followed. During this period a folk idiom called the blues gained popularity. An urban adaptation soon paralleled its rural development, associated especially with the work of composer W. C. Handy. Versions of the blues influenced by both streams became a repertory staple of black professional musicians in the 1910s and 1920s, especially such noted singers as Bessie Smith. Like Smith, most of the working, urban blues singers were women. For communities restricted in their choice of profession

by bigotry and stereotype, music (and later sports) became an important solution to the problem of survival, a solution at once integral and imposed.

Meanwhile, jazz developed in the longer-established black urban communities. Although its precise origins were disputed and subject to fable, jazz is agreed to represent a primarily instrumental musical confluence of ragtime, military brass band, minstrelsy, popular song, and social dance music. As the singing and playing of Louis Armstrong convincingly show, the predominant influence on jazz phrasing and rhythm is the vocal blues, with subsidiary influence from the music of the black churches. While ragtime and Handy's written blues form had already gained some attention in the northern United States, jazz captivated the entire country during the 1920s and after. LeRoi Jones (later known as Amiri Baraka) has argued that black innovations in music continued to reach the larger public primarily in attenuated white forms. The rise of jazz in concert, broadcast, and recording did, however, present direct contact for white Americans with African American musical expression. Musicians including Armstrong and Duke Ellington were national figures, and soon international musical celebrities, too.

Reactions and Interactions. Jazz quickly became an international symbolic expression of American culture. Intellectuals admired it and saw in it the vitality of a young nation. Others denounced it as a symptom of decadence and moral decline. British critic Constant Lambert praised Duke Ellington's imaginative exploits as a way out of the deadlocked situation of European composition, while countless moral guardians shrieked that jazz was the devil's music.

Both reactions find their roots in a longer history. In describing the development of U.S. folk music, American musicologist Charles Seeger posited four stages in the cultural encounter with an alien musical tradition: hostility, satirization, admiration, and adoption. White Americans initially regarded African American music as incoherent savagery. Soon the striking accomplishments in performing (neo-)European music by Northern freedmen and select slaves caused wonder. Almost from the outset, the crude depictions of African Americans in minstrel shows were mixed with sentimental portrayals of tender feeling and sensibility. These shows seldom offered any accurate musical reflection of their subjects, satirizing an imaginary musicality. By the Civil War some abolitionists with direct experience of black music came to a deep respect for it, if not a real understanding. The important volume *Slave Songs of the United States* (1867) speaks with reverence and frankly admits its authors' inability to represent the musical richness of what they have heard.

A substantial portion of the populace came to share in this admiration through the concert spirituals of the Fisk Jubilee Singers. The earliest forms of emulation of black music by white Americans can be traced back to the rural South. The most striking demonstration of this process is the history of the banjo. Originally an African string instrument, almost entirely abandoned by modern African Americans, it has become emblematic of white Southern bluegrass and hillbilly string music. Large-scale adoption of black music styles began at the turn of the twentieth century, as the emergent cauldron of Tin Pan Alley turned to black music. Sometimes this attention amounted to little more than a title such as "blues" or "rag," or the odd syncopation. Nevertheless, the composers began to listen and were soon followed by the performers. By the 1920s most professional musicians outside the concert hall likely had some direct aural experience of black music performance, at least through recordings or broadcasts. Jazz was the first type of substantially African American music to be adopted completely by some white musicians as their primary or even sole form of music making. Groups such as the New Orleans–based Original Dixieland Jazz Band, which became the first group to make a jazz recording in 1917, played jazz (and its parent musics) exclusively.

Although all four of Seeger's stages can be discerned today, the admiration and emulation of African American music has been a world phenomenon for many decades. Perhaps the most striking single innovation of African American music has been the development of the rhythm section, which combines the drum kit—military snare, bass, and tom-tom drums with various Middle Eastern cymbals—in close cooperation with a bass instrument such as the tuba, plucked string bass, or electric bass guitar. The rhythmic foundation of this seemingly limitless combination is a common factor in virtually every secular form of African American music outside the church (and, often enough, inside it as well). Today, most kinds of popular music in the world employ some textural variant of the rhythm section. African popular musics, too, have widely adopted this innovation.

Modern Developments. The key factors in twentieth-century African American musical growth continued to be urbanization and professionalization. The period of World War I saw an immense northern migration by black Americans. These new Northerners brought fresh inspiration from the flourishing blues styles, yet paradoxically they also tended to discard these traditional inclinations as vestiges of a crude, haunted past. During the 1920s and 1930s, the predominant professional forms of black music were small-group jazz and large-band swing, respectively, both of which digested rural influence to the point of complete assimilation. Recordings of early blues legends such as Blind Lemon Jefferson or Mississippi John Hurt were marketed largely to Southerners, who by the 1920s could often afford the small cost of a gramophone. Similarly, recordings of gospel groups and other religious music tended toward a demographic niche position in the industry.

Even such localized and specialized markets afforded many more African Americans the opportunity of a musical profession. Like their white counterparts in hillbilly music (as it was then termed), many musicians made a living by combining agricultural or urban labor with music performance, highly variable conditions in both fields permitting. Gradually but inexorably, rural musical values in all idioms declined in favor of urban professionalism—more consistent performances, disciplined arrangements, and performance standards, less casual surrender to the inspirations of the moment.

FRANK DRIGGS COLLECTION/ARCHIVE PHOTOS

Bandleader Cab Calloway in a pre–World War II performance.

The story of the blues is characteristic. During the Great Depression, record sales plummeted and many musicians were forced out of the business altogether. The postwar period saw the music revitalized in a new form. In the cities of both North and South, urban blues was played with electric guitars and bass, the standard drum kit of jazz bands, and a regularized song format of twelve bars replacing the freer stanza practice of earlier blues singers. At first popular largely within urban black communities, urban blues soon exploded as a dominant force in rock and roll and, especially through the adulatory efforts of young British musicians, in rock music as well. Though at times rejected within the black community as an embarrassing reminder of a peasant past—Muddy Waters was booed in Harlem in the late 1950s—the huge blues revival of the 1960s embraced black musicians and audiences as well. Leading exponents such as James Cotton, Buddy Guy, and Junior Wells found an enthusiastic public, if not the huge financial success of their white rock contemporaries. Like blues, black gospel music survives both autonomously and in countless transformed adaptations.

Jazz and Swing. Despite the Depression, the decades after World War I were largely good ones for black musicians. As the popularity of so-called hot jazz peaked and began to fade, larger dance bands playing swing music took their place in popular attention. LeRoi Jones's argument that white musicians profited from black creativity seems especially trenchant in the case of swing, but overlooks some significant developments of the period. Black and white musicians performed together publicly under the aegis of white bandleaders including Artie Shaw and Benny Goodman, who used their immense audience appeal in part to wrest a revolution in social mores. The swing era broadened the appeal of African American music to all Americans, in direct and indirect forms. Created almost entirely by musicians reading music notation, swing also brought the general skills of black and white musicians closer and paved the way for black participation in the lucrative recording-studio industry after the war.

Ironically, just as these homogenizing tendencies peaked, a genuine upheaval shook jazz. The mid-1940s "bebop" of Charlie Parker, Dizzy Gillespie, and Thelonious Monk was complex, intense, often very fast, highly oriented to improvisation and spontaneity, and initially baffling to many music lovers, black and white. In particular, bop broke the most obvious links to social dance

© DIANE WALKER/LIAISON AGENCY

Singer Lena Horne performing in 1983.

UPI/CORBIS-BETTMAN

Jazz great Dizzy Gillespie performing at a concert in Carnegie Hall in June 1988.

music, popular song, and church music. The one clear traditional holdover was the blues, which was never far from either the repertory or the musical styling of the boppers. Although earlier jazz had been admired as an artistic music, bebop made this status bluntly undeniable.

As the controversies died down in the next decade, they mollified the apparent breaches with the past, and even gospel gestures were audible in the "soul" jazz of Horace Silver, Julian Adderley, and others. Later developments in jazz extended these possibilities in many directions, for example, heightening the dimension of intellectual and artistic self-expression (1960s free jazz) and reclaiming some of the popularity of dance music (1970s fusion). Broadly speaking, postbop jazz represents the artistic wing of African American music.

Postwar Popular Musics. The striking influence of blues on virtually all forms of jazz was replicated in other popular forms. Early rock and roll was heavily based on black blues, and itself a form of black music, in the guise of popular innovators Little Richard, Fats Domino, and Chuck Berry. Rock and roll's rhythmic energy stemmed in part from swing, especially the "jump" style of Louis Jordan,

and from the dance style broadly termed rhythm and blues (R&B). The name points to the lively dance energy that led the record industry to bestow this name, and to the twin staples of the repertory, the twelve-bar blues and the thirty-two bar standard form of George Gershwin's "I Got Rhythm." If R&B and rock and roll were secular, adolescent dance musics, the influence of church returned in the 1960s. Aretha Franklin and James Brown, major figures of "soul" music, were well versed in a variety of musical styles, but both were strongly shaped by gospel singing.

A flexible fusion of church vocalizing, strong dance beat, tight ensemble playing, and blues phrasing held sway through the succession of popular black musics in the next few decades. With the success of Berry Gordy's Motown label, black music became a firm and direct part of the music business. The most notable shift was the rise of rap and hip-hop in the 1980s and 1990s. Initially owing to poverty, these musics drastically pared down the ensemble texture, sometimes employing just a drum beat and the scratch of a turntable needle. The emphasis in these styles was on poetic declamation, intensely styled by an aggressive groove. Often defiantly political, hip-hop is explicitly concerned with and addressed to the social issues of the urban black community.

Conclusions. Eugene Genovese has stressed the parallels of the African American experience to that of other Americans. Despite unique hardships endured by the African American community, past and present, the double-barrelled name points to a common identity. North American civilization is the greatest experiment in acculturation in human history, a vast exercise in improvised cultural self-generation. Like all other Americans, the black community has been obliged to invent itself. If persecution and tragedy have marked their social condition in that process, the result of their effort has been vital to the national whole. No definition of "American" can get further than a few words without mentioning the contribution of black Americans.

[See also HIP-HOP.]

BIBLIOGRAPHY

Allen, William Francis, Charles Pickard Ware, and Lucy McKim Garrison, *Slave Songs of the United States* (Applewood Bks. 1995).

Conway, Cecelia, *African Banjo Echoes in Appalachia: A Study of Folk Traditions* (Univ. of Tenn. Press 1995).

DeVeaux, Scott, "Constructing the Jazz Tradition: Jazz Historiography," *Black American Literature Forum,* 25 (1991):525–560.

Genovese, Eugene D., *Roll, Jordan, Roll: The World the Slaves Made* (Pantheon Bks. 1974).

Jones, LeRoi, *Blues People: Negro Music in White America* (Morrow 1963).

Lambert, Constant, *Music Ho! A Study of Music in Decline,* with an intro. by Arthur Hutchings, 3d ed. (Faber 1966).

Oliver, Paul, *Savannah Syncopaters: African Retentions in the Blues* (Studio Vista 1970).

Russell, Tony, *Blacks Whites and Blues* (Stein & Day 1970).

Seeger, Charles, "United States of America, II: Folk Music," vol. 19 of *The New Grove Dictionary of Music and Musicians,* ed. by Stanley Sadie (Grove Dictionaries of Music 1980).

Small, Christopher, *Music of the Common Tongue: Survival and Celebration in Afro-American Music* (Riverrun Press 1987).

Southern, Eileen, *The Music of Black Americans: A History,* 3d ed. (Norton 1997).

Southern, Eileen, ed., *Readings in Black American Music,* 2d ed. (Norton 1983).

MICHAEL W. MORSE

African Americans in Film and Theater

African American actors and actresses, appearing on stage or in movies, have symbolized black experience in the United States. Plays, television, and films have featured blacks in starring or supporting roles and explored racial themes. These media have had a powerful influence on Americans' perception of blacks. Nineteenth-century dramatic performances were mostly controlled and contrived, representing white views of African Americans. Gradually, during the first part of the twentieth century, some black actors and actresses expressed themselves independently. The Harlem Renaissance and 1930s federal relief programs enabled African Americans to gain access to creative opportunities. After the Depression, however, conservative elements of society reinforced racism, and blacks continued to play mostly stereotypical roles. Although the civil rights movement of the 1960s achieved educational and legal guarantees of equality, America's drama community assigned few roles to blacks in mainstream productions. By the 1980s several television series and movies had featured black families and protagonists, but not many actors and actresses were recognized with major awards for their talents. Almost two decades later, African Americans criticized the television and movie industries for consistently excluding minority actors and actresses from primetime shows and blockbuster films.

Milestones regarding Broadway and Hollywood's inclusion of African Americans cite specific actors and actresses achieving firsts. For example, Sam Lucas was the first African American to perform as a lead actor in a movie when he starred in the silent picture *Uncle Tom's Cabin* in 1914 (he also was the first black actor to play Uncle Tom on stage in 1878). Hattie McDaniel was the first African American Oscar winner when she was chosen best supporting actress for her performance in *Gone with the Wind* (1939); in 1954, Dorothy Dandridge was the first African American woman nominated for a best-actress Oscar; and Sidney Poitier was the first African American actor to win best actor for the 1963 movie *Lilies of the Field,* in which he was the sole black cast member. Black theater also had significant firsts, such as Charles Gardone, the first African American playwright to win a Pulitzer Prize for drama in 1969 for *No Place to Be Somebody,* and Charles Sidney Gilpin and Ethel Waters, who were the first blacks to play leading roles on major American stages. Willis Richardson was the first African American playwright to have a play produced on Broadway (*The Chip Woman's Fortune,* 1923).

The Metaphorical Silence of Early African American Drama.

African American drama began in antebellum America, primarily in the form of traveling minstrel shows featuring white actors in blackface or African American groups such as the Ethiopian Serenaders and Georgia Minstrels. Free blacks in the North enjoyed theater. In 1821 the African Company began performing in New York City, and two of that company's distinguished actors, James Hewlett and Ira Aldridge, became prominent Shakespearean performers in England. One of the African Company's notable plays was Henry Brown's *The Drama of King Shotaway* (1823).

In the South enslaved blacks were forbidden to read and write, limiting their opportunities for public expression. Also, strict labor demands and black codes prevented many African Americans from having recreational time to travel to theaters. Blacks in slave quarters may have informally performed dramatic skits, often based on folklore and oral tradition, representing their daily experiences and dreams of freedom.

Nineteenth-century white playwrights rarely included black characters except to provide comic relief or emphasize white characters' superiority by comparison. Most theater managers believed that white audiences would not be interested in African American issues and thus encouraged theatrical troupes to omit those parts or only present patronizing images. Whenever possible, African American drama groups presented vaudeville and ragtime routines at both mainstream and black theaters. The Pekin Theater, which opened in Chicago in 1905, was the first stage owned and managed by African Americans.

As film technology advanced in the late nineteenth century, African Americans remained on the periphery. Thomas Edison invented the Kinetoscope, which was used to make short silent films shown mainly in nickelodeons. Racist reels disrespectfully portrayed blacks, such as the 1894 film *Pickaninnies*. Black actors and directors were subtly present, often as extras, during the silent-film era (an ironic metaphor for the imposed social silencing of African Americans) but lacked substantial creative control. American movies mostly excluded blacks as actors, writers, and crew members through the 1940s. Many filmmakers believed that white audiences would be apathetic toward African American movies or be uncomfortable with Af-

rican American subject matter and themes, especially if blacks represented authority figures.

When black characters were shown, such as Stepin Fetchit, played by Lincoln Perry, they were depicted as servants, comical simpletons, or unsavory oafs demeaningly caricatured as passive, feeble-brained, and irrationally relying on illogical beliefs and folk tales. Initially, white actors in blackface portrayed African Americans in early films. White directors used black characters to reinforce racist imagery, represent blacks as puerile or villainous, and suggest to audiences that African Americans preferred being subjugated by whites. Most films that included blacks presented contradictions, for example showing only negative traits and emphasizing comedy while ignoring drama. Many talented actors, such as Nina Mae McKinney, the first African American leading lady, were unable to express fully their dramatic abilities.

D. W. Griffith created films that included black characters (played by white actors) to perpetuate his bigoted biases. *His Trust* and *His Trust Fulfilled* (1911), set during the Civil War, depicted a loyal black slave willingly and devotedly sacrificing his best interests to serve his masters. Griffith's best-known movie is *The Birth of a Nation* (1915), a white-supremacist propaganda piece that displayed such intense racism and radical characterization of blacks that a public backlash resulted in fewer black roles in mainstream movies, except for minor parts. *The Birth of a Nation* also was the catalyst for the establishment of a separate African American film industry that made and marketed "race films" specifically for African American audiences. Exploring themes of social persecution, panic, and helplessness, these movies, in addition to plays, realistically portrayed African American issues and attempted to correct the lies perpetuated in Griffith's film. While trying to improve the quality of life and respect within the African American community, black filmmakers were also interested in profiting financially like their white counterparts.

Actor Noble Johnson formed the Lincoln Motion Picture Company, the first African American movie studio, in 1916. The Lincoln Motion Picture

Company consisted almost entirely of black actors and crew members and produced several movies that were notable for being the first film portrayals of African Americans as ordinary people with realistic daily problems and concerns. The company's first film, *The Realization of a Negro's Ambition* (1916), follows the tribulations of a young engineer who left his family farm after graduating from the Tuskegee Institute in Alabama. More than three hundred African American extras were hired for the filming of *A Trooper of Troop K* (1917), about the massacre of black Army troops affiliated with the Tenth Cavalry in the 1916 campaign against Mexican outlaws. Noble Johnson's brother George promoted the movies for viewing in African American churches, schools, and segregated movie houses, but white financial backer P. H. Updike was concerned about monetary gains. George Johnson reserved an auditorium and marketed showings of *By Right of Birth*. Despite large attendances, the Johnsons and Updike determined that white audiences were not interested in African American movies and that such widespread support was necessary for the company to survive. The Lincoln Motion Picture Company closed in 1921.

From the late 1910s through the 1940s, Oscar Micheaux became a prominent African American filmmaker. He produced approximately thirty-five silent and sound movies, primarily using black performers. African American actors who began their careers with Micheaux included Paul Robeson in *Body and Soul* (1925). A novelist, Micheaux had discussed film production of his books with the Johnson brothers. Unwilling to relinquish creative control, Micheaux decided instead to form an independent film company and became one of the most successful African American film producers, showing blacks in nonstereotypical situations and expressing universal human emotions. His characters questioned the politics of racism between blacks and whites and between blacks and blacks. Assimilation was a theme that Micheaux broached. He also depicted black characters who were authority figures and commanded respect from people of all races.

Micheaux's first movie, *The Homesteader* (1919), portrays rural experiences on the American prairie. He then distributed *Within Our Gates* (1919), which graphically depicts a lynching and a rape. Although many contemporaries thought that this movie represented Micheaux's response to *The Birth of a Nation*, he insisted that the film chronicled the racism that confronted African Americans. His images were so powerful that Chicago church leaders, both black and white, attempted to halt screenings of the movie in that city because they were scared that race riots, which had occurred earlier that year, might flare up again. Additional censorship efforts resulted in Micheaux eventually pulling the film from public viewing.

The Lincoln Motion Picture Company and the Micheaux Film Corporation inspired other independent African American filmmakers to establish businesses to produce race films in large urban centers as well as in smaller cities such as St. Louis, Missouri, and Jacksonville, Florida. These studios included the Big New Colored Company and Colored Players Film Corporation. In 1929 there were 461 segregated movie houses in the United States. The term *midnight ramble* was coined to refer to the late hours that films were shown for African Americans in some public theaters. By the 1930s, Hollywood recognized the potential for financial gain and started to produce movies specifically for African Americans. Most black filmmakers could not compete with entrenched movie moguls, and Micheaux was one of the last African American distributors of race films working in the 1940s.

Black stage actors and playwrights experienced similar struggles. African American theaters, including New York City's Apollo, featured such outstanding performers as Charles Sidney Gilpin, who became the first black actor to star in a major dramatic role in a mainstream theater when he appeared in *The Emperor Jones* (1920). The Harlem Renaissance gave voice to African American playwrights and actors. Black playwrights Willis Richardson, Angelina Grimké, and Langston Hughes crafted scripts especially for African American performers. Alain Locke promoted the establishment of a national African American theater movement, and college and high school theater groups participated in drama competitions. Community theater became popular in black neighborhoods, and the Federal Theater Project, sponsored by the Works Progress Administration from 1935 to 1939, enabled blacks to explore dramatic expression. African American stage actors successfully crossed over to film roles, and some whites, such as Orson Welles who directed a black cast in a version of *Macbeth* set in Haiti, at Harlem's Lafayette Theatre, invested time and money in black stage productions. White theater fans often attended plays performed by African American companies.

Sound Bites of Modern African American Drama. The antebellum-era epic *Gone with the Wind* (1939) paradoxically perpetuated stereotypes of African Americans as being servile, silly, and helpless, while also representing a transition of black actors and actresses securing more significant roles in mainstream films and plays. This trend continued during World War II because the federal government wanted to encourage African Americans to assist the war effort. Movies such as *The Negro Soldier* (1944) tried to increase the black community's pride in African Americans participating in military service despite segregation. All-black musicals, such as *Stormy Weather* (1943) and *Cabin in the Sky* (1943), on film and on Broadway, featured Lena Horne, Bill "Bojangles" Robinson, Cab Calloway, and jazz musicians who boosted patriotism. Paul Robeson became the first African American to play Othello with a white cast in 1943.

Fewer stereotyped characters were portrayed on film during the 1940s, and black actors became more vocal in protesting racist scenes and dialogue. African Americans playing supporting roles, such as the part of Sam in *Casablanca* (1942), were freed from some traditionally held racial expectations of white directors including Otto Preminger. An African American boxer in *The Set Up* (1949) was shown to be the opposite of the greedy, corrupt whites associated with that sport. Other movies from the post–World War II era, such as *Intruder in the Dust* (1949) and *To Kill a Mockingbird* (1962), attempted to explore authentically and sensitively racial views and

interactions between blacks and whites. African American stars such as Sidney Poitier achieved success with mainstream audiences during the 1960s and 1970s. Charles Lampkin was the first African American actor with a significant role in a science-fiction film, appearing in *Five* (1951). African American movies began to receive major awards, including *Porgy and Bess* (1959), with Dandridge, Poitier, Sammy Davis, Jr., and Pearl Bailey, winning a Golden Globe for best musical and an Oscar for best music.

Independent filmmakers and theater companies consistently produced the most truthful accounts of African Americans. Scored with African American blues and jazz (and sometimes choreographed with traditional dance steps), these performances had cultural integrity lacking in other productions. A recognizable black genre had emerged by the 1970s. Gordon Parks's *Shaft* (1971) featured Richard Roundtree in the title role, the first African American private detective and superhero to appear in film. Sometimes the term *blaxploitation* was used to describe such movies because critics felt that black actors and themes were exploited by the white movie industry. Warner Brothers distributed Melvin Van Peebles's *Sweet Sweetback's Baadasss Song* (1971), which critics found to symbolize the rage and frustration of African American filmmakers striving to maintain creative independence from societal restraints.

The civil rights and black power movements resulted in more African Americans working in Hollywood, but few blacks were attaining authority positions to make decisions. Van Peebles was one of the first black filmmakers to attract white viewers. Although blacks often were included in movies, sitcoms, and plays during this period, their roles primarily remained minor, stereotyped, and spurious representations of African American experiences. White filmmakers created such movies as *Sounder* (1972) and *Lady Sings the Blues* (1982) about black characters, which, to achieve commercial success, portrayed white, more than black, cultural realities. Many filmmakers were faced with the dilemma of how to make movies that would appeal to mainstream audiences yet accurately describe Af-

ALFRED EISENSTAEDT/LIFE MAGAZINE © TIME, INC.

Gordon Parks, photographer, filmmaker, composer, and writer, was awarded a National Medal of Arts in 1988.

rican American themes and identities. Some films, attempting to provoke viewer reaction, were didactic forms investigating black and white perceptions of how African Americans are treated in the United States, including *A Minor Altercation* (1977). Other films pushed the edge, including *Guess Who's Coming to Dinner?* and *In the Heat of the Night* (1967) with Sidney Poitier, and *The Great White Hope* (1970) with James Earl Jones.

The black arts movement of the 1960s and 1970s witnessed the creation of such outstanding dramatic groups as Barbara Ann Teer's National Black Theater. African American theatrical performances continued to receive mainstream critical acclaim. The first African American woman to write a Broadway show, Lorraine Hansberry created *A Raisin in the Sun* (1961), which won praise for the performances of its cast, including Poitier, Ruby Dee, and Louis Gossett, Jr. August Wilson wrote interconnected plays exploring African American identity in the twentieth century and accurately depicting the vernacular and brutal reality of inner city life. The notable women who emerged during the 1980s were Ruby Dee, the first black actress invited to perform at the American Shakespeare Festival, and

Maya Angelou, a pioneering black female playwright and Tony Award–winning actress. Other significant productions during this period include *The Wiz* (1978), an African American version of *The Wizard of Oz,* and the televised movie *Roots* (1977), based on Alex Haley's novel of the same name, which captured America's attention because of its focus on ancestral origin.

Mainstream movies such as *Ghosts of Mississippi* (1996) continued to feature white heroes rescuing black victims from racism and injustice, thus minimizing white violence. The white leads were in the forefront, while blacks were pushed to the background. African Americans expressed outrage when *The Color Purple* (1985), based on Alice Walker's novel, did not win Academy Awards. Some gains were made, however. Euzham Palcy became the first female African American director of a major film (*A Dry White Season,* 1989), and John Singleton was the first black film director to be nominated for an Oscar (*Boyz 'N the Hood,* 1991). Actors and actresses including Denzel Washington, Laurence Fishburne, Wesley Snipes, Ossie Davis, Whoopi Goldberg, Angela Bassett, Cicely Tyson, Danny Glover, Morgan Freeman, Cuba Gooding, Jr., Vanessa Williams, and Oprah Winfrey starred

UPI/CORBIS-BETTMANN

Playwright August Wilson, author of the award-winning plays *Fences* (1987) and *The Piano Lesson* (1990).

in movies that appealed to racially mixed audiences and were recognized with industry honors.

Director Spike Lee brought an authentic voice to his film representations of modern African American culture, society, and experiences. He portrayed fully developed, realistic black characters who were devoid of stereotyping; his films featured topics that interested the black community. Because of his directing skills and creativity, Lee, who also acted in his films, became a significant and influential filmmaker. He won awards at the Cannes film festival and was nominated for Academy Awards, earning recognition from mainstream cinematic leaders. Although critics mostly praised his work, especially the films *She's Gotta Have It* (1986), *School Daze* (1988), *Do the Right Thing* (1989), and *Clockers* (1995) and the documentary *4 Little Girls* (1997), Lee has also been criticized for stereotyping Hispanics. Also, some African Americans protested Lee's direction of *Malcolm X* (1992), disagreeing with his presentation of violence and describing his work as exploitative. Other blacks were uncomfortable with Lee's depiction of discrimination within the black community.

Lee applied his film technique to music videos and commercials and promoted products and books related to his films. He proved that films produced and directed by African Americans with black actors and themes could earn box-office profits and appeal to audiences of all races. In addition, he showed the film industry the marketing importance of black movie patrons. Because of Lee's success, young African American filmmakers benefited from more opportunities, and some black figures such as Malcolm X became mythic to many filmgoers. Lee's films were the catalyst for several African American actors' successful film careers.

Scholarly studies and documentaries on the evolution of African American theater and film have included *Small Steps, Big Strides: The Black Experience in Hollywood (1903–1970)*. Black film centers and archives exist at Howard University, Indiana University, and Wayne State University, among others. Many of these schools also sponsor Internet sites with information, documents, movie trailers, and links. Founded in 1973, the Black Filmmakers Hall of Fame in Oakland, California, has strived to empower African Americans with culturally authentic dramatic images and to preserve films and artifacts about blacks working on and off stage.

BIBLIOGRAPHY

Anderson, Lisa M., *Mammies No More: The Changing Image of Black Women on Stage and Screen* (Rowman & Littlefield 1997).

Cripps, Thomas, *Making Movies Black: The Hollywood Message Movie from World War II to the Civil Rights Era* (Oxford 1993).

Gray, Christine Rauchfuss, *Willis Richardson, Forgotten Pioneer of African-American Drama* (Greenwood Press 1999).

Hamalian, Leo, and James V. Hatch, eds., *The Roots of African American Drama: An Anthology of Early Plays, 1858–1938,* foreword by George C. Wolfe (Wayne State Univ. Press 1991).

Jones, G. William, *Black Cinema Treasures: Lost and Found* (Univ. of N.Tex. 1991).

Moon, Spencer, *Reel Black Talk: A Sourcebook of 50 American Filmmakers* (Greenwood Press 1997).

Turner, Darwin T., ed., *Black Drama in America: An Anthology,* 2d ed. (Howard Univ. Press 1994).

ELIZABETH SCHAFER

African American Dance

African American dance is unique to the United States because it draws together performing styles that, until the 1920s, were aesthetically, racially, politically, and socially divided. Following the Civil War, cultural suppression and economic repression prevented black Americans from performing in dance venues considered high art: the opera, ballet, and artistic dancing. The training of pre-twentieth-century dancers was linked to European classical ballet. But this training was closed to slaves who, if agile and adept, were trained to blend tribal rhythms and ballroom rhythms, work songs and spirituals along with ballroom quadrilles and marches. A decisive strutting, stomping dance style, which evolved from the cakewalk, was originally a prize dance that became indigenous to blackface minstrels and vaudeville.

Fayard Nicholas (*left*) and Harold Nicholas, the tap dancing team of stage and screen.

By the 1840s, a minstrel format of the olio act evolved, similar to a variety show, with an emphasis on lowbrow satire and slapstick burlesque. At first most of the troupes, such as the Christy Minstrels, were white performers in blackface makeup. Not until the 1880s did all-black shows, such as *The Creole Show,* begin to emerge. Dances coming from these showcases were the Cake Walk, Juba, Pigeon Wing, and Possum Walk. Today, one can recognize the West African and Trinidadian origins of early dances. From these dances tap dancing evolved, a staple of vaudeville and musical-comedy productions to this day.

Many black dancers and musicians migrated in the 1920s to Europe, where they were popular attractions and where there was little of the overt stereotyping or bigotry that was rampant in the United States. Black entertainers in the United States were demeaned through white popular-culture acts based on racial stereotypes and a format satirizing plantation life and African customs. Early American films, notably D. W. Griffith's *Birth of a Nation* (1915), heightened the varied fears many whites had concerning the freed slave population. Consequently classical dance venues were closed to blacks, al-

though middle-class black families provided European-influenced training in dance and music to their children.

Throughout the twentieth century a black aesthetic was assimilated into mainstream American culture. Certain characteristics of an African American style of concert performance emerged, later regarded under the rubric of African American dance, a specific genre of concert dance. In African-inspired dances, a synergy between the rhythmic pattern and feel in the music and the detailed movements of the body establish a dialogue (usually in call-and-response form). Such dancer-music dialogues are recognized even today in African-inspired social dances that can be traced to particular tribal rituals, particularly those of West and East Africa.

In African American dance the whole body is involved, with an emphasis on movement within the central core of the torso and pelvis. Movement flows through the body like water and makes visual the dancer's physical effort by sharply contrasting postures, gestures, and focus. Historically, male and female movements and gestures are gender coded, differing in intention, style, focus, and dynamics. Jacqui Malone writes, "A tendency to 'dance the song' in traditional African cultures was preserved in the secular and sacred expression of U.S. slaves. Spirituals were always sung with some degree of body motion." In contrast, European-style social dances were formally codified to emphasize a comparatively upright posture with a less active central core of the body. The movements are differentiated by varied step patterns that underscore the music's underlying rhythm, form, and style more than the emotions of the music.

African American dancers maintain a grounded connection to the floor or earth. Natural body postures diminish the artificiality of theatrical illusions and gather the audience's emotions into the dance. It is an intimate, personal experience. Viewers and dancers feel the movement coming from the floor as though it were a huge drum beaten by the feet. The dancer is not so concerned with presenting formal beauty as he or she is with feeling and expressing the radiation of energy in a deeply personal way. The supple sensuality of the body, emanating boldly from a fully articulated spine and pelvis to the ends of the limbs, involves the viewer in a visceral experience. Black historian Edward Thorpe writes, "The beauty of Black dance lies in its total lack of inhibition."

However, not until 1921, with the advent of the Harlem Renaissance, did the first all-black production, *Shuffle Along,* open on Broadway. Several other musicals featured black dancers and singers, so blacks began to move from the entertainment venues into the theater. Such dances as the Big Apple, Charleston, one step, buzzard's lope, Suzie Q, lindy hop, camel walk, and others that grew from the social dances in dance halls, speakeasies, public ballrooms, and marathon dances appear, for example, in F. Scott Fitzgerald's 1920s classic, *The Great Gatsby.* Black colloquial dance terms merged with the American vernacular. *Jazzin' it, bebop, jitterbug, cuttin' a rug, goose bumps, time step, shim-sham, in the groove,* and *swing* are just a few examples. Blacks were welcomed by American modern dancers, many of whom were ardent socialists. In turn, black dancers embraced the philosophies and practices of American modern dance. Particularly compelling were those modern dance themes of the 1930s associated with the social activism and the symbolic expressionism of dancer Martha Graham.

The first professional black American dance company was the Hampton Creative Dance Group, which toured to New York City in 1928. In 1931 Chicago-based dancer Katherine Dunham organized a troupe called Ballet Negre, soon renamed the Chicago Dance Group. That was followed by Eugene Von Grona (a white student of Mary Wigman in Germany) who founded the American Negro Ballet (ANB) in 1934; he was intrigued by the spirit and dance energy of black dancers performing in Harlem clubs. The company was the first to receive critical review and draw media attention. Yet, it was not a classical ballet company; rather the ANB performed modern dances choreographed by Von Grona in the German expressionistic style tinged by the social consciousness prevalent in New York.

In 1933 the Negro Art Theatre Dance Group appeared in *Run L'il Chillun* in a dance choreographed by white modern dancer Doris Humphrey. Later Hemsley Winfield choreographed the operatic version of Eugene O'Neill's *The Emperor Jones.* From the mid-1930s African American dance received exposure and support from President Franklin D. Roosevelt's New Deal.

Musicals of the 1930s blended black dance styles into the choreography of white choreographers and the performances of white dancers who were often coached by uncredited black dancers. Movies educated white audiences about the spectacular virtuosity and rhythmic physicality of African American dance with featured solos by such dancers and singers as Lena Horne, Bill Robinson, Ethel Waters, Whitey's Lindy Hoppers, Cab Calloway, and the Nicholas Brothers. Beginning in the 1960s television shows such as *Soul Train* and later *MTV* (Music Television) provided to American postwar youth similar crossover exposure to new black rhythm and blues, Motown, and rock and roll music and dances.

The connection between social protest and the emergence of an African American concert style was fostered through the socialist New Dance Group in New York, where black dancers were welcomed and nurtured. Pearl Primus's first work, *African Ceremonial,* was performed in 1943 along with two Depression-era dances of protest, *Strange Fruit* and *Hard Time Blues.*

Teacher-choreographer Edna Guy and black colleges, such as Spelman College, Fisk University, and Howard University, organized creative dance groups. The New Dance Group was a gathering place for serious black and white dancers who worked with the great modern dancers of that time: Anna Sokolow, Donald McKayle, Helen Tamiris, Daniel Nagrin, Jack Cole, Talley Beatty, Eleo Pomare, and many others. They built on the inspiration of Asadata Dafora who had immigrated to the United States from Trinidad in 1929 to perform African tribal-based plots and African instruments. His *Kykunkor* (1934) was a revelation to black and white audiences and dancers. Each dance contributed to the text, depicting various village events and moods.

Katherine Dunham (*center*), dancer, anthropologist, and choreographer, in 1936.

It crossed a threshold making it possible for dancers to move away from exploited idiosyncrasies and codified stereotypes to portray real characters.

At the same time Katherine Dunham established the New Negro Art Dancers for an evening of ceremonial dances and Guy's dance spirituals. Soon after, Dunham returned to Chicago to direct the Negro Unit of the Federal Theatre Project. Back in New York, after successful national touring, Dun-

ham organized another dance troupe and a studio, spurred by her Broadway and film successes, such as *Stormy Weather* and *Cabin in the Sky*.

In 1943 Dunham, holding a degree in anthropology, choreographed one of her masterworks, *Rites de Passage*, a dance inspired by her study and life in Haiti, which celebrates the role of ceremonials to mark important transitions in human experience. In her memoirs of her years in Haiti, *Island Pos-*

sessed (1969), Dunham writes, "Of my kind I was a first—a lone young woman easy to place in the clean-cut American dichotomy of color, harder to place in the complexity of Caribbean color classifications." When she opened her New York studio in 1945, Dunham's mission was to "develop a technique that will be as important to the white man as to the Negro. . . . To take our dance out of the burlesque—to make it a more dignified art." In 1946 *Bal Negre* opened in New York, and Dunham was called "the best dancer in America today" by the *New York News.* Her autobiography, *A Touch of Innocence,* appeared in 1959.

In 1943 one of Dunham's dancers, Donald McKayle, created *Games,* a modern dance work that showed how urban children of all nationalities and races create their own little societies. In 1947 Talley Beatty's riveting solo, *Mourner's Bench,* was drawn from episodes in which murdered black farmers were buried by moonlight and mourned in secret. In the 1950s black choreographers more graphically and angrily attacked racism and made inroads into the deeply segregated theater world. McKayle's career was boosted when he assisted Jerome Robbins on the choreography for *West Side Story* in 1958. The following year McKayle choreographed *Rainbow 'Round My Shoulder,* a dance inspired by dramatic, emotional themes of labor camps in Alabama and Mississippi.

According to Brenda Dixon-Gottschild, "much of the vilification of Africanist culture . . . is focused on the black body, the dancing body, the grounded, freely articulated body [that is] charged with tension." Slowly black dancers broke through the barriers of racially biased aesthetic standards. These barriers were rigidly framed by body image, acceptable genres, themes, choreographic structures, performance style, and costumes. Another dancer-anthropologist, Pearl Primus, and Percival Borde created *Dark Rhythm,* a work influenced by Primus's research in West Africa. Primus's mission was unique in that she sought to "discover, restore, revive, and expand African dance and allied cultures." Following in her footprints, in the 1960s modern dancer Chuck Davis traveled to West Africa to study his ancestral roots and to intertwine tribal tradi-

tions and artmaking into a style later found in his company, the African-American Dance Theatre. Through his company, Davis has committed his personal life to promote "interest in and teach young black people the art of classical ballet, modern, and ethnic dance."

Alvin Ailey's *Blues Suite* (1958) looked at the social life in the inner city and in *Revelations* (1960) he explored the deeply felt spirituality that was born in the church to express the pain, yearning, and hope of African American people. Unlike Ailey, McKayle, Primus, and Dunham, all of whom sought themes that would speak universally, educate audiences, and inspire black children, other choreographers were more angry in their works, emphasizing the social politics of the black power movement. These choreographers faced the issues of dynamic racial conflict that charged the political and cultural arenas: Rod Rogers, Eleo Pomare, Talley Beatty, Bill T. Jones, Blondell Cummings, and Ulysses Dove.

During the 1940s Dunham was joined by black ballet companies both in New York and California. In 1947 Joseph Rickard, a white ballet master, organized the First Negro Classic Ballet, which toured the West Coast. In the 1950s the New York Negro Ballet, and later Ballet Americana, performed and toured Europe. Between 1951 and 1954 Janet Collins was the first black ballerina with New York's Metropolitan Opera Ballet (in Beatty's words, "She was the best in the world"). In 1963–1964, Dunham's choreography for *Aida* marked the first time a black person choreographed for New York's Metropolitan Opera Company. Ten years later she choreographed the reconstruction of Scott Joplin's *Treemonisha* for the Houston Opera.

It was not until Arthur Mitchell was invited by George Balanchine to join the New York City Ballet in 1956 that black dancers began to find their way permanently into white-dominated classical ballet; however, his performing career was eclipsed in 1968 by the assassination of Martin Luther King, Jr. That same year Mitchell founded the Dance Theatre of Harlem (DTH). An aesthetic parallel to the civil rights movement, DTH challenged the structure of ballet, as defined by the dominant culture, by documenting the core strength and power of ballet as open and universal. Under Mitchell's direction, Virginia Johnson joined Janet Collins as a ranking American prima ballerina. By the end of the 1960s, dancers of color integrated a number of dance companies. Some of these pioneers include Matt Turner, Mary Hinkson, and Clive Thompson with the Martha Graham Dance Company; John Jones with the Joffrey Ballet; Louis Johnson with the New York City Ballet; and Carmen de Lavallade with Ballet Theatre.

Nine years earlier, in 1960, Alvin Ailey's American Dance Theatre struggled into existence as a voice and venue for the work of almost lost black choreographers, such as Dunham, Primus, Beatty, Rod Rodgers, McKayle, and Ailey himself. Outstanding dancers included Dudley Williams, Judith Jamison, Thelma Hill, Lavallade, and Georgia Collins. Ailey's *Blues Suite*, set to jazz music, and *Revelations*, performed to Negro spirituals, established a tone for the African American choreographic voice. Through the choreography and performances of Ailey's mixed-race company, consistent attributes of African American concert dance style and themes were richly textured with issues of the human spirit, communal and conversational culture, gender-influenced gestures and movement, deep physicality, emotion-rich dramas, and African-influenced rhythms.

By the end of the 1960s, black female dance teachers played key roles in fostering regional companies. In Dallas, Ann Williams formed the Dallas Black Dance Theatre; in Dayton, Ohio, Jeraldyne Blunden organized the Dayton Contemporary Dance Company; Joan Myers Brown founded Philadanco in Philadelphia; and Cleo Parker Robinson formed the Cleo Parker Robinson Dance Theatre in Denver, Colorado. A more recent addition is Willa Jo Zollar's Urban Bushwomen.

By the 1970s, with the support of the National Endowment for the Arts and state and local agencies, black dance performance spread across the United States, particularly in urban centers heavily populated by black Americans. Black pride, community, and diaspora themes characterize the 1970s

and 1980s. Geoffrey Holder created *Dougla Suite* for Dance Theatre of Harlem, which depicts a Trinidadian wedding ceremony, while Beatty's *The Stack-Up* depicts cool youths partying until the neighborhood pusher entraps them into another form of social oppression. The Bill T. Jones/Arne Zane Dance Company, originally the American Dance Asylum, encouraged mixed-race communal companies.

American culture in the 1980s was more inclusive in that African American dance was a recognized style, mixed-race dance companies were commonplace, and contemporary black repertory had diversified considerably. The democratic pluralism of dance in the 1960s inspired a new generation of black dancers who no longer felt the need to define African American dance as a category of dance practice, or to assert the dignity of the black dance artist. Mitchell juxtaposed the motif of marriage from two different cultural traditions by restaging the romantic ballet master work, retitled *Creole Giselle*. Since the 1980s his choreography addressed issues of personal identity and asserted more individual credos. Jones worked with issues of myth and death in *Still/Here*. David Rousseve merged contemporary dance with African American pop music, singers, and family coming-of-age rituals. Bebe Miller danced resoundingly to African drum rhythms, as did Kariamu Welsh Asante, Zollar, and Chuck Davis. Zollar's company, Urban Bushwomen, synthesizes the spiritual influences of her upbringing with a concern for the history and day-to-day life of African Americans; and Blondell Cummings focuses on the disparity between the promise of equality and the reality of African American women.

Although black history and studies were prevalent at most universities, not until 1982 did dancers convene for the first Black American Dance Festival at the prestigious Brooklyn Academy of Music. This event was followed by the American Dance Festival sponsorship of the Black Tradition in American Modern Dance project, later a major repository of black dance-performance history.

At the beginning of the twenty-first century, black choreographers remain concerned with the human condition, expressed through works that describe the unique black experience and draw audiences in to a collective humanity through shared experiences. Sean Curran, a white dancer who performed with the Bill T. Jones/Arne Zane Company for eight years, observed how the sense of community and a concern for individual dancers within the company spilled over into the choreography and vice versa.

The role of the elder in society is mirrored in the role of the choreographer, or artistic director, who, as a kind of griot, is a respected, wise storyteller and myth-maker. Black American concert dance rarely centers on sheer entertainment, although rebelliousness, rhythmic sassiness, and physical pleasure in syncopated and polyrhythmic movements create a dialogue with the music to build an of-the-people authenticity, a key aesthetic element. Individual choreographers inspire with tightly formed works in what is now considered the African American style. These choreographers include the late Ulysses Dove, Cummings, Jamison, Jones, Zollar, Garth Fagan, Davis, and Rousseve. When Jones's partner, Arnie Zane, died of complications from AIDS (acquired immune deficiency syndrome), Jones's works took on a deeper resonance of grief; the first piece he made following Zane's death, *Absence* (1988), outed the issue of homosexual love. Another issue that Jones blasted open included that of the body and its mass. He writes, "My dancing is leaping over a terrain that keeps changing."

Many contemporary dance artists, particularly Cummings, Zollar, Dove, Donald Byrd, and Rousseve, focus their works as explanations of black heritage and of the deep, prevailing hurt caused by years of enslaved degradation while ennobling unique attributes and positive values for black audiences. Jones's *The Last Supper of Uncle Thomas* is an unusual mix of symbols, including Leonardo Da Vinci's painting *The Last Supper* and Harriet Beecher Stowe's troubling antislavery novel, *Uncle Tom's Cabin*. Dove's *Vespers* exemplifies the empowered black woman. Feminist black dancers helped to amplify the mission of the women's liberation movement beyond the white woman's experience to embrace women of color. They contextualized the black struggle with gender-specific issues.

How is African American dance a specific genre of expression? The deep connection between dancers and the music bursts across the footlights to engulf the audience. The audience directly participates. Soul, emotion, and the black experience in America set a tone for another unique dialogue (one with a deep spiritual reality), whether that be with the Christian church, with ancestral rituals, or with the downtrodden and lost souls who populate the inner city's seedy clubs and music joints. The dances of Jamaican choreographer Garth Fagan, like those of Holder, combine formal modern dance and ballet with resonating black themes, especially in *Griot New York*. And Rennie (Lorenzo) Harris's hip-hop-based choreography for Pure Movement has drawn in a young generation to continue the earthy improvisation and street-savvy insolence of urban dance forms. Harris's background in black vernacular break dancing and street dance places his style as a fusion of hip-hop with postmodern concert dance.

Although the tone of African American dance has evolved since the 1960s, issues of difference persist. Edward Thorpe's strident remark that "the continent from which the West first received Black dance contains a political system which separates whites from Blacks both on and off stage" seems off putting in today's inclusionary environment. The feeling of separation persists, yet in a way that helps Americans to realize the changes in society, culture, and art. Fagan emphasizes the natural dimensions of separation: "My roots are Black, but it's a cultural thing, not a racial thing. . . . Dance is a testament to people." African American dance is infused with the musical forms (blues, jazz, gospel, spirituals, soul, rap, and funk) associated with the African diaspora. It has exerted a considerable force in American concert dance, from ballet to musical theater and contemporary postmodern dance.

[See also AILEY, ALVIN.]

BIBLIOGRAPHY

Ailey, Alvin, and A. Peter Bailey, *Revelations: The Autobiography of Alvin Ailey* (Carol Pub. Group 1995).

Stearns, Marshall, and Jean Stearns, *Jazz Dance: The Story of American Vernacular Dance* (Schirmer Bks. 1979).

Thorpe, Edward, *Black Dance* (Overlook Press 1989).

Toll, Robert, *Blacking Up: The Minstrel Show in Nineteenth Century America* (Oxford 1974).

Welsh Asante, Kariamu, and Molefi Kete Asante, eds., *African Culture: The Rhythms of Unity* (Greenwood Press 1985).

JANICE LaPOINTE-CRUMP

African American Visual Art

Past studies of African American art have generally focused on the ways in which black artists have advanced in a white-dominated art world using Western media (for example, oil on canvas) and conventions (for example, portrait painting). Africa's vital craft and ritual traditions, which had flourished for centuries and inform much African American art, are only now being recovered and integrated into the mainstream.

Until the early twentieth century most successful African American artists imitated the styles and conventions of European art. The enigmatic Joshua Johnson is regarded as the first professional African American artist. Probably a former slave from the West Indies, Johnson was a portrait painter in the region around Baltimore, Maryland, around the turn of the nineteenth century. The fact that only two of his sitters were black suggests that African Americans had neither the freedom nor the means to commission portraits. Notable exceptions are the paintings that appear as decorations in the Louisiana Melrose Plantation House (circa 1833), the only surviving plantation house built by an African American family in the South. Other important black portraitists include William E. Simpson (1818–1872), Robert Douglass, Jr. (1809–1887), and David Bowser (1820–1900). Julien Hudson (1811–1844), working in New Orleans in the 1830s and 1840s, trained in Paris, then returned to his native city where he taught art and produced portraits. His *Self-Portrait* (1839, Louisiana State Museum) is the earliest known self-portrait by an African American. In an age when American art was broadening in scope and accessibility, Patrick Reason, born in

New York in 1817 of Haitian parents, was an important printmaker.

Black artists generally followed the same route to professional success as did their white counterparts. In the nineteenth century this often meant training in Europe—painters to Paris and sculptors to Italy. There they learned their crafts as well as styles then in favor. Many African American artists experienced prejudice at home and a kind of awed curiosity abroad. Edmonia Lewis (1845–1911), of African and Native American descent, is regarded as the first professional black sculptor. Some of her works addressed African American themes, such as a bust of Colonel Robert Gould Shaw, leader of the first all-black regiment in the Civil War, and a *Freedwoman*. Eugene Warbourg (1826–1859) trained in Rome and, like Lewis and most American sculptors of this period, worked in a neoclassical style.

Robert S. Duncanson (1817–1872) is regarded as a major figure in nineteenth-century landscape painting. The first African American artist to achieve international recognition, the cosmopolitan Duncanson painted in a Romantic style akin to the contemporary Hudson River landscape tradition. The landscape artist Edward Mitchell Bannister (1826–1901), who was born in Nova Scotia, took up painting after reading a newspaper article asserting that blacks could appreciate but not create art. He was the first black artist to win a national award, and he was a founding member of the organization that eventually became the Rhode Island School of Design. Bannister was also the first accomplished African American artist to be trained in the United States and not in Europe.

The most renowned African American artist of the nineteenth century is Henry Ossawa Tanner (1859–1937). The son of a minister, Tanner studied with Thomas Eakins at the Pennsylvania Academy of Fine Arts in Philadelphia. To escape prejudice and to further his training, Tanner left for Paris, where he remained for most of his life. Though he made perceptive genre paintings of African American life, it was his religious imagery that won him prizes and recognition. Tanner's first solo exhibition—perhaps the first by a black artist—was at the

American Art Galleries in New York in 1908. The following year he became the first African American to be elected to the National Academy of Design, setting a precedent for black artists in the world of academic art.

The Harlem Renaissance of the 1920s was the most intense expression of African American visual culture in the twentieth century. Artists such as Aaron Douglas (1899–1979), Malvin Gray Johnson (1896–1934), William E. Scott (1884–1964), and Palmer Hayden (1890–1973) flourished in its atmosphere. The professional photographer James Van Der Zee (1886–1983) recorded the people and events of Harlem in a career that spanned a half-century. Philanthropic projects significantly publicized African and African American art at this time. The historian and bibliophile of African and Puerto Rican descent, Arturo Alfonso Schomburg, began organizing exhibitions in Harlem in the early 1920s; the Schomburg Center for Research in Black Culture continues to this day. Similarly, the Harmon Foundation, begun by white philanthropist William Harmon, mounted shows and published catalogs of the works of African American artists. It has since become a seminal archive and repository of artworks.

The Depression brought the Harlem Renaissance to a close. But Franklin D. Roosevelt's New Deal programs—specifically the Federal Arts Project under the Works Progress Administration (WPA)—generated public commissions for African American muralists. Sometimes attempting African-inspired subjects and treatments, artists such as Scott, Hale Woodruff (1900–1980), Charles White (1918–1979), and Charles Alston (circa 1907–1978) painted large-scale images on library, school, and post office walls. Besides painting murals, Archibald J. Motley (1891–1980) has become famous for his modernistic depictions of jazz clubs and African American dance and music. Depression-era programs gave black artists greater access to printmaking. Robert Blackburn opened a printmaking workshop in 1949—the first by an African American—which still exists.

Although they segregated the accomplishments of blacks, fairs and expositions of the modern era nevertheless heightened public awareness of African American art. The 1907 Tercentennial Exposition in Jamestown, Virginia, for example, included a "Negro Building," which displayed African American crafts and included nearly five hundred artworks. That it included none by renowned black artists indicates that its intent was more ethnographic than aesthetic. Still, African Americans were being given ambitious projects in this period. For the "Negro Pavilion" of the New York World's Fair of 1939, sculptor Augusta Savage (1892–1962) produced a large-scale ensemble of singing figures arranged in the shape of a harp. Selma Burke (1900–1995) won a competition sponsored by the federal government for a portrait bust of President Franklin Roosevelt; it was later adopted for use on the U.S. dime coin. The American Negro Exposition in Chicago in 1940 was the site of a very important exhibition: Art of the American Negro, 1851–1940. The serious study of African American art began at about this time.

A major figure from this generation is Jacob Lawrence (1917–2000), whose style is a combination of folk-inspired forms and modernist principles. He applied his brightly colored, splintered forms to themes of emancipation, migration, and to such heroes from African American history as Harriet Tubman, Toussaint-L'Ouverture, and John Brown. These comprise large series, such as the sixty-panel *Migration of the Negro* (1941; Washington, D.C., Phillips Collection and the Museum of Modern Art). An important teacher, Lawrence taught at Black Mountain College in North Carolina in 1947, at the Art Students League in New York for many years, and retired as professor emeritus from the University of Washington at Seattle. The collages of Romare Bearden (1911–1988), at once modernist and vernacular, are inspired by jazz and the visual landscape of African American culture. The painters Elmer Simms Campbell (1906–1971), Eldzier Cortor, born in 1915, and Frederick Flemister, born in 1916, belong to this generation of sophisticated artists. They blended a Harlem Renaissance earnestness with the formal stylizations of modern art. After study at Howard University, then the only black college offering a degree in art, the sculptor

Three Folk Musicians, a collage by Romare Bearden.

and printmaker Elizabeth Catlett, born in 1915, went to Mexico City where she established a gallery and became intimate with the Mexican muralists.

In the 1950s and 1960s some African American artists worked in contemporary modes such as abstract expressionism or color-field painting, styles not racially identifiable. The works of Sam Gilliam, a Washington, D.C., artist, often include hanging and draped folds of canvas. Committed to avant-garde styles, African American artists expressed a sense of solidarity in this period by working collectively. The New York–based Spiral group was founded in 1963 by Bearden and Norman Lewis and included the jazz singer and artist Richard Mayhew. Another member, Woodruff, later became an influential teacher at several black colleges in the South. African American photographers also made important inroads in this period. Roy DeCarava sensitively documented Harlem life and became the first African American to win a Guggenheim Fellowship (1952). This project culminated in the book *The Sweet Flypaper of Life* (1955), a collaboration with the celebrated poet Langston Hughes. DeCarava founded A Photographer's Gallery in New York in 1954 and in 1963 the Kamoinge Workshop, devoted to teaching young black photographers. In the 1940s the renowned photojournalist Gordon Parks made important images for government photography departments under Roy Stryker. Though many periodicals turned him away on racial grounds, as a staff photographer for *Life* magazine (1948–1961) he flourished, and he made some of the most memorable images of twentieth-century blacks (including Duke Ellington, Malcolm X, and Martin Luther King, Jr.). Many regard this author-musician-filmmaker as the first professional African American photographer.

In the postwar period, African American sculptors made works of great formal accomplishment but with little overt reference to racial identity. The Chicagoan Richard Hunt has made several dozen important public commissions, his art combining graceful organic and abstract shapes. Sculptors Barbara Chase-Riboud and Juan Logan use a wide range of material, including metals and fabrics, in complex formal rhythms. One of the most renowned artists in contemporary art, Martin Puryear works in natural materials to create large-scale, postminimalist sculptures. They allude to objects of broad cultural memory—traps, decoys, hoopskirts, brooms, dolls, totems, and the like. Cleverly addressing issues of race perception, the conceptual works of David Hammons employ cast-off materials (chicken wings, for example) to challenge derogatory stereotypes of African Americans.

Black expressionism was a product of the struggle-filled 1960s and was an artistic response to the civil rights movement. Distinct from art being produced by venerable modernists such as Bearden and Lawrence, black expressionism utilized spirited ethnic themes in a passionate style. Favorite subjects include images of Muhammad Ali, anti–Vietnam War slogans, and the Black Panthers. Aiming to incite activism, recurring motifs include slogans relating to black empowerment and the human figure in bright, strident colors, sometimes the red and green of the black nationalists' flag. The American flag often appears, but as a symbol of hatred or cowardice. Noteworthy black expressionist artists include Malcolm Bailey, Murry DePillars, Melvin Edwards, Phillip Mason, Joe Overstreet, and Vincent Smith. The multifaceted Faith Ringgold is sometimes linked to black expressionism because

Forward, by Jacob Lawrence, is a tempera painting depicting Harriet Tubman.

of the militant content of some of her art. She was one of the first artists to challenge discrimination against women in art exhibitions. Her favorite themes are family, maternity, and neighborhood. Working in an enormous range of media (quilts, most notably), she has collaborated on pieces with her mother, the noted fashion designer Willi Posey.

An important expression of black expressionism was the black neighborhood mural movement of the 1960s. In Chicago, then later in other cities, brightly painted popular images began appearing on buildings in African American communities. It was art for the street, made for an audience that knew or cared little for the modern art shown in "uptown" museums. A seminal example is the *Wall of Respect and Community as One* (1967; Chicago), depicting black heroes, painted by the Visual Arts Workshop of the Organization of Black American Culture (OBAC). A group of artists from OBAC later broke off to become the African Commune of Bad Relevant Artists (AfriCobra). Their murals, by artists such as Barbara Jones-Hogu and Jeff Donaldson, employed shrill colors and are filled with prideful slogans. In an attempt to bring accessible art to black households, AfriCobra produced inexpensive prints. In the 1960s Harlem was once again the site of a flourishing African American artistic movement. The group *Weusi Nymuba Ya Sanaa* (Swahili for "Black House of Art") established an art school and gallery (1967–1978) that promoted African sub-

jects and values. Many of its members converted to African religions and abandoned their American "slave names." Ademola Olugebefola was an important *Weusi* artist and the group's spokesman.

The affluent 1980s witnessed a resurgence in the commercial art scene and a heightened interest in New York's urban environment. It was in this milieu that the brief but intense career of Jean-Michel Basquiat (1960–1988) occurred. Of mixed Puerto Rican and Haitian descent, the middle-class Basquiat moved in circles that included street-life and graffiti, but also upscale venues and art-world stars. His art—originally words on buildings, T-shirts, and postcards, then canvases and murals—appears crude but is very sophisticated. It often included references to African American culture and to black heroes such as Charlie Parker and Muhammad Ali. The texts that appear in his works challenge stereotypes and refer to Basquiat's own identity and experiences.

African Americans also figure largely in the history of folk and outsider art (art made by untrained individuals). Art of this sort is unrefined but intricate, often profusely decorated with text and fashioned from junk materials. Favorite subjects include animals, biblical themes, and figures from American history, such as Abraham Lincoln and Martin Luther King, Jr. It reflects the spirit of African art, especially in its intuitive production and in the magical energy of the object. Born a slave, Bill Traylor (1854–1947) began making the iconic colored drawings for which he is known in his eighties while living like a hobo. The crudely powerful paintings of Horace Pippin (1888–1947), the first acclaimed African American folk artist, were "discovered" by important dealers and avidly collected afterward. Mose Tolliver began painting in his sixties after a work-related accident forced him to retire. Other members of the Tolliver family are also renowned outsider artists.

Since the 1960s more than a hundred museums dedicated to African American art have appeared and have begun emphasizing the role of African craft traditions and visual culture. Traditional art museums have intensified their efforts to acquire and exhibit the works of historical and contemporary African American artists. Current studies are beginning to recognize the complexity of how a subdominant culture makes art that asserts its own values while conforming to received standards.

[See also BLACK ARTS MOVEMENT.]

BIBLIOGRAPHY

Bearden, Romare, and Harry Henderson, *A History of African-American Artists: From 1792 to the Present* (Pantheon Bks. 1993).

Black Art Ancestral Legacy: The African Impulse in African-American Art (The Dallas Museum of Art; dist. by Abrams 1989).

Harlem Renaissance: Art of Black America (Abrams 1987).

Patton, Sharon F., *African-American Art* (Oxford 1998).

Perry, Regenia, *Free within Ourselves: African-American Artists in the Collection of the National Museum of American Art* (Smithsonian Inst. Press with Pomegranate Art Bks. 1992).

Robinson, Jontyle Theresa, *Bearing Witness: Contemporary Works by African-American Women Artists* (Rizzoli Int. Pub. and Spelman College 1996).

Stuckey, Sterling, *Going through the Storm: The Influence of African American Art in History* (Oxford 1994).

MARK B. POHLAD

African American Folklore and Humor

There is a close relationship between African American folklore and humor. African American humor is not only an integral part of folklore but, in turn, it draws on the content and themes of folklore. This symbiotic relationship fosters an in-group feeling during performances by African American humorists, whose material often plays on the different meanings their humor has for white and black audiences. African American comedians are keenly aware of this fact. The comedian Chris Rock, for example, gained Howard University's permission to publish a humor magazine along the lines of the *Harvard Lampoon,* which will encourage material on all aspects of African American humor.

Awareness that humor will be interpreted differently by different audiences goes back as far as the days of slavery. Daryl Cumber Dance's 1998 collection of African American women's humor demonstrates the manner in which humor was used to comment on relations between blacks and whites while reflecting on the singular and universal in African American life. Moms Mabley, the Delany sisters, and Zora Neale Hurston share space with lesser-known humorists, but their material shows a consistency of experience and identity, the expression of which owes a good deal to the shared common folklore.

Such sharing, however, does not preclude individuality and difference within that general identity. The diversity within African American female humor, for example, is as great as that within male comedy. Slave narratives, as well as modern humor from such people as Gloria Naylor and Terry McMillan, demonstrate the manner in which humor both promotes subversion of accepted social reality and promotes tolerance and acceptance of life as it is.

African American Folklore. African American folklore provides a corrective lens to the manner in which African Americans are generally portrayed by whites. Even when white culture has taken notice of black folklore, it has generally misunderstood its meaning by ignoring its context. There are, furthermore, many aspects of folklore: folktales, folk dance, folk beliefs, folk music, and even folk medicine. Folklore refers to that which is traditional among a people, mainly referring to customs, tales, and other art forms, as well as medicine and "superstitions." Therefore, by its very nature folklore is somewhat amorphous; it is hard to pin down its exact ancestry. Since folklore reflects elements common to "the folk," that is, ordinary people, similar stories are found in similar conditions around the world.

The issue of the origins of African American folklore becomes important in light of racism. Too many things that are seen as valuable in African American culture are attributed directly or indirectly to outside influences. The fact is, however, that what is significant is not the borrowing of items but a people's interpretation of those items and their integration with other cultural elements. Thus, African American folklore has an overall West African base. African Americans borrowed some European elements and adapted the whole to reflect their experiences in America. Folklore enabled African Americans to mitigate and resist their forced assimilation into European American culture. Although overt expression of African religion and even, at times, music was prohibited by slave owners, African oral tradition, adapted to the American scene, survived. There might be a combination of Nigerian and Ghanaian material but the basic ethos of the cultures survived the adaptation. The folktales helped essential ethical and cosmological attitudes survive.

The "Uncle Remus" stories are perhaps the best-known African American folktales. Joel Chandler Harris freely acknowledged that these folktales were not his creations. He "borrowed" them from slaves. In fact, *Remus* is an American adaptation of a Hausa word for a slave foreman in the northern area of what is now Nigeria. Harris managed to retain the basic symbolism of these tales. The trickster rabbit—in West Africa it was either a hare (Nigeria) or a spider (Ghana)—needs to use his wits to survive against the superior forces of the fox and bear. Interestingly, even these enemies referred to one another as "brother" (brer).

Brer Rabbit represented the weaker African Americans in their struggle against the more powerful white masters. That struggle did not end with the abolition of slavery just as oppression did not end with the Thirteenth, Fourteenth, and Fifteenth Amendments. Old Massa found a new incarnation in the new power structure of the South. Thus, Brer Rabbit also found a new incarnation in folktales, that of the trickster, John. Like Brer Rabbit, John used his wits to defeat the "boss man."

Folk music has also reflected basic African American themes. Moreover, it would be difficult to find even the most ardent racist denying the impact that African American music has had on American music as well as world music. Call-and-response patterns, the use of drums, and what is really not syncopation but cross-rhythms mark both African and African American music. Just as folktales oper-

ate on many levels and praise the wily underdog who manages to use wits to conquer power, so, too, folk songs, including spirituals and other religious music, contain a message of subversion of the oppressive system. Thus, religious songs about Moses or the River Jordan generally spoke of escape from slavery and oppression. Additionally, music, like the tales, is a means for recording the history of the people.

The manner in which African American folklore is constructed also carries a message to its African American audience. There are certain cultural master frames that resonate in the African American community. Thus, David Maines provides an example of the conspiracy and contamination narrative structure. He discusses the rumors about Church's Chicken that circulated in certain areas of the country. Contaminated chicken was presumably served in African American areas. Maines offers the narrative to demonstrate that the believability of the story is related to its racialized structure.

Perhaps that is why African American folklore has had such a great impact on African American literature, most famously in the work of Zora Neale Hurston. Hurston is both a folklorist and novelist. She is not, of course, the only folklorist who specializes in African American folklore. James Mason Brewer, Elsie Clies Parson, Patricia Turner, John Vlach, and Lawrence Levine are but a few others who contributed to the field. There were also many other novelists, poets, and literary figures who used African American folklore in their works. Ralph Ellison's use of blues lyrics in *Invisible Man* (1952), for example, is well known.

Humor. Humor, in the basic tradition of the African American folktale, subverts the conventional view of the white-dominated American social structure. It forces a rethinking of what is "appropriate" to humor as well as the general Western tradition of humor as passed on through Greco-Roman ideas from rhetorical theory. African American humor forces a rethinking of black-white relationships, and its subject matter consists of reflections of the multiple audiences it has. Moreover, these audiences are divided along racial lines. Those lines, however, cannot keep the races apart, no matter how unequal their relationships might be.

Much of the style of African American humor comes from West Africa, including punning and other wordplay, signifying, mocking the relatives of one's enemy, the trickster, ridicule verses (sung and chanted), and a form of aggressive joking that hones quick wit in participants. There are various mentions of African American humor stretching back to the earliest days of the American colonies. There were African American street entertainers who employed characteristics found in later African American humor: William Henry "Juba" Lane's tap dancing and Signor Conneali's (Old Cornmeal) use of a rich baritone and a contrasting high falsetto to amuse people. There was also John "Picayune" Butler who played a banjo and inserted clowning into his act.

There were also African American minstrels. The Seven Slaves, for instance, traveled to Massachusetts and New York in 1855. Charles "Barney" Hicks, an African American, led the Georgia Minstrels, an integrated group with a majority of white members. The most famous African American minstrel, however, was Billy Kersands (1842–1915), who performed for many luminaries, including Queen Victoria. He exaggerated the size of his mouth, telling the queen that if God wanted his mouth to be any larger he would have had to move his ears. Kersands found that he earned the enmity of people such as W. E. B. Du Bois who felt that such catering to racial stereotypes demeaned efforts by blacks to improve their image. Kersands's dilemma regarding whether or not to make money through exaggerating and thereby mocking racial stereotypes has plagued other comedians who came after him.

Despite many criticisms of minstrelsy, however, the majority of African Americans frequented minstrel shows with black stars, seeking out those that African Americans owned. Bert Williams (1876–1922), for example, came from a minstrel background and rose to great prominence, although he was often criticized for playing up to racial stereotypes. Williams was an all-around entertainer who

often performed in white night clubs. He also may have been the first African American vocalist to be recorded. Williams even starred in the *Ziegfield Follies,* an otherwise all-white show.

Stepin Fetchit (1896–1985), who was born Lincoln Perry in Jamaica, did what many others had done; namely, he exaggerated racial stereotypes and became a star. However, he suffered because he was too successful. Stepin Fetchit portrayed the bewildered, superstition-ridden "darky" too well. While white audiences howled, many African Americans winced. Such behavior would be fine for an all-black audience but it opened up the race to ridicule. Fetchit became embittered when he saw his popularity drop after World War II because his style of humor did not help promote racial pride. He maintained that he paved the way for the comedians who came after him. He took pride in being the first African American to work at major Hollywood studios and also the first to become a millionaire movie star.

There were a number of other African American stars who did not get their full due working at the same time as Stepin Fetchit. Jackie "Moms" Mabley (1897–1975), for example, finally made it big with white audiences when she was about seventy. Moms was an irreverent grandmother figure, who delighted in shocking her audiences only to find that they were so much on her side that they were unshockable. Unfortunately, Pigmeat Markham (1904–1981) never crossed over to a broader audience, although his material did. His "Here comes de judge" routine made a sensation on television's *Laugh-in,* performed by Flip Wilson and Sammy Davis, Jr.

Ironically, the most famous "black" comic show was really performed by white actors. *Amos 'n' Andy* ruled the airwaves from the 1930s through the 1940s. On television, African American actors replaced their white counterparts. However, *Amos 'n' Andy* lasted only two years. Protests over its racial stereotypes helped end the show. It did, however, pave the way for later African American comedians to become popular. And in the 1950s a number of other comics made the grade. Eddie

Anderson (1905–1971) came to television from radio. He was Jack Benny's sidekick, Rochester, who served as his conscience. Nipsey Russell, Sleepy White, and Bill Cosby made their breakthroughs in the 1950s.

Dick Gregory appeared on the scene at about the same time. Gregory worked to put his mainly white audiences at ease before beginning with his racial humor. He made his points by winning his audience over without sacrificing his dignity. Godfrey Cambridge, Flip Wilson, and others soon followed. Wilson (1933–1998) was hailed as "television's first black superstar." Wilson introduced white audiences to a number of stock characters from the African American repertory. He made sure however that audiences knew that these were characters, not the real thing. Moreover, he took care to provide the characters with some basic dignity amid the shenanigans.

The Cosby phenomenon, however, surpassed even that of Flip Wilson. Bill Cosby used stand-up comedy and comedy record albums to vault his way into television as the first African American comedian to appear in a starring role on television. Cosby's accomplishments are fairly well-known: a doctorate in education, work on *The Electric Company*, a number of hit television situation comedies, beginning with *I Spy* (1965–1968) and including the enormously successful *Cosby Show* (1984–1992).

Perhaps the greatest comic genius of the age was Richard Pryor, who managed to combine various strains of black comedy as well as the Jewish perspective of Lennie Bruce, and George Carlin's Irish take on the world. Pryor was unpredictable on stage, and at his peak he could do it all. He forced people to take a fresh look at revealed wisdom. White and black audiences loved him and his filmed concerts did well in theaters.

After Pryor and other comedians had paved the way, the floodgates seemed to open for such hugely popular comics as Jimmy Walker, Whoopi Goldberg, Eddie Murphy, Martin Lawrence, Will Smith, Arsenio Hall, Chris Rock, and the Wayans family. Interestingly, white America joined African American audiences in its enjoyment of black humor. The basic question is, of course, do they understand the same performances in the same ways? Just as Louis Armstrong appeared to cater to white audiences while performing white popular songs but changed from a "servile" person to a trickster while reinventing the songs, so, too, have many African American comics provided alternate perspectives on white culture in such a way that whites often have not noted the manner in which the humor subverts notions of white superiority and dominance.

BIBLIOGRAPHY

Abernethy, Francis Edward, et al., eds., *Juneteenth Texas: Essays in African-American Folklore* (Univ. of Tex. 1996).

"African American Humor," in *Encyclopedia of 20th-Century American Humor,* ed. by Alleen Pace Nilsen and Don L. F. Nilsen (Oryx Press 2000).

Brewer, J., *American Negro Folklore* (Quadrangle Bks. 1968).

Dance, Daryl Cumber, ed., *Honey Hush!: An Anthology of African American Women's Humor* (Norton 1998).

Dundes, A., *Mother Wit from the Laughing Barrel: Readings in the Interpretation of Afro-American Folklore* (Prentice-Hall 1972).

Gordon, Dexter B., "Humor in African American Discourse: Speaking of Oppression," *Journal of Black Studies* 29 (1998):154–276.

Maines, David R., "Informational Pools and the Racialized Narrative Structures," *Sociological Quarterly* 40 (1999):317–326.

Nicholls, David G., "Migrant Labor, Folklore, and Resistance in Hurston's Polk County: Reframing Mules and Men," *African American Review* 33 (1999):467–485.

Ogunleye, Tolagbe, "African American Folklore: Its Role in Reconstructing African American History," *Journal of Black Studies* 27 (1997):433–455.

Prahlad, Anand, "Guess Who's Coming to Dinner: Folklore, Folklorists, and African American Literary Criticism," *African American Review* 33 (1999):565–580.

Spalding, H., ed., *Encyclopedia of Black Folklore and Humor* (Jonathan David Pub. 1972).

FRANK A. SALAMONE

African American Religions

From its origins in traditional African societies to its contemporary manifestations, religion has permeated every dimension of African American history and culture—from art, music, and literature

An African American family celebrates Kwanza, inspired by African harvest festivals.

to the formation of social institutions, economic collectives, and political philosophies. Understanding the religious history of African peoples in North America and the larger African diaspora is imperative for any genuine analysis of the African American experience. As anthropologist Melville J. Herskovits argued in his classic text *The Myth of the Negro Past* (1941), "Religion is vital, meaningful and understandable to the Negroes of this country be-cause, as in the West Indies and West Africa, it is not removed from life, but has been deeply integrated into the daily round."

Religion before and during African Enslavement. Early scholarship on African American religion was largely fixated on investigating the institutional history of "the Negro Church" (the unofficial aggregation of African American Protestant denominations). Such a narrow perspective has tended to render African American religiosity as merely a derivative of European Christianity without any regard for the unique history of religion for people of African descent. Later scholars significantly contributed to the study of religion in the African American experience by focusing on the proliferation of indigenous African religious traditions that predated European colonization and the Middle Passage, and the resulting syncretisms in the Americas.

Prior to the incursion of Europeans into sub-Saharan Africa, most Africans participated in religious practices that were not only indigenous to the continent but were also specific to their family or kinship group and society. While each group had its own practices, prayers, and ideas concerning spirituality, African communities did share certain core principles: a Supreme Being or Creator, the veneration of ancestral and natural spirits, the primacy of family, the use of religious artifacts and symbols (fetishism), and the significance of liturgical and ritual practices. Although it is difficult to reconstruct precisely the religious ideas of early Africans, it is important to note that many traditional African languages lack a word for religion per se because religion is inextricably linked to African cosmology, or way of life. In the wake of forced relocation of Africans to America resulting from the Atlantic slave trade, these varied religious traditions ultimately served as the foundation for the subsequent establishment of African American religion in the New World.

Africans encountered Islam and Christianity long before the Middle Passage. Muslim traders traveled from Arabia to North Africa between the seventh and eighth centuries, and their attempts at widespread religious conversion throughout the region had mixed results. Although Islam was very successful in the North, Africans below the Sahara were more hesitant to relinquish their existing religious traditions in favor of this new faith. Overall, Africans refused to become Muslim if it meant sacrificing their own native beliefs and traditions. Christianity emerged concurrently with Islam in the northernmost reaches of Africa; however, its popu-

larity was minimal until the Portuguese began Christian missionary efforts in southern Africa in the 1500s. The contradictory behavior of Europeans who preached the Christian gospel while forcing Africans to endure the terror of being kidnapped, shipped overseas, and enslaved in the Americas greatly circumscribed the spread of Christianity. Enslaved Africans arriving in the New World often embraced Christianity in tandem with their indigenous religions in the hopes of preserving their culture and overall humanity.

Africans imported to North America and enslaved from 1619 to 1808 sought to create communal and kinship networks within the context of slave traders and slaveholders who deliberately separated families and exacerbated intraracial differences among enslaved populations. Religion soon became the means to galvanize people of African descent into a more cohesive cultural entity. On one hand, the retention of African traditional religions in the Western Hemisphere has been evident in the persistence of such religious practices as spirit possession, "river baptisms" (total immersion), the "ring shout," call-and-response, conjuring practices, and cross-cultural identification of African divine spirits with Roman Catholic saints. Early African American religion was, therefore, an effort by enslaved Africans to safeguard themselves against the disruption of their religious worldview. On the other hand, enslaved Africans gradually merged their composite African religiosity with western European notions of Christianity through a complex process of acculturation, adaptation, and assimilation. Whether enslaved or free, African American converts to Christianity of the early 1800s subordinated European sacred rhetoric to their own hermeneutical interpretation of personal salvation, conviction of sin, charismatic praise and worship, the equality of all peoples, and the divine promise of heaven.

The emergence of a sizable and increasingly autonomous African American Christian populace became a reality both during and after the Revolutionary War. Although many free African American Christians belonged to interracial congregations in the late 1700s, by the early 1800s, owing to the rising tide of racism among formerly egalitarian white

THE BLACK CHURCH'S FIVE FORMS OF POLITICAL MINISTRY

Political Orientation	Moral Means	Moral Ends	Theological Justification (God as)
Pragmatic Accommodationism	Social Order	Cooperation	Creator
Prophetic Radicalism	Social Justice	Confrontation	Liberator
Redemptive Nationalism	Separate Nation	Opportunistic Engagement	Redeemer
Grassroots Revivalism	Personal Salvation	Indifference	Savior
Positive Thought-Materialism	Individual Property	Opportunistic Engagement	Provider

preachers and congregations, African Americans were ousted from their churches. However, with the pioneering work of African American preachers such as David George and George Liele preceding the American Revolution, as well as the founding of the First African Baptist Church of Savannah, Georgia, by Reverend Andrew Bryan in 1788, the institutional roots of the black church were officially established. This growing African American Christian populace played a key role in the resistance of enslaved African Americans in the American South. Frightened by the invocation of Christian beliefs to incite slave insurrection, such as those led by Gabriel Prosser (1800), Denmark Vesey (1822), and Nat Turner (1831), white Southerners used legislation as well as brute force to crush any sense of religious freedom among African Americans during the nineteenth century. Consequently, the vast majority of African Americans were forced to practice their newfound Christianity in an underground manner in an environment wherein open professions of faith could lead to torture and even death.

The Black Church in America. The black church in America can be defined in two ways. Most generally and popularly, the black church is any Christian congregation predominately populated by blacks, including all European founded and governed Christian congregations (that is, Southern Baptist, American Baptist, Presbyterian, Episcopalian, Lutheran, Roman Catholic, Seventh Day Adventists, Assembly of God, Pentecostal, and so on). Additionally, the black church can be defined as a Protestant denomination that was created, founded, governed, and populated by blacks, reflecting an organized religiosity that merges Protestant doctrines of faith with an unapologetic cultural and political awareness in order to be intentionally relevant to the social and spiritual plight

of African American peoples. This would include, for example, the National Baptist Convention (1895), National Baptist Convention of America (1915), Progressive National Baptist Convention (1961), African Methodist Episcopalian (1787), African Methodist Episcopalian Zion (1820), Christian Methodist Episcopalian—formerly Colored Methodist Episcopalian—(1870), Church of God in Christ (1897), and Full Gospel Baptists.

Theologian Paul Tillich defined religion as that which reflects "our ultimate concern." By applying this truth to the black church, it is clear that the struggle for black empowerment was inextricably bound to the Christian message. The means to attain black religious empowerment differ from one denomination to another and from one congregation to another. It is crucial to locate the varied paradigms within the black-derived denominational black churches. According to Robert Franklin, the black church has a number of responses to the social crisis African Americans confront in America. As his model illustrates, the black church merges theological beliefs with moral values and political needs. Thus, the sociopolitical goals of the church and its definition of God are seen as directly corresponding to one another.

Pragmatic Accommodationists. The leaders and clergy of the larger denominations of the black church, such as the National Baptist Convention and the African Methodist Episcopal Church, practice pragmatic accommodationism as their expression of black empowerment. The theological justification of God as the sovereign creator mandates that God has supplied all that is needed for accommodationist clergy to attain fair treatment and distribution of goods but that it is up to church members to cooperate with the political system in order to attain the provisions for their congregations. Toward this end, pragmatic accommodationist black churches seek to conform to the political climate of American society. Unsurprisingly, these churches are the most frequently visited by political campaigners and officials.

Prophetic Radicals. Prophetic radicals, such as Martin Luther King, Jr., Adam Clayton Powell, Jr., and, later, Jesse Jackson, represent leaders within the black community who believe that to assimilate to the political climate in which black Americans find themselves is to become coconspirators with the evil structures of racial and class oppression. Instead, prophetic radical congregations, such as the Progressive National Baptist Convention, find themselves accentuating black empowerment by wresting power from the forces in society that consign blacks to second-class citizenship. Understanding God as the divine force that seeks to liberate all oppressed people, the prophetic radical tradition has been a catalyst for social change in black America since the slave revolts of Denmark Vesey and Nat Turner, the civil rights movement, and later protests from Jackson and others. Prophetic radicals believe that it is their Christian duty to confront social sin in order to ensure a climate of social justice and liberation.

Redemptive Nationalists. Black nationalists have sought to reclaim a sacred and separate nation for black people to secure their inalienable rights and racial pride. Although such black leaders as Malcolm X and Nation of Islam leader Louis Farrakhan come to mind, there are black Christian nationalists who proclaim a redemptive nationalist agenda (Albert Cleage, founder of the Shrine of the Black Madonna in Atlanta and Detroit, is a prime example). The unapologetic aspirations of creating a separate black nation are evident in the retention of Afrocentric expressions in dress and language during worship and the emphasis that is placed on the ownership and control of businesses by and for black people in their own communities. Redemptive nationalists understand God as one who seeks to guide people to their full potential. Such expression of black empowerment seeks to affirm,

validate, and redeem black people and to restore the unity that existed before the African diaspora. Redemptive nationalists only interact with America and its systems in an opportunistic way to get closer to their goal of ethnic purity without seeking any loyalty or unity with the United States and its structures.

Grassroots Revivalists. Pentecostal black churches, in particular the Church of God in Christ (COGIC), represent the second largest constituency of the black church. This group is referred to as grassroots revivalists because its leaders reach their urban masses through cultural energy rather than through a theological education as do many prophetic radicals. By holding church services in storefront buildings or private homes, this grassroots congregation seeks total detachment from worldly concerns. Rather, grassroots revivalists focus on the spiritual world of personal salvation. Understanding God as one who will save people from this mundane world, revivalists seek to generate a religious practice that is sanctified (set apart) from any earthly trappings.

Positive-Thought Materialists. The legendary personalities of Daddy Grace and Father Divine, the black vocal religious personas of the Depression era, represent the smallest constituent of the black church's political ministry. Much like redemptive nationalists, positive-thought materialists emerge as leaders in the black church and community when black people are most threatened economically. Clergy such as Daddy Grace, Father Divine, or radio personality Reverend Ike espoused a message of material health, wealth, and success. Detached from concerns of social order, justice, ethnic purity, or personal salvation, these materialistic practitioners merely sought opportunistic means to advance individual prosperity. Referring to God as Jehovah Jireh ("the one who provides"), positive-thought materialists seldom concern themselves with the traditional themes of Christianity and thus find themselves marginalized by the majority of black Christians.

Contemporary Alternative African American Religions. Whereas black Protestantism remained the chief religious identification within the African American experience, in the twentieth century a number of groups made significant increases in their overall membership and social visibility. Those groups included Roman Catholics, Muslims, and practitioners of African-derived traditional religions. Each movement underwent considerable change, very much in the spirit of African American religion writ large.

Black Catholics. From the era of slavery until the heyday of the civil rights movement, the Roman Catholic Church had actively sought to baptize and convert African Americans through segregated and race-specific clerical and lay organizations. Founded in 1931, Xavier University in New Orleans became the first Catholic school among historically black colleges and universities. Furthermore, the increased presence of African American priests, nuns, and brethren, as well as the incorporation of "jazz masses" into the traditional liturgy in the 1960s, marked a more responsive posture toward African American Catholics by the Vatican. In 1979 American bishops met and officially decreed that racism was a sin.

Despite such efforts, there has been a schism within the Catholic Church between the "white" church and African American Catholics caused by the reassertion of the unique cultural aesthetics and concerns of black men and women. George A. Stallings left the Roman Catholic Church in 1989, denouncing its enduring racist attitude toward people of color. Soon thereafter Stallings founded the Imani Temple in Washington, D.C., leading to the formation of the African American Catholic Congregation, which infused Catholic ritual with Afrocentric music, dance, and sacred customs. With churches in seven cities in the United States, Stallings's movement currently claims over seven thousand members.

Nation of Islam and Black Muslims. Islam made a substantial resurgence within the African American experience during the first half of the twentieth century. The Ahmadiyya movement, the Moorish Science Temple of America, and the Muslim Mission of America helped inspire a greater awareness of the Islamic faith among African Americans. Founded by Wallace D. Fard and under the leadership of Elijah Muhammad, the Nation of Islam grew into the most recognizable manifestation of African American Islam since the 1930s. During the early 1960s the Nation of Islam's level of popularity and controversy was largely fueled by the fiery rhetoric and sharp social critique of its national spokesperson, Malcolm X. In the wake of the death of Muhammad and the assassination of Malcolm X, the Nation of Islam was split between the original group under the direction of Warith Deen Muhammad, who espoused Islamic orthodoxy, and the black-nationalist group led by Louis Farrakhan since the 1970s. In 2000, the two factions made attempts at reconciliation in the hopes of embracing orthodox Islam as the basic faith of African American Muslims. According to recent estimates, at least one million African Americans identify themselves as Muslims.

African-Derived Religions. The last group of African American religiosity involves the emergence of African-centered movements. These manifestations of African American religion have taken two emphases: direct appropriations of African traditional religions and the practice of Afrocentric forms of worship. On the one hand, the immigration of Africans to the United States since the 1960s has reintroduced traditional beliefs (most notably Yoruba and Akan groups) in the United States. On the other hand, the second half of the twentieth century also witnessed the importation of African-derived belief systems from the Caribbean and South America. Although Santería from Cuba and Vodun from Haiti have been the most stereotypically misunderstood of these religious traditions, there are numerous other religions arising from the combination of African beliefs, folk European Catholicism, and indigenous American cosmologies, resulting in localized hybrid expressions such as Candomblé and Umbanda (Brazil), Kumina (Jamaica), Shango (Trinidad and Grenada), María Lionza (Venezuela), and Boni (French Guiana). The existence of these African-inspired religions in the United States represents the intrinsic multiculturalism and adaptability of religion within the African American experience. In turn, understanding these and other forms of African American religion dramatically expands the scope of American studies as a field of inquiry.

[See also KWANZA.]

BIBLIOGRAPHY

Cone, James, *Martin and Malcolm and America: A Dream or a Nightmare?* (Orbis Press 1991).

Franklin, Robert M., *Another Day's Journey: Black Churches Confronting the American Crisis* (Fortress Press 1997).

Higginbotham, Evelyn Brooks, *Righteous Discontent: The Women's Movement in the Black Baptist Church, 1890–1920* (Harvard Univ. Press 1993).

Lincoln, C. Eric, and Lawrence Mamiya, *The Black Church in the African American Experience* (Duke Univ. Press 1990).

Raboteau, Albert, *Slave Religion: The "Invisible Institution" in the Antebellum South* (Oxford 1978).

JUAN FLOYD-THOMAS *and* STACEY FLOYD-THOMAS

African American Speech and Language

Arguments over black English (also styled Black English and Black English Vernacular) are longstanding and often bitter. They encompass a number of areas, including whether there is such a linguistic entity as black English. If it exists, there is an argument as to whether it is simply illiterate or incorrect English or a legitimate descendant of African speech and the pidginization and creolization of languages that occurred under slavery. Moreover, if it is held that black English is related to African speech, there is a further controversy over what constitutes black English, specifically, over what is known as Ebonics. Somewhere in the controversy is the older consideration of the Gullah people of the Sea Islands, off the coast of South Carolina and Georgia. Africanisms deeply influence their language.

All these arguments are not simply squabbles in the academic community over linguistic theory and practice. Neither are they but another round in the culture wars over political correctness. There are substantive pedagogical issues at stake regarding the legitimacy of the manner in which African Americans are taught in schools and the consequences of these methods on their achievements. The Ebonics controversy brought these issues to the front and center in the educational arena.

Black English. Robert L. Williams coined the word *Ebonics* in 1975 in his book of the same name, shaping the new term from the words *Ebony* and *phonics*. Ebonics is defined by Williams as a language spoken by African Americans that is not a variety of English but a separate language with its own mode of expression and rules of grammar. It is seen as coming from West African languages such as Yoruba, Ewe, Fula, Igbo, and Mandinka. Williams is joined in his theories by John Baugh, John R. Rickford, Peter Sells, and Tom Wasow of the Stanford University linguistics department; William Labov of the University of Pennsylvania; Ralph Fasold of Georgetown University; Walt Wolfram of North Carolina State University; Geneva Smitherman of Michigan State University; Lisa Green of the University of Texas at Austin; and Orlando Taylor of Howard University, a consultant to the Oakland, California, school board.

It is important to note, as Margalit Fox does, that "from a linguistic viewpoint all dialects are equally complicated and equally good." It is also true that in people's minds, however, the social status of a group that speaks a dialect helps determine the way in which that dialect is evaluated. The fact that black English, or Ebonics, is tied to African Americans has led to many white Americans devaluing its importance. Thus, two separate issues are under discussion: the fact of the existence of a black English dialect, and the manner in which people judge it.

As stated above, there are those scholars who do not believe that Ebonics is black English. Others agree that it is neither a dialect of English nor a separate language but simply ungrammatical English. It is argued that Ebonics is "an African-based linguistic system using English words." Indeed, there is clear evidence that the term has been used for a number of years and that there is a strong linguistic case for treating Ebonics as a separate language. In the opinion of some scholars there is "no genetic kinship between it and the Germanic family that produced English." Their conclusion is that African Americans who are described by educators as being language-deficient are really speaking a separate language. Therefore, they deserve to have a bilingual education program in which English is seen as their second language.

An article in *The Economist* magazine stated the case for the opposition. It characterizes Ebonics as deriving primarily from inner-city speech patterns. Teachers wish to use Ebonics to teach African American students so that they will perform better academically. The article notes that those who support the use of Ebonics in schools claim that "it derives from the structures of Niger-Congo African languages and marks the persistent legacy of slavery." However, a number of Ebonics usages are relatively recent. When the Oakland board of education sought to implement Ebonics in the school in 1997, it made the mistake of stating that Ebonics is "genetically based." They should have said that it was based on long-established linguistic structures.

The furor in Oakland led many to believe that Ebonics had emerged in 1997 as a new idea, when, in fact, it had been around for quite some time. Even the argument over its use in instruction is not new. In 1981, for example, Michigan had sought to define Ebonics as a separate language. The Reagan administration responded that black English "is a form of English." In other words, they denied that it was a separate language. In 1981 the California department of education put a standard English program into place to aid African American students in learning. In fact, as *The Economist* points out, "Since 1991 the Los Angeles school board has recognized Ebonics, and has tried to make a special effort with black pupils as a result." Oakland, however, was the first board of education to suggest that Ebonics be treated as a classroom language having a unique "legitimacy and richness."

Granting Ebonics official recognition as a separate language rather than a dialect of English would open up a flood of money for bilingual education to help African American students, something a number of African American parents want. They believe it would offer their children the same aid given to Latino students in Oakland. African American parents hold that their children suffer from linguistic problems deriving from structural differences in their spoken language just as Latino children do. More money to aid them in learning "standard English" would help solve a number of problems. Certainly, according to *The Economist* article, the availability of more money to aid students at a disadvantage is an objective that both supporters of Ebonics as a separate language and those who reject that notion can get behind.

Steven Fox states the matter rather clearly. He notes that the current reality is that Standard American English (SAE) is the "money language." Black English is identified with poverty and, therefore, holds a great stigma. Many African American students do not wish to be associated with it. He holds with many linguists that black English is a variety of English, not a separate language. It is a dialect like Australian or various regional dialects in America. Linguists, as reported in *The Chronicle of Higher Education*, support the efforts of the Oakland school board to use Ebonics to aid in student learning. They generally do not agree that it is a separate language, although it does have certain rules that differ from SAE.

Fox points out that "speakers of SAE cannot truly say that they find Ebonics unintelligible; neither can speakers of Ebonics claim that they cannot understand SAE." Some grammatical features of Ebonics contradict the rules one learns in the standard dialect, so that the expression "He don't got none," for example, causes some purists to say that Ebonics is wrong. But in the Ebonics dialect the double negative is used for emphasis. The fact that many listeners unfamiliar with Ebonics have not sorted out its regularities does not mean that it has none. The media have stressed that Ebonics is a highly rule-based dialect, and speakers of Ebonics do not carelessly drop the verb "to be," for example, or word endings or any number of other features one associates with SAE. Because Ebonics and other varieties of English, such as SAE, are mutually intelligible they are dialects of English, not separate languages. Fox thus takes a compromise position on the issue.

There are, of course, other scholars who are far less sympathetic with the entire issue of Ebonics. Leon W. Todd, Jr., states, "*Ebonics* is a politically correct term for dysfunctional speech. Legitimizing poor language habits will not help children find a job nor take control of their affairs later in life." Todd argues that good jobs require the use of standard English. No amount of political correctness will compensate for a lack of basic language skills. Teaching children in a degraded form of language will not enhance their future employment opportunities, no matter how good it may be for their self-esteem. It will only place them at a disadvantage in their future work competition.

The Gullah. The Gullah people live in the South Carolina and Georgia Sea Islands. It is universally agreed that their language and culture have retained a large percentage of Africanisms. Indeed, that percentage far exceeds retentions found among other African Americans. The word *Gullah* has no acceptable origin. It first appeared in an article in the 1739 *South Carolina Gazette*. According to Bijan C. Bayne, the article made reference to a runaway slave named Golla Harry.

However they obtained their name, the Geechie people are descended from slaves who were abducted from the area of West Africa around Sierra Leone. Today they number about one hundred thousand. According to Sherman Pyatt, the word *Gullah* refers to the language and customs of the Geechie people. The Gullah language was forged through the mixing of English vocabulary with African pronunciation, grammar, syntax, and vocabulary. The first linguist to study the language was Lorenzo Turner, who found over four thousand African words. Joe Opala, an anthropologist, has found a significant tie between Gullah and Mende and Krio, languages spoken in Sierra Leone.

The links between Sierra Leone and the Sea Islands are not accidental. There was a need to find slaves familiar with rice growing for which the Low

Country of South Carolina is so well suited. Sierra Leone was an area in which experienced rice farmers flourished. Since over forty percent of all Africans brought to America passed through South Carolina, the Carolina planters had little trouble choosing the type of skilled labor they required for rice farming. Indeed, until the 1920s the majority of South Carolina's population was African American, a factor important in the preservation of African language and tradition. So well preserved have been elements of Sierra Leonean languages that in the 1990s a group of Geechie people visiting Africa discovered that Sierra Leoneans could carry on a mutually intelligible conversation without a translator.

Conclusion. There is little doubt among reasonable people that African language and culture have had a deep and persistent influence on African Americans. There is also little doubt that black English, or Ebonics, exists. Whether Ebonics is a separate language or a dialect of English, its grammatical construction, vocabulary, pronunciation, and overall style are influenced by Africa. Like jazz, which Ebonics has influenced along with hip-hop, blues, and other musical styles, however, Ebonics has its own particular take on the conventional American wisdom and it is a vital means for subverting that wisdom. It has been a vehicle for preserving Africanisms and group identity. Even such masters of Standard American English as Martin Luther King, Jr., could and did easily slip into the black vernacular to express that which could be similarly stated in SAE. As the old song says, "It ain't what cha do, it's the way that cha do it!"

BIBLIOGRAPHY

Bayne, Bijan C., "Gullah Festivities," *American Visions* 12, no. 2 (April–May 1997):45–48.
Foster, M., "Sociolinguistics and the African-American Community: Implications for Literacy," *Theory into Practice* 31, no. 4 (1992):303–310.
Fox, Margalit, "Dialects," *New York Times Magazine* (Sept. 12, 1999):40 col. 2.
Fox, Steven, "The Controversy over Ebonics," *Phi Delta Kappan* 78, no. 3 (Nov. 1997):237–240.

Pollitzer, William S., *The Gullah People and Their African Heritage* (Univ. of Ga. Press 1999).

Pyatt, Sherman, *A Dictionary and Catalog of African American Folklife of the South* (Greenwood Press 1999).

Romaine, Suzanne, *Language in Society: An Introduction to Sociolinguistics* (Oxford 1994).

Todd, Leon W., Jr., "Ebonics Is Defective Speech and a Handicap for Black Children," *Education* 118, no. 2 (Winter 1997):177–180.

Williams, Robert L., *Ebonics: The True Language of Black Folks* (Inst. of Black Studies 1975).

FRANK A. SALAMONE

AFRO

The "Afro," or "natural," a full-bodied, rounded hairstyle primarily worn by African Americans, was popular from roughly the mid-1960s to the late 1970s. The hairstyle did coincide with the wearing of long hair by white youth as a counterculture statement, but black wearers of the Afro were often making a black power statement as well. As Robin D. G. Kelley writes in "Nap Time: Historicizing the Afro," "The political contexts in which the Afro reached popularity, and the particular meaning that black political activists, hairstylists, and ordinary proud black folks gave the Afro, led to a rewriting of the history of black hair and a new style of politics that required omissions, revisions, and new myths." Angela Davis and her "basket" natural remains an enduring icon for late 1960s black radical politics, as do the Afros worn by members of such black nationalist organizations as the Black Panther Party for Self-Defense. Of course, some form of the Afro has always been worn, as the cover of the March 1925 *Survey Graphic* edited by Alain Locke during the Harlem Renaissance makes clear. And while the Afro became popular in the 1960s, it was actually predated by the late 1950s–early 1960s "au naturel" style made fashionable by women including Miriam Makeba, Abbey Lincoln, and Nina Simone. This style was also politically aligned with the black freedom movement and African liberation, but the immense popularity and political implications of the Afro in the 1960s has served to rewrite the earlier origins of the hairstyle.

By the early 1980s Hollywood, the advertising industry, and the demise of the black power movement—along with the ongoing urge for the "new"—all combined to render the Afro passé. Beginning in the mid-to-late 1980s, the post-civil-rights movement generation of artists and writers began to spoof and critique the Afro in such films as *Hollywood Shuffle* and *I'm Gonna Git You Sucka*, plays such as George Wolfe's *The Colored Museum*, books including Lisa Jones's *Bulletproof Diva: Tales of Race, Sex, and Hair*, and in various music videos (particularly from a rap group actually named The Afros). Ultimately, in much the same way "samples" of songs from previous eras dominated black rap and hip-hop music at the turn of the twenty-first century, the Afro returned as a viable hairstyle, albeit in a retro or ironic fashion, among many contemporary hairstyle possibilities.

[See also FASHION.*]*

BIBLIOGRAPHY

Caldwell, Paulette M., "A Hair Piece: Perspectives on the Intersection of Race and Gender," *Duke Law Journal* (1991):365–396.

Jones, Lisa, *Bulletproof Diva: Tales of Race, Sex, and Hair* (Doubleday 1994).

Kelley, Robin D. G., "Nap Time: Historicizing the Afro," *Fashion Theory* 1, no. 4 (1997):339–352.

Mercer, Kobena, "Black Hair/Style Politics," in *Out There: Marginalization and Contemporary Cultures,* ed. by Russell Ferguson et al. (MIT Press 1990).

BERTRAM D. ASHE

AFRO-CARIBBEAN CULTURE

Afro-Caribbean culture is a result of the forced diaspora of West African peoples. The concept of a diaspora is dependent on the recognition of a boundary between a homeland and those who belong to that homeland but are separated from it. People in the diaspora define themselves as being different from those in their host society. They maintain identification with their homeland and keep up cultural and social practices from that area. The more that people in the host country disparage the homeland, the stronger its symbolic meaning as a

© CARL JUSTE/MIAMI HERALD

Haitian American children from Florida perform a traditional Haitian dance.

lost ancestral homeland grows. Afro-Caribbean communities kept alive the meaning of Africa as their ancestral homeland and preserved and extended African worldviews and cultural practices.

Afro-Caribbean culture is a mixture of West African and European culture, with traces of various Native American elements. The African diaspora began with the European incursion into Africa in the mid-fifteenth century. For three hundred years Europeans enslaved Africans from the continent and spread them over the continents of North and South America. European capitalism demanded cheap raw materials and labor. Guns and ships aided in the conquest of Africa and its depopulation through the slave trade.

These transported peoples brought their cultures and ideas of social organization with them and held on to a good portion of their African identity. In other words, it is essential to emphasize "the central place of Africa in the slave experience," as the historian Paul Lovejoy notes. It is vital to note that enslaved Africans had their own understanding of the political issues of their own predicaments. Moreover, as Lovejoy stresses, " . . . individual colonies in the Americas often received slaves from the same places in Africa, thereby updating information, re-

kindling memories, and reinforcing the African component to the cultural adaptations under slavery." There was, therefore, a continuous influx of Africans who renewed the cultural identity of Africans in the Afro-Caribbean area and saw themselves as preserving and adapting African culture and society to a new area. As Lovejoy notes, Africans in Brachia, Brazil, regarded themselves as following a living tradition through their Islamic rituals. They saw themselves as active members of a living community, not as struggling to keep remnants of their former culture alive.

It is patently clear that the Afro-Caribbean communities were quite African in their orientation. There was a combination of elements from various parts of West Africa and a great deal of investigation is necessary to discern specific influences in any individual case. However, an overall West African culture permeates the Afro-Caribbean area. There are monuments, sacred sites, cemeteries, carnival and Santería festivals, and other cultural activities that clearly demonstrate African cultural connections. As a familiar song has it, "Anywhere you come from, as long as you're a black man, you're an African."

Since the nineteenth century there has been a return of Afro-Caribbeans to West Africa, especially to Sierra Leone. Other areas in West Africa also have witnessed the return of free men, mainly merchants. These settlements have also kept the connection between the Caribbean and West Africa and facilitated the flow of cultural information between the two areas. There are a number of traits that are obviously African found in Afro-Caribbean society: marketing behavior, credit institutions, religious rituals, naming practices, funeral ceremonies, various festival traits, and, of course, music. However, Lovejoy argues that careful study will reveal specific connections between individual Afro-Caribbean communities and their counterparts in West Africa.

Moreover, the racism and consequent racial stereotypes that were perpetuated by slave owners and later whites who lumped all Afro-Caribbeans together helped promote a common identity. The more that whites disparaged Africa, the greater became its cultural value and the Africanness of the Afro-Caribbean community. According to Lovejoy " . . . the 'Africanness' of the diaspora emerged in tandem with the evolving racism that provided the moral and liminal means of upholding the enslavement of blacks." In return, Africans in the Caribbean subordinated ethnic differences among themselves to foster a common Creole identity to oppose the white European identity of their oppressors.

There was, therefore, a conscious effort to maintain ties with Africa and to promote a sense of African identity through the development of African practices and culture, including music, religion, and political organization. These practices were replenished by new arrivals. After the end of slavery there were intensive relationships with West Africa. All of these ties kept African awareness alive and fresh in the Caribbean. Lovejoy says, "The pursuit of African history into the diaspora demonstrates how slaves could create a world that was largely autonomous from white, European society."

Too often historians and others have presented the history of Afro-Caribbeans as a passive reaction to events outside their control. They either have ignored the fact of the conscious shaping of their history on the part of Africans in the Caribbean or failed to take into account the historical contexts of their actions. Africans found many ways to assert their own identities in the midst of white control. For example, religion, music, cooking, naming, kinship, ethnicity, and other cultural and social aspects of their lives reflect a clear desire to preserve African identity. These actions reflect a conscious aspect not found in the notion of survival. The practice of people risking death in attempting to return to Africa by boat offers a stark example of the deep meaning of Africa in the lives of Africans in the Caribbean.

Ethiopianism. Much of the felt connection between Afro-Caribbean people and Africa has been expressed through Ethiopianism, a socioreligious movement that, in the words of Kevin A. Yelvington, "sought to identify personages and events in the Bible as 'African.'"

Ethiopianism stood traditional denigration of Africa on its head and found great favor in the Caribbean, where African American preacher George Liele founded the first Baptist church in Jamaica in 1784, named the Ethiopian Baptist Church. Edward Wilmot Blyden, better known than Liele, was born in the Danish West Indies. Blyden used Ethiopian emperor Menilek II's victory over the Italian army at the Battle of Adwa in 1896 as a means to connect the modern world and the era of Ethiopia's past glories. Bénito Sylvain, a Haitian pan-Africanist, went to Ethiopia to see Menilek and sought his support for the pan-African movement. Ras Tafari Makonnen, who became the Emperor Haile Selassie I in 1930, stirred up a great deal of interest in the Caribbean. His coronation led to the emergence of the Rastafarian religion in Jamaica.

Marcus Garvey invoked Ethiopia in his pan-African movement. Indeed, the Universal Negro Improvement Association (UNIA) produced a catechism that used biblical passages demonstrating the sacred nature of many places in Ethiopia. Garvey wrote, "We, as Negroes, have found a new ideal. Whilst our God has no color, yet it is human to see everything through one's spectacles, and since the white people see their God through white spectacles, . . . we shall worship Him through the spectacles of Ethiopia." Garvey and his followers hailed Ethiopia as the land of their fathers. Garvey had a great impact both in the Caribbean and in Africa, especially among the middle classes.

The Italo-Ethiopian War promoted a racial unity in the Caribbean. Ethiopia became associated with Africa in general, and the war was used to promote working-class solidarity. As Yelvington writes, "In Haiti, it was argued that there were three races in the world, and that Ethiopians were part of the black race, the Cushite and Hamitic branch." François Duvalier and Lorimer Denis used their ethnological authority to weigh in on the subject, affirming that "Ethiopians belong to the great black race," and, therefore, "our sympathy for the actual Ethiopians is not a case of geographical sentimentalism, but moreover one of the mysterious appeals of Race." Similar talk emerged in Jamaica, and Afro-Caribbean movements to aid Ethiopia found great support. Haile Selassie's distancing of himself from black leaders led to his disparagement by many who felt betrayed. Blyden, for example, took him to task for his betrayal and accused him of racial disloyalty.

Immigration into the United States. Caribbean immigration has not always been to the metropolitan centers of the United States, Great Britain, and Canada. Caribbean peoples became used to immigration as a result of local migration in the early periods of their history. In fact, migration had become a rite of passage, so that interregional migrations prepared people for what they termed *regional unity,* a concept stressing the cultural integrity of the Caribbean.

Afro-Caribbean immigration into the United States brought a number of influences that proved significant. Among them were various musical contributions including Latin, calypso, and reggae; cooking; religious ideas and practices; pan-African notions and other political ideas; and a host of other Africanisms that added to and reinforced those already present in the United States. Many of the luminaries of the Harlem Renaissance, for example, such as Claude McKay, came from the West Indies. Puerto Rican and Cuban musicians such as Tito Puente, Chano Pozo, and Paquito D'Rivera, to name only a few, had an impact on the development of American music.

The "radicalism" of many early immigrants from the Caribbean is explained by the deep racism they met in the United States in the early twentieth century. It was a racism that produced the lynching of innocent blacks as well as the everyday humiliation (and denial of rights) concomitant with segregation. Caribbean immigrants were not prepared for these outrages to their dignity. Claude McKay, a sophisticated and worldly immigrant, and one aware of American race prejudice and discrimination, found himself unprepared for its depths. McKay wrote in 1918, six years after his arrival, "It was the first time I had ever come face to face with such manifest, implacable hate of my race, and my feelings were indescribable. . . . I had heard of prejudice in America but never dreamed of it being

so intensely bitter." McKay had expected that he would encounter an English style of prejudice, one that hid behind a mask of civility and was more class than color based. What he encountered was the presence of

strong white men, splendid types, of better physique than any I had ever seen, exhibiting the most primitive animal hatred towards their weaker black brothers. In the South daily murders of a nature most hideous and revolting, in the North silent acquiescence, deep hate half-hidden under a puritan respectability, oft flaming up into an occasional lynching—this ugly raw sore in the body of a great nation. At first I was horrified, my spirit revolted against the ignoble cruelty and blindness of it all. Then I soon found myself hating in return but this feeling couldn't last long for to hate is to be miserable.

Out of his conviction that "to hate is to be miserable" came an outpouring of literature that contributed to the Harlem Renaissance.

The Caribbean-based Rastafarian movement contributed to the pan-African and black pride movements in a number of ways. Its roots can be traced to a number of early sources of African cultural pride, identification, and resistance, particularly that of Jamaica's Maroons. Maroons are slaves who escaped in the Caribbean area and established independent communities based on African social structures and cultural principles. The very basis of the Rastafarian movement is the idea that Africans outside Africa are in exile. It is a conscious acknowledgment of the fact of the African diaspora. Many of the ideas of the Rastafarian movement have become familiar to people through the reggae music of Bob Marley and his followers. Marley's music of protest spread the Rastafarian message, while also presenting another form of African music to the world. Along with the music, the "roots culture" of Rastafari has extended from the Caribbean to North America, Europe, and Africa. The increase in migration of Jamaicans has spread the message of Rastafari along with the music.

Indeed, since the 1990s the great increase in the number of migrants from Caribbean island nations has led to a growth in their influence within the United States and elsewhere. These island nations have a population of 35 million people and have sent one-sixth of their population, legally and illegally, into the United States since the 1990s, establishing a vast kinship, ethnic, and employer network across the United States, which has become an alternate homeland for many people from the Caribbean.

As is the case with other areas, high emigration from Caribbean countries has cost the homelands greatly while benefiting the United States. There has been a brain drain of professionals into the United States. During its long period of troubles, Haiti, for example, has lost a large number of its educated elite to the United States, where over 12 thousand of its professionals live. The English-speaking countries, such as Jamaica, Trinidad, and Tobago, find themselves most at risk for losing professionals. Out of a combined population of about 3.8 million, over 38 thousand of their professionals dwell in the United States.

Recent immigration figures from the United States Immigration and Naturalization Service (INS) attest to the continuing migration of people into the United States from Caribbean countries. These people will continue to influence the development of African American life in particular and American life in general.

[See also CENTRAL AMERICAN AND CARIBBEAN IMMIGRANTS; AFRICAN AMERICANS, articles on AFRICAN AMERICAN LITERATURE, AFRICAN AMERICAN DANCE, AFRICAN AMERICAN RELIGIONS, AFRICAN AMERICAN MUSIC.]

BIBLIOGRAPHY

Brereton, Bridget, and Kevin A. Yelvington, eds., The Colonial Caribbean in Transition: Essays on Postemancipation Social and Cultural History (Univ. Press of Fla. 1999).

Cashmore, Ellis, "Ethiopianism," in Dictionary of Race and Ethnic Relations, ed. by Ellis Cashmore with Michael Banton, et al. (Routledge 1994).

Chevannes, Barry, Rastafari: Roots and Ideology (Syracuse Univ. Press 1994).

Clifford, James, "Diasporas," Cultural Anthropology 9, no. 3 (1994):302–338.

Drake, St. Clair, The Redemption of African and Black Religion (Third World Press 1970).

Drake, St. Clair, Black Folk Here and There: An Essay in History and Anthropology, 2 vols. (Univ. of Calif. Press 1990).

Frey, Sylvia R., and Betty Wood, Come Shouting to Zion: African American Protestantism in the American South and British Caribbean to 1830 (Univ. of N.C. Press 1998).

Garvey, Marcus, The Philosophy and Opinions of Marcus Garvey, or, Africa for the Africans, ed. by Amy Jacques Garvey (1923; Majority Press 1986).

Magubane, Bernard Makhosezwe, The Ties That Bind: African-American Consciousness of Africa (Africa World Press 1987).

FRANK A. SALAMONE

AFROCENTRISM

The influential scholar Molefi Kete Asante rejects the term Afrocentrism as too ideologically bound; he prefers the term Afrocentricity, which he defined in The Afrocentric Idea (1980). Nonetheless, most proponents and critics of the Afrocentric movement use the terms interchangeably.

Asante defines the Afrocentric perspective as "placing African ideals at the center of any analysis that involves African culture and behavior." In other words, one should not analyze the peoples and cultures of Africa—and, by extension, those of the African diaspora—using the values and assumptions of western Europe and North America. Afrocentrists argue, moreover, that American culture draws from Africa far more than most Americans recognize or acknowledge. Therefore, by understanding and valuing African thought and culture, Americans can interpret U.S. history and culture in ways that avoid overemphasizing their European roots.

Afrocentrism seeks to integrate holistically—in ways ostensibly modeled by African peoples—the natural and supernatural, the mind and the body, the past and the present, the storyteller and the listener, and other traditionally European and American dichotomies. Students of all world cultures, therefore, can benefit from an Afrocentric perspective, according to its proponents. At the very least an Afrocentric perspective leads to the recognition that the unquestioned assumptions and values of a European tradition (emphasis on linear rather than ambiguous, circular narratives in literary studies, for example) limit American self-understanding and devalue non-European thought, culture, and ultimately, people. Because it fosters alternative perspectives based on ideas and values of nondominant peoples, some proponents of multiculturalism in American studies embrace Afrocentricity.

As Asante points out, critics' obstinate use of the term *Afrocentrism* (the "ism" suffix supposedly denotes a political ideology) reveals their belief that an Afrocentric perspective stems from a radical dogma, which they deride as politically correct. Such critics assume that a traditional perspective avoids ideology and remains free of personal values. Rather, Asante contends, an Afrocentric perspective competes with a Eurocentric perspective, which is as ideologically bound as any analytical perspective.

Regardless of whether or not Afrocentricity's critics misunderstand Asante's ideas, they are vocal in their opposition. Some have attacked what they believe are false contentions of Afrocentric history, such as the notion that the ancient Greek religion and philosophy was modeled on African cosmology, religion, and philosophy as asserted in Martin Bernal's *Black Athena*. Others claim that Afrocentrists' research often lacks rigor, and still others decry what they see as a radical attempt to cut American universities from their intellectual and structural moorings.

Despite the controversy, many scholars apply Afrocentric perspectives to a variety of studies, from Africa-centered world histories to analyses of African American images depicted by mass media. Others have developed Afrocentric school curricula intended to improve black children's self-esteem and learning, and health-care models better suited to African American beliefs and values.

As American studies broadens its geographic scope in the twenty-first century, more scholars seeking to understand American culture will look to other continents, including Africa, and to other continents' influences within America's borders. Debates about Afrocentricity, therefore, are likely to expand within the discipline.

[*See also* AFRICAN AMERICANS; BLACK POWER; BLACK PANTHERS; BLACK NATIONALISM; BLACK ARTS MOVEMENT.]

BIBLIOGRAPHY

Asante, Molefi Kete, *The Afrocentric Idea,* rev. and exp. ed. (Temple Univ. Press 1998) [the seminal text about Afrocentricity].

Bernal, Martin, *Black Athena: The Afroasiatic Roots of Classical Civilization* (Rutgers Univ. Press 1987) [embraced by many Afrocentrists, although neither Asante nor Bernal himself call this author an Afrocentrist].

Hamlet, Janice D., ed., *Afrocentric Visions: Studies in Culture and Communication* (Sage 1998) [a collection of Afrocentric research in a variety of disciplines].

Howe, Stephen, *Afrocentrism: Mythical Pasts and Imagined Homes* (Verso 1998) [a critical analysis].

Lefkowitz, Mary, *Not Out of Africa: How Afrocentrism Became an Excuse to Teach Myth as History* (Basic 1996) [an often-cited critique of Afrocentricity].

DAVID GOLDSTEIN-SHIRLEY

AGRARIANS

The meaning of the word *agrarian* goes back to Latin roots related to fields or land. Historically, agrarianism has referred to land tenure issues, and particularly strategies or laws needed to break up land monopolies. Thus, agrarian reform has often involved a radical attack on entrenched privileges.

Because of its expanse of land, and very low rents, the United States has not faced much agrarian agitation. Thomas Jefferson embraced a mild agrarianism in his unsuccessful effort to get Virginia to grant every child a birthright of fifty acres (20 ha). Thomas Paine advocated death taxes to regain for society the rent value of land. The new United States made illegal any entailed land, or what in England had been a prop for land monopoly. In all such mild efforts, the working principle was that land, unlike productive tools, was not created by human labor. The most important implication of the right to property was the right of every person to have access to what God made.

Exclusion from nature and its productive power reduced one to a state of dependence and servility.

Briefly, after 1825, the most radical agrarian schemes in American history gained rather broad public support. Urban artisans, threatened by factory production, organized workingmen's parties and often argued that easy access to land would provide a safety valve for a surplus of city workers. In 1829 one of the leaders of New York workingmen, Thomas Skidmore, advocated the most radical agrarian reform in American history. He reacted in anger to a developing land monopoly in New York and, in *The Rights of Man to Property,* asked the state to acquire title to all property and provide equal shares to all citizens, so that each could have an equal start in life. Few wanted such a radical redistribution of wealth, but in the wake of the workingmen's movement a milder agrarianism survived. Eventually led by George Henry Evans, the movement grew from an early Agrarian League into the National Reform Association (NRA), which gained members all over the country in the years before the Civil War. The leaders of the NRA believed that a land-rich United States could attain agrarian justice by two relatively simple programs—state laws restricting the amount of land any one person could own and a federal program that would offer any family who wanted it a free, nonalienable (one could not sell the land) homestead of 160 acres (65 ha). This crusade contributed to the enactment of the Homestead Act of 1862 (it violated agrarian principles by allowing owners to sell and mortgage such land).

Agrarianism lived on after 1865 but never again gained broad support. The most radical latter-day agrarian was Henry George, who wanted to tax away all the rent value of land (the single tax). Such a tax would end land speculation, and in a sense socialize access to land. George's impact would be greater in Europe than in America. Many scholars have misleadingly referred to Populism as an agrarian movement, but in fact it was largely led by farm owners hostile to land reform. In the 1930s a group of Vanderbilt University professors offered what they called an agrarian philosophy to challenge industrialism. For the most part these Southern Agrar-

ians celebrated farm life, not land reform, but in the Depression they did support tenant-purchase programs and the breakup of large plantations. In the twentieth century the amount of cultivated land steadily declined, even as production per acre soared. This plenitude made most agrarian schemes seem irrelevant. Thus, it has been in Latin America and other parts of the world that agrarian reform has remained a vital political issue.

BIBLIOGRAPHY

Chase, Malcolm, *The People's Farm: English Radical Agrarianism, 1775–1840* (Clarendon Press 1988).

Conkin, Paul, *Prophets of Prosperity: America's First Political Economists* (Ind. Univ. Press 1980).

Montmarquet, James A., *The Idea of Agrarianism: From Hunter-Gatherer to Agrarian Radical in Western Culture* (Univ. of Idaho Press 1989).

Scott, William B., *In Pursuit of Happiness: American Conceptions of Property, from the Seventeenth to the Twentieth Century* (Ind. Univ. Press 1977).

Skidmore, Thomas, *The Rights of Man to Property* (A. Ming 1829).

PAUL CONKIN

AGRICULTURE

The romantic view of agriculture is deeply ingrained in the American psyche. It was given its classical literary expression in the writings of James Fenimore Cooper who was deeply influenced by the agrarian teachings of President Thomas Jefferson and the Marquis de Lafayette. In this view the strength of the country lay in its independent farmers, the "yeomen." Democracy could only flourish when based on the holding of independent land and the production of food. Industry was perceived as the enemy of democracy because it concentrated wealth in the hands of a few affluent merchants and bankers.

This simple Jeffersonian faith in the virtue of the American farmer has become a staple of American political life. Cooper's Leatherstocking Tales, with their romantic images of American independence and ingenuity, captured the American imagination and helped give focus to Jefferson's agrarian myth. The classic academic study of the agrarian dream

Iowa's fertile farmland encourages increasing productivity.

is Seymour Lipset's *Agrarian Socialism* (1950; revised 1968), in which he developed his theory of elite systems and politics and the manner in which American political and economic life developed in opposition to Jefferson's agrarian dream. In *The Economic Origins of Jeffersonian Democracy* (1915), Charles Beard placed somewhat greater emphasis on the philosophical context of Jefferson's political struggles with Alexander Hamilton, but he also stressed the significance of economic interests in governmental action.

Much of the philosophical foundation for the liberal agrarian movement, the basis of Jeffersonian democracy, came from the writing of John Taylor (1753–1824) of Caroline county, Virginia. Taylor was a leader of the movement for a liberalization of democracy in America. He favored religious disestablishment, greater dissemination of voting rights, and fairer representation. Taylor opposed a strong central government and fought the ratification of the U.S. Constitution. *An Inquiry into the Principles and Policy of the Government of the United States* (1814) and *Construction Construed and Constitutions Vindicated* (1820) defended agrarian democracy from attacks by a strong central government and the mercantile classes. Taylor fought the idea of a strong Supreme Court, which was able to declare state ac-

tions null and void. He fought any congressional restrictions on the expansion of slavery into the territories.

Jeffersonian Republicans formed the first opposition political party in the United States around the notions of agrarian democracy. It gained power nationally in 1801 and held it until 1825. It drew its members from the Anti-Federalists, those who opposed adoption of the United States Constitution. These Anti-Federalists began to form a coherent party in opposition to the fiscal programs of Alexander Hamilton, Washington's secretary of the treasury. Jefferson drew around him people who opposed a powerful central government. His party also opposed the loose Constitutional interpretation of the Federalists. The Republicans favored states' rights and strict constructionist interpretation of the Constitution.

The party chose the name "Republican" to emphasize its opposition to what it considered the monarchical bent of the Federalists. The party had been influenced by the ideals of the French Revolution. Hamilton favored the wealthy mercantile class at the expense of the average man according to the Republicans. The strengthening of the central government threatened, in Jefferson's view, the future of American democracy.

The strong central bank chartered in 1791 by the U.S. Congress focused the opposition of the Republicans on Hamilton's policies. The debate over this bank was largely responsible for the emergence and shaping of the first political parties in the United States. Although Jefferson did not manage to "kill" the bank when he became president, his opposition kept it from being rechartered in 1811. Interestingly, even as most policies of the Federalists gained favor in contrast with the agrarianism of the Republicans, the central bank remained controversial and a focus of opposition to the Federalist program.

As agrarianism became "agrarian populism," especially in the South and West and among the poor in all regions of the United States, opposition to the Second Bank of the United States, chartered in 1816, became formidable. The bank became a symbol of wealth with its notions of aristocratic privilege. People termed the bank "the monster," and they came to see it as the enemy of the common people. Andrew Jackson, who became president in 1829, united opposition to the bank. Jackson resisted Congress's attempt to renew the bank's charter through vetoing the new charter. The "Bank War" that followed, in which Jackson withdrew federal government money from the bank, was a victory for the notion of agrarian democracy.

The 1828 presidential election was a major event in U.S. political history. Historians see it as a victory for the West and a signal that power had shifted to the frontier. In line with the growing spirit of democracy in the country, Jackson had appealed directly to the people of the United States for his election. Although eventually quite wealthy, Jackson was the first president born in poverty. Thus, the inherent agrarian distrust of the wealthy mercantile class came to him naturally.

As the "embodiment of American democracy," Jackson had to embrace issues that appealed to the mass of voters. These issues tended to be much the same as those that were part of agrarian democracy; namely, opposition to the National Bank and favoring the extension of democracy, and opposition to mercantile interests while favoring those of farmers and independent workers. Jackson, in sum, opposed the centralization of power and tended to favor regional interests, especially those of the South and West.

Jackson's followers believed that he represented the principles of agrarian democracy. They saw in his rise to power the victory of the self-made man, which they believed demonstrated the strength of popular democracy. His rise to power in some way represented the power of the people. To his friends and foes he represented opposition to property and order. His victory was that of the people against entrenched interests. Those special interests were virtually the same ones that Hamilton and the Federalists had supported.

Farmers had already begun to develop the language of class that dominated much of the early political battles of the republic. Farmers believed that their own improvements brought value to the land. They had little use for the romantic notions of nostalgic pastoralism that the rural gentry (the wealthy landowning class) embraced. Farmers tended to use this notion of productive labor as the basis for American democracy over Hamilton's theories of speculative investment.

The "fathers" of the agrarian notion were the Gracchi brothers. Tiberius and Gaius Gracchus were Roman political leaders who participated in Roman politics in the second century B.C. These brothers came from a distinguished Roman aristocratic family, which had held high political office for over a century. The brothers were well educated in the Greek system, which stressed literature, oratory, and philosophy. Tiberius was murdered by his political opponents and Gaius took up the cause.

Tiberius and Gaius moved to reform Roman agrarian law, and that championing of the agricultural element of Roman republicanism stirred up fierce opposition. Gaius became tribune and united the knights to his cause against the aristocracy in the senate, combining the middle-class knights with the poorer citizens. This coalition could carry out radical reforms. Gaius sought to reform Roman government but he remained an aristocrat who led the populace, a model for the Jeffersonians who were for the people but not of them. Similarly, the Jeffersonians were influenced by Gaius's understanding of the agrarian foundation for Rome's strength and his attempted political reforms, including his opposition to the growing power of the courts.

The populist movement in the United States in the late nineteenth century was one more manifestation of a politically oriented coalition of agrarian reformers in the Midwest and South. These reformers advocated a wide range of economic and political reform legislation. These reforms echoed those of presidents Jefferson and Jackson. The farmers' alliances that sprang up in the Midwest and South tapped into the discontent of farmers over crop failures, falling prices, and poor marketing and credit facilities. These alliances were organized on a local level and won significant regional victories. However, they were unable to transfer their power to a national level.

In 1892 leaders of the alliances organized the Populist (or People's) Party, replacing the farmers' alliances. Although the Populist Party attempted to woo labor and other disenfranchised groups, they remained almost entirely agrarian-oriented. Their program included demands for an increase in the amount of money in circulation through the unlimited coinage of silver, a graduated income tax, government ownership of the railroads, a tariff for revenue only, and the direct election of U.S. senators. Their program sought to strengthen political democracy and give farmers economic equality with business and industry.

The party managed to win more than one million votes for its presidential candidate in the election of 1892 and to join the Democrats in some states in electing candidates who supported their platform. In 1896 the Populists merged with the Democratic cause since both parties supported the Free Silver movement. William Jennings Bryan, the candidate, lost the election, leading to the collapse of the Populist Party.

In the last thirty or so years of the twentieth century there was a movement among American historians and students of popular culture to focus on the importance of the agrarian myth in understanding American history and culture. The pull of the agrarian myth is still strong in American society. For example, scholars have examined the literary agrarian movement that originated in Nashville, Tennessee, which, in common with other similar movements, advocated a return to preindustrial society as a reaction to the emptiness of modern industrial culture.

Modern agrarian movements, however, have adapted to the exigencies of contemporary demands. Agrarian fundamentalist Henry A. Wallace, for example, witnessed the industrial revolution that swept American agriculture and rural life in the 1950s and changed American farm life. While increasing farm productivity, it diminished the number of farm workers and the number of independent farms. Wallace attempted to increase the number of independent farmers through his own use of technology, including a new form of hybrid

© JEFF ZARUBA/ALLSTOCK/PICTUREQUEST

A Wisconsin dairy farm.

corn; however, he soon realized that this was hopeless. Therefore, he began to preach the value of agriculture in the foundation of American power.

This myth, however, has been used against the interests of the American farmer. Agricultural interests, for example, that did not want to pay for the protection of farm workers appealed to the myth of the independent American farmer. The archetypal American farmer, in this view, is honest, self-reliant, and willing to do a hard, tiring job. Thus, the agrarian myth has led many to believe that society owes a debt to farmers.

Moreover, there is still a substantial belief that agrarianism can cure the ills of industrial society. Agrarianism is a radical idea that argues that the economy should be decentralized and based on land. It urges a return to the Jeffersonian ideal of a republic based on small landowners. The key to true democracy is the spread of small, independent farmers. As more individuals own their own small parcels of land, so the argument runs, care of the land will improve. Self-sufficiency will return to American life.

Much of the political policy after World War II was shaped by the myth of the agrarian past. Former president George H. Bush, for example, noted that "a good country song is like a Norman Rockwell painting. It captures the essence of the American spirit and portrays experiences that those who work hard and play by the rules can identify with. It is devoid of cynicism and can make you laugh or cry. To me, the same timeless qualities that make country music so appealing have also made our nation great." The images of country music, of course, reflect rural farm values, believed by many to be the essential American spirit. This folk Americanism still lies deep in the American psyche.

Much of the flavor of this American agrarianism has been articulated for Americans in the works of talented writers. The problems of California farming in the 1930s, for example, found brilliant social critics who used neo-Jeffersonian assumptions. These critics attacked the capitalism that marked Depression-era California agriculture, challenging the laissez-faire capitalist creed of California agribusiness. These critics include Carey McWilliams, John Steinbeck, and Paul S. Taylor, who revealed the unseen ugliness and human exploitation beneath the outer beauty of agribusiness.

In *Factories in the Field* (1939), for example, McWilliams recalled a rural past that no longer existed. That past featured family farms and thriving villages. "[T]here seem to be no farms in the accepted sense," McWilliams states. "One looks in vain for the incidents of rural life: the schoolhouse . . . the comfortable homes, the compact and easy indolence of the countryside. . . . The impression gained is one of vast agricultural domains, huge orchards, and garden estates, without permanent occupants."

The Works Progress Administration and Farm Security Administration of the 1930s provided opportunities for talented artists to produce works that emblazoned images of honest farmers exploited by the system in the American mind. James Agee and Walker Evans's *Let Us Now Praise Famous Men* (1941), Paul Taylor and Dorothea Lange's *American Exodus* (1939), and Pare Lorentz's films, notably *The Plow That Broke the Plains*, perpetuated the ideas the agribusiness practiced unhealthy farming. Talented novelists such as Erskine Caldwell (*Tobacco Road*, 1932, and *God's Little Acre*, 1933) and John Steinbeck (*The Grapes of Wrath*, 1939) put a face on the inhumanity of agribusiness. Real-life people suffered under the heel of greedy interests that threatened to distort American democracy and take it away from the people.

[See also FARMS; AGRARIANS.*]*

BIBLIOGRAPHY

Berry, Wendell, "Back to the Land: Arguments for Agrarianism and Local Economy," *The Amicus Journal* 20:4 (Winter 1999):37.

Clark, Christopher, "Rural America and the Transition to Capitalism," *Journal of the Early Republic* 16:2 (Summer 1996):223 [special issue on "Capitalism in the Early Republic"].

Cochrane, Willard W., *The Development of American Agriculture: A Historical Analysis,* 2d ed. (Univ. of Minn. Press 1993).

Danbom, David B., *The Resisted Revolution: Urban America and the Industrialization of Agriculture, 1900–1930* (Iowa State Univ. Press 1979).

Danbom, David B., *Born in the Country: A History of Rural America* (Johns Hopkins Univ. Press 1995).

Dufou, Ronald P., "The Agrarian Origins of American Capitalism," *Journal of Social History* 28:2 (Winter 1994):420 [book review].

Ebeling, Walter, *The Fruited Plain: The Story of American Agriculture* (Univ. of Calif. Press 1979).

Flamm, Michael W., "The National Farmers Union and the Evolution of Agrarian Liberalism, 1937–1946," *Agriculture History* 68:3 (Summer 1994):54.

Hurt, R. Douglas, *American Agriculture: A Brief History* (Iowa State Univ. Press 1994).

Kelsey, Timothy W., "The Agrarian Myth and Policy Responses to Farm Safety," *American Journal of Public Health* 84:7 (July 1994):1171.

Kirkendal, Richard S., "Reflections of a Revolutionary on a Revolution [Henry A. Wallace], " *Journal of the West* 31:4 (October 1992):8.

Knoblock, Frieda, *The Culture of the Wilderness: Agriculture as Colonization in the American West* (Univ. of N.C. Press 1996).

Kulikoff, Alan, *The Agrarian Origins of American Capitalism* (Univ. Press of Va. 1992).

McWilliams, Carey, *Factories in the Field* (Little, Brown 1939).

Vandeman, Ann, "The Political Economy of the Family Farm: The Agrarian Roots of American Capitalism," *Review of Radical Political Economics* 26:3 (September 1994):150 [book review].

FRANK A. SALAMONE

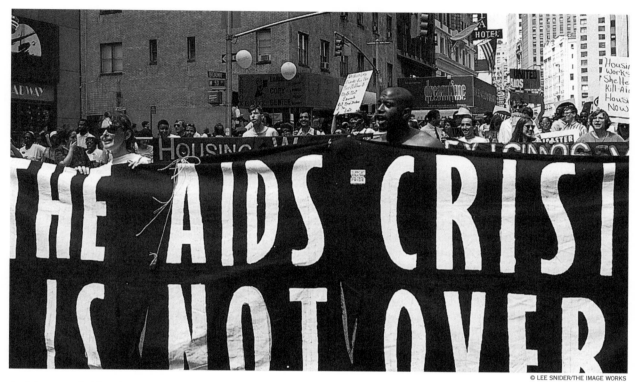

© LEE SNIDER/THE IMAGE WORKS

Activist group holding banner, "The AIDS Crisis Is Not Over," marches for the United for AIDS Action during the 2000 Democratic presidential convention in New York City.

AIDS

From its early identification in the United States as *gay related immune deficiency* (GRID), acquired immune deficiency syndrome (AIDS) has demonstrated the powerful impact of identity on scientific research, social service provision, media representation, and community organizing. The initial list of the Centers for Disease Control (CDC) that identified risk groups for AIDS (hemophiliacs, Haitians, homosexuals, and heroin or intravenous drug users) suggested that only some kinds of people were at risk for human immunodeficiency virus (HIV) infection. In the mass media, such terms as *general public* and *innocent victim* conferred stigma on those with AIDS and justified the lack of an adequate response by the government. National and racial identity also were used in attempts to assign blame, perhaps most blatantly in widely reported efforts to place the origin of HIV first in Haiti and

subsequently in central Africa. These theories led to the spread of rumors within some communities that AIDS was a government plot to target African Americans and homosexuals. Although the CDC ultimately removed Haitians from the list of risk groups, the association of AIDS with particular national identities continued to trouble immigration policy. Ultimately, under activist pressure to articulate a policy more in line with the known facts about HIV transmission, public health officials shifted their discussion from "risk groups" to "risk practices." This approach seemed to avoid arbitrarily targeting entire population groups, while more accurately addressing people whose behavior might put them at risk, an issue raised in research on men who engaged in sex with other men but who did not identify themselves as homosexual.

The AIDS epidemic has been characterized by a strong activist response. Many activists adopted the phrase "AIDS crisis" to describe AIDS as a state

71

of emergency demanding immediate action at all levels. Two key activist projects in the first years of the epidemic were the creation of AIDS service organizations, which stepped forward to provide practical care and social support in reaction to widespread discrimination and inadequate social services, and the organization of the National Association of People with AIDS, which promoted the "person living with AIDS" as an alternative identity to media representations of "AIDS victims." Other AIDS organizing took place within existing community groups, particularly in communities of color. The NAMES Project AIDS Memorial Quilt, established in 1987, challenged the practice of reducing people with AIDS to statistics. The quilt remains a powerful if controversial symbol of the epidemic, raising complex questions about the politics of memorialization. AIDS activists explored the politics of representation in a variety of media, both deconstructing mainstream images of the syndrome and producing new alternatives. Video became an effective method of activist production, particularly as a way to disseminate information about safer sex practices. Such efforts attracted the opposition of conservative politicians, who consistently attempted to block funding for materials perceived as obscene. In addition to explicit sex-education material, needle exchange became a hugely controversial public issue, pitting public health findings against legal status in the problematic "war on drugs." The question of criminalization also affected outreach to and among sex workers. In 1987 the founding of the AIDS Coalition to Unleash Power (ACT-UP) introduced a new confrontational style of cultural politics. ACT-UP, a loose federation of local chapters, produced a number of highly publicized direct actions, creating political street theater to illustrate the failures of important institutions (including the churches, the Food and Drug Administration [FDA], the CDC, and the New York Stock Exchange). Some participants in ACT-UP pursued treatment activism, challenging research protocols and demanding swifter access to new treatments. Although chapters of ACT-UP struggled with issues of race, class, and gender, participants also brought these issues to a broader public. For

example, women challenged the CDC's definition of AIDS, arguing that it failed to include opportunistic infections commonly experienced by women, leading to a revised case definition in 1990.

In the 1990s, reports on the epidemiology of AIDS provoked discourse on the "changing face of AIDS," as the epidemic affected increasing numbers of poor women of color. These changes provided new challenges for AIDS service and activist organizations that were founded, staffed, and located in primarily white, middle-class, gay communities. Rural service providers also raised issues about reaching geographically dispersed populations. As the epidemic continued into a second decade, debate erupted in the gay community about how to sustain safer sex practices after research showed that following a brief period of decline, HIV infection was again rising, particularly among young people. Gay writers explored issues such as support for HIV-negative men, and sex without condoms. "Public sex" became an important activist issue, as commercial sex venues and other areas of public sexual expression came under attack, in part in the name of AIDS prevention. In the 1990s, AIDS provided a justification for policing the boundaries of human sexuality. Sexual practice and HIV transmission were studied in terms of space, in response to some activists and critics who suggested that such places as commercial bathhouses provided community forums that might promote and sustain changes in sexual behaviors.

The development of new treatments in the 1990s further exacerbated the politics of class. For economically advantaged people who could afford and tolerate these drugs, the "triple cocktail" protease inhibitor combinations caused a dramatic decrease in mortality, leading some to speculate about a future in which AIDS might be a chronic, but manageable, condition, and to predict the imminent "end of AIDS." Others pointed to earlier cases in which widely heralded drugs failed to deliver in the long run. The price of these drugs remained a difficult issue, as public assistance programs struggled to meet their staggering annual expenses. The high cost of treatment also raised troubling questions about the global pandemic. The propensity of AIDS to cross national borders highlighted the importance of situating the American epidemic within a global context, making the inaccessibility of more successful treatments for many people around the world an issue for the United States. Effective public health cannot be conducted solely within national borders; the flow of people, images, and capital around the world represents a critical area for cultural analysis in relation to AIDS.

[See also GAY AND LESBIAN MOVEMENT; PUBLIC HEALTH.*]*

BIBLIOGRAPHY

Browning, Barbara, *Infectious Rhythm: Metaphors of Contagion and the Spread of African Culture* (Routledge 1998).

Murphy, Timothy, and Suzanne Poirier, eds., *Writing AIDS: Gay Literature, Language, and Analysis* (Columbia Univ. Press 1993).

Patton, Cindy, *Fatal Advice: How Safe-Sex Education Went Wrong* (Duke Univ. Press 1996).

Stoller, Nancy, *Lessons from the Damned: Queers, Whores, and Junkies Respond to AIDS* (Routledge 1998).

Sturken, Marita, *Tangled Memories: The Vietnam War, the AIDS Epidemic, and the Politics of Remembering* (Univ. of Calif. Press 1997).

MEREDITH RAIMONDO

AILEY, ALVIN

Alvin Ailey, Jr., was a pioneer in popularizing black American dance as a vital American dance style. Ailey organized the first black repertory dance company in 1958, which toured extensively and came to the forefront during the civil rights movement. His most famous work, *Revelations*, first performed in 1960, is considered an anthem to the faith and strength of black people. Although his choreographic output was not large, his company, the Alvin Ailey American Dance Theatre (AAADT), remains a performing base for seminal black choreographers and dancers, a repository of classic and new black choreography. According to Judith Jamison, a leading dancer who remained in Ailey's company for fifteen years, "he made sure that your influence was eclectic, but that you realized what your roots were."

© JACK VARTOOGIAN

Alvin Ailey (*center*) rehearsing the dance *Hermit Songs* with Clive Thompson (*left*) and Dudley Willcoms.

Ailey, a child of the Depression, was both outrageous and courageous. Equipped with brilliant energy, good humor, and a sense of community, Ailey broke many barriers in the theater world. His dances, bridging black and white cultures, rewrote the choreographic canon by intertwining European American linear styles with black Africanist qualities and structures. He demonstrated that a dance language accessible to a broad public has important artistic value. Throughout Ailey's fifty-nine years, he strived for the rightful place of black dance and culture in America: "Treat us like something that's worthwhile, like something that contributes to the culture of the country."

Born on January 4, 1931, in Rogers, Texas, north of Austin, Ailey and his mother, Lulu, were abandoned by his father. Ten years later his mother preceded him to Los Angeles, a city that promised work for blacks during the war effort. As a teenager Ailey began wandering the city's movie houses, the theatrical and nightclub scenes, and seeing performances by the Ballet Russe de Monte Carlo and Katherine Dunham and her Tropical Revue. It made him curious about the creative potential of dance. Two of his friends, Fred Crumb and Carmen de Lavallade, drew the seventeen-year-old to Lester Horton's studio where he started his dance studies. After graduation from high school, Ailey enrolled at the University of California at Los Angeles, interrupting his dance training. An indifferent student, in 1950 he transferred to Los Angeles City College where he found time to dance, quickly moving into the advanced class.

Ailey enrolled at San Francisco State University in 1952. He danced briefly with Anna Halprin and partnered another dancer, Marguerite Angelos (now, Maya Angelou), in a nightclub act known as Al and Rita. Another show, directed by Lou Fontaine, introduced Ailey to jazz music and dancing. Soon the act was booked into Los Angeles and Ailey returned to the Horton studio.

In 1953, with high hopes, the Horton troupe drove to New York to perform, only to find their concert badly advertised and under reviewed. The company recovered with a strong season and a successful debut at Jacob's Pillow summer dance festival in Massachusetts. Invited back to the Pillow for a two-week engagement, the company's euphoria crashed with Horton's sudden death. Leadership of the company went to Ailey.

The following year Ailey returned to New York to dance in the chorus of *Carmen Jones,* choreographed by Herbert Ross. Back in Los Angeles, Ailey proclaimed that the artist must create "his own unity according to his own experience and belief." He worked collaboratively on *Morning Mourning* and *According to St. Francis,* two dances from this experimental period as director of the Horton company.

In New York to dance in *House of Flowers,* another musical choreographed by Herbert Ross, Ailey, only twenty-four, was a hit. Critic Carl Van Vechten enthused: "Alvin Ailey has all the attributes of a great dancer." John Martin likened him to a "svelte, nervously alert animal." Ailey remained in New York making his new dance home the New Dance Group, a collective where black and white dancers congregated. After *House of Flowers* closed, he danced with Anna Sokolow, Donald McKayle, and Sophie Maslow. Ailey taught at different locations between 1955 and 1956, and he appeared in

the Off-Broadway play *The Carefree Tree;* toured with Harry Belafonte's show *Sing, Man, Sing;* danced in *Caribbean Calypso Carnival,* directed by Geoffrey Holder; and did a pilot for a television show, *The Amos and Andy Music Hall.* In 1957 there was another calypso part for him in *Jamaica,* choreographed by Jack Cole.

Dismayed at the few opportunities for black dancers to do good work in New York, Ailey organized a concert of black dancers in 1958. His dances included *Blues Suite, Redonda (Five Dances on Latin Themes),* and a solo tribute to Lester Horton, *Ode and Homage.* Warmly received at Jacob's Pillow, his dancers began to feel like a real company. In 1960, at the premiere of Ailey's *Revelations,* the dancers were surprised by a cheering standing ovation. Performed to an anthology of Negro spirituals, the work is direct, theatrical, unabashedly fun, autobiographical, and yet captures the human spirit in a way that speaks to all people. A long-time friend, dancer James Truitte once remarked that *Revelations* is "a dance that contains the history of blacks in America."

A point of view well in hand, Ailey envisioned two innovative ideas for his young company: first was a modern-dance repertory company not fixed to the aesthetic of a single choreographer; the second was to produce regular showcases of new choreography. The company prepared for its first major tour in 1962. Sponsored by the U.S. Department of State, the international tour brought the ten-dancer company to Australia. For the program Ailey wrote: "From his roots as a slave, the American Negro—sometimes sorrowing, sometimes jubilant, but always hopeful—has touched, illuminated, and influenced the most remote preserves of world civilization. I and my dance theater celebrate this trembling beauty."

By the mid-1960s the nation was reeling in the turmoil of the civil rights movement. Support for AAADT eroded owing to charges that Ailey's choreography was not legitimate and was too commercial. To counteract the criticism, Ailey sought out signature works by his peers without consideration of the ethnicity of the choreographer. New works in 1966 included *Antony and Cleopatra,* a commissioned opera by Samuel Barber for the opening of Lincoln Center in New York, and *The House of Bernarda Alba (Feast of Ashes).*

Ailey created *Masekela Langage* and *La Strada* in 1969. Two years later *Streams* was choreographed to a score by Miloslav Kabelac, and *Gymnopédie,* to Erik Satie's piano score, rounded out the season. Jennifer Dunning called this period Ailey's "golden years." Just when success was at his fingertips, Ailey shocked the dance world by dissolving the company. He was demoralized and tired because the tour of the Soviet Union arranged by the state department had failed to materialize. Just as suddenly, the tour was back on for the fall, convincing Ailey to reinstate his company. At the same time, he was creating his first plotless ballet, *The River* (with a Duke Ellington score) for American Ballet Theatre.

Following seasons in the Soviet Union and in England, the company returned to New York to more success. Fascinated with the ballet idiom, in 1971 Ailey created *Flowers* starring British ballerina Lynn Seymour. *Cry,* a dance for Judith Jamison, was dedicated to Ailey's mother and to "all black women everywhere." In this period Ailey's dances demonstrated a passionate relationship to the music, quickening the emotions of the dance and establishing his role as a storyteller.

Ailey choreographed Leonard Bernstein's religious opera, *Mass* (1972). He received an honorary degree from Princeton University, was invited to perform for the twenty-fifth anniversary of the American Dance Festival at Connecticut College, and was commissioned to create the dances for *Carmen* at the Metropolitan Opera Company. His first television special, *Alvin Ailey: Memories and Visions,* aired in 1974. Three years later Ailey received one of the first long-term residency awards from the National Endowment for the Arts. This allowed the company to remain in such towns as Atlanta (1977), Los Angeles (1983), and Kansas City (1984 and 1986). More dances poured forth: the sultry *Night Creature* (1975) and *The Mooche* (1974), honoring five great black female singers, were created for a television program honoring Duke Ellington.

In 1977, to celebrate the company's twentieth anniversary, Ailey produced a festival honoring Duke Ellington. He was one of the first dancers to receive the Mayor's Award of Honor in Arts and Culture, followed in 1979 with the Capezio Dance Award. The death of his former partner, Joyce Trisler, resulted in a moving tribute, *Memoria,* but his own world was unraveling. In 1980 Ailey was arrested for criminal trespass and held for psychological testing at New York's Bellevue Hospital. Nevertheless, in 1984 he choreographed *For Bird—With Love* to music by Charlie Parker, Dizzy Gillespie, Count Basie, and Jerome Kern.

The company's thirtieth anniversary in 1988 was not joyful, for Ailey was in failing health. Feted at the Kennedy Center's annual honors, Ailey and the company were featured in another television special, hosted by Bill Cosby. Ailey enthused: "I am overwhelmed by these people—it's always been the people."

Four nights after receiving New York City's Handel Medallion for cultural achievement, Ailey entered the hospital and was diagnosed with AIDS (acquired immune deficiency syndrome). Although weakened, he maintained his work pace. But by the summer of 1989, Ailey was forced to reduce his schedule. He flew to Kansas City where he witnessed, unannounced, the performance at the end of the first AileyCamp for underprivileged youth, the culmination of a long-held dream. It was his last public appearance. Ailey died on December 1, 1989, and was buried in Whittier, California. His company has survived him, directed by his longtime dance partner and assistant, Judith Jamison.

[See also AFRICAN AMERICANS, *article on* AFRICAN AMERICAN DANCE.]

BIBLIOGRAPHY

Dunning, Jennifer, *Alvin Ailey: A Life in Dance* (Addison-Wesley 1996).

Gold, Sylviane, "Thirty Years with Alvin Ailey, the Ailey Generations," *Dance Magazine* (Dec. 1988):40–43.

Jamison, Judith, *Dancing Spirit: An Autobiography* (Doubleday 1993).

Latham, Jacqueline, *A Biographical Study of the Lives and Contributions of Two Selected Contemporary Black Male*

Artists, Arthur Mitchell and Alvin Ailey—in the Idioms of Ballet and Modern Dance, Respectively, unpublished diss. (Texas Woman's Univ. 1973).

Long, Richard, *The Black Tradition in American Dance* (Rizzoli Intl. Pubns. 1989).

Thorpe, Edward, *Black Dance* (Overlook Press 1990).

Warren, Larry, *Lester Horton, Modern Dance Pioneer* (M. Dekker 1977).

JANICE LAPOINTE-CRUMP

History's first powered flight, photographed in 1903. Orville Wright is the pilot, as his brother Wilbur watches.

AIRPLANES AND AVIATION

As an American invention, the airplane is a symbol of the United States's emergence as a twentieth-century superpower. It has linked the communities of the nation and the world for trade, travel, and communication, while also increasing the destructiveness of modern warfare and accelerating debate about the place of machines in contemporary American life.

Early Development. Early American flight experiments copied the advances of European inventors, most notably in hot air balloons. But powered, winged flight was an impossibility until December 17, 1903, when Orville and Wilbur Wright, bicycle manufacturers from Dayton, Ohio, successfully piloted the first motor-powered airplane. Of that day's three flights near Kitty Hawk, North Carolina, Wilbur's 528-foot (161-m) hop was the longest.

Slowly, visionaries from several fields recognized the airplane's potential. The U.S. War Department bought its first airplane in 1909. The Wright brothers themselves directed the first commercial flight in 1910. In 1913 Florida entrepreneurs began experimenting with the airplane as a form of public transportation. Stunt fliers and barnstormers performed in traveling exhibitions throughout the early decades of the twentieth century, demonstrating the possibilities of flight to a public that relied largely on the railroad for long-distance travel and the horse-drawn wagon for shorter trips. And in 1915 President Woodrow Wilson created the first government agency to oversee the aeronautics industry, the National Advisory Committee for Aeronautics (NACA).

World War I. As World War I began, however, the U.S. airplane industry lagged far behind its European counterparts. In addition to Germany's mighty fleet of dirigibles, France, England, and Germany all developed warplanes for reconnaissance, bombing, and aerial dogfights. American manufacturers scrambled to catch up. Between 1917 and 1919, the industry more than doubled its production. Although U.S. involvement in the war was brief, aerial warfare provided the nation with new heroes. Dashing pilots such as Eddie Rickenbacker, who notched twenty-six battle victories, inspired a series of imitations in popular culture, from comic strips such as "Smilin' Jack" to such movies as *Wings,* winner of the 1928 Academy Award for best picture of the year.

The interwar years were a time of great expansion for the airplane industry. The U.S. Air Mail Service, created in 1918, delivered transcontinental mail a full day faster than railroad carriers. The Air Service of the Army utilized airplanes in forest-fire control and border patrol. And in 1927 Charles Lindbergh completed the first nonstop transoceanic flight, when he piloted *The Spirit of St. Louis* from Long Island, New York, to Paris. Lindbergh became an international celebrity, and his flight proved that the airplane could create a powerful link between nations.

Female Aviators. At the same time American women proved to be formidable partners and competitors in the aeronautics industry. Air show headliners such as Katherine Stinson and long-distance record breakers such as Ruth Law paved the way for the most famous aviatrix of the era, Amelia Earhart, who in 1932 was the first woman to fly solo across the Atlantic Ocean. Later fliers, including the Women Airforce Service Pilots (WASPs), who completed crucial transport and trade missions during World War II, and Sally Ride, who in 1983 became the first American female astronaut to travel in space, continued the successful tradition of women in aeronautics.

World War II. In spite of the advances of the interwar years, U.S. aeronautic capabilities once again lagged behind Europe at the start of World War II. The German Luftwaffe and the British Royal Air Force were better trained and equipped than the U.S. Navy, and the army air force was depleted after the Japanese attack at Pearl Harbor. Nevertheless, domestic mobilization efforts—such as the conversion of Ford automobile plants into airplane factories—produced dramatic results. By 1943 U.S. planes were winning important victories over Europe and American aircraft carriers were fighting off Japanese bombers over the Pacific. But the United States revealed the destructive power of warplanes in early 1945, when B-29 Superfortresses firebombed the cities of Dresden, Germany, and Tokyo, Japan. Then, on August 6, the B-29 *Enola Gay* dropped an atomic bomb on the city of Hiroshima, Japan, killing 280 thousand civilians and 43 thousand Japanese soldiers. Three days later, another B-29 dropped a second atomic bomb on Nagasaki, Japan, killing fifty-four percent of its inhabitants.

Following such devastation American artists and intellectuals began to question the legacy of the airplane in human history. Books and films, includ-

ing Joseph Heller's *Catch-22* (1961) and director Stanley Kubrick's *Dr. Strangelove* (1963), presented airplanes as sinister weapons of mass destruction.

The Postwar Years. Airplanes were put to more constructive uses in the late 1940s when they carried supplies to citizens of Wyoming, South Dakota, and Nebraska during the blizzard of 1949, and, during the Berlin Airlift, to Berliners trapped behind a Soviet blockade. The airplane's image also improved with the arrival of a new hero, Charles E. "Chuck" Yeager, who broke the sound barrier in a rocket-powered Bell X-1 in 1947.

Yeager's achievement marked a turning point in American aeronautics history. Forty years after Kitty Hawk, American pilots finally had mastered the lower atmosphere. Now, the nation set its sights on outer space. In 1958 the National Aeronautics and Space Administration (NASA) replaced NACA and dedicated the nation's resources to spaceflight. In constant competition with the Soviet Union, the U.S. space program soon amassed a list of aeronautics heroes, including Alan Shepard, John Glenn, and Neil Armstrong. The link between airplanes and spaceflight was strengthened in the early 1980s when a fleet of space shuttles inaugurated the age of reusable spacecraft.

The mid-twentieth century was a time of great successes in commercial flight. Jet airliners, including the Boeing 707 and jumbo jets such as the 747, made flying cheaper and faster than ever before. The longer runways and larger terminals necessary to accommodate the larger planes and increased traffic led to the construction of grand-scale airports in rural areas outside American cities, such as Chicago's O'Hare Field, changing the interaction between cities and suburbs and escalating the phenomenon of urban sprawl.

At the same time, such military advances as the high-altitude U-2 spy plane and the Huey high-performance helicopter played major roles in international politics, particularly during the Cuban missile crisis and the Vietnam War. But Vietnam also represented a continuation of the techniques of total war, as American warplanes dropped napalm and defoliants on the Vietnamese jungle.

BOEING COMPANY ARCHIVES

The first Boeing 707 jetliner, before it was tested in 1954.

In the early 1980s the deregulation of the commercial airline industry led to a steep drop in ticket prices and a sharp increase in the number and variety of flights and destinations, making possible an increasingly interconnected world made even smaller by the supersonic transport. Successful military operations (centered on "surgical strikes") in Iraq and Yugoslavia during the 1990s restored public faith in the airplane as a tool of national defense. Yet while the popularity of such books as Tom Wolfe's *The Right Stuff* (1979) and the 1986 film *Top Gun* sustained a romantic optimism about flight, patrons of commercial airlines found themselves increasingly squeezed into uncomfortably small seats, on planes that were more often delayed than not in taking off and landing. The airplane had become by the twenty-first century an indispensable means of transportation but one that more and more people were coming to dislike.

[See also TECHNOLOGY, AN OVERVIEW.*]*

BIBLIOGRAPHY

Bilstein, Roger E., *Flight in America 1900–1983: From the Wrights to the Astronauts* (Johns Hopkins Univ. Press 1984).

Dupuy, Trevor, ed., *International Military and Defense Encyclopedia* (Brassey's 1993).

Goldstein, Laurence, *The Flying Machine and Modern Literature* (Ind. Univ. Press 1986).

Howard, Fred, *Wilbur and Orville: A Biography of the Wright Brothers* (Knopf 1987).

Wolfe, Tom, *The Right Stuff* (Farrar, Straus 1979).

JOHN TESSITORE

ALGER, HORATIO

Raised by a Unitarian clergyman to become a Unitarian clergyman, Horatio Alger, Jr., changed course and found a bully pulpit in juvenile fiction. After his death Alger's name would become synonymous with the vision of American boys going from "rags to riches" on the merits of honesty, pluck, perseverance, and thrift.

Born in Revere, Massachusetts, on January 13, 1832, Alger was educated in the classics but read romances voraciously. After graduating from Harvard in 1852, he published poetry, stories, and essays in now-forgotten periodicals such as the *Monthly Religious Magazine* and the *True Flag.* Schoolteaching paid the bills while Alger wrote for small pay under pseudonyms. Between 1857 and 1860 he studied for the ministry while keeping up his literary work; when the Civil War broke out, and

COURTESY, JOHN HANCOCK FINANCIAL SERVICES

A painting by Stevan Dohanos depicts writer Horatio Alger with fictional characters from his books.

myopia made him ineligible for the Union Army, Alger wrote war-ballads and his first juvenile novel. *Frank's Campaign* (1864) is the story of a youngster who runs the family farm so that his father can go to fight the Confederacy. Also in 1864 Alger was hired by a church in Brewster, Massachusetts. He left two years later, after being accused of "unnatural familiarity with boys."

Desperate to escape exposure Alger dropped the title "Reverend" and concentrated on a writing career. He moved to New York City and became interested in the "street arabs" (homeless people, especially young boys) there. Alger's single most successful book, *Ragged Dick: or, Street Life in New York* (1867), describes a boy who works hard to pull himself out of the dead-end jobs of selling matches and peddling papers. Readers loved this book and critics praised it genially. Yet in its wake, and impelled by the low remuneration for juvenile fiction, Alger wrote too much, too quickly.

Noting Alger's classical training, Carol Nackenoff argues that formulaic plots and characters allowed Alger to preach, in a way that young readers found acceptable, on topics such as benevolent capitalism, the dangers of industrialization, and individual virtue. Gary Scharnhorst and Jack Bales note, however, that when Alger's sales figures fell, he resorted to sensationalist techniques. To refute those who charged him with vitiating young readers' taste, Alger wrote a biography of the recently slain president, James Garfield. *From Canal Boy to President* (1881) supported Alger's contention that America was a land of opportunity for the industrious, honest, and shrewd.

After Alger died, on July 18, 1899, in Natick, Massachusetts, the sales of his books soared. Scharnhorst and Bales find that "[t]he phrase *Horatio Alger hero* obtained popular currency in the language during the 1920s," the decade in which a "hoax" biography raised much Freudian speculation about Alger's motivations. In 1946 the American Schools and Colleges Association established the Horatio Alger Awards for upholders of political or religious orthodoxy. Later scholars in U.S. literature and American studies have examined Alger's works of fiction in the context of late-nineteenth-century concerns such as masculine sexuality, labor unrest, and homeless children.

[*See also* AMERICAN DREAM.]

BIBLIOGRAPHY

Cawelti, John, *Apostles of the Self-Made Man* (Univ. of Chicago Press 1965).

Moon, Michael, "The Gentle Boy from the Dangerous Classes: Pederasty, Domesticity, and Capitalism in Horatio Alger," *Representations* 19 (Summer 1987): 87–110.

Nackenoff, Carol, *The Fictional Republic: Horatio Alger and American Political Discourse* (Oxford 1994).

Scharnhorst, Gary, and Jack Bales, *The Lost Life of Horatio Alger, Jr.* (Ind. Univ. Press 1985).

Trachtenberg, Alan, *The Incorporation of America: Culture and Society in the Gilded Age* (Hill & Wang 1982).

BARBARA RYAN

ALI, MUHAMMAD

Born in 1942, Cassius Marcellus Clay, Jr. (named after both his father and the famous Kentucky abolitionist and politician), was one of the most gifted athletes of his time. In 1960 the handsome, gregarious boxer became a media star when he won a gold medal at the Rome Olympic games. Clay stunned the sports world in 1964 by beating heavily favored Sonny Liston to win the world heavyweight title, and he shocked America by announcing immediately after the fight that he had joined a militantly racialist, isolationist religious sect, the Nation of Islam, popularly known as the Black Muslims (seated ringside during the fight was the Nation of Islam's fiery orator Malcolm X). Shortly afterward the young fighter announced that he was changing his name to Muhammad Ali. The press and the white public roared disapproval, saying that Ali had joined a hate group, that the Black Muslims would take all of his money, that he should be stripped of his title, that he was not a loyal American, nor was he an appreciative black. His notoriety was such that, at one point in the mid-1960s, he had a series of title defenses outside the United States, in Canada (George Chuvalo), in London

(Brian London and Henry Cooper), and in Germany (Karl Mildenberger).

Ali was a national hero in the cold-war era, despite the fact that he was a black who, having grown up in Kentucky, lived under an entrenched system of racial segregation. Ali may or may not have been a particularly complex man, but he is a complex symbol. The fame of the brash young prizefighter from Louisville certainly eclipsed that of nearly every other major African American athlete including Jesse Owens, Joe Louis, Wilma Rudolph, Wilt Chamberlain, Jim Brown, Bill Russell, and Jackie Robinson. Certainly, he is remembered as the heavyweight boxer who generated the most drama both in and out of the ring.

Opposed to the draft, Ali refused to serve in the Vietnam War. He was convicted of violating the Selective Service Act in 1967 and stripped of his titles. He was also banned from boxing anywhere, since his boxing license was universally revoked. Far from diminishing his stature, Ali's stance against the war and his willingness to go to prison garnered him a new level of respect among many of the white press who had formerly castigated him. He also became a darling of the white Left, although he shared virtually no other political views with them. Ali appealed his conviction, and it was overturned by the Supreme Court on a technicality. On one hand, Ali's political views as a member of the Nation of Islam would have been viewed by a leftist, black or white, as parochial, even reactionary. On the other hand, to nationalist blacks he was a Third World hero, a Pan-Africanist hero, because he was, clearly, the most famous Muslim in the world and the most publicized athlete to speak out about the nature of race relations in the United States.

Returning to boxing in 1970 after a three-and-a-half-year layoff, Ali lost his heavyweight title to Joe Frazier in 1971 in one of the biggest boxing matches in history. He eventually reclaimed his title by beating George Foreman in Zaire in October 1974, a victory that was rejoiced throughout the United States, even among many whites, who thought that Ali had been treated unfairly and deserved to win the title back. Ali continued to box throughout the 1970s

(far past his prime as an athlete) largely because he was earning huge sums to do so. He retired from the ring in 1981 with a record of fifty-six victories and five losses.

Following Ali's remarkable appearance at the torch-lighting ceremony that opened the 1996 Summer Olympic Games in Atlanta, some blacks commented that Ali is loved by whites now only because of his Parkinson's-like illness, which has left him unable to speak. For these commentators, the elevation of Ali's status to hero, no doubt bolstered by the 1996 Academy Award–winning documentary about him, *When We Were Kings*, is in direct ratio to his having become a harmless, even a maimed presence, the beat-up, has-been fighter walking on his heels. There is some justification to this view but it simplifies greatly the complex levels at which Ali operates as an athletic, political, racial, and national icon, sometimes in stages and sometimes simultaneously. Ali remains a hero for many today because he seems (more than any other figure from that era) to embody the virtues of the antiestablishment, civil rights era, revolutionary 1960s and the success-oriented, narcissistic hedonism of the 1970s.

[See also BLACK MUSLIMS.*]*

BIBLIOGRAPHY

Early, Gerald, ed., *The Muhammad Ali Reader* (Ecco Press 1998).

Gorn, Elliot, ed., *Muhammad Ali: The People's Champ* (Univ. of Ill. Press 1995).

Hauser, Thomas, *Muhammad Ali: His Life and Times* (Simon & Schuster 1991).

Remnick, David, *King of the World: Muhammad Ali and the Rise of an American Hero* (Random House 1998).

Sammons, Jeffrey, *Beyond the Ring: The Role of Boxing in American Society* (Univ. of Ill. Press 1988).

GERALD EARLY

ALTERNATIVE MEDICINE

The term *alternative medicine* has come to encompass any form of medical treatment not known or readily accepted by conventional or "allopathic" medical practitioners. Alternative techniques include

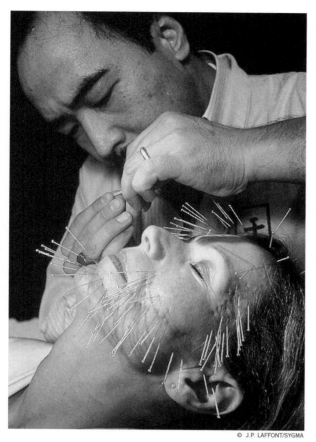

© J.P. LAFFONT/SYGMA

Acupuncture treatment uses thin sterile needles.

many states to repeal medical licensing laws by the 1840s. Alternative medicine treatments became so popular that they appeared in many home medical guides, thus allowing the general population to treat itself.

The development by drug companies of effective and easily administered remedies for illnesses in the twentieth century made it easier for doctors to prescribe antibiotics than to find a good homeopathic remedy. Homeopathy faded into near nonexistence until the 1970s, when it was once again seen for its virtues. Today most homeopathic remedies are approved by the Food and Drug Administration (FDA) and produced by drug companies.

Chiropractic began in 1895 and has become the largest nonmedical healing art in the United States. This evolving health profession focuses on the diagnosis, treatment, and prevention of disorders of the musculoskeletal system. Approximately ten percent of the American population seeks chiropractic care annually. On the surface chiropractic appears to be mainstream, yet in 1980 the American Medical Association (AMA) made the referral of patients to chiropractors unethical, in large part owing to the exaggerated claims of successful chiropractic practices. Later the AMA lifted the prohibition when challenged in a successful antitrust suit. Many companies now offer employees health coverage for chiropractic treatment.

Different from many other alternative medicines, holistic medicine emphasizes the cooperative relationship between all those involved in achieving and maintaining a person's optimal levels of physical, mental, emotional, social, and spiritual health. Holistic medicine emphasizes the need to explore the well-being of the whole person.

The primary roadblock to the full acceptance of alternative forms of medicine as viable for treating aliments is the presumption by conventional Western medical culture that alternative medicine modalities are not scientific. The difference between traditional and alternative lies in the practice of the latter drawing from daily testing and refinement on patients rather than Western medicine's stan-

noninvasive, nonpharmaceutical practices such as medicinal herbalism, acupuncture, homeopathy, chiropractic, and others. In addition, alternative medicine has evolved to encompass any experimental drug or nondrug technique that is not accepted by conventional medical practitioners. Noninvasive, nonpharmaceutical methods that become popular or "accepted" by the medical community are not considered alternative.

Arriving in the United States in the mid-eighteenth century, homeopathy was the first of the popular medical movements and could be practiced by the novice at home. It was so popular that by the end of the century there were many practicing homeopaths. The 1832 cholera epidemic fueled the surge of the homeopathic movement. The belief that every person could be his or her own doctor led dard practice of developing abstract theory tested in controlled laboratories.

The National Institutes of Health (NIH) recently endorsed acupuncture as an effective treatment for certain conditions. The endorsement by the NIH cleared the way for acupuncture to move off the list of "experimental medical devices," opening the door for widespread insurance coverage and greater public acceptance.

Emphasis on prevention and maintenance continues to foster the popularity of alternative forms of health care. Conventional medicine's incorporation of prevention and maintenance alongside cures to ailments will only aid in pushing the complementary and alternative medicine of today into the conventional medicines of tomorrow.

[See also MEDICINE; HOSPITALS AND ASYLUMS; PUBLIC HEALTH.]

BIBLIOGRAPHY

Cassileth, Barrie R., *The Alternative Medicine Handbook: The Complete Reference Guide to Alternative and Complementary Therapies* (Norton 1998).

Gevitz, Norman, ed., *Other Healers: Unorthodox Medicine in America* (Johns Hopkins Univ. Press 1988).

Gordon, Rena J., Barbara Cable Nienstedt, and Wilbert Gesler, eds., *Alternative Therapies: Expanding Options in Health Care* (Springer Verlag 1998).

GINGER LEE BLACKMON

AMERICA

[Scholars often distinguish between the concept and the reality of America. Accordingly, the subject is divided here into three separate articles. The first, THE IDEA OF AMERICA, *examines the contradictions involved in founding and sustaining the nation on the basis of a particular set of ideals, or ideological constructions, ranging from Puritanism to cultural pluralism.* AMERICAN CULTURE ABROAD, *the second entry, looks at the global impact of the symbols and practices that uniquely define the United States. The last article in the group,* AMERICA PERCEIVED, *explores the United States as an object of contemplation and confusion among foreign and domestic observers.]*

The Idea of America

Historically, it has been commonplace for many schoolchildren in the United States to attribute the "discovery" of America to Christopher Columbus and its naming to the explorer and mapmaker Amerigo Vespucci. Of course, there was always some talk of Leif Erikson, but never a real challenge to Columbus. At the beginning of the twenty-first century, no one questions whether or not Columbus made the famous voyage, but the idea of "discovery" has come under some scrutiny, as has the nomenclature. What does it mean to "discover" a continent that was already populated? And what entitles the United States to claim for itself the designation America?

Significantly, several centuries had passed in the New World before 1492 was marked as a beginning and Columbus canonized as a founding hero. With the emerging nation's quest for independence came the need for national heroes and an originary moment. The intervening years had witnessed a proliferation of incarnations for the New World, symbolically diverse and often contradictory. To early modern Europe, "America" represented a variety of opportunities, social, economic, political, and even religious. "In the beginning," wrote the influential English philosopher John Locke in 1690, "all the World was 'America.'" For Locke the land on the other side of the Atlantic came closer than any part of the known world to a "state of nature," a world in which the codes of civilized nations did not yet exist. To a variety of explorers and colonizers, to travelers who were seeking class mobility, religious freedom, or new markets, "America" meant possibility.

Yet, accounts of the New World penned by those who had seen it, as well as pamphlets printed for emigrants and others who had an interest in its settlement and development, do not present a consistent depiction. The veritable Garden of Eden peopled by children of nature in some accounts contrasts dramatically with reports of the harsh wilderness populated by dangerous cannibals in others. Running through all depictions, however, is a theme captured with particular vividness in Theodore

Galle's famous engraving, *The Arrival of Vespucci in the New World* (circa 1600). In this depiction Europe, personified by Vespucci rather than Columbus, awakens a sparsely clad woman (representing savage America) to the benefits of civilization. To the lush world with its naked "savages" and strange wild animals, the superiority of European civilization is beyond dispute. Whatever advantages this brave new world might offer, it could not do so without Europe. The very utopian fantasies that were set in the New World well into the sixteenth century, although antidotes to the decay of European civilization, resembled the Old World rather than the New World in social, economic, religious, and political structure.

While the geographical entity that would come to be known as the United States bears the imprint both of its indigenous inhabitants and of a variety of early settlers and adventurers (especially French, Spanish, and Dutch), it was the English colonizers who would have the greatest impact on its political formation. The settlements, which they called plantations, were as varied as the motives through which they were founded. To such avid proponents of colonization as Richard Hakluyt the Younger, the most famous of the early promoters, the English had an obligation to this New World that the earlier Spanish colonizers had not realized. From Hakluyt's perspective, the greed of the Spanish had led them to barbarous acts of cruelty and exploitation toward the indigenous peoples: not the least of their sins was bringing their religion, Catholicism, rather than Anglicanism, to the indigenes. Other motives for settlement did not preclude the great mission that, he argued, history had bequeathed to the English people. Indeed, the political and economic advantages that settlement would confer on England (the enumeration of which dominates Hakluyt's account) would strengthen the reach and power of the Church of England as well. Historian Jack P. Greene sees the roots of American exceptionalism— the idea that the nation developed uniquely, independent of global influences, because of its geographical isolation and geological specificities—in celebrations, such as Hakluyt's account, of the expanse and resources of the New World, which pre-

sumably offered opportunities for self-realization and social development unlike those that existed anywhere else.

For other cultural historians, however, including Sacvan Bercovitch and Perry Miller, American exceptionalism stemmed from the Puritan conviction that the New World was going to be the fulfillment of the Christian promise, the gospel's city shining upon a hill with the eyes of the world on it. The seeds of the Christian ideal would surely thrive in the rich soil of this New World if, as John Winthrop, the first governor of the Massachusetts Bay Company, assured his fellow pilgrims, they understood that they had a covenant with God. The idea of the covenant, or contract with God—the idea, that is, that they would prosper if they lived up to certain spiritual expectations—would prove formative for the idea of America. But, of course, there was not yet any America; the colonists saw themselves as Christians and, in most cases, English, fleeing the corruption of England to found a New Jerusalem, the fulfillment of God's promise on earth.

By the time the Declaration of Independence announced the birth of a new nation, the idea of America had come to reflect Puritan and Enlightenment (as well as other philosophical and political) influences. Penning the draft of the document that would officially declare the colonies' break from England, Thomas Jefferson knew that he had to wage a battle on two fronts. He had to justify the decision to the nations of Europe, themselves colonial powers, and he had to persuade the people in the colonies, many of them content to be English, to accede to the consensus from which the document allegedly drew its authority: that it was "in the name, and by the authority of the good people of these colonies" that the declaration was issued. At the heart of the document is the Enlightenment idea on which the new political entity, the nation, would be founded: "that all men are created equal; that they are endowed by their creator with certain inalienable rights; that among these are life, liberty, and the pursuit of happiness: that to secure these rights, governments are instituted among men, deriving their just powers from the consent of the governed. . . . " And the principle of consensus, with its implicit invocation of a covenant, found expression in the very name by which the document christened the new entity: the United States of America.

Yet the contradictions that trouble this idea are evident in the very document that sets them forth. Among the "men" who are "created equal," the founders included neither "the merciless Indian savages," as the Declaration named them, nor the enslaved Africans. Two paragraphs concerning the enslaved population had to be excised from Jefferson's original draft; he had counted the slave trade among the many abuses with which he charged the king, but his colleagues understood the contradictions that such a charge entailed: while England already had begun the arduous processes leading to abolition, the slave trade was escalating in the colonies, and the issue threatened to destroy their fragile unity. The contradiction was written into the very fabric of the nation with the drafting of the U.S. Constitution, which, in setting the terms for determining the population of a state, excluded "Indians" and to the number of "free Persons, including those bound to Service for a Term of Years" added "three fifths of all other Persons." In effect, each enslaved person counted as three-fifths of a person; convention reflected this expression of the law, since enslaved persons were effectively denied the "inalienable rights" of personhood. The presence of human beings who were excluded from the legal terms of personhood thus haunted the idea of America from its inception.

Among the other inflammatory political issues that the Constitution could not resolve was the urgent question of the nature of the union itself: did "the United States" name a powerful political entity with a central government or a loose confederation of states united in something resembling a treaty? Many issues, economic and social, threatened the union with dissolution before the question of the enslavement of Africans finally led to war between the Northern and Southern states. The designation under which each side fought expressed the idea of America that it embraced in its very name: those who fought for the Confederacy prioritized the states, while those who fought under the Union's banner favored a strong central government.

More than any other document, the address that Abraham Lincoln delivered at the dedication of a cemetery in Gettysburg, Pennsylvania, in 1863 articulates the idea of America that emerged from the Civil War. Returning to the principles of the Declaration of Independence, Lincoln marked 1776 as the birth date of the "new nation, conceived in Liberty, and dedicated to the proposition that all men are created equal." With these words the president, who, ironically, had not been the featured speaker at the event, powerfully affirmed the principle that the Declaration of Independence had first set in motion: that this new political entity arose not from the history of tribal migrations and negotiations, as had the European nations, but from a proposition, an idea. It was the nature of that particular origin that, according to Lincoln, made the United States different from European nations. And both the Puritans' sense of mission (the founding of the city on a hill) and the Enlightenment ideals of the rights of man resonate in Lincoln's conception of the Civil War as a test of "whether that nation, or any nation so conceived and so dedicated, can long endure." At Gettysburg, Lincoln reinvigorated the idea of America and charged the nation with its survival.

Yet neither Lincoln's powerful words nor the Union's victory could erase the contradiction that the Constitution had written into the law of the land. Speaking at the dedication of a monument to Lincoln more than a decade after his assassination, the prominent African American orator and writer Frederick Douglass called Lincoln the "white man's president" and insisted on the distinction between white Americans who were "the children of Abraham Lincoln" and black Americans who were "at best only his step-children, children by adoption, children by force of circumstances and necessity." The idea of America for which the Civil War had ostensibly been fought was not yet realized, he argued, for children of non-European descent.

Although the Civil War settled the question of the nation's political structure, it did not resolve the contradictions implicit in the idea of America. They had always surfaced with particular force at moments of cultural encounter. Central to the idea in the early nineteenth century, for example, was the doctrine of Manifest Destiny, which held that the westward expansion of the European peoples across the continent of America was preordained. However, when the Europeans encountered resistance from the indigenous peoples, they had to adjust the founding principles to be compatible with colonization and genocide. And when at the end of the nineteenth century western settlement left no continental frontier and the nation's manifest destiny appeared to be abroad, the principles of universal equality had to be reconciled with the practices of imperialism. Among the many critics who called attention to these contradictions was Cuban exile Jose Martí, whose powerful 1891 essay "Nuestra America" ("Our America") challenged the imperialism evident even in the United States's usurpation of the name *America*.

Similar contradictions surfaced at home with the unprecedented immigration and domestic migration at the century's end. Critics of immigration and urbanization decried the influence that a large-scale influx of peoples might have on American culture and values, but even those who argued that it would reinvigorate the native stock agreed on the need for a clear definition of Americanism. Thus, at the turn of the century the idea of America was once again at the center of public debate centered on the question of assimilation: Who could become an American, and what had to be relinquished or embraced for them to do so? In a public lecture and, subsequently, widely circulated essay, "True Americanism" (1894), Theodore Roosevelt declared that Americanism was a "faith" rather than a "birthright," and while he conceded that some groups of people might be unassimilable, there was room enough for most immigrants, provided that they were willing to renounce their affiliations with their countries of origin. Roosevelt was delighted by the metaphor of the melting pot popularized by English writer Israel Zangwill in 1909 to describe the

alchemistic nature of assimilation: prior affiliations melted away as each individual was forged anew in the cauldron of America. For cultural critic Horace Kallen, the renunciation called for by Roosevelt was neither possible nor desirable; he coined the term *cultural pluralism* to describe the coexistence of people from diverse backgrounds.

Multiculturalism is the contemporary heir to both Kallen's and Martí's critiques, and it bears witness to the continuing struggle to define America, and to the social, political, and economic stakes of that struggle. Ongoing debates about bilingual education, for example, or classroom curricula, or even about the likelihood of electing a president who is not a white Christian male are at their base about the "idea of America." The rise of ethnic studies and women's studies in the universities in the 1960s and the 1970s directly responded to students' perceptions of the discrepancy between a popular idea of America and the lived experiences of many Americans whose race, gender, class, sexuality, religion, or political beliefs compromised their opportunities. From the outset the idea of America has offered the promise of inclusion and struggled with its reality. Increasing recognition of the tension between the promise and the struggle has helped to bring about important social and political changes as it has raised questions about the very idea of America.

[See also AMERICAN CHARACTER; AMERICAN DREAM; AMERICANIZATION.]

BIBLIOGRAPHY

Bercovitch, Sacvan, *The Puritan Origins of the American Self* (Yale Univ. Press 1976).

Greene, Jack P., *The Intellectual Construction of America: Exceptionalism and Identity from 1492 to 1800* (Univ. of N.C. Press 1993).

Kaplan, Amy, and Donald Pease, eds., *Cultures of United States Imperialism* (Duke Univ. Press 1993).

Mancall, Peter C., ed., *Envisioning America: English Plans for the Colonization of North America, 1580–1640* (St. Martin's Press 1995).

Miller, Perry, *Nature's Nation* (Belknap Press 1967).

Saldívar, José David, *The Dialectics of Our America: Genealogy, Cultural Critique, and Literary History* (Duke Univ. Press 1991).

© MELVYN CALDERON/THE LIAISON AGENCY

Children eating at a McDonald's restaurant in the Philippines.

Thelen, David, and Frederick E. Hoxie, eds., *Discovering America: Essays on the Search for an Identity* (Univ. of Ill. Press 1994).

Wills, Garry, *Inventing America: Jefferson's Declaration of Independence* (Doubleday 1978).

PRISCILLA WALD

American Culture Abroad

When people discuss the topic of American culture abroad, the word *Americanization* is likely to enter the conversation. The word first appeared in the French language in the mid-nineteenth century, at the time when the United States literally manifested itself on French soil with a display of its technical and entrepreneurial prowess during the 1855 *Exposition universelle* (Universal Exposition) in Paris. A little earlier a famous French observer, Alexis de Tocqueville, had noticed other aspects of America's daring leap into modernity, this time as a great experiment in democracy and republican life. America, in its various manifestations, seemed to offer a glance into a future that might also lie ahead for Europeans, a future geared toward the dictates and tastes of the multitude rather than the elite, exerted through the mass market and the arena of mass politics. Europeans watched in awe, but never without a sense of foreboding. They feared that a future under American auspices would level established taste hierarchies in culture, and through the standardization of mass production and mass politics would cater to the lowest common denominator of lifestyles, political preferences, and consumption behavior that prevailed among the multitude. Europeans were at the same time stunned by an American cultural attitude that could never leave well enough alone, but always tampered with what reached American shores, taking it apart, and reassembling the constituent parts as Americans saw fit. For example, some milk in America is as much human-made as it is cow-produced, with some ingredients taken away and others added.

Of course, Americanization had taken place in America itself before it could begin to affect cultures elsewhere. Generation after generation of immigrants underwent the process when they entered a space of experiences and dreams unlike any they had ever known before. Political ideas and ideals as well as notions of economic production and organization received, like immigrants, the imprint of an "American Way." Europeans still recognized the family resemblance, but also were keenly aware of a systematic transformation imposed by a cultural and social mold that to them typified America. It is a process that still goes on. What reaches foreign markets and becomes visible as typically American, either as an intrusion or a welcome widening of an existing cultural range, is often a matter of products taken from other cultural contexts and given an American twist. Italian pizza, Japanese sushi, and Mexican tacos have all undergone the fast-food touch; varieties are added, production is standardized, and brand logos are invented.

American culture knows no borders. It has spread from its home base to encompass the globe; it penetrates the everyday environments of people everywhere; it invades their fantasy worlds, if it has not actually, as German filmmaker Wim Wenders once ruefully put it, colonized their subconscious. Increasingly, along with the internationalization of American culture itself, American studies has internationalized its perspective and approach. Research now more than ever before focuses on questions of the transmission and reception of forms of American culture, and on the ways in which they are adopted and adapted abroad. America has thus become a provider of ingredients for stores of cultural self-expression elsewhere. America is only one among many sources, of course. More often than not, the American option serves as a counterpoint to established repertoires, providing groups with the expressive means for cultural opposition and for revolt against a prescribed mold of cultural affiliation.

In that sense a long history exists of the reception and rejection of American culture. That history has always appeared within national settings, in the guise of a continuing reflection, if not a polemic, on the national identity and the main tenets of a national culture. Groups outside of the United States rejecting American culture, seeing it as a threat to the core values of their own particular national cultures, always find themselves in opposition to enemies within the gate, who hold up elements of American culture as much-needed counterpoints to the established cultural ways of a nation.

One crucial element in American culture that has always perplexed foreign critics, while at the same time appealing to those who welcomed American culture, was its aspect of a successful mass culture. More radically so than any other culture, American culture took its central cues, in the ways it was produced, disseminated, and received, from the secular process of democratization. From the early stage of republican enthusiasm on, Americans agreed that American culture, in order to be American, had to be democratic. The mission for America's cultural production was to appeal to the many, not the few, and to reflect the lives of the general citizenry at large rather than those of elite groups in its midst. In this way it set standards for others to follow.

In their critique of American culture, many cultural and political conservatives in Europe may have grudgingly paid tribute to the democratic aspirations of American culture. What troubled them, however, was that culture as they observed it in America appeared as not only democratic but also as unashamedly commercial. If the American mode of cultural production and reproduction was geared to the many, it was also geared to the market. It also implied that Americans were less reluctant than many Europeans to adopt methods of mass production through mechanical reproduction and of cultural dissemination through mass marketing, employing advertising techniques, and new developments in mass communication. Americans were less in thrall with a European, Benjaminian sense of the aura surrounding culture, of a deference that is by its very nature at odds with the vulgarity of the mass market. European critics, whether on the Left or the Right of the political spectrum, chose to look at this potent brew of democratic and commercial instincts as a clear case of the commodification of culture. Others in Europe, though, welcomed American culture precisely for its blithe irreverence toward standards that cultural gatekeepers in Europe rallied to defend.

There Are No Borders. Many are the explanations for the worldwide dissemination of American mass culture. There are those who see it as a case of cultural imperialism, as a consequence of America's worldwide projection of political, economic, and military power. Others, broadly within the same critical frame of mind, see it as a tool rather than a consequence of this imperial expansion. Behind the globalization of American culture they see an orchestrating hand, whetting foreign appetites for the pleasures of a culture of consumption. Undeniably, though, part of the explanation of the worldwide appeal of American mass culture will be found in its intrinsic qualities, in its blend of democratic and commercial vigor. In particular cases the mix of these two elements may differ. At one extreme the commercial component may be nearly absent, as in the worldwide dissemination of jazz, rock and roll, and blues music. At the other extreme, however, the commercial rationale may be the central carrying force, as in American advertisements.

In a couple of examples of advertisements from the early 1860s, two tobacco brands, Washoe and Westward Ho, used images of the American West, in addition to more general American imagery, embodied in representations of the goddess Columbia. The advertisements featured vast stretches of open country, a pot of gold brimming over, an American eagle, a bare-breasted Columbia loosely enveloped in an American flag, galloping forth on elk-back. This is not Europa being abducted by Jupiter; this is a modern mythology of Columbia, much like American culture, carrying everything before her. At the time, clearly, an abundance of mythical markers was needed to tie Virginia tobacco to the beckoning call of the West. Today such explicit references are no longer necessary to trigger our store of images concerning America as a dream and a fantasy.

The Freedom of Movement and the Freedom of Choice. In January 1995 huge posters were pasted all across the Netherlands advertising Levi's 508 model denim jeans. The posters showed the lower half of a seminude male torso, covered from the waist down by a pair of Levi's. The text, in English, mentions four freedoms: the freedom of expression; the freedom of thought; the freedom of choice; and finally, following the words "Levi's 508," the freedom of movement. Clearly, the poster playfully recycles cultural memories: the cover of the Rolling Stones's *Sticky Fingers* album, designed by Andy Warhol, as well as the cover photograph of Bruce Springsteen's album *Born in the USA.* It also plays on the classic Rooseveltian four freedoms, assuming a rather high level of cultural and political literacy among the public it addresses. Yet it does more. The fourth freedom, political though it may sound, is meant to convey the greater room of movement provided by the fuller cut of the 508. The picture graphically illustrates the point by showing the unmistakable bulge of a male member in full erection, casually touched by the hand of its owner. Nor do the double entendres and the resonance of intertextuality end there. The third freedom, the freedom of choice, has a ring that is political and commercial at the same time. It evokes the freedom of the citizen as well as of the consumer. Also, the freedom of choice may have added resonance for those aware of the cultural war in the United States regarding abortion, and its clashes between the pro-life and pro-choice groups.

What is to be made of this poster? As it turns out, it was produced by a Dutch advertising agency solely for the Dutch market. The piece of merchandise it advertises may be American, and so may the political rhetoric it draws on. The language may be English, yet the semantic games being played are Dutch. The liberties taken with the freedom of movement, and the way the poster visualizes this freedom, do betray a jocular attitude about things sexual that one would not easily find displayed on walls in American cities. More generally one could argue that advertising in Europe takes the semiotics of American commercial strategies to lengths that are inconceivable in America. From the point of view of American culture traveling abroad, in many cases the exploration of cultural frontiers is pushed farther or given twists beyond anything one might see in America.

While Europe may have been more daring than America in its "pursuit of happiness," earlier on America may have been less hesitant than Europeans to explore the continuities between the political and the commercial. For example, a commercial message broadcast by Cable News Network (CNN) International makes the point that without advertising everyone would be worse off, getting less information through the media, whether the press or the electronic media. Advertising is presented as a necessary prop for the continued existence of a well-informed public in a functioning democracy. The little civics lesson offered by the commercial (and paid for by the Advertising Council in London) ends with the slogan: "Advertising—The Right to Choose." This blending of the rationale of capitalism and democratic theory is not new. Something similar happened in the early 1940s in America when, on the eve of U.S. participation in World War II, President Franklin D. Roosevelt made his powerful contribution to American public discourse with his "Four Freedoms" speech, a rallying cry in which he called on his countrymen to fulfill an American world mission as he saw it. In all likelihood he picked up the "four freedoms" as a rhetorical figure in the public domain of American mass culture. The Four Freedoms, as a group of four statues erected along the main concourse of the New York World's Fair of 1939–1940, had already left their imprint on the millions of visitors to the fair. Working on his final draft of the state of the union address, Roosevelt briefly toyed with the idea of five freedoms, but in order for his words to reverberate among the larger public, he needed to draw on a popular image that was already established. After the address, the link with political views among the larger public was further reinforced through Norman Rockwell's series of four oil paintings, each representing one of the four freedoms. Using his appeal as an artist who had succeeded in rendering a romantic, small-town view of life cherished by millions of Americans, Rockwell gave the same endearing touch to Roosevelt's message. Through the mass distribution of reproductions, including, later, a series of four U.S. postage stamps, Rockwell's *Four Freedoms* facilitated the translation and transfer of Roosevelt's high-minded call to a mass audience.

If this is an illustration of American political culture as an element of American mass culture, of political rhetoric as it emanates from the public domain and returns to it, it was as yet unaffected by the rationale of business. If anything had to be sold at all, it was a matter of political ideas; if a sales pitch was needed at all, it was a matter of public suasion, explaining the world to a larger democratic public and calling on it to take appropriate action. Yet it was not long before Roosevelt's four freedoms would be joined by a fifth, in an advertisement by the Hoover Vacuum Cleaner Company in a 1944 issue of the *Saturday Evening Post*. It was an ad illustrated in the style of Norman Rockwell. The setting is recognizable and the faces are familiar: an old woman, a middle-aged man, and a young girl ("people from the neighborhood"). They look upward into a beam of light; providence, if not the good provider, is smiling on them. In their arms they hold an abundance of packages, all gift-wrapped. This is Norman Rockwell country. With a difference, though: Rockwell's mythical small-town people, carriers of democratic virtue, now appear in the guise of Americans as consumers. Three years after Roosevelt had decided that there were four, not five, freedoms, the Hoover advertisement

reminded Americans that "the Fifth Freedom is Freedom of Choice." If America had joined the struggle to safeguard democratic values, this implied safeguarding the freedom of choice. By a simple semantic sleight-of-hand, the (con)text of the advertisement shifted the meaning of freedom of choice: the "signified" was no longer the realm of politics, but the freedom of choice for the citizen in his or her role as consumer. Thus spheres of freedom smoothly shaded into one another.

And they still do. The Hoover Company may have chosen to use language popular at the time, and to speak of a freedom. The CNN message is cast in the language of rights, reminding the viewer of his or her right to choose, with all the current resonance of that term. In either case, what is happening is the commodification of political discourse. The language of political ideals, of rights and freedoms, is being hijacked in order to dress purposeful commercial action in stolen clothes. Whether dressed as a freedom or a right, a commodifying logic appears as an act of self-legitimation, in almost pure form to the point of being unconnected, as in the CNN example, to any particular product. The implied message may well read: "No choice of freedom without the freedom of choice," or more cynically, no political freedom without unhindered consumerism. This logic has been seen at work in particular cases, tying the promise of freedom to cigarettes or blue jeans. It is a logic that commodifies, and pedestrianizes, political ideals by putting them at the service of commercial salesmanship. In that sense, then, this is just another instance of the vulgarizing impact of American culture, corroborating a point made by generations of European critics of American culture. Europeans, though, have become as adept as Americans at using these commercialized forms of political language. After all, it was a Dutch advertising agency that made the "freedom of movement" the selling point of the Levi's 508. And at about the same time, the French national airline, Air France, introduced "passenger rights" in a large ad in the *International Herald Tribune*. Next to a photograph of a beautiful woman, the epitome of French feminine elegance, is the message "The chances of her being seated next to you are so slim that you won't regret the extra space between our seats." Two separate captions refer to *"L'espace Europe"* ("Europe Space") and to "The Right to Privacy." In one stroke the advertisement commodifies yet another political right, while at the same time trying to Europeanize the seductive qualities of America's "open space." If it works for the Marlboro Man, why not for Air France? Or for that matter, if it works for an American cigarette, why not for European rivals, such as a German cigarette simply calling itself West, or an Anglo-American cigarette introducing the slogan "There are no borders"?

Exploring frontiers of freedom, of children rebelling against parental authority, of sexual freedom, of freedom in matters of taste and styles of behavior, American consumer goods have been instruments of political and cultural education, if not of emancipation. Generations of youngsters, growing up in a variety of settings in Europe, West and East of the Iron Curtain, vicariously enjoyed the pleasures of cultural alternatives conjured up in commercial vignettes. Simple items such as a pair of blue jeans, Coca-Cola, or a cigarette brand thus acquired an added value that helped these younger generations give expression to an identity all their own. They used American cultural language and made American cultural codes their own. To that extent they became Americanized. To the extent, though, that they "did their own thing," while drawing on American cultural repertoires, Americanization is no longer the proper word for describing what has gone on. If anything, those at the receiving end of American mass culture have adapted it to make it serve their own ends. They have woven it into a cultural language, whose grammar, syntax, and semantics, metaphorically speaking, are still recognizably French, Italian, or Czech. All that the recipients have done is make new statements in such a language.

There are many instances of such recontextualization. Surrounded by jingles, posters, neon signs, and billboards, all trying to convey their commercial exhortations, one ironically recycles these messages. One quotes slogans while bending their meanings; one mimics voices and faces familiar from radio and television and weaves them into conversations, precisely because they are shared repertoires. Used in this way, two things happen. International repertoires become national, in the sense that they are given a particular twist in conversations, acquiring their new meanings only in particular national and linguistic settings. Second, commercial messages stop being commercial. A decommodification takes place in the sense that the point of the semantic transaction is no longer a piece of merchandise or any particular economic deal. In the ironic recycling of the commercial culture one becomes its master rather than its slave.

The Freedom of Reception. Many things have happened along the way since American culture started traveling abroad. American icons may have become the staples of a visual lingua franca that is understood anywhere in the world, yet their use can no longer be dictated solely from America. For one thing, it is clear that European commercials made for European products may draw on semiotic repertoires initially developed in and transmitted from America. Yet, in a creolizing freedom not unlike America's modularizing cast of mind, Europeans in their turn now freely rearrange and recombine the bits and pieces of American culture. They care little about authenticity. T-shirts produced in Europe are as likely to say "New York Lions" as they are "New York Giants." What is more, American brand names, like free-floating signifiers, may even be decommodified and turned into carriers of a message that is no longer commercial at all. Admittedly, the T-shirts, leather jackets, and baseball caps sporting the hallowed names of Harley Davidson, Nike, or Coca-Cola still have to be bought. Yet what one pays is the price of admission into a world of symbols shared by an international youth culture. Boys or girls with the words *Coca-Cola* on their T-shirts are not the unpaid peddlers of American merchandise. Quite the contrary. They have transcended such trite connotations and restored American icons to their pure semiotic status as messages of pleasure and freedom. Within this global youth culture, the icons youngsters carry are like the symbol of the fish that early Christians drew in the sand as a code of recognition. They are the members of a new "international," geared to a postmodern world of consumerism rather than to an early-modern one centered on values of production.

There are many ironies here. What is often held against the emerging international mass, or pop culture, is precisely its international, if not cosmopolitan character. Clearly, this is a case of double standards. At the level of high culture, most clearly in its modernist phase, there has always been the dream of transcending the local, the provincial, the national, or in social terms, to transgress the narrow bounds of the bourgeois world, and to enter a realm that was nothing if not international: the transcendence lay in being truly "European," or "cosmopolitan." But clearly what is good at the level of high culture is seen as a threat when a similar process of internationalization occurs at the level of mass culture. Then, all of a sudden, the defense is not in terms of high versus low, as one might have expected, but in terms of national cultures and national identities imperiled by an emerging international mass culture. There is a further irony in this construction of the conflict, contrasting an emerging global culture seen as homogenizing to national cultures seen as havens of cultural diversity. In the real world, of course, things are different. There may be a hierarchy of taste cultures, yet it is not a matter of the higher taste cultures being the more national in orientation. It seems to be the case that this hierarchy of taste cultures is itself transnational, that indeed there are international audiences who at the high end all appreciate Beethoven and Bartók or at the low end all fancy Madonna or Prince. Yet in a replay of much older elitist tirades against low culture, advocates of high art see only endless diversity where their own taste is concerned and sheer vulgar homogeneity at the level of mass culture. They have no sense of the variety of tastes and styles, of endless change and renewal in mass culture, simply because it all occurs far beyond their ken.

[See also AMERICANIZATION.*]*

BIBLIOGRAPHY

Barber, Benjamin R., *Jihad vs. McWorld* (Ballantine Bks. 1996).

Cowan, Paul, *The Making of an Un-American: A Dialogue with Experience* (Viking 1970).

Friedman, Thomas, *The Lexus and the Olive Tree* (Thorndike Press 1999).

Herman, Edward S., *The Global Media: The New Missionaries of Corporate Capitalism* (Cassell 1997).

Hollander, Paul, *Anti-Americanism: Critiques at Home and Abroad, 1965–1990* (Oxford 1992).

Huizinga, J., *Amerika Levend en Denkend—Losse Opmerkingen* (Tjeenk Willink & Zoon 1926) ["America Living and Thinking—Loose Observations"].

Kroes, Rob, *If You've Seen One, You've Seen the Mall: Europeans and American Mass Culture* (Univ. of Ill. Press 1996).

Kroes, Rob, *Them and Us: Questions of Citizenship in a Globalizing World* (Univ. of Ill. Press 2000).

Kroes, Rob, and Maarten van Rossem, eds., *Anti-Americanism in Europe* (Free Univ. Press 1986).

Kuisel, Richard, *Seducing the French: The Dilemma of Americanization* (Univ. of Calif. Press 1993).

Lacorne, Denis, Jacques Rupnik, and Marie-France Toinet, eds., *L'Amérique dans Les Têtes* (Hachette Littérature 1986) ["America in Our Heads"].

Lutz, F. A., ed., *Amerika-Europa: Freund und Rivale* (Eugen Rentsch 1970) ["America-Europe: Friend and Rival"].

Maase, Kaspar, *BRAVO Amerika* (Junius 1992).

Pells, Richard, *Not Like Us: How Europeans Have Loved, Hated, and Transformed American Culture since World War II* (Basic Bks. 1997).

Stead, W. T., *The Americanization of the World, Or, the Trend of the Twentieth Century* (H. Markley 1901).

Tomlinson, John, *Cultural Imperialism: A Critical Introduction* (Pinter Pub. 1991).

Wagnleitner, Reinhold, *Coca-Colonization and the Cold War: The Cultural Mission of the United States in Austria after the Second World War,* tr. by Diana M. Wolf (Univ. of N.C. Press 1994).

Wagnleitner, Reinhold, and Elaine Tyler May, eds., *Here, There, and Everywhere: The Foreign Politics of American Popular Culture* (Univ. Press of New England 2000).

Watson, James L., ed., *Golden Arches East: McDonald's in East Asia* (Stanford Univ. Press 1997).

ROB KROES

America Perceived

America existed in the imagination of the peoples of Europe, North Africa, and West Asia long before the voyages of Christopher Columbus. In Egyptian mythology as well as in classical, biblical, and medieval legends a lost land, a promised land, was imagined beyond the western seas. The "discoveries" of Columbus were seen as fulfillment of this ancient prophecy.

Naming these lands the New World created two metaphors simultaneously—Europe was immediately transformed into the Old World in contrast to the "virgin" land across the ocean. The metaphor of the New World had several connotations: it meant new in the sense of young, fresh, innocent, and full of possibility, and, as such, it represented the past of the Old World, a lost youth, as well as an opportunity to start anew. It was also seen as new in the sense of being immature, rude, vulgar, and uncivilized compared with the mature cultures of the Old World.

Whether a commentator stressed the positive or negative aspects of the newness of America was usually more telling about the speaker than about America. From its beginnings to the present, it has been the case that America is praised or denounced, often for the identical trait, depending on the political, social, or cultural orientation of the observer. Thus, America perceived is a reflection of the perceiver.

The optimistic metaphor of the New World was dominant in the seventeenth and eighteenth centuries, receiving memorable expression in *Letters from an American Farmer* (1782), in which Jean de Crèvecoeur answered the question he posed ("What then is the American, this new man?") by extolling the freedom and the perfect society of pre-Revolutionary America. However, by the eighteenth century there were instances of anti-Americanism in Europe, including the first anti-American riot in front of the American Embassy in The Hague in 1787. As J. W. Schulte Nordholt pointed out, some of the earliest examples of anti-Americanism of a more philosophical nature can be traced to the theories of the French naturalist Count de Buffon who claimed that the climate of the New World condemned that land to a backward condition. The Romantic poets and philosophers admired the vast and unspoiled wilderness of America but had only contempt for its society and inhabitants—save the "noble" Indians. American society was materialistic, it was not organic, and it lacked history—all sins in the eyes of the Romantics, who also complained about the absence of castles, cathedrals, and ruins.

Nineteenth-century visitors to the United States, such as Frances Trollope and Charles Dickens, entertained their British readers with descriptions of the raw and uncivilized aspects of the New World, while Crèvecoeur's compatriot, Alexis de Tocqueville, saw in the New World not an unsullied, idealized past of the Old, but its future. The theme of the United States as the future of the world would transform the concept of newness, and in the course of the nineteenth century, the ruling metaphor for America would become that of modernity.

Modernity, like newness, had both attractive and repellent aspects, depending on the eye of the beholder. While scientific progress could be admired, the social changes connected with mass society were regarded with alarm in some European intellectual circles. Members of the European working and peasant classes, however, saw opportunity in the very social changes that distressed the elites, and they voted with their feet by moving to what they regarded as a land where the social distinctions and disadvantages of the Old World could be left behind. Even among European intellectuals, divergent views emerged. The Italian futurists reveled in the very excitement of the modern metropolis, which led Dutch cultural conservatives to reject America.

Modernity would continue to be the dominant metaphor for America until late in the twentieth century, when it was replaced with postmodernity and hyperreality. As the symbol of the modern, America would play a role in political, social, and intergenerational conflicts throughout the world. The idea of America would be embraced or resisted by opposing groups in other countries, who would use the metaphor as well as its cultural manifestations (music, film, food, politics, clothing) as weapons in their own local struggles for cultural, social, or political dominance.

But whether America represented the New World, the modern world, or hyperreality, a core group of national stereotypes—both positive and negative, with the negative attribute often the pendant of some positive trait—has remained remarkably stable over time and across continents. Americans are seen as open and curious, and at the same time immature and naive. They are regarded as optimistic, friendly, dynamic, and pragmatic, but also superficial, shallow, materialistic, and lacking culture. The ready smile with which Americans greet friends and strangers alike has been taken not only for a symbol of openness, and superior dentistry, but also as an indication of a fundamental shallowness and insincerity. Observers often remark on the paradoxical combination of American freedom and conformity, of license and puritanism. An observer for whom the negative traits outweigh the positive traits perceives America as a threat, particularly if America is also seen as the embodiment of the future.

Such views of America and Americans were not the exclusive province of the Old World but could also be found within the New World itself. From Latin America came voices identifying the Anglo-Saxon Northerners with such unflattering attributes as vulgarity, excess, and sensationalism, while the Latin cultures were characterized by delicacy of feeling and nobility of mind. In his essay "Ariel" Uruguayan writer José Enrique Rodó, using Shakespearean analogies, compares the United States to uncouth Caliban while reserving for his fellow Latin Americans the spiritual qualities of Ariel.

Perceptions of American cultural achievements, whether high or low, often differed abroad from the value given the same products on home ground, reflecting the receiving rather than the sending culture. In the nineteenth century Europeans greatly admired the writings of James Fenimore Cooper and Edgar Allan Poe and eagerly embraced the Western and the detective genres, first in literature

and later in film. Mark Twain, Jack London, and later Sinclair Lewis were all acclaimed in Europe. Outsiders, critics, and members of racial minorities often received earlier and more positive critical reception abroad than at home, as exemplified by the Parisian embrace of Richard Wright. During the cold war the list of approved works of American literature in the Soviet bloc countries included proletarian novels such as those by Howard Fast and Albert Maltz, as well as the works of such naturalist writers as Theodore Dreiser, Jack London, and Frank Norris, and the novels of Upton Sinclair.

The perception of America has relied not only on works of literature, published accounts of literary travelers and observers, and the promotional efforts of steamship companies and railroads but also on millions of individual letters and cards sent to family and friends "back home" in every part of the globe from ordinary travelers and immigrants who were eager to share their own personal confrontations with this mythical land, the Promised Land, the "gold mountain." With changing technology, these letters were supplemented with or replaced by telephone calls, e-mail, snapshots, slides, and home videos. In this way the American dream has been propagated throughout the world, as those left behind are invited to share the experience. The perception of America as a land of economic opportunity was broken only during the years of the Great Depression. The unrelenting demand from all continents for U.S. immigration and work visas, as well as the increasingly ingenious methods used by illegal immigrants to enter U.S. territory, testify to the continuing attraction of the American economy.

With the postwar occupations of Germany, Austria, and Japan, and the stationing of U.S. troops in North Atlantic Treaty Organization (NATO) countries and at bases in Asia, even those who never traveled could get a firsthand view of American culture, because such products as Coca-Cola and American music always accompanied the GIs. American tourists traveled to every part of the globe, often demanding and receiving U.S. styles of food, lodging, and amenities, in effect bringing

© JOHN AND BINI MOSS/BLACK STAR

A Peace Corps volunteer works with tribesmen in Tanganyika.

America in their wake. The behavior of these tourists and soldiers was often perceived as insensitive, if not arrogant, and such perceptions were then projected onto the United States as a whole, feeding the image of the "ugly American." Beginning in 1961 U.S. Peace Corps volunteers brought yet another image of America to Asia, Africa, and Latin America and, after 1990, to eastern and central Europe. The U.S. government made a conscious effort to influence the perception of the United States abroad, implementing through the U.S. Information Agency an ambitious program of radio broadcasts, magazine publications, overseas libraries and cultural centers, book translation programs, and cultural tours to cultivate, particularly among foreign elites, a favorable view of American culture and policies.

However, this official projection of U.S. culture paled in significance when compared with the enormous export of commercial culture of all kinds. Not only Coca-Cola and Hollywood but brand-name sportswear, television, including MTV and programs such as *Baywatch,* the National Basketball Association, Levi's jeans, Disneyland, and McDonalds were by the end of the twentieth century everywhere recognizable. The two Michaels—basketball star Michael Jordan and pop star Michael

Jackson—became known all over the globe. While there was no debating the ubiquity of these cultural exports, the value and the implications of their universal penetration were contested.

In nearly every society the importation of American popular culture was resisted by conservative, nationalistic, religious, or establishment forces. Paradoxically, Marxists, both in eastern and western Europe, joined forces with conservative elements to object to U.S. popular culture. Equally paradoxically, those conservatives who objected to the influx of the products of Hollywood or rock and roll often supported the foreign policy and economic leadership of the United States. It was the youth in every part of the globe who enthusiastically embraced popular culture in all its manifestations (food, fashion, music, sports, films) even while objecting to U.S. foreign policy. The idea of America was thus a battleground in an intergenerational struggle, which the rebellious youth were bound to win, just as an earlier youthful generation had embraced jazz over the objections of their parents.

The perception of America in Soviet bloc countries deserves special mention. The official media of the Soviet bloc relentlessly portrayed the United States as an imperialist, war-monger nation, populated by drug addicts. Propaganda from Radio Free Europe and Radio Liberty extolled a land of wealth and freedom. Supporters of the Marxist regimes held unrelievedly negative views of the United States, while some of their opponents held untenably rosy images, which could not be sustained after the political changes of 1989. As the films, publications, and cultural and consumer products of North America and Western Europe flooded the markets of Budapest, Moscow, and Warsaw, the same groups that had most fiercely championed the United States and its allies in the fight against communism were often the most critical of what they saw as a cultural and commercial invasion of vulgar, even pornographic, entertainments. This process was denounced as Americanization, regardless of the country of origin of the offending material.

The perception of America abroad has rested not only on its cultural and commercial aspects but also on its political ideals. The Declaration of Independence and the American Revolution became, for many, compelling symbols of liberty and were consciously recalled in revolutionary and anticolonial struggles throughout the world. The independence of the United States became a reference point for the Spanish colonies of the New World, which appealed to their Northern neighbor for aid in their own independence wars. The New World revolutions, in turn, served as both rallying cries and refuges for the failed nineteenth-century revolts in Germany, Poland, Greece, and Italy.

In Japan, in the period of the Meiji Enlightenment of the late nineteenth century, as well as in the post–World War II constitution, the words and spirit of the Declaration of Independence served as inspiration. In 1876 the supporters of the people's rights movement in Japan explicitly drew on the American example of 1776 by calling on their fellow citizens to resist oppressive laws in the manner of Patrick Henry. The 1911 Chinese revolution led by Sun Yat-sen was also directly influenced by ideas of the Declaration of Independence, which was first published in Chinese in 1901, while the most prominent symbol displayed in Beijing's Tiananmen Square in 1989 was modeled after the Statue of Liberty.

The antiapartheid struggle in South Africa drew on eighteenth-century political ideals of America but more directly on their twentieth-century manifestations in the U.S. civil rights movement. Film screenings and readings of Martin Luther King, Jr.'s "I Have a Dream" speech from the 1963 March on Washington were common in black townships throughout the 1980s. Dissidents in Eastern and Central Europe during the cold-war era found inspiration in American ideals of freedom and rebellion expressed not only in American political writings but also in popular culture forms such as jazz and rock and roll. The U.S. Constitution became a model for many of the states formed in the postcolonial era, particularly in cases where a federal system was perceived as a useful construct for dealing with geographically and ethnically diverse regions within a nation.

While at certain times and in certain places the dominant image of America is as a symbol of liberty, the concept of American imperialism is also a component of the perception of the United States. Sometimes these two faces of America have been directly linked in opposition, as was the case when the official media of the Warsaw Pact states repeatedly denounced the "bourgeois capitalist imperialists" at the same time the political dissidents were embracing both the political and cultural aspects of American freedom. In other countries it was not uncommon to find those protesting American imperialism, particularly in the years of the Vietnam War, wearing the same style of jeans and singing the same protest songs as their American counterparts, adopting U.S. culture while rejecting its foreign policy.

The concept of American imperialism includes: a literal period of colonial rule of the Philippines and the Panama Canal Zone; dollar diplomacy and military interventions to secure American investments, particularly in Latin America; covert as well as open cold-war operations to support friendly regimes or to overthrow perceived opponents; efforts to force open foreign markets to American goods and services; the charge of "cultural imperialism" used to condemn the export of American films, television programs, fast food, fashion, theme parks, sports, and language; and less tangible cultural exports such as the concepts of human rights and feminism, and American techniques of political polling and campaigning.

Each of these varieties of imperialism has produced reactions and counterforces, in the United States as well as abroad. By the end of the twentieth century, the accusation of cultural imperialism had largely been replaced by the concept of globalization, a more diffuse omnidirectional force. While the resistance to globalization was often as fierce as that against Americanization, the target for protests became multinational organizations such as the International Monetary Fund, the World Trade Organization, or the World Bank, rather than uniquely the United States. American overseas military involvement at the end of the twentieth century also had a multinational character, as exemplified in the missions in Bosnia and Kosovo.

BIBLIOGRAPHY

Baudrillard, Jean, *America*, tr. by Chris Turner (1988; Verso 1989).

Eco, Umberto, *Travels in Hyperreality*, tr. by William Weaver (Harcourt 1986).

Kroes, Rob, *If You've Seen One, You've Seen the Mall: Europeans and American Mass Culture* (Univ. of Ill. Press 1996).

Kroes, Rob, and Maarten van Rossem, eds., *Anti-Americanism in Europe* (Free Univ. Press 1986).

Kuisel, Richard, *Seducing the French: The Dilemma of Americanization* (Univ. of Calif. Press 1993).

Pells, Richard, *Not Like Us: How Europeans Have Loved, Hated and Transformed American Culture since World War II* (Basic Bks. 1997) [contains useful bibliographic essay].

Wagnleitner, Reinhold, *Coca-Colonization and the Cold War: The Cultural Mission of the United States in Austria after the Second World War*, tr. by Diana M. Wolf (Univ. of N.C. Press 1994) [originally published in 1991 as *Cocacolonisation und Kalter Krieg*].

KATE DELANEY

AMERICAN CHARACTER

David Potter (*People of Plenty*, 1954) argues that historical explanations of national character have followed three distinct paths. The oldest approach assumed that God had assigned different missions to different groups and that each nation would ultimately fulfill its divinely appointed task.

The second approach was more sophisticated. It sought to explain national character in terms of environmental influences and generally assumed that nurture was more important than genetic shaping of behavior. Frederick Jackson Turner's work on the American frontier (1893) was a case in point. As Alexis de Tocqueville (*Democracy in America*, 1835, 1840) had done before him, Turner sought to explain American character by examining the environmental matrix in which American values and institutions had developed.

The third approach to national character studies shifted the focus from the environment to genetics. Demagogues on both sides of the Atlantic, in the period between the two world wars, placed primary emphasis on the assumed genetic makeup of racial and national groups. As Potter has noted, the end result put all national character studies in disrepute.

Yet national entities were too important to ignore. Potter demonstrated that anthropologists, sociologists, and psychologists had begun, even before World War II, to study a variety of cultures and group behaviors. What they found was that it was possible to discover significant similarities in the ways that different groups of people were socialized into the societies in which they lived, and that some of those similarities followed national boundaries.

Between 1940 and 1970 studies of United States character flourished. Their purpose was not so much to increase national pride as to foster self-understanding. Most of the works pointed to the fact that the strengths and weaknesses of the culture were interrelated. For example, Margaret Mead (*And Keep Your Powder Dry*, 1942) noted that Americans were all third generation, and that mobility was both a source of strength and insecurity.

The most influential midcentury study was David Riesman's *The Lonely Crowd* (1950). Riesman's study postulated the existence of three modes of conformity that had emerged in distinct historical and cultural circumstances. "Tradition direction" flourished in illiterate societies, which experienced little change from generation to generation. "Inner direction" marked societies that were experiencing rapid growth and mobility. Such societies tended to be productivity and achievement oriented. The third mode of conformity, "other direction," arose in a consumer-oriented society in which success depended on peer group approval. These modes of conformity, although arising in different time periods, all pointed to behavioral styles that simultaneously created security and insecurity, strength and weakness, courage and fear. In Riesman's view, the ideal character type was an autonomous individual who knew what society wanted and was fully capable of filling society's demands, but who chose, on the basis of heightened self-knowledge, whether to conform or not. Thus Riesman suggested that most of those who achieved autonomy came from the ranks of those who mastered the skills and techniques required by current standards of conformity.

Riesman's study had wide-ranging effects on midcentury scholarship and on popular attitudes as well, because it accepted the reality of a consumer-oriented society and also spoke to the loneliness and insecurity that increasing numbers of people felt. In 1954 Potter argued that the twentieth century had spawned a new social institution equal in its socializing power to that wielded by school, church, and family—namely, the institution of advertising. Advertising's strength was measured not only by the size of its budget but also by the fact that it had a clear vision of the kind of person it wanted to nurture—a person who was, above all, a good consumer. Two years later William Whyte wrote *The Organization Man,* and in 1964 Leo Marx wrote *The Machine in the Garden.* In quite different ways these works explore the issue of whether and how even successful individuals could translate their success into meaningful and satisfying lives. In the mid-1960s, when Lyndon Johnson announced a War on Poverty, and the goals of the eighteenth-century liberal democratic revolution seemed to be within reach, scholars on the cutting edge of American studies scholarship probed beneath the surface of American prosperity and laid bare the anxieties and insecurities that seemed to go hand in hand with increasing prosperity.

The 1960s also produced grassroots revolts. As long as there was little hope of changing the discriminatory patterns ingrained in American society, minority citizens were hesitant to act in ways that would rock the boat. As discriminatory patterns began to change, however, voices of protest mushroomed in the 1960s and 1970s. Some opted out of a society whose racism, sexism, and imperialism seemed incurable. Others demanded a new equality and a voice in the power structures of their society. While identity issues remained important, there was a growing awareness of the many diversities that characterized United States society as well as a growing conviction that identities that mattered had to do with one's race, class, gender, or

ethnic background. Simultaneously, scholars found it increasingly difficult to make generalizations about Americans that included enough segments of the nation to be significant.

One important study that appeared in the 1980s was done by Robert Bellah and four colleagues at the University of California (*Habits of the Heart,* 1985). The authors found a measurable erosion of the resources Americans had for making sense of their lives, a deteriorating sense of community, and a growing reliance on the language of therapy, which assumed that a free self could muster the resources to solve any and all problems. They believed, however, that communities of memory linked the lives of various groups of people in potentially meaningful ways, and they held out some hope that Americans might still find a viable balance between their commitments to individualism and to a larger community.

Clearly Bellah and his colleagues were worried about the health and well-being of modern American society. And they were not alone. Christopher Lasch's *The Culture of Narcissism* (1979), Richard Sennett's *The Uses of Disorder* (1970), Daniel Yankelovich's *New Rules* (1981), Martin Seligman's *Research in Clinical Psychology: Why Is There So Much Depression Today?* (1989), and John McKnight's *The Careless Society: Community and its Counterfeits* (1995) are but a few of the works that raise serious questions about whether Americans can lead satisfying lives in the world they inhabit.

Leinberger and Tucker (*The New Individualists: The Generation after the Organization Man,* 1991) argued that a great transfer of power was taking place as the baby boomers replaced the "organization men." Offering a kind of postscript to Robert Jay Lifton's "protean man," the authors suggested that members of the new generation had subject-oriented identities, which were nothing more than the sum-total of the identities derived from the roles they played. Their analysis describes a fragmented and pluralistic society.

Yet such a narrative is incomplete. Although Americans live and work in an increasingly diversified society, they are still subject to forces that exert widespread pressures to conform. Indeed, the booming prosperity of the 1990s together with the technological revolution nurtured by computers made the analyses of Riesman, Potter, and Marx more relevant than ever. A computerized society offers enormous possibilities of decentralization and individual choice, but the choices are all subject to increased knowledge about the ways in which other people make their choices. A prosperous economy greatly increased the ranks of the affluent, but it simultaneously raised the level of expectations and made more terrible the consequences of being left behind or out. Prosperity also increased the illusion that individual autonomy is possible while magnifying the fact of our interdependence.

The 1980s and 1990s rightly directed the attention of American studies scholars to neglected people and subjects. Scholars have not adequately understood or appreciated the ways in which race, poverty, gender, and ethnicity have shaped American identities and communities. But there remains a national context in which personal and collective struggles are carried out. Thomas Wolfe recognized in 1934 (*You Can't Go Home Again*) the existence of a "lonely crowd" in America as well as the suffocating pressures to conform, which resulted from modern technology and mobility. Richard Wright described in *American Hunger* (1977) the effects of "the American dream" on those who were excluded from its pursuit and questioned whether, indeed, the dream was worth pursuing. Arthur Miller's play *Death of a Salesman* (1949), which depicted individuals who had been seduced by their culture into pursuing the wrong dreams, enjoyed a spectacular revival in 1999. Yet the dreams continue.

Indeed it was clear that there also existed a spirit of patriotism and hopefulness even in the midst of senseless violence and outrageous inequalities that existed in the 1990s. To watch an immigrant conductor of the Boston Symphony Orchestra dance exuberantly to the strains of "The Stars and Stripes Forever" on the Fourth of July was to glimpse a joyful, still-flourishing side of American character. It also suggested that there really are "communities of memory" linking Americans' lives in unsuspected ways.

[*See also* AMERICANIZATION; AMERICAN DREAM.]

BIBLIOGRAPHY

Hague, John A., "Whither American Cultural Studies," in *An American Mosaic: Rethinking American Culture Studies,* ed. by Marshall Fishwick (Am. Heritage Custom Pub. 1996).

McClay, Wilfred M., "Where Have We Come since the 1950s? Thoughts on Materialism and American Social Character," in *Rethinking Materialism: Perspectives on the Spiritual Dimension of Economic Behavior,* ed. by Robert Wuthnow (Erdmans 1995).

Wilkenson, Rupert, *The Pursuit of American Character* (Harper 1988) [the above three items contain reviews of the literature dealing with United States character studies in the second half of the twentieth century].

Erikson, Erik, *Childhood and Society,* 2d ed. (Norton 1964) [this remains a classic way of relating biological, psychological, and sociological materials].

Erikson, Kai T., *Everything in Its Path: Destruction of Community in the Buffalo Creek Flood* (Simon & Schuster 1976) [a trenchant study of what happens when a community disappears].

Hsu, Francis L. K., *Americans and Chinese: Two Ways of Life* (Cresset Press 1955) [a fine comparative study].

Lipset, Seymour Martin, "A Changing American Character," in *The First New Nation* (Basic Bks. 1963) [Lipset describes a polarity of value orientations that has proven to be remarkably stable. These last four items are classic studies whose approaches offer seminal ways of looking at the study of United States character].

JOHN A. HAGUE

AMERICAN DREAM

The interpretation of the good life in the United States, commonly referred to as the American dream, is an evolving concept that has frequently been redefined through the course of American history. The main features of the American dream were often exclusionary to minority groups, but by the end of the twentieth century the notion had become significantly more comprehensive and accessible. Despite its changing nature, two constants have formed the core of the American dream: property and economic security.

For many of the original colonists, the promise of economic opportunity was the prime motivating factor in immigrating to the British territories in North America. This promise of a better life was represented by the potential to gain land. In an effort to encourage emigration the headright system of the mid-Atlantic colonies offered individuals as much as 50 acres (20 ha) of land for either coming to the colony or for paying the transport costs of a family member or an indentured servant (who would then be free to obtain land after a seven-year period of servitude). The headright system remained the most common manner to gain land in many of the colonies throughout the seventeenth and early eighteenth centuries. The push for new land led to armed conflict with the Native American tribes of the eastern seaboard. British efforts to curtail westward expansion were one of the contributing factors in the Revolutionary War.

The importance of property and the right of citizens to own and acquire property were incorporated in the Declaration of Independence and formed one of the hallmarks of American political culture. In an effort to secure the frontier, successive administrations in Washington encouraged resettlement in the West by opening territory to settlers, often granting land rights for minimal costs or even for free. Following the War of 1812 westward expansion greatly accelerated, and after the acquisition of California in the 1840s, the movement to fill in the interior of the nation was accelerated both by the economic promises of the California gold rush and by encouragement in the popular media, where prominent newspapermen such as Horace Greeley urged Easterners to "Go West" to seek their fortunes and the promise of a better life. Migration was encouraged by events such as the Oklahoma land rush. The government opened up some 3 million acres (1.2 million ha) of land to settlers in 160-acre (65-ha) plots for whites at the expense of the Native American tribes living in the territory.

Concurrent with the movement West there began to emerge a significant leisure class in the settled East. The dramatic growth in wages and increased urban services created improvements in the quality of life. The materialism of the period had a significant impact on literature and art. Social Darwinism and the traditional American emphasis on individualism reinforced class stereotypes. Quality of life was defined by wealth. While works such as Mark Twain and Charles Dudley Warner's *The Gilded Age* (1873) criticized the unbridled greed of the time, popular magazines such as the *Saturday Evening Post* and *McClure's* expounded on the virtues of economic success. Meanwhile the publications of Horatio Alger (who wrote 130 works and sold millions of novels) made the "rags to riches" theme one of the central components of American culture.

For Americans at the onset of the twentieth century, the "good life" was marked by economic success. Nonetheless, the economic disparities created a backlash against the most extravagant displays of wealth. Within the emerging middle class many developed a nostalgia for the small-town lifestyle. The rise of monopolies, widespread poverty, and corruption in politics challenged the ideas of equality. Despite the reforms of the Progressive Era, the American dream remained beyond the reach of the millions of poor. Reformist writers, known as muckrakers, worked to expose the falsity of the American dream. For instance, Upton Sinclair's novel *The Jungle* (1906) emphasized the abuses in the meatpacking industry and helped spur reforms, including the passage of the Pure Food and Drug Act. Meanwhile, segregation in the South and anti-immigrant sentiment in the Northeast and California further alienated groups within the United States.

The importance of economic success to perceptions of the good life was augmented by the economic boom of the 1920s. The rise of the consumer culture broadened the definition of the American dream to include not only property but various material items as well. Possession of automobiles, radios, and other consumer products became hallmarks of prosperity. The widespread use of advertising reinforced the public's desire for these new products, while the availability of credit made ownership more practical and easier to accomplish with limited household budgets. Chain stores such as J. C. Penney and Woolworth's offered consumers the same products on a national basis. As Americans bought the same merchandise, saw the same advertisements, and listened to the same radio programs or saw the same movies, regional differences began to fade and there arose conformity in fashion and lifestyle. This growing uniformity was brilliantly criticized by Sinclair Lewis in his 1922 novel, *Babbitt*. Lewis presented a satirical look at the fictional George Babbitt, who personified the materialism, closed-mindedness, and devotion to passing fads that marked the era.

The Great Depression and the war years of the early 1940s ended, or at the very least delayed, the aspirations of millions of Americans for any degree of prosperity. However, the end of World War II ushered in both the dramatic rise of consumerism and the subsequent emergence of the middle class as the dominant force in American culture. Hence the preferences and values of that group came to be absorbed into the mainstream as the modern "American dream." The latter comprised a number of key objects of desire, including, besides a family and a career, a house in the suburbs and various material possessions, such as an automobile, a television, and an array of electric appliances.

Many of the trends begun in the 1920s reasserted themselves in the 1950s. In the United States, the gross national product (GNP) and real wages doubled from 1945 to 1960. There was a dramatic revival of consumerism as a wave of new products, including televisions and other electric appliances and automobiles, fueled the economy. Real gains in consumer purchasing power, easy credit, and price declines resulting from improved manufacturing made such products easily affordable. Mass production and the proliferation of chain outlets continued the growing conformity of American society. Stores such as the fast-food retailer McDonald's and the hotel chain Holiday Inn had spectacular success in meeting the needs of certain markets, while suburban malls created shopping megasites for consumers. Middle- and upper-class Americans traveled extensively and began to frequent such entertainment sites as Disneyland.

© SUPERSTOCK

A family of the 1950s watches a program on their new television set, living the American dream.

The second main component of the American dream (property) also reemerged in the late 1940s. New means of construction led to a rapid expansion in the housing industry. By the 1950s approximately two million new homes were being built each year for the forty million Americans who fled the urban areas for the new suburbs. The expansion of the federal highway system made it possible for some ninety percent of workers to drive to their places of employment. Yet the growth of the suburbs further segregated society as the white middle class left urban centers. The loss of this purchasing power and tax base led to a lessening of services and commerce. The overall urban decline in the United States of the late 1960s and 1970s continued to accentuate the difference between the prosperous groups and the growing urban poor.

The main features of the American dream were vividly presented to the American people through the medium of television. Programs such as *The Donna Reed Show* and *Father Knows Best* presented images of American life that emphasized home ownership and the importance of material possessions. Advertising reinforced these impressions and promoted new products as well as the conspicuous consumption fueled by the notion of "keeping up with the Joneses." This notion spurred consumers to be the first to own new products or new versions of goods.

Yet television also documented the civil rights movement and the overall struggle by minority groups to gain access to the good life. Televised, for example, was the violence encountered by people such as the Freedom Riders in their effort to overturn segregation and prompt social acceptance of the Supreme Court decisions of the 1950s and the civil rights legislation of the 1960s. This would be followed by the emergence of the counterculture in the 1960s. Movements within the counterculture rejected the materialism and conformity of the American dream and instead adopted alternative lifestyles. The traditional notion of family composed of a husband, wife, and two to three children also began to break down with the rise in divorce rates. Communal property and a refusal to participate in the mainstream workforce marked the hippie culture that originated in San Francisco. The economic downturn of the 1970s, led by the loss of industrial jobs, put the American dream further out of the reach of many Americans.

Despite the problems, however, the main ingredients at the core of the American dream remained consistent. Home ownership and material possession continued to be prized. In the 1980s there emerged a renewed emphasis on the accumulation of wealth and material items. Ownership of name-brand clothing or status-symbol cars continued to be seen as a mark of success. For many, the strong economy at the turn of the twenty-first century brought elements of the prized life within reach.

BIBLIOGRAPHY

Daleiden, Joseph L., *The American Dream: Can It Survive the 21st Century?* (Prometheus Bks. 1999).

Kaiser, Charles, *1968 in America: Music, Politics, Chaos, Counterculture, and the Shaping of a Generation* (Weidenfeld & Nicolson 1988).

Marchand, Roland, *Advertising the American Dream: Making Way for Modernity, 1920–1940* (Univ. of Calif. Press 1985).

Merk, Frederick, *History of the Westward Movement* (Knopf 1978).

Salmon, Emily J., ed., *A Hornbook of Virginia History,* 3d ed. (Virginia State Library 1983).

Schaller, Michael, Virginia Scharff, and Robert D. Schulzinger, *Present Tense: The United States since 1945* (Houghton 1992).

Wright, Esmond, *The American Dream: From Reconstruction to Reagan* (Blackwell 1996).

TOM M. LANSFORD

AMERICAN EAGLE

The national bird of the United States, the bald eagle (*Haliaeetus leucocephalus*) is the only eagle unique to North America. The common name dates from a time when *bald* meant "white," not hairless. The bald eagle ranges over most of the North American continent, from the northern parts of Alaska and Canada to northern Mexico.

This eagle was chosen on June 20, 1782, as the American emblem, owing to its long life, great strength, and majestic looks, and also because it was then believed to exist only in North America. The bald eagle, with outspread wings, appears on the backs of American gold coins, silver dollars, half-dollars, and quarters. The eagle is also found on the great seal of the United States. The great seal shows an eagle with its wings spread, facing

White-headed Sea Eagle, or Bald Eagle.

Painting by John J. Audubon of a bald eagle, the national bird.

front, with a shield on its breast featuring thirteen perpendicular red and white stripes, surmounted by a blue field with the same number of stars. In its right talon the eagle holds an olive branch, in its left, a bundle of thirteen arrows, and in its beak it carries a scroll inscribed with the motto *E Pluribus Unum* ("From Many, One").

There were some dissenters to the selection of the bald eagle as the national bird. Benjamin Franklin wrote that the eagle was "a bird of bad moral character, he does not get his living honestly; you may have seen him perched on some dead tree, where, too lazy to fish for himself, he watches the labor of the fishing-hawk, and when that diligent bird has at length taken a fish, and is bearing it to its nest for the support of his mate and young ones, the bald eagle pursues him and takes it." Franklin favored the humble wild turkey as a symbol of America.

When European settlers first sailed to America's shores, eagles soared, nested, and fished along the Atlantic, from Labrador to the tip of south Florida, and along the Pacific, from Baja California to Alaska. Eagles inhabited every large river and concentration of lakes in the interior of the continent. They nested in what would later become forty-five of the lower forty-eight states. The bald eagle population would steadily decline, owing to a number of complex reasons. Essentially, eagles and humans were in competition for the same food, and humans, with guns and traps at their disposal, had the upper hand. By the 1930s public awareness of bald eagles and their plight began to increase, and in 1940 the Bald Eagle Act was passed and eagle populations began to rebound. However, at the same time DDT (dichloro-diphenyl-trichloroethane) and other pesticides began to be widely used, and these had a disastrous effect on birds of prey. Bald eagles were officially declared an endangered species in 1967 in all areas of the United States south of the fortieth parallel, under a law that preceded the Endangered Species Act of 1973. Federal and state government agencies, along with private organizations, successfully sought to alert the public to the eagle's plight and to protect its habitat.

Only a handful of species have fought their way back from the United States's endangered species list: the California gray whale, the American alligator, and the bald eagle are a few. Once endangered throughout the United States, the bald eagle's status was upgraded to "threatened" in 1994, two decades after the banning of DDT and the passing of laws to protect both eagles and their nesting trees.

BIBLIOGRAPHY

Beans, Bruce E., *Eagle's Plume: The Struggle to Preserve the Life and Haunts of America's Bald Eagle* (Scribner 1996).

Laycock, George, *Autumn of the Eagle* (Scribner 1973).

Stalmaster, Mark V., *The Bald Eagle* (Universe Bks. 1987).

BRIAN BLACK

AMERICAN LANGUAGE

In the spirit of federalism and enterprise following the founding of the United States of America, Noah Webster undertook a patriotic mission to establish independent standards for the English language in America. For almost a half-century he produced and promoted writings on language including spelling books and a series of dictionaries, the largest of which was *An American Dictionary of the English Language* (1828). By his death in 1843 at the age of eighty-five, Webster was recognized throughout the expanding nation as the authority in matters of language.

Shortly after World War I American journalist and cultural critic H. L. Mencken reasserted the linguistic independence of North America from Great Britain in *The American Language* (1919). Its immediate popularity caused Mencken to enlarge and revise it twice by 1923. He convinced readers of the energy and creativity of American English with examples of place names, terms for food, regional expressions, euphemisms, nicknames, and the lingoes of various marginal groups. In addition, his notion that the English language in America would soon develop into a separate language from that of the British Isles appealed to Americans who desired to repudiate inherited British artistic and literary norms in favor of a new and distinct American culture. *The American Language* appeared in four editions and two large supplements during Mencken's lifetime, and this is still available in a one-volume abridged edition with annotations and corrections by Raven I. McDavid and David W. Maurer (1963). It stands as the basic compendium of American English.

Mencken's prediction that American and British would shortly diverge into separate languages has not come to pass. Rather, these two major varieties now form the two mutually intelligible bases of the rapidly expanding international English language. To be sure, differences between oral American and British English in pronunciation, placement of stress, and intonation are clearly noticeable. The most general contrast is in the pronunciation of the vowel *a* in words such as *bath, fasten, half, plaster,* and *reprimand.* Differences in the placement of word stress are numerous but unpredictable, as in British ad**ver**tisement, **bal**let, con**tro**versy, re**search**, and week**end** as compared with American adver**tise**ment, bal**let**, **con**troversy, **re**search, and **week**end. In contrast to the overwhelming percentage of vocabulary common to both British and American English, the list of vocabulary differences is short. For instance, British *ring road, sweets, biscuit, torch, petrol, removal van,* and *trainers* are equivalent to American *beltway, candy, cookie, flashlight, gasoline, moving van,* and *sneakers.* Sentence structure and other grammatical features are largely the same in the two varieties. Except for some spelling differences (for example, British *draughty, pretence,* and *tyre* versus American *drafty, pretense,* and *tire),* in written form British and American English are much like each other. Such uniformity sometimes makes it difficult to discern from a written text whether its author is a native speaker of English from York in England, York in Canada, or York in Pennsylvania. Some international varieties of English are modeled on British English and some on American English. One debate within the profession of teaching English to speakers of other languages is which dialect to teach to international learners abroad. Because of a long tradition of teaching English in Britain's far-flung colonial empire, materials and methods based on British English are more widely and firmly established. The professionalization of teaching English to nonnative speakers is more recent in the United States, occasioned mainly by Hispanic and Asian immigration.

The American language that Mencken described with such passion was in fact English. From the earliest days of the colonies that were later to form the United States, a monolingual English-speaking society was taken for granted both by English-speaking settlers and by others who joined them in the British colonies. The languages of the Native Americans were virtually ignored by the colonists, except for taking into English from them nouns for unfamiliar plants, animals, and foods (such as *hickory, raccoon,* and *hominy*) and thousands of place names (for example, *Potomac, Manhattan,* and *Niagara*). At the time of European contact, more than five hundred languages were being spoken by the indigenous population of North America. The number today is around two hundred. In terms of de facto public language policy, the languages of non-English-speaking immigrant groups fared little better. Becoming American meant speaking English. From the early 1600s to the present, the dominant pattern has been for the grandchildren of immigrants who spoke only a foreign language to speak only English. Nonetheless, in their transition to Americanness, immigrants have left their mark on the national language through vocabulary. For instance, from Dutch the vocabulary of American English has acquired *cookie* and *Santa Claus,* from Spanish *corral* and *plaza,* from French *prairie* and *portage,* from German *delicatessen* and *pretzel,* and from Yiddish *chutzpah* and *schlep.* Including words acquired in international military and commercial contexts (such as *tycoon* from Japanese, *sauna* from Finnish, and *robot* from Czech), American English has acquired thousands of words from hundreds of languages. In the twentieth century the rate of acquiring words from foreign sources decreased and American English became the major exporter of vocabulary to other languages. Later American English satisfied its voracious appetite for new words by using words already in the language in new ways. *American Speech,* the quarterly journal of the

American Dialect Society, carries a limited record of new vocabulary in each issue in "Among the New Words."

The numbers and social status of non-English-speaking immigrants have caused some to advocate an amendment to the Constitution of the United States designating English as the official language. Several states have passed resolutions recognizing English as the official language of the state. Such pronouncements are largely without consequence. On the endangerment of English in the face of large numbers of speakers of foreign languages, the history of the United States is clear. Millions of speakers of foreign languages have given up their native language, often at the price of losing family connections and their cultural heritage. A small percentage retained their ancestral languages by living in socially or geographically isolated communities, as did French-speaking Acadians in southern Louisiana until World War II, for example. Among those who did not remain separate from English-speaking America, some maintained bilingualism through family, religious, or cultural affiliations. Within the overall picture of English as the language of the nation, a remarkable amount of language diversity has existed, as shown by essays in *Language in the USA* by Charles A. Ferguson and Shirley Brice Heath (1981).

Despite predictions that the mass media would homogenize American English, regional dialects persist. They are most fully documented in a set of linguistic atlases in which sounds and distinctive words and expressions used by carefully selected individual speakers are recorded on maps. A thorough review essay by Michael Montgomery at the completion of the *Linguistic Atlas of the Gulf States* in 1992 (*American Speech,* Fall 1993) evaluates the contributions and prospects of this geographical approach to dialect. A more accessible record of regional variation is the *Dictionary of American Regional English* (*DARE*), based at the University of Wisconsin under the editorship of Frederick Cassidy and, recently, Joan Houston Hall. Since 1985 three volumes, comprising the letters A–O, have been published. The linguistic atlases and *DARE* are for the most part based on the speech of longtime residents of small cities and towns and on fieldwork conducted decades ago. Innovative work by William Labov in New York City in the 1960s expanded the study of regional diversity to include the complexities of urban areas. With sophisticated computer equipment and programs, Labov and his co-workers on the research project Phonological Atlas of North America at the University of Pennsylvania have identified and are tracking some rapidly developing changes in the pronunciation of vowels taking place in New York, Philadelphia, Detroit, and Chicago—an orderly series usually called the Northern Cities Shift. Labov has also described a different set of shifts currently taking place in the South.

Geography is only one factor that correlates with dialect variation. Socioeconomic class, ethnicity, education, and gender also are important in shaping speakers' linguistic habits and allegiances. The most familiar and widespread set of social dialects in North America is African American Vernacular English (AAVE). AAVE is a rule-governed linguistic system, not a collection of haphazard deviations from a standard English. The designation *vernacular* indicates that AAVE is almost always oral, rarely used in writing except in literary or other creative works intended to convey the sound of speech. Words and expressions used by AAVE speakers in the 1990s are collected in Geneva Smitherman's *Black Talk* (1994). The popularity of rap music among American adolescents has made many AAVE expressions part of the casual speech of young people throughout the nation. Examples are *da bomb* (the best); *D. L.* (down low, or in a sly manner); *front on* (deceive); *G* (noun of address to a male: "what's up, G?"); *phat* (excellent); *skeezer* (person who has sex indiscriminately); *T. C. B.* (take care of business); *wigga* (white youth who identifies with African American youth culture). Scholars debate whether AAVE is part of a continuum with Creole spoken in the Caribbean and how its distinct grammatical features can be explained historically. Educators and parents debate whether African American children should be encouraged to use AAVE for purposes of self esteem and community solidarity or discouraged from using it because it might be an impediment to mastering standard English. African Americans themselves hold a range of views about AAVE.

Correctness is a perennial American concern. Books of advice on vocabulary and grammar are issued and reissued, and mistakes in the use of English are decried almost daily by nationally syndicated newspaper columnists. At the beginning of the twenty-first century, however, Americans are much more concerned about abusive terms than they are about standard vocabulary and grammar. At the same time that explicit vocabulary referring to sex is regularly heard from television, films, and celebrities—breaking a long-standing taboo against such vocabulary in public settings—the public use of vocabulary that negatively pictures minority groups can bring dire consequences. A new vocabulary of cultural sensitivity has arisen, which proscribes older uses such as *Negro* and *colored*, favors *African American*, and prefers *Asian* to *Oriental*, *disabled* to *crippled*, and so forth.

[See also AFRICAN AMERICANS, *article on* AFRICAN AMERICAN SPEECH AND LANGUAGE; NATIVE AMERICANS, *articles on* NATIVE AMERICAN LANGUAGES, NATIVE AMERICAN LITERATURES; JEWISH AMERICANS, *article on* JEWISH AMERICAN SPEECH AND LANGUAGE.]

BIBLIOGRAPHY

Carver, Craig, *American Regional Dialects: A Word Geography* (Univ. of Mich. Press 1987).

Crystal, David, *The Cambridge Encyclopedia of the English Language* (Cambridge 1995).

Flexner, Stuart Berg, and Anne H. Soukhanov, *Speaking Freely: A Guided Tour of American English from Plymouth Rock to Silicon Valley* (Oxford 1997).

McDavid, Raven I., "American English: A Bibliographic Essay," *American Studies International* 17 (Winter 1979):3-45.

Merriam-Webster Dictionary of English Usage (Merriam 1989).

Preston, Dennis, ed., *American Dialect Research* (Benjamins 1993).

Wolfram, Walt, and Natalie Schilling-Estes, *American English: Dialects and Variation* (Blackwell 1998).

CONNIE EBLE

AMERICAN STUDIES

[The two articles grouped under the present heading deal with two closely related but nevertheless distinct topics. The first, AN OVERVIEW, *provides an introduction to the nature, scope, and history of American studies as an academic discipline. The second,* APPROACHES AND CONCEPTS, *focuses more specifically on the analytical tools and methods employed by scholars in the field.]*

An Overview

The term *American studies*, often treated as a singular rather than plural noun, has been most conventionally used to refer to the seven-decade-old institutionalized academic movement devoted to the multi-, inter-, and transdisciplinary study, both in and outside the United States, of U.S. society and culture. Those institutional arrangements now include undergraduate and graduate degree-granting and other programs in over four hundred colleges and universities worldwide; curricula in numerous high schools; academic journals in a dozen countries; American studies sections in academic publishers' booklists; offices in various governmental agencies, private foundations, museums, and research libraries; and professional American studies associations in Europe, Asia, Africa, the Middle East, Latin America, the South Pacific, Canada, and the United States, the oldest and largest of which is the U.S.-based American Studies Association (ASA).

In addition to this conventional use of the term, *American studies* has also at times been applied to over three centuries of self-conscious commentary on American life. Ranging from nationalistic celebration to antinationalist critique and constantly being augmented by new and rediscovered texts in print, electronic, and other media, this massive commentary is a continuous reminder that academic American studies depends in profound ways on the discursive and institutional worlds outside its own academic borders.

A third use of the term *American studies* has recently assumed some prominence, particularly among academic activists, and proceeds from a sharp critique of versions of American studies that focus exclusively or primarily on an analysis of the United States. Although, from the eighteenth century to the present, "America" has been conventionally applied in its singular form primarily to the United States, critics have increasingly attacked such application as symptomatic of nationalist chauvinism. Equally important, their argument for a broader, pannational use of "America" and "American" stems from a critique of the value of using nation-states as units of analysis and explanation.

Although academic American studies can be called a movement, it may be more accurate to say that it is constituted by a variety of movements, embedded in a wide range of practices, positions, and groups. From its outset, academic American studies has offered sites for myriad debates and negotiations over content, theory, method, structural arrangements, and membership. In general, the history of academic American studies can be seen as an unevenly developing and often contested movement toward enlarging the content of the field, diversifying the theories and methods brought to bear on that content, strengthening the often unstable institutional arrangements for the field, and achieving greater cultural diversity among the field's participants and leaders.

American studies' development in the United States both reflected and refracted most of the major changes animating the nation during the twentieth century. If some of this development can be captured imperfectly in "representative" moments, it can also be viewed in part in terms of the five or six overlapping generations of academics who have come, in varying degrees, to identify themselves with the movement or some of its aspects.

Most of the U.S. "founders" of academic American studies were born within a decade on each side of 1900. Like others of their era, they experienced the pressures of rapid urbanization, massive immigration, corporatization, professionalizing of higher education and other institutions, and dramatic changes in transportation, communication, and other technologies that were transforming the physi-

cal, social, and cultural landscape of the United States and other societies. They too were affected by the complex ideological and discursive legacies of the Progressive movement, World War I, and the immediate postwar era, and they negotiated the myriad and often contradictory impulses—utopian, pragmatic, internationalist, nationalist, populist, elitist, futuristic, nostalgic—emanating from such experiences. Some of this first generation labored in relative isolation from other kindred spirits. But most academic Americanists of the 1920s and 1930s undertook their work in a context of scholarly conversation and collaboration. Such cross-institutional and, to an extent, cross-disciplinary collaborations offered one important seedbed out of which an institutional American studies was to spring.

Arguably the most important proximate catalysts for institutional American studies were the Depression and President Franklin Roosevelt's New Deal. If the Depression created a widespread sense of cultural as well as economic and political crisis in the United States and elsewhere, the crisis also stimulated new and recently established academics in their twenties and thirties to inspect the social processes, values, and patterns of thought that had led to the crisis and to examine the social and cultural traditions and contemporary resources possessed by the nation that might lead the nation out of the crisis. The New Deal's pragmatic and improvisatory approach to the reconstruction of the economy and public morale paralleled curricular experiments, and academic writing focused, like many New Deal social programs, on bringing people together across boundaries (in the case of American studies, across departmental boundaries) and on highlighting the relationship of national traditions and contemporary problems. Even when many U.S.-focused courses of this period were historically oriented, they developed themes that self-consciously linked past and present. Like the Progressive historians, philosophers, and social theorists, many academic Americanists of the 1930s stressed the practical contemporary value of knowing about the national past. Also influential among Americanists of the 1930s were New Deal cultural projects that promoted not only attention to American literature and the arts but to local histories, folkways, and the celebration of ordinary Americans' lives. In addition to generating materials usable by scholars and teachers as well as others, these projects also implicitly taught the value of organized approaches to the study of American life. And the projects offered models for a handful of academics among the first generation of Americanists who were searching for effective ways of being public intellectuals, both speaking and listening to audiences outside the academy.

By 1940 this first generation of academic Americanists had founded a few formal American studies programs and had been joined in the nascent enterprise by the beginnings of a second generation, one that had entered college during the mid and late 1930s, taken recently inaugurated undergraduate and graduate courses in American social, literary, cultural, and intellectual history from the first generation, and been influenced by the liberal and left-wing currents of the decade. Whether they interrupted their academic lives when World War II broke out to serve in the military or stayed and studied on the home front, many in this generation emerged from the war with both nationalist and internationalist perspectives on the perils confronting democracy and capitalism, and they began to embody those perspectives in their teaching and writing in academic American studies.

A survey of the growing number of American studies undergraduate and graduate programs in 1948 found institutional patterns not surprising for a new academic enterprise. Most depended entirely or heavily on courses offered by established departments. In some could be found a small core of multi- and interdisciplinary courses sponsored by the American studies program itself. Faculty teaching these courses typically had their primary homes in an established department or held a dual department-program appointment. Some "interdisciplinary" courses were at the outset more so in title than in content and method. But, increasingly, often by focusing on "themes" or case-study "problems," a more or less distinctive self-labeled "American studies" curriculum became fairly widespread in programs of the 1950s.

The American studies movement of the postwar decades was tugged at by a number of often conflicting tendencies that Americanists at a number of specific institutional sites attempted, with varying degrees of success and self-consciousness, to negotiate. The preeminent political and economic power and assertiveness of the United States in the immediate postwar period, further heated by cold-war politics and rhetoric, undoubtedly affected in complex ways the character of the movement's development both in and outside the United States. For example, international postwar politics stimulated the United States's active effort, as a part of its foreign policy, to develop American studies programs, libraries, research institutions, associations, and publications abroad, to send U.S. Americanists abroad to teach and lecture, and to help foreign scholars from a variety of "free" and "developing" countries come to the United States to study. Most leaders of the first and second generation of U.S. Americanists had been overseas on Fulbright scholarships or private-foundation grants by the mid-1960s. For some scholars, such overseas experiences further stimulated an interest in cross-national comparative studies that had already been present in prewar American studies. The opportunity to travel abroad as a result of governmental and corporate largesse also carried its pressures and temptations. Even while not usually instructed explicitly by federal authorities to be evangelists of the American way of life, and even while they might criticize various aspects of American society and culture while abroad, many Fulbrighters and academic United States Information Agency (USIA) consultants nonetheless felt some obligation to be goodwill ambassadors of their nation.

Closer to home, American studies programs were beneficiaries of the unevenly distributed prosperity of postwar U.S. society, rapidly growing college enrollments, and a widespread although by no means unanimous celebration of "American" products, institutions, people, and values. Undergraduates looking for fresh kinds of courses—perhaps in the same way that they were drawn to postwar films, music, and the new medium of television and to a desire to discover and explain themselves in a rapidly changing world—found an outlet for their curiosity and restlessness in American studies programs. And a few of these undergraduates found their way into the steadily growing number of American studies graduate programs.

Most Americanists of the second generation, like those of the first, functioned more or less comfortably in the academic culture of the era. If many used American studies to pursue what they considered a progressive academic agenda, they for the most part dressed and spoke and socialized like most other faculty of the era. Still, this was the era in which the first large group of working-class, Jewish, second-generation "ethnic" American, and other nonmainstream students moved into elite institutions of higher education. American studies was one of the beneficiaries of the social ambitiousness and sometimes fresh perspectives they brought into the schools they attended.

In the course of the late 1950s and early 1960s, the first and second generations of Americanists were joined gradually by a third generation. Many American studies Ph.D.'s of the period participated in what might be thought of as a diasporic movement, migrating from their parent programs to other colleges and universities at which they founded or helped build new American studies programs. In the process they both imported and transformed the models of social and cultural analysis that they had learned in graduate school. The result was a range of postwar American studies programs, scholarship, and other Americanist activity that was much more various than can be captured by reductive characterizations of the period as one dominated by "myth-and-symbol," "consensus," or "high culture" analysis. The agendas of local programs depended often on the personalities, interests, and skills of their core faculty as well as on the ethos, structures, and resources of their individual schools. Similar dynamics were also creating a variety of American studies programs abroad.

Despite these often striking local differences, most of the major themes, aspirations, and tensions in the postwar American studies movement in the United States were eventually felt and negotiated

in what became its most prominent institutional manifestation, the ASA. Formed in 1951 at meetings in Washington, D.C., and Philadelphia by a small group of prominent first- and second-generation Americanists, the ASA began as a loosely federated structure and to that extent reflected the diverse agendas and local institutional bases of the postwar American studies movement. For its first two decades, the ASA's national council—a rather clubby group if its minutes are to be trusted—consisted of the ASA's officers (elected by the council itself), several council-elected at-large members, and one representative from each of the growing number of regional American studies groups (gradually to become known as ASA "chapters"). Regional chapters organized regular conferences and other activities with little assistance from ASA, and some guarded their relative independence from the national body in language that often reminds one of states' rights or populist rhetoric.

With a small although steadily growing membership (from slightly over three hundred in 1952 to nearly twenty-three hundred in 1966) and very modest dues, ASA depended heavily in its early years on federal and foundation grants and on the generosity of a few universities, most notably the University of Pennsylvania (Penn), which housed the ASA's offices and provided other support for better than three decades. ASA focused its slender budget and part-time staff on a limited number of activities, most notably on joint sessions at annual meetings of well-established disciplinary associations. Perhaps the ASA's most defining early act was its designating as its official journal the *American Quarterly*, which had been founded at the University of Minnesota in 1949 and then migrated to Penn in 1951. Symptomatic of the limited powers of the early ASA, Penn owned the *Quarterly* until 1985, and the journal's editors were members of the Penn faculty. Penn's substantial assistance, although essential to ASA's growth, was not free of the strains often attendant on relationships between unequal partners. Some historians of ASA have thus termed the decades at Penn the *colonial* phase of the ASA's development.

The leadership of the ASA during the 1950s and 1960s was drawn almost entirely from the now well-established first and second generation of the movement. Not surprisingly, the primary goal pursued by many although not all of ASA's leaders during this period was to use Americanists' publications, curricular initiatives, conference papers, grant- and Fulbright-getting skills, and hard-won savvy at institutional negotiations to gain academic respectability for American studies. Although some scholars continued to argue for the importance of a more public role for American studies, the national leadership for the most part avoided a sustained debate of this question. Also avoided was a sustained discussion of the possibility of the ASA's sponsoring its own national conventions. When ASA finally sponsored its first national conferences—in Kansas City in 1967, Toledo in 1969, and Washington, D.C., in 1971—the association stuck at first to the East and Midwest.

But the very decision in 1965 to launch national meetings (if with a cautiousness reflected in the fact that, for two decades, the meetings were biennial rather than annual) suggested a growing institutional self-confidence, one fueled by a variety of dynamics in and outside the movement. ASA membership and the number of established local American studies programs had gradually reached a number, by the mid-1960s, sufficient to make a national meeting seem likely to draw a large enough audience and come close to paying for itself. The first wave of the postwar baby boom was reaching higher education by the early 1960s and causing an expansion of enrollments in Americanist courses in many academic fields, including American studies, with the concomitant need for new faculty. Although not yet central for the most part to the national ASA leadership, many of the postwar American Studies Ph.D.'s, augmented by American studies graduate students of the 1960s, were eager to interact with each other, confirm their common professional status, and consider ways to further strengthen the movement they shared.

In 1965 few of these Americanists could have anticipated that such national meetings would become focusing sites of other far-reaching political

and social forces that were beginning to cause a seismic shift in the national landscape, and that those meetings in turn would become catalysts of often dramatic changes in the movement itself. As the shock waves from the civil rights movement had slowly pressed into the academy, beginning in the late 1950s, some of American studies' early if imperfectly institutionalized concerns—for bringing people and ideas together across artificial barriers, for relating past and present, for studying the lives and perspectives of ordinary people as well as dominant opinion makers, for speaking to and with publics beyond the academy—began to assume renewed prominence in some American studies classrooms in the form of greater attention to such topics as African American history and culture, urban studies, and critiques of corporate capitalism. And some American studies graduate students began to press the faculty to make the curriculum more relevant to pressing contemporary political and social problems and to open up the academic decision-making structure to students' participation.

Interestingly, the same increasingly flexible modes of communication and interaction that made possible the first national conventions of the ASA also made possible the national organizing of left and liberal student activism in the movement. At ASA's second national convention in 1969, surrounded by sharp memories of recent assassinations, urban race riots, antiwar protests on and off campus, and often violent police and military retaliation against demonstrators, a tense ASA council faced the demands of a newly formed group of American studies graduate students and young faculty who called themselves the Radical Caucus. Although its members tied their goals to larger movements for social justice, the caucus's demands were most notable for focusing primarily on American studies itself. Drawing perhaps unconsciously on an older if muted impulse in American studies, the caucus argued for the need to bring passion and commitment into the academy. It called on the ASA and *American Quarterly* to pay much more attention to contemporary popular culture and to the pressing social and political crises of the late 1960s.

It called for more academic work in ethnic, women's, urban, developing-world, and ecological studies, and for sharper critiques of dominant United States and transnational political economic structures. But it also wanted the association to play a more active role in helping them find academic jobs. And it criticized many established Americanists for not asserting forcefully enough that American studies was a distinctive field of study rather than mainly a collection of the "American" aspects of other disciplines.

In addition to opening up subsequent ASA conventions to numerous workshops on these issues, sponsoring several summer institutes in the early 1970s, and publishing a journal (*Connections* and *Connections II*) for several years, the caucus pressed successfully for the addition of several student members to the national council. Although it faded as an organized group by the late 1970s, the Radical Caucus succeeded in accelerating the opening of the national leadership of the movement to the third and beginnings of a fourth generation of academic Americanists (one symptom of which was the decreasing average age of ASA presidents and council members) and making contemporary social and cultural analysis a much more important part of the movement's agenda. The caucus's call for a more public agenda was also reflected in the short-lived National American Studies Faculty, funded by a National Endowment for the Humanities (NEH) grant, that during the 1970s sent Americanists on pro-bono cultural missions into high schools, libraries, museums, and other sites. The democratizing agendas of the caucus also manifested themselves in revisions of ASA's constitution in 1978 that, among other things, made the president and vice president electable by the entire association membership and, in a change protested by some loyal regional chapter members, that replaced chapter representatives to the council with nationally elected representatives nominated with an eye to drawing on the membership's diverse backgrounds and interests.

In addition to students, perhaps the single largest group of initial beneficiaries of such activism was women. At a meeting of the twenty-eight-member ASA national council in December 1969, the only woman on the council presented the body with a series of resolutions on the status of women adapted from a similar series just presented to the leadership of the American Historical Association. At its next meeting, the council formally agreed to state its opposition to discrimination against women in admissions, employment, and other areas and to establish a Committee on the Status of Women. Throughout the decade a feminist presence, taking energy from the larger U.S. women's movement, began to make its influence strongly felt in the work of the association and in the American studies movement as a whole. In 1975 the association elected its first female vice president. By the early 1980s close to half of the council was female, and feminist topics were prominent in the association's national meetings, as they had become in American studies classrooms and in the major Americanist journals. Not until 1986 did ASA elect its first female president. Since then, eleven women have served in that office.

While students, social activists, and women were steadily transforming the agendas and operations of American studies, another social transformation in the movement was more slowly taking shape. At the 1977 ASA convention, for example, the dozen black scholars on the program constituted less than five percent of the program roster. Despite the activism of the 1960s and early 1970s, the coming of faculty and students of color into the work of American studies, at both local and national levels, had been very slow. In 1967, John Hope Franklin was elected president of ASA and presided over its first national meeting; but he was only one of less than a handful of African Americans or other scholars of color to appear on the national council's roster before the mid-1980s. At both the undergraduate and graduate levels, most American studies programs diversified their curricula well before they diversified their faculty and students, and many students of color continued to see American studies as an enterprise unresponsive to their needs and interests.

Nevertheless, the increasingly cross-ethnic integrative efforts in some local American studies programs began slowly to yield greater diversity in the movement and gradually percolated up to the national level. In 1985 at the national convention in San Diego, as a result of vigorous recruiting by some members of the program committee, several dozen African American, Latino, and Asian American faculty and graduate students gathered for the first time. The association formed a special committee on minority affairs that evolved in the late 1980s into the Minority Scholars Committee. Scholars of color began to be elected in significant numbers to ASA's national council and to make their presence felt in all the association's standing committees. In 1996 a prominent African American scholar became president of ASA; and in 2000 the association's members elected their first Latino president. Such leaders have focused the association's attention, as they have local programs' attention, on building alliances with and actively supporting the work of ethnic studies programs and organizations. A recent sign of this multicultural and feminist activism was the council's decision in 1996 to refuse to hold its annual conventions in any state that had passed an antiaffirmative-action statute.

During six decades of national and international crises, transformations, conflicts, and shifting alliances, the American studies movement itself was thus transformed dramatically, if in fits and starts. Among numerous other factors resulting in the closing of some local American studies programs (as well as a temporary decline during the 1970s in ASA's own membership, and even in some loyalists' belief that the movement was in institutional and intellectual crisis) were: post-Vietnam and post-Watergate disillusionment; periodic recessions, such as those in the late 1970s and early 1990s; college budget cuts; ups and downs in the job markets for liberal arts Ph.D.'s; retirements and defections of some early Americanists; competition from emerging women's, ethnic, media studies, and other interdisciplinary programs; and expanded cultural-studies portfolios of established disciplines. In the 1990s, following the end of the cold war, additional challenges to American studies were raised by voices in the university arguing that area-studies programs (seen as ideological agents of U.S. cold-war foreign policy) and nation-based analyses of social, political, and cultural questions were no longer defensible explanatory models. Furthermore, in a world economy dominated by transnational corporations, massive movements of goods and people, and lightning-fast, globe-spanning modes of communication and representation, transnational modes of analyses were seen as the inevitable wave of the future.

In the face of these challenges, the American studies movement overall has nonetheless prospered, often as a result of the stimulus presented by the challenges. By the late 1970s, for example, ASA itself had begun to benefit, if not without internal debate, from pursuing the agendas of the third and fourth generation of academic Americanists. Its membership began to increase as it threw its weight more vigorously and systematically behind multicultural, popular culture, and ideological studies. In a gesture of institutional self-confidence in the mid-1980s, it purchased *American Quarterly* from the University of Pennsylvania, settled a large debt to Penn, and moved its offices and the *Quarterly* to Washington, D.C., under the sponsorship of a consortium that included five universities, a major academic press, and the Smithsonian Institution.

Americanists' work at all levels was dramatically facilitated in the last two decades of the twentieth century by such dramatic technological transformations as the burgeoning computer-based global electronic network. Such Americanist Web sites as the Crossroads Project and H-Amstdy facilitated more rapid exchange of scholarship, syllabi, and programmatic strategies. International American studies, and its transnational and comparativist proclivities, was further strengthened by the general and often dramatic expansion and transformation of universities abroad and the emergence of large waves of younger international scholars fluent in English, well-traveled, and highly knowledgeable about contemporary U.S. society as well as about other parts of the globe.

Academic American studies has thrived in large part because its participants have been able to choose and negotiate multiple identities for themselves, identities that are often tactical and among which "Americanist" is only one. If a committed core of true believers in American studies has been crucial to the movement's survival in bad times as well as good, the movement has also gained bite and energy from the critiques of various loyal oppositions, the goodwill of fellow travelers, and even the occasional consumers of its conventions and publications. In all its own diverse manifestations and agendas, the movement continues to offer an array of students and scholars a supportive home for their work. Key to its present strength is its flexibility, its willingness to treat challenges to its agendas as opportunities to engage in enlightening dialogue, its willingness to welcome new perspectives and participants as full partners. In their most idealistic moments, Americanists still set for themselves the difficult and never-completed task of modeling in the movement itself a just, creative, and humane "America" and helping make that imagined community a responsible partner in a just, creative, and humane world.

BIBLIOGRAPHY

American Studies 40 (Summer 1999), special issue on "American Studies: A Critical Retrospective."

Davis, Allen F., "The Politics of American Studies," *American Quarterly* 41 (September 1989):353–374.

Kerber, Linda, "Diversity and the Transformation of American Studies," *American Quarterly* 41 (September 1989):415–431.

Lauter, Paul, "Versions of Nashville, Visions of American Studies: Presidential Address to the American Studies Association, November 20, 1994," *American Quarterly* 47 (June 1995):185–203.

Lucid, Robert E., ed., "Programs in American Studies," *American Quarterly* 22 (Summer 1970):430–605.

Maddox, Lucy, ed., *Locating American Studies: The Evolution of a Discipline* (Johns Hopkins Univ. Press 1999).

Radway, Janice, "'What's in a Name?' Presidential Address to the American Studies Association, November 20, 1998," *American Quarterly* 51 (March 1999):1–32.

Walker, Robert H., ed., *American Studies Abroad* (Greenwood Press 1975).

Wise, Gene, ed., "The American Studies Movement: A Thirty-Year Retrospective," *American Quarterly* 31 (1979):289–447.

MICHAEL COWAN

Approaches and Concepts

Studies of America are at least as old as the age of exploration. European artists, philosophers, cartographers, theologians, investors, and adventurers were trading depictions of America for centuries before there was anything very cohesive, much less well known to them, about the place. As a discrete field of learning, though, American studies is relatively young. Most of the modern disciplines of the liberal arts professionalized in the last quarter of the nineteenth century, but even isolated references to American studies (also known as Americanistics or American civilization) cannot be found much before 1920. The first regular supply of degrees, conferences, and publications bearing the name dates from the mid-1930s. A full academic infrastructure (curriculum, scholarly associations, journals, departments or programs, publication series, and professional positions specific to the field) took another twenty years to develop. In the United States the growth of American studies only became a recognizable movement in colleges and universities in the early 1960s. With some important exceptions it developed elsewhere (in secondary schools and museums in the United States and in higher education outside the United States) in the 1970s.

Despite its youth American studies has several histories. Accounts of its aims have varied greatly. In some parts of the world, especially in universities in the United States since the mid-1950s, the field seems perpetually in an identity crisis. Scholars are both eager to be counted part of the field and loath to define it. Many of the field's leaders have treated the mere mention of "method" as if it were a threat to intellectual liberty. Humanists, who increasingly dominate the field in the United States, particularly worry about the prospect of creeping "methodolatry" (Joel M. Jones's word for it) whereby robotic regimens supplant creativity and common sense. Instead, method could be understood, as the founder of sociology Émile Durkheim recommended, to indicate a more general, articulate but evolving disposition. Any collective endeavor might be expected to nurture a particular quality of curiosity. But method in U.S. American studies has more often been considered a tool of scientist totalitarians. In this respect U.S. Americanists defend their liberty in a stereotypically "American" way. The freedom to act as an individual, independent of a group, is more precious than the freedom to act as a member of one.

U.S. publications on American studies method hence have an elusively scrappy or passive-aggressive tone. Authors conjure, disavow, demonize, or resurrect intellectual spirits so discreetly that it is hard to know precisely what is at stake. Readers new to this literature are apt to wonder what all of the fuss is about. At issue is the definition of the field, the identity, purpose, tolerance, and capacities of its teachers and students.

In most of the rest of the world, especially where English is a foreign language, the actual practice of American studies has varied even more widely but rallied more readily around a single, broad aim: understanding a place called "America." Commencing with the onset of "the American century" and accelerating rapidly during the cold war with encouragement from the United States Information Agency and the Fulbright program, American studies in most places has meant considering "American stuff," America-related topics and materials of any variety in any way. Outside the United States, then, American studies has consistently supported regular exchanges with a larger range of fields: business, policy, and social sciences as well as humanities. Any one set of topics or one discipline or a few of each may dominate the practice of American studies in a school or a whole nation or region of the globe for a time. In Spain, for example, American studies has emphasized the long history, literature, and culture of its former colonies (especially Mexico), while in China the field has stressed recent diplomatic, strategic, and trade relations with the United States. In many secondary schools outside the United States the name *American studies*

means, in effect, instruction in English as a second language, possibly enriched by the inclusion of popular-culture texts. In U.S. high schools it may be just a new name for the traditional survey of domestic history and government, but sometimes an American literature teacher and an American history teacher will team-teach an American studies course.

Since in the late twentieth century the United States gained powers that could scarcely be ignored anywhere on the planet, it would seem an unproblematic focus, a perfectly sensible academic target. But at least since the mid-1980s, U.S. scholars and others moved by colonial experience or postcolonial theory have worried greatly about a residue of ambiguity in this conception of the field, in particular, in the word *American*.

For some scholars, the word *America* refers to a geographic site, a locale that could be fixed on a map. Unfortunately, it rarely is. It might be as large as both halves of the Western Hemisphere, only the northern half, or the portion that lies roughly between the forty-ninth parallel and the Río Bravo. For other scholars (or the same ones on different occasions), *America* is a political designation, a shorthand for the jurisdiction of the United States of America (and the governments that it has subsumed). For yet other scholars or purposes, *America* is a symbol, a social construction that people associate with a geopolitical terrain. It is their sense of the place. It is a concocted, contestable, and mobile entity, more like a set of beliefs or ways of life than a tangible or legal object. It might be bounded by nothing more substantial than sentiment (or as Alexis de Tocqueville would have it, a "habit of the heart"), with familiarity on one side and estrangement on the other. Its contents can be shaped not only by topography, law, and power but also by word-of-mouth, ritual, the circulation of goods, arts, amusements, flights of fancy, and acts of will. This is the sense of the word to which more plainly controversial terms such as *Americanism* or *Americanization* appeal. Given this variation in usage, whether defined spatially, politically, or symbolically, the "America" that American studies scholars aim to understand is itself an elusive target.

For most of the history of the field most Americanists, like most nonacademics, have assumed that these senses of the word *America* actually do or ought to converge. They suppose that the U.S. terrain, its government, and the ways of life of its people compose a single, even if conflicted, whole—a culture—that is distinguishable from the cultural contributions of annexed territories, populations, and polities. For better or worse, America is supposed to be unique. When assembled on North American soil, subject to an American government, citizens supposedly participate in the making of a New World. Scholars have long disagreed about the extent to which the United States actually has achieved such a special prospect, but there has seldom been much doubt that (also for better or worse) it has one.

In the 1950s and early 1960s, U.S. scholars from a broad range of humanities and social sciences lent this notion—"American exceptionalism"—academic credibility. Among the most renowned were Ethel Albert, Gabriel Almond, Daniel Bell, Ray Allen Billington, Daniel Boorstin, Henry Steele Commager, Cora Du Bois, Erik Erikson, Richard Hofstadter, Francis Hsu, Orin Klapp, Florence Kluckhohn, Clyde Kluckhohn, John Kouwenhoven, Harold Laski, Max Lerner, Seymour Lipset, F. O. Mattheisson, Margaret Mead, Perry Miller, David Potter, David Riesman, Arthur Schlesinger, Henry Nash Smith, and William Whyte. But there are also much older precedents. Such pioneering scholars as Constance Rourke and Vernon Parrington published theories of American distinctiveness in the 1920s and 1930s, as Henry Adams and Frederick Jackson Turner did in the early 1890s, Tocqueville in the 1830s, or for that matter, John Winthrop in 1630. Proponents of American exceptionalism can be found throughout international literature for centuries.

In documenting that distinctiveness they cite a bewildering array of influences: God's grace, Puritan theocracy or the separation of church and state, early colonists' military might or their resistance to diseases that they spread, the timing and composition of particular waves of immigration, the "availability" of arable land, continental abundance or regional shortages of resources, free enterprise or slavery, the spirit of science or unfettered individualism, political liberty or the suppression of dissent, technological prowess or omnivorous consumerism, mobility, individualism or conformity, pragmatism or idealism, relative peace and prosperity or racism and violence. Whatever the explanation, at issue has been less whether there is anything distinctly American (a culture uniquely associated with a population, a setting, and a nation-state) than deciding the best way to describe and evaluate it.

Beginning in the late 1960s, in response to intensifying demands for self-determination at the U.S. borders and among domestically oppressed groups, attention shifted to the relationships among these various senses of the term *American*. Since the label has both an ambiguous referent and political connotations, scholars have become more sensitive to the consequences of designating anything in or out of it. Since, too, the label can be either honorific or pejorative, people in and around the United States have good reason to be wary. Depending on the generalization in question, they might insist on being included or excluded from it. By focusing on allegedly mainstream or dominant traits, Americanists risk signaling that these people—in total, the majority of Americans by any definition—do not count.

Scholars, especially in the United States, now tend to argue that faithfulness to the historical record and basic fairness require a more measured, less ambiguous and presumptuous use of the word *American*. At the very least scholars expect more demographic precision. By the early 1990s U.S. Americanists demanded careful attention to ways that gender, race, ethnicity, sexuality, region, and class, as well as chronology, condition their generalizations. With each passing year, as the global circulation of goods and communications intensifies, it becomes harder to think of America as a free-standing whole or to imagine that it ever was one.

The *studies* part of the name of the field has also encompassed significant variation. In general the term has signaled an approach that is vaguely interdisciplinary. Exactly which disciplines are broached or how they are bridged remains uncertain. Regardless, American studies, especially in the United States, is proudly not disciplinary, at least not in the same way as fields with which it most often trades: language and literature, history, political science, art, sociology, communications, film, museology, folklore, music, and anthropology. American studies may engage people or interpretive strategies from these "regular" disciplines but it remains in some ways smaller (in its focus on but one place) and larger (in its methodological eclecticism) than any one of them. It shares this hybrid quality with other fields that have *studies* in their names.

Between the 1930s and 1950s the first of them ("area studies") in the United States were chiefly defined around parts of the world that seemed culturally or strategically distinct in relation to western, industrialized states. Beginning in the late 1960s their number rapidly multiplied and their principle of definition changed. Focusing mainly on U.S. "minorities" with organized, articulate advocates, these programs were a low-budget, curricular response to social movements (for example, the civil rights movement, the women's movement, the gay rights movement) and demands for "social relevance" and recognition of diversity on U.S. campuses. Americanists generally supported the development of these kindred African, Native, Latino and Latina, and Asian American, women's, ethnic, gender, sexuality, queer, and environmental studies programs. Although relations among these programs were often troubled, they similarly styled themselves as young and rebellious when compared to "regular" liberal arts. Although they differ greatly in official favor, subject matter, and approach, they share, at least, pride in their difference from academic business as usual. In many cases, that is all that the word *studies* (and by implication, *interdisciplinary*) is taken to mean.

The most common way that American studies relates to affiliated disciplines is as a bricolage. Candidates for an American studies degree are ordinarily required to take America-oriented courses in several academic departments. The selection and

sequence is seldom stipulated. United States Americanists are expected to be comfortable with more than one of the media (sources of "texts") that traditionally distinguish areas of expertise (for example, novels or artifacts as well as archival records, or paintings and music as well as polls). Although print is favored, any supplement will do. Scholars who augment the definition of sources favored in their home discipline might thereby consider themselves "interdisciplinary" without ever leaving home. Or their purpose may be more ambitiously transdisciplinary, a deliberate, discipline-crossing quest for methods and materials that complement each other.

More commonly, however, Americanists boast of borrowing insights hither and yon. While "regular" disciplines might demand high regard for the epistemology and pedigree of each of their approaches, Americanists are apt to grab and mix anything that works. Theirs is a can-do spirit—"a kind of principled opportunism," Henry Nash Smith dubbed it in 1957. Ever since, U.S. Americanists have been willing to face the charge that they are dilettantes, if the compensation includes insights that academic sectarianism and meta-theory would impede.

The oldest line of methodological discussion in American studies revolves around the promise of just such integration: Can or even should American studies develop a method of its own? For most of its history, the answer has been a resounding No. After all, most people who "do American studies" are already responsible to the rigors of a home discipline. Back in regular departments there is no shortage of methods for Americanists to borrow (and better employment opportunities). The vitality of the field, most argue, depends on improvisation, the mixing of ingredients that are as diverse as possible. Leave it to the disciplines to develop them. Strategies can be cobbled to fit the particular interpreter, curiosity, and source material at hand. It is through the absence of a regimen that American studies has earned its distinction.

One problem with this view is that in hindsight it has been relatively easy to detect regimens in the field. Both outside the United States and inside it (at least through the mid-1950s), such regimens were generally those of individual, contemporary liberal arts. There has been nothing particularly transdisciplinary or even "not disciplinary" about it. Even the pioneers of improvisation just basted a couple of methods together and left the edges unhemmed.

For example, when preparing his classic *Main Currents in American Thought*, Vernon Parrington chose an unconventional mix of sources—a sample of U.S. literature and history. At the time (the 1920s) most English departments belittled American (versus British) literature, as history departments did the arts. Rather than finding a ready-made position at an East Coast university, Parrington had to earn his living, among other things, coaching football at the University of Oklahoma. As Gene Wise, the most credited chronicler of the field, has argued, Parrington's work on *Main Currents*—its range, passion, and critical edge—inspired subsequent generations of Americanists. To this day, introductory American studies courses in the United States draw from the well that he dug.

But the way he dug, his mode of research, was hardly original. He more or less sorted readings conventional in one discipline into a chronology conventional in another. He interpreted literature (stressing belles lettres) as if it expressed the sociopolitical vision of its authors. He then classified those visions as tacking through time, periods of looking forward and then back, in the manner of the then-fashionable "progressive" historians of American politics. Furthermore, at least since the early eighteenth century, Western philosophers have consulted both history and the arts to assess national achievement. The strategy was less controversial than the standard of judgment. At issue then, and in some measure still, is whether critics should advocate "achievement" by standards that owe more to the Enlightenment (universalizing, rational; the French *civilisation*) or Romanticism (localizing, spiritual; the German *Kultur*). It is perhaps telling that an alternative name for the field—American civilization—fell into disrepute in the 1960s precisely because of its Enlightenment implications.

The first, and by some accounts the only, truly distinctive method ever to be fully developed and hegemonic in U.S. American studies was a variant on these precedents. First centered in the 1950s at the University of Minnesota, Harvard University, and Amherst College, the approach became known (ten to fifteen years later) as "myth-and-symbol." Its sources for analysis were primarily drawn from literature and history. The evolution in patterns of particularly complex, evocative ("powerful") images and stories ("symbols" and "myths") in those sources was taken to reflect the course of dominant ideas in their time. The ideas that drew attention, then, were mainly matters of national political dispute that were evident at once in public letters and public affairs. These ideas, in turn, became the object of Americanists' criticism, generally from a cold-war liberal point of view. They aimed to distinguish the best from the worst propensities of "the American mind."

The earliest and most celebrated example of myth-and-symbol was *Virgin Land*, published by Henry Nash Smith in 1950. Like many who were inspired by his work, Smith focused on the way that Europeans and their descendants established dominion over the continent (albeit, with scant reference to New Spain, slavery, the Civil War, people of color, or women of any sort). Although they normally insist on their individuality, scholars associated with this school of thought (during its heyday, roughly the 1950s to the mid-1970s) include not only Smith but also Daniel Aaron, Allen Guttman, Leo Marx, Alan Trachtenberg, R. W. B. Lewis, Roy Harvey Pearce, and John William Ward. The first heady era of the "American studies movement" took place in the shadow of their work.

Since the late 1970s, however, it has been the subject of devastating criticism. To have one's teaching or research likened to myth-and-symbol is now to stand accused of serious errors. Among the first that leap to mind are those associated with American exceptionalism. Myth-and-symbol classics in general slight diversity and dissent in the United States as well as international relations. They slight women and people of color in particular, a bias with special sting given the subsequent strength of social-justice movements on college campuses. As Nina Baym has explained, myth-and-symbolists' orthodox taste in source material and their propensity to highlight struggles for individuation may better bespeak the authors' worries about their own "manhood" than anything else. Other critics lambaste the epistemology of the approach (the facile, conceptual leaps from text to writing, publishing, reading, thought, and action), its anachronisms (the projection of modern assessments of literary power onto prior periods), its conception of culture (idealist, homogeneous, autotelic), or its taste for irony and tortured platitude.

Nevertheless, despite their reputation as cold-war-accommodating, myth-and-symbol works emphasize national flaws. They find America's myths unsustainable and its realities grim. But since the nation's people, with the exception of gifted artists and, presumably, their myth-and-symbol promoters, are supposedly so governed by delusion, there is not much to be done beyond wringing hands. The lesson is often excruciatingly fatalistic and condescending. Hence—when compared (also anachronistically) to "post-1960s" academia—myth-and-symbol is remembered as "elitist" and "conservative." Americanists in the United States have subsequently demanded ever more "radical" remedies to these methodological flaws. What they mean by "more radical" is the subject of continuing dispute in the United States and mystery in other parts of the world.

Among the first orthodoxies to lose credibility were those privileging whole categories of source material. After the 1970s, as pop art helped discredit "mass-culture," Frankfurt-school fogies, mass-marketed entertainment became fodder for the field. Ever since, U.S. Americanists have tended to consider items of "popular culture" (best-selling novels, top-forty music, Hollywood film, television, advertisements, amusement parks, snapshots, kitchen gadgets, and the like) better indicators of cultural currents than the canonical literature whose "power" so impressed myth-and-symbolists. Waves of interpretive strategies reigning in departments of English subsequently made the rounds through popular culture by way of American studies: structuralist, Marxist, feminist, deconstructionist, reader-response, poststructuralist, postmodern, and later "cultural studies."

Likewise, the sorts of documentary sources that early Americanists had shared with the two, then chic branches of U.S. history—political and intellectual—fell out of favor. Social records, particularly those pertaining to the history of women and other oppressed groups (subalterns), took their place. By the late 1980s, women's history was the most common specialty in the field in the United States. While myth-and-symbolists scored debating points against national leaders, their descendants unmasked brute injustice in domestic and intimate, no less than civic, affairs. They focused on social formations that privilege and resist the white, wealthy, heterosexual, and male.

In so improvising on its past, American studies has flourished. In the 1990s, for example, the membership of the U.S. professional association (the American Studies Association [ASA]) soared. Credit for this growth mainly belongs to the recruitment of humanists and cultural historians new to American studies. Some Americanists charge that many of the conceptual flaws of myth-and-symbol (for example, its bookish bias and epistemological incoherence) remain or that U.S. Americanists are losing touch with the social or natural sciences and international norms. Some lament that, after so many years, the proportion of Americanists trained in and primarily committed to the field (versus English or history) remains so small. But to resurrect questions of interdisciplinary method—visions of a more clearly defined, distinct, and transdisciplinary field—still raises in the United States the old specter of methodological tyranny. Such are the gains and losses of the field's liberty.

BIBLIOGRAPHY

Bercovitch, Sacvan, *The Rites of Assent: Transformations in the Symbolic Construction of America* (Routledge 1993).

Ceaser, James W., *Reconstructing America: The Symbol of America in Modern Thought* (Yale Univ. Press 1997).

Greene, Jack P., *The Intellectual Construction of America: Exceptionalism and Identity from 1492 to 1800* (Univ. of N.C. Press 1993).

Gunn, Giles, *Thinking across the American Grain: Ideology, Intellect, and the New Pragmatism* (Univ. of Chicago Press 1992).

Horwitz, Richard P., ed., *Exporting America: Essays on American Studies Abroad* (Garland 1993).

Kammen, Michael, *Mystic Chords of Memory: The Transformation of Tradition in American Culture* (Knopf 1991).

Kuper, Adam, *Culture: The Anthropologists' Account* (Harvard Univ. Press 1999).

Lipsitz, George, *Time Passages: Collective Memory and American Popular Culture* (Univ. of Minn. Press 1990).

Maddox, Lucy, ed., *Locating American Studies: The Evolution of a Discipline* (Johns Hopkins Univ. Press 1999).

Madsen, Deborah L., *American Exceptionalism* (Univ. Press of Miss. 1998).

Rothenberg, Paula S., ed., *Race, Class, and Gender in the United States: An Integrated Study*, 4th ed. (St. Martin's 1998).

Shumway, David R., *Creating American Civilization: A Genealogy of American Literature as an Academic Discipline* (Univ. of Minn. Press 1994).

Tate, Cecil F., *The Search for a Method in American Studies* (Univ. of Minn. Press 1973).

Wilkinson, Rupert, ed., *American Social Character: Modern Interpretations from the '40s to the Present* (IconEditions 1992).

Wise, Gene, *American Historical Explanations: A Strategy for Grounded Inquiry*, 2d ed. (Univ. of Minn. 1980).

RICHARD P. HORWITZ

AMERICANIZATION

More than any other concept Americanization marks the instability of the term *American*. Oscillating between a state of mind and a geographical entity in the work of would-be Americanizers, *America* alternatively names a nation into which foreigners may be inducted as citizens and a set of principles and ideals in which every "true American" must believe. While the term *Americanization* was most commonly invoked in the early decades of the twentieth century to describe the processes through which immigrants were assimilated into the culture of the United States, there are recorded uses of it as early as the late eighteenth century; it is, in other words, nearly as old as the nation, and in the subtle shifts in the meaning of the term are registered the changes in the United States itself.

In a 1797 letter, the prominent political figure John Jay wrote to a colleague of his "wish to see our people more *Americanized,* if I may use that expression; until we feel and act as an independent nation." In the wake of the Revolutionary War, the nation's founders faced the task of unifying a disparate group of people and uniting colonies across profound social, economic, and geographical differences. Here Jay dubs that process *Americanization,* and implicit in the term is the other major obstacle to developing a national culture: how to declare cultural as well as political independence from England. Americanization in the United States thus named the processes through which the complementary tasks of unification and distinction would be accomplished. In England, however, the term was commonly used with disdain to refer to a lack of taste and a crass materialism. For the first half of the nineteenth century, it continued to be appropriated both by political and cultural nationalists and by the new nation's (usually foreign) detractors.

By the middle of the nineteenth century, *Americanization* and, even more, *Americanism* had entered common parlance. While the latter term referred to practices and behaviors, it was most often associated with the Americanization of the English language. When John Witherspoon coined the term *Americanism* in 1781, through direct analogy with Scotticism, he intended it precisely to distinguish U.S. linguistic features from those of Britain. Aware of the relegation of Scottish English to the "provincial" and "barbaric," U.S. colonists including Benjamin Franklin first defended American English as the more pure form of English because it had not yet splintered into dialects such as those in England. By 1828, when Noah Webster published his *American Dictionary of the English Language,* the innovations of American English ranked among the key distinctive features in the bid for cultural independence in the United States, as well as the source of contempt and criticism in British grammars, which warned of possible "infection" by American English. *Americanism,* while occasionally used in late-twentieth-century British journals to describe fashionable language, is still generally a term of reprobation in England for corrupted language.

The terms *Americanization* and *Americanism* both proliferated and mutated in the decades following the Civil War. The most immediate cause of these renovations was the massive influx of immigrants from southern and eastern Europe, although many Northerners who went South after the war saw themselves as Americanizers as well. The concept assumed a new urgency with the efforts to articulate a unified national culture that could encompass former military and ideological rivals, a migrating population of freed men and women, an increasingly deracinated urban population, and immigrants who were characteristically peasants from powerful non-Protestant religious backgrounds. Although they registered the need to consolidate a heterogeneous population, Americanization initiatives were characteristically directed specifically at the immigrants.

By the 1890s Americanization had become an important political issue. In his 1894 essay "True Americanism," Theodore Roosevelt warned that "alien elements, unassimilated, and with interest separate from ours" would prove "mere obstructions to the current of our national life," and educator John Dewey, in 1902, cautioned that "unless we Americanize them they will foreignize us." There was, however, little agreement about how to go about *Americanizing* the immigrants or even about what that term actually meant. For anthropologist Franz Boas, it named the physiological improvements enjoyed by the children of immigrants to the United States.

With the beginning of World War I, loosely conceived Americanization initiatives began to crystallize into a full-fledged Americanization movement. Education was the focus of the earliest efforts to systematize these initiatives. Deeming traditional classes in English, U.S. history, and civics no longer adequate to address the needs of immigrants, the Americanization movement introduced specific curricular innovations. Anthologies of American literature and textbooks of U.S. history proliferated, as did outreach to private businesses whose owners

were willing to offer classes for their employees. Pamphlets on naturalization procedures also appeared with greater frequency. Gradually, men and women who established outreach programs among the immigrants—known as settlement houses—began to address the immigrant women who were not usually in the schools or businesses. Settlement workers, recognizing the centrality of these women to their families and therefore to the potential success of Americanization initiatives, set about trying to turn them into American housekeepers. American women were pivotal in outreach efforts, drafted for them by such militant Americanizers as Frances A. Kellor. From the efforts of Kellor and others emerged the celebrated National Americanization Committee in New York City in 1915. Among the committee's initiatives was Americanization Day, which was typically held on or around July 4 and became a popular institution around the country.

As World War I progressed, many cultural commentators leveled allegations of insufficient patriotism and national spirit against the general citizenry, attributing the lack partly to a weak national culture. The war, they argued, had thrown into relief both the importance of nationalism and its absence in the United States. In particular, some contended that the effort surrounding the war had shown how unintegrated many of the immigrants were—how much they had retained their Old World loyalties, prejudices, and rivalries. Accordingly, books and essays on the topic of Americanization abounded in the late years of the war and into the postwar period.

While politicians and pundits gave the topic lip service, the task of figuring out what *Americanization* meant fell to the settlement workers and their more academic counterparts, the sociologists. The discipline of sociology was new to the United States at the turn of the century, and the concepts of assimilation and Americanization helped to define it. Although the settlement workers and sociologists had different approaches, both groups worked from the assumption that a better understanding of the immigrant experience could yield deeper insights into the practices and beliefs of the nation, and that this knowledge in turn could help them better understand, and thereby facilitate, the difficult process of Americanization. Assimilation and Americanization were among the most popular topics for study in the first three decades of the *American Journal of Sociology*, founded at the University of Chicago in 1895.

Like the public in general, sociologists were divided not only about the desirability but even about the definition of Americanization. At one extreme were outspoken proponents of immigration restriction who believed that the failure to close the national borders would have terrible consequences for the nation, particularly for "white America." That doctrine, known as "race suicide," was put broadly into circulation by sociologists including Edward Arlington Ross and Henry Pratt Fairchild. Both, however, recognized that even restriction would not address the problem of the immigrants who had already arrived in hitherto unprecedented numbers. Accordingly, they sought to spell out the most fundamental principles of America and to explore the strategies through which the immigrants could be most quickly *Americanized*, a word Fairchild believed was new and that he, like Ross and others, understood to mean a complete renunciation of any prior national identity.

The difficulty of achieving that renunciation is captured poignantly by immigrant writer—and enthusiastic assimilationist—Mary Antin in the introduction to her 1912 paean to America, *The Promised Land*. Antin describes her impossible longing to forget her past and tells her tale, she explains, "in order to be rid of it."

However, there were reformers, including settlement workers and immigrant activists, who genuinely believed in what cultural critic Horace Kallen called "cultural pluralism," a model of assimilation that celebrated cultural difference and the mutual transformation of immigrants and the host culture. Most characteristic, however, was the middle ground represented by the sociologists of the influential Chicago school, who, while celebrating the folk culture of immigrants and other marginalized groups, nonetheless articulated in their work the

inevitability and even desirability of their conforming to the culture and institutions of the mainstream United States.

Although the 1920s were the heyday of *Americanization* movements, the term and the concept have circulated throughout the politics of the twentieth century. In the legacy of the movements of the 1920s, Americanization, although never unambiguously defined, typically emphasizes conformity to a dominant white, middle-class U.S. culture and, especially when used in reference to foreign policy, to the political ideals officially espoused by the nation. When used abroad it is with the conventional overtones of the crass materialism and the commercialization associated with twentieth-century U.S. cultural imperialism. All too frequently, it has been invoked to justify discrimination against nonwhite populations.

In the 1960s rebellion on university campuses against the practices and policies of Americanization, at home and abroad, resulted in the transformations of culture and curriculum that came to be known as multiculturalism. Among its many critiques, multiculturalism offered important revisions of U.S. history while it sought to connect social and political inequities to the suppression of cultural expression. Not surprisingly, opponents of the movement accused the students and their supporters of being un-American and warned, in ominous tones that echoed their early twentieth-century predecessors, that multiculturalism was divisive and would lead to the nation's downfall. At the center of their counterinitiatives were curriculum and language reforms.

In later decades, language has become the contemporary focus of Americanization issues. Concerns about the lack of official status for English tend to flare during periods of high immigration or national crisis. These years have seen both dramatic growth in the Spanish-speaking population in the United States and a highly organized push for official English both at the state and federal levels. The rhetoric surrounding language legislation is familiar within the context of Americanization efforts: it is said to be in the best interests of immigrants to learn English as quickly as possible and critical to the integrity of the nation to be unified by one language. At the beginning of the new millennium, bilingual education programs are being cut and the courts remain unresolved on language discrimination cases. The role of multilingualism in the multiculturalism that is coming to be accepted as an integral part of America remains a source of tension. While the English language clearly continues to flourish, worries over its status and use reflect larger concerns about the social, cultural, political, and linguistic ties that bind Americans as a nation.

Americanization initiatives record the permutations of a nationalism that has never been fully articulated and theorized; biases have flourished under their rubric, often in spite of the most conscientious and progressive intentions. While these initiatives have shifted their focus and form throughout history, they have been motivated by the ongoing desire and perceived need to define America both as a culture and as a nation.

[See also NATIONALISM; AMERICAN STUDIES; AMERICAN LANGUAGE.]

BIBLIOGRAPHY

Berkson, Isaac B., *Theories of Americanization: A Critical Study with Special Reference to the Jewish Group* (Columbia Univ. 1920).

Carlson, Robert A., *The Quest for Conformity: Americanization through Education* (Wiley 1975).

Roosevelt, Theodore, "True Americanism," *The Forum* (April 1894):15–31.

Tamura, Eileen H., *Americanization, Acculturation, and Ethnic Identity: The Nisei Generation in Hawaii* (Univ. of Ill. Press 1994).

Wolfram, Walt, and Natalie Schilling-Estes, *American English: Dialects and Variations* (Blackwell 1998).

ANNE CURZAN *and* PRISCILLA WALD

ANGEL ISLAND

Angel Island, now an idyllic state park in California's San Francisco Bay, was once the point of entry for over a million Asian immigrants who came to America from across the Pacific Ocean between 1910 and 1940. Its historical and cultural significance, however, is tied to the story of approximately 175 thousand Chinese immigrants who risked everything to journey to the United States in search of a better life. Modeled on New York's Ellis Island, Angel Island was used as the detention headquarters for immigrants awaiting decisions on the outcomes of medical and immigration examinations. However, whereas most European immigrants were processed through cursory examinations at Ellis Island in a few hours, Chinese immigrants were locked up at Angel Island for weeks and even months and subjected to grueling cross-examinations because of the Chinese Exclusion Act of 1882.

Passed at a time of economic depression and rampant racism, the Exclusion Act barred the further immigration of Chinese laborers to the United States, marking the first time in U.S. history that any group of laborers was denied entry on the basis of race or national origin. Other exclusionary laws that followed profoundly affected all Asian immigration as well as that from southern and eastern Europe. Exclusion, however, did not stop the Chinese from coming. Desperate to escape political chaos and grinding poverty in China, they came as "paper sons" and "paper daughters," falsely claiming to be related to a legal resident or a U.S. citizen. The burden of proof fell on their shoulders since immigration officials at Angel Island scrutinized their papers and testimonies in an effort to bar the Chinese from entering the United States.

The average stay for Chinese detainees at Angel Island was from two to three weeks. On passing the medical examination, they were locked up in dormitories segregated by sex to await hearings on their applications. To prevent collusion, the Chinese were allowed no visitors, except missionaries, prior to interrogations. Women were sometimes taken outside for walks, and men were allowed to exercise in a small, fenced-in yard. Otherwise, confined inside, men passed the time gambling, reading, or listening to records while women sewed, knitted, played dominoes, or chatted among themselves. Three times a day, the detainees were taken to the dining hall for meals, which, although cooked by Chinese staff, were barely edible. The interrogation usually lasted two or three days, and a prospective immigrant's testimony had to be corroborated by witnesses. For those whose applications for entry were rejected, the wait could stretch to as long as two years while they awaited appeals to higher authorities in Washington, D.C. Although similar to the experience of European immigrants at Ellis Island (where only five percent of those denied were ever deported), the situation was much worse for the Chinese at Angel Island, who were subjected to a process different not only in degree but also in kind.

While waiting for the results of their appeals, many Chinese immigrants chose to vent their frustrations and anguish by writing or carving Chinese poems on the barrack walls. Left behind as a testimony to the indignities they suffered at Angel Island, the poems speak of the immigrants' voyage to America, their longing for families left behind, and their outrage and humiliation at the harsh treatment accorded them. The poems, some of which are still visible at Angel Island, occupy a unique place in the literary culture of Asian America. Often haunting and poignant in their directness and simplicity of language, they express an indomitable spirit never before identified with Asian immigrants. Along with the Angel Island Immigration Station, which has been designated a National Historic Landmark, these poems are a vivid fragment of America's cultural legacy as a nation of immigrants and a reminder that the United States has yet to live up to the democratic tenets on which the country was founded.

[See also ELLIS ISLAND; IMMIGRATION AND IMMIGRATION LAW; ASIAN AMERICANS.]

BIBLIOGRAPHY

Lai, Him Mark, "Island of Immortals: Chinese Immigrants and the Angel Island Station," *California History* 57 (Spring 1978):88–103.

Lai, Him Mark, Genny Lim, and Judy Yung, *Island: Poetry and History of Chinese Immigrants at Angel Island, 1910–1940* (Chinese Culture Foundation 1980; Univ. of Wash. Press 1991).

Yu, Connie Young, "Rediscovered Voices: Chinese Immigrants and Angel Island," *Amerasia Journal* 4, no. 2 (1977):123–139.

Yung, Judy, "'A Bowlful of Tears': Chinese Women Immigrants on Angel Island," *Frontiers: A Journal of Women Studies* 2, no. 2 (1977):52–55.

JUDY YUNG

ANGLO-AMERICANS

Anglo-Americans have played an important role in the social, cultural, and political history of the United States, particularly because of the large-scale English immigration to the North American continent beginning in the seventeenth century. Among the earliest motivations for this migration was the exploratory urge that had infected Elizabethan England. Richard Hakluyt, for example, argued for an English claim to American land as a way to secure material and political advantages: resources for ship building, solutions for domestic unemployment, and ballast against Spanish expansionism. Furthermore, John Smith, a leader in the Jamestown colony (founded in 1607), encouraged settlement in the area he named New England. Following his advice, groups of dissenters against the English Church arrived in what later became Massachusetts. This movement began in 1620 with the Pilgrims (who had already removed themselves from England to Holland) and in 1630 with the Puritans.

In addition to religious differences and general social dissatisfaction at home, greater agricultural and industrial opportunities abroad led many English people to leave for America. At first, economic destitution was not the main cause (as it was for many other immigrants) yet by the mid-nineteenth century, overpopulation, rural poverty, and technological unemployment in England prompted emigration. Moreover, certain political conditions within the United States, such as the American Civil War, influenced this movement: the blockade of the South brought a cotton shortage to English textile mills and an unemployment crisis; U.S. factories needed to replace workers fighting in the Union army; and America's expanding postwar industry then demanded even more overseas laborers. The population of English immigrants increased through the 1870s (the third highest behind Germany and Scandinavia) before reaching its peak in the 1880s.

Whereas many quickly joined the original Pilgrim and Puritan settlements (fourteen thousand to twenty-one thousand between 1629 and 1640), more English arrived in America after 1870 than in the previous 250 years. Overall, the number of English settlers throughout the expanding United States was often not as high as other immigrant groups. The 1870 census revealed that they made up only 1.5 percent of the U.S. population. However, in the Utah territory at that time, 18.5 percent of the population was British Mormon—the highest percentage of English-born people anywhere in the United States—and their presence there marked the largest religious-based migration since the Puritans.

Continued English immigration and presence in the United States assisted in the evolution of Anglo-American economic, cultural, and social status. Economically, financial success often followed quickly for the many eighteenth- and early-nineteenth-century English immigrants who arrived with agricultural and industrial skills, a large portion seeking new employment freedom in America's Old Northwest: Illinois, Indiana, Ohio, Michigan, and Wisconsin. By the mid-nineteenth century, over twice as many English had settled there in the New England states. Those arriving later in the nineteenth century were often less skilled, but they brought with them elements of British working-class radicalism that helped reform American labor. British immigration also promoted Anglo-American cultural development. For instance, nearly all major sports played in the United States during the nineteenth century had been brought from Great Britain, including cricket and soccer (by English textile-mill workers and coal miners), curling and golf (by the Scottish), and baseball (derived from the old British game of rounders). Furthermore, English immigrants often experienced social and cultural advantages over other foreign-born immigrants because they shared the language and the religious beliefs that continued to be dominant in American life. These beliefs still followed a Puritan ethic that was usually not, ironically, tolerant of different religious and political views. The English immigrants' relatively easy assimilation led to the belief that Americanization should be based on an Anglo-Americanism, a cultural form that other immigrants quickly recognized as a model.

An inevitable result of such a standard for American assimilation was a sense of Anglo-American ethnic "invisibility": members of this group did not have as distinguishable an ethnicity as other nationally identified groups. An equivalent to the "Irish" vote, for example, did not exist for those with English ancestry. To strengthen Anglo-American ethnic affiliation, many joined fraternal organizations such as the Masons and the Order of United Americans. Yet complicating the goal of solidifying group identity, "Anglo-Americanism" itself faced an internal contradiction. Anglo-Americans were often reluctant to fully Anglicize American culture because of previous efforts to separate themselves from their place of origin: historical moments of religious dissent (the original Pilgrim and Puritan settlement) and political struggle (the American Revolution) remained as crucial benchmarks for their identity. Therefore, Anglo-Americans often participated in fraternal organizations not to emphasize culture or "blood" ties (as other ethnic groups often did), but to focus on a shared commitment to republican ideals and virtues.

Hence, such Anglo-American social activity disclosed the combination of cultural and political goals that undergirded Anglo-American identity and affected American culture more broadly. For example, Benjamin Franklin worried that the Pennsylvania Germans would Germanize America rather than become Anglified themselves, and thus he valorized a pure "white" race based on an Anglo-American model. Yet, his interest was not simply in cultural superiority, but in a perceived threat to a particular body politic (Anglo-American) that he and others felt stood alone as the one that was fit for republican self-government. Subsequent political activity demonstrated this emphasis on an Anglo-American foundation for U.S. politics, including the 1790 Naturalization Act, which restricted citizenship to "free white persons," and nineteenth-century organizations such as the American Party (the Know-Nothings) and the Immigration Restriction League. Both of these organizations represented forms of nativism that stressed the necessity of an

Anglo-Saxon and Protestant foundation to sustain American political and cultural traditions. While definitions of the "white" race changed over the years—becoming more inclusive of others of European descent, for instance, following African American migrations north and west—such racializations continued to be driven by the notion that Anglo-Americanism was the "true" American nationality. This pattern eventually led to the eugenics movement of the 1910s and 1920s and the quota system behind the Immigration Act (the Johnson-Reed Act) of 1924.

Despite these social and political movements, some observers have suggested that, as the twentieth century continued, the white Anglo-Saxon Protestant model of the ideal American has been undercut by an increasingly multiethnic America. Yet Anglo-American culture has continued to be a clear force in American society, retaining power, for instance, in the highest levels of both government and business. This status illustrates the hegemonic characteristic of Anglo-Americanism: once it was understood as the American norm—a condition supported by the strength of its economic and religious position—this culture has been legally inscribed as dominant through political, economic, and cultural means. Consequently, the Anglo-American model remains central to the way "Americanism" is popularly imagined.

[See also EUROPEAN AMERICANS; WASP; AMERICANIZATION.]

BIBLIOGRAPHY

Erickson, Charlotte, *Leaving England: Essays on British Emigration in the Nineteenth Century* (Cornell Univ. Press 1994).

Hill, Douglas, *The English to New England* (Potter 1975).

Jacobson, Matthew Frye, *Whiteness of a Different Color: European Immigrants and the Alchemy of Race* (Harvard Univ. Press 1998).

Knobel, Dale T., *America for the Americans: The Nativist Movement in the United States* (Twayne 1996).

Thompson, Roger, *Mobility and Migration: East Anglian Founders of New England, 1629–1640* (Univ. of Mass. Press 1994).

PETER KVIDERA

© THE EVERETT COLLECTION

The Arthurian legend inspired Disney's *Sword in the Stone*.

ANIMATION

Animation, or the art of making drawings or three-dimensional inanimate objects appear to move almost magically on screen, can be traced in America to the work of J. Stuart Blackton, who in 1906 brought simple chalk drawings to life in the Vitagraph film *Humorous Phases of Funny Faces*. Using the technique of stop-motion photography, Blackton underscored a key characteristic of animation: unlike live-action films, which are filmed continuously, animated films are typically shot frame by frame. His work and that of Émile Cohl in France, whose dancing match-stick figures in *Fantasmagorie* (1908) delighted audiences, paved the way for America's first animation genius, Winsor McCay. A New York newspaper cartoonist known for his imagination and ability to draw quickly, McCay drew each frame individually for his first animated cartoon, *Little Nemo* (1910), based on his popular comic strip. He later incorporated a cartoon, *Gertie the Dinosaur* (1914), into a popular vaudeville act. McCay is also remembered for a series of fantasy films titled *Dreams of a Rarebit Fiend* and for *The Sinking of the Lusitania* (1918), based on a tragic, real-life event.

Contemporaries of McCay's, J. R. Bray and Earl Hurd, approached animation differently. While McCay was most interested in the art of animation, Bray and his associates conceived of it as an assembly-line business and sought to patent time-saving animation techniques that would make production more efficient and profitable. In 1913 the Bray Studio produced *The Artist's Dream,* which reflected experimentation with cel animation, a technique of drawing animated figures on transparencies, painting them, and then placing the sheets atop others depicting the background prior to photographing, thereby eliminating the need to redraw an entire character or background for every frame. This labor-saving technique, patented by Hurd in 1914, was particularly useful for film series, such as Bray's *Colonel Heeza Liar* and Hurd's *Bobby Bumps,* which required repeated drawings of the same characters and backgrounds. Many talented artists who would later establish their own animation studios, such as Max Fleischer, Paul Terry, and Walter Lantz, received their early training with Bray.

During the silent-film era, several popular comics provided subject matter for animated films, among them *Mutt and Jeff, The Katzenjammer Kids,* and *Krazy Kat.* This was also a period when animated films benefited from a growing audience (becoming part of the standard motion-picture experience) and from new techniques. In 1919 Max and Dave Fleischer created the first of their *Out of the Inkwell* films starring Koko the Clown, a graceful, mischievous animated character who interacted with actors in a live-action setting. Part of Koko's appeal was the fluidity of his movements, made possible by Max Fleischer's invention of the rotoscope. This device enabled animators to trace over a live-action model, creating a cartoon character that moved and gestured realistically, like a live actor. Also appearing for the first time in 1919, *Felix the Cat,* produced by Pat Sullivan and drawn by Otto Messmer, exhibited a fully developed personality, loosely patterned after Charlie Chaplin. Felix's distinctive facial expressions and anatomical resource-

fulness helped to make him the greatest cartoon star in silent film.

Various animators experimented with color and soundtracks in animation in the 1920s, but it was not until Walt Disney released *Steamboat Willie* in 1928 that animation entered a new era. The first animated film with synchronized sound and the first to feature the character Mickey Mouse, *Steamboat Willie* catapulted Walt Disney to the forefront of American animation, and his studio has remained there ever since. A visionary with gifts for storytelling, organization (his studio was the first to use the storyboard to plan films), and motivating people, Disney oversaw the production of *The Silly Symphonies* (such as "The Skeleton Dance" [1929]) with synchronized movement, and "Flowers and Trees" [1932] in Technicolor) and the creation of popular characters such as Donald Duck, Goofy, Pluto, and Minnie Mouse. The early cartoons were characterized by "rubber hose" animation, where characters stretched their arms or legs to absurdly long, loopy proportions. In later years this style gave way to a more realistic technique, "squash and stretch," where animated characters compress and extend their bodies showing the effects of weight, plasticity, and tension. In 1937 the Disney Studio released *The Old Mill,* showcasing a new technology, the multiplane camera, which shot through many separate layers of drawings, creating depth and perspective. That same year Disney unveiled another animation milestone, *Snow White and the Seven Dwarfs,* the first feature-length animated film. Other features—including *Pinocchio* (1940), *Fantasia* (1940), *Dumbo* (1941), and *Bambi* (1942)—followed, solidifying Disney's commitment to a sentimental, naturalistic animation style combined with memorable musical soundtracks and establishing Disney as the leading producer of feature-length animated films.

While Disney embraced new technologies in feature films, other studios focused on developing cartoon series and characters of lasting appeal. Max Fleischer's Betty Boop, Popeye, and Superman; Paul Terry's Heckle and Jeckle, Deputy Dog, and Mighty Mouse; and Walter Lantz's Woody Woodpecker are a few examples. Most notable, however, was the

Warner Brothers Studio, which employed some of the most talented animators in the history of the profession, including Chuck Jones, Tex Avery, Bob Clampett, Friz Freleng, and Frank Tashlin, and produced a stable of stunning characters, including Bugs Bunny, Daffy Duck, Porky Pig, Elmer Fudd, Yosemite Sam, Wile E. Coyote and Roadrunner, Sylvester and Tweety, Pepe LePew, Foghorn Leghorn, and Speedy Gonzales. The Warner Brothers Studio adopted a very different animation style from Disney—zany, bold, and irreverent—and perfected techniques such as the chase, the gag, and the visual pun, creating a perfect vehicle for a new animation audience: television viewers. Another studio to adopt a decidedly different look from Disney was United Productions of America (UPA), founded in 1943 by Steven Bosustow, who had left the Disney fold following a strike by animators seeking more artistic control. Reflective of the style of modern painters such as Paul Klee and Joan Miró, UPA animation in the 1950s, as seen in the *Gerald McBoing Boing* and *Mr. Magoo* cartoons, was characterized by simple, stylized figures grouped in patterns and by more sophisticated themes, such as the danger of conformity.

Since the 1960s animation has continued to flourish, affected by artistic, economic, and technological innovations. While short cartoons are no longer part of the moviegoing experience, animated features have continued to draw diverse audiences to theaters. *Yellow Submarine* (1968) featured the colorful, op-art style of Peter Max and the music of the Beatles; Ralph Bakshi's *Fritz the Cat* (1972) became the first animated feature to carry an X rating; Walt Disney's *Lion King* (1994) earned over 300 million dollars, making it a marketing phenomenon and the most profitable animated feature ever; and Pixar's *Toy Story* (1995), directed by John Lasseter, broke ground as the first fully computer-generated feature-length film. On the small screen, Hanna-Barbera succeeded with the first prime-time animated show, *The Flintstones*, characterized by limited animation (movement is reduced to a bare minimum) and the theme of suburban life. Animation has remained a mainstay on Saturday morning and after-school television, spawned the Cartoon Network, and become cutting-edge, prime-time fare, as evidenced by *The Simpsons, Beavis and Butt-Head,* and *South Park.* Will Vinton's Claymation, Tim Burton's stop-action animation, and Pixar's computer animation represent facets of an art form continuously in flux, responding to the audience's continuing desire for new forms of entertainment and creative expression.

[*See also* DISNEY, WALT; FILM, *articles on* FILM AND HISTORY, FILM TECHNOLOGY, FILM AND REALITY; INDEPENDENT FILM; HOLLYWOOD.]

BIBLIOGRAPHY

Barrier, Michael, *Hollywood Cartoons: American Animation in Its Golden Age* (Oxford 1999).

Kanfer, Stefan, *Serious Business: The Art and Commerce of Animation in America from Betty Boop to Toy Story* (Scribner 1997).

Maltin, Leonard, *Of Mice and Magic: A History of American Animated Cartoons,* rev. ed. (New Am. Lib. 1987).

Solomon, Charles, *Enchanted Drawings: The History of Animation,* rev. and updated ed. (Wings Bks. 1994).

KATHY MERLOCK JACKSON

ANTI-CATHOLICISM

Anti-Catholicism is a term that describes any discriminatory attitude, policy, or practice directed against individuals or organizations on the basis of their affiliation with the Roman Catholic Church; its expressions range from pejorative discourses to attacks on people, symbols, rituals, or artifacts associated with Roman Catholicism. In the history of the United States, anti-Catholic sentiment dates to the early English colonial period. Although a numerical-minority Christian sect, Roman Catholics have been accused of, at best, dual and, at worst, treasonous political allegiance to the pope in Rome. Dating to the 1559 "Oath of Supremacy" and the "Act for the Better Discovering and Repressing of Popish Recussants [*sic*]," early colonial opposition to Roman Catholicism was structural and pervasive. Although Maryland is believed to have been the most tolerant among the English colonies toward Catholicism, it was nonetheless necessary for the Assembly (largely Catholic at the time) to pass the Maryland Act for Church Liberties in 1640, providing for legal freedom to all churches. The challenge posed to Roman Catholics at the turn of the eighteenth century was whether their political allegiance was determined by religious or civic identity. Thus, Catholics were required to prove their loyalty in ways that other Christians were not.

The intensity of anti-Catholic sentiment has varied over time and could be gauged over the last century and a half by manifestations during times of political, economic, and military hardship or prosperity. As is true for all social phenomena, its expressions were complex and often self-contradictory. For example, during the Mexican War, not only was there an increased number of "pretexts for Protestant attacks on Catholicism," but also a simultaneous diminution of anti-Catholic sentiment, partly owing to the patriotism demonstrated by Catholic immigrant soldiers.

Historic prohibition of Catholics from certain organizations, educational institutions, and places of residence or recreation has made some of their experiences of discrimination and exclusion similar to those experienced by other numerical minorities in the United States. However, the effects of anti-Catholicism on Catholics as a group have never extended to practices such as the genocides and forced dislocation and reservation living experienced by Native Americans; nor have Catholics been subject to laws such as the Chinese Exclusion Act of 1882, which established a ten-year prohibition against immigrant Chinese laborers.

Anti-Catholic sentiment has occasioned neither the legally sanctioned oppression that blacks experienced under chattel slavery, nor the deprivation of civil liberties enforced under Jim Crow laws. Similarly, consequences of anti-Catholicism have never reached extremes such as Presidential Order 9066, which established official disenfranchisement, dispossession, and internment of citizens of Japanese ancestry in the western United States during World War II. Despite the persistence of anti-Catholicism, Roman Catholics have attained notable status in education, business, and civic life, including representation in the highest ranks of the three branches of government, achieving the ranks of U.S. senator, justice of the Supreme Court, and president of the United States.

[See also ROMAN CATHOLICISM.]

BIBLIOGRAPHY

Curran, Francis X., S.J., *Catholics in Colonial Law* (Loyola Univ. Press 1963).

Dulce, Berton, and Edward J. Richter, *Religion and the Presidency, A Recurring American Problem* (Macmillan 1962).

Salyer, Lucy E., *Laws Harsh as Tigers: Chinese Immigrants and the Shaping of Modern Immigration Law* (Univ. Of N.C. Press 1995).

Zanca, Kenneth J., ed., *American Catholics and Slavery, 1789–1866: An Anthology of Primary Documents* (Univ. Press of Am. 1994).

FRANCES WOOD

ANTI-INTELLECTUALISM

The term *anti-intellectualism* was popularized by the historian Richard Hofstadter in *Anti-Intellectualism in American Life* (1963), a personal response to the "distaste for intellect" exhibited by Joseph McCarthy and other right-wing demagogues of the 1950s. Hofstadter defined this term as "a resentment and suspicion of the life of the mind and of those who are considered to represent it; and a disposition constantly to minimize the value of that life." Through a series of case studies—he called them exhibits, as though prosecuting a legal case—drawn from the American 1950s, Hofstadter portrayed anti-intellectualism as an idea, an attitude, and a historical subject that illustrated the milieu or atmosphere of a particular period of American life. His analysis relied on "impressionistic devices" directed at American culture rather than political history, making his work a contribution to American studies scholarship of the post–World War II generation.

The resentment and suspicion to which Hofstadter alluded can be traced through the length of Euro-American experience. However, it is frequently unclear whether Hofstadter's "anti-intellectualism" is an active idea or attitude or merely a description of disparate ways in which theorizing has been overwhelmed by practicality in American cultural life. Is this anti-intellectualism or non-intellectualism? The vernacular tradition, as described by John Kouwenhoven (*The Arts in Modern American Civilization,* 1948) and others of Hofstadter's generation, presents practicality as a hallmark of American culture. But this favoring of "intelligence" over "intellect," to use two of Hofstadter's terms, could manifest an indifference to pure thought rather than an overt hostility to the life of the mind.

Anti-intellectualism was most effectively used by a self-conscious class of intellectuals that formed in the cultural foment of fin-de-siècle France and czarist Russia. The notion of "an oppositional elite of necessary dissenters" then migrated to the United States to replace a genteel, "mugwump" (Hofstadter's term) community of thinkers and writers of which William Dean Howells was a representative. The first generation of self-proclaimed intellectuals, represented by Van Wyck Brooks, Randolph Bourne, and other writers for magazines such as *The Seven Arts,* sought cultural leadership for their class and were disdainful of such thinkers as John Dewey, whose pragmatic philosophy sacrificed intellectual principles for active participation in the quotidian world of civic life.

Writings directed by self-conscious twentieth-century intellectuals toward the larger American culture frequently juxtaposed words including *intellectual, liberal,* or *radical* with *middlebrow, mainstream,* and *conservative.* Most often the accusation of anti-intellectual behavior was thrust by the Left toward the Right. The word *culture* often sharpened the Right's riposte. As a rhetorical device, the anti-intellectual label forced the accused to disprove a negative. Perhaps Hofstadter's contemporaries, the most likely to use this specific term, appreciated the force of such an attack, having been menaced, or even impaled, by the "anti-American" campaigns of the 1950s. In any case, the language surrounding anti-intellectualism became value-laden and invidious because it was deployed to defend intellectual territory against attacks by the larger culture. Contextualization of the term within a specific cultural moment is both essential and enlightening.

Hofstadter's work, for instance, emerged from cold-war circumstances and appeared on bookshelves during the New Frontier of the Kennedy administration. Defining an oppositional class of intellectuals loyal to American ideals, a familiar project in 1950s culture, was an important task. At the same time Hofstadter had to take into account the seeming acceptance of intellectuals into national political life by a new administration that had invited the poet Robert Frost to read at the 1961 inauguration and regularly raided Ivy League departments for highly visible government posts. Hofstadter saw a facile acceptance of erudition and the trappings of culture that masked a deeper ambivalence about the inclusion of the intellectual in the American mainstream. Contemporary intellectuals were recognizable civic figures only because they resembled more familiar types, such as the businessman, a surrender to commercial culture that Van Wyck Brooks had already condemned before World War I. Hofstadter left open the question of whether intellectuals could participate fully in civic life. Must one be alienated from society to lead the life of the mind?

So, where is the intellectual to stand? In his 1987 book *The Last Intellectuals,* Russell Jacoby traces the virtually complete ingestion of the intellectual class by the knowledge industry of the post–World War II American university. The comfortably oppositional spaces created during the 1950s by the *Partisan Review*'s symposia, such as "Our Country, Our Culture," for example, was fleeting and rare. Critics have now become professors, Jacoby claims, with their own systems of value and their chain-gang shuffle toward tenure. Where is the younger generation of intellectuals, he rhetorically asks, and how can they be heard outside university walls? This is a good question, but it is artificially limited to traditional cultural terrain that has in fact shifted in contemporary American culture.

Much of twentieth-century discussion of anti-intellectualism has presumed large, collective units: the intellectual, the public, one American culture. Culture at the start of the new millennium is manifested in specific sites that attract particular public audiences. As Dolores Hayden points out in *The*

Power of Place, these are provocative, intellectually stimulating, and socially engaged locations that often question the qualities, or even the existence, of an American culture. The work of many minority scholars likewise attacks unitary views of cultural terms. Viewed in these ways, debates over anti-intellectualism can appear myopic or even inconsequential. One could theorize definitions of the public or one could simply engage the culture in the public realm without being consumed by thoughts of nomenclature. Could it be, in short, that the effective life of anti-intellectualism is bracketed by two end-of-the-century periods of cultural transformation?

In any case, present-day definitions of *anti-intellectualism* must take into account the many destabilizations that have occurred since the 1960s. Ironically, while the end of the cold war has lessened the potency of accusations of anti-Americanism, postcolonial theorists have called into question the definition of "America" itself. The radical pluralism of multicultural America has fractured the class solidarity of intellectuals. No longer, Andrew Ross points out in *No Respect,* can one posit the existence of a universalized "intellectual." As Hofstadter's own study shows, the intellectual is too frequently constructed as white and male. In postmodern America, the line between high culture and popular culture, so carefully maintained by previous generations of intellectuals, has broken down, throwing those leading the life of the mind into contact with a facet of culture that, by tradition and temperament, they have been least prepared to engage. Poststructural analysis also reveals the link between knowledge and power and makes suspect the seemingly dispassionate analyses of culture by self-proclaimed intellectuals. Finally, the intellectual Hofstadter had viewed as a secular cleric has now become, for the most part, a knowledge worker; within American universities, at any rate, the production of "intellect" has become thoroughly commodified.

It is tempting to see anti-intellectualism as a major theme in American life at century's end. Hofstadter traced the devaluation of intellect to the strong, fundamentalist enthusiasms that were running through American religious life. His examples may be more than matched by present-day rejections of evolutionary theory, for example, or the fulminations against modern culture mouthed by televangelists. Hofstadter bemoaned the vocationalization of American education. The "right-sizing" of contemporary universities and the widespread attacks on the liberal-arts core in the name of cost effectiveness he would have found even more appalling than the situations he describes in the mass universities that were emerging during the post–GI Bill boom of the 1950s.

Conservative critiques of the multicultural Left, such as E. D. Hirsch's *Cultural Literacy* (1985), are consistent with Hofstadter's view: Americans simply do not have a common body of cultural knowledge. One of the most memorable episodes of *Anti-Intellectualism in American Life* is set in a Senate hearing, in which the Eisenhower administration's ambassador-designate to Ceylon congenially proves that he cannot locate that country on a map. Twenty years later Hirsch enumerates case after case of what he terms *cultural illiteracy* ranging from geographical to literary know-nothingism. "Anti-intellectualism" is now an accusation directed from each to each, across political and cultural spectra.

By defining the intellectual as a person for whom thought is both work and play Christopher Lasch, a Hofstadter student and himself an eminent intellectual historian, characterizes a habit of mind, a disposition toward the world that informs both ideas and actions. In contemporary culture there is work aplenty to test the equanimity, if not the playfulness, of such thinkers. Certainly, examining the social positions of such intellectuals is as important as extirpating anti-intellectual tendencies in the fractious culture of everyday life. As Andrew Ross rightly asserts, "The need to search for common ground, however temporary, from which to contest the existing definitions of a popular-democratic culture has never been more urgent."

[See also INTELLECTUAL HISTORY, AMERICAN; INTELLECTUALS.]

BIBLIOGRAPHY

Hayden, Dolores, *The Power of Place: Urban Landscapes as Public History* (MIT Press 1995).

Hirsch, E. D., Jr., *Cultural Literacy: What Every American Needs to Know* (Houghton 1985).

Hofstadter, Richard, *Anti-Intellectualism in American Life* (Knopf 1963).

Jacoby, Russell, *The Last Intellectuals: American Culture in the Age of Academe* (Basic Bks. 1987).

Lasch, Christopher, *The New Radicalism in America 1889–1963: The Intellectual as a Social Type* (Knopf 1965).

Ross, Andrew, *No Respect: Intellectuals and Popular Culture* (Routledge 1989).

ERIC J. SANDEEN

ANTI-SEMITISM

Anti-Semitism, a term for the hatred of Jews and Judaism, was coined in the 1870s by German journalist Wilhelm Marr. Although anti-Semitism was never as interwoven into American culture as it was elsewhere in the world, it flourished nevertheless. Anti-Jewish prejudice in the American colonies sprang from feelings European settlers brought with them. Anti-Semitism persisted owing to the widely held belief that America was and should be a Christian nation and the characterization of Jews as Christ killers. At varying times since the seventeenth century, Jews were not allowed to vote, hold public office, buy land, work as artisans, practice law, or worship publicly. But they continued to work toward success, often finding opportunities by running their own businesses, leading to a perception that Jews did not create anything but simply managed and lent money. The arrival in the United States of over 1.6 million Jewish immigrants beginning in 1890 led to calls for immigration restriction in the belief that morally degenerate Jews were destroying American culture.

During and after World War I, Jews were considered unpatriotic and they were linked negatively in the public imagination to Russian socialism. In 1915 in Atlanta Leo Frank, a Jew, was unjustly convicted of murdering a thirteen-year-old employee in his pencil factory; when the governor commuted his execution to life imprisonment, a mob hanged Frank. A 1920 book, *The Protocols of the Elders of Zion,* accused Jews of conspiring with the devil to overthrow world Christianity. Automaker Henry Ford filled his newspaper, the *Dearborn Independent,* with circulation-boosting anti-Semitic articles that caused a decrease in the enrollment of Jewish college students nationally, limited immigration, and revitalized the Ku Klux Klan in America.

American anti-Semitism peaked in the 1930s, with Americans blaming Jews for their economic problems, a hatred fueled by the rise of Nazis in Germany. The Silver Shirts, headquartered in Asheville, North Carolina, and led by William Pelley, was one of over a hundred anti-Semitic groups formed during the 1930s. Father Charles Coughlin, a Catholic priest and host of a popular radio show, became America's most vocal anti-Semite. Coughlin's call for the creation of a Christian Front led to roving gangs who attacked and harassed Jews at work and worship.

Anti-Semitism in the United States eased somewhat after the end of World War II because of increased economic prosperity, revelations of Hitler's atrocities, and many veterans' distaste for bigotry, though widespread discrimination still existed. In 1945 Bess Myerson became the first Jew to be crowned Miss America. *Gentleman's Agreement*, a book by Laura Z. Hobson about anti-Semitism, was made into a film and received the 1947 Academy Award for best picture. Hotels that would not accept Jews faced boycotts by rejected guests and their supporters.

But anti-Semitism survived. In the South it resurfaced after the 1954 *Brown* v. *Board of Education* Supreme Court decision to end segregation. Many African Americans pointed to Jews as the cause of their problems, an attitude exacerbated by high-profile incidents such as Andrew Young's forced resignation as America's ambassador to the United Nations after he met secretly with the Palestine Liberation Organization in 1979 and Jesse Jackson's derogatory reference to Jews as "Hymies" during his 1984 presidential campaign. At the end of the twentieth century, despite periodic inflammatory incidents, overt anti-Semitism continued to diminish in the United States, home to almost six million Jews, nearly one-half of the world's Jewish population.

[See also JEWISH AMERICANS; PREJUDICE.*]*

BIBLIOGRAPHY

Dinnerstein, Leonard, *Antisemitism in America* (Oxford 1994).

Gerber, David, ed., *Anti-Semitism in American History* (Univ. of Ill. Press 1986).

Jaher, Frederic Cople, *A Scapegoat in the New Wilderness: The Origins and Rise of Anti-Semitism in America* (Harvard Univ. Press 1994).

Quinley, Harold E., and Charles Y. Glock, *Anti-Semitism in America* (Free Press 1979).

Sachar, Howard M., *A History of the Jews in America* (Knopf 1992).

EVELYN BECK

ARAB AMERICANS

Arabs have immigrated to the United States in three main groups. Most early immigrants (from 1885 to 1945) were Christian minorities of Eastern rite sects from Greater Syria, largely from Mount Lebanon. Multiple factors led to their immigration, ranging from poverty, famine resulting from the blockade of the Syrian coast during World War II, the breakdown of Syria's silk trade after the opening of the Suez Canal, and the indirect encouragement of missionaries, tourists, and returning emigrants.

Until World War II, most Arab immigrants were village farmers or artisans. At first they were primarily young single males. But the ratio of women to men increased rapidly, so that by the turn of the twentieth century, one out of every three Syrian immigrants was female. The early immigrants' central motive for immigration was economic opportunity. Pack peddling was their most common trade. All of the occupations that were open to Syrian men were open to Syrian women. Although most early immigrants intended to acquire wealth and return to their country of origin, the majority eventually became permanent U.S. residents. No accurate records exist, but it is estimated that by 1916 one hundred thousand Arabs had immigrated to the United States, and by 1924 the Arab population in the United States reached two hundred thousand.

But confusion developed because pre–World War II immigrants were classified according to multiple, conflicting social categories. The early immigrants primarily were identified according to family, kinship, village affiliation, or religious sect. However, because they migrated from an Ottoman province (Syria) they were classified as Turks, the same appellative applied to Greeks, Albanians, Armenians, and other Eastern groups. In 1899 officials began to classify the early immigrants as a separate "Syrian" ethnic group. But the census of 1910 continued to include Syrians under the category "Turkey in Asia." Newspapers and magazines of this period referred to the Syrians as (and conflated them with) Arabians, Armenians, Assyrians, or Turks.

From early on, the "Syrians" occupied a precarious position within the U.S. racial system. In 1914 a South Carolina judge ruled that while Syrians may be Caucasian, they were not that particular free white person to whom the act of Congress had denoted the privilege of citizenship—a privilege that was intended for persons of European descent. When this court decision was reversed in 1923, an ethos of "Americanization" and "assimilation" shaped immigrants' loyalty to the United States and halted the development of a visible Arab American social identity. In developing a strong civil allegiance to America, immigrants and their successors tended to view solidarity with their countries of origin as a liability. Many switched from speaking Arabic to English, anglicized their names, and restricted their ethnic identity to the private sphere, thus participating in the process of cultural and ethnic erasure. By the early twentieth century, the transition between immigration and settlement was underway. Many early immigrants and their children gave up peddling to become grocery-store owners, and a new Syrian middle class emerged.

Significant political and demographic shifts among immigrants of the second period (1945–1967) complicated their "Americanization" process. The second immigrant wave was distinguished by its large number of Muslims and females, refugees displaced by the 1948 Palestine War, others driven by particular political events, and many professionals and university students. By midcentury, Arab Americans were one of the best-acculturated ethnic groups in America. But when Arab nations had achieved a certain level of political autonomy from Western rule, Arab immigrants, who brought new and specific forms of Arab nationalism to the United States, began to self-identify according to the classification "Arab."

During the third period (1967 to the present) relaxed immigration laws and increased war and upheaval in the Arab world contributed to a rapid influx of immigrants, increased religious and geographic diversity among immigrants, and altered immigration patterns. Scholars estimate that in the 1990s, the U.S. population tracing their roots to the Arab world was between two and two and a half million. They were distinguished from their predecessors by a greater number of Muslims than Christians, a stronger sense of Arab nationalism, heightened criticism of U.S. policy, a rise in ethno-political consciousness, weaker civic identification, and the maintenance of cultural and religious traditions.

The declaration of Israel's independence instigated the beginning of the social, political, and cultural marginalization of Arab Americans and the emergence of a war waged by the U.S. media against Arabs in the United States and in the diaspora that has distorted the meaning of the term *Arab* and further complicated Arab American identity. After the Arab-Israeli War of 1967, the U.S. media began to conflate the categories Arab, Middle Eastern, and Muslim, and to portray Arabs according to three primary images, all of which reinforce the idea of a generic, inferior, "Arab Middle Eastern Muslim" enemy/Other. The first image portrays generic Arab Middle Eastern Muslim men as irrationally violent, particularly toward women. The second portrays generic Arab Middle Eastern Muslim women as supra-oppressed in comparison with white American women, who are idealized to represent equality, democracy, and justice. The third focuses on the absent Arab woman, juxtaposing Arab men and white women while keeping Arab

women entirely absent from the scene. These media portray Arab Middle Eastern Muslim culture as cruel and violent; sensationalize the mistreatment of Arab women; equate Arabs, Middle Easterners, and Muslims with barbarism; and portray the West as superior to the entire Arab world. Repeated images of excessively oppressed Arab Middle Eastern Muslim women are implicitly used to justify Western intervention in the Middle East on the grounds that "Arab Middle Eastern Muslim" society is backward and is therefore in need of Westernization or civilization.

Heightened awareness of political conflict between the United States and the Arab world, experiences of social and political marginalization, and the 1960s ethos of ethnic revival in the United States culminated in the development of a distinct Arab American identity that tends to perceive the cultural, political, and religious values of their homeland in tension with the majority U.S. culture. Since the late 1960s, many Americans of Arab descent who had previously identified according to country of origin or religious affiliation, or as generically American, began uniting under the label "Arab American." Community activists have spearheaded the process of pan-ethnic unification by developing pan-ethnic community organizations focused on combating racism, maintaining cultural traditions, and increasing Arab Americans' political voice.

Racist attacks against Arab American individuals and community organizations are generally linked to U.S. crises in the Middle East and the media images that sensationalize them, often resulting in racism, discrimination and violence against Arab Americans in their everyday lives. When conflicts arise between the United States and an Arab country, anyone identified as an Arab, Muslim, or Middle Easterner living in the United States may be targeted as a terrorist-enemy. This instills fear in Arab Americans, leading many to conceal their ethnic identity and to avoid participation in Arab American community organizations, thereby halting the community's political development and silencing its voice within the larger North American society.

For example, after the 1985 Trans World Airlines (TWA) jet hijacking in Lebanon, members of the Roxbury, Massachusetts, branch of the American Arab Anti-Discrimination Committee (ADC) found a pipe bomb in front of their office and the ADC's West Coast regional director Alex Odeh was assassinated. After the Odeh murder, ADC closed its New York City office, where its director, Bonnie Rimawi, had been harassed and threatened for months. On January 26, 1987, the Los Angeles Eight (L.A. 8), seven Palestinians and one Kenyan, were arrested in Los Angeles, publicly labeled a "terrorist threat," and threatened with deportation for selling newspapers and participating in Arab American community events, even though such legitimate activities are protected by the First Amendment.

A Justice Department contingency plan was revealed during the L.A. 8 court proceedings that provided a blueprint for the mass arrest of ten thousand Middle Eastern U.S. residents, in the event of war with certain Arab states, and provisions for their detention in camps in Louisiana and Florida and their possible deportation. These incidents, and events that followed them (including ongoing Federal Bureau of Investigation harassment and airport profiling of Arab Americans), demonstrate the U.S. government's attempt to instill fear in Arab Americans and others who participate in Arab American community affairs. In response to phone calls from Arab Americans concerned that they could be arrested for attending Arab dances and programs, Mark Rosenbaum, an American Civil Liberties Union attorney, stated "What the U.S. government is saying to Arabs is Shut Up or Get Out of This Country."

Arab Americans' paradoxical position within the U.S. racial system contributes to their marginalization. The U.S. census bureau defines Arab Americans as whites or Caucasians. However, in many social contexts they are perceived and defined as nonwhites, rendering them "white—but not quite." Currently, a heated debate among Arab American scholars and activists concerns whether Arab Americans should seek minority nonwhite status or remain classified as whites or Caucasians.

But the question of Arab Americans' racial and ethnic classification is no simple matter. While many Arab Americans pass as white, phenotypically, some live racially marked lives. Others make conscious decisions to self-identity as nonwhites or as persons of color to distinguish themselves from European American whites, to politically align themselves with other racially marked groups, and to claim their rights in the face of racial, ethnic, or religious discrimination. Many Arab Americans identify as *Arab, Arab American, Middle Eastern,* or *Muslim,* reclaiming and redefining the meaning of these terms in the face of state and media distortion. A few introduce themselves according to non-Arab racial and ethnic labels, such as Greek, Italian, Puerto Rican, or generically American, in order to avoid the stigmatization often associated with the label *Arab.*

The Arab American community faces pressing new challenges. Violence, racism, and discrimination against Arab Americans is rapidly increasing and Arab Americans' "white—but not quite" status within the U.S. racial and ethnic system renders them "invisible." But if "visibility" requires that Arab Americans occupy a more distinct place within the U.S. racial and ethnic system, what that place should be remains a matter of debate.

[See also ISLAM.]

BIBLIOGRAPHY

Aswad, Barbara, and Barbara Bilgé, eds., *Family and Gender among American Muslims: Issues Facing Middle Eastern Immigrants and Their Descendents* (Temple Univ. Press 1996).

Naber, Nadine, "Ambiguous Insiders: An Investigation of Arab American Invisibility," *Journal of Ethnic and Racial Studies* (January 2000).

Naff, Alixa, *Becoming American: The Early Arab Immigrant Experience* (Southern Ill. Univ. Press 1985).

Kadi, Joanna, ed., *Food for Our Grandmothers: Writings by Arab-American and Arab-Canadian Feminists* (South End Press 1994).

Samhan, Helen, "Politics and Exclusion: The Arab American Experience," *Journal of Palestine Studies* 16, no. 2 (1987):20–28.

Shakir, Evelyn, *Bint Arab: Arab and Arab American Women in the United States* (Praeger 1997).

Suleiman, Michael, and Baha Abu Laban, eds., *Arab Americans: Continuity and Change* (Assn. of Arab-Am. Univ. Graduates 1989).

NADINE NABER

ARCADE GAMES

During each era of human civilization, arcade has included an escape from the everyday. In ancient societies, the arcade was a shopping area; at the start of the twenty-first century, it is a place for electronic games. Since the late nineteenth century, the arcade has been linked to leisure activities, which became more and more mechanized until the computer age allowed people to bring icons of the arcade into their homes and offices. This process began with an effort to humanize the machines reserved for business and industry. Once this had taken place, the arcade connected Americans to a culture of gaming that spanned from mechanical pinball to laser tag.

While arcade-like atmospheres existed at most fairs, carnivals, and other such gatherings, their structure became formalized with the 1893 World's Columbian Exposition in Chicago and the amusement park tradition that it inspired. Often, these amusement sites were linked to urban areas by elec-

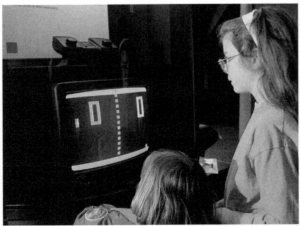

© MIKE DERER/AP/WIDE WORLD PHOTOS

The special units required to play Pong and other early video games on the home television set were expensive and sometimes difficult to set up.

tric trolleys and railways. Many such parks became important outlets for surplus electrical power, which was normally controlled by the traction companies that ran the rail lines and brought in customers. Most important, parks such as Coney Island, Atlantic City, and others were among the first to use electric lighting as well as power to create amusing rides. Finally, electric power was also brought into the arcade. Kinetoscopes in penny arcades gave suggestive glimpses of the female anatomy, while other games used electricity to reward participants with the bells, lights, and noises of the new electric era. Trolley parks, as well as the arcades that followed, were one of the first cultural institutions in the United States to function as a mediating influence between economic classes and ethnic groups.

Pinball is one of the most enduring of the early electronic games; yet it was not always powered. Games similar to pinball date back to ancient Greece, where a popular outdoor game featured round stones and holes dug in a hillside. In the eighteenth century in France, the game of bagatelle, a mechanical ancestor of the pinball machine, was developed. Generally, pinball games are coin-activated electromechanical devices, found in such places as candy stores, arcades, malls, and bars. Earlier machines were simply mechanical and used marbles. By about 1930 electrical circuitry was added and the marbles were replaced with steel balls. To play, a player releases a plunger to drive a steel ball up an alley along the side of a glass-enclosed, semi-inclined playing area. After it reaches the top of its arc, the ball descends into the playing area, which is filled with gates, bumpers, posts, and holes of various kinds. The ball's contact with these items increases the point score, which is recorded on a lighted vertical panel at the top of the machine. Scoring is accompanied by ringing bells and flashing lights: the age of electronic arcades had begun.

A new stage for pinball began in 1981 when computer versions of the game were first developed. The market for computerized arcade games officially began with large manufacturers in the United States and Japan. One historical footnote reveals how closely related the evolving technologies were. Assigned to construct a television, Ralph Bauer, a young engineer, created a primitive space adventure game, but his managers did not know what to do with the product. Similar fates befell other inventors who created crude versions of such games as Space Invaders and Asteroids. Marketing and consumer interest would need to be mobilized before the games could truly succeed.

Computers and computer games revolutionized arcade entertainment after 1980. This shift was governed by the Atari Corporation beginning in the 1970s with its simple video game, Pong. With the release of Pong into arcades, bars, and restaurants in 1972, a seven-billion-dollar industry was born. Although Pong games were little more than a novelty, with this foothold Atari sought to release Pong for home use in 1975. Originally Atari planned to build 50 thousand units, but Sears, Roebuck and Company and other dealers demanded more. By December 1975, 150 thousand Atari units had been sold to consumers.

Games such as Pong, Tank, Outlaw, Missile Command, Donkey Kong, and Pac Man defined a shift to computer games in arcades—even changing the common name to video arcade. Atari also released such games for home use on video computer systems and orchestrated the connection between arcade and home use. Slowly Americans grew more and more willing to consider the idea of a home video arcade. Manufacturers Nintendo and Sega ultimately developed this market further, creating handheld electronic games, such as Game Boy and Game Gear.

Computer gaming became the next frontier in 1981 as the personal computer (PC) became prevalent in most American homes. This change greatly influenced the quality and intensity of arcade games as well. Stimulated by the end of the cold war, new technology made computer games (such as flight simulators, for example) better than ever.

Ultimately, the most popular post-cold-war release in gaming breathed life back into the video arcades. Virtual reality and laser tag games combined computer imagery with fully active player participation. The leisure amusement of the origi-

nal penny arcades reached a totality of experience in the twenty-first century that its inventors could have never imagined. In virtual reality the arcade's voyage from reality seems complete.

[See also POPULAR CULTURE; CYBERCULTURE; VIOLENCE; VIDEO AND COMPUTER GAMES; YOUTH CULTURE.*]*

BIBLIOGRAPHY

Dery, Mark, ed., *Flame Wars: The Discourse of Cyberculture* (Duke Univ. Press 1994).

Geist, Johann Friedrich, *Arcades: The History of a Building Type* (MIT Press 1983).

Holtzman, Steven, *Digital Mosaics: The Aesthetics of Cyberspace* (Simon & Schuster 1997).

Kasson, John F., *Amusing the Million: Coney Island at the Turn of the Century* (Hill & Wang 1978).

Provenzo, Eugene F., *Video Kids: Making Sense of Nintendo* (Harvard Univ. Press 1991).

BRIAN BLACK

ARCHITECTURE

[The subject of American architecture is addressed in the encyclopedia in a series of separate articles, grouped together under the present heading. The first article, AN OVERVIEW, *provides an introduction to the principal movements and figures in the field, highlighting stylistic innovations and exemplary works in their historical contexts. The remaining six entries focus on individual areas of architectural activity. Their titles are as follows:*

COMMERCIAL ARCHITECTURE

DOMESTIC ARCHITECTURE

PUBLIC BUILDINGS

RELIGIOUS ARCHITECTURE

URBAN ARCHITECTURE

VERNACULAR ARCHITECTURE*]*

An Overview

Architecture can provide important insights into the culture that produces it. The architecture of the United States is no exception. It reflects the traditions, innovations, and setbacks of a young developing nation. While American architecture often exhibits strong ties to European culture, the buildings also reveal an innate pioneering spirit since designers created architectural forms to best meet the unique physical and social conditions of the United States. The rich backgrounds and the incredible innovations of architects have resulted over the years in an extensive variety of American building forms.

Colonial America. Colonial buildings in the New World, whether constructed by German, French, Dutch, British, or Spanish builders, typically echoed the native architecture of the immigrant group's homeland. In many cases, however, builders had to simplify the designs because of a dearth of trained craftsmen. Different climates and a limited choice of available building materials also contributed to modifications of Old World architectural forms. The design of early colonial buildings tended to focus on function, with only minimal effort given to nonfunctional, decorative details.

Colonial architecture in the Southwest was a blend of Spanish and Native American designs. The builders of seventeenth-century Catholic missionary churches, such as San Estevan in Acoma, New Mexico (1629–1642), attempted to copy European designs. The buildings typically included long naves, bell towers, and, later, simplified baroque details. Because the Spanish did not bring skilled craftsmen with them, the churches were usually constructed out of adobe or stone by Native Americans, who often incorporated their own symbols and forms into the designs.

At the same time the Spanish were establishing themselves in the Southwest, British immigrants began settling along the eastern seaboard. Regional differences between the architecture of the New England and the Southern colonies were primarily the result of the dissimilar climates of the areas and different circumstances of the colonists. The earliest New England immigrants came from a lower class of English society and settled in small, self-governing communities. Their architecture tended to be unpretentious, reflecting their puritanical background. The square-shaped meetinghouse, which developed out of the English market hall, was the major public building form. It was used for both religious and secular functions. Houses in New England showed little variation from traditional English practices. Wattle and daub placed between heavy wood framing was covered with clapboard siding to insulate interior spaces from harsh New England winters. The basic floor plan included two major rooms on the first floor, the parlor and the all-purpose hall, which were separated by a central chimney. The addition of a one-story lean-to on the back of a two-story house created the distinctive "saltbox" form.

In contrast to New England, the Middle-Atlantic states were settled by immigrants more interested in commerce than religious freedom. Over time they developed vast tobacco plantations with large manor houses and small outbuildings. While wood was the most common building material along the East Coast, the colonial buildings in the South that survive today are those that were built out of brick or stone. In residential architecture, chimneys were typically located on the short ends of the house rather than in the center to allow for cross breezes and to help eliminate excess heat. Simple classical and Gothic details appeared in a few prominent Southern colonial designs, such as St. Luke's in Isle of Wight County, Virginia (1632; 1657), which was modeled after English parish churches.

Once colonists had achieved a degree of stability in their new homeland, they could begin to expend energy on the creation of more fashionable buildings. The colonists looked primarily to England for precedents of architectural taste. In most cases, however, there was a time lag between when a building trend was popular in Europe and when it first appeared in the colonies. Published architectural sources, however, became more and more available to American builders during the eighteenth century. Books, including architectural treatises such as Colen Campbell's *Vitruvius Britannicus* and translations of the sixteenth-century work *Quattro libri dell' architettura* by Andrea Palladio, helped generate great interest in the architectural designs of the Italian Renaissance.

In an effort to achieve the grandeur of English baroque country houses, wealthy colonists adapted

Mission San Carlos de Río Carmelo in California constructed of adobe in a Spanish style.

designs from British publications. These Georgian designs, like that of Westover in Charles City County, Virginia (William Byrd, 1730–1734), were characterized by rigid symmetry, sash windows, pitched roofs with dormers, and classical details. Builders modeled the designs of new meeting-houses and churches on the classical churches designed by Christopher Wren and James Gibbs for London after the Great Fire of 1666. These designs, like the Old North Church in Boston, Massachu-setts (William Price, 1723), were topped by large towers and spires.

Early American Architecture. After the Revo-lution, American designers began searching for a style of architecture that would better epitomize their new independence from England. They began looking more directly at ancient architectural de-signs. Their major sources, however, were still Brit-ish publications. Interest in ancient Greek and Roman culture had spread to England in the mid-eighteenth century with the rise in popularity of the Grand Tour. Books, such as *The History of the Art of the Ancients* by Johann Joachim Winckelmann (1764), provided a popular source of ancient building forms for English and, later, American builders. The result were designs in the United States, often referred to as Federal or Adamesque, that had lower roof lines and more refined classical details than the earlier Georgian buildings. The first Harrison Gray Otis House in Boston (1796), designed by Charles Bulfinch, is a good example of the Federal style.

In 1785 Thomas Jefferson, the most notable gentleman architect in the United States, wrote that he was appalled with the current state of American architecture. He realized that architecture could serve as a major instrument for social and political reform, but he felt that no American building yet exemplified the greatness that he envisioned for the new nation. Jefferson rejected earlier sources of British colonial designs. Instead he favored ancient Roman architecture, particularly classical designs as interpreted through Palladio, as the style most appropriate for the new republic. While serving as minister to France in the 1780s, Jefferson visited Roman ruins in that country and experienced firsthand recent works of the French neoclassicists. His deep conviction regarding the importance of architecture to the education of young Americans is reflected in his design for the University of Virginia. Jefferson, who began contemplating the design for a university as early as 1805, wrote that he included the "choicest samples" of the orders of architecture for each front facade of the ten pavilions in his "Academic Village" as examples of good architecture for the students to study. The interconnected pavilions lined two sides of a rectangular open space. At one short end, Jefferson placed a multipurpose building modeled after the ancient Roman Pantheon. He left the other end open to symbolize both the infinite opportunities the new nation offered and the vast expanse of the country, recently doubled in size by the Louisiana Purchase.

While Jefferson favored Roman sources for American architecture, other designers, for example his friend architect Benjamin Latrobe, felt that Greek architecture was more appropriate for the United States. Archaeological investigations in the early nineteenth century sparked a great interest in Greek architecture. A major source for Greek-revival designers was James Stuart and Nicholas Revett's book, *The Antiquities of Athens* (1761), which included detailed drawings of classical Greek monuments. William Strickland, a former student of Latrobe's, designed the exterior of the Second Bank of the United States in Philadelphia (1818–1824) as a small, simplified version of the Parthenon, which was illustrated in Stuart and Revett's book. The Greek-revival style quickly grew in popularity and was used for buildings ranging from public institutions in the form of carefully detailed archaeological reproductions, such as Strickland's bank, to simple farmhouses that included only a few classical elements. While the style peaked between 1825 and 1835, Greek-revival buildings continued to be constructed for the next several decades throughout the heartland of the country.

Picturesque Movement. During the early nineteenth century the English picturesque movement, an aesthetic doctrine that focused on the Romantic qualities of the beautiful and the sublime, had spread from writing to landscape painting to garden design and finally to architecture. The earliest picturesque buildings were classical temple ruins, grottoes, and rustic Gothic cottages located in natural-looking, constructed gardens. As in England, architects in the United States began looking to other eras of the past for creative inspiration for their picturesque building designs. The result was a long series of fashionable historic styles during the nineteenth century, one superseding another.

Medieval Gothic churches, typically built of irregular forms and constructed over many years, served as design sources for picturesque architecture. Early practitioners of the picturesque movement favored Gothic designs, because they were more flexible than classical forms. The first Gothic-revival churches in America, however, were classical in composition but included identifiable Gothic details such as pinnacles, pointed windows, and buttresses. In England the symbolic meaning behind Gothic-revival designs became more profound when the influential writings of the English critic A. W. N. Pugin were disseminated. Pugin believed in a close connection between morality and Gothic architecture. He believed that those who worshipped and lived in Gothic designs would, as a result, be morally good people. Pugin's writings reached the United States in the 1840s and influenced such architects as Richard Upjohn, who produced religious buildings that he closely derived from medieval Gothic designs.

The use of the Gothic revival peaked on the East Coast in the 1840s and 1850s but remained popular through the 1880s in small Midwestern towns, owing in a large part to architectural books by American writers that promoted the use of picturesque variations of the style. Andrew Jackson Downing, a landscape architect and architectural critic, published several books, including *Cottage Residences* (1842), that expounded the benefits of the Gothic revival. Unlike Pugin, he did not advocate copying authentic Gothic designs, but instead favored a simplified form of the style for America. Following Downing's advice, many houses across the country were built of wood with token Gothic details. These dwellings, often referred to as Carpenter's Gothic, were characterized by the presence of vertical board-and-batten siding, decorative scrollwork, and pointed arch windows.

Downing also helped to popularize the Italianate style as part of the picturesque movement. He recommended villa designs based on vernacular architecture from the countryside of Tuscany, because he felt that the irregularity of their massings would result in extremely picturesque outlines. One of the most popular forms of the Italianate style in the United States consists of a three-part massing that includes a central tower with a porch on one side and a pedimented wing on the other. Additional characteristics included wide overhanging eaves with large double brackets, tall grouped windows with crown moldings, and restrained classical details, such as on the Morse-Libby House in Portland, Maine (Henry Austin, 1859). By the 1860s, Italianate had overshadowed Gothic-revival designs

to become the dominant architectural style for the upper class in the United States through the 1870s.

Industrial Revolution. Building activity in the United States slowed considerably after a depression in 1857 and did not pick up again until after the Civil War. America then went through a period of rapid economic growth and expansion, punctuated by depressions, as it began evolving from a rural, agrarian society to an urban, industrial one. The result was a need for larger, and more complex, specialized buildings. American architects continued to search for appropriate styles in which to design both traditional and new building types. Design influences from Europe, however, were still prominent as the succession of historic architectural styles continued.

During the second half of the nineteenth century, the discipline of architecture became more professionalized. Prior to this time, architects were typically either self-educated, like Thomas Jefferson, or had received training in Europe prior to immigrating, like Benjamin Latrobe. Beginning with Richard Morris Hunt in 1848, a growing number of American designers received formal architectural training either at the École des Beaux-Arts in Paris or, after 1860, through one of the early architectural programs offered in engineering departments at American universities. Hunt and other architects who had attended the École often set up educational studios, known as ateliers, in their offices to pass on their knowledge to young designers. In 1857 Hunt and twelve other architects founded the American Institute of Architects, to this day the major professional organization for architects in the United States.

The rise of industrialization led to the introduction of new building materials and techniques. The Crystal Palace in London (Joseph Paxton, 1851), built for the first international exposition, ushered in the industrial age for architecture. The iron and glass building was the first large structure to be constructed of prefabricated materials using modern assembly processes. Two years later a building of similar construction was built for the Exhibition of the Industry of All Nations held in New York.

Many contemporary critics did not consider these iron and glass buildings architecture, since their decorative qualities primarily derived from the exposed structure of the building. In contrast, the tall dome of the United States Capitol (Thomas Walter, 1855–1864), in which the iron structure was hidden by a shell of classical details, was viewed as a more acceptable architectural solution.

Although American designers integrated the use of new building processes and materials in their work, they continued to borrow from European sources. The French Second Empire style, characterized by its steep, double-sloping mansard roofs, and the English Victorian Gothic, with its multicolored Venetian voussoirs, were used for a variety of new building types in America, such as museums, train stations, and office buildings. Advances in manufacturing made possible the inclusion of a profusion of mass-produced details on building facades, such as on the Second Empire exterior of the State, War and Navy Building (now referred to as the Old Executive Office Building), in Washington, D.C. (Alfred B. Mullett, 1871–1875). Some architects during this period combined both contemporary English and French sources with additional decorative details to create distinctively American designs, such as architect Frank Furness did in his design for the Academy of Fine Arts in Philadelphia (1871–1876).

Still another nineteenth-century style was the Romanesque revival, popularized in the 1870s by Boston architect Henry Hobson Richardson. Heavily influenced by the French Romanesque buildings that he visited while attending the École des Beaux-Arts, Richardson felt Romanesque designs combined the best elements of both Roman and Gothic architecture. Not particularly interested in new materials, Richardson favored the use of heavy, rough-faced stone. Other characteristics of the Romanesque revival, as seen in his design for Trinity Church in Boston (1873–1877), include deep window openings, gabled roofs, towers, dormers, and round, arched entrances. The style was used by American architects for a wide range of building types, including libraries, railroad stations, and county courthouses.

The 1876 Centennial Exhibition in Philadelphia awoke Americans to their own past. Designers began to look at America's architectural heritage for inspiration, particularly at colonial British designs. While some colonial revival houses were accurate copies of earlier buildings, most borrowed only details from the past. Shingle-style designs, such as the Isaac Bell House in Newport, Rhode Island, by McKim, Mead and White (1882–1883), incorporated several American architectural traditions. From the colonial revival, designers borrowed lean-to additions, classical columns, and Palladian and casement windows; from earlier Victorian designs, they included wide porches, shingled surfaces, and asymmetrical forms; and from the Romanesque revival, they incorporated rounded arches and massive stone foundations.

The rise of an industrial society led to the growth of cities and a need for larger buildings. With the invention of the passenger elevator, the economics of tall buildings changed significantly, as upper floors became more desirable rental space. The introduction of a skeletal steel frame, meanwhile, allowed the construction of even taller buildings. These towering office buildings, soon referred to as skyscrapers, represented the first uniquely American architectural form. Their soaring forms symbolically reflected the growing importance of capitalism in American society, replacing church steeples as the dominant building feature of urban skylines.

The aesthetics of tall buildings were a major issue for architects. The first tall office buildings were designed like massive houses with oversize details. The Tribune Building in New York City by Richard Morris Hunt (1875), topped by a mansard roof several stories high, was a gigantic adaptation of the mansions he was concurrently designing for the Vanderbilts and other members of the American nouveau riche. As buildings grew to heights of over ten stories, however, the "big house" concept began to look more and more ridiculous. Economics, as well as taste, led to the eventual elimination of picturesque details in favor of flat roofs.

Much of the development of skyscrapers in the last decades of the nineteenth century took place

Biltmore, the Vanderbilt mansion near Asheville, North Carolina, designed to resemble a French chateau.

in Chicago after the city was devastated by fire in 1871. The need to rebuild provided great opportunities for architects and engineers to explore new ideas. The Home Insurance Building in Chicago by William LeBaron Jenney (1883–1885), usually considered the earliest skyscraper, was the first tall office building of fireproof construction to include a skeletal steel frame and a passenger elevator.

American architects continued to search for better aesthetic, as well as technical, solutions for skyscrapers. In 1896 Chicago architect Louis Sullivan published his design solution in the essay "The Tall Office Building Artistically Considered." He stated that the tall office building should be treated like a column, with a base, shaft, and capital. Sullivan's design for the Wainwright Building in St. Louis (1890) illustrates this approach. The building's two-story "base" housed retail spaces, its central "shaft" consisted of identical office floors, and the "capital," consisting of the top floor and cornice, provided space for mechanical systems.

Toward the end of the century, a new wave of classicism spread across the United States. Some of the earliest corporate architectural firms with Beaux-Arts-trained principals, such as McKim, Mead and White, favored the use of Roman and Italian Renaissance sources. A unified scheme of white, neoclassical, faux-marble pavilions dominated the fairgrounds of the 1893 World's Columbian Exposition. The popular success of the event contributed to the widespread use of classical forms for a growing number of stately residences and numerous new museums, libraries, and other civic buildings being constructed in emerging American cities. Even steel-framed skyscrapers, such as the Reliance Building in Chicago (D. H. Burnham & Co., 1894–1895), were clad in classical details. The adaptation of Roman monuments, however, often incorporated modern materials and forms, for example, Pennsylvania Station in New York City (McKim, Mead and White, 1902–1911). The classical design of the massive railway station, largely based on Bernini's colonnade at St. Peter's and the Roman Baths of Caracalla, complete with a vast, tepidarium-shaped waiting room, contrasted sharply with its iron and glass concourse.

The bold massing and intricate, colorful detailing of Louis Sullivan's Transportation Building at the 1893 Exposition contrasted dramatically with the neoclassical pavilions. Sullivan and other progressive Midwestern architects felt strongly that classical forms were inappropriate for modern America. Influenced by nature and the writings of the transcendentalists, Sullivan closely united function, structure, and artistic form in his attempt to create a democratic American architecture that captured the unique spirit of the place and age. Nature provided the basis for his system of organic ornamentation, which combined foliage and geometrical forms, and served as an integral part of his building designs.

During the second half of the nineteenth century, middle-class families, attempting to escape the filth of industrial cities, began building their homes in commuter suburbs, such as Riverside, Illinois (Frederick Law Olmsted and Calvert Vaux, 1868), on the outskirts of urban centers. Progressive designers, most prominently Frank Lloyd Wright in Chicago and the Greene brothers in California, followed Sullivan's lead and rejected the use of historical elements as they searched for more fitting architectural forms for American suburban homes. Influenced by Japanese art and architecture and the English Arts and Crafts movement, these architects reacted against the shoddy quality and poor design of many mass-produced products resulting from the Industrial Revolution. Like Sullivan, they sought instead to create buildings that exhibited a close integration of materials, structure, and function while respecting the natural surroundings. Wright and his Midwestern colleagues' solution was the prairie house, which included low-pitched or flat roofs with wide projecting overhangs, reflecting the horizontal lines of the prairie. Other characteristics, found, for example, in the Ward Willits House in Highland Park, Illinois (Wright, 1901–1902), included central chimneys, rows of windows, Roman brick or stucco siding with dark wood banding, a lack of applied ornament, and a close integration of furnishings and decorative objects.

The Twentieth Century. After World War I, progressive American designers searched for an architectural vocabulary expressive of a rapidly changing, modern age. Designers and critics became involved in heated debates concerning the definition of modern architecture and the future direction of building design. The result was the appearance of a wide range of concurrent architectural ideologies and building forms in the United States.

The 1925 Exposition Internationale des Arts Décoratifs et Industriels Modernes in Paris had a major impact on American architecture, particularly in the design of movie theaters and skyscrapers, such as the Chrysler Building in New York City (William Van Alen, 1926–1930). Art deco ornamentation consisted of a "machine-age aesthetic" with flattened, abstract designs reflecting the energy of the Jazz Age. The angled lines of art-deco detailing were soon replaced, however, by the curving forms of streamlining as the country moved from the roaring twenties into the Great Depression of the 1930s. Promoted by industrial designer Norman Bel Geddes, the aerodynamic teardrop forms and triple speed lines of streamlining, used on both moving and stationary objects, such as the Coca-Cola Bottling Plant in Los Angeles (Robert Derrah, 1936), reflected the increasing pace of life during the Automobile Age.

Many Americans, however, continued to favor historical building forms. The rise of Hollywood movies and the construction of extravagant mansions (complete with entire rooms extracted from European castles) by the extremely wealthy, such as William Randolph Hearst's San Simeon (Julia Morgan, 1919–1939), contributed to a desire among the less affluent to own their own palaces. In an attempt to meet this market, builders constructed neighborhoods of smaller residences with stagelike facades presenting miniature versions of English country houses, French chateaux, and Spanish haciendas. While the designs often came from plan services, such as the Architects' Small House Service Bureau, in some cases, complete houses were constructed from kits, such as those available from Sears, Roebuck and Company.

Historical forms also continued to be used for larger buildings. A new generation of classical civic buildings included simplified versions of neoclassical elements reduced to only a few symbolic, angular lines, such as on the Folger Shakespeare Library in Washington, D.C. (Paul Cret, 1928–1932). The winning design in the prominent Chicago Tribune skyscraper competition (Howells and Hood, 1922) was Gothic in character, complete with flying buttresses. Finnish architect Eliel Saarinen's second-place entry, which included more delicate Gothic details, consisted of a tall, step-pyramid form reflecting the aesthetic influence of the New York Building Zone Resolution of 1916. The ordinance required skyscrapers to include setbacks to ensure that adequate sunlight reached the streets. Other European entries in the competition, such as that by Walter Gropius and Adolf Meyer, foretold of the more austere, functional modern designs heralded a decade later in the influential International style show held at the Museum of Modern Art (MoMA) in 1932.

The MoMA show, curated by Henry-Russell Hitchcock and Philip Johnson, promoted a restrictive, formal definition of modern architecture primarily based on the flat, unadorned facades of avant-garde European buildings such as those designed by architects involved with the German Bauhaus. This definition, however, only superficially encompassed a small segment of the innovative architecture being produced in the United States at this time. In contrast, the Century of Progress International Exposition, held in Chicago the following two years, presented a more complete picture of the wide range of design ideologies in American architecture. The exposition's design commission based their definition of modern architecture on the use of new building materials and processes rather than a specific formal vocabulary. Most of the major fair pavilions were constructed out of recently introduced, manufactured building materials, such as Masonite and gypsum board—prefabricated products made possible by advances in scientific laboratories. The architects primarily relied on innovative uses of color and electrical lighting to create interest in their modern building designs.

Reacting to poor housing conditions and the growing congestion of urban centers in the 1920s and 1930s, architects began exploring new models for the design of modern cities. Early planned, self-sufficient communities, such as Radburn, New Jersey (begun in 1928), were based on the garden-city ideas of Ebenezer Howard. Frank Lloyd Wright, who believed that the telephone and car would make dense cities obsolete, created Broadacre City (1932–1950s), a model, decentralized, automobile community. Reflecting the American ideal of land ownership, every resident would be guaranteed an acre of land along with a car. Wright was able to realize his housing concept for Broadacre City in his Usonian House designs. These modest dwellings, designed specifically for the modern American family, were small, one-story houses built on a gridded concrete slab and had flat roofs and horizontal board-and-batten walls. Wright's Usonian concepts strongly influenced later residential designs, particularly in the unification of living and dining areas.

The production of modern prefabricated building materials allowed for the construction of millions of residences during the twentieth century. After World War II, great prosperity and the GI Bill created the need for the assembly-line construction of large suburban developments, such as William Levitt's Levittowns, begun in the mid-1940s, as young families, mimicking their idealized counterparts on television, desired their own pseudocolonial, detached, single-family homes. Progressive architects, however, continued to market modern alternatives to historic residential designs. For example, the publication *Arts and Architecture* sponsored a series of low-cost prototypes, known as the Case Study houses, to promote the use of new standardized materials and building techniques. Architect Charles Eames's own Case Study house in Pacific Palisades, California (1945–1949), incorporated a steel frame, industrial sashes, and prefabricated panels of a variety of colorful modern materials into its design.

Post–World War II was a period of tremendous commercial growth in America. The ideal corporate architectural image was the glass and steel box-shaped office tower. The German immigrant architect Ludwig Mies van der Rohe, a former head of the Bauhaus, had developed this architectural vocabulary for his universal design concept, which he based on the belief that building designs should be flexible enough to adapt easily to the rapidly changing functional needs of modern life. The result was that the designs of his tall office buildings, such as the Seagram Building in New York City, which he designed in collaboration with Philip Johnson (1954–1958), were almost identical in basic detailing to his other building designs, whether for an architecture school, an apartment complex, or a governmental building.

Despite the influence of European modernism on architectural fashion, the plurality of American architecture continued. In contrast to the plain, functional office buildings, other solutions for postwar architecture consisted of freer, more organic building forms. A number of architects explored the expressive abilities of modern building materials, in particular reinforced concrete. Eero Saarinen, for

example, created several innovative concrete shell designs, including a sculptural, birdlike form for the Trans World Airline Terminal in New York City (1956–1962).

Architect Louis Kahn was also interested in the expressive potential of modern building materials. In contrast to Mies's universal spaces, he attempted to express the specific function of a building in its form. Kahn's designs also took advantage of the aesthetic effects of natural lighting. This is clearly evident in his Kimball Art Museum in Fort Worth, Texas (1972), in which diffused daylight delicately illuminates the intimate gallery spaces.

For some architects and critics the 1972 implosion of the once-heralded Pruitt-Igoe public housing project in St. Louis (Minoru Yamasaki, 1958) symbolized the failure of modern architecture in America. The apartment complex was one of many austere, high-rise housing projects built as part of slum-clearance efforts after World War II. These massive, communal apartment blocks, which incorporated European modernist ideals in efficient living, never replaced the American dream of the suburban home. Cheap construction methods and a lack of a feeling of ownership among residents led to the rapid decay of these sterile buildings, which in many cases evolved into centers of urban crime.

Realizing the limitations of the "orthodox modern architecture of the white box," architects and critics began searching for alternatives to modernism in the 1960s. In their search, designers began exploring the meaning of symbolism in architecture. Robert Venturi, a student of Kahn's at the University of Pennsylvania, wrote *Complexity and Contradiction in Architecture* (1966), a criticism of modernism that served as the foundation of postmodern architecture. Venturi and other postmodernists, adapting ideas in contemporary literary theory, set out to exploit then-current ambiguity in the symbolic meanings of architectural forms. Their goal was to design architecture (such as the house Venturi designed for his mother in Chestnut Hill, Pennsylvania, 1964) that could both speak to an educated elite and appeal to the masses. Postmodern buildings often were referred to as "decorated sheds," as their facades typically had little to do with the building's structure or interior program. Postmodern architects, such as Michael Graves, drew from historical languages of architecture with little regard to substantive meaning. The attention-attracting facades of Graves's designs, including the Portland Public Service Building in Portland, Oregon (1980–1983), with its gigantic swags and ribbons, were little more than colorful billboards with only minimal relationship to interior function.

A second group of architects reacting to the limitations of modernism looked to the deconstructive literary theories of Jacques Derrida and started "deconstructing" architecture to create sculptural building forms. Beginning with his own small traditional house in Santa Monica, California, in 1978, Frank Gehry, one of the leaders of the deconstructivists, dissected building designs and then, using industrial materials, reassembled the fragments into animated formal compositions. A decade later an exhibition on deconstructive architecture at MoMA publicized this elite, intellectual movement to the public. Deconstructivism borrowed some of the basic vocabulary of the short-lived Russian constructivist movement earlier in the century, including the practice of creating tension in designs through the dynamic use of structural forms. While early deconstructive buildings favored sharp, angular forms, Gehry eventually went on to design exploding assemblages of visually softer, sculptural building components, such as in the design of the stainless-steel Whitney Art Museum in Minneapolis, Minnesota (1990–1994).

Although American architecture continued to encompass a variety of design ideologies, the change in Gehry's basic design forms was reflective of a general trend in American architecture toward the end of the twentieth century. Many designers moved away from the highly expressive gimmicks of postmodernism and severe forms of deconstructivism in favor of more organic and sensitive building designs. Both the neighborhood communities designed by New Urbanists, which recalled romantic visions of nineteenth-century small towns, and the individual designs created by practitioners of Critical Regionalism, which respect the local con-

ditions and traditions of the site, reflect this change. Architects including Antoine Predock, Will Bruder, and Steven Holl began exploring innovative uses of building materials, color, and lighting in their creation of sculptural building forms that respect the unique qualities of the site. Even modernist Richard Meier, who had made a career out of exploiting the potential of the basic white box, softened his design forms. Dramatically situated high above the sprawl of the city, the six large pavilions of his Getty Center in Los Angeles (1997) formed one of the most talked-about works of architecture at the end of the twentieth century. In designing the buildings, Meier went beyond carrying out an exercise of light and space to create an exquisite, sculptural setting for a remarkable collection of art.

American architecture, like other art forms, is still evolving as architects search for aesthetic solutions to new design challenges that meet changing social needs and, along the way, adopt new technological developments. As in the past, the growing complexity of American society will guarantee rich variety in future architectural designs in the United States.

[See also MALLS; NATIVE AMERICANS, *article on* NATIVE AMERICAN ARCHITECTURE AND DESIGN; WRIGHT, FRANK LLOYD; VENTURI, ROBERT; HISTORIC PRESERVATION; DESIGN, COMMERCIAL AND INDUSTRIAL.*]*

BIBLIOGRAPHY

Andrews, Wayne, *Architecture, Ambition, and Americans: A Social History of American Architecture,* rev. ed. (Free Press 1978).

Condit, Carl, *American Building: Materials and Techniques from the First Colonial Settlements to the Present* (Univ. of Chicago Press 1968).

De Long, David G., Helen Searing, and Robert A. M. Stern, eds., *American Architecture: Innovation and Tradition* (Rizzoli Intl. Pubns. 1986).

Gelernter, Mark, *A History of American Architecture: Buildings in Their Cultural and Technological Context* (Manchester Univ. Press 1999).

Handlin, David P., *American Architecture* (Thames & Hudson 1985).

Jordy, William H., *Progressive and Academic Ideals at the Turn of the Twentieth Century,* vol. 3 of *American Buildings and Their Architects* (Oxford 1972).

Jordy, William H., *The Impact of European Modernism in Mid-Twentieth-Century Architecture*, vol. 4 of *American Buildings and Their Architects* (Oxford 1972).

Le Blanc, Sydney, *Twentieth Century American Architecture: A Traveler's Guide to 200 Key Buildings* (Whitney Library of Design 1993).

Mumford, Lewis, *Roots of Contemporary American Architecture: A Series of Thirty-Seven Essays Dating from the Mid-Nineteenth Century to the Present* (Dover 1972).

Pierson, William H., Jr., *The Colonial and Neoclassical Styles*, vol. 1 of *American Buildings and Their Architects* (Oxford 1970).

Pierson, William H., Jr., *Technology and the Picturesque: The Corporate and Early Gothic Styles*, vol. 2 of *American Buildings and Their Architects* (Oxford 1978).

Roth, Leland M., *A Concise History of American Architecture* (Harper & Row 1979).

Scully, Vincent, *American Architecture and Urbanism*, rev. ed. (H. Holt 1988).

Whiffen, Marcus, *American Architecture since 1780: A Guide to the Styles*, rev. ed. (MIT Press 1992).

Wiseman, Carter, *Shaping a Nation: Twentieth-Century American Architecture and Its Makers* (Norton 1998).

LISA D. SCHRENK

Commercial Architecture

For nearly two hundred years, commercial architecture has been a key component in defining American towns, cities, and metropolitan areas. An increasingly prosperous, consumption-oriented society has led to a proliferation of specialized buildings in which much of the population works, shops, procures services, and engages in recreational pursuits. In their physical dimension, these buildings collectively are representative of the size and character of concentrated human settlement. Few components of the landscape are more reflective of Americans' interests and identity.

An architecture designed explicitly for commercial purposes barely existed at the time of the Revolutionary War. The distribution of goods centered on the public market, which was little more than a covered shed even in the few cities that were of substantial size. Most goods were made or processed and sold in buildings that also served as residences for the merchants and others. In communities of all sizes the prevailing scale and building form was domestic.

Following independence the introduction of free trade, accumulation of large amounts of capital, territorial expansion, immigration, and, soon, the rapid embrace of mechanized production led to an unprecedented pace of urban development. Established centers grew exponentially; new ones, farther west, arose; smaller communities, new and old, aspired to the same goal of city building. A commercial architecture evolved quickly to address the proliferation of emerging requirements: retail spaces, large and small, for food, dry goods, hardware, pharmaceuticals, furniture, jewelry, and dozens of other categories; offices for physicians, attorneys, jobbers, architects, manufacturers, journalists, and more; spaces for financial transactions; hotels of a grand sort and of more modest varieties; theaters, concert halls, and other gathering places for diversion; restaurants, tea rooms, bars, and additional places of refreshment; lofts for business activities of every kind.

The primary purpose of all such building was (and still is) to secure a profitable real estate investment irrespective of whether the project was designed for the specific needs of the occupant or whether it was built on speculation for multiple tenants. As the requirements for commercial building became ever more particularized, they were also subject to frequent change. Tenants could come and go, or they could find that the amount and kinds of space they needed changed over time. As a result, most retail, financial, and office buildings, as well as those constructed as lofts, were essentially neutral containers, vessels of space that allowed for maximum flexibility. Commercial architecture also was, and remains, closely tied to amenities and fashion and thus becomes quickly dated. Newness, in terms of both the latest equipment and appearances, has always been important in marketing commercial space to prime tenants and to the pubic alike. In the last decades of the twentieth century, buildings given the imprimatur of "historic" have also become marketable, but only after extensive, often conspicuous, rehabilitation that allows them to compete with new construction.

If practical considerations have dominated commercial architecture, aesthetics and other attributes that generate a strong symbolic presence have also figured prominently in examples that cater to a major portion of the consumer market. The retail store building must convey stylishness; the office block, prominence and respectability; the theater, fantasy; the hotel, luxury to secure a substantial trade. A building may also symbolize the achievements of the entrepreneur who creates it, the standing of the company that owns and occupies it, or the prominence of the community in which it rests. But unlike many examples of governmental and institutional architecture, the identity of most commercial buildings is collective rather than individual.

The emergence of commercial districts, distinct in function and appearance from other places, began with the rise of cities in the United States at the turn of the nineteenth century. Within a few decades not only had a large central precinct, downtown, formed in major cities, but that area was often divided into zones according to function (such as retail and finance), and also according to the class of patronage. The smaller the community, the less extensive and clearly demarcated the divisions; yet the basic structure was much the same. In its formative stages, the downtown could be somewhat crude and chaotic in both appearance and organization. The second generation of its growth, when most existing buildings were replaced and many new ones added, tended to bring a greater sense of order and purpose to the precinct. Even before it matured, the downtown became an indication of a community's growth, its progress, and its potential.

At first, commercial buildings tended to present restrained, even plain, exteriors owing to economic considerations and the prevailing tastes of the early nineteenth century. By the 1850s, however, exuberant ornamentation became the preferred mode, a trend that intensified over the next several decades. Between the 1890s and the 1930s, new approaches to design were taken to bring a greater sense of order and unity to commercial buildings, but the belief that product should embody the best of urban values remained constant.

The scale of many commercial buildings changed during the nineteenth and early twentieth centuries, too. Into the 1870s most commercial buildings extended from two to four stories, with another five to six stories common in the largest cities. Advancements in technology, such as the introduction of the passenger elevator, iron-, then steel-frame and reinforced-concrete construction, and a range of improvements in plumbing, artificial illumination, and ventilation, led to growth in the construction of multiple-storied buildings through the 1920s. Downtown began to be defined to a significant degree by its tall commercial buildings, or skyscrapers, which grew ever more pronounced in form and in the 1920s were rendered as soaring, sculptural towers. Escalating land values and the increasingly complex requirements of occupants led to larger floor areas as well. In the 1850s a building with one hundred feet (30 meters) or more of street frontage was the exception, but such dimensions were commonplace a half-century later.

Mass transportation systems had a profound impact on commercial development. The horsecar and especially the electric streetcar, as well as the elevated railroad and subway in the largest cities, not only enabled the expansion of downtown but also spawned galaxies of secondary and tertiary centers around key stations and transfer points. At first, such nucleations mainly catered to the basic needs of nearby residents. By the early twentieth century, however, some were assuming characteristics of downtown in miniature, affording a wide range of goods and services. This trend accelerated through the 1920s, when it began to be supplanted by patterns related to a new form of transportation, the motor vehicle. Between that decade and the mid-twentieth century, the impact of the automobile and the motor truck was sweeping and profound. Decentralization of commercial functions, especially in the retail and recreational spheres, became ever more prevalent as motorists sought to avoid the hassle of downtown congestion, preferring to have such outlets close to home. Ease of access by car and the availability of large parking lots became increasingly important determinants of location and design. In appearance, too, many

© NORMAN MCGRATH

The interior of the Netherland Plaza Hotel in Cincinnati, Ohio, is decorated in the art-deco style.

commercial buildings began to possess forms and motifs that were by design calculated to attract the fleeting glance of the motorist. The neighborhood business center along the trolley lines was being supplanted by the more diffuse and seemingly amorphous automobile strip.

In the late twentieth century the continued growth of outlying retail areas in many cases all but replaced commerce in the core of towns and cities. Although they are convenient, retail strips seldom are seen as significant definers of a community, nor are they otherwise assigned the symbolic importance once given to downtown.

Prior to World War II most business functions, save some medical and legal services, remained downtown; thereafter they too joined the decentralizing trend. By the late 1960s large new office centers began to appear in peripheral locations, on occasion extensions of, but often independent from, retail concentrations. These new workplaces have become competitors with the city center but have not begun to replace it. To the contrary, since the early 1960s many city centers have experienced an enormous increase in office building density, with skyscrapers several times the height and bulk of their pre-Depression forebears.

Many aspects of commercial building design have changed substantially since the 1930s. Reflecting the tenets of modernism, architecture has become abstract in both form and detail. Refinement of air conditioning has permitted many retail buildings to be without windows, save for display, to improve merchandising space, and many office towers to be almost entirely glazed to maximize views.

During the second half of the twentieth century, too, many commercial developments were comprehensively planned. The shopping center (from the modest neighborhood complex to the great regional mall) is among the most ubiquitous manifestations. Later, office parks became common as well. Yet the majority of work remains the product of numerous, often competing, initiatives. The resulting diffuse, multifaceted, and often visually cacophonous nature of contemporary commercial districts is perhaps no less indicative of values at the beginning of the twenty-first century than the concentrated, sometimes congested, prideful urban centers of earlier generations.

BIBLIOGRAPHY

Bluestone, Daniel, *Constructing Chicago* (Yale Univ. Press 1991).

Boyer, M. Christine, *Manhattan Manners: Architecture and Style, 1850–1900* (Rizzoli 1985).

Francaviglia, Richard V., *Main Street Revisited: Time, Space, and Image Building in Small-Town America* (Univ. of Iowa Press 1996).

Leach, William, *Land of Desire: Merchants, Power, and the Rise of a New American Culture* (Pantheon Bks. 1993).

Liebs, Chester, *Main Street to Miracle Mile: American Roadside Architecture,* reprint ed. (1985; Johns Hopkins Univ. Press 1995).

Longstreth, Richard, *City Center to Regional Mall: Architecture, the Automobile, and Retailing in Los Angeles, 1920–1950* (MIT Press 1997).

Longstreth, Richard, *The Drive-in, the Supermarket, and the Transformation of Commercial Space in Los Angeles, 1914–1941* (MIT Press 1999).

Longstreth, Richard, *The Buildings of Main Street: A Guide to American Commercial Architecture,* updated ed. (1987; AltaMira Press 2000).

Naylor, David, *American Picture Palaces: The Architecture of Fantasy,* reprint ed. (1981; Prentice-Hall 1991).

Rifkind, Carole, *Main Street: The Face of Urban America* (Harper 1977).

RICHARD LONGSTRETH

Domestic Architecture

Domestic architecture in the United States is associated with the American ideal of a nation of families, each in its own house. But in actuality there are no universal standards in the United States for houses, which comprise dwellings of many sorts. Free-standing houses, typically designated "single family houses," are very common. Multiple-family dwellings range from duplex, or "two family" houses, to triple-deckers or three-flat buildings, to larger apartment buildings with four, forty, or more domestic units within. While dwellings typically are identified by the number of "families" within, it would be more accurate to call groups of dwellers "households," since many households are not properly families; the term *households* includes everything from families of related people to a single person to groups of unrelated dwellers.

Dwellings of one, two, or three stories predominate in the United States, yet towers of apartments are commonplace in major urban centers for both rich and poor. Along with a wide range of sizes in the architecture of dwellings is a range of tenancy or ownership models. Some house dwellers own their houses and the land on which they sit; others rent land and houses from local or distant landlords; some units in multiple-dwelling buildings are rented, while others (condominiums, for example) are owned by their residents. In spite of this diversity, American tax codes favor house ownership over renting, and mortgage practices favor free-standing, single-family houses over other forms of dwellings.

© STEPHANIE MAZE/WOODFIN CAMP & ASSOCIATES

A Victorian-style house in Savannah, Georgia, showing the ornate woodwork and other decorative elements typical of such houses in the region.

In the formative years of the United States, the physical forms of domestic architecture depended on the period's current building technology, a region's available building materials, and an owner's resources, customs, and tastes. Early settlers in the New England region tended to build with wood, the most readily available material, and to use building practices brought to the New World from their towns of origin in England. Spanish colonists in the American Southwest and California built houses of adobe brick made from the earth of the region, and they created towns based on orthogonal gridded layouts influenced by Spanish colonial policies governing land distribution. Immigrants from Germany, Holland, or Sweden in the seventeenth and eighteenth centuries also used traditional methods of handling wood and brick materials and shaping domestic spaces that were familiar from their native countries.

The history of organizing the interior space within domestic architecture in the United States is one of separating and dividing. Sometimes spatial divisions are based on function, sometimes on hierarchy of meaning (parents' rooms more important than children's or parlors more important than kitchens), and divisions always relate to changing ideas about what should be private and what should be shared. Interior space in seventeenth-century houses commonly was divided according to the rank of uses and users. One-room houses, common in all settlement areas, separated undifferentiated storage and sleeping space in the attic from the more important social and housework activities of the house's one main room. Interiors of twentieth-century houses tended to be divided by functions such as bedrooms for sleeping, kitchens for cooking and eating, and sometimes dining rooms for dining. Nonetheless the privileges of rank persist in such spatial concepts as "master bedroom."

Also accompanying the history of domestic architecture are distinctions between what belongs inside a dwelling and what goes elsewhere, what is the responsibility of householders and what is to be undertaken by neighborhood, town, or commercial enterprise. For example, in many early settlements there was one central baking oven shared by the individual householders; later houses typically had their own baking ovens in fireplaces, cookstoves, and kitchen ranges. Bachelor apartment houses in New York City around 1900 did not have kitchens since it was expected that bachelors would have meals at their clubs or at friends' dinner tables; by the end of the twentieth century only hotel rooms or lodging houses lacked kitchen facilities. Early twentieth-century houses had automobile garages containing repair equipment and gasoline storage tanks before such facilities were relocated to commercial gas stations. Later, entertainments that once took place in movie theaters became commonplace in the average home. The shifting boundary that locates some activities within the home and others outside it is one key to observing the development of American houses.

A characteristic house of the seventeenth-century New England elite is the Parson Capen House (1683). Built of wood, its heavy timber frame is exposed on the interior. Two rooms on the ground floor (the hall and the parlor) served for all household work, reception, and sleeping. The parlor contained the better furniture, valuable household textiles or silver, and the parents' bed—the highest ranking people and objects. The hall was used for lower ranking activities such as cooking (in a great fireplace), spinning and other household work, and sleeping (probably on pallets on the floor). Two second-floor rooms, reached by a narrow boxed stair, served for storage of foods and household goods and for sleeping quarters for the rest of the household. Functions in each room were mixed; again, it was the rank of household members and activities that governed spatial divisions.

Inventories from the seventeenth century show that families used strikingly few pieces of furniture or other consumer goods, which were expensive to import. Household goods expanded in number and value by the middle of the eighteenth century, as some colonists prospered and elites began to display their wealth through a newly enriched architecture of houses. A well-to-do family in the mid-eighteenth-century Chesapeake region might have lived in a three-story brick house with additional rooms in wings on either side of the main house and separate service buildings behind; however, in the same period, average town or farm families of the region could afford only one- to four-room houses. Slave dwellings were smaller than those of modest farmers; a single room often housed several slaves. Sometimes plantation owners built freestanding houses for slaves but many slaves occupied leftover space on the upper floors of outbuildings.

Industrialization shifted the terms of house construction. New building technologies, national distribution of materials, broad access to architectural knowledge through print media, and dwellers' desires to fit into community standards contributed to less ethnically and regionally specific house forms in the nineteenth and twentieth centuries. Ethnic building traditions and customs were often in conflict with modern, efficient production and fashionable architectural styles. The physical forms of this era's dwellings and their spatial configurations tend to approximate national norms, and only in individual room uses and furnishing patterns do ethnic traditions survive.

A characteristic upper-middle-class house of the nineteenth century was divided into many rooms, each for its own purpose, and into several floors to create various zones of privacy. On the ground floor a social caller would wait in an entrance hall or reception room before being escorted by a servant to the social space of the house. One or two parlors, and perhaps also a music room, a library, or a sitting room, comprised the social array of rooms. Adjacent to these reception rooms was a formal dining room. Houses such as this were popularized by architectural pattern books including those by Calvert Vaux, Andrew Jackson Downing, and others. Middle-class builders found stylish ideas for both exterior ornament and interior layout in these pattern books, which propagated the same set of eclectic styles across the United States.

The several floors of many nineteenth-century houses divided dwellings into private and public areas and differentiated the social ranks of participants in domestic life (parents, children, servants). Kitchens, designed for servants, might be located at the back of houses or in basements or separate outbuildings. Cooks depended on stored foods kept in basements and attics, smokehouses, ice-houses, and root cellars. Servants also occupied the attic floors of houses where their bedrooms shared space with work rooms and cisterns; their beds were fitted in beside stored household goods. The second and third floors of such nineteenth-century houses were laid out in chambers, which contained family members' beds, clothes storage, and seating furniture for visiting family. These floors also held bathrooms with fixed plumbing, nurseries and children's playrooms, and sometimes billiard rooms or additional sitting rooms.

The organization of the interior space in houses depends on the availability of various technologies used for heating, lighting, food preparation, plumbing and water supply, and other aspects of housekeeping. Builders of seventeenth- and eighteenth-century houses in cooler climates arranged living spaces around a fire, and dwellers did not expect to be warm once they moved away from the direct heat source (stories of tea frozen in cups beyond the reach of the fireplace remind us of the difficulty of using all the space that even heated rooms might have offered). The development of central

151

The lifelong home of President Franklin D. Roosevelt in Hyde Park, New York, was built around 1800.

heating and the distribution of heat through pipes or ducts in the nineteenth century allowed more freedom both in the room layout of the dwelling and in the use of space in the rooms. Twentieth-century advances in air-conditioning allowed a similar flexibility in the use of rooms formerly overheated in summer. Climate-control technology makes houses less permeable to the outdoors; porches and verandas, once essential to most houses as shaded and airy gathering places in the warm weather, are no longer necessary. Beginning in the nineteenth century electric pumps brought water to indoor faucets and toilets, making the outdoor or back-porch privy and its mate, the chamber pot, obsolete.

Indoor lighting also underwent enormous changes both in technology and in expectation. The small seventeenth-century house had received minimal light from a few tiny windows, and since most work was done out-of-doors and most evening hours were spent sleeping, indoor lighting seemed less essential. Eighteenth-century houses had expanded window areas, vastly improving indoor illumination during the day; lightweight furniture of the period made it easy to move, say, a sewing table near a window to see. Candles used in sconces and chandeliers illuminated parties and dinners at night. As industrial cities in the early nineteenth century adopted street lighting and the night was reinterpreted as usable work time, lighting for houses improved. A variety of gaslight devices were used to illuminate house interiors, and by the end of the nineteenth century electric light appeared in public buildings, commercial establishments, and urban dwellings. Rural electrification made electric light available to most regions of the country by World War II. House designs incorporated even larger areas of glass in the picture windows of the postwar suburbs, even as better artificial illumination decreased dwellers' dependency on natural light. Smaller and more efficiently organized dwellings run by electricity, machine-like in their rationalized functionalism, were mass-marketed to a postwar generation. Regional and economic differences dissipated with industry's ability to produce and the homeowner's desire to have a modern set of utilities and tools in the dwelling.

Technologies that improved the speed and quality of wood-milling and the production of cast- and wrought-iron elements led to industrially produced prefabricated houses. Starting in the mid-nineteenth century, prefab houses were available for missionaries to take with them into less developed areas and for prospectors to load aboard ships bound for the California gold rush. At the turn of the twentieth century, numerous companies sold precut lumber so that frugal customers could assemble their own houses. Sears, Roebuck and Company sold hundreds of small- to-medium-size houses that were erected all over the United States.

Following World War II an enormous increase in families inspired a building boom. Small, efficient houses were produced by the thousands by commercial developers such as the Levitt Brothers on the East Coast and the Eichler firm in California. Small houses condensed the elaborate nineteenth-century array of rooms into just a few, containing both costs and the needs of the nuclear family whether their exterior styles were traditional or modernist. A fully equipped kitchen with modern electric and gas appliances included an eating area, a living room satisfied needs for social space, and a bedroom for the boy children, one for the girl children, and one for the parents allowed families with minimum resources to become house owners. Architects such as Frank Lloyd Wright shifted their attention from servant-run, large houses to small, efficient, servantless ones in the 1930s and 1940s. Wright's Usonian houses merged kitchen, dining, and living spaces into modern flowing space, using clean, modern geometries and natural materials.

A characteristic larger house of the affluent middle class in the United States at the beginning of the twenty-first century might include the following: a large, ground-floor, eat-in kitchen stocked with modern appliances (refrigerator and freezer, oven and cooktop, microwave oven, sink, garbage disposal, and dishwasher). This kitchen is often linked to an open, informal dining and socializing area called the family room or great room. Most houses contain a living room for entertaining (in some houses this space is very small, since most active entertaining happens informally in kitchens and family rooms). A formal dining room may be eliminated from some house plans since meals are often served in the kitchen. In addition, each child in the family has a separate bedroom, and in more expensive houses every bedroom has its own bathroom. Bedrooms usually are on the second floor in two-floor houses. A master bedroom suite often includes a large bathroom, a dressing room, and perhaps a small sitting room for reading or watching television. Sometimes the master bedroom is located at the opposite end of the house from the children's rooms for privacy. Ground-floor or basement laundry and utility rooms are essential for the washing machine and clothes dryer, the hot water tank, and the furnace, although a popular trend located the washer and dryer on the bedroom level where dirty clothes could go directly from body to wash.

Although responsibility for producing dwellings in the United States has never been viewed as the state's domain, in periods of extreme need, the government has sometimes stepped in to assist. In the 1930s, 1950s, 1960s, and 1970s, federal and state housing initiatives produced multiple-family dwellings and in the 1990s some single-family dwelling units for the poor. These units incorporated all the expected services that middle- and upper-class dwellings had, such as electricity, hot and cold running water, central heating, modern kitchen appliances and bathrooms, and separate rooms for cooking, socializing, and sleeping. Such spatial variety supported by such modern technology had been within reach only of the wealthy a mere half-century earlier.

BIBLIOGRAPHY

Cromley, Elizabeth, *Alone Together: A History of New York's Early Apartments* (Cornell Univ. Press 1990).

Franck, Karen, and Sherry Ahrentsen, *New Households, New Housing* (Van Nostrand Reinhold 1991).

Groth, Paul, *Living Downtown: The History of Residential Hotels in the United States* (Univ. of Calif. Press 1994).

Lanier, Gabrielle, and Bernard Herman, *Everyday Architecture of the Mid-Atlantic: Looking at Buildings and Landscapes* (Johns Hopkins Univ. Press 1997).

Upton, Dell, and John Vlach, *Common Places: Readings in American Vernacular Architecture* (Univ. of Ga. Press 1986).

Wright, Gwendolyn, *Building the Dream: A Social History of Housing in America* (Pantheon Bks. 1981).

ELIZABETH C. CROMLEY

Public Buildings

America is a vast country with a decentralized government, hence it is not surprising that its public buildings number in the thousands and are found throughout the land. With one federal government, fifty state governments, and more than eighty thousand local and tribal governments, the number and variety of governmental structures are enormous. They include capitols, courthouses, county buildings, city halls, post offices, fire stations, airport terminals, customs houses, public schools, public libraries, health clinics, penitentiaries, and museums. In addition are many thousands of administrative office buildings occupied by employees at all levels of government, in all sizable communities.

The earliest noteworthy American public buildings were the colonial capitols on the eastern seaboard. These were a combination of "government house" in the British colonial tradition and a set of rooms in which colonial assemblies could gather. A prime example is the Virginia Capitol in Williamsburg, originally constructed in 1701–1705 and the first building in America to bear the name *capitoll*. This term was inspired by Capitoline Hill in ancient Rome and given also to the Congress House in Washington by Secretary of State Thomas Jefferson, who wished to identify the new nation with the Roman republic. In New England colonial headquarters were called colony houses or state houses, which in several instances also provided space for courts and local government. Examples still extant are Newport Colony House in Rhode Island and the Old State House in Boston. Local courts also had their own structures, such as the elegant Hanover County Courthouse north of Richmond, Virginia.

In the period between the American Revolution and the Civil War many new public buildings were built in the capital cities and other urban areas. In the newly formed District of Columbia, the President's House, modeled after an aristocratic mansion rather than monarchical palace, was burned by the British in 1814, as were the partially built Capitol and first Treasury and War Offices. After defeating the British at New Orleans, the national government expressed its new sense of confidence by reconstructing these buildings and erecting new ones, including Robert Mills's massive Greek Revival–style Treasury. Meanwhile several new state capitols were erected that also resembled the temples of antiquity, becoming objects of popular amazement in their frontier locations. As local government jurisdictions grew they too needed new quarters. City Hall in New York City dates from 1811 and is the oldest U.S. municipal building still in use. It is an ornate French Renaissance composition, but small compared to the great town halls of Europe.

The period following the Civil War was a heyday for construction of elaborate, large-scale governmental buildings. The U.S. Capitol was largely complete a few years after the war. Construction of a majority of state capitols ended between 1869 and 1917. Ornate city halls on a European scale were built during the Gilded Age in Baltimore, Cincinnati, Cleveland, Louisville, Milwaukee, Minneapolis, Newark, Oakland, Philadelphia, Pittsburgh, Providence, St. Louis, and San Francisco. Other no-

The San Francisco Museum of Modern Art, designed by Swiss architect Mario Botta, opened in 1995.

table structures erected in this era are the Boston Public Library; New York Customs House; and the State, War and Navy Building in Washington. The latter two Second Empire edifices, with their imposing mansard roofs and elaborately carved facades, reflected the country's new industrial might and international status.

The vast majority of public buildings in use in the United States were built later in the twentieth century. Handsome public libraries were erected in numerous cities and towns owing to the philanthropy of Andrew Carnegie. During the New Deal many post offices and state and local structures were constructed as part of federal works programs. After World War II the International Style influenced much public architecture, yielding windowed boxes indistinguishable from private-sector office buildings. Yet, despite generally conservative government attitudes toward architecture, examples of exciting work appeared in the public sector, such as art deco city halls in Buffalo and St. Paul, Frank Lloyd Wright's Marin County Courthouse, Bertram Grosvenor Goodhue's Nebraska State Capitol, Eero Saarinen's Dulles International Airport, and I. M. Pei's East Wing of the National Gallery of Art.

Stylistically American public buildings do not differ greatly from what was popular at the time in Europe and the British Isles, for example, Georgian, Greek Revival, Second Empire, Richardsonian Romanesque, Beaux Arts, classical revival, art deco, international, and, to some extent, postmodern. An enduring theme until late in the twentieth century was the classical temple portico, with its line of columns topped by triangular pediment and reached by massive stairs. This assemblage, the most important architectural symbol of authority in the Western world, became integral to the American image of government.

Innovations occurred in the New World, however. One was to add a rounded dome (taken from the Renaissance church) to the top of a parliament house laid out in cruciform shape, thus creating the capitol building type. This and the skyscraper are American architectural inventions that then spread around the world. Another innovation was to create regional styles to fit the distinctive cultures of the far corners of the country, most notably Native American–inspired forms in the Southwest and Pacific Islander concepts in Hawaii.

When considering the relationship of these buildings to the democratic American society an ambivalent picture emerges. On the one hand, large-scale public buildings with their temple fronts, elaborate facades, and high domes can provoke awe. They add a European flavor to American cityscapes, underscoring the presence of governmental authority and tying that authority to an ancient heritage of legitimacy. Particularly good examples of such visual impact are the Philadelphia City Hall, San Francisco City Hall, Connecticut and Illinois state capitols, and Federal Triangle in Washington, D.C.

On the other hand, in contrast to this seemingly antidemocratic, authoritarian impulse is the easy approachability of many U.S. public buildings. Most of the courthouses, city halls, and post offices that grace the public squares of America do not so much alienate as provide an orienting landmark and give the community an identity. In addition to being large and richly adorned, the national and state capitols constitute objects of pride that attract countless visitors. The fact that most American public buildings are surrounded by lawns or city sidewalks, rather than formal malls or complexes of ministry buildings, further diminishes their ability to intimidate. Because of safety concerns federal office buildings are often heavily guarded and protected by street barriers, while state and local public buildings for the most part remain open, protected by invisible television cameras rather than overt security measures.

BIBLIOGRAPHY

Craig, Lois A., et al., *The Federal Presence: Architecture, Politics, and Symbols in United States Government Building* (MIT Press 1978).

Goodsell, Charles T., *The American Statehouse: Interpreting Democracy's Temples* (Univ. Press of Kans. 2000).

Hitchcock, Henry-Russell, and William Seale, *Temples of Democracy: The State Capitols of the U.S.A.* (Harcourt 1976).

Lebovich, William L., *America's City Halls* (Preservation Press 1984).

Pevsner, Nikolaus, *A History of Building Types* (Princeton Univ. Press 1976).

CHARLES T. GOODSELL

Religious Architecture

Religious architecture in its structure and form visually manifests a religious community's understanding of the divine-human relationship. This relationship between the spatial environment and the definition of God becomes apparent in those religious traditions such as High Church Episcopalianism, exemplified in the Cathedral Church of St. Peter and St. Paul (National Cathedral) in Washington, D.C., in which a transcendent God is central and therefore the religious edifice is monumental with an emphasis on verticality, signifying the distance between the God above and the humans below. By contrast, for such religious traditions as

Quakerism, in which an immanent concept of God was paramount, the religious building (the meetinghouse) had a low ceiling with an emphasis on horizontality, symbolizing the mutuality between the presence of God and of humans. Unique to the American experience are the myriad ways in which religious architecture reflected the national origins of various groups of settlers and immigrants and ultimately the development of a clearly "American" architecture. Further, the American commitment to the separation of church and state and the development of a civil religion have colored the evolution of religious architectural spaces in American cultural history.

Colonial architecture, just like colonial society, emphasized the importance of religion and thereby of the church building. Beyond certain common denominators in style and intent, in New England and in the South the emerging styles of colonial ecclesiastical architecture bespoke both the characteristics of the varied settlers and the local climates, thereby beginning the development of what would become identifiable regional styles within the new nation's first centuries. For example, Spanish colonial mission architecture in the American Southwest was as dependent on the availability of adobe and the warm arid climate of the region as it was on the baroque spirituality of the Roman Catholic missionaries. Following this architectural mode of simple exteriors and detailed interiors were San Esteban Del Rey Mission Church in Acoma, New Mexico (1629), and San Miguel Mission Church in Santa Fe (1670). Meanwhile, St. Luke's Church (1632–1638) in Smithfield, Virginia, combines an early-Gothic brick exterior with the simple interior of an English parish church, characterizing colonial religious architecture in the South. The earlier and simpler Romanesque-style building, creating a functional interior space for religious and secular activities, characterized the New England meetinghouse design of religious edifices such as the Old Ship Meeting House (1681) in Hingham, Massachusetts.

The early-eighteenth-century diversity of national styles, represented by King's Chapel in Boston, Touro Synagogue in Rhode Island, Mission Concepcion and Mission San José in San Antonio, and St. Paul's Chapel in New York City, surrendered to the development of American revolutionary values in the eighteenth century. These later architectural forms reflected the evolution of nationalist attitudes and the contrast between Roman Catholic and Protestant religious values as seen in the diversity of architectural styles. New England religious architecture emerged from the designs of the British architect Christopher Wren. These rectangularly shaped churches, ornamented with pilasters and Palladian windows, such as St. Paul's Church (1707) in Wickford, Rhode Island, contrasted with the New England meetinghouse style of Old North Church and St. Stephen's Church in Boston. These functional, auditory spaces featured white interiors, clear glass windows, high pulpits, and modestly sized altars in contrast to the more liturgically ornate architecture of Roman Catholicism in the late eighteenth and early nineteenth century found in the Cathedral of Baltimore and the San Francisco de Asis Church in Ranchos de Taos, New Mexico.

Early-nineteenth-century religious controversies led to the search for an American architecture that would witness the diverging views of worship. Mainstream Protestantism had striven for a classicism whose internal simplicity and spaciousness visually emphasized the theological realities of preaching and hearing, just as the increasing height of the exterior steeple became the architectural focus and symbol for "heaven," as found in Christ Church in Cambridge, Massachusetts, and Christ Church and Burton Parish in, respectively, Alexandria and Williamsburg, Virginia. These forms gave way in the early nineteenth century to the temporary or seasonal structures required by the emerging religious values of the "American" camp meetings and evangelical gatherings.

The emergence of spiritual domesticity and the theology of Christian nurture in the antebellum period, combined with the religio-cultural concept of the home as a "religious center," was the beginning of American Gothic religious architecture and of the identification of "America" with Protestantism rather than with the Roman Catholicism of the

Southwest or of the non-English immigrants. Thus the moral spirit of the nation combined with artistic competence to dictate architectural styles and to recognize the direct connection between the fabric of society and identifiable architectural styles. The simple architectural interiors and Gothic exteriors of antebellum ecclesiastical architecture signified the renewed interest in the centrality of the Eucharist and its liturgical mysteries evidenced by the influence of the Oxford Movement and the Camden Ecclesiological Society.

The Great Age of American cathedrals paralleled the age of Reconstruction and the ensuing era of the Social Gospel, Protestant liberalism, and the waves of immigration in the later nineteenth century. This architectural trend toward the high-Gothic style emerged with a new interest in liturgical mystery and awe, symbolizing the movement away from the verbal tradition central to earlier forms of American Protestantism. This was the era during which the detailed exterior and elegant interiors of St. Patrick's Cathedral and the Cathedral of St. John the Divine, located in New York City, and the Basilica of the National Shrine of the Immaculate Conception and the National Cathedral, located in Washington, D.C., simultaneously sought to reaffirm the values of both American religion and American cultural identity.

Stylistic changes in twentieth-century religious architecture in America continued to reflect both immigrant influences and transformations in religious values. The American modernist movements in the arts paralleled the emergence of liberal Christian theologies and the neoorthodoxy of the post–World War I ethos. Frank Lloyd Wright's architectural innovations symbolize this time and are manifested in his design for the Annunciation Greek Orthodox Church in Wauwatosa, Wisconsin. The growing globalization of cultural and religious values that may be said to begin with the post–World War II and Korean War periods clearly comes into its own in the post–Vietnam War global culture. Ecumenical chapels such as the Rothko Chapel in Houston, Texas, originally designed by Philip Johnson and completed by Howard Barnstone and Eugene Aubry, and the Erol Beker Chapel of the Good Shepherd, designed by Louise Nevelson, in New York City reflect these changing architectural, religious, and cultural milieus, as affirmation of functionality in liturgical space and of individuality in religious experience characterizing late-twentieth-century American religious architecture.

BIBLIOGRAPHY

Dillenberger, John, *The Visual Arts and Christianity in America: From the Colonial Period to the Present* (Crossroad 1989).

Kennedy, Roger G., *American Churches* (Stewart, Tabori & Chang 1982).

Taylor, Joshua C., *America as Art* (Smithsonian Inst. Press 1976).

DIANE APOSTOLOS-CAPPADONA

Urban Architecture

Urban architecture in the United States is informed by the social, economic, and political conditions that constitute the process of urbanization. As such, urban architecture can express in physical form particular socioeconomic conditions as well as serve as a forum where competing discourses about local or national identity occur. In this process regional variation often exists within larger, national movements (in terms of style, patronage, and building cycles, for instance). Architecture fundamentally shapes space; although everyday encounters with architecture may make it seem as if it is simply the end result of market demands and personal desires (or conversely, an esoteric and abstract medium of artistic expression), it is a process that involves a host of social networks. Furthermore, architecture is not confined solely to the era of its production; while political and ideological regimes may change, the buildings and cityscapes associated with them often remain.

The forms of the architecture of a particular city are dependent on a number of interrelated factors including, but not limited to, the age of the city; its mix of races, classes, and ethnicities (and the balance of power among them); the (often changing) primary mode of economic organization; restrictive climatic and geographical conditions; and the

An interior view of St. Patrick's Cathedral in New York City.

historical prevalence of large-scale disasters (fires, earthquakes, floods) that provide opportunities for citywide redevelopment. In addition to these influences, the rise and fall of various architectural styles and trends plays a central role in defining the character of a city's public and private buildings. Needless to say, style and form can also be influenced by technological innovations, which provide new methods for the construction of buildings as well as stimulate the economic activity required to fund new construction.

In the United States modern cities largely came into existence after the Civil War with the rise of industrialization. Before then most American cities were centers of mercantile activity, and most of the population lived in rural areas. The urban architecture in such centers of mercantile activity as Boston, Philadelphia, and New York was usually in one of many revival styles, for example, Greek or Gothic. Noteworthy and influential early urban structures include Benjamin Henry Latrobe's Bank of Pennsylvania in Philadelphia (1798–1800) and

Baltimore Cathedral in Maryland (1804–1821). Latrobe, who at one time was the supervising architect on the construction of the U.S. Capitol, created designs in a neoclassical style, with particular reference to Roman temples. At the same time, other architects in the United States turned to another form of neoclassical architecture, Greek Revival. One reason for its lasting influence and popularity is that one of its earliest practitioners was Thomas Jefferson. His Virginia State Capitol in Richmond (1785–1789), designed with Charles-Louis Clerisseau, is an early example of the Greek Revival form that gained fuller and more complete expression in such works as William Strickland's Second National Bank of the United States in Philadelphia, Pennsylvania (1818–1824); in Boston, Massachusetts, the Sears house (1816) and Quincy Market (1825–1826), both by Alexander Parris; and Alexander Jackson Davis's La Grange Terrace, or Colonnade Row, in New York City (1830–1833). Symbolically, Greek Revival architecture appealed to the political and economic elite for its ability to communicate an image of American society as the rightful heir to an older, uncorrupted classical tradition. The style was suggestive of stability (these buildings were in general built of stone), democracy (the political tradition the United States ostensibly inherited from the Greeks), and the Enlightenment (whose rational, scientific thought is reflected in the geometry of the Greek Revival style). In an obvious counterpoint, the style did not address contemporary and divisive political or social issues such as slavery, conflicts with Native Americans, or the disenfranchisement of women and the poor.

By the 1890s the expansion of industrialization had propelled urban growth to previously unimagined levels. Two of the more significant developments of this period were the rise of the City Beautiful movement and the coalescence of the Chicago school of architecture. Both are expressive of a search for order; the latter received much of its impetus from technological developments and capital accumulation, while the former was an attempt by city leaders to limit the rising influence of new immigrant communities and to quell threats of urban disorder.

The rise of the Chicago school was preceded by (between the late 1850s and the late 1880s) the inventions of the passenger elevator, reliable incandescent lighting, the telephone, mimeograph, and typewriter. In addition the widespread availability of affordable steel had a profound influence on the changing form of commercial urban architecture. These innovations, combined with a growing speculative real estate market based on the sale or rent of office and commercial space and rising land values, helped propel the development of the skyscraper. William Le Baron Jenney's Home Insurance Building in Chicago, Illinois (1883–1885), is generally credited with being the first skyscraper, although it is only ten stories high. It was, however, the Reliance Building in Chicago (1889–1891; 1894–1895), designed by Daniel Burnham and John Wellborn Root, that developed an ordered exterior design expressive of the interior steel frame that held the building up. With its "Chicago" windows (one wide fixed pane with double hung sashes on either side), projecting bays, and strong vertical lines, the Reliance Building established many of the design characteristics associated with the Chicago school. Another important structure from this period is Louis Sullivan and Dankmar Adler's Wainwright Building in St. Louis, Missouri (1890–1891). The Wainwright incorporates most of the elements of structure and form associated with the modern skyscraper and is an example of Sullivan's belief that a well-designed building should allow one to read from the appearance (or form) of the building its purpose (or function). This theory, and its attendant maxim "form follows function," would come to dominate much of the commercial and public architecture of the twentieth century.

Where the Chicago school crafted order through architectonic means, the City Beautiful movement sought to restore a lost harmonious social order by establishing a neobaroque aesthetic that would dominate not only the design of individual buildings, but also the layout of cities as a whole. The historical roots of the movement were the construction of the Vienna Ringstrasse and Georges-Eugène Haussmann's reorganization of Paris for Napoleon III. The designs of the City Beautiful movement conspicuously embraced hierarchies of race and class, often ignoring the pressing need for housing, schools, and sanitation. Instead, in such prototypical City Beautiful projects as Daniel Burnham's 1909 Plan for Chicago, an ideal city aesthetic existed hand in hand with an imagined future for Chicago in which immigrant machine politics had been expelled and proper Anglo-Saxon order restored.

Urban construction in the twentieth century was slowed or halted at times owing to restrictions placed on new building by the materials rationing put into effect during World Wars I and II and by that great shudder of capitalism, the Depression. This led to a number of periods during which urban architecture was built at a breathtaking pace. Between 1925 and the stock market crash of 1929 (Black Monday), for instance, office space in New York City increased by ninety-two percent. The construction boom of those four years included the start of the Empire State Building (1929–1931), designed by Richard Shreve, Thomas Lamb, and Arthur Harmon; the Chrysler Building (1926–1930), designed by William Van Alen; and Rockefeller Center (1927–1935), designed by Raymond Hood and Associates, among others. A similar boom in urban construction occurred through the late 1940s and 1950s, when corporations were expanding rapidly and the federal government underwrote a number of sizable public housing projects.

In addition to being significant because of the rate of construction, the late 1920s and immediate post–World War II era were also the years when modernism (and particularly what is often called the "International Style") came to prominence in the United States. Prior to the late 1920s, architect Raymond Hood employed a historical style for his winning entry for the Chicago Tribune Tower competition; by 1929, however, as evidenced by his McGraw-Hill Building (1929–1930) and Daily News Building (1930) in New York City, Hood had turned decidedly toward modernism. Clients also were turning toward modernism: commissions that had in the past been awarded to architects working in historical styles were now being offered to architects whose designs were deeply indebted to the formal (if not social) aspects of modernism pio-

COURTESY, GEORGE EASTMAN HOUSE

A worker helps to construct the Empire State Building.

neered by such European architects as Walter Gropius and Ludwig Mies van der Rohe. The Philadelphia Savings Fund Society building in Philadelphia (1929–1932), designed by George Howe and William Lescaze, illustrates this trend, since both architect and client had, until 1929, been relatively conservative in their aesthetic preferences.

After World War II modernist architecture continued to dramatically reshape the landscape of most cities in the United States. Some well-known examples of urban corporate architecture from this period include Pietro Belluschi's Equitable Savings and Loan Association Building in Portland, Oregon (1944–1948); Skidmore, Owings and Merrill's Lever House in New York City (1951–1952); and Mies van der Rohe's Seagram Tower in New York City (1954–1958). By the late 1960s and early 1970s, deindustrialization and the flight from urban centers of the white middle class (both private and corporate) ravaged the economic and social base of cities across the nation. Resentment grew toward the modernist planning and architecture epitomized (in the minds of some) by such public housing complexes as Pruitt-Igoe in St. Louis, Missouri (1950–1954), designed by Minoru Yamasaki. Many contemporary critics attacked Pruitt-Igoe, and modernist architecture and planning in general, as cold and im-

© MASIMO MASTRORILLO/THE STOCK MARKET

The Sears Tower, the world's tallest skyscraper from 1974 to 1996, rises high above the Chicago skyline.

personal. They portrayed the designs of these complexes as an alienating architectural style that failed to address the dramatic problems facing the American city. Recent scholarly reevaluations of developments such as Pruitt-Igoe, however, suggest that long-standing and deeply entrenched economic and racial divisions affected the success or failure of public housing to a far greater degree than style ever did. Taking the demolition of Pruitt-Igoe in 1972 as a rallying point of sorts, postmodern architecture began to appear on the urban scene in the late 1970s. Its arrival had been prefigured by Robert Venturi's Guild House in Philadelphia (1960–1965), and the style (if postmodernism can be said to have a singular one) gained popularity with the construction of works such as Philip Johnson's American Telephone and Telegraph Building in New York City (1979); Michael Graves's Portland Building in Oregon (1980–1983); and Charles Moore's Piazza d'Italia in New Orleans, Louisiana (1975–1979).

Forces beyond aesthetics shape urban architecture in the United States. The virulent and active legacy of residential segregation, the razing of poor and minority neighborhoods in the name of urban renewal and highway development, and the relent-

less pressure of the speculative real estate market (particularly in the form of gentrification) all play a part in shaping American cities.

BIBLIOGRAPHY

Davis, Mike, *City of Quartz: Excavating the Future in Los Angeles* (Verso 1990).

Hall, Peter, *Cities of Tomorrow: An Intellectual History of Urban Planning and Design in the Twentieth Century* (Blackwell 1996).

Hayden, Dolores, *Redesigning the American Dream: The Future of Housing, Work, and Family Life* (Norton 1984).

Upton, Dell, *Architecture in the United States* (Oxford 1998).

The WPA Guide to New York City: The Federal Writers Project Guide to 1930s New York (Pantheon Bks. 1982).

BENJAMIN FLOWERS

Vernacular Architecture

According to architect Amos Rapoport ninety-five percent of the world's structures qualify as examples of *vernacular* buildings, if what is understood by the term are those structures that are not designed by professional architects. Even in the most technologically advanced nations, somewhere between eighty and ninety percent of all buildings still go up without the benefit of an architect's design or an engineer's specification. Because the term *architecture,* like the word *art,* generally designates a small set of exceptional buildings that are usually monumental in size and lavish in their decoration, attempts to connect architecture with the notion of the vernacular have proved problematic. The major textbooks for architectural history brim with images of grand buildings—palaces, cathedrals, and other public buildings along with a generous selection of photographs of the homes of the rich and famous. Vernacular structures, looking like the wallflowers at the dance of civilization, are presented chiefly in negative terms as the collective foil to works of architecture. They are seen either as early forms from the distant past or as the crude and unsophisticated structures in preindustrialized nations. Vernacular buildings are frequently referred to as non–high style, non-academic, not designed by professional architects, unsophisticated, and mere

A pioneer family in a sod house near Cobury, Nebraska, in 1887.

building. This emphasis on the negative reveals a strategy aimed at entrenching a canon of elite taste that does little to clarify the definition of the vernacular.

While one can point to several pioneering studies of American vernacular buildings that were published during the first decades of the twentieth century, the most important work was undertaken in the 1970s. These efforts, inspired to a great extent by the breakthrough scholarship of geographer Fred B. Kniffen, tended to focus chiefly on recording old buildings, developing accurate typologies and chronologies, and identifying general patterns of use. But this body of scholarship, when viewed collectively, still provided a less-than-satisfying definition. One could easily have concluded that the study of American vernacular architecture was merely an

antiquarian pursuit for those interested mainly in the interpretation of old farmhouses.

Later scholarship, which focused on challenging received hierarchical assumptions, offers a sweeping revisionist critique that reframes the interpretation of built form. Students of vernacular architecture in the United States are just as inclined to study high-style buildings designed by professional architects as they are to consider log cabins or fast-food restaurants. Assuming that every building is both culturally dynamic and historically situated, students are as concerned with design processes as they are with the resulting structures. Students of vernacular architecture probe the formation of a sense of place as they document the key stages in the creation of a building. They are interested in how a building might express both a collective cultural statement and the desires of a particular individual. An inclusive theory of design, construction, and reception is evolving in which all contributions to a given environment are fully credited. Such an approach significantly directs attention toward the creative interactions that regularly occur across canonized class lines. Rejecting the notion that vernacular buildings are only of marginal importance, students of vernacular architecture routinely examine settings wherein it can be readily demonstrated that information moves upward just as often as it trickles down.

Research conducted in the last few decades of the twentieth century revised perceptions of everyday life in America. Investigations of the multicultural origins of the American scene have shown, for example, that there is no single or representative American house. Rather, each immigrant group had its own perceptions regarding an optimal home and they built ethnically marked structures in their communities. Over time some of these ethnic buildings were transformed into symbols of regional identity. The so-called Creole house of Louisiana can be traced back not merely to France but to Normandy, the precise homeland of many Cajun families. Similarly the landscape of southeastern Pennsylvania contains numerous examples of a type of German house prominent in the Rhine valley called an *earnhaus*. Featuring an irregular three-room floor plan and an off-center fireplace and entry, these houses are easily distinguished from the homes of the English-speaking majority, which have balanced plans and facades organized around a central hallway. The influence of Africa and the Caribbean shows up in the shotgun house, the earliest examples of which appeared in New Orleans during the first decades of the nineteenth century and from there spread all across the South. Students of Midwestern housing have uncovered numerous examples of buildings that were transplanted from the Old World to the New World.

Construction techniques often are regarded as the exclusive domain of the specialist. Discussions of arcane procedures are frequently determined by the close inspection of telltale marks made long ago that usually prove incomprehensible to all but the

THE MASSILLON MUSEUM/AMERICAN HERITAGE

A barn raising near Massillon, Ohio, in 1888.

most dedicated expert. Yet there are some features of the building process that can convey powerful messages regarding cultural intention. English settlers of Virginia, for example, built their houses without foundations, suggesting their tentative commitment to the colony. These so-called earthfast dwellings were expected to crumble into ruins within a generation. That even the wealthy built their houses this way shows that they regarded the colonial enterprise as a temporary venture. The heavily framed houses of New England, by contrast, reveal the desire to create a durable legacy that would be left for future generations. The Virginian plan, as revealed by their buildings, was to amass a quick fortune and then leave.

Scholars interested in domestic routines have found the social role of women concretely manifested in house plans. When the status of women was low, the kitchen—generally assumed to be a woman's space—was located at the back of the house behind the rooms where men congregated. Cultural transformations leading to degrees of social, if not political, enfranchisement for women saw the kitchen moved to a flanking wing of the house. From this more forward position, a woman was at least afforded a view of the public world. In twentieth-century suburban tract homes the kitchen was often placed in the middle of a rambling string of rooms and provided with a view of the back yard. The plan of a typical rambler thus attempts to promote domestic efficiency by providing a strategically located "command center" where cooking, washing, and supervising children at play can be done all at the same time. Clearly, vernacular architecture, when viewed over time, can bring issues linked to gender and the shifting status of women into sharper focus.

Vernacular builders are not immune to the influence of fashion trends. Indeed, all the major aesthetic shifts seen in monumental architecture show up in domestic buildings as well. One can easily identify the sequence of styles: Georgian, classical revival, Gothic, Italian, and Queen Anne. But local builders tend to behave cautiously, choosing to sample only a few of the features of the latest style, such as ornamental woodwork along the eaves or the moldings around windows and doors. If structural modification is needed, it may be confined only to the roof, for example, when a steeply pitched dormer is added to provide a house with a visual allusion to a morally uplifting Gothic spire. The results of such experiments may strike the purist as an ad-hoc hodgepodge, but the builder will have successfully negotiated a delicate balance between the seductive pull of fashion and the restraining tug of custom. By confining all of the changes to the building to the exterior of the house, the comfortable inner workings of a traditional routine remain in force. The house is updated but none of the domestic functions is changed at all. For the analyst, when an owner or builder flirts with fashion in this way, the house becomes a telling barometer of the true impact of national styles. The kinds of changes made will suggest which fashions are really significant and which are only the claims of publicists and promoters.

Late-twentieth-century scholars of vernacular architecture aim to explore how the social identity of a particular place is manifested in built form. The way that the distinctive inflection of place is established and maintained or transformed thus constitutes a core focus in much research. One can, for example, infer from the fluid, ever-changing connections between location and inflection that the more secure a group is about its identity, the more fixed and routinized are its architectural conventions. If, as is the case for much of the United States, there are diverse claims on a community's allegiances, commonplace buildings will be not only highly varied but probably short lived as well. Regardless of where along a spectrum of possibilities—ranging from clarity to confusion, permanence to perishability, collective assent to personal desire—a particular architectural act happens to fall, it is assumed that its connection to a complex human saga is worthy of investigation and study.

BIBLIOGRAPHY

Carson, Cary, et al., "Impermanent Architecture in the Southern American Colonies," *Winterthur Portfolio* 16, nos. 2–3 (1981):135–196.

Glassie, Henry, *Folk Housing in Middle Virginia: A Structural Analysis of Historic Artifacts* (Univ. of Tenn. Press 1975).

Gowans, Alan, *Styles and Types of North American Architecture: Social Function and Cultural Expression* (HarperCollins 1992).

Kniffen, Fred B., "Louisiana House Types," *Annals of the Association of American Geographers* 26, no. 4 (1936):179–193.

McMurry, Sally Ann, *Families and Farmhouses in Nineteenth-Century America: Vernacular Design and Social Change* (Oxford 1988).

Rapoport, Amos, *House Form and Culture* (Prentice-Hall 1969).

Upton, Dell, "Outside the Academy: A Century of Vernacular Architecture Studies, 1890–1990," in *The Architectural Historian in America*, ed. by Elisabeth Blair MacDongall (National Gallery of Art 1990).

Upton, Dell, and John Michael Vlach, *Common Places: Readings in American Vernacular Architecture* (Univ. of Ga. Press 1986).

JOHN MICHAEL VLACH

ART MUSIC IN THE EUROPEAN TRADITION

While music making is as old as culture, classical music is a more recent development. It originated in the early nineteenth century when lovers of serious music—music thought to inspire moral, spiritual, or aesthetic growth, cultivated tastes, or reflection—distinguished it from popular or vernacular entertainment. Only occasionally have its defining principles, if not its attendant elitism, been challenged. But while the tradition itself has survived, it has enjoyed myriad expressions in which can be seen some of the richness of American cultural life.

Classical Music Grows Serious. European music accompanied white settlement. From earliest days, psalm singing filled most churches, and balladeering and fiddling were popular entertainments. Among the elite of the Tidewater South, mastery of an instrument was a mark of good breeding and the first music society appeared in Charleston in 1762.

Churches were music's primary performance sites and by the 1770s a significant number of composers were engaged in the writing of hymns. The most famous member of the "First New England School" was William Billings (1737–1800), whose fuguing tunes and psalms would inspire a host of classical composers. Billings was a natural talent, a vigorous self-promoter, and a patriot, but not a writer of art music. As with many highly gifted, self-taught people, his works are at once original and homespun, designed not to tax the amateur choirs that sang them.

During Billings's time, vocal music (ballad opera and oratorio) was a popular art form and was widely performed to paying audiences. In contrast instrumental music, in America as in Europe, was an elite luxury and was generally written for private entertainments. In the 1780s Francis Hopkinson (1737–1791) became the new nation's first composer of this genteel music, writing highly derivative and ornamental pieces for the "republican court circle."

But despite differences in performance venue, no systematic effort was made to distinguish the classical from the vernacular. Though much fine music had already been recognized in Europe, few conceived an idiomatic difference between Arne's or Handel's scores and those of Colley Cibber. Theater music, especially, was enjoyed by the wealthy who filled the boxes, the middling classes who oc-

cupied the pits, the blacks and poor whites in the galleries, and the prostitutes who advertised from the third tier.

The most popular theater music of this period was Italian opera. This music was vibrant, melodramatic, and somewhat scandalous, peopled with libertines, unwed mothers, adulterers, and girls who sleepwalked into men's rooms. Before the Civil War it drew a large and socially diverse audience and was popular everywhere. New Orleans had three opera companies in 1836, and New York, in 1864, was home to six. Even some American composers began mimicking the Italian style, and the operas of William Henry Fry (1813–1864) were closely modeled on Bellini's.

After 1850, however, the popular and the classical more openly diverged. The old federalist elite, disturbed by the spreading market culture and the empowerment of the middling class, worked more assiduously to distinguish themselves. Boxes at the opera or, more effectively, a new theater that charged prohibitive prices, such as the Philadelphia Academy of Music (built in 1857), was one means of securing status. Another lay in the cultivation of a new approach to music.

Change first became apparent in music education. Lowell Mason (1792–1872), cofounder of the Boston Academy of Music, patron of the Handel and Haydn Society, and author of an influential musical education handbook, spearheaded the destruction of the "singing school" tradition of such composers as Billings. He did so by disparaging as amateurish New England hymnody and initiating the canonization of European court music.

The arrival in the 1840s of middle-class Germans fleeing political repression furthered this impulse to define the classical. German immigrants carried with them the belief that music was an element in *Bildung* ("self-development"). Influential thinkers and writers, such as Boston's John Sullivan Dwight (1813–1893), embraced this idea and promoted music as "a beautiful corrective of our crudities . . . the finer the kind of music heard or made together, the better the society." This was serious business, and not one suited to either balladeering or Italian opera.

Those conceiving music's function in terms of self-improvement embraced the German classics and criticized Italian music as "sentimental" and "superficial." This new attitude ripped music culture apart even as the popularity of Italian opera peaked. In 1850–1851, the promoter P. T. Barnum (1810–1891) managed a tour by one of Europe's leading sopranos, Jenny Lind (1820–1887). Lind sang a mixture of religious songs, ballads, and opera arias to huge and socially diverse crowds, but she also made clear her resentment at being mass-marketed as "any other one of [Barnum's] monstrosities." At the same time, William Fry, once considered a "serious" composer, found himself criticized as a popularizer. In self-defense, Fry offered a series of public lectures in which he urged musicians not to "allow the name of Beethoven or Handel or Mozart to prove an eternal bugbear." Equally ill at ease in the developing music culture, America's magnificent piano virtuoso Louis Gottschalk (1829–1869) felt compelled to choose between the classes and the masses and, in the 1860s, as one contemporary put it, "exhausted" his talents "playing before the multitude."

After the Civil War America's gentry swelled as a new business elite emerged and married into it. As this new money shed some of its newness it adopted the social pretensions of the old, building monuments to itself such as New York's Metropolitan Opera (the Met) in 1883. The idea that serious music was different because only the initiated could understand it proved to be attractive to this elite in pursuit of self-definition. Although the rich were not the only people attending concerts, classical-musical life was now capitalized by them, and its popularity shrank to involve few beyond the well-to-do.

Germany became the destination for anyone wanting professional music training. The leading home-grown talents were composers of sentimental songs, operettas, and marches, such as Stephen Foster (1826–1864), the blackface minstrel Daniel

Emmett (1815–1904), and John Philip Sousa (1854–1932). Unashamed of their roots in the vernacular, they wrote music that was distinctly American in character, but they were not considered "serious" composers.

Still, few lamented the absence of an indigenous art music. The excellence of the European canon; the fact that the big performing organizations were almost exclusively peopled with Germans; the shortage, until late in the century, of enough wealthy patrons willing to support native composers; and the need for the urban elite to distinguish its taste had all served to encourage a culture of imitation and importation.

Music: The Manly Calling. In the last decades of the nineteenth century, American classical music established itself as an outcropping of German *Kultur*. Italian opera lost its appeal, the mass audiences drifted away, and musical life developed under the patronage of the wealthy. And yet art music also gained in definition and professionalism. A group of New Englanders, including John Knowles Paine (1836–1906), George Chadwick (1854–1931), Arthur Foote (1853–1937), Horatio Parker (1863–1919), and Amy Beach (1867–1944), together with Edward MacDowell (1861–1908) of New York, emerged in the 1880s as the first recognizable school of American classical composers. Their music, grounded in the German tradition, was warm, melodic, and well crafted. It lacked originality, but it achieved what it sought: emotionality without vulgarity and passion without sentimentality.

The notion that music was the language of the emotions originated in German Romanticism. Music, it was argued, liberated the soul and, in so doing, sensitized it. By the 1880s Romanticism's sensual melodies, especially those of the German opera composer Richard Wagner, exercised a commanding influence. One contemporary, George Santayana (1863–1952), suggested in the *Genteel Tradition* that this music was therapy for well-to-do people "who cannot or dare not express their unfulfilled ideals." And there was some truth in this: music lovers did hope, through sound, to experience an emotional catharsis.

Bourgeois women appeared to be the most profoundly affected by Romantic music. At a time when propriety contained women's emotional expression, the concert provided a socially sanctioned environment for the ritualized expression of passion. The great Romantic conductors, Anton Seidl (1850–1898) and Arthur Nikisch (1855–1922), became cult figures. They were mystical, distant, and sensitive; under their batons the orchestral pulse was continually modified, volume levels exploited, and climaxes built impulsively. Seidl, observed the *Musical Courier*'s critic, so excited audiences that "middle-aged women in their enthusiasm stood up in their chairs and screamed their delight."

But as manliness came, toward the turn of the century, to be increasingly associated with martial virtue, with competition, racialism, and the physical body, Romanticism began to appear feminine and sentimental. Even in the 1880s some professional musicians had had difficulty accepting the feminization of their art. Theodore Thomas (1835–1905), while conducting a great deal of Romantic music, was no Seidl. Thomas was a man of vigor who took icy baths, practiced gymnastics, and was a disciplined time-keeper. Boston conductors Emil Paur (1855–1932) and Wilhelm Gericke (1845–1925) were even more mechanical and academic in their manners.

Already ailing, Romanticism suffered a mortal blow during World War I. In Chicago the Grand Opera stopped performing German works in 1917 and Frederick Stock (1872–1942), the German-born conductor of the orchestra, retired prematurely. The conductor of the Boston Symphony, Karl Muck (1859–1940), was harassed and finally interned, as was the conductor of the Cincinnati Symphony. Overall, there was a drop of some twenty percent in the amount of German music performed by the major orchestras.

The war closed an era that was already waning by 1917. A post-Romantic generation of New England composers had already emerged that was rebelling against Romanticism and penned music that expressed a new spiritual ideal. Charles Ives (1874–1954) was not alone in dismissing the Romantics

as "Sissies" and "Pussies." To Ives and his contemporaries music was not about emotion or even sound; its goal was to express febrile intensity, the bones and sinew behind nature, the earthy depth of reflective thought. Music was a manly art.

Shunning the middling class the Romantics had courted, composers including Daniel Gregory Mason (1873–1953), Charles Ives, and Carl Ruggles (1876–1971) embraced a muscular elitism. As Ives (the most gifted and original of this centennial generation of composers) observed, a day in a Kansas wheatfield did more for a musician than three years' study in Rome. These musicians idealized the natural life while refusing to write music ordinary people would appreciate. Stylistically, however, their work took many forms. Conservatives such as Mason wrote dry, disciplined works that looked defiantly back to Brahms; modernists such as Ruggles labored on miniatures containing intense, grinding dissonance, flexible melodies, and thick textures; while Ives chaotically juxtaposed the sound-fragments of a small-town life remembered. Ives's music, like Ruggles's, is brilliant, dense, rhythmically asymmetrical, and polymelodic.

If, in the wake of World War I, Romanticism was considered degenerate, feminine, Germanic, and too popular, the new music was disciplined, morally clear, and spiritually invigorating. The leading conductors of the postwar period embodied this martial spirit. Serge Koussevitsky (1874–1951), Arturo Toscanini (1867–1957), Leopold Stokowski (1882–1977), and Fritz Reiner (1888–1963) were all disciplined and tyrannical drill sergeants. Ironically, all of them were also deeply impetuous, childish, and temperamental. But, with the partial exception of Stokowski with his flowing mane and mastery of dark, sensual sound, none of them was a romantic figure.

The manly music culture of the interwar years proved oppressive for those who did not conform. In the 1940s the magnetic young composer and conductor Leonard Bernstein (1918–1990) felt the need to project heterosexuality in order to prevent talk that might ruin his career. So too did the experimentalist composer Henry Cowell (1897–1965), for whom marriage offered redemption after four years in prison for sodomy with a minor. Similarly, Koussevitsky's homophobia kept the brilliant conductor Dimitri Mitropoulos (1896–1960) from succeeding him at the Boston Symphony. Hardly surprisingly, the new cult of manhood also affected women. Where an earlier generation had acknowledged the compositions of, for example, Amy Beach, after World War I it became more difficult for women to be heard. Between 1910 and 1930 the number of female music teachers and professionals fell from sixty percent of the total to forty-seven percent. Works by such exceptional composers as Ruth Crawford (1901–1953) were not only seldom performed but were dismissed as mere "transcriptions of someone else's ideas" (in this case her husband's). As late as the 1940s most professional orchestras refused to employ women.

Opera also rejected Romanticism. With the high-blown passions of Wagner now out of favor, the Italians made their glorious return. With such stars as Enrico Caruso (1873–1921), Beniamino Gigli (1890–1957), Giovanni Martinelli (1885–1969), Rosa Ponselle (1897–1981), Elisabeth Rethberg (1894–1976), Lawrence Tibbett (1896–1960), and Ezio Pinza (1892–1957) as house staples between 1903 and 1945, the Met had what was arguably history's finest assemblage of Italian operatic talent. The Verdi, Puccini, Bellini, and Donizetti that these artists sang was intensely human: real sorrow, real joy; human in its scale and intensity. Even Verismo, which raised emotions to a fever-pitch, still grounded its virile tragedy in ordinary life. In this, Italian opera was fundamentally different from German Romanticism and it would not be until the 1930s that Wagner would enjoy a renaissance. But it was not the same Wagner. The great German singers who inspired the revival, Kirsten Flagstad (1895–1962) and Lauritz Melchior (1890–1973), had resplendent voices, but they rarely lived a part. The drama and energy were there, but not the passionate sublime.

A new mood dominated American music after 1910. For a time audiences fell away again, as the Romantic's longing after passionate release lost its social relevance. Music now presented emotion in strenuous ways and it was no longer privileged

among the arts. Concertizing found itself in direct competition with other entertainments (movies, theater, and radio) in its quest for consumer dollars, and, suffering under the pressure, it was compelled to reinvent its relevance.

Composing America. Although American composers of the centennial generation inherited an aversion to nationalism, they broke with the Romantics in making greater use of indigenous material. In this, many post-Romantic composers were following Antonín Dvořák (1841–1904), whose brief tenure in New York had inspired his *From the New World* Symphony. Dvořák urged composers to embody their Americanness in music, which he argued meant rediscovering their Aboriginal and African American roots. Some American composers of the early 1900s, including African American artists Will Marian Cook (1869–1944) and Henry T. Burleigh (1866–1949), as well as Henry Gilbert (1868–1928) and Rubin Goldmark (1872–1936), accepted his call and penned a series of forgettable works on Native American and African American themes.

But World War I, Wilsonianism, and America's emergence as an international power fueled the quest for a national sound. In the 1920s the goal became to write a music for the modern age and not one that looked backwards as Dvořák had suggested, to a folk tradition. Postwar Wilsonian internationalists were interested in compositions that, as Aaron Copland explained, "would speak of universal things in a vernacular of American speech and rhythm."

Still fleeing Germanism and still convinced that a proper musical education brought one to Europe, composers searching for a style descended on the Paris studio of the pedagogue Nadia Boulanger. Here they found music that was deeply emotional, yet cooly classical; tonally ambiguous, odd in its chord combinations, and exotic in its rhythms. Already French impressionism had transfixed such American composers as John Alden Carpenter (1876–1951), but in the 1920s the floodgates opened.

Boulanger educated a generation of American composers, among them Copland (1900–1990),

Walter Piston (1894–1976), Roy Harris (1898–1979), Virgil Thomson (1896–1989), Elliott Carter, and Marc Blitzstein (1905–1964). This group of gifted young men was searching, as their predecessors had generally refused to do, for a contemporary American voice. They were in Paris at a time when American movies, American advertising, and American jazz were saturating Europe. If America was emerging as an icon in popular culture, why not also in the refined arts?

In the 1920s the young composers experimented with a variety of styles, from dadaism to Stravinskyan neoclassicism, but the work they composed in America in the 1930s would ensure their reputations. The Depression encouraged young composers to adopt a more socially conscious purpose, arousing, as Copland noted in *The New Music,* "a wave of sympathy for and identification with the plight of the common man." While the soloists recorded stacks of digestible encore pieces, and such conductors as Toscanini and Stokowski broadcast to the millions over the National Broadcasting Company (NBC) or were featured in Hollywood movies, the composers wrote for and about the people. Even Virgil Thomson, the witty composer of the dadaist opera *Four Saints in Three Acts,* accepted commissions to write lyrical music for such films as *The Tender Land* and *The Plow that Broke the Plains.*

The ideal of capturing America's sound fit perfectly with the goal of inspiring a nation in misery. What was called for was a new music "evocative of the [contemporary] American scene." Copland was the most durable of the populists and in celebrated works including *Billy the Kid, Rodeo,* and *Appalachian Spring* he presented memorable tunes in inventive, easily assimilable forms. But none grasped at America's essence more firmly than Roy Harris. Harris's was Mount Rushmore nationalism. American music, he wrote, must manifest the "vast and elemental"; the "wonderful, young, sinewy, timorous, browbeaten, eager, gullible" society; the "smoking, jostling, clamorous cities of steel"; the "rolling plains, wind-swept prairies, gaunt deserts, rugged mountains, forests of giant redwoods and pines, [and] lonely rockbound shores." Harris's music, and in particular his immensely popular

Third Symphony, imparts its Americanness through awkwardly loping melodies, irregular rhythms, and harmonies dominated by open chords.

Copland, Harris, Thomson, and Blitzstein were also all on the Left politically and in the 1930s they flirted with communism. Musically, they sought to blur the ninety-year-old distinction between the popular and the classical by composing appealing works of patriotism, uplift, and celebration. Blitzstein went further and conceived of music as agitprop, and his iconoclastic Brechtian opera *The Cradle Will Rock* was a triumph despite attempts to block its production.

As the lines separating popular and classical music blurred in the 1930s, some writers from Tin Pan Alley also took up "serious" composing. The irrepressible George Gershwin (1898–1937) dreamed, like Blitzstein, of creating a new music that might marry the vernacular with the highbrow. Works such as *Rhapsody in Blue, An American in Paris,* and the *Concerto in F* may suffer from Gershwin's difficulty with sustaining and developing ideas, but they are a joy to hear. And yet, as an outsider, Gershwin was rejected by the classical-music crowd, and his great sprawling opera *Porgy and Bess* with its African American cast and pastiche of spirituals, Tin Pan Alley tunes, and late Romantic arias, was roughly treated when it opened.

Sadly, though increasing numbers of composers now saw jazz as holding the essence of the American spirit, the people who had created that music were unable to gain training or acceptance. There were few black classical composers, since the conservatories were expensive and those musicians who did graduate tended to get low-paid jobs in segregated schools. Most black musicians were prevented from performing before white audiences, forcing the determined to find work in Europe. In the 1930s the composer William Grant Still (1895–1978) was a rare victor over music's caste system, possibly because his conservatism and picturesque use of black musical forms (blues, spirituals, jigs) failed to challenge racial perceptions.

The search for money and relevance did, however, induce orchestras and opera houses to became more innovative in their programming, and they began to offer a small if steady diet of American music. Taken together, between 1925 and 1945 American music's share of the orchestral repertoire rose from under two percent to six percent, although only a handful of composers had their pieces performed more than once. The New Deal orchestras, established under the Work Projects Administration (WPA) to provide temporary employment for jobless musicians and subsidized entertainment for the masses, were significantly better in this regard: in the 1930s those orchestras performed over seven thousand works by some two thousand American composers.

American classical music appeared to have "come of age" in the interwar period. Not only was a more distinctive sound produced, but a new social purpose had been discovered. Sturdy masculine values, populism, patriotism, and social activism all flowed together to invigorate musical life. Important too was the fact that orchestras and opera houses, having lost their wealthy patrons in the Depression's crunch, were increasingly dependent on government assistance and public ticket sales. These factors stimulated the interest of professional musical organizations in the works of American composers. The intrinsic marginalization of serious music in the post-Romantic era appeared to have been overcome.

The Center Does Not Hold. Not all composers in the 1930s wanted, however, to abandon classical music's principles and write works that could be broadly appreciated. Princeton University's Roger Sessions (1896–1985) found "musical nationalism . . . [as] dangerous to the development of a healthy music culture . . . as the erection of 'accessibility' or 'audience appeal' into a kind of dogma." Populism's critics tended to be associated with universities, and the music they wrote was jarringly difficult. Where the populists had broken with the intellectualizing of Ives and Mason, the academicians preserved that tradition.

Their cause received a boost from the Nazis. Ideologues of the Third Reich had denounced some modern music, and particularly the serialist work of Arnold Schoenberg (1874–1951) and his disciples, as racially degenerate. Under Schoenberg's system the standard organizational principle of western music—the octave scale organized around a dominant tone—was replaced by a twelve-tone series in which all pitch intervals were considered equal. Serialism eliminated the harmonic relationships that made for tonality and supplanted conventional melody. Fleeing to America in the 1930s, Schoenberg and the serialists found work on university campuses and their highly academic and mathematical approach soon triumphed. The very unpopularity of atonality in Nazified Europe gave it an added cachet, as the music the Nazis hated became gospel to the postwar generation.

The most influential American serialist was Milton Babbitt, who taught mathematics before succeeding Sessions on the music faculty at Princeton. Babbitt's compositional method involved applying set theory to pitch organization and serial procedures to rhythm, meter, and dynamics. Not untypical is his *Relata II*, which contained six hundred measures, no two of which are alike. The product, while impressive and challenging, sounds not unlike a conglomeration of unrelated notes.

Even as the serialists captured the academies, the cold war shifted the political mood decisively to the Right. The vision of the Roosevelt years—the ideal of a people's music—began to be suspected as leftist and subversive. Wallingford Riegger (1885–1961), Marc Blitzstein, Aaron Copland, and Roy Harris were all named by the House Un-American Activities Committee. Harris, for example, was investigated for dedicating his *Fifth Symphony* to the people of the Union of Soviet Socialist Republics and for supporting the Composers' Collective and the Musicians' Committee to Aid Spanish Democracy, both Communist-front organizations.

The absurdity of the situation and the gloom that accompanied the cold war turned many composers inward. Copland followed Igor Stravinsky (1882–1971) and began to write serialist works, while Blitzstein found communicating with an audience increasingly disheartening. Roy Harris remained the most defiant of the popularizers, but his inspiration was gone. Even Leonard Bernstein appeared unable to sustain the marriage of the popular and the classical and his postwar "serious" works are short on charm.

Elliott Carter also gave up composing people's music and, in the words of his biographer, "liberated himself from the tyranny of the audience." Carter married Babbitt's notion of "partitioning" to something he called metric modulation, by which he broadened or shortened the value of the notes to alter the pulse. The result is dazzlingly hard to follow: each instrument speaks in its own voice and at its own speed. Carter acknowledged the difficulty this posed to listeners but declared: "To hell with the public and the performers too."

The artistic thrust that had (from the New England Romantics through the folklorists to the populists) kept mainstream American classical music if not popular then at least abreast of public tastes had dissipated. By the 1950s most composers rejected the public and composed for ever more specialized audiences. Cliques formed and in time even the serialists came under attack as hidebound and dogmatic. While some composers explored non-Western forms and instruments (Alan Hovhaness blended Armenian folk music with American schmaltz; Lou Harrison wrote extensively for the Javanese gamelan; George Crumb prepared works involving crystal goblets and conch shells), others denied the very principles that separated music from noise.

The most important postwar experimentalist was John Cage (1912–1992), who developed French-born composer Edgar Varèse's (1885–1965) notion that sound was spatial. Cage's best-known works deny sequential thinking: the sounds coexist, they do not progress. Further, like Varèse, Cage made no distinction between music and noise and welcomed improvisation and chance in performance. In *Landscape No. 4* for twelve radios, Cage indicated the frequencies, the dynamic levels, and the length of time each radio should be played, but he did not control the content. His compositions open out like natural phenomena, for, as he explained it, his "purpose is to eliminate purpose."

While the initiates of serialism battled the experimentalists, and the populists capitulated, the broader music public lost interest. This was sad, because the 1960s were good years for classical music in America. New performing halls were built everywhere and, with the creation of the National Endowment for the Arts in 1965, many of music's financial worries seemed over. But the European masterworks still dominated the repertoire, and the most popular American pieces were those composed during the 1930s and 1940s. Artistic directors, their eyes on the patron state, and on the large endowments that subsidized their ever more expensive industry, did try to feature some contemporary works. Composer-in-residence programs were established and new pieces were commissioned, but the public was seldom interested. In the 1960s only such conservative holdovers as Samuel Barber (1910–1981) and Gian-Carlo Menotti enjoyed substantial audience support.

Contemporary music's problems brought a reaction of sorts in the 1980s as a new generation of neo-Romantic composers emerged. Champions of tonality and melody including David del Tredici, William Bolcom, and Ellen Taaffe Zwilich began to attract enthusiastic audiences. John Corigliano's noisy and self-indulgent *First Symphony*, for example, received two recordings within five years; his long-winded operatic pastiche, *The Ghosts of Versailles,* was premiered by the Met in 1991 and was also promptly recorded. In 1999 Corigliano won an Academy Award for the film score to the *Red Violin.*

But no neo-Romantic composer matched the popularity of the other disciples of tonality, the minimalists. Drawing on Indonesian, West African, and Indian influences, minimalists stripped music down to its harmonic and rhythmic skeleton, which they then revealed in almost imperceptibly changing phrase repetitions. Though the music often seems eventless, audiences responded to the chugging rhythms and warm harmonies. Moreover, as time passed and minimalism's popularity grew, its creators wrote ever more engagingly, introducing unpredictable elements and even recognizable melodies. In the 1990s the young minimalist John Adams gravitated toward neo-Romanticism with his opera *The Death of Klinghoffer* (1991); later Philip Glass found inspiration in the rock compositions of David Bowie.

The postwar fracturing of classical music culture created multiple fissures. Among younger musicians, homosexuality was more openly expressed; and women and African Americans enjoyed greater opportunities as performers and composers. But in other ways the wind in the closing decades of the century blew less freely. Orchestras that hired adventuresome conductors in the 1970s gravitated back to well-known Germans in the 1990s. Opera, in the meantime, suffered the collapse of its repertory company system and a rapid inflation in soloists' salaries. The result was atavism in choice of repertoire as singers on tight schedules had little time for rehearsals. Opera singers sang too much, too often, and in too many places, making real ensemble a thing of the past. Increasingly, what came to distinguish one opera from another was not the house and cast but the direction, sets, and costumes.

Still, for all its problems, classical music remains a vital, vast, and diffuse cultural industry. Questions involving its contemporary relevance, its financial viability, its quality and ability to cope with fast-changing competition from other entertainments will continue to be asked, as they must be asked. But the classical-music tradition, in all its elitist splendor, remains vibrant despite predictions to the contrary. One can only assume that American composers and performers will continue to be, for good and ill, as varied and contentious in their development of that tradition as they have been in the past.

[*See also* MUSIC.]

BIBLIOGRAPHY

Broyles, Michael, *Music of the Highest Class: Elitism and Populism in Antebellum Boston* (Yale Univ. Press 1992).

Davis, Ronald, *A History of Music in American Life,* 3 vols. (Krieger 1981).

Dizikes, John, *Opera in America: A Cultural History* (Yale Univ. Press 1993).

Gamm, Kyle, *American Music in the Twentieth Century* (Schirmer Bks. 1997).

Griffiths, P., *Modern Music: The Avant Garde since 1945* (Dent 1981).

Hitchcock, H. Wiley, *Music in the United States: A Historical Introduction,* 3d ed. (Prentice-Hall 1988).

Hitchcock, H. Wiley, and Stanley Sadie, eds., *The New Grove Dictionary of American Music,* 4 vols. (Grove 1986).

Kingman, Daniel, *American Music: A Panorama* (Schirmer Bks. 1979).

Moore, Macdonald Smith, *Yankee Blues: Musical Culture and American Identity* (Ind. Univ. Press 1985).

Mussulman, Joseph, *Music in the Cultured Generation: A Social History of Music in America, 1870–1900* (Northwestern Univ. Press 1971).

Struble, John, *The History of American Classical Music: MacDowell through Minimalism* (Facts on File 1995).

Sullivan, Jack, *New World Symphonies: How American Culture Changed European Music* (Yale Univ. Press 1999).

Tawa, Nicholas, *A Most Wondrous Babble: American Art Composers, Their Music and the American Scene, 1950–1985* (Greenwood Press 1987).

Tawa, Nicholas, *The Coming of Age of American Art Music: New England's Classical Romanticists* (Greenwood Press 1991).

Tischler, Barbara, *An American Music: The Search for an American Musical Identity* (Oxford 1986).

Zuck, Barbara, *A History of Musical Americanisms* (UMI Res. Press 1980).

DAVID MONOD

ART, SOCIETY, AND CULTURE

American art used to refer in a self-evident manner to art produced by Americans. Since the 1960s this relative clarity has become muddled. Now, as never before, the meaning of the term *American* is under dispute and riddled with contradictions. And so is the term *art*.

From the early nineteenth century through the middle of the twentieth, American art surveys typically opened with the British colonial period and barely touched on the artistic contributions of either Native Americans or the French, Dutch, and Spanish colonists. Likewise, Africans, Asians, and Europeans who came to American shores unwillingly as slaves, indentured workers, or refugees in transit were generally ruled out as producers of

"American art," their production of visual images and objects relegated instead to the status of folk crafts.

Needless to say, such acts of exclusion are ideological in nature. Who counts as an "American" and what counts as "art" are determinations that derive legitimacy from assessments ultimately having less to do with aesthetics than with politics. By and large, art was what was produced by members of culturally dominant groups in forms and media that had already been sanctioned, often for centuries, by elite European arbiters of taste.

That is, American art, with only an occasional exception, meant painting, drawing, sculpture, architecture, and, later, photography modeled on dominant European aesthetic codes but produced in the United States by Anglo-American men. Furthermore, most of these were men who came from or worked in New England, New York, or in urban centers farther south along the eastern seaboard.

Such criteria of selection, though rarely put forth explicitly, excluded vast numbers of actual producers of visual art because they did not fit into the prescribed categories. Not only was the object-making of African American, Asian American, and Native American artists left out of the mix, but so too was the visual-arts production of virtually all women, as well as that of working-class men. Indeed, the list of those makers of visual images not included under the rubric of "American artists" would appear to be practically endless: quilt-makers, cartoonists, comic strip artists, graffiti spray-painters, commercial illustrators, set designers, fashion designers, costume designers, landscape architects, furniture makers, automobile stylists, and so forth.

In the late twentieth century, serious academic studies materialized on all of these object- or image-making professions and on the object- or image-making of a variety of socially or politically marginal groups, including preadolescent children, alienated teenagers, felons, and the mentally disabled. Tattooing, hair styling, fashion styling, body-piercing, motorcycle ornamentation, album-cover design, cyber-graphics, video-game construction, computer animation, and Hollywood special effects were now routinely talked about by their partisans as "art forms" and were sanctioned in the marketplace of ideas by academic treatises and seminars, art gallery installations, and art museum retrospectives.

This apparent democratization of American art, or, more specifically, the expansion of definitions and categories as to what constitutes American art, would seem to be a direct outcome of a variety of social changes occurring in the postwar era of the 1950s and 1960s. The most obvious of these would be the increased visibility and political viability of previously dispossessed groups, among them racial and ethnic minorities, gays and lesbians, and women as a class.

A related change was the breakdown of traditional hierarchies. Just as the political, religious, and educational leadership of America ("the Establishment") was repeatedly assailed by populists and radicals during this period and found wanting in moral authority, so too was the traditional art hierarchy subjected to attack. Critics charged that this putatively universal, that is, politically and economically disinterested, scale of values actually abetted the special interests of the establishment by fostering aesthetic distinctions that sustained social inequality. The traditional art hierarchy was condemned as being nothing more than an insidious propaganda arm of the dominant class hierarchy.

In the traditional value scheme, elite art was better than popular art, academic better than folk, high better than low, noncommercial better than commercial, individually produced better than mass-produced, and that which demanded serious intellectual contemplation better than that which, allegedly, induced passive amusement. This system also generally valued art of the metropolis over that of the provinces, Eastern over Western, Northern over Southern, masculine over feminine, straight over gay, white over black or brown, and Protestant over Catholic, Jewish, or otherwise. Revisionists in the late twentieth and early twenty-first century sought to overturn each of the separate hierarchies within the overall hierarchical system, either to replace them with counter-hierarchies or, what appears to be conceptually impossible, to dispense with hierarchy altogether.

Another social change leading to the widespread reevaluation of American art was the exponential expansion of higher education in the United States in the postwar era. The GI Bill of Rights provided low-cost college and university educations for millions of American veterans in the aftermath of World War II. Of these millions, thousands who most likely would not have done so without such assistance went on to pursue careers as art educators, art historians, art critics, and professional artists. Hundreds of thousands if not millions more of the new generation of university students took art-history or art-studio classes during their transit through the halls of academe and came away after four or five years with a cultural indoctrination known euphemistically as "art appreciation."

With an even greater mushrooming of the college and university student population in America during the 1960s, thanks to the so-called baby boom, the numbers of "art lovers" swelled throughout the land. This, hand-in-hand with the most affluent national economy theretofore seen in America, a lessening of working hours, and a concomitant increase in leisure time, led to a rapidly expanding industry in art production and sales. It also led to a greatly increased demand for more art dissertations, monographs, and art-museum exhibitions, often on previously unknown or overlooked artists or for already canonical artists seen in a new light, whether that of formal analysis, iconographic studies, or social and political history. Moreover, art history as a scholarly discipline lost its exclusive franchise on the close study of visual images during this period. Rival academic disciplines such as anthropology, comparative literature, English, and sociology and interdisciplinary fields such as American studies, film studies, material culture studies, and visual culture studies all claimed their own stake in the analysis and interpretation of visual materials.

Since 1945 the advent of new technologies of reproduction also contributed in a major way to the overturning of the traditional artistic hierarchy. These technologies included inexpensive means of publishing and photocopying illustrated hardcover and paperback books; low-cost, low-maintenance, and high-quality 35-mm photographic equipment; the library copy-stand for transfer of book and magazine illustrations to color slides for classroom projection; and television, video, laser disc, compact disc, digital video display (DVD), and the Internet. In addition, improved technologies of travel, such as the interstate highway system and the passenger jet, both introduced during the 1950s, and new financial technologies, such as the credit card (also dating from the 1950s), caused a surge in popular travel.

Thus it was now vastly easier than at any previous time to see and study, whether firsthand or in reproduction, the work of image-makers from any period in U.S. history, any region of the country, any medium of production, any race, class, or gender of producer. Under these circumstances rigid definitions of what counted as art and who counted as an artist were bound to bend if not snap. The widespread diffusion of knowledge led inevitably to a confusion of standards regarding the evaluation of art, since now any one authoritative pronouncement was certain to be offset by a slew of others from opposing points of view.

This democratization of American art and its redefinition toward all-inclusiveness might well be considered a good thing, especially from a populist perspective. But one need not be an elitist to worry that what goes here by the name of democratization and greater inclusiveness actually has less to do with the triumph of democracy than with the ever-expanding reach of the huge, multifaceted, and decentralized network of commercial and informational systems known as the culture industry. Since World War II, the culture industry in the United States has grown so enormous in power and influence that it dips into virtually every conceivable pocket of the American population to extract payment for artistic products and services rendered. Regardless of whether such products and services are identified as high or low, academic or folk, urban or rural, contemplative or active, masculine or feminine, straight or gay, white or black, they now are all up for sale in the great twenty-four-hour-a-day emporia of American culture.

Academic tomes, blockbuster museum exhibitions, high-priced art auctions, glossy magazines and coffee-table volumes devoted to the visual arts, picture postcards, art-lovers' videos, art calendars, postage stamps celebrating American art and artists, introductory art courses, art tours, and even encyclopedia essays about art such as this one—all of these endeavors service the art industry or are themselves services it provides to its actual or potential customers. Art forms that were previously not regarded as art forms and countless artists who were previously obscure, forgotten, or relegated to craft status have now been elevated ("hyped") by an art marketplace and intellectual service industry that is ever in need of new products and producers to designate as art and peddle to art-hungry consumers.

In previous periods the art hierarchy excluded from serious consideration all but a minuscule fraction of the visual images and objects produced at any given time. Almost by definition, products that were mass-marketed stood outside the realm of "art." But now, in the omnivorous realm of the culture industry, "mass-market art" is no longer an oxymoron. Conversely, art that sets out to be difficult and unpopular can nevertheless be sold to millions of consumers around the world who, purchasing access to such works through the latest technologies of mechanical reproduction, seek to affirm their own individuality and proclaim their free-thinking independence.

Various observers have been troubled by the implications of this rampant deregulation of art and breakdown of traditional protocols of evaluation. Those on the Right decry the jettisoning of traditional standards of evaluation that once purportedly enabled viewers of visual artifacts to discern the good from the bad, the beautiful from the ugly, the substantial from the meretricious, and so forth. When truth was beauty and beauty truth, the theory goes, works of art were at once beautiful objects and conveyors of universal human truth. Such

works adhered to, embodied, and safeguarded aesthetic and philosophic objectivity. But now that virtually anything can lay claim to being a work of art, beauty becomes arbitrary, in the eye of the beholder, and hence the so-called objective truths of the human condition also appear arbitrary and subjective. When any object or visual pattern made by just about anyone can be regarded as art, art ceases to function as a conveyance of timeless or universal truth, these critics lament, and thus can no longer provide moral authority.

Observers on the Left view the situation from a different angle. Their concern is that the culture industry has so absorbed and commodified every facet of art production and distribution that art has lost whatever ability it ever may have possessed to resist political and corporate hegemony. From this perspective the problem is not that art has ceased to explore and reinforce universal truths about the human condition (which many on the Left regard as specious truths anyway). The problem, rather, is that in assuming a place within the commodity system, artists, art critics, art historians, and art foundations have in effect laid down their arms against it.

Hence the phenomenon of "radical chic," in which members of the art world advance polemics against the so-called establishment even while seeking and receiving largesse from that establishment, in which instance the recipients' bite of the hand that feeds them tends to be more tempered than their bark. Art that has attempted to circumvent the commodity system or self-reflexively note its own complicity with it (as in the happenings and pop art of the 1960s or the conceptual and punk art of the 1970s) has been notoriously unable to detach itself from the system it strives to critique. All too quickly on the heels of an emergent audience for such art come various forms of economic sponsorship, which seem inevitably to deform the nature and intent of the artist's original, presponsored product.

Corporate and nonprofit institutions subsidize the arts because of the cultural legitimization that redounds to such institutions. Yet strings almost invariably come attached, given (often unstated) imperatives not to offend shareholders and trustees in the case of corporations, overseers in the case of philanthropies, and voters and legislators in the case of government-funded arts organizations. Artists, art galleries, and art museums are forced to react, whether defiantly or by self-censorship, and the age-old dialectic between art patron and art producer is filtered through a largely impersonal and bureaucratized labyrinth of grant applications, funding events, and development campaigns. Of course, those corporate entities that specifically cater to the youth market or other consumer groups that have been identified as socially progressive or "alternative" are often happy to support art of a shocking or offensive nature. By endlessly extending the horizons of tolerance as to what constitutes art (and thus endlessly extending what may now be marketed as art) the multinational behemoths of the culture industry have helped make it all but impossible for art today to be seriously radical, difficult, or shocking. For a slight extra fee, there's always a gallery guide, audio-tour, or CD-ROM close at hand to explain what it all means, put it in context, and defuse its threat.

In the anything-goes, everything-for-sale world of the pluralistic culture industry, would-be radicals are reduced to making flamboyant gestures of religious blasphemy, sexual voyeurism, and even political incorrectness in an effort to create a stir. In this regard, their worst enemies (those who object most obstreperously to these gestures) are their best friends, because art does not register in the public mind as radical unless there are "reactors" (not necessarily reactionaries) around to lodge vociferous protest against it. Cultural conservatism stifles radical or progressive art in obvious ways. But cultural liberalism, too, has a stultifying effect. In a commercial, democratic society in which liberal tolerance of all points of view is the arch virtue, it is difficult to find genuinely radical art—that is, art that actually changes people's minds and alters their ways of seeing and living instead of art that merely preaches to the converted.

At the start of the twenty-first century, Americans are filled to the bursting point with man- and woman-made visual images and objects that they can hardly stop themselves from ingesting, even when they so desire. Americans are said to live in a "society of the spectacle" or in a state of "media saturation." It becomes difficult for any one particular visual image to capture and sustain the attention of an audience that is forever being bombarded with new generations of images to replace the old. The turnover is dizzying but it also makes the audience ravenous for more; yesterday's vivid picture is already stale and must give way to that which will be stale by tomorrow.

Those visual images and objects that prove to have staying power in the public imagination (exceedingly famous photographs or internationally recognized monuments or astronomically priced paintings) are so ubiquitously recirculated by electronic media of reproduction that they have passed beyond the realm of art itself. Despite their original merits, they have become "pseudo-events," artifacts celebrated for nothing so much as their hypercelebrity. Viewers are transformed into starstruck fans, awed by the enormous fame of such images, which have become virtually impossible to see on their own terms, arriving before the audience as they do, already familiar, venerated, prepackaged, and predigested.

The current state of affairs can better be understood by contrasting it to earlier periods in the history of American art, when infinitely fewer artists, not to mention art authorities, were at hand to muddy the waters. The market for art was far less ubiquitous than today, and public agreement on the meaning and value of a work of art was, if not routinely predictable, at least relatively uniform, despite occasional storms of controversy.

Moreover, image-glut was simply not a problem in premodern colonial America. Artistic representation in the earliest days of the colonies was primarily practical or religious in nature. Painted signs identified the presence of a shop or tavern, and tombstone carvings announced the presence of the departed in the bosom of God. As the colonies became more worldly and affluent, itinerant artists found employment painting individual or group portraits of the well-to-do, who displayed such portraits in their homes as testaments to status and success or shipped them back to the mother country for the benefit of family members left behind. The portraits that survive from this period attest not only to the design sensibilities of the anonymous limners who executed them but also to that of the apparel-makers and furniture-fabricators whose handicraft is prominently and proudly exhibited in these portraits as props, costumes, and setting.

Throughout the seventeenth century little or no distinction was made between artists and artisans (a portrait painter's social status was no greater than that, say, of a cabinetmaker). Over the course of the following century, however, a clear demarcation was established. Though artists and artisans alike worked with their hands to produce aesthetic objects, the former were considered more cerebral, more attuned to matters of the intellect and the spirit, than the latter, whose concerns were thought to be primarily of a practical and materialistic nature. This division reflected the idealist ideology of the European art academies, which, established and sustained by royal patronage and devoted to aristocratic privilege, vaunted the life of the mind.

The royal academies taught that painting, drawing, and sculpture were "noble" arts precisely to the extent that they did not serve practical functions, whereas the lesser arts (metalworking, cabinetmaking, and so on) did serve such functions. Architecture proved an anomalous case, in that buildings were expected to be beautiful according to classical standards and yet functional as well. But even in this case function had to be subordinate to form if the building in question was to be considered artistic.

Painting itself was divided into several graduated levels or branches. At the top were historical and mythological painting, which provided viewers with moral edification by recreating celebrated scenes of the distant past or dramatically envisioning instructive tales from classical mythology. Portraiture was a lesser branch, although a portrait of a great and noble man was thought to be of higher aesthetic value than one of an ordinary man of commerce. After landscape painting came the bottom branches of the tree: scenes of common, everyday life (genre painting) and pictures of common, ordinary objects (still life painting).

The academic system thus legislated and policed a hierarchy of artistic values that unambiguously defined which cultural products counted as art and which did not, and, of those that counted, which were to be the more highly esteemed. Aesthetic distinction provided an allegory for social distinction; refined taste in art bespoke refinement of an aristocratic nature. Thus in America, which was in theory without hereditary aristocracy, one of the chief means by which one could lay claim to aristocratic status was by endorsing and enforcing so-called aristocratic taste.

Academic values were imported to America by merchants and landowners who traveled abroad and by English artists who immigrated to New England, New York, and the Mid-Atlantic colonies in the early eighteenth century. Schooled in the techniques of the baroque, these artists portrayed the burghers of America as gentlemen of noble mien and deportment and their wives as well-bred ladies of leisure. In the latter half of the century, the most promising young artists born in America went to England for firsthand training in the academic-aristocratic technique. Instilled by their mentors with an allegiance to lofty patrician sensibilities, those artists who chose to return to America often found such sensibilities to be disappointingly at odds with the brusque pragmatic realities of an increasingly nouveau-riche business society bereft of a longstanding aristocracy.

The first schools of art instruction in America, which emerged in Philadelphia and New York at the close of the eighteenth century and opening of the nineteenth, adhered to academic orthodoxy and accorded privilege of place to painting, sculpture, and engraving. The so-called lesser arts, as practiced by artisan laborers or household workers, were simply excluded from consideration. As the Romantic cult of imagination and disdain for practicality gained acceptance among the American elite, artists were increasingly distinguished from (and elevated above) artisans. Art, as such, provided patrons and collectors of the era a social distinction superior to that attained from the possession of mere artifacts, however colorful, decorative, or costly.

In the early republic the leading American artists were those who had trained in Europe and dedicated themselves to a thoroughly Europeanized aesthetic practice. Such artists were often connected to the channels of political power by means of the patronage afforded them. Though they themselves did not determine public policy, they moved in circles that did. By the end of the first quarter of the nineteenth century, however, this ceased to be the case. In the era of antebellum nationalism, those painters, sculptors, and engravers who were oriented toward dominant European aesthetic codes were politically marginalized, their work deemed suspiciously elite and un-American.

More congenial to public taste were the so-called Hudson River school landscape artists, whose paintings celebrated the wilderness glories of the westward-expanding nation. Similarly appreciated were the genre-scene painters whose halcyon depictions of horse traders, riverboatmen, scullery maids, and harvesters satisfied a need for idealized representations of American common folk. Such works were promulgated in the middle decades of the century through organizations known as art unions that dispersed art to middle-class audiences across the nation by means of art lotteries and inexpensively priced graphic reproductions.

In the economically expansionist era following the Civil War, as enormous private fortunes were established and U.S. industry and agriculture made a significant impact on world markets, visual art became one of the nation's primary sources of conspicuous consumption. Gilded Age millionaires hired architects to build their mansions and commissioned painters and sculptors to furnish them with opulent decoration. In a renewed affiliation with the Old World, they imported art from Europe and financed the training of local artists in European art centers.

Visual design proliferated during this period. Newspaper and magazine engraving, book illustration, studio and snapshot photography, machine decoration, housing ornamentation, and shop-window and shop-counter display all developed into full-fledged commercial enterprises. Once wordy and devoid of visual images, advertising copy in newspapers and handbills became reliant on visual imagery in order to pitch its wares. Also during this time manufacturers of household goods realized that products swathed in colorful and brand-labeled packages sold better than those wrapped nondescriptly. By the end of the nineteenth century, America was awash in visual imagery, and even citizens who lived far from urban centers were immersed in the plentiful visual imagery of the readily available mail-order catalogs.

It was in this period that pictorial aestheticism or "art for art's sake" found wide acceptance not with the general public, which continued to think of art in terms of moral instruction, but with sophisticated critics, collectors, dealers, and artists. The proponents of aestheticism insisted on art's autonomy from didactic meaning and commercial popularity, whereas their adversaries contended that art not recognizably concerned with the moral edification of the viewer and the enhancement of public virtue, although it may have been attractive to the eye, was not true art.

Of various controversial events and scandals that have highlighted this ongoing clash of expectations with regard to the basic nature and purpose of art, the 1913 Armory Show in New York is perhaps the most instructive. Featuring numerous works of avant-garde European modernism that flouted traditional academic values and refused to be easily or conventionally interpreted, the Armory Show insisted that a work of art be judged solely on its own aesthetic terms rather than for its ability to soothe, inspire, or edify the viewer. Outraged observers, however, would have nothing of this sea change in standards and heaped calumny on the pictures (and artists) in question for having failed to be morally accountable.

Less controversially, the art-for-art's-sake aesthetic of the late nineteenth century had a significant impact on the design of furniture and other household goods. American designers joined the international Arts and Crafts movement, which sought to revive the handicrafts in an era dominated by mass production. Here the independent artisan of the Middle Ages was the idealized role model, a worker supposedly not alienated from his or her work, as was the case with industrial laborers, but instead wholeheartedly devoted to it and spiritually recompensed by it.

The movement lost momentum after it became apparent that customized craft was a luxury only the rich could afford. But the Arts-and-Crafts ideology had a lasting effect on the way that artists, art collectors, and art critics conceived of the nature and purpose of art. The movement made it possible for its successors to claim that moral worth inhered in pure, nonnarrative form (in color, materials, and design) and in the professional dedication and integrity of the artist.

That is to say, the Arts and Crafts movement legitimized the ideology of art-for-art's-sake by popularizing the notion that the true morality of an art or craft object resided not in its overt content or subject matter but rather in its internal structure. An artifact that was, for example, "true to materials" did not pretend to be made of anything other than what it was and thus was to be regarded as honest and straightforward, not an instance of fakery, hypocrisy, or dissimulation. Likewise, effusive Beaux Arts architectural ornamentation could be deemed decadent, and paintings that strove to render three-dimensional, single-perspective representations of reality could be reproved as falsifications that, in misleading the eye, misled the viewer. In effect, art-for-art's-sake (aestheticism) provided a new form of artistic morality in an age of therapeutic consumerism, wherein "good objects" were those that gave properly trained consumers either soothing or stimulating sense impressions amid the nerve-jangling or nerve-deadening environments of modern urban society.

The leading modernists of the early twentieth century generally disdained the art-for-art's-sake ideology as old-fashioned, frivolous, and effete, and they dissociated themselves from it. Nevertheless they showed themselves to be heirs to this ideology when they spoke of the intrinsic morality of pure form and truth to materials, which they contrasted to the extrinsic (and thus ersatz) morality of Victorian and neo-Victorian art. Rebelling against the ironclad authority of older generations, many of the most influential modernists were themselves powerful or charismatic authority figures who, whether as painters, designers, architects, photographers, gallery impresarios, or critics, established dominant codes of aesthetic value that prevailed throughout much of the twentieth century. To these modernist titans and their followers, the highest form of personal morality for an artist was to create works of art that transcend mundane facts, pragmatic necessities, and easy comprehension. This also meant that art (and artists) should be strictly divorced from any sort of direct involvement in contemporary politics.

To a certain degree, modernism in America faltered in the decade of the Great Depression. During this period numerous artists sought to produce political art, whether in a watered-down modernist idiom or in more conventional and realist terms, and in so doing contribute to the alleviation of widespread social dislocation and inequality. Many of them worked under the auspices of the Federal Art Project of the Works Progress Administration (WPA), established as a cultural arm of the New Deal administration. Some formed Left-leaning organizations such as the short-lived American Artists Congress. Some took up membership in the American Communist Party. Others steered clear of political parties, congresses, and organizations but strove nevertheless to respond to real-world crises with art of a satirical, social realist, or surrealist nature.

With the end of the Depression and World War II, however, modernism surged in America and abstraction in particular achieved critical hegemony. One explanation for this has been that by eradicating real-world references and sticking strictly to those of an internal or formal nature, left-wing artists, critics, and collectors safeguarded themselves from political stigmatization by right-wing zealots in an era of fervent anticommunism. An alternative explanation is that these artists, critics, and collectors found in abstraction a viable means of turning inward (or to the Right), away from the political passions and commitments of which they had grown weary or that now struck them as jejune. Additional explanation could be found by looking at the postwar booms in the economy, population, and higher education addressed earlier in this essay. As never before, the market was now driven by an increasingly affluent and college-educated middle class that sought to distinguish itself from previous generations, as well as from other social classes, by displaying a bold predilection for "progressive" or "advanced" forms of art and design.

Given this market situation, in which works of art, like detergents, seemed to sell better if labeled "bold," "revolutionary," and "startlingly new," abstraction could not remain the dominant idiom for long. The turnover of artistic products, and not only of the objects themselves but the books, magazines, and exhibitions devoted to them, required a turnover of artistic styles. (But not necessarily of artistic heroes. The canonical heavyweights of the twentieth century were established as and have since remained the enduring giants of the art industry's belated mimicking of the star system pioneered by the film industry.) Various forms of figurative and realist art, overtly political or not, came back into and again went out of fashion during the 1960s and 1970s, as did varieties of abstract, minimal, and optic art. By the close of the 1990s it seemed as though every artistic style of the twentieth century had been mined, rejected, appropriated, deconstructed, forgotten, and mined all over again in an endless loop. Artists, critics, and collectors of any and every stripe deemed *their* art of choice a socially or morally valuable contribution to the collective human endeavor, regardless of whether it addressed topics of social concern directly or indirectly.

Yet by the start of the twenty-first century, it had become difficult to sustain the modernist conviction in the inherent morality of forms (that is, that a creative and serious-minded arrangement of colors, textures, and shapes can be beneficial for society at large). This was not so much because of the ever-renewed attack by conservatives who demanded from art that it be overtly moral and emphatically serve patriotic and religious causes. Rather, it was because of the dwindling faith of those on the Left who used to believe that nominally apolitical art could nonetheless play a genuine role in the struggle for social equality and justice because of its dedication to internal truth and authenticity. Moreover, the modernists themselves (despite their continuing superstar aura) are now judged in historical hindsight to have been authoritarian, intolerant, and elitist in their beliefs and behavior and are criticized for a lack of social inclusiveness (having little room in their various canons for art by women and nonwhites). Alternatively, art with an overt social or political agenda is likewise viewed as suspect, either for being too serious and lacking in irony, or so full of irony that it thoroughly undercuts itself and fails to point in a viable way toward social action.

With the collapse of modernist goals and standards of evaluation, the democratization (and, in effect, overproduction) of art-making, art-collecting, and art-appreciating, the ever-tightening hegemony of a narrowly circumscribed liberal-conservative consensus, and the ever-widening embrace of free-market, therapeutic consumerism, which blandly commodifies and thus defuses work that is aesthetically or politically difficult, American art is at once more active and more moribund than ever. Never before has art been so highly prized (or priced) in American life yet so irrelevant to the daily lives of most Americans.

[See also HISTORICAL SUBJECTS IN PAINTING AND SCULPTURE; ENVIRONMENTAL ART; FEMINISM, *article on* FEMINIST ART; PAINTING; POP ART; SCULPTURE; WARHOL, ANDY; POLITICAL CARTOONS.*]*

BIBLIOGRAPHY

Adorno, Theodor W., *The Culture Industry: Selected Essays on Mass Culture,* ed. with an intro. by J. M. Bernstein (Routledge 1991).

Barzun, Jacques, *The Culture We Deserve,* ed. by Arthur Krystal (Wesleyan Univ. Press 1989).

Becker, Howard S., *Art Worlds* (Univ. of Calif. Press 1982).

Benjamin, Walter, "The Work of Art in the Age of Mechanical Reproduction" (1936), in *Illuminations,* ed. by Hannah Arendt, trans. by Harry Zohn (Harcourt 1968).

Boorstin, Daniel J., *The Image: A Guide to Pseudo-Events in America* (Vintage 1992).

Danto, Arthur C., *After the End of Art: Contemporary Art and the Pale of History* (Princeton Univ. Press 1997).

Frank, Thomas, and Matt Weiland, eds., *Commodify Your Dissent: Salvos from the Baffler* (Norton 1997).

Frascina, Francis, ed., *Pollock and After: The Critical Debate* (Harper 1985).

Gans, Herbert J., *Popular Culture and High Culture: An Analysis and Evaluation of Taste,* rev. and updated ed. (Basic Bks. 1999).

Harris, Neil, *The Artist in American Society: The Formative Years, 1790–1860* (Braziller 1966).

Harris, Neil, *Cultural Excursions: Marketing Appetites and Cultural Tastes in Modern America* (Univ. of Chicago Press 1990).

Hobbs, Stuart D., *The End of the American Avant Garde* (N.Y. Univ. Press 1997).

Hughes, Robert, *Culture of Complaint: The Fraying of America* (Oxford 1993).

Jameson, Frederic, *The Cultural Turn: Selected Writings on the Postmodern, 1983–1998* (Verso 1998).

Lears, T. J. Jackson, *Fables of Abundance: A Cultural History of Advertising in America* (Basic Bks. 1994).

Lears, T. J. Jackson, *No Place of Grace: Antimodernism and the Transformation of American Culture, 1880–1920* (Pantheon Bks. 1981).

Levine, Lawrence W., *Highbrow/Lowbrow: The Emergence of Cultural Hierarchy in America* (Harvard Univ. Press 1988).

Lubin, David M., *Picturing a Nation: Art and Social Change in Nineteenth-Century America* (Yale Univ. Press 1994).

Lynes, Russell, *The Tastemakers: The Shaping of American Popular Taste,* reprint of 1954 ed., with new afterword (Dover 1980).

Mills, C. Wright, "The Cultural Apparatus," in *Power, Politics and People: The Collected Essays of C. Wright Mills,* ed. by Irving Louis Horowitz (Oxford 1963).

Morgan, Robert C., *The End of the Art World* (Allworth Press 1998).

Orvell, Miles, *The Real Thing: Imitation and Authenticity in American Culture, 1880–1940* (Univ. of N.C. Press 1989).

Postman, Neil, *Amusing Ourselves to Death: Public Discourse in the Age of Show Business* (Viking 1985).

Susman, Warren, *Culture as History: The Transformation of American Society in the Twentieth Century* (Pantheon Bks. 1984).

DAVID M. LUBIN

ASIAN AMERICANS

[The place of Asian Americans in the culture and history of the United States is here treated in several separate but related articles. The first entry, AN OVERVIEW, *points to the rich diversity inherent in the term* Asian American *and discusses the groups and histories it is meant to designate. Following this introduction are three more specialized pieces concerning the contributions of Asian Americans to various fields of activity. These are as follows:*

ASIAN AMERICANS IN FILM AND THEATER

ASIAN AMERICAN ART AND LITERATURE

ASIAN AMERICAN POLITICS

For related articles in the encyclopedia, see also ANGEL ISLAND; AMERICANIZATION; VIETNAMESE AMERICANS; SOUTH ASIAN AMERICANS; KOREAN AMERICANS; ORIENTALISM.*]*

An Overview

Asian Americans are those groups and individuals in North America (some prefer to expand the scope of the term to include all countries of the two Americas) who trace their ancestry back to Asia. Asian Americans by this definition include all Chinese, Japanese, Korean, Filipino, East Indian, Pakistani, Sri Lankan, Malaysian, Indonesian, Vietnamese, Cambodian, ethnic Lao, Hmong, Thai, and all other Americans with ethnic backgrounds in Asia. Many include Pacific Islanders under the rubric of "Asian Pacific Americans," so that Samoan Americans and Tongan Americans, for example, are included in the mix.

Ever since Chinese sought out the "Gold Mountain" in the California gold rush, Asians have been coming to America in significant numbers. Once America opened its doors—although at times halfheartedly or reluctantly—to Asian immigration, Americans of Asian descent experienced lives as diverse as their backgrounds. Many live in communities with such names as Chinatown, Koreatown, Little Tokyo, and Little Saigon. From western railroads to New York City's Chinatown, from Alaskan canneries to hospitals in New York and New Jersey, from California's Silicon Valley assembly lines to high-technology laboratories of Route 128 in Massachusetts—people of Asian descent have contributed much to the building of society and the development of culture in America.

Chinese and Filipino mariners of the Spanish galleons jumped ship at Acapulco during the 1600s, and this may have initiated the first immigration toward what would become the United States. Filipinos made their way to present-day Louisiana and established settlements in the Barataria Bay area. The first wave of migration began in the mid-nineteenth century with the arrival of 195 Chinese contract laborers in Hawaii and more than 20 thousand Chinese in California. Gold is what drew Chinese to California in 1848, and work in the sugar plantations attracted Chinese contract laborers to Hawaii beginning in 1851, thanks largely to the efforts of the Hawaiian Sugar Planters' Association. The Chinese were followed by 149 Japanese laborers shipped to Hawaii in 1868 and dozens of Japanese seeking their fortunes in California to work in the Wakamatsu Tea and Silk Colony. Large numbers of Japanese laborers, contracted under the Irwin Convention, came to Hawaii in 1885 and continued to do so until 1894. The newcomers were welcomed coldly in other parts. The 1878 ruling in the case of Ah Yup determined the ineligibility of Chinese for citizenship. In 1894 the circuit court in Massachusetts confirmed the ineligibility of the Japanese for U.S. citizenship; this finding did not, however, prevent Shinsei Kaneko from becoming the first to be naturalized in California in 1896.

A second wave of Asian immigration began in the first decade of the twentieth century. The initial group of Korean laborers joined the Hawaiian plantation workforce in 1903. That same year sponsored Filipino students called *pensionados* came to study in American colleges and universities. During this period hundreds of East Indian Sikhs, mainly from the Punjab region, made their way to the Pacific Northwest. They met with hostility and exclusion in both Canada and in the United States, where legislation in 1917 finally closed off the influx of the so-called turban tide.

The reception of Asians arriving in American lands was not usually congenial. Quite the opposite. In 1850 California imposed a Foreign Miners' Tax, with discriminatory impact on the Chinese miners who had come to join the gold rush in that state. Discriminatory legislation was often directed against Asian Americans. The justices in the 1854 case of *People* v. *Hall* ruled that a Chinese person could not give valid testimony in court cases. Some 12 thousand Chinese were contracted to work for the Central Pacific Railroad Company. When 2 thousand of the Chinese workers went on a week-long strike for equal pay and better work conditions, the company broke the strike by cutting off the strikers' food supply. Discriminatory legislation included the California law of 1858 prohibiting the entry of Chinese and those classified as "Mongolians."

Immigration and "Becoming American." America opened its doors, but not so widely to some immigrant groups. Whereas Chinese and Mongolians were shut out by the 1858 California law, the commercial Burlingame-Seward Treaty of 1868 allowed Chinese to immigrate. Chinese sweat and blood built the first transcontinental railroad beginning in 1865, when the Central Pacific Railroad Company employed Chinese laborers to grade, dig, and lay tracks.

Everywhere they moved, Chinese and Japanese immigrants met with discrimination and exclusionary practices. In 1870 the San Francisco Board of Supervisors voted to charge a fee to laundries using no horses, thus setting up a discriminatory ordinance targeting the Chinese laundries. Anti-Chinese mob violence broke out in Los Angeles in 1871; in Chico, California, in 1877; and in Washington Territory in 1885. The Page Law of 1875 prohibited the immigration of Chinese, Japanese, and Mongolian laborers, especially targeting felons and women perceived to be destined for prostitution. The Chinese Exclusion Law blocked the entry of Chinese immigrant labor from 1882 to 1892. In 1892 the Geary Law required registration of all Chinese immigrants. A 1902 police raid in Boston's Chinatown resulted in the arrest of nearly 250 Chinese immigrants without certificates. With the Organic Act of 1900 extending U.S. law to Hawaii, the flow of contract labor ended and many Japanese sought work on the U.S. mainland. But there they met with hostility and distrust. In 1913 California passed a series of alien-land laws designed to prevent "aliens ineligible for citizenship" from buying agricultural property.

A landmark event in Asian American history was the internment of Japanese Americans during World War II. Executive Order 9066 authorizing the army to carry out the relocations was signed March 18, 1942, by President Franklin D. Roosevelt. All told, some 120 thousand Japanese Americans were interned in ten relocation camps throughout the interior western United States.

Amy Ling calls Asian America a "borderland," one that is "rich in its variety of permutations of ethnicity, race, and culture, and in the paradoxes of multiculturalism, multivocality, and multinationalism." But in order to reach this borderland, Asian Americans had to struggle against tremendous odds. Institutionalized racism took form early on. In 1854 the Supreme Court ruled in *People* v. *Hall* that the killer of a Chinese man could not be convicted on the testimony of a Chinese, whose testimony could not be admitted in court. The road to becoming American was beset with other kinds of obstacles as well. In 1880 Section 6 of California's Civil Code was enacted to ban marriages between whites and nonwhites, the latter category including those of Mongolian descent.

Self-Definition and Cultural Assertion.

Asian American history tells more than stories of exploitation, and Asian American culture offers more than reactions to victimization. Asian Americans, from their beginnings as newcomers to their acceptance as integral members of American society, proved time and time again their creativity and resourcefulness as the agents of their own history

and makers of their own identity. Self-definition took multiple forms of resistance to oppressive conditions collectively and individually. Many Asian immigrants formed mutual benefit associations such as San Francisco's Sam Yup and Sze Yup Associations in 1851 and the Chinese Six Companies, a loose federation of six Chinese district associations in San Francisco in 1862. In 1884 the parents of Chinese American student Mamie Tape sued the San Francisco board of education to allow their child to attend public school.

The first trade association among the Japanese, the Japanese Shoemakers' League, was established in 1893 in San Francisco. Also in San Francisco, the Japanese founded in 1898 the Young Men's Buddhist Association, and in the following year Nishi Hongwanji priests in California established the North American Buddhist Mission. In 1909 the Korean Nationalist Association was formed, and in 1911, Pablo Manlapit began and organized the Filipino Higher Wages Association in Hawaii.

In Oxnard, California, in 1903 15 hundred Japanese and Mexican sugar-beet workers joined in a strike, and the following year Japanese sugar laborers in Hawaii carried out their first organized strike. The Caballeros de Dimas Alang, a fraternal and nationalist organization founded in Manila in 1906, established a San Francisco branch in 1921.

Asian Americans continued to fight for admission and citizenship. They encountered a setback in 1923, when in *United States* v. *Bhagat Singh Thind* the Supreme Court ruled that Asian Indians could not be naturalized as citizens. Despite such obstacles, Asian Americans persisted in seeking acceptance into American society. The Japanese American Citizens League, founded by young professionals and businesspersons, advocated "that Nisei [second-generation Japanese] should become 200 percent American" and thus promoted the American model of individualism and entrepreneurship.

Significant events in later years have affected Asian American communities. In 1965 the Hart-Cellar Act removed national-origins quotas for immigration to allow entry to preferred groups: refugees, needed professionals, and family members related to citizens. A nine-month student strike at San Francisco State University and the University of California at Berkeley, in 1968–1969, led to the creation of ethnic-studies programs on those two campuses. The 1974 Supreme Court ruling in *Lau v. Nichols* determined the right to bilingual education, which reaches many Asian American children. The triumph of Communist governments in Southeast Asia drove more than 130 thousand from that region to migrate to the United States in 1975. The 1976 Health Professionals Education Assistance Act reduced the flow of foreign health professionals into the country. In 1979 the resumption of Sino-American diplomatic relations allowed Chinese families to be reunited. In 1980 a Congressional Refugee Act was passed to order and regulate the influx of refugees. In 1988 the U.S. Congress approved the Amerasian Homecoming Act, permitting entry to children conceived by American fathers in Vietnam. In 1992 President Bill Clinton signed a bill for reparation of 25 thousand dollars to each survivor of the Japanese American internment.

Many are the stereotypes that continue to limit the possibilities and opportunities of Asian Americans. Such widely diffused stereotypes involve labels such as "yellow peril," which sees Asians in general as aggressive and diabolical enemies in war and aggressive and unscrupulous rivals in business; the "model minority," which assumes Asian Americans to be inherently oriented toward achieving success in school and work while working within the existing sociopolitical system, thanks to a traditional work ethic, family discipline, and adaptation to the social order; the "household eunuch," which regards Asian men as apt to perform as asexual domestic servants; and the "lotus blossom" and the "dragon lady," which relegate Asian-descended women either to the category of submissive plaything for men or to that of the seductive, yet emasculating and manipulative, dominatrix.

Asian American studies began as an academic discipline on San Francisco and Berkeley campuses in 1968. Its field of inquiry includes representations of Asians in literature and media, citizenship and assimilation, trans-Pacific relations, and the global economy.

Out of 600 thousand immigrants arriving each year in the United States, about half are Asian, contributing to the fact that Asian Americans make up the fastest growing minority group in the United States, at a rate of 95 percent in the last two decades of the twentieth century. In 1960, only 877,934 Americans were of Asian ancestry. By 1990, according to the U.S. Census, there were 7,273,662 Asian Americans in the United States, or nearly 3 percent of the total population, including 1.6 million Chinese, 1.4 million Filipinos, 847 thousand Japanese, 815 thousand East Indians, 800 thousand Koreans, 593 thousand Vietnamese, 147 thousand Laotians, and 149 thousand Cambodian Americans. By the year 2000 the Asian American population reached 10 million. It is expected that by the year 2050, Asian Americans will constitute 10.7 percent of the U.S. population. In 1989, 35 percent of Asian American households earned an annual income of 50 thousand dollars or more.

"Close to 50 percent of Asian Americans under 35 are marrying non-Asians," wrote Eric Liu in 1998, "which promises rather quickly to change the meaning of the race." This fact emphasized the hybrid significance of the term *Asian American*. In the aftermath of the Japanese American internments, the Japanese American Citizens League encouraged intermarriage as a means of gaining acceptance and assimilation. United States military involvements and interventions in Asia also promoted intermarriage between soldiers and women from Korea, Japan, the Philippines, and Vietnam—the so-called war brides. California lifted the remaining barrier to intermarriage with Asian Americans in 1948 when it repealed its antimiscegenation laws.

The scope of Asian American experience should not be limited solely to that of Asian immigrants and their spouses and descendants, however. Rather, it is a collective history that connects both sides of the Pacific Ocean, one that involves Asians of diverse national origins and Americans of other than Asian descent, which inevitably entails the social processes of transnationalization and cultural transformation.

Amy Ling asserts the value of an Asian American perspective because "it calls to account those in positions of power and shines a light on the discrepancy between word and deed, between democratic ideals and discriminatory practices." Along the same lines, Gary Okihiro argues that "the deeper significance of Asians, and indeed of all minorities in America, rests in their opposition to the dominant paradigm, their fight against 'the power,' their efforts to transform, and not simply reform, American society and its structures." Indeed, their struggle for admission, recognition, livelihood, and equality has meaning for the entirety of American society, inasmuch as "Asians resisted their exclusion and marginalization and thereby enlarged the range and deepened the meaning of American democracy."

BIBLIOGRAPHY

Chan, Sucheng, *Asian Americans: An Interpretive History* (Twayne 1991).

Cao, Lan, and Himilce Novas, *Everything You Need to Know about Asian American History* (Plume 1996).

Hagedorn, Jessica, ed., *Charlie Chan Is Dead: An Anthology of Contemporary Asian American Fiction,* with a preface by Elaine Kim (Penguin 1993).

Liu, Eric, *The Accidental Asian: Notes of a Native Speaker* (Random House 1998).

Okihiro, Gary Y., *Margins and Mainstreams: Asians in American History and Culture* (Univ. of Wash. Press 1994).

Takaki, Ronald, *From Exiles to Immigrants: The Refugees from Southeast Asia,* adapted by Rebecca Stefoff, with Carol Takaki (Chelsea House 1995).

Yang, Jeff, et al., eds., *Eastern Standard Time: A Guide to Asian Influence on American Culture from Astro Boy to Zen Buddhism* (Houghton 1997).

Zia, Helen, *Asian American Dreams: The Emergence of an American People* (Farrar, Straus 2000).

EUGENIO MATIBAG

Asian Americans in Film and Theater

While distinctly different disciplines with separate histories, Asian American film and theater are linked by their similar development and existence as a response to, if not in opposition to, mainstream American film and theater. The image of the Asian has long been a subject of fascination in American film and theater; from the dawn of the era of the silent movie and the minstrel show, Asians have been depicted on the American screen and stage. The stage convention of Caucasian actors portraying Asian characters later became accepted in film; a cavalcade of noted actors including Katharine Hepburn, Fred Astaire, Louise Bremer, Marlon Brando, Sidney Toler, Greta Garbo, Peter Sellers, David Carradine, Jonathan Pryce, Ricardo Montalban, and Bette Davis are among those who donned "yellow face" to create enduring and stereotypical images, such as the submissive geisha, the humble peasant, the emasculated servant, the exotic prostitute, the inscrutable sage, the comic sidekick, the evil dragon lady, and the diabolical villain—images that continue to inform the popular imagination and media.

The emergence of Asian American film and theater is intrinsically tied to the Asian American movement, which was catalyzed by the civil rights and anti–Vietnam War movements. The monolithic, mythologized "Oriental" was appropriated and subverted in the term *Asian American* as a source of political power for diverse communities of Asian descent. According to William Wei:

> The concept of Asian American implies that there can be a communal consciousness and a unique culture that is neither Asian nor American, but Asian American. In defining their own identity and culture, Asian Americans bring together previously isolated and ineffective struggles against the oppression of Asian communities into a coherent Pan-Asian movement for social change.

Films made by Asian Americans began in this spirit of community activism in the 1970s. Filmmaking emerged that both redressed damaging media images and addressed pressing issues in the Asian American community, such as urban renewal and the plight of Asian communities. Documentary films, far more economical to produce than feature films and the ideal vehicle with which to probe social issues, have been the predominant genre of Asian American filmmaking. They have earned Asian American filmmakers deserved critical attention, while serving to further activist efforts concerning such issues as reparations for Japanese American survivors of internment in Loni Ding's *The Color of Honor* (1987), a chronicle of Japanese American participation in the U.S. military in World War II against the backdrop of Japanese American internment; and racial violence against Asian Americans in Christine Choy's *Who Killed Vincent Chin?* (1989). Documentaries by Asian American filmmakers have made a neglected history visible and probed stories from a previously unheard perspective. Among the documentary films that have won critical acclaim (and Academy Awards) are Steven Okazaki's *Days of Waiting* (1991); Freida Lee Mock's *Maya Lin: A Strong Clear Vision* (1995); and Jessica Yu's *Breathless* (1996). Other significant documentary filmmakers include Renee Tajima, Thi Thanh Nga, Lee Mun Wah, Arthur Dong, Lise Yasui, Robert Nakamura, Felicia Lowe, Rea Tajiri, Paul Kwan, Janice Tanaka, Sharon Jue, Renee Cho, John Esaki, Deborah Gee, Valerie Soe, and Curtis Choy.

Similarly, the early Asian American theater movement was begun by actors and writers, such as the Academy Award–nominated actor Mako and playwright and novelist Frank Chin, both of whom were frustrated by the limited opportunities available in the mainstream theater. Earlier individual efforts can be cited, particularly in Hawaii from 1920 through 1940. However, it was the 1970s that marked the birth of a sustained movement and evolving contemporary body of work in both theater and film. Theater also sought to fill in a historical void, addressing such issues as the Japanese American internment camp experience through such plays as Momoko Iko's *Gold Watch* (1970) and Wakako Yamauchi's *12-1-A* (1981); the immigration experience, as exemplified in Genny Lim's *Paper Angels* (1978); and the unique stories of hidden communities in Velina Houston's *TEA* (1983), Philip Gotanda's *The Wash* (1983), and *The Kamiya Family Trilogy* by Ed Sakamoto.

The development of Asian American film and theater in the crucible of activism also had a bearing on the creation of institutions, which have sustained and steered these disciplines beyond the initiatives of individual artists. Recognizing the marginal position of Asian Americans in the society at large and the limited probability of distribution, Asian Americans established (international) film festivals in San Francisco, New York, Los Angeles, and Seattle and advocacy networks, such as Visual Communications in Los Angeles; Asian Cine Vision in New York, founded in 1976; and the National Asian American Telecommunication Association in San Francisco, founded in 1980. These organizations developed audiences, created networks of communication and distribution, and also defined the context and content of the field.

The pioneering Asian American theaters (East West Players in Los Angeles, founded in 1965; Kumu Kahua in Honolulu, founded in 1971; the Asian American Theater Company in San Francisco, founded in 1973; the Pan Asian Repertory of New York City, founded in 1977; and the Northwest Asian American Theater in Seattle, founded in 1976) have been joined over the years by theaters that have sprung up as the changing Asian American population demographic has defined new communities. These include Theater Ma-yi in New York City; Theater Mu in Minneapolis; Teatro Ng Tanan (Theater for the People) in San Francisco; and Pom Siab Hmoob Theater, formerly the Hmong Theater Project in Minneapolis. Many works that engage new aesthetics and emerging Asian American communities are being performed at theaters (such as Theater Mu) that are not located in the historic centers of Asian immigration but in areas of the country where newer immigrants have arrived. Theaters that embrace a multiracial or multiethnic vision include New World Theater in Amherst, Massachusetts, and Pangea World Theater in Minneapolis. In 1999 the Northwest Asian American Theater Company organized the first national convention of Asian American theaters, which concluded that the previous focus on works exploring the histories of people who came to this country at the turn of the century will increasingly give way to the vital new materials and aesthetics of recent Asian immigrants.

While Asian American film and theater have been consistently developed, sustained, and promoted within the aforementioned institutions and organizations that provide a continuum of Asian American activism, it is important to note that there have always been individual artists operating independently, in alternative settings or within the mainstream, or in a combination of all of the above. The independent Asian American filmmaker has pushed boundaries in experimental film and addressed fresh themes while creating new audiences. Important independent and experimental filmmakers include Shu Lea Chang, Trinh T. Minh-ha, Peter Wang, Gregg Araki, and Kayo Hatta. Increasingly, independent filmmakers have made headway in crossing boundaries. Wayne Wang, whose independently produced *Chan Is Missing* (1982) was the first critically hailed film utilizing an all Asian American cast and crew, has gone on to direct projects under major studio sponsorship, with Asian and non-Asian themes, such as *The Joy Luck Club* (1993) and *Smoke* (1995). Taiwanese American Ang Lee was nominated for an Academy Award for best foreign language film for *The Wedding Banquet* (1993) and in 2001 won that award for *Crouching Tiger, Hidden Dragon*. He has also directed several acclaimed films with non-Asian themes, including the Civil War epic, *Ride with the Devil* (1999). The presence in festivals and distribution networks of Asian and Asian diasporic filmmakers, particularly from Hong Kong, Canada, and the United Kingdom, has placed Asian American filmmaking within a global context.

David Henry Hwang, who won the Tony Award for *M. Butterfly* in 1988, has had other works produced on Broadway and in regional theater, while retaining his ties to the Asian American theater through production and mentoring new writers. Hwang, as well as playwrights Philip Gotanda, Lane Nishikawa, Chay Yew, and Velina Hasu Houston, has worked both in the Asian American theater, regional theater, and film. Other theater artists such as Ping Chong, Han Ong, and Jessica Hagedorn have found affinity and support in alter-

native and experimental performance venues while writers such as Diana Son and Naomi Iizuka have developed work not necessarily tied to an ethnically specific voice. The work of many solo performance artists, such as Dawn Akemi Saito, Dan Kwong, Denise Uyehara, Jude Narita, Amy Hill, Brenda Wong Aoki, Nicky Paraiso, Shushir Kurup, and le thi diem thuy, has been developed independently, in experimental venues and in Asian American theaters. Still other artists, such as Nobuko Miyamoto of Great Leap Incorporated, have founded their own organizations to support their work and the work of others. Finally, a plethora of independent ensembles, particularly sketch comedy, improvisation, and experimental groups, have brought younger audiences into the theater.

The fluidity with which individual artists are able to work between mainstream, Asian American, and experimental theater is less a matter of desire than of the whims and fashions of the marketplace at any given moment. Writing about a spate of Asian American–themed films, a short-lived situation comedy, and the fleeting presence of a few Asian Americans in major television roles in the 1990s, George Toshio Johnson observed, "Every decade, Hollywood and Asian Americans have had a fling that bloomed with great promise—and resulted in broken blossoms. The '90s were no different." Jun Xing poses incisive questions about the nature of Asian American film and video, which have equal relevance to Asian American theater. He asks:

> Does the term *Asian American* refer to the ethnicity of the filmmaker or the topic of the film, regardless of who makes it? Would a film made by an Asian American in Asia or elsewhere—such as Ang Lee's *Eat Drink Man Woman* (1994), made in Taiwan, or Tran Anh Hung's *The Scent of Green Papaya* (1993), filmed in France—be considered Asian or Asian American? How do we categorize an Asian American–directed "non-ethnic" movie, such as Wayne Wang's *Smoke* (1995) and *Blue in the Face* (1995) or Ang Lee's *Sense and Sensibility* (1995) and *The Ice Storm* (1997)?

Where do we draw the boundaries? Do films with a clear Asian American theme, but shot by a multiracial crew—such as Oliver Stone's *Heaven and Earth* (1993) and David Cronenberg's *M. Butterfly* (1993)—qualify as Asian American?

A 1990 reader's poll in *A Magazine* underscored these questions as readers freely mixed Asian and Asian American screen stars and films in their choices. As the future of each discipline is considered, these questions become increasingly relevant in terms of demographic shifts (both changes in the composition of Asian communities and the increase in racial and ethnic hybridity), the movement of Asians and Asian Americans transnationally, and the positive impact that the Asian American movement has on social institutions, attitudes, and cultural expectations.

BIBLIOGRAPHY

Berson, Misha, ed., *Between Worlds: Contemporary Asian-American Plays* (Theatre Communications Group 1990).

Choy, Christine, "Images of Asian-Americans in Films and Television," in *Ethnic Images in American Film and Television,* ed. by Randall Miller (Balch Inst. 1978).

Feng, Peter, "In Search of Asian American Cinema," *Cineaste* 21 (1995):1–2.

Houston, Velina Hasu, ed., *The Politics of Life: Four Plays by Asian American Women* (Temple Univ. Press 1993).

Houston, Velina Hasu, ed., *But Still, Like Air, I'll Rise: New Asian American Plays* (Temple Univ. Press 1997).

Johnson, George Toshio, "'Hope Floats': Hollywood's Latest Fling with Asian America," *A Magazine* (November 30, 1990):52–54.

Lee, Josephine, *Performing Asian America: Race and Ethnicity on the Contemporary Stage* (Temple Univ. Press 1997).

Leong, Russell, ed., *Moving the Image: Independent Asian Pacific American Media Arts* (Univ. of Calif. Press 1991).

Perkins, Kathy, and Roberta Uno, eds., *Contemporary Plays by Women of Color* (Routledge 1996).

Tajima, Renee, "Lotus Blossoms Don't Bleed: Images of Asian Women," in *Making Waves: An Anthology of Writings by and about Asian American Women,* ed. by Asian Women United of California (Beacon Press 1989).

Uno, Roberta, ed., *Unbroken Thread: An Anthology of Plays by Asian American Women* (Univ. of Mass. Press 1993).

Wei, William, *The Asian American Movement* (Temple Univ. Press 1993).

Wong, Eugene F., *On Visual Media Racism: Asians in the American Motion Pictures* (Arno Press 1978).

ROBERTA UNO

Asian American Art and Literature

Asian American literature and art cannot be explained by one set of aesthetics or a single method or approach. The sheer diversity of the artists and their backgrounds and even the variety and change within the oeuvre of an individual artist simply defy neat categorization. Some artists emphasize personal experience and reflection; others reflect on historical occurrences and cultural phenomena; others tend toward sheer experimentation with forms of expression and types of media or discourse.

Literature: Major Themes. Asian American authors have explored issues central to the Asian American experience: the legacy of the past; the encounter of diverse cultures; the challenges of racism, discrimination, and exclusion; and the dreams achieved and dreams deferred of an immigrant nation. In the process of developing and defining itself, then, Asian American literature speaks to the very heart of what it means to be American. The authors of this literature above all concern themselves with identity, with the question of becoming and being American, of being accepted, not "foreign." Elaine Kim characterizes Asian American literature as mainly one of "protest and exile, a literature about place and displacement, a literature concerned with psychic and physical 'home'—searching for and claiming a 'home' or longing for a final 'homecoming.'"

Distinguished Asian American authors and works include Korean American Younghill Kang's *The Grass Roof* (1931) and his book about life in New York, *East Goes West* (1937); Chinese American Louis Chu's *Eat a Bowl of Tea* (1961), also about life in New York; Filipino American Carlos Bulosan's experiences as a migrant worker in *Letters from America* (1942) and *America Is in the Heart* (1946); and Korean Canadian writer and video artist Theresa Hak

© ROBERT FOOTHORAP/BLACK STAR

Novelist Amy Tan in Guilin, China, where part of the movie version of *The Joy Luck Club* was filmed.

Kyung Cha's acclaimed *Dictée* (1982). Chang-Rae Lee, of South Korea, won the PEN Hemingway Award for the Best First Novel in 1995 for *Native Speaker* (1995).

Other celebrated works are Maxine Hong Kingston's groundbreaking and widely acclaimed memoirs, *The Woman Warrior* (1976) and *China Men* (1980); Frank Chin's coedited Chinese Japanese American anthology, *Aiiieeeee!* (1974) and his novel *Donald Duk* (1991); Cynthia Kadohata's account of Japanese Americans in the post-internment years in *The Floating World* (1988); Amy Tan's best-selling family chronicles, *The Joy Luck Club* (1989, the basis for the 1993 film) and *The Kitchen God's Wife* (1991); Garrett Hongo's poetry collections *Yellow Light* (1988) and *The River of Heaven* (1989); David Henry Hwang's drama, *M. Butterfly* (1988), the first play by an Asian American to be produced on Broadway; Gish Jen's comic novel *Typical American* (1991); Laurence Yep's young adult fictions *Child of the Owl* (1977) and *Dragon of the Lost Sea* (1982); Hisaye Yamamoto's collection *Seventeen Syllables and Other Stories* (1988); Shawn Wong's novels *Homebase* (1979) and *American Knees* (1995); and M. Evelina Galang's stories in *Her Wild American Self* (1995).

Eminent anthologies of Asian American writing not only indicate the emergence and coalescence of a body of literature that could be called Asian American, but also signal the form by which that body of literature can be recognized by the reading public and assigned as reading in academic settings. Such anthologies include the aforementioned *Aiiieeeee! An Anthology of Asian American Writers* (1974), edited by Jeffrey Paul Chan, Frank Chin, Lawson Fusao Inada, and Shawn Wong. This anthology, devoted exclusively to Chinese American and Japanese American works, was followed by the more inclusive *The Big Aiiieeeee!!!* (1991), whereas Jessica T. Hagedorn's *Charlie Chan Is Dead: An Anthology of Asian American Fiction* (1993) showcases imaginative prose representative of all the major immigrant groups, with the exception of Southeast Asia. Garrett Hongo edited *The Open Boat, Poems from Asian America* (1993). All of the erotic stories and poems of *On a Bed of Rice* (1995), an anthology edited by Geraldine Kudaka, contradict the racist notion that Asian Americans are asexual or passive in their sexuality.

Artistic Genres. Art has many meanings and diverse significance for those who create it or behold it or in some way participate in it. It is difficult to define one universally Asian American aesthetic or artistic ideology, yet some generalizations can be ventured. There exists a sense in this emergent Asian American culture that "art" is not the special province of the professional artist, not something merely to be seen and consumed. Art, somewhat like Asian-based religious practice and spirituality, forms a part of everyday life. Art belongs to people and not to a special class of artists and artisans. Nor can the category of Asian American art be limited to that produced exclusively by Asian Americans, for it must embrace as well those works that originate in Asian countries but are imported and translated or otherwise adapted for American reception.

Artistic contributions to American domestic culture abound, as seen in the distinctly Japanese plantings of bonsai and ikebana; Chinese brush painting; the calligraphy of China, Korea, and Japan;

Chinese ceramics and Japanese porcelains; rugs from Turkey, the Caucasus, Persia, the Turkoman of Central Asia, India, Tibet, and China and, of course, the celebrated Asian American culinary arts. Many Americans are familiar with the art of Japanese paper folding called origami. In Japanese-influenced decor one might find the thick bedding consisting of mattress and cover called futon, shoji screens, and tatami mats. Mass and popular culture have been permeated by Anime and Pokéman cartoons, Manga comic books, the Sanrio "Hello Kitty" merchandise, Nintendo video games, the Power Rangers television series, and martial-arts action movies featuring Bruce Lee, Jet Li, and Jackie Chan, for example. Martial arts have gone mainstream as well, with the proliferation of programs and classes in karate, aikido, judo, Korean tae kwon do, Japanese jujutsu, Thai muay thai (or kickboxing), and Filipino kali (or arnis).

Renowned among architects are Minoru Yamasaki, chief architect of the 110-story twin towers of the World Trade Center in New York City; Arata Isozaki, who designed the Museum of Contemporary Art of Los Angeles; Maya Lin, whose Vietnam Veterans Memorial provoked reflection and controversy; and internationally known Tadao Ando, whose minimalist style is characterized by concrete surfaces and geometric figures. Chinese American architect I. M. Pei is best-known for designing the Rock and Roll Hall of Fame and Museum in Cleveland, Ohio; the glass pyramid entrance to the Louvre in Paris, France; the John F. Kennedy Library in Massachusetts; New York City's Jacob K. Javits Convention Center; and the East Wing of the National Gallery of Art in Washington, D.C.

Perhaps the best-known Japanese graphic and clothing designer today is Eiko Ishioka, who won the 1992 Academy Award for best costume design. She is one of numerous Asian American clothing designers who have mixed cultural motifs and sensibilities to create the kind of art that is worn. The international fashion world came to appreciate Josie Natori's beaded and embroidered bustiers as well as Vera Wang's wedding dresses and evening gowns.

© B. BISSON/CORBIS-SYGMA

Architect I. M. Pei outside the new entrance to the Louvre museum in Paris, France.

Musicians who have drawn both applause and critical acclaim are Paris-born cellist Yo-Yo Ma; Korean American violinist Kyung-Wha Chung; Japanese and American violinist Midori; and conductors Zubin Mehta, born in Bombay, India, and Seiji Ozawa, born in Shenyang, China. Other musicians include singer-songwriter-artist Yoko Ono, widow of John Lennon. The Japanese American rock group Shonen Knife and the Filipino American singing groups Kai and Pinay have drawn packed crowds of admirers.

Other collaborative artistic projects have produced works and performances that challenge the mainstream views of race and culture. The art network *Godzilla* has created links of communication among Asian American artists. Based in New York and cofounded in 1990 by Ken Chu, Godzilla has sponsored discussions and debates on the notion of an "Asian American aesthetic." Group exhibitions such as *Yellow Peril: Reconsidered,* which toured Canada in 1990 and 1991, and the Godzilla-sponsored *The Curio Shop* in New York in 1993 displayed the images and artifacts by which Asian Americans have been stereotyped. In both of these exhibitions, artists and installers performed a negative critique

191

Cellist Yo-Yo Ma (*center*), with violinist Isaac Stern (*left*) and conductor Zubin Mehta in 1991.

of mainstream essentialism that has marginalized and dehumanized the image of the Asian in American culture.

Korean American artist Nam June Paik has drawn wide attention for multimedia electronic installations that incorporate videorecorders, television circuitry, and avant-garde musical performance in works that include the *Electronic Superhighway* and the *Information Wall*. Sculptor Isamu Noguchi's creations of interior and exterior works include items of furniture, the Akari Japanese lanterns, the design of the gardens for the United Nations Educational, Scientific, and Cultural Organization (UNESCO) headquarters in Paris, the sunken garden of the Beinecke Rare Book and Manuscript Library at Yale, and the Philip A. Hart Plaza in Detroit. Among performance artists, Hmong American rapper Tou Ger Xiong brings his family history to audiences with a blend of storytelling and slides. One of his performances, given at Iowa State University in 1999, was titled "Snoop Doggy Dogg Meets Bruce Lee."

Arts and Identities. Inasmuch as being Asian American means to find one's own identity as multiply originated and diversely situated, many productions of Asian American art must seek a com-

ing-to-terms with an inherently plural selfhood. Asian Americans have attained a critical mass and achieved a self-consciousness of their agency in the making of history. Coming from specific countries of origin, from diverse religious, ethnic, and linguistic groupings, they know the dangers of generalization and self-ghettoization. Accordingly, most artists are wary of pinning themselves down to anything that could be called an Asian American aesthetic. Many works aim to create a change in social consciousness. For example, Sung Ho Choi's 1993 installation of burnt-out wood, photographs, awning, and living plants titled *Choi's Market* vividly recalls the 1992 riots of south central Los Angeles, in which Korean storekeepers became the targets of racial enmity.

The crossing of borders and the creation of hybrid spaces are obsessions of many Asian American artists. One of Rirkrit Tiravanija's installations in New York's 303 Gallery in 1995 consisted of a "meditation area" complete with a camping tent, a couch, an audio tape of a Hmong radio program, and a video on Hmong appliqués. This art of dislocations and thresholds brings together cultures and technologies and engages viewers in the examination of their own social frameworks. In 1994 artist Michael Joo videotaped himself swimming in two thousand pounds (907 kg) of monosodium glutamate, addressing with this, as with other performances, stereotypes of Chinese culture and the "economic" circulation of meanings and identifications. Xu Bing's *A Book from the Sky* offered a view of sheets and sheets of paper—some hanging from the ceiling, some bound up in books, some hung on the walls—inscribed in authentic-looking but invented "Chinese" characters. This 1995 installation examined the crisis of meaning involving Chinese tradition and modernity, expression and silence. Art critic Alice Yang has called Bing Lee's 1994 show "an imaginative foray into chance operation," by which, beginning with a blank wall, the artist adds drawings to it each day, creating an array that amounts to a "pictodiary" that stages a sort of surrealist automatism as it performs a Buddhist meditative notation marking the subject's emptying-out. Cultures cross again in Chen Zhen's 1996 "Daily

Incantations," composed of 101 Chinese wooden chamber pots arrayed and suspended in the fashion of Bronze Age chime bells. By so merging the physical and the spiritual, Chen's installation indicates the cycles of consumption, assimilation, and expulsion that transcend the national dramas.

Aesthetics and Social Import. As this brief overview has indicated, Asian American writers and artists in general have undertaken a twofold task: that of creating art works while displaying true originality and combining elements of European American and Asian cultures; and that of transcending or subverting the ethnocentricism of the dominant culture, offering in its place a transpacific aesthetic, a new racial and cultural synthesis, and a renewed vision of art's possibilities.

BIBLIOGRAPHY

Hagedorn, Jessica, ed., *Charlie Chan Is Dead: An Anthology of Contemporary Asian American Fiction,* with a preface by Elaine Kim (Penguin 1993).

Kim, Elaine, *Asian American Literature: An Introduction to the Writings and Their Social Context* (Temple Univ. Press 1982).

Liu, Eric, *The Accidental Asian: Notes of a Native Speaker* (Random House 1998).

Okihiro, Gary Y., *Margins and Mainstreams: Asians in American History and Culture* (Univ. of Wash. Press 1994).

Yang, Jeff, et al., eds., *Eastern Standard Time: A Guide to Asian Influence on American Culture from Astro Boy to Zen Buddhism* (Houghton 1997).

EUGENIO MATIBAG

Asian American Politics

Politics, for Asian Americans, covers a host of concerns that hold in common a challenge to racialization beyond a black-white paradigm, a critique of the persistence of discrimination and exclusion, a recognition of their group's increasing numbers and diversity, and a desire to empower their communities. The term *Asian American* was an internally defined political label that arose as a consequence of the civil rights movement but was elaborated as a specific expression of anti-imperialist, antiracist, and antiexploitation agendas that bound together ethnonational groups whose origins could be traced back to Asia. Even though Chinese Americans, Japanese Americans, Filipino Americans, Korean Americans, and others previously regarded themselves (and were also regarded by society) as distinct and competing groups, political activists in the 1960s realized the advantages of intergroup mobilization to fight for common demands.

Such a panethnic formation has had important consequences for building political consciousness among very diverse populations. Not only were Asian Americans able to appreciate their common geographical origins but their political efforts also have become more recognized as intimately connected to common historical and contemporary experiences of disenfranchisement and violence, mainly because of perceptions that they are a "model minority," are threats to society, or are foreigners. This panethnic label has also been used by the state primarily for census purposes and resource distribution. However, this way of lumping for convenience has, at times, perpetuated unfair treatment.

An important occasion that resulted in Asian American political mobilization occurred in the wake of the murder of Vincent Chin in 1982. Chin, a Chinese American, was targeted as an Asian foreigner responsible for lost or diminishing job opportunities in Detroit. His case is evidence of the power of coalition politics as a response to racism. Such politics have further called for a more complex consideration of race relations beyond those that include only African Americans and European Americans, the ways in which Asian Americans challenge dominant assimilationist demands imposed on them, the advantages of forging ties with other minoritized groups, and the quest to be regarded as equal members of American society.

Because the Asian American population has grown exponentially and changed dramatically with different immigrant groups since the 1960s, questions about the viability of panethnic grouping have arisen. Among the issues being debated are the inclusion of Pacific Islanders into the fold, the position to take on affirmative action, and the directions that national and international political agendas need to take. Panethnic politics, however, have been steadily galvanized by a strong concern for the attainment of political power—something long denied to Asian Americans as evidenced by their continuously low representation in public office. Redistricting, voter registration, and a strong voice in policy-making are the primary concerns in this area. Beyond these are related political issues that Asian Americans face both as members of ethnic-specific groups within the label and as people who are pejoratively treated as "racially the same" by society. These include policies on immigration, language use, labor, education, health, cultural production, gay rights, women's rights, and crime.

BIBLIOGRAPHY

Aguilar-San Juan, Karin, ed., *The State of Asian America: Activism and Resistance in the 1990s* (South End Press 1994).

Espiritu, Yen Le, *Asian American Panethnicity: Bridging Institutions and Identities* (Temple Univ. Press 1992).

Hu-DeHart, Evelyn, ed., *Across the Pacific: Asian Americans and Globalization* (The Asia Society/Temple Univ. Press 1999).

Leadership Education for Asian Pacifics (LEAP), Asian Pacific American Public Policy Institute and UCLA Asian American Studies Center, *The State of Asian Pacific America: Policy Issues to the Year 2020* (LEAP/Univ. of Calif. Press 1993).

Wei, William, *The Asian American Movement* (Temple Univ. Press 1993).

RICK BONUS

ASSASSINATIONS

Assassins have repeatedly targeted American presidents since 1835, when Andrew Jackson was saved from death by the misfiring of his assailant's gun. Four serving presidents have been killed, and other leading political figures also have been assassinated. The most notable deaths, including those of Presidents Abraham Lincoln and John Kennedy, resulted in huge displays of public mourning and became the inspirations for numerous artistic works and

THE GRANGER COLLECTION

Charles Guiteau shot President James A. Garfield in 1881.

kitsch. They were also to become the subjects of speculation and investigation when people sought to blame the deaths on wide-ranging conspiracies. Under the auspices of the Central Intelligence Agency (CIA), the American government has also utilized assassination as a means of conducting foreign policy.

Abraham Lincoln, the first American president to be assassinated, was shot by pro-Confederate actor John Wilkes Booth in Ford's Theater, Washington, D.C., on April 14, 1865. On the same night an accomplice stabbed Secretary of State William Seward, while a third conspirator failed in his assignment of attacking Vice President Andrew Johnson. After shooting Lincoln, Booth broke his leg leaping from the presidential box before making his escape. Troops found him two weeks later, when he was killed in a burning barn in Virginia. Eight accomplices were later convicted for their parts in the plan, four of whom were hanged.

In July 1881 a second president was killed when Charles Guiteau shot James Garfield in the Washington railway station. Unlike Lincoln, Garfield lingered for a number of weeks before dying, in September. Guiteau was motivated by the deluded belief that Garfield had promised him a prestigious position within the new administration. Despite his

UPI/BETTMAN

A mule-drawn caisson carries the casket of assassinated leader Martin Luther King, Jr., in April 1968.

clear insanity, Guiteau too was hanged. Twenty years later anarchist Leon Czolgosz shot President William McKinley at the Pan-American exposition in Buffalo, New York. Poor medical treatment was a major factor in McKinley's death, but Czolgosz was executed in the electric chair just fifty-three days afterward.

The 1960s saw a spate of assassinations, of which the pinnacle was the death of President John F. Kennedy, as America endured its most politically turbulent decade since the Civil War. Kennedy was shot while being driven through Dallas, Texas, in November 1963. Lee Harvey Oswald was soon arrested in connection with the assassination, but he was never tried because he was himself shot by Jack Ruby, a minor underworld crime figure. Oswald claimed that he had been set up as a patsy, but a subsequent presidential commission under the chairmanship of Chief Justice Earl Warren concluded that he had acted alone, a conclusion repeat-

195

edly challenged by conspiracy-theory advocates in the following years.

Parallels can be drawn between the deaths of Lincoln and Kennedy because both presidents were advocates of liberal (racial) reforms, which were greatly opposed by conservatives, especially Southerners. Both deaths also caused widespread mourning; for example, a million people saw Lincoln's coffin as his funeral cortege traveled to his hometown of Springfield, Illinois. This expression of public grief also influenced the works of contemporary artists and writers, including Walt Whitman, whose poems "O Captain! My Captain!" and "When Lilacs Last in the Dooryard Bloom'd" were moving expressions of his and America's sorrow. In the 1960s Kennedy's death caused similar reactions and famously inspired a series of silkscreens by pop artist Andy Warhol.

Kennedy's assassination has retained the public's interest because conspiracy theorists have accused many groups of complicity in it, including the Mafia, Cuban exiles, rogue elements of the government, and leading members of the military-industrial complex. Lincoln's death raised similar theories with the defeated Confederacy, Secretary of War Edward Stanton, and Catholics all being blamed. Modern historians reject these ideas, but Lincoln is still seen as a fallen martyr and just leader worthy of huge commemorations in both Washington, D.C., and Mount Rushmore. Many early films promoted this image (for example, *Abraham Lincoln*, 1908), although few were as brilliant as D. W. Griffith's reconstruction of the assassination in *Birth of a Nation* (1915). The most important film based on the Kennedy assassination is Oliver Stone's *JFK* (1991), which reawakened the controversy by producing a "countermyth" to challenge the Warren Report's conclusions. The controversy has also led to the publication of numerous books, including works by William Manchester (*Death of a President*, 1967), Norman Mailer (*Oswald's Tale*, 1995), and Don DeLillo (*Libra*, 1989).

Kennedy's death caused consternation in America, but it was only part of a series of assassinations throughout the 1960s. In June 1963 Medgar Evers, a leading civil rights figure, was shot and killed in Mississippi, but his death would be overshadowed by those of Malcolm X and Martin Luther King, Jr. Malcolm X, a leading member of the Nation of Islam, was shot by some of his former followers in Harlem, New York, in September 1965, after he had broken with the group. In April 1968 King was shot on a hotel balcony in Memphis, Tennessee, by James Earl Ray. Ray pleaded guilty to the murder but later claimed that he had been part of a wider conspiracy, an argument that the King family came to support. Two months after King's death, Robert Kennedy, the late president's brother, was assassinated in a California hotel as he celebrated winning the state's vital Democratic presidential primary. The gunman, Sirhan Sirhan, was a Palestinian who was angered by Robert Kennedy's Middle East policies. Further victims of shootings were George Rockwell (the leader of the American Nazi Party, who was killed in 1967) and George Wallace (the segregationist governor of Alabama and presidential primary candidate, who was paralyzed after being shot in Maryland in 1972). President Ronald Reagan was also shot, and his press secretary, James Brady, was critically injured in an assassination attempt in 1981. John Hinckley, the gunman, was tried but found "not guilty by reason of insanity," a verdict that caused nationwide reforms to insanity tests in court cases.

This series of assassinations was part of the reason for the post-Watergate "intelligence flap" of 1975, which uncovered CIA assassination plots against a number of foreign leaders. Congressional investigation under the chairmanship of Senator Frank Church revealed that Cuban leader Fidel Castro had been repeatedly targeted through Operation Mongoose from 1959 to 1962 and that the CIA had plotted against Rafael Trujillo of the Dominican Republic and Patrice Lumumba of Congo. (Both were killed without CIA involvement.) The CIA has also been linked to assassinations carried out by the supporters of General Augusto Pinochet of Chile.

[*See also* VIOLENCE; LINCOLN, ABRAHAM.]

BIBLIOGRAPHY

"Alleged Assassination Plots Involving Foreign Leaders" (An Interim Report of the Select Committee to Study Government Operations with Respect to Intelligence Activities), *Senate Report,* 94th Cong., I sess., no. 94–465 (Nov. 20, 1975).

Clarke, James W., *American Assassins: The Darker Side of Politics,* rev. ed. (Princeton Univ. Press 1990).

Peterson, Merrill D., *Lincoln in American Memory* (Oxford 1994).

Sifakis, Carl, *Encyclopaedia of Assassinations* (Facts on File 1991).

Simon, Art, *Dangerous Knowledge: The JFK Assassination in Art and Film* (Temple Univ. Press 1996).

Zelizer, Barbie, *Covering the Body: The Kennedy Assassination, the Media, and the Shaping of Collective Memory* (Univ. of Chicago Press 1992).

NEIL DENSLOW

ASSIMILATION

Assimilation refers to the act or process by which a minority or subordinate group gradually becomes indistinguishably integrated into dominant mainstream society. The term's usage in American social-science theory is in reference to a process by which members of immigrant ethnic or racial groups come to America and shed their original culture over time in favor of the host society's culture. This process is measured in terms of adaptation or acculturation—the groups' ability to fit in with and be a part of the cultures of dominant society so that they eventually become "American." An "assimilated" person, therefore, is someone who has absorbed the elements of mainstream American culture. Perhaps the most dominant ways of studying and thinking about American ethnic and racial communities have been framed largely by the perspectives offered by assimilation theory. For a number of years, however, such a framework has been disputed and challenged principally for its inapplicability to nonwhite groups, its Eurocentric bias, and its conceptual inadequacies.

The origins of the assimilation framework can be traced to the progressive scholarship of the Chicago school of sociology under the influential leadership of Robert E. Park. Responding to the xenophobic sentiments of immigration restrictionists around the turn of the twentieth century and into the 1920s, Park and his colleagues challenged the then-prevailing view that race was biologically determined and that racial hierarchies (in which whites were on top) were naturally preordained. They instead proposed that race was a socially constructed category whose meanings changed over time, so that racialized groups could then be understood to have the capacity, and even possess the desire, to integrate into mainstream society. Park argued that all immigrant groups go through a "race relations cycle" that comprises four stages: contact (the initial experience of migration), competition (conflict over resources and opportunities), accommodation (adjustment to new situations that may include compromises), and assimilation (incorporation into the new society). This schema of intergroup experience is assumed to be linear (or one-way), irreversible, inevitable, desirable, and available to all.

The desirability of the assimilation process in American society was reinforced by Gunnar Myrdal's *An American Dilemma: The Negro Problem and Modern Democracy* (1944), the result of a study of U.S. race relations undertaken and published in the 1940s under the auspices of the Carnegie Commission. In this landmark text Myrdal and his team of scholars concluded that assimilation and, hence, integration of blacks into America's "modern democracy" ought to be the only solution to the nation's problems with racial inequality and injustice. Fundamentally Myrdal's work, in parallel to Park's, challenged the ideology of the assumed genetic inferiority of blacks (and by extension, the biological distinctions between races) by proposing the elimination of racial prejudice and institutional discrimination. Later works, particularly Milton Gordon's *Assimilation in American Life* (1964) and Nathan Glazer and Daniel Patrick Moynihan's *Beyond the Melting Pot* (1970), extended and refined the parameters of assimilation theory to account for the various patterns of incorporation found in other ethnic and immigrant groups, as well as the competing

197

consequences of the assimilation process (Anglo conformity, cultural pluralism, or melting pot, among others).

Social scientists and scholars engaged in the study of American society and culture have used assimilation theory to explain as well as critique the ideological assumptions and political agendas implicit in such a framework. In spite of its original intent to dislodge the biologically determinist ideology of racial hierarchies, Park's thesis ignores the qualitative differences between the experiences of white and nonwhite groups. Not all groups are subjected to the same conditions, afforded the same opportunities to integrate, and equally accepted as "Americans," even after integration. Michael Omi and Howard Winant, in their book *Racial Formation in the United States* (1986), refer to some of these critiques using the term *bootstraps model*. In the bootstraps model they argue that the experiences of racialized minorities are not qualitatively analogous to the experiences of other European immigrants (who have been perceived as able to assimilate well because they "pulled themselves up by their own bootstraps") owing to the presence of institutional barriers, such as institutionalized racism in the judicial system and limited access to economic opportunities on the basis of race, beyond their control that hinder their successful adaptation to mainstream American society. To be sure, the works of Myrdal, Gordon, and Glazer and Moynihan have addressed some of the inadequacies in Robert Park's theory. But the central tenet has remained the same for these scholars: the assimilation framework is predicated on a Eurocentric bias that forces conformity to the cultures and values of a more powerful group while devaluing others.

To a good extent, therefore, assimilation theory may be said to contain a political prescription, rather than an innocent description. It fails to consider racism as a central feature of the life experiences of, and conditions faced by, communities of color in the United States. It places the burden of adaptation solely on the marginalized groups as it discounts the impact of structural barriers to mobility, thus preserving and reinforcing unequal relations of power in society. And it ignores or undervalues the various strategies of resistance to acculturation and the numerous alternatives to American community formation that minority groups have deployed over the years. Others have questioned the framework's conceptual and methodological flaws. In some applications of assimilation theory that are still in use, for example, research subjects are asked to identify on a scale the degree to which they are either "foreign" or "American," as if processes of identity formation and notions of belonging can be quantified. In such a framework, dominant and nondominant cultures are assumed to stay as they are, as if they do not affect one another, and as if ideas and practices of being an "American" are not changing. Assimilation theory in these cases, then, has been utilized not only to explain social mobility but to critique it. Many scholars of contemporary race relations view these assumptions as inaccurate, given the current and continuing demographic transformations of American society.

[See also AMERICANIZATION; MELTING POT.*]*

BIBLIOGRAPHY

Glazer, Nathan, and Daniel Patrick Moynihan, *Beyond the Melting Pot: The Negroes, Puerto Ricans, Jews, Italians, and Irish of New York City,* 2d ed. (MIT Press 1970).

Gordon, Milton M., *Assimilation in American Life: The Role of Race, Religion, and National Origins* (Oxford 1964).

Myrdal, Gunnar, *An American Dilemma: The Negro Problem and Modern Democracy* (1944; with new intro. by Sissela Bok, Transaction Pubs. 1996).

Omi, Michael, and Howard Winant, *Racial Formation in the United States: From the 1960s to the 1990s,* 2d ed. (Routledge 1994).

Park, Robert E., *Race and Culture* (Free Press 1950).

RICK BONUS

ATOMIC BOMB

The atomic bomb in America began as an immigrant project and ended as the product of a vast consortium of large-scale institutions: corporate, military, and governmental. The fundamental scientific discoveries necessary to the development of an atomic weapon occurred primarily in Europe,

A close-up of the atomic bomb dropped on Nagasaki, Japan.

in the decade before the beginning of World War II. Fleeing Nazi and Fascist persecution, a number of high-level theoretical physicists brought their knowledge and training to the elite American universities, along with a deeply personal antipathy to the Axis powers and an awareness that weapons that applied atomic discoveries might well be developed in German labs. Working in the United States, Enrico Fermi, Edward Teller, Leo Szilard, and Eugene Wigner concluded that an atomic bomb was feasible and, in August 1939, persuaded Albert Einstein to write a letter directly to President Franklin D. Roosevelt warning of the possibility of a Nazi superweapon and urging vigorous pursuit of the weapon by the Allies.

Over the next two years progress was agonizingly slow; the need to combine scientific knowledge, industrial and manufacturing sophistication, managerial expertise, and commitment by both the military and the government made for a unique exercise in the formation of a new sort of collective organization. By the end of 1942 the army had succeeded in taking control of the program, in a rapidly expanding bureaucratic entity known as the Manhattan Engineer District. In December of that year, the first controlled atomic reaction occurred in the famous reactor built under the squash courts at the University of Chicago; within three months a sequestered scientific-technological colony had been organized and moved to the ultrasecret site of Los Alamos, New Mexico, where physicist J. Robert Oppenheimer presided over a collection of émigré scientists and young Americans from the top academic centers, in a complex and often contentious relationship with military technicians and ad-

ministrators, overseen by the gruff, uncompromising and unpopular General Leslie R. Groves.

Los Alamos was but one of three sites essential to the program. Oak Ridge, Tennessee, was the administrative headquarters for the Manhattan Engineer District and the site of a vast industrial facility devoted to producing purified weapons-grade uranium in a series of factories run or supplied by the major names in American industrial production. In Hanford, Washington, E. I. du Pont de Nemours & Company administered the conversion of plutonium for a second type of bomb. Final components for both types of weapon were fabricated or assembled at Los Alamos. Beyond these three principal sites, however, a network of smaller locations sprawled across the continent and into Canada, supplying information, design, experimental evidence, raw materials, and physical components: uranium from the Navajo reservation; heavy water from Trail, British Columbia; housing designs from Chicago and Spokane, Washington; mathematical computations from the Massachusetts Institute of Technology and the University of California at Berkeley; and medical procedures from the University of Rochester, for example.

By 1944 the atomic scientists were confident their theories would result in a viable weapon. By then military control over the project was complete and opposition to any civilian influence unyielding; scientist Leo Szilard summed up the situation when he called the major global scientists "employees" of a vast new consortium of military, corporate, and governmental interests. Added to this institutional collective were the largest unions, which came to represent the vast numbers of workers on the project—150 thousand at its height, probably close to 300 thousand over the life of the program. The Manhattan Project, as it came to be called, was a top-secret program, and to maintain security, army officials engaged in steadily more draconian measures. Their efforts were, however, finally unsuccessful; while they sought to control every aspect of life, speech, and even thought within the boundaries of the Manhattan Engineer District, they could not create a net tight enough to ensure that no information leaked out, not least because many of the scientists and workers on the program considered England and the Soviet Union to be allies rather than enemies, and while they might never have given information to Nazi or Axis powers, scientists believed they might work in the interests of lasting world peace by giving information to representatives of the Allied Powers.

Early in 1945 the gigantic factory complexes at Oak Ridge and Hanford began producing weapons-grade uranium and plutonium, and the scientific and technical personnel at Los Alamos devised two bomb designs, one for each fuel. Confident the uranium system would work, the military went ahead with fabrication of the weapon that would come to be known as Little Boy. The plutonium weapon (Fat Man) was more speculative, and military officials decided a test was necessary. Choosing the relatively empty desert region of southern New Mexico, the Manhattan District moved onto the site, evacuating most residents, building roads and bunkers, and then, in July, importing a cadre of scientists, administrators, and military personnel to observe the experiment known as Trinity. On July 16, 1945, a plutonium bomb was exploded; its force was far greater than most had predicted, and this first-ever mushroom cloud unleashed a torrent of radioactivity and a cloud of contaminated materials, later named "fallout," that rose, plumed, and then dispersed across uninhabited and inhabited regions alike. An ordnance success—it neither failed to explode nor set off an uncontrolled chain reaction that burnt up the atmosphere and unleashed a global catastrophe—the Trinity test in New Mexico revealed a Pandora's box of unforeseen and uncontrollable consequences, primarily medical, environmental, and social.

With the European war over, jockeying for control of the postwar world began; meanwhile stubborn intransigence on the part of Japanese military and governmental figures promised a protracted and bloody endgame to the Pacific conflict. In early August 1945, President Harry S. Truman ordered the deployment of atomic weapons on Japan. On August 6, 1945, a uranium bomb exploded in the sky over Hiroshima, resulting in wholesale destruction of the city and the immediate death of more

U.S. ARMY, FROM THE LIBRARY OF CONGRESS

The mushroom cloud over Nagasaki, Japan, after an atomic bomb was dropped on the city in August 1945.

than 140 thousand, eventually rising to 200 thousand as long-term effects took their toll: more than half the civilian population. With the Japanese chain of command in disarray, failure to submit to unconditional surrender caused Truman to order a second atomic strike, using the plutonium weapon; on August 9, an atomic explosion over Nagasaki caused an equal swath of destruction, and Japanese authorities swiftly surrendered.

Historians continue to argue whether the use of atomic weapons was directed primarily at ending the Japanese campaign or at tilting the postwar balance of power against the Soviet Union by a decisive show of military might with an unprecedented new superweapon. Most scholars, however, agree that both factors played into the decision; in any case, the American control of atomic weapons had a decisive effect on the spheres of influence that would be carved out by the two superpowers following the war. Within two years after the end of the war, the United States had instituted a campaign of highly publicized "atomic tests," first conducted in the South Seas and then in the American desert regions of Nevada. American control over the technology was short-lived, however, as the Soviet Union detonated its first atomic weapon in August 1949.

In the United States, as throughout the world, atomic weaponry generated a culture of fear, amplified and directed by mass media, which seemed to bombard readers and viewers with a barrage of essays, speeches, statements, and images, many of them drawn, directly or indirectly, from government sources. Attitudes toward the atomic age clustered around certain positions. Military figures tended to argue that the atomic bomb was simply an extension of conventional warfare and that its technology could be "harnessed" to other, utopian peacetime ends, from the generation of electricity to the carving out of irrigation channels and the making of great earthen dams. At the other extreme were those scientists, physicians, philosophers and humanists, and ordinary citizens who shared the position that the atomic age represented an unprecedented rupture in nearly every aspect of global life. Popular culture argued both these positions, often simultaneously; science-fiction writings especially focused on the complex implications of the atomic age, while movies generated new icons of monsterdom and mastery from the forces unleashed in the atomic age. Mass-market magazines such as *Life* presented the worried faces of Americans confronting the possibility of nuclear annihilation and the responsibilities of a nuclear arsenal; journals including *Popular Mechanics* and *Popular Science* described the dangers of atomic warfare and trumpeted the promise of atomic cars and planes, houses, and cities. Atomic fear changed the debate about the role of American power around the globe and altered the face of warfare during the Korean conflict, as public and secret arguments raged over the moral and tactical utility of using atomic weapons in war arenas. By the mid-1950s, new American rituals and icons had appeared: the fallout shelter, whether in the backyard or the school basement; barrels of water in public places, emblazoned with the sign of the Civil Defense Administration; such self-preservation procedures as "duck and cover" taught in elementary schools; and, perhaps most prevalent of all, the mushroom cloud itself, which appeared in its terrible beauty on a weekly and sometimes daily basis in mass journalism, as the American and Soviet governments engaged in regular, public displays of atomic testing designed not simply for scientific and military purposes but also toward the goal of intimidating the enemy with a show of strength and resolve. As atomic weapons gave way to hydrogen superbombs, and intercontinental bombers and elaborate missile-delivery systems appeared and were trumpeted by military and political figures as the insurance of superiority, the sky above America seemed full of atomic weapons waiting to explode, and the doctrine of "mutually assured destruction" became the dominant policy in a battle for hegemony over the globe.

By the end of the 1950s, such displays had contributed to a resolute and growing public movement to regulate and eventually eliminate nuclear weapons. The American scientific community, especially, took on an activist stance in arguing for control and limitation of nuclear weaponry. The 1957 founding of the Committee for a Sane Nuclear Policy, represented a crucial moment in the institutionalization of antinuclear sentiment. Mass protest marches and rallies, public advertisements, and the prominent appearance of celebrities, perhaps most notably the "nation's pediatrician," Benjamin Spock, all contributed to the growing momentum of the ban-the-bomb movement. A limited nuclear test-ban treaty was signed in 1963, but the next decade saw a paradoxical proliferation of nuclear weaponry around the world even as the major superpowers signed increasingly stringent treaties to limit nuclear testing, weapons production, and deployment.

By the 1990s the power of the atomic bomb as an icon of modern life had receded, though the continuing presence of atomic weaponry and the proliferation of its technology remained live issues. Increasingly, awareness of the environmental consequences of atomic-weapons production replaced the older fear of atomic warfare. At sites such as Hanford, Washington, decades of ill-considered technological and manufacturing decisions made in an atmosphere of impunity generated by the secrecy of the industry and the massiveness of its bureaucracy, military and civilian, had resulted in vast wastelands of contamination; the "atomic accidents" at nuclear power plants including Three Mile Island, Pennsylvania, in 1979 and Chernobyl in the Ukraine in 1986 contributed to the antinuclear activism of Americans. By the end of the twentieth century, the consequences of a vast stockpile of aging atomic and nuclear weapons, and the decaying facilities that had built, maintained, and stored those weapons, became the dominant issues of the atomic age.

[See also TECHNOLOGY, AN OVERVIEW, *and article on* CRITIQUES OF TECHNOLOGY; NUCLEAR ENERGY.*]*

BIBLIOGRAPHY

Boyer, Paul, *By the Bomb's Early Light: American Thought and Culture at the Dawn of the Atomic Age* (Univ. of N.C. Press 1994).

Hales, Peter Bacon, *Atomic Spaces: Living on the Manhattan Project* (Univ. of Ill. Press 1997).

Rhodes, Richard, *The Making of the Atomic Bomb* (Simon & Schuster 1986).

Rhodes, Richard, *Dark Sun: The Making of the Hydrogen Bomb* (Simon & Schuster 1995).

Schwartz, Stephen I., ed., *Atomic Audit: The Costs and Consequences of U.S. Nuclear Weapons since 1940* (Brookings Inst. 1998).

Weart, Spencer, *Nuclear Fear: A History of Images* (Harvard Univ. Press 1988).

PETER BACON HALES

AUDUBON SOCIETY

The Audubon Society is America's first national grassroots conservation group. It dates back to the sportsman George Grinnell's short-lived club for bird protection, which lasted from 1886 to 1888. But the organization was reborn securely in 1896, when two Boston women, Harriet Hemenway and Minna Hall, founded the Massachusetts Audubon Society to combat the hugely popular use of birds and feathers to decorate women's hats. The campaign spread state by state, when these bird hats ignited the first widespread public outrage over a conservation issue.

Women founded most of the Audubon clubs— the state societies enjoyed strong ties to the expansive, late-1800s middle-to-upper-class network of women's groups, who worked for a wide range of social causes. Joining with male scientists and civic leaders, these female activists brought members, tactics, and an emphasis on education. Propelled by women's Victorian-era mandate to uphold the morals of American society, the clubs above all converted the nascent calls for conservation into a supremely moral crusade.

After just four years Congress passed the Lacey Act, the first federal legislation to protect wildlife, and set aside the first national wildlife refuge. The Audubon campaign had laid the foundation for a twentieth-century nature-lover tradition, in which affluent Americans used nature education and experiences to foster aesthetic and moral values. The clubs augured moral convictions but also moral rigidity in debates on the natural world, and they established the pivotal role of private organizations in modern conservation politics.

The Audubon Society went on to play a prominent role itself in both the appreciation and the politics of wild nature. In the early 1900s the state clubs united into a national federation, which funded refuge wardens (and backed landmark legislation to ban commercial game and plumage sales and placed migratory birds under federal protection). The society launched its own refuge system in the 1920s and in the next two decades started Audubon camps and spearheaded major research and protection programs to save whooping cranes and other endangered bird species.

After World War II the Audubon Society widened its focus from birds to work prominently on national campaigns for wilderness preservation, bans on pesticides, and population control. It built nature centers and revived the state and local branches to do grassroots advocacy work. In 1984 it launched the *World of Audubon* television specials, while its magazine *Audubon* (which began as *Bird-Lore* in 1899) promoted environmental protection and a reverence for wild things in equal measures.

Since the 1980s the Audubon society has had to respond to criticisms of its size, corporate support, ties to government, mainstream views, and lack of ethnic and class diversity. In the last decade of its first century, the group engaged in a struggle with its own history, as some leaders and members feared that the group was too old-fashioned, while others countered that Audubon lost its distinctive mission amid the host of late-twentieth-century environmental groups. The society will continue to redefine itself. But this pioneering, heavily funded organization of lands, lobbyists, education programs, hotlines, research, media, and bird walks will always have its origin in middle-to-upper-class experience, Victorian gender roles, moral conviction, and fierce politics.

[See also NATURE.]

BIBLIOGRAPHY

Buchheister, Carl, and Frank Graham, Jr., "From the Swamps and Back: A Concise and Candid History of the Early Audubon Movement," *Audubon* 75 (January 1973):7–45.

Doughty, Robin W., *Feather Fashions and Bird Preservation: A Study in Nature Protection* (Univ. of Calif. Press 1975).

Graham, Frank, with Carl W. Buchheister, *The Audubon Ark: A History of the National Audubon Society* (Univ. of Tex. Press 1992).

Price, Jennifer, *Flight Maps: Adventures with Nature in Modern America* (Basic 1999).

JENNIFER PRICE

AUTOBIOGRAPHIES, MEMOIRS, AND DIARIES

Intimate and public, self-exploratory and self-protective, personal and historical, forthright and playful: autobiographies, memoirs, and diaries of different kinds pepper the American literary scene from its beginnings, with a special flowering in the twentieth century. The term *autobiography* includes memoirs and diaries, so that the three genres exist in a continuum and can overlap. Nonetheless, important distinctions between the three forms exist.

Autobiographies, like biographies, tend to aim toward completeness and historicity: a whole life from ancestry through old age. Like biographies, they tend to read as factual: the truth and nothing but the truth, with as little embellishment as possible. But, of course, all writing involves embellishment and few biographies, let alone autobiographies, meet the standard of pure factuality. Like novelists, writers of autobiography choose where the story starts and where it ends. Such choices always give the writing a distinctive form and control its meanings.

When Henry James wrote *A Small Boy and Others* (1913), he intended to write two subsequent volumes, though he never wrote them. *A Small Boy and Others* grew from a nineteenth- and twentieth-century sense that, as Wordsworth said, "the child is father to the man." James saw himself as part of a lineage: he came, of course, from a famous family. But, as an adult looking back, he saw himself also as among "others"—and not completely comfortable in their midst. James's claim, the autobiographer's typical claim, is that his experience differs. But a successful "life" must suggest connections to other lives (so that Michael Moon, in a later critical book, which has its own autobiographical elements, takes James's book as a prototype for gay childhood). Good autobiographies need to stake claims simultaneously to uniqueness and to typicality. Perhaps especially in the United States, no one need write an autobiography, but anyone can—and get it read—if the writers' achievements seem, or can be made to seem, notable enough.

In the United States, politicians and diplomats write autobiographies. Actors and celebrities write autobiographies, too—by the late twentieth century, perhaps especially actors and celebrities, often with the help of a ghostwriter. But a writer's autobiography remains a special thing, an extension of the writer's craft and a narrative of how the writer came to art.

A prolific novelist who is also a prolific autobiographer often feels a profound sense of roots: for example Reynolds Price, who explores his North Carolina upbringing and probes his childhood family. For Price, the autobiographical impulse motivated early fictions. As his fictions became populated by imagined lives quite different from his own,

Price moved also more toward autobiography: *Clear Pictures* (1989), for example.

Other modern masters of the writerly autobiography include Gertrude Stein, Zora Neale Hurston, and Norman Mailer. Some writers have been notoriously averse to autobiography: William Faulkner, Vladimir Nabokov, J. D. Salinger, Joyce Carol Oates, and Thomas Pynchon, to name a few. Nabokov could never resist pulling his critics' legs, sending them off in search of red herrings. But he made a significant contribution to autobiography in *Speak, Memory* (1951), perhaps because he wanted to cover aspects of his own life before a biographer did.

Speak, Memory is subtitled *A Memoir*. Like many books, it hovers between autobiography and memoir. Unlike autobiographies, memoirs do not aspire to completeness nor do they require a strict adherence to fact. Memoirs choose a particular slice of the writer's experience and organize the life around a focal point or theme. They leave out many things that a biographer would want to include. In practice, the line between autobiography and memoir can be awfully thin. Themes in memoirs vary, but theme comes through more clearly in memoir than in autobiography.

In *Colored People* (1984), Henry Louis Gates, Jr., writes about growing up African American in an aspiring West Virginia family, and the force of the memoir depends largely on who the narrator became, despite the odds; it omits and includes to make racial themes clear. Similarly, Alice Kaplan's *French Lessons* (1993) describes the writer's special love for France and its language. Richard Rodriguez's *Hunger of Memory* (1982) describes his experience being Hispanic and gay. In the United States, memoir gravitates especially to themes of identity, often ethnic identity, especially when the writer is first or second generation.

Autobiography looks back to such classic models as St. Augustine and Rousseau. But because autobiography as a form came into its own in the eighteenth century, it has been a part of the American literary scene from the start. Many early autobiographies focused on religious or spiritual roots, but the theme persists, such as in Kathleen Norris's book *Dakota* (1993). Many American autobiographies focus on the grounding of an individual in a community, a grounding not always easy or comfortable. Protagonists of memoirs tend to perceive themselves as outsiders and to present themselves that way.

One key boundary between autobiographies and memoirs is often the writer's level of fame prior to writing. History, rank, and the public record seem to demand autobiography, while a memoir must justify itself more by the quality of the writing. Someone famous who has had an illness or accident, for example, might write either an autobiography or a memoir. The more intense the focus on the illness or accident (quite intense in Reynolds Price's *A Whole New Life*, 1994, or Gretel Ehrlich's *A Match to the Heart*, 1995), the more one is in the realm of memoir. But it would be rare for someone previously unknown to publish a full-fledged autobiography instead of a memoir. To put it a different way: autobiography often results from a life exceptional in its overall contours or achievement; memoir makes the importance of the writer's life clear on the basis of a particular plot or theme.

Autobiographies give names and dates. Similar to biographies, they aspire to history. Memoirs depend more frankly on memory to create a mood and an ambiance. It would make little sense for an autobiographer to change names, hide identities, alter facts, or reconstruct dialogue; in some cases, such changes might even be scandalous. But memoirists hide identities, alter facts, and reconstruct dialogue all the time—within limits. Autobiographies are not completely factual: writers often misremember or embellish to create a persona. But memoirists use the resources of fiction, the molding of a persona, as their stock in trade. For this reason, memoirs seem a quintessentially American form of life writing—an equal-opportunity employer, and a creative one.

Unless they are fictional (a possible genre), diaries often begin in the privacy of the home and with the attempt to record daily, quotidian emotions and experience. Great American diarists, like great American autobiographers, often focus on spiritual life. The genre lends itself to spirit. But diarists, like memoirists, can also focus on a specific experience: the details of a journey, a wedding, parenthood. Annette Kolodnoy collects women pioneers' diaries in *The Land before Her* (1984). Like autobiography, diaries depend on chronology, but even more strictly, since when diaries skip months or years, readers feel the pressure of life omitted, a curiosity about what happened between the lines.

As in autobiography, the known greatness of the writer can make a diary come to life. But the diaries of pioneer women, of slaves, of plantation owners' wives, of spiritual questers, of prisoners have also proven to have strong literary mettle. One might make a comparison here between diaries and memoirs. Diary writers may not necesarily be famous people; they become known because they published a diary. The text may add to the historical record, but the writer's role in history is small, save for the power of the writing.

Autobiographies, memoirs, and diaries dominate life writing in the United States. But they do not exhaust the category. Confessions are like autobiographies and memoirs, except that they court the edge, often presenting the protagonist as someone risky, and even dislikable at times. Journals are like diaries (the two terms are often synonymous), but journals often are records of a writer's process, of how a work came to be. Henry James kept extensive journals of his work, which helped to generate the sense that modern writers pursue writing as a craft.

Autobiographies, memoirs, and diaries flourished in the twentieth century and will likely flourish in the twenty-first. All three require a faith in the construction of identity and a willingness to build it, word by word. All three psychologize the writer, a process which, as Sigmund Freud well knew, could take place long before psychology as a discipline existed. But perhaps because they cut their teeth on psychology and on a sense of the importance of their own generation, baby boomers love to read, and to write, autobiographies and memoirs.

Yet there is, and always has been, a certain unpredictability about when life writing will flourish and what forms it will take, and also about the vexed question of what gets read, and why and how. In early American literature, captives who had spent time with Indians often wrote to teach moral lessons, but also because they felt compelled by the experience. Former slaves and, later, African American leaders such as Malcolm X wrote politically to further a cause, but also because they needed to share their experiences and ideas from a personal perspective. In American literature, as in most traditions, life histories of the rich and famous remain legion. But perhaps most characteristic of life writing in the United States is its persistence and variety, and its appearance in places where people might not always have put pen to paper. Autobiographies, memoirs, and diaries depend on confidence that experience can be put into words, confidence that special lives deserve telling, and also a belief in the American idea that all lives can be special.

[See also LITERATURE, AN OVERVIEW, *and articles on* LITERATURE AND THE CONSTRUCTION OF IDENTITY, LITERARY CANON, CRITICAL APPROACHES TO LITERATURE; RELIGIOUS WRITING AND SERMONS; NATURE, *article on* NATURE IN LITERATURE AND THE ARTS.]

BIBLIOGRAPHY

Anderson, Linda, *Women and Autobiography in the Twentieth Century: Remembered Futures* (Prentice Hall 1997).

Bjorklund, Diane, *Interpreting the Self: Two Hundred Years of American Autobiography* (Univ. of Chicago Press 1998).

Conway, Jill K., *When Memory Speaks: Reflections on Autobiography* (Knopf 1998).

Foster, Frances Smith, *Witnessing Slavery: The Development of Ante-Bellum Slave Narrative* (Greenwood Press 1979).

Freedman, Diane P., Olivia Frey, and Frances Murphy Zauhar, eds., *The Intimate Critique: Autobiographical Literary Criticism* (Duke Univ. Press 1993).

Lee, Robert A., ed., *First Person Singular: Studies in American Autobiography* (St. Martin's 1988).

Olney, James, ed., *Studies in Autobiography* (Oxford 1988).

Smith, Valerie, *Self-Discovery and Authority in Afro-American Narrative* (Harvard Univ. Press 1987).

MARIANNA DE MARCO TORGOVNICK

AUTOMOBILES AND RECREATIONAL VEHICLES

No other technological development transformed the twentieth-century American landscape, culture, economy, and psyche more profoundly than did the automobile. Although largely a European invention, the "horseless carriage," powered by an internal combustion engine, first became an integral part of modern society in the United States. From the beginning of America's frontier society, geographic movement was associated with individual freedom and social mobility; when the invention of the automobile offered a new means of travel that was more individual and flexible, Americans seized it and made it their own. But the vicissitudes of American society quickly transformed the auto from a merely useful machine of transportation to a cultural icon.

Owing to its high price, the early automobile was available to only the wealthy; for average Americans it became a symbol of the arrogance of wealth. However, the dream of a cheap car for the masses was realized by Henry Ford, who introduced his Model T in 1908. This tough, reliable, and simple car, whose price fell throughout its twenty-year history, helped to extend auto ownership across the class spectrum, making it a symbol of democracy and equality. In popular films of the era the auto was portrayed as a means by which ordinary people could overcome class barriers to achieve upward mobility. But the gains Ford offered the American masses through access to the automobile were paid for by losses in their working lives. In order to lower car prices, Ford and other manufacturers introduced between 1905 and 1913 the assembly line and other methods of mass production that compartmentalized, mechanized, and simplified jobs, ultimately destroying the industry's skilled trades. As Ford production systems spread throughout industrial America, there was also a cultural casualty, the work ethic. Routinized, deskilled labor could no longer provide Americans with evidence of their skills, efforts, or moral worth.

Around 1913 the mass production of automobiles caused a wave of working-class protests. Al-

BROWN BROTHERS

A family poses with its new Model T Ford, circa 1915.

though scholars dispute whether the goal of autoworkers was a return to shop-floor control or merely higher wages, the result of these conflicts was clearly the latter. Led by Ford's Five Dollar Day program of 1914, automakers gave workers higher wages and benefits in exchange for their acquiescence in mass-production methods. With their higher pay workers in the automobile and other industries began to embrace a new ethic of increased consumption of mass-produced goods to compensate for their loss of identity, freedom, and individuality.

In the 1920s consumer goods in America were increasingly defined by their symbolism, not their function. Once again the auto industry led the way, concentrating less on the mechanics and more on the aesthetics or styling of a car. The leader in auto styling was General Motors Corporation, whose head, Alfred Sloan, pioneered the industry's practice of annual style redesign and the corporate model hierarchy, which offered an array of car models graded by price and accessories. These policies offered automobile consumers the illusion of newness and individuality, while keeping the mass-produced mechanical parts of the car standardized and unchanged. To implement these policies, Sloan hired the first automobile stylist in the industry, Harley

Earl, whose design philosophy was to give consumers an escape—a little vacation—every time they got into the car. To do so he camouflaged all signs of assembly-line monotony with exciting new surfaces that evoked individuality, freedom, and power.

The Great Depression, which many Americans believed was caused by mass production, temporarily tarnished the image of the automobile and its industry. In cultural works, from Charlie Chaplin's film *Modern Times* (1936) to Diego Rivera's *Detroit Industry* (1932–1933) murals, the assembly line was critically portrayed. Deteriorating work conditions in auto factories led to landmark sit-down strikes, which not only helped unionize the industry but also pioneered the collective bargaining system that came to dominate big industry. Yet even during the Depression the car did not lose its centrality to the American psyche. Robert and Helen Lynd reported in *Middletown in Transition* (1937) that destitute Americans would give up every other possession before relinquishing their cars. By the early 1940s wartime production, utilizing Fordist methods, had revived the economy as well as dreams of automotive abundance.

The decade of the 1950s saw the zenith of the nation's automobile culture. Postwar prosperity expanded car ownership to unprecedented proportions. Style reigned supreme at the automakers; cars became not only bigger and more powerful but also the embodiment of escapism and entertainment. In some designs aeronautical-style tail fins and exhaust nozzles were appended to earthbound vehicles. In these dream machines masses of Americans left behind industrial cities for the new suburbs, where they pursued privatized consumerism. City and countryside alike were reconfigured to accommodate throngs of commuting Americans, and the landscape became divided between affluent suburbs and decaying cities.

The tumultuous 1960s saw the first widespread questioning of America's infatuation with the auto since the 1930s. With increasing traffic, accidents, and pollution on overburdened roads, the promise of automotive escape from America's problems rang hollow. In popular films the automobile was

© GENDREAU/CORBIS-BETTMANN

The dream machine of the 1950s, a Cadillac convertible.

just as likely to be depicted as a menace as it was to be portrayed as a savior. Pressured by popular movements such as environmental and consumer, the government began to enact safety and pollution regulations and, in the wake of the 1973 oil embargo, fuel economy standards. These measures, along with an ailing economy, sent a chill of sobriety throughout the automobile industry, and the 1970s saw cars become smaller, and more efficient and functional. The economic recovery that began in the mid-1980s reinvigorated consumerism and with it a return to the traditional automotive values of bigness and escape.

By the end of the twentieth century, oversized cars, known as sports utility vehicles (SUVs), and light trucks became hugely popular. Although designed for functions such as hauling and off-road driving, SUVs served mainly the symbolic goals of power, prestige, and retreat from bureaucratic monotony. As America's model of consumer capitalism continues to spread over the globe, the social, economic, and environmental limits of the automobile culture will surely be tested.

[See also HIGHWAYS; MASS TRANSIT.]

BIBLIOGRAPHY

Flink, James J., *The Automobile Age* (MIT Press 1988) [the best and most comprehensive history of the automobile from America's foremost automotive historian].

Gartman, David, *Auto Opium: A Social History of American Automobile Design* (Routledge 1994).

Lewis, David L., and Laurence Goldstein, eds., *The Automobile and American Culture* (Univ. of Mich. Press 1983) [a wide-ranging collection of scholarly essays, fiction, poetry, and images on America's automobile culture].

Rae, John B., *The Road and Car in American Life* (MIT Press 1971).

Silk, Gerald, ed., *Automobile and Culture* (Abrams 1984) [a collection of images and essays focusing on the car as an art object].

DAVID GARTMAN

AVANT-GARDE MOVEMENTS

There is debate over what counts as an American avant-garde movement. Some maintain there was a "historical avant-garde" in New York from 1909 through the 1920s, but that sometime between the 1930s (with the Depression, the Moscow trials, and the Nazi-Soviet pact) and the 1960s (after World War II, with the widespread institutionalization of earlier avant-garde movements), the avant-garde died. Others counter that the avant-garde is very much alive, although there are different opinions on whether there is a historical lineage (and if so, what) from early-twentieth-century through more contemporary movements.

Critical disagreements stem from divergent conceptions of what constitutes an (or the) *avant-garde*. The term as a description of radical, political artistic activity originated in early-nineteenth-century France, first used by the utopian socialist Henri de Saint-Simon. The military image makes clear the historical link between an artistic avant-garde and activism. Renato Poggioli's seminal theory from the 1960s defines the avant-garde sociologically and offers four aspects of avant-garde movements: activism, antagonism, nihilism, and agonism. Most theorists align the emergence of the avant-garde with social and cultural alienation including that resulting from the institutionalization of art and agree that the twentieth-century avant-garde includes both activism and alienation from the common idioms and social fabric of the day. Insofar as the first generation of American avant-gardists, the modernists, have been incorporated into the common idiom (of everything from advertising—one thinks

UPI/CORBIS-BETTMANN

Writer Gertrude Stein (*left*) with her companion, Alice B. Toklas, in 1934.

of Reebok's 1996 sneakers, the "Avant Guards"—to museums, including the Museum of Modern Art, to educational institutions), it is difficult to imagine how alienated or oppositional a contemporary avant-garde that insists on a modernist lineage could be.

On the other hand, those who argue for the continued existence of an American avant-garde point to a constantly reincarnated spirit, an aesthetic of process, and a lineage based on modernism defined not as a formal style (the way art critic Clement Greenberg retrospectively defined modernism) but as content, including an openness that locates art's work in its audience and based on strains of modernism other than those now canonized. This "other" line of modernism usually is said to run from such figures as Gertrude Stein, the New York and French dadaists, William Carlos Williams or Ezra Pound, and various forms of jazz, to the 1931 objectivist and 1950 projectivist manifestos and the artists who gathered at Black Mountain College during the 1940s and 1950s (Charles Olson, Merce Cunningham, John Cage, Willem de Kooning, Robert Creeley), sometimes including the abstract expressionists and New York poets (Barnett Newman, Robert Motherwell, Jackson Pollock, Frank O'Hara,

208

© RUDOLPH BURCKHARDT

Artist Jackson Pollock at work on one of his abstract expressionist "action paintings."

John Ashbery), the beats and participants in the San Francisco Renaissance (Jack Kerouac, Allen Ginsberg, Gary Snyder, Kenneth Rexroth), and later to practices such as performance art, oral poetry, earth art, ethnopoetics, language poetry, or postmodernism.

In the 1910s and 1920s, drawing on the work of both French and expatriate American writers, overlapping American avant-garde circles clearly flourished, especially in New York. Alfred Stieglitz's *Camera Work* reproduced for American audiences both French post-impressionism and writings on Picasso and Matisse by Gertrude Stein; Stieglitz's gallery, 291, like the salons that gathered, for instance, in the New York apartment of Louise and Walter Arensberg, formed centers for artists, filmmakers, writers, and musicians interested in experimentation in the arts. French artists such as Marcel Duchamp who came to New York as a result of World War I further fostered the international cross-fertilization characteristic of American modernism, as did the spread of small (mostly short-lived) magazines such as *Rogue, Others, The Blind Man, Secession, Broom,* or *transition.* The manifestos from these various avant-garde circles—surrealist, dadaist, cubist, imagist, and futurist, among others—

generally state their resistance to official (genteel) culture and their view of art as cultural criticism or activism, and they also imply that the early American avant-garde defined itself according to the original metaphor as mapping terrain it hoped would redefine American culture. These movements further raised questions about the boundaries of various arts and genres, spawning exchanges and collaborations, sometimes seen as defining features of any avant-garde, such as those among Stein's prose portraits, Marius de Zayas's and Francis Picabia's object portraits (including Picabia's "portrait" of Stieglitz), Charles Demuth's 1920s portrait posters, and poems by such writers as Marianne Moore, Wallace Stevens, and William Carlos Williams.

While many members of this first American avant-garde continued to produce art through at least the 1950s, their shared sense and shared rhetoric of an oppositionalist alliance of arts and styles, from the machine aesthetic of precisionism or dadaism to the more fluid surrealist or futurist aesthetics, did not survive the Depression. Moreover, by 1941 museums were featuring retrospective shows by avant-garde artists. Questions, thus, now arise: is the avant-garde dead because it by definition should be new, and the avant-garde is now canonized? Or because there is now no "garde" to be "avant"? In America it can be argued that centralized venues for legitimizing art were consolidated along with the historical avant-garde between the late-nineteenth and the mid-twentieth centuries in such institutions as museums, universities, the mass media, and publishing and no longer existed in the increasingly pluralistic late twentieth century. Or is the concept of the avant-garde incoherent because commercial culture so easily commodifies rebellion as a fashionable status marker, making it impossible to theorize the social importance of avant-garde work or set it apart from some mainstream works, as emphasized by figures such as artist and filmmaker Andy Warhol or formations such as radical chic or even the appearance of a Norton anthology of postmodern poetry (when the historical avant-garde, through the 1960s, defined itself as antiacademic)?

Alternatively, the opening of the academy following the GI Bill may have shifted the nature of the university as much as the nature of the arts, and it may even be that the arts' separation from power and alliance with commerce was always a feature, if not a precondition, of the avant-garde. If so, perhaps one can still identify contemporary avant-garde movements, despite the codification of the concept in places such as this encyclopedia. The question remains open.

[See also BEAT WRITERS; LOST GENERATION; POETRY; LITERATURE, articles on LITERARY CANON, LITERATURE AND THE CONSTRUCTION OF IDENTITY; PROLETARIAN LITERATURE; WRITERS AND POLITICS.]

BIBLIOGRAPHY

Bürger, Peter, *Theory of the Avant-Garde,* tr. by Michael Shaw (Univ. of Minn. Press 1984) [a translation based on the second edition of the 1980 *Theorie der Avantgarde* and the 1979 essay "Theorie der Avantgarde und Theorie der Literatur." Bürger responds to Poggioli, being more historically concrete in his theory of the avant-garde, although he does not focus on American culture].

Hobbs, Stuart D., *The End of the American Avant Garde* (N.Y. Univ. Press 1997) [a historian's analysis of the avant-garde in the United States, with a useful bibliographical essay, and offering a useful foil to Sayre's arguments about the persistence of an American avant-garde].

Mann, Paul, *The Theory-Death of the Avant-Garde* (Ind. Univ. Press 1991) [while Mann unfolds a highly theoretical argument, in the process he offers one of the most comprehensive overviews of the various, contesting histories and theories of the avant-garde to date, drawing on earlier theorists and particularly work by critic Marjorie Perloff].

Poggioli, Renato, *The Theory of the Avant-Garde,* tr. by Gerald Fitzgerald (Harvard Univ. Press 1968) [the first, and (together with Bürger) the major, theorist of the avant-garde, although not focused on American materials].

Sayre, Henry M., *The Object of Performance: The American Avant-Garde since 1970* (Univ. of Chicago Press 1989) [covers a number of arts (dance, performance, photography, visual arts, poetry) in a clear and historically informed manner and offers one of the clearest theoretical defenses of a contemporary avant-garde].

LISA STEINMAN

B

BABY BOOM

The baby boom that began during World War II and continued for two decades was one of the most remarkable demographic phenomena of the twentieth century. From a low of 2.4 million births in the United States in the depths of the Depression, the number rose to 2.9 million in 1945. After the war the birthrate skyrocketed, reaching 4.3 million births at the peak of the baby boom in 1957. The two decades of the baby boom reversed nearly two centuries of declining fertility. The boom ended in the early 1960s, and the birthrate sank back down to the point where it began in the early 1940s.

A number of factors contributed to the baby boom. Part of the boom can be explained by the drop in the marriage age between 1930 and 1950 (to 21.5 from 24.5 for men and to 20 from 22.5 for women). But a lower marriage age would not necessarily result in a higher birthrate. In fact, during the first few decades of the twentieth century, the marriage age and the birthrate both declined. Nor did the baby boom result from a dramatic rise in the number of children per family; the increase was rather modest. Women coming of age in the 1930s had an average of 2.4 children, compared with 3.2 children for those who reached adulthood in the 1950s. What made it a baby boom was that the increase occurred after a decline in the birthrate for 150 years, and that it occurred among all social groups. Variables such as race, ethnicity, education, and income did not affect fertility trends. Although the birthrate varied from one group to another, the pattern, that is, the rise during the 1940s and the decline during the 1960s, prevailed for all social groups. Americans behaved with remarkable demographic conformity during these years. They married young and had an average of at least three children. Most women who married in the 1940s and 1950s completed their childbearing by the time they were in their late twenties. Thus, the smallest birth cohort of twentieth-century women, those born in the 1930s, had the largest birth cohort of children: the baby boom.

A major causal factor was the intense and widespread endorsement of pronatalism—the belief in the positive value of having several children. This accompanied a powerful ideology of domesticity that located the "good life" in the nuclear family, with a male breadwinner and a homemaker mother. Most Americans at the time believed that the best route to happiness was marriage and parenthood.

211

Childlessness was considered deviant, selfish, and pitiable. Nearly everyone believed that family togetherness, focused on children, was the mark of a successful and wholesome personal life. The government poured resources into the expanding suburbs to support the nuclear family ideal.

The baby boomers became the youth of the 1960s, sparking the civil rights, feminist, and antiwar movements. They have carried tremendous economic and political power, coming of age at a time of relative affluence. As they age their numbers have brought attention to the concerns of the elderly. The baby boomers have transformed the demographic, political, and economic realities of the nation. No doubt their influence will continue well into the twenty-first century.

© M. BABEL/WELLS FARGO HISTORICAL SERVICES

Customers at a Wells Fargo Bank in 1922.

BIBLIOGRAPHY

Cherlin, Andrew J., ed., *The Changing American Family and Public Policy* (Urban Inst. Press 1988).

Coontz, Stephanie, *The Way We Never Were: American Families and the Nostalgia Trap* (Basic Bks. 1992).

Light, Paul Charles, *Baby Boomers* (Norton 1988).

May, Elaine Tyler, *Homeward Bound: American Families in the Cold War Era,* 2d ed. (Basic Bks. 1999).

Skolnick, Arlene, *Embattled Paradise: The American Family in an Age of Uncertainty* (Basic Bks. 1991).

ELAINE TYLER MAY

BANKS AND BANKING

The development of the U.S. banking system has been distinctive and unique. The unique label applies when the financial system is considered in an international context. Since its emergence in the late eighteenth century, commercial banking has been a structurally diffuse economic sector—a legacy of Jeffersonian ideology, which feared concentrations of political and economic power. In other advanced economies around the world, banking was invariably a highly concentrated sector dominated by a few large financial institutions. In the United States, by contrast, tens of thousands of commercial banks with offices in thousands of cities and towns, large and small, operated independently under either a state or a federal charter. The American commer-

cial banking sector has always been more decentralized than its counterparts overseas.

The nation's investment banking sector, centered in the Wall Street area of New York City, was tightly concentrated from the outset, following the prevailing patterns in other advanced economies. The main function of investment banks has been to help corporations float new issues of bonds and stocks. Investment bankers typically earned fees for identifying and soliciting buyers for these securities. The most notable American investment banker was John Pierpont (J. P.) Morgan, who aided powerful railroads in the flotation of millions of dollars' worth of new security issues in both domestic and European capital markets.

The U.S. banking sector is distinctive because, on balance, it has performed the role of financial intermediary extremely well over the past two centuries. Few other nations in the world have benefited so greatly from the strength and inclusiveness of their financial services sectors. The fundamental function of commercial banks has been to marshal the savings of individuals and businesses and then, in turn, to lend those funds to a varied group of borrowers. Banks loaned money for many purposes—for example, to businesses that required financing to carry inventories and customer debts; to farmers who needed seed and fertilizer for the growing season; and to households for the purchase of homes. In the twentieth century banks loaned money to millions of individuals who held credit cards. Contrary to the rhetoric of many critics, commercial banks were rarely enterprises with extraordinarily high rates of profit, and they were certainly not businesses that benefited from the economic misfortunes of their customers. Instead, banks profited when their customers and their local economies grew and prospered.

Despite their overwhelmingly positive contributions to the promotion of economic growth, banks have often been a target of harsh criticism by political leaders and social commentators. Commercial bankers were often scapegoats caught in an impossible quandary whenever the economy went into a sustained tailspin. In an effort to preserve the claims of trusting depositors during difficult times, bankers typically recalled their outstanding loans, refusing the pleas of borrowers for renewals. In a major depression, this action drove thousands, if not millions, of borrowers to the edge of bankruptcy. If too many borrowers defaulted on their loan repayments, bankers faced a worst-case scenario. When banks could not generate a sufficient inflow of funds to pay off depositors, everybody lost—very often including investors in the common stock of the bank itself. When the economy was stable, banks got little credit for their contributions to society, but when conditions deteriorated, bankers were frequently vilified by disappointed depositors, by cash-strapped borrowers, and by politicians of all stripes.

In colonial North America organized banking institutions did not exist. Before independence persons seeking loans to improve farm properties or to buy artisan tools usually borrowed from relatives, friends, or wealthy neighbors. Merchants involved in foreign trade obtained their financing through a chain of credit originating in London. Domestic merchants and storekeepers typically generated extra sales by extending seasonal book credit to farmers, with the expectation of receiving payment after the harvest.

Periodically, the colonial legislatures entered the marketplace by establishing governmental loan offices. In the eighteenth century these offices were called land banks, but the name was a misnomer because no deposits were accepted. These offices made loans secured by first mortgages on real estate to a wide spectrum of property holders. In most colonies the loans were amortized over periods of five to twelve years, and most borrowers met their obligations on schedule.

The first chartered institutions with a full range of financial services emerged after political independence. The Bank of North America received a charter from the Confederation government in 1784. It operated in Philadelphia on a modest scale and set a precedent for the subsequent expansion of the banking sector. The two largest business enterprises in the economy from 1792 to 1836 were the two federally chartered commercial banks. The First Bank of the United States was the inspiration of Secretary of the Treasury Alexander Hamilton. The two national banks were controversial throughout their twenty-year charter periods not so much because of their operating policies, which were generally safe and sound, but because a majority of citizens feared any large institution that seemingly had the potential of breeding a powerful financial elite.

President Andrew Jackson believed a large national bank was a public danger, and in 1832 he vetoed a congressional bill designed to extend the life of the Second Bank. For the next eight decades, unlike most other advanced economies around the world, the United States had no large financial institution with the resources to play the role of central banker or that possessed enough power and influence to alleviate the boom and bust cycles in the broad economy.

Meanwhile, the growth of commercial banks chartered by the several states continued apace during the first half of the nineteenth century. Most banks were strictly local institutions, which conformed with the Jeffersonian ideal of a geographically diverse and atomistic commercial system. Some investors created commercial banks to help

An 1828 cartoon shows Andrew Jackson battling the many-headed monster, the Bank of the United States.

finance their own industrial projects, especially in the New England region. During the first quarter-century of operations (1785–1810), the commercial banking system was fundamentally safe and sound. Bankers were prudent in their lending, and they held substantial reserves against their outstanding liabilities. Only one small bank failed prior to 1810, and that failure was linked to fraud rather than to unfavorable economic conditions.

Thereafter the commercial banking system proved vulnerable to temporary collapse during the financial panics that periodically wracked the economy after the War of 1812. The Panic of 1819 was a forerunner of future catastrophes. Panics in 1837, 1839, and 1857 took their toll. Borrowers could not repay outstanding loans on their maturity dates, and without a steady inflow of cash banks could not meet the demands of customers to convert cur-

214

rency and deposits to gold and silver. Many banks closed their doors and suspended operations; some never reopened. These chaotic episodes increased the doubts of many skeptics about the soundness of the financial system. A few states temporarily banned all banks except publicly owned institutions; some Midwestern states prohibited banking altogether.

The inherent problem for commercial bankers was the difficulty of balancing the twin goals of maintaining customer safety and promoting economic efficiency by granting loans for worthy projects. Some banks were faulted for failing to respond adequately to the needs of citizens; critics claimed these institutions were too conservative because bank managers refused to approve all the loan requests of local residents. At the other end of the spectrum, some banks were accused of engaging in irresponsible lending, which threatened, in turn, the safety of their noteholders and depositors.

The issue of customer safety was tackled in two major governmental reform initiatives. During the Civil War, Congress passed laws permitting the establishment of thousands of local commercial banks operating under federal charters. One feature of the new legislation made the nation's paper currency completely safe. All circulating banknotes were fully secured by federal government bonds; as a result paper money always maintained its face value in exchanges for silver and gold. The second initiative came at the nadir of the Great Depression. One of the New Deal laws enacted in 1933 created the Federal Deposit Insurance Corporation (FDIC). The FDIC guaranteed that individual depositors would never lose a single penny even if managers made a rash of bad loans and the bank became insolvent.

The creation of the Federal Reserve System (the Fed) in 1913 gave the commercial banking system greater stability and uniformity without changing its fundamental structure. The central bank was granted the power to intervene in financial markets to prevent panics and to smooth out boom and bust business cycles. Unfortunately, the central bank failed to take effective action to avoid the depths of the Great Depression. In the post–World War II

era, the Fed had a better record, but bouts of high inflation and frequent recessions were common. In the 1990s the economy enjoyed a long period of sustained economic growth, and the enlightened monetary policies of the Fed under the leadership of Alan Greenspan were widely praised.

In the second half of the twentieth century, the states liberalized their branch banking laws, and a few commercial banks created regional or national networks. Nonetheless, small- and medium-sized local banks continued to thrive; the United States continued to have a more decentralized commercial banking system than any other nation. Many banks broadened their base of borrowers to include not just business enterprises but private households. Automobile loans and credit card debt mushroomed. Automatic teller machines (ATMs) became popular with millions of depositors in thousands of nontraditional locations.

Meanwhile, the investment banking sector expanded dramatically after 1840. Investment bankers initially aided railroads in securing millions of dollars for new construction. After 1880 the capital markets became more accessible to industrial and service sector firms. The nation's most prominent investment banker, J. P. Morgan, was often the target of social criticism because so many of his peers deferred to his judgment during financial panics. Populist politicians often included investment bankers—along with grain dealers, railroads, and Jews—in their search for economic villains and conspirators.

The Great Depression devastated the investment banking sector. The creation of the Securities and Exchange Commission (SEC) in the 1930s, which increased the transparency of the capital markets, helped revive the confidence of investors. In the second half of the century, investment bankers sponsored thousands of new issues of stocks and bonds for corporations, and the collective sum ran into the billions of dollars. Investment bankers on Wall Street made New York City the largest market for investment capital in the world, surpassing London and other European money centers.

New laws enacted by Congress in the 1990s gave both commercial banks and investment banks greater latitude in offering customers a broad range of financial services. As a result the entire financial services sector had the opportunity to engage in the type of comprehensive integration commonly found in other advanced nations. Indeed, some of the largest U.S. financial institutions negotiated mergers with banks in western Europe.

Given the reforms enacted over the past two centuries to protect customers and the broader services available to businesses and households, public criticism of the banking system subsided in the last quarter of the twentieth century. Banking institutions were seen less often as potential threats to the political system and the social order. The fear of concentrated power in the hands of a narrow financial elite seemed less ominous in the increasingly global economy of the late twentieth century than it had to suspicious Jeffersonians and Jacksonians in the prior century.

In the literary field most prominent authors have portrayed bankers in an unflattering light. One exception was Louis Auchincloss, a New York lawyer and fiction writer in the second half of the twentieth century, who treated powerful figures on Wall Street in a sympathetic manner. Most films with financial executives in their narratives have presented these characters in an unfavorable manner. The movie *Wall Street* (1987), directed by Oliver Stone and featuring an unscrupulous, avaricious character played by Michael Douglas, is a prime example of that trend.

[See also CREDIT CARD.*]*

BIBLIOGRAPHY

Klebaner, Benjamin, *American Commercial Banking: A History,* 2d ed. (Twayne 1990).

Perkins, Edwin J., *American Public Finance and Financial Services, 1700–1815* (Ohio State Univ. Press 1994).

Timberlake, Richard H., *Monetary Policy in the United States: An Intellectual and Institutional History* (Univ. of Chicago Press 1993).

EDWIN J. PERKINS

COURTESY, MATTEL INC.

The original Barbie doll was dressed in a swimsuit in 1959. Later versions (here from 1987 and 1994) kept pace with fashion trends and with the expanding roles of women in the workplace.

BARBIE

The most popular and widely recognized doll in the history of the toy industry, Barbie was first introduced to the public in 1959 by the Mattel Company at a major toy fair. Barbie was initially packaged as a "Teen Age Fashion Model," despite some reservations about her "adult" features. In that first year some 350 thousand Barbies were purchased at three dollars each, a remarkable initial sale for a new doll.

Since then Barbie has become an international phenomenon, marketed in over 140 countries. By the late 1990s more than one billion Barbies had been sold. Equally important are the countless outfits designed to clothe her; over one hundred new costumes debut each year. Mattel also sells to-scale houses and furniture, cars, and other effects to accommodate her lifestyle. As a point of reference, in 1999 Barbie and all her related products generated almost two billion dollars for Mattel. It is estimated that in the United States alone nine out of every ten girls ages three to ten possess at least one piece of Barbie paraphernalia. These items are usually sold in "paks" for easy identification, complete with official pink Barbie labels to protect against imitators.

Despite her associations with American life and fashions, Barbie's roots are European. She is modeled on Lilli, a 1950s German doll patterned after a comic-strip character appearing in the newspaper *Bild Zeitung*. Clearly intended for adults, Lilli came with suggestive clothing and had proportions remarkably similar to Barbie's. In fact, Ruth Handler, the then-president of Mattel and creator of Barbie, freely admits that she copied the eleven-and-a-half-inch (29-cm) figure from Lilli but sagely keyed her appeal to young girls. Handler also devised the sophisticated marketing strategies that have made a simple latex doll into a complex icon of popular culture.

Like Lilli, her American counterpart possesses long legs, a tiny waist, an obvious bosom, painted nails, and a detailed face. Barbie is "really" Barbie Millicent Roberts, a name derived from that of Handler's daughter. Over the years, Barbie has gone from a solitary figurine to a veritable family of dolls. Boyfriend Ken came along in 1961 and was named after Handler's son. His wardrobe, while no rival to Barbie's, is nonetheless extensive and ever-changing. Assorted relatives, friends, and pets have since appeared—along with the ubiquitous line of accessories. In addition Barbie and her cohorts frequently display the logos of many well-known companies through product tie-ins, thereby familiarizing their young owners with international consumerism at an early age.

Beginning in 1980 the first African American Barbie was introduced. This version was soon followed by a number of other ethnically identifiable Barbies that continued to multiply throughout the 1990s. Likewise, the clothing has grown more diverse. Barbie does not predict fashions but instead reinforces what is popular. Basically, her many costumes reflect that which is new, stylish, and elegant, and her designers seldom miss a trend.

In keeping with the vogue for collectibles, a "Limited Edition" line appeared in 1986. Made of porcelain, these were hardly toys; they were in-tended for display. The 1990s went one step further with a "Designer Series"—Barbie wearing the clothing of some of the world's best-known couturiers. As a result a subculture of collectors has evolved, swapping and selling their Barbies on television shopping channels, through magazines and newsletters, flea markets, and numerous other venues. Some of the rarer or more unusually clothed dolls can fetch astronomical prices.

Barbie is a toy that symbolizes adulthood in a youngster's imagination. The act of dressing up Barbie and her friends is play, but the need to have all the latest dolls and accessories places an emphasis on real possession. With her instant name recognition, Barbie represents the consumable, the beautiful, the world of appearances.

[See also CONSUMERISM.]

BIBLIOGRAPHY

Fennick, Janine, *The Collectible Barbie: An Illustrated Guide to Her Dreamy World* (Courage Bks. 1994).

Motz, Marilyn Ferris, "'Seen through Rose-Tinted Glasses': The Barbie Doll in American Society," in *Popular Culture: An Introductory Text,* ed. by Jack Nachbar and Kevin Lausé (Popular Press 1992).

Rogers, Mary F., *Barbie Culture* (Sage Pubs. 1999).

Tosa, Marco, *Barbie: Four Decades of Fashion, Fantasy, and Fun* (Abrams 1998).

WILLIAM H. YOUNG

BASEBALL

Sports historians long ago discredited the legend that a Civil War general by the name of Abner Doubleday invented baseball as a boy in 1839 in rural upstate New York. Yet this story remains the game's "official" history. Its endurance is a testimony to the powerful mythologies that have surrounded the game since its formation. As this legend suggests, baseball is as important for the ideals it has evoked as the "national pastime" as it is for the records players have set or the victories that teams have won.

Baseball developed from the English children's game of rounders during the first half of the nineteenth century. By the mid-1840s urban men began

Babe Ruth hitting a home run at Yankee Stadium.

A major league baseball game in 1887.

to create formally organized baseball clubs in New York City, often in association with a working profession or a skilled trade. Clubs grew from urban voluntary associations that provided a link between less affluent male artisans and middle-class males who could provide resources for their membership. Baseball clubs were social organizations that not only played the sport but also sponsored events or donated proceeds to charity, social services, or union treasuries.

By 1857 a number of clubs formally organized into the National Association of Base Ball Players (NABBP) when games, particularly those pairing the best teams of two respective clubs, began to attract larger groups of spectators, and when the popular press began covering baseball games with increasing frequency. At this time the press also began keeping statistics. The NABBP also compiled the game's first formalized rules with the publication of its initial guidebooks in 1860.

Before the Civil War cricket was as popular a sport in the United States as baseball, but during the early 1860s baseball became much more popular when players and sportswriters began to recognize it as a more "American" game during a time of intense nationalism. The association of baseball with national identity has been one of its greatest sources of contention. Warren Goldstein has argued that the game's promoters attempted for a long time to portray baseball as representative of democratic ideals they have associated with the United States; however, they also labored hard to make participation in baseball an exclusive enterprise that connoted middle-class culture of white, native-born Americans.

These tensions emerged clearly during the game's early professionalization. In the 1860s clubs began to pay and recruit their best players, first covertly and then explicitly with the 1869 Cincinnati Red Stockings. The National League, formed in 1876 to wrest control of professional baseball away from players and toward investors, worked to present the game as a "respectable" one for middle-class audiences by forbidding alcohol consumption at the ballpark and banning games on Sundays.

This "respectable" national community envisioned by the founders of baseball and the major leagues also excluded African Americans. The NABBP banned African Americans from playing in 1867, and the highest levels of professional baseball officially banned African American players in the mid-1880s. Even during the nineteenth century baseball presented a nostalgic image of national pride, one that celebrated the values of republican community and of independent producers. Craftsmen and artisans associated such independence with "whiteness." The game's founders created a "national pastime" that resisted the regimentation of the industrial time clock and the alienation of the modern workplace. However, they also set this national vision so powerfully against blacks that African Americans were uniquely barred from playing in major league baseball between the mid-1880s and 1947.

Yet African Americans still played the game during this period, creating semiprofessional "sandlot" leagues, barnstorming teams, and all-black major leagues, popularly known as the Negro Leagues. Many of the all-black teams that would emerge over the next half-century operated under white financial management, since African Americans usually lacked the financial resources, political connections, and access to public-relations outlets that could enhance their profitability.

Even with their lack of resources, some African American entrepreneurs did move into and exercise control over black baseball. Black sports entrepreneurs including Rube Foster and Gus Greenlee created and maintained the Negro National League (NNL) between 1920 and 1947. Yet because of financial instability teams and leagues often existed for short periods of time. Perhaps as important as the better-known NNL were the numerous sandlot and barnstorming teams that flourished during the 1930s and 1940s. Players on these clubs often played baseball at its highest level but did not receive a regular salary and often did not play in an organized league. Instead, they "barnstormed," meaning that they spent most of their time on the road performing in often hastily arranged exhibitions against numerous teams throughout North America. Even franchises that were part of the NNL played many of their games outside the league in exhibitions against local teams or even against white major league teams.

NATIONAL BASEBALL LIBRARY, COOPERSTOWN, NY

Leroy "Satchel" Paige, one of baseball's most memorable pitchers.

Early founders of baseball associated the game they played with masculinity just as they had with whiteness. They worked to prove that baseball was a manly game, distinguishing it from rounders, which was known as a game for children. They changed the rules to make baseball more difficult and therefore more "manly." Either as members of an emerging middle class or as part of a growing working class of wage earners, many men felt that the new social formations of modern life undermined their authority as men, and they responded to this situation by attempting to symbolically revitalize their masculinity. Sports, and particularly baseball, were part of this movement.

During World War II women entered this "man's world" at the same time that many women in the United States were working in occupations traditionally reserved for men. Drawing from widespread interest in women's softball during the 1930s and 1940s, major league owners formed the All American Girls Baseball League (AAGBL). Although women in the league played a game long associated with manliness, the league also required them to live according to a "femininity principle," wearing makeup and skirts while playing, attending charm school, and appearing in a way that was both sexually appealing and "respectable." Susan Cahn argues that the founders of the AAGBL actually highlighted the tension between the feminine appearance of players and their masculine skills because it provided a conservative social vision of women doing "men's" work in a way that did not fundamentally challenge traditional gender relationships.

When men returned to baseball after World War II, the women of the AAGBL found it hard to compete against the attention fans paid once more to men's baseball. The women's league continued for several years but ended up folding in 1954. Yet the 1950s became one of the most turbulent decades in the history of mainstream baseball, largely because of television.

Before the 1950s many communities treated minor league teams almost as regional major leagues, particularly in the West and South. Television, however, worked to focus the attention of baseball fans almost entirely on the major leagues, dramatically changing the ways that people experienced the game by the end of the decade. Hundreds of minor league teams folded during the decade, and major league teams moved to new cities with greater television markets.

During the 1980s there was an outpouring of popular nostalgia for baseball. Ironically, many yearned for the game as it was played and experienced during the 1950s. Adult males, for example, returned in large numbers to the hobby of baseball-card collecting, which had developed into a widely popular boyhood hobby during the 1950s. Nostalgia for the baseball of the 1950s overshadowed the instability that actually characterized baseball during that decade. More profoundly, it masked dislocations that characterized the decade itself while it helped to recycle images of nuclear-family stability, suburban tranquility, and affluence that many associated with that time period. Themes of simplicity and stability were common within popular representations of baseball that reemerged during the 1980s and early 1990s. For example, baseball films of the 1980s represented a return to more nostalgic themes that had been expressed in the hey-day of baseball movies produced during the 1940s and 1950s, and publishers flooded the market with nostalgically poetic books about the game by such writers as W. P. Kinsella, George Will, Roger Angell, and the late baseball commissioner A. Bartlett Giamatti. Films and books celebrated baseball as emblematic of innocence and simplicity.

Despite the outpouring of nostalgic sentiment, baseball became a less centrally important sport than it once was in the United States. This was particularly evident after 1994, when major league owners broke off negotiations with the Major League Players Association during contract negotiations. This "lockout" interrupted the season in August and for the first time since 1905 forced the cancellation of the World Series. When the season resumed the following spring, there was a dramatic drop in attendance, evidence of the bitter disillusionment that many fans expressed.

Ironically, major league teams that had fought to exclude African Americans from the game now fought to attract black fans to the ballpark, many of whom were simply not interested in a game that for so long defined itself against blackness. At the same time, baseball might best be described as the "transnational pastime," becoming as popular in Asian countries and in Latin America as it is in the United States. Although many still hold on to the notion of baseball as the national pastime, the idea of nation and the meaning of sports remain socially contested.

[See also SPORTS, AN OVERVIEW.]

BIBLIOGRAPHY

Adelman, Melvin L., *A Sporting Time: New York City and the Rise of Modern Athletics, 1820–1870* (1986; Univ. of Ill. Press 1990).

Bloom, John, *A House of Cards: Baseball Card Collecting and Popular Culture* (Univ. of Minn. Press 1997).

Cahn, Susan, *Coming on Strong: Gender and Sexuality in Twentieth-Century Women's Sport* (Free Press 1994).

Goldstein, Warren, *Playing for Keeps: A History of Early Baseball* (Cornell Univ. Press 1989).

Kimmel, Michael S., "Baseball and the Reconstitution of American Masculinity, 1880–1920," in *Sport, Men, and the Gender Order: Critical Feminist Perspectives,* ed.

by Michael A. Messner and Donald Sabo (Human Ki-
netics Bks. 1990).

Levine, Peter, *A. G. Spalding and the Rise of Baseball: The
Promise of American Sport* (Oxford 1985).

Ruck, Rob, *Sandlot Seasons: Sport in Black Pittsburgh*
(Univ. of Ill. Press 1987).

JOHN BLOOM

BEAT WRITERS

Every era has its avant-garde. In the 1950s the "official" America of Dwight Eisenhower, Joseph Mc-
Carthy, and nuclear domesticity also possessed its
share of critics—civil rights activists, alternative religious groups, radical social theorists, abstract expressionists, and, most conspicuously, the beat writers. While the term *beat* is usually associated with
the writers Jack Kerouac, Allen Ginsberg, and William S. Burroughs, it embodies a distinct literary
sensibility shared by a wide range of artists: New
York writers such as John Clellon Holmes, Gregory Corso, LeRoi Jones (Amiri Baraka), and Diane
Di Prima as well as West Coast poets Gary Snyder,
Michael McClure, Philip Whalen, Philip Lamantia,
Bob Kaufman, and Lawrence Ferlinghetti, among
others. While it is important to keep in mind the
very real differences that separate the works of, say,
Burroughs and Snyder, beat serves as a useful designation for a specific cross section of the American literary avant-garde in the middle of the twentieth century.

What bound the beat writers together in common cause were their deeply felt suspicions about,
and interrogations of, the "American way of life,"
which celebrated domestic consumption, geopolitical dominance, and technological innovation as pre-
scriptions to quell the anxieties of cold war culture.
Much of beat literature elicits an emotional sympathy from the reader for either a dissenting narrative voice or a protagonist. For example, in Ginsberg's *Howl and Other Poems* (1956), Kerouac's *On
the Road* (1957), and Burroughs's *Naked Lunch* (1959),
there exists a search for an alternative way of life
against the current of the cultural majority. Ironically, many beat writers committed themselves to
both a pastoral ideal and the traditional history of

© ALLEN GINSBERG. COURTESY OF FAHEY/KELIN GALLERY, LOS ANGELES

Jack Kerouac at the Battery, New York City, in 1953, photographed by fellow beat writer Allen Ginsberg.

America even as they questioned its present state.
Their personal experiences, observations, and confessions imbued their work with an adversarial
tenor, but also with a certain pathos. While the beats
questioned the dominant culture, that is, the system of generalized goals and values that maintained
the social order, they were simultaneously rebellious and beholden to the mythic language of America, suspicious of its content but committed to its
general form. Such suspicions necessitated alternative ideas of both self and country, new ways to
live, and, most important, a new conception of the
artist, describing an America he or she could feel
and imaginatively grasp but not fully inhabit. However, to appreciate the aesthetic, political, and religious dimensions of this literary movement, one
must keep in mind its origins.

William Burroughs, Jack Kerouac, and Allen
Ginsberg came together in New York City at a sub-
cultural crossroads: the intersection of Times Square
addicts and petty criminals, Greenwich Village bo-
hemia, and Columbia University intellectual circles.
Soon after their first meeting in 1944, they were

sharing an apartment and had become, in Kerouac's words, a "libertine circle." Because of their close association during the 1940s and 1950s, these writers first garnered the label of "beat," a self-descriptive adjective that Kerouac first applied to the entire generation of postwar American youth. During the deluge of criticism and media hyperbole that accompanied the publication of their works, beat lost its religious connotation—beaten down but capable of overcoming oppression through religious transcendence.

In the previous decade, however, these writers had initiated a collaborative project of literary and spiritual development, which they termed the *new vision*. Out of an array of idioms (including the prophecies of Oswald Spengler, the psychology of Wilhelm Reich, the semantic theories of Alfred Korzybski, drug experiences, the writings of Rimbaud and Yeats, the jazz cadences of Charlie Parker and Lester Young, the kinetic energy of their muse Neal Cassady, and the stoicism of Times Square hustler Herbert Huncke), Burroughs, Kerouac, and Ginsberg fashioned a religious platform for belief and action. The "new vision"—borrowed, stolen, and invented out of the fabric of their everyday surroundings—became the context for their criticism of mainstream culture. As John Clellon Holmes noted in his 1952 *New York Times* piece "This Is the Beat Generation," this accumulation of insights also sustained their "perfect craving to believe" in America's promise of absolute freedom.

Given their desire to participate in an alternative social reality, many beat writers sought to realize new means of perception and expression, or rather, a new means of expression as perception. To the extent that the boundaries dissolved between subject and object, conscious and unconscious, description and explanation, their poetics sought to achieve an uninterrupted and complete account of reality. In their attempt to unearth the unspeakable visions of the individual, beat writers rejected both the literary standards of the academy and middle-class decorum. Burroughs's "factualism" and later, his cut-up technique; Kerouac's spontaneous compositions; Ginsberg's attention to the individual breath; and Michael McClure's physically based po-

© FRED W. MCDARRAH

Allen Ginsberg at the Living Theatre, November 23, 1959, reading from an early poem, "Song: Fie My Fum."

etics were all experiments in achieving a form of confessional honesty, a way to interrogate the conditioning power of language in the name of social change. The political charge of this style derived from the fact that they believed that there was an organic relationship between the individual and society.

The beat writers left an indelible mark on the tradition of American arts and letters. While failing to institute "religions of perception" in the leg-

222

islature, beat writers did have a profound impact on popular culture. In the 1960s their work informed both the symbolic, individualistic politics of the New Left and the stylized alienation of youth culture. Some of the beat writers have since influenced or collaborated with artists such as Bob Dylan, Tom Waits, Patti Smith, Philip Glass, and Laurie Anderson. In the 1990s there was yet another revival of the beat sensibility in popular culture: eulogies for Herbert Huncke, Ginsberg, and Burroughs; The Gap Incorporated clothing ads featuring pictures of a smiling, khaki-wearing Jack Kerouac; a spate of biographies, memoirs, academic studies, and recordings; a revival of spoken-word poetry and slam competitions involving a blend of improvisatory theater, debate, and hip-hop style; movie chronicles and documentaries such as David Cronenberg's *Naked Lunch* and Chuck Workman's *The Source;* as well as a host of Web sites dedicated to any number of beat-related items. In a culture where dissent has become the norm, the legacy of the beat writers continues to set the standard.

[See also LITERATURE, AN OVERVIEW, *and articles on* LITERARY CANON, LITERATURE AND THE CONSTRUCTION OF IDENTITY; AVANT-GARDE MOVEMENTS; PROLETARIAN LITERATURE; LOST GENERATION; POETRY; WRITERS AND POLITICS.*]*

BIBLIOGRAPHY

Belgrad, Daniel, *The Culture of Spontaneity: Improvisation and the Arts in Postwar America* (Univ. of Chicago Press 1998).

Charters, Ann, ed., *The Portable Beat Reader* (Viking 1992).

Davidson, Michael, *The San Francisco Renaissance: Poetics and Community at Mid-Century* (Cambridge 1989).

Lardas, John, *The Bop Apocalypse: The Religious Visions of Kerouac, Ginsberg, and Burroughs* (Univ. of Ill. Press 2000).

Tytell, John, *Naked Angels: The Lives and Literature of the Beat Generation* (McGraw-Hill 1976).

JOHN LARDAS

BEAUTY CONTESTS

The concept of the beauty contest dates from early Greek mythology, when the goddesses Athena, Aphrodite, and Hera competed for the prize of beauty, judged by the Trojan prince Paris. He chose Aphrodite because she promised him the most beautiful woman in the world as his consort. That woman was Helen, the wife of Menelaus, king of Sparta; Helen's subsequent elopement with Paris supposedly caused the Trojan War. The connection between the beauty of women and the violence of men continued in European folk tales such as "Beauty and the Beast," with beautiful women viewed alternately as the provokers or tamers of male wildness. In the medieval era, queens of beauty were often selected to preside over tournaments. In addition beauty queens were selected during the ancient celebrations of Twelfth Night, which honored the magi's visit to the baby Jesus, and as part of May Day festivities.

The first commercial beauty contest in the United States was held in 1854 by Phineas T. Barnum in his American Museum. When no contestants appeared, however, Barnum bowed to Victorian prudery and agreed that applicants need only submit photographs for judging. (No records exist of either the photos or the winners.) By the 1890s newspapers throughout the nation adopted the photographic beauty contest as a promotional device, especially after circus entrepreneur Adam Forepaugh's photographic beauty contest in 1888 to crown a "Ten Thousand Dollar Beauty" drew eleven thousand applicants for the grand prize.

In 1905 the promoters of the St. Louis Exposition formed a consortium of twelve newspapers nationwide to solicit photographs from which to choose the exposition's beauty queen; some forty thousand entries were received. A standard variation on these photographic newspaper contests were city and state competitions conducted through the newspapers to find beautiful women to be models for civic sculptures erected at the many expositions and centennials of the turn-of-the-century period.

City festivals also often included contests to select queens, especially when the New Orleans Mardi Gras (their esteemed progenitor) added a queen in 1871 and the Philadelphia Centennial Exposition of 1876 held a beauty contest that drew two thousand applicants. Festivals such as these often func-

The swimsuit competition at the first Miss America Pageant, held in Atlantic City, New Jersey, in 1921. The winner was sixteen-year-old Margaret Gorman (*second from left*).

tioned as promotional events for cities, as in the Pasadena Tournament of Roses, which was first held in 1889, and in the Portland, Oregon, rose festival, which was first held in 1909. During the Denver Festival of Mountain and Plain, the ancient contest of the Greek goddesses for the prize of beauty was reenacted.

By the 1880s promotional beauty contests also were being employed at dime museums and at carnival midways. So ubiquitous was the phenomenon that in 1898 the Elks' Clubs of Akron, Zanesville, and Canton, Ohio, awarded a prize to the township sending the most attractive wagonload of women to their jointly held carnival.

Both the Chicago Columbian Centennial of 1893 and the Atlanta International Cotton Exposition of 1895 held "Congresses of Beauty." The first beach beauty contest was held at Rehoboth Beach, Delaware, in 1880, setting the scene for the first Miss America pageant, held in Atlantic City, New Jersey, in September 1921, as an attempt to prolong the summer season. The most famous and long-running of American beauty contests, the Miss America Pageant, has been held each year in Atlantic City, except for a hiatus between 1928 and 1935.

The beauty contest solidified its hold on American culture through the additions of cheerleaders, song girls, and homecoming queens at football games. Moreover, the general objectification of women's beauty to sell commercial products played a role in the growing popularity of beauty contests, as did a variety of local and regional beauty contest competitions in the mid-twentieth century, such as one in the Japanese American section of Los Angeles designed to choose a queen of the Little Tokyo festival and the general beauty contest circuits for young girls. These children's circuits gained notoriety in 1995, following the brutal killing of six-year-old JonBenet Ramsey of Boulder, Colorado, who was a regular winner in these contests.

Competition is a hallmark of modern capitalist cultures, and beauty contests most often function as secular ritual events to harness the powers of young women in modern society to the status quo. Contestants usually enshrine the dominant ideal of beauty of the era. Yet sometimes beauty contests serve the purpose of overturning societal norms as a means of protesting them or obversely of containing protest by dissipating it through parody. Parodies include the burlesqued beauty contests often held at feminist events in the 1970s; the "voguing" contests held at transvestite balls; and such events as the Slum Goddess Pageant of Bloomington, Indiana, where drag queens compete in a contest designed to mimic standard beauty contest rituals.

Because beauty contests have been criticized as little more than displays of women's bodies, their organizers have attempted to legitimize their contests with added talent competitions and speeches about humanitarian interests. Vanessa Williams, an African American actress who is one of the most successful Miss Americas in the history of the pageant, was stripped of her title when it was discovered that *Penthouse* magazine had published nude photographs of her. Public feminist protests against beauty contests have not been extensive, although the one held in 1968 outside the Miss America contest, in which protesters threw into a trash can such artifacts of oppression as bras, hair curlers, and makeup, is often cited as one of the founding events of second-wave feminism.

[*See also* FASHION; BEAUTY PARLORS; FEMINISM, AN OVERVIEW; GIBSON GIRL; MOVIE STARS; PHYSICAL CULTURE.]

BIBLIOGRAPHY

Banet-Weiser, Sarah, *The Most Beautiful Girl in the World: Beauty Pageants and National Identity* (Univ. of Calif. Press 1999).

Banner, Lois W., *American Beauty* (Knopf 1983).

Tzu-Chan, Judy, "*Loveliest Daughter of Our Ancient Cathay! Representations of Ethnic and Gender Identity in the Miss Chinatown U.S. Beauty Pageant,*" *Journal of Social History* 31 (Fall 1978):5–31.

LOIS W. BANNER

BEAUTY PARLORS

The beauty parlor represents a predominantly female refuge in the American cultural imagination, a place where the odors of hairspray and nail-polish remover blend with the laughter and conversation of the women who form a unique community. Annie S. Barnes's 1975 study, which suggested that lower-class African American women in the southern United States frequented the beauty parlor even more than women of the middle and upper classes, provides evidence that the beauty parlor offers far more than a well-groomed coiffure. Similarly, Ray Oldenburg notes that in America's much more privatized and individualistic society, informal public meeting places are more difficult to find than, for example, in Europe or Japan. Because Americans are encouraged to solve their problems on their own rather than in a shared social environment, such community centers as the beauty parlor can have enormous value for the "regulars" who gather there to exchange news and engage in dialogue, fostering an intimacy unavailable to them in another setting. Yet other scholars, skeptical of the so-called democratization of beauty that the beauty parlor claims to offer women, warn about overly romanticizing that institution and suggest that the beauty parlor once notoriously housed unlicensed "quack" surgeons who unscrupulously encouraged women to undergo dangerous and unnecessary plastic surgeries.

Frida Kerner Furman's *Facing the Mirror* explores the significance of beauty-parlor culture for elderly Jewish American women, finding that it is composed of an "unintentional community" of women whose bonds are forged primarily on the basis of storytelling. Whether sharing the details of a recent illness, consoling one another about a loss, or joking affectionately about their appearances, these women share their lives in order to combat loneliness and the prejudices of ageism and to celebrate their achievements as older women surviving in a youth-obsessed culture that tends to ignore or ridicule the elderly. Furman's initial concern that the topic was not serious enough for academic inquiry suggests one reason for the lack of scholarship on this phenomenon, which has been taken up for the most part by artists and filmmakers.

In 1980 visual artist Michael Dorsey began a mixed media work entitled *Historical Beauty Parlor Series,* which was based on his childhood experiences in his family's beauty parlors in Findlay, Ohio, and portrays the beauty parlor in a variety of settings. From the "Prehistoric Beauty Salon," which features four women draped in animal skins beneath the cave-painted bulls of Lascaux, France, to the "Gothic Beauty Parlor," in which one woman offers what appears to be a church indulgence exempting her from a conformist hairstyle, Dorsey's work stresses the public nature of the beauty parlor and situates it as a dynamic, historicized space deeply affected by cultural, religious, and political processes and events. Eudora Welty's short story "The Petrified Man" and the 1989 film *Steel Magnolias* provide further proof that the beauty parlor

holds a tremendous imaginative and symbolic power in American culture.

[*See also* FASHION.]

BIBLIOGRAPHY

Barnes, Annie S., "The Black Beauty Parlor Complex in a Southern City," *Phylon: The Atlantic University Review of Race and Culture* 36, no. 2 (1975):149–154.

Furman, Frida Kerner, *Facing the Mirror: Older Women and Beauty Shop Culture* (Routledge 1997).

Gootkerk, Paul, "The Beauty Parlor Mirror: Reflections of Tradition," *Journal of American Culture* 11, no. 2 (1988):11–16.

Haiken, Elizabeth, *Venus Envy: A History of Cosmetic Surgery* (Johns Hopkins Univ. Press 1997).

Oldenburg, Ray, *The Great Good Place: Cafés, Coffee Shops, Community Centers, Beauty Parlors, General Stores, Bars, Hangouts, and How They Get You through the Day* (Paragon House 1989).

D. RAE GREINER

BIBLE

No single book has had a more profound influence on American culture than the Bible. In a country with unusually strong commitments to literacy and publishing, the Bible has remained a best-seller. Even at the end of the twentieth century, ninety percent of Americans said they owned a Bible, and forty percent stated that the Bible was important to them. The Bible's influence on American society has been so pervasive that it has touched every area of American life, including education, literature, law, politics, and, of course, religion.

The Bible's initial importance in colonial America was primarily evident in the Northeast, where large populations of Puritans settled. The Puritans centered their religious beliefs on the teachings of the Bible, using it as the standard by which they guided their private, social, and political worlds. The Puritan commitment to the Bible inspired, in 1642, the colony of Massachusetts to enact a law requiring that all children be taught to read, for if the Bible was the standard by which one was to live one's life, one needed to be able to read it. While the Bible has lost its primacy in American public education (in large part owing to several court decisions beginning in the late nineteenth century upholding a strong view of separating church and state), it was read regularly in most classrooms up through the early part of the twentieth century.

It should be no surprise that much of American literature is deeply inflected with biblical resonances. The famous politician and orator Edward Everett argued for the existence of a uniquely American literature in the early nineteenth century by pointing to the vast corpus of American religious writings. Whether these religious writings were sermons, poems, or histories, they were all rooted in the biblical text. A host of American writers continued to use the Bible as a crucial touchstone for their work, including Herman Melville, Harriet Beecher Stowe, Louisa May Alcott, Mark Twain, William Faulkner, John Updike, and John Irving.

The Bible served as a cultural anchor—a text so well known by so many Americans that it provided a common set of ideas, characters, and narrative conventions—well beyond the field of literature as seen in its ubiquitous presence in American law and politics. Countless American laws and political debates are rooted in various themes of the biblical narrative, including slavery, monogamy, qualification to hold political office, prohibition, divorce, and abortion. The Bible has also significantly influenced the rhetoric of political debate in the United States. Abraham Lincoln could call the nation away from being a "house divided" and later Ronald Reagan, George H. Bush, and Bill Clinton could all invoke their favorite image of the United States like "a city upon a hill" because the Bible provided Americans with a common set of ideas, characters, and narrative conventions.

The Bible remains central to many of the United States's largest and fastest growing religious communities. Whether it be the Jehovah's Witnesses, the Church of Jesus Christ of the Latter-day Saints (Mormons), or more mainstream Protestant denominations, such as Southern Baptists or Assemblies of God, the Bible continues to play an absolutely pivotal role in how these communities view themselves and the world around them. Issues that define the belief structures of these bodies, such as race relations, gender roles, the place of science and technology in society, and the nature and purpose of the family, are all addressed according to differing interpretations of the Bible.

Finally, while various biblical interpretations have long exercised a profound influence on differing segments of the country's national, regional, and local life, it is critical to understand that along with a diversity of biblical interpretation has come a diversity of biblical production. While the centrality of the Bible to early Americans' spiritual lives has won them the nickname of "people of the Book," it would be more accurate to call late-twentieth-century Christians in America "people of the Books." Literally millions of Bibles in thousands of different editions have circulated in the United States since the seventeenth century.

Different editions of the Bible feature varied formats, illustrations, appended material, and, perhaps most important, translation work. Over 450 English-language translations of the Bible have appeared in the United States in the past three hundred years, not including the various foreign language and Native American translations. These different translations have often altered the way the core biblical text is interpreted, spawning new social movements and religious traditions. The Bible is a work of infinite complexity both in terms of its central narrative and in how that narrative has been interpreted by the millions of Americans who have made it, and continue to make it, the country's most popular written text.

[See also RELIGIOUS WRITING AND SERMONS; POPULAR RELIGION; FUNDAMENTALISM; RELIGION AND RELIGIOUS MOVEMENTS, AN OVERVIEW.]

BIBLIOGRAPHY

Frerichs, Ernest S., ed., *The Bible and Bibles in America* (Scholars Press 1988).

Gutjahr, Paul C., *An American Bible: A History of the Good Book in the United States, 1777–1880* (Stanford Univ. Press 1999).

Hatch, Nathan O., and Mark A. Noll, *The Bible in America: Essays in Cultural History* (Oxford 1982).

Hills, Margaret Thorndike, *The English Bible in America: A Bibliography of Editions of the Bible and the New Testament Published in America, 1777–1957* (Am. Bible Soc. 1962).

Thuesen, Peter Johannes, *In Discordance with the Scriptures: American Protestant Battles over Translating the Bible* (Oxford 1999).

PAUL GUTJAHR

BICULTURALISM

Is there a homogeneous and recognizable American culture? If there is such a thing, is it possible to maintain healthy connections to both that culture and another, the culture of one's history and ancestry? These are the central questions embodied in the study of biculturalism, which considers all the issues related to the combination of a home culture, acquired and practiced in family and ethnic groups, with a national culture, to which adherence is expected if one is to be accepted and respected as a citizen. In the United States, where most citizens can trace family origins to other countries, the search for balance between respect for ancestral ties and commitment to the broader community is an essential facet of the national character. At its best, this ongoing personal and political struggle has led to widespread respect for diversity and the expectation that people of all national origins are entitled to the full rights and responsibilities of citizenship; at its worst, awareness that many American citizens have unsevered ties to other communities has been the cause of much fragmentation, conflict, exclusion, and bigotry.

The practice of adding qualifying information to the identification of American nationality, combining recognition of one's present national identity with mention of an ancestral culture, is a familiar demonstration of the complexity of American culture. Evolving choices of self-assigned labels can show changes in the sense of connection to a culture: immigrants may call themselves "Irish," while their children may be "Irish-American," and later generations simply "American"; similarly, the willingness of others to label a person or group as "American," without qualification, is an indication of perceived assimilation into the broader society. The phenomenon of the "hyphenated American," bearing a label such as "Polish-American" or "Japanese-American," draws attention to the importance of even such a small item as a hyphen in validly describing a person's relationship to two cultures. The difference between "Mexican-American," suggesting active connections to both nations, and "Mexican American," where "Mexican" may be an indication of cultural syncretism or a descriptive adjective no stronger than "tall" or "young," only begins to show the possible approaches to describing Americans' complex cultural allegiances. Some labels, such as "Chicano," may describe a combined culture that is uniquely American; others, such as "Hispanic," imply that a common linguistic heritage is enough to define and unite Americans of widely varied national origins.

The intertwined nature of language and culture leads to frequent use of the term *bilingual/bicultural* to describe educational efforts and community programs that attempt to communicate in the ways most acceptable to their participants, most of whom are assumed not to be native speakers of American English. Such projects may be undertaken in order to provide efficient exchange of information, minimizing participants' need to struggle with linguistic and cultural obstacles to understanding; programs organized within ethnic communities sometimes use bilingual/bicultural techniques to provide a connection to their own American-born young people. Often, however, bilingual/bicultural education is viewed as a temporary situation, designed to eliminate itself as rapidly as possible by accelerating assimilation and conformity to the majority culture, which includes the English language. As with other cultural practices, such as religion and dress, there is no nationwide legislation designating the majority language, English, as the official language of the United States; still, concern over the difficulty of fully sharing a culture without sharing a language has motivated many attempts to formalize the status of English, sometimes accompanied by efforts to forbid the use of other languages in the workplace.

Assimilation, the process of absorbing newcomers into the majority culture, acts in opposition to biculturalism by pressuring individuals to abandon cultural practices that may distinguish them from their established and successful "real American" neighbors. In the interest of accelerating assimilation, some evidence of national origin, such as distinctive dress or cuisine, may be consciously limited to the private sphere or set aside altogether; the degree of willingness to do so may predict the ease with which an individual will be accepted by others less conscious of their own immigrant roots. Willingness to assimilate, however, is not always enough to smooth the way to acceptance. Physical evidence of national origin, such as skin color or eye shape, cannot be set aside in the interest of fitting in with the majority, although cosmetic industries have been fueled by attempts to do so; for individuals whose appearance obviously differs from that of the majority of Americans, nonnational, bicultural designations such as "Asian-American" or "African-American" are likely to be applied no matter how strongly their cultural practices conform to those of the majority.

United States foreign policy is often influenced by bicultural Americans who remain deeply interested in events in their ancestral homelands and expect their elected representatives to share their interest. By insisting that decisions be made with the good of both nations in mind, bicultural Americans contribute to the creation and maintenance of strong national alliances. Immigration policy is also of vital interest to bicultural Americans, many of whom wish to have their extended families join them. Although most Americans are aware of some family origins in other countries, many have lost any personal connection to those countries or their own immigrant pasts; in what has been called a "nation of immigrants," bicultural Americans serve as living links not only to other nations but also to the history of the United States.

While many individuals, families, and communities may be considered bicultural, assimilation and intermarriage create many others that are more properly termed *multicultural*, combining elements of several ancestral cultures into a mixture that is uniquely their own. As distance from an immigrant past and connection to the present of a diverse American community increase simultaneously, a bicultural identity may be only one of several possibilities. Persons may move from feeling themselves displaced members of another culture to describing themselves as bicultural Americans to describing a multicultural background as "mixed" rather than attempting to account for all of its components. Such persons may also come to think of themselves as ordinary Americans who, like many of their fellow citizens and like the nation itself, have a complex and interesting history that draws strength from many sources.

[See also MULTICULTURALISM; AMERICANIZATION.]

BIBLIOGRAPHY

Anzaldúa, Gloria, *Borderlands/La Frontera: The New Mestiza* (Aunt Lute Bks. 1999).

Darder, Antonia, *Culture and Power in the Classroom: A Critical Foundation for Bicultural Education* (Bergin & Garvey 1991).

Namias, June, ed., *First Generation: In the Words of Twentieth-Century American Immigrants* (Univ. of Ill. Press 1992).

Reimers, David M., *Unwelcome Strangers: American Identity and the Turn against Immigration* (Columbia Univ. Press 1998).

Takaki, Ronald, *A Different Mirror: A History of Multicultural America* (Little, Brown 1993).

ROSEMARIE L. COSTE

BILINGUAL EDUCATION

Bilingual education literally refers to a curriculum that teaches literacy in two distinct languages. The term, however, is extended to any instruction in a child's native language other than English and encompasses the rights of any immigrants to have their child instructed in his or her native language.

Bilingual education in the United States dates to the early nineteenth century, when a number of states supported education in German or French. However, during World War I there was a strong suspicion regarding the loyalty of German-speaking immigrants. That suspicion was extended to other immigrant groups, especially those who ran schools in their own languages. Mistrust of those who do not speak English in the United States has a long history and periodically erupts into view.

The nineteenth-century nativist movement, for example, viewed English-language skills as the path to assimilation. There are still a number of Americans who adhere to that way of thinking. Interestingly, there is evidence that many Hispanics support English-only instruction, believing that bilingual education confines them to second-class citizenship.

Bilingual education was essentially dead in the United States by the 1920s. This practice went along with the predominant Americanization view of the country. One function of schools was to assimilate new immigrants into the country, to teach them basic citizenship. New immigration was severely restricted by the United States government, partially to enable any immigrants already in the country to be assimilated.

During the 1960s the influx of Cuban immigrants and the new migrants resulting from the Kennedy reforms, enacted under President Johnson, opened the immigration gates again. Many new bilingual programs emerged, basically with the support of the federal government.

In 1968 Congress passed the first federal bilingual education law. Given subsequent opposition, it is interesting to note that the vote was unanimous in both houses of Congress. However, programs did not get started until the Supreme Court ruled in 1974 in *Lau v. Nichols* that such programs were constitutional. Kenny Kinman Lau was a first-grade student. The class-action lawsuit argued against the "sink or swim" philosophy, which stated that a child had to learn English in normal classrooms, calling this approach "a violation of the children's right to an equal education." The court refused to lay out specific plans for schools but mandated that schools develop plans for bilingual education programs. Over strong and often bitter opposition, schools did so.

In the 1980s many immigrants from Southeast Asia and Central America came to the United States fleeing political oppression. States such as California witnessed a 220 percent increase in the number of students who were not fluent in English. This increase taxed the ability of many schools to live up to bilingual education requirements. There were not, for example, teachers with the required training for these classes nor were there sufficient classrooms available for students.

Opposition to bilingual education has continued to grow. Many parents, including a number of Latino parents, believe that such programs hinder the progress of their children and relegate them to inferior educational resources and poorer colleges. Many parents maintain that their children suffer because too many resources are diverted for too little gain. Children, they argue, are kept in these programs well beyond what is necessary, in order to support a bureaucracy and teachers with an entrenched interest in maintaining them.

[See also EDUCATION, *article on* EDUCATION AND PUBLIC POLICY; BILINGUALISM; AMERICANIZATION.*]*

BIBLIOGRAPHY

Claire, Elizabeth, *ESL Teacher's Activities Kit* (Prentice Hall 1988).

Krashen, Stephen D., *Under Attack: The Case against Bilingual Education* (Language Educational Assoc. 1996).

Kuykendall, Crystal, *From Rage to Hope: Strategies for Reclaiming Black and Hispanic Students* (National Educational Service 1992).

Tabors, Patton O., *One Child, Two Languages: A Guide for Preschool Educators of Children Learning English as a Second Language* (Paul H. Brookes Pub. 1997).

VIRGINIA SALAMONE

BILINGUALISM

The term *bilingual* means two languages that are spoken by an individual or a group or taught within a school. One of the myths of bilingualism is that a bilingual child has two equally well developed languages. This idealized notion of a balanced bilingual or ambilingual speaker is inapplicable to the majority of bilinguals throughout the world. Studies of the different social circumstances in which a child becomes bilingual suggest there are four broad types of bilingualism: elite bilingual (children who are purposefully instructed in and exposed to a desired language); children from linguistic majorities; children from bilingual families or communities; and children from linguistic minorities. Some scholars have distinguished between the term *bilingualism*, referring to the state of a linguistic community in which two languages are in contact resulting in both being available for use, and the term *bilinguality*, referring to the psychological status of an individual who has access to more than one language. Although individual bilingualism historically has been categorically defined, current research suggests that it is a relative process wherein a child attains degrees of competency in two languages. At one end of the scale is fluency in both languages and at the other is minimal communicative skill in a second or foreign language.

Bilingualism and Code Switching. A bilingual speaker has access to two languages, each capable of being used to encode meaning into a message and provide options to the speaker when conceptualizing, structuring, or expressing these meanings. Bilingual speakers have the competence to select from either code depending on their situational context or intent. This process is called code switching, which is a common, rule-governed feature of bilingual speech. The most common form of code switching occurs when a word from one language is substituted for a word in the other. Tag switching involves the insertion of a question from one language into an utterance that is otherwise completely in the other language, for example, This is the restaurant, *n'est-ce pas* ("is it not")? A more advanced form, though commonly used by children, is intersentential switching, where a phrase or sentence from one language is inserted at the sentence boundary of the other. An English and French example: I want the book; *Donnez-le moi s'il vous plaît* ("give it to me if you please"). An even more advanced form, common among bilingual adults, is intrasentential switching, where insertion occurs within the sentence or phrase. A Sudanese Arabic and English example: *Walahi yakhi* ("by God my brother"), I'm very happy *min ziarah bitak* ("from

your visit"). Bilinguals have been shown to engage in code switching in a purposeful manner as they utilize the entirety of the grammar and vocabulary at their disposal to express themselves.

Educational Issues. In the United States the major assumptions about bilingual programs have arisen out of two camps: the English-only and the English-plus movements. In the English-plus camp are advocates of bilingual programs in which students are encouraged to learn in their native language. The primary justification given for native language instruction is that for the development of a full range of proficiency skills in English, literacy is best developed in the native language, which also allows immigrant parents to participate in the acquisition of mutually beneficial language skills. In the English-only camp are advocates of immersion programs that reinforce learning in English, while avoiding the student's native language. Advocates of this approach view the United States as a monolingual society to which immigrants should pledge their full allegiance by substituting English for their original language. English-only supporters often cite measures that claim bilingualism has a negative effect on intelligence, while English-plus advocates argue that these same measures improperly compare the performance of dissimilar bilingual and monolingual speakers.

The comprehensive reviews comparing the effectiveness of bilingual to monolingual education conducted since the 1960s and 1970s largely concluded that bilingual programs were preferable if they led to language minority children becoming fluent in both the majority and minority language. The trend in the research seems to support early total immersion programs for children whose first language is a majority language. For example, an English and Italian speaker in the United States would do better if immersed in English rather than in Italian. And despite opposition from the advocates of English-only, there is a trend toward supporting programs that maintain the native language, citing advantages for minority children. For example, studies on intellectual and cognitive functioning show that bilinguals operate at higher synthesizing and multidimensional levels, and cultural and political studies have shown that bilinguals are more interested in and sensitive to other cultures.

Sociolinguists have argued that since language is used for communication, bilingual instruction should be in the parameters of communicative competence. The assumption is that by examining utterances in their situational contexts the educator can better assess the language-specific perceptions, skills, and deficits of a bilingual speaker. The situational context informs the appropriateness of a response, not just its grammatical correctness, and can provide nuances of words or expressions that are unavailable in the abstract. For example, the English word *teacher* translates to *ustadh* in Arabic, the latter term connoting not only an individual with certain technical skills and training, as it does in English, but also a lofty and select human being. In Arabic *teacher* is used as a title similar to the use of *doctor* in the English-speaking world. The Arabic speaker when using or interpreting the English word *teacher* might mean something different than would an English speaker. The latter case could lead to an inappropriate usage for an Arabic and English bilingual who might generate an English sentence such as: Teacher Wilson, how are you today? The contextual teaching and learning of words and phrases in the social context in which they are used by speakers of the language have been shown to be key to an effective bilingual program.

Language Policy and Bilingualism. In communities that have large numbers of bilinguals, governments often enact policies to maintain or change the relationship between the majority and minority languages. For example, the government selects which language (usually the majority language) would be the medium of instruction and which minority languages are to be taught in schools. If speakers of a minority language lack prestige within the society for racial or cultural reasons, their language will also lack prestige. Children attending school where their cultural background is not supported will encounter difficulties. This is true of children speaking the majority language, of those speaking a dialect significantly removed from the majority language standard, and especially true of children from a linguistic minority.

No other country has been host to more bilingual immigrants than the United States, but each new generation has seen a decline in their mother tongues since mastery of English is associated with success. Though most Americans descend from ancestors whose cultural heritage has included languages other than English, foreign language requirements have been persistently reduced at all educational levels. Sociolinguists have claimed that there has been a tendency to uphold the ideal of monolingualism in the midst of an increasingly multilingual population. Economists have asked whether this reluctance to develop language resources is not giving away competitive advantages to other countries where our trading partners are often multilingual and fluent in English. Sociologists hold that promoting "English plus other languages" will better prepare students for world citizenship while reducing cultural conflict. Some argue as well that the generational conflict within immigrant families would also be lessened if parents did not feel pressured to teach their children English at all costs. The controversies over policies concerning bilingualism and bilinguality are unlikely to mitigate as the United States continues to welcome new groups of immigrants speaking foreign languages.

[See also BICULTURALISM; BILINGUAL EDUCATION.]

BIBLIOGRAPHY

Arias, M. Beatriz, and Ursula Casanova, eds., *Bilingual Education: Politics, Practice and Research* (Univ. of Chicago Press 1993).

Gonzalez, Virginia, ed., *Language and Cognitive Development in Second Language Learning: Educational Implications for Children and Adults* (Allyn 1999).

Hakuta, Kenji, *Mirror of Language: The Debate of Bilingualism* (Basic Bks. 1986).

Romaine, Suzanne, *Bilingualism,* 2d ed. (Blackwell 1995).

Williams, James D., and Grace C. Snipper, *Literacy and Bilingualism* (Longman 1990).

ERNEST B. JOHNSON

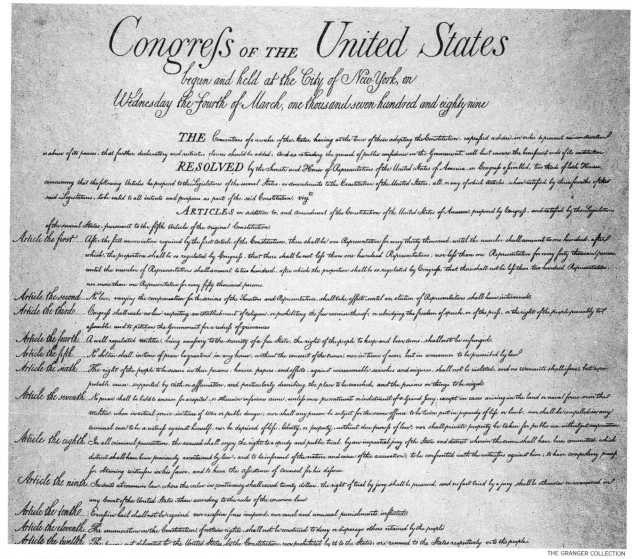

Top half of the first page of the Bill of Rights drafted in 1789 and proposed to the states for ratification.

BILL OF RIGHTS

The first ten amendments to the U.S. Constitution guaranteeing certain rights to the people are known collectively as the U.S. Bill of Rights. Britain's constitutional arrangement adopted various protections for British subjects in the Magna Carta (1215), the Bill of Rights of 1689, and English common law, while many of the colonial charters also contained protections for various customary rights. None of

these proclamations of rights could prevail against a legally omnipotent act of Parliament, however.

The American Declaration of Independence proclaimed that persons were "endowed by their Creator with certain unalienable Rights," including "Life, Liberty, and the Pursuit of Happiness," but the Declaration of Independence gave no practical protections for these rights. The Articles of Confederation contained no bill of rights, although the body of the Articles contained the mandate that states extend to the citizens of other states the liberties and immunities enjoyed by their own citizens. Most state constitutions produced in the Revolutionary and post-Revolutionary periods contained bills of rights, which enshrined a wide variety of protections for the individual.

When the Constitutional Convention met in Philadelphia in 1787, the rights of citizens were a deep concern of the framers, and the text of the Constitution contained a number of entrenched protections: the writ of habeas corpus was given special protection (Article I, section 9, paragraph ii), bills of attainder and ex post facto laws were banned for both the federal government (Article I, section 9, paragraph iii) and the states (Article I, section 10, paragraph i), trial by jury for federal criminal offenses was guaranteed (Article III, section 2, paragraph iii), the scope and punishment of treason were restricted (Article III, section 3), citizens were guaranteed the privileges and immunities of every state (Article IV, section 2, paragraph i), and states were forbidden to impair the obligation of contracts (Article I, section 10, paragraph i). In addition, religious tests for federal office were perpetually forbidden (Article IV, paragraph iii).

Despite the inclusion of these rights, several delegates thought a more substantial bill of rights advisable. In the end, however, the arguments of Alexander Hamilton and others prevailed, for they held that the Constitution with its federalism of reserved and delegated powers as well as its tripartite federal structure with its separation of powers and checks and balances constituted a bulwark of liberty. In addition, Hamilton and others maintained that a bill of rights could do positive harm, since by the ordinary rules of statutory construction the enumeration of certain rights would necessarily imply that no other rights existed. Furthermore, the grant of a right against a federal power not enumerated in the Constitution would imply that absent that protection, the federal government would have enjoyed that power—thus promoting a loose constructionist view of the Constitution.

During the ratification debates and in the various state ratifying conventions, Federalists and Anti-Federalists argued over the wisdom of including a basic charter of liberties. Several states, including New York, made their ratifications of the Constitution conditional on the ultimate adoption of a Bill of Rights.

It was James Madison's conversion to a supporter of a Bill of Rights in the first Congress that insured its adoption and gave it the particular form that it was to enjoy. Several drafts of the Bill of Rights were proposed, with the amendments constantly reworked. Phrases were added, withdrawn, and altered; some amendments were divided, while others were combined for clarity and concision.

In the end, on September 25, 1789, Congress proposed twelve amendments to the states for ratification. By 1791, the requisite number of states had ratified ten of the proposed amendments (three–twelve), which became the first ten amendments to the Constitution and are collectively known as the U.S. Bill of Rights.

Madison had intended that Congress should propose an amendment applying some of the rights of the Bill of Rights to the actions of state governments, but Congress demurred, holding that a state's own bill of rights ought to be sufficient to restrain a state's excesses. As a result of this congressional choice, the Bill of Rights did not originally restrict the states, as the Marshall court found in *Barron* v. *Baltimore* (1833). It was not until *Gitlow* v. *New York* (1925) that the Supreme Court embraced the incorporation doctrine, which held that the Fourteenth Amendment had applied selected portions of the Bill of Rights to the states.

By the Ninth and Tenth amendments, Madison sought to solve the problems originally raised in Federalist objections to a Bill of Rights. The Ninth Amendment, which refers to other unenumerated "rights retained by the people," precludes any attempt to interpret the Bill of Rights' listing of rights as in any way exhaustive. As a practical matter, however, scholars are unclear as to what unenumerated rights might be alluded to by the amendment, and the courts have generally avoided using this amendment as the basis for any decisions. The Tenth Amendment enshrined the doctrine of delegated powers, preserving federalism against an extreme loose constructionist hermeneutic that might have interpreted the Constitution as bestowing on the federal government all powers not specifically denied to it by the Constitution.

In the First Amendment the framers set up a number of rights of citizens beginning with "the free exercise [of religion]"; combining this with the injunction that "Congress shall make no law respecting an establishment of religion," often labeled as "the separation of church and state." When originally adopted, of course, several states already had established churches that continued under the Constitution as before, since the First Amendment bound only the federal government. Beginning in the 1940s, in decisions such as *Cantwell* v. *Connecticut* (1940), the Court applied the free-exercise standard against state action under the incorporation doctrine, and in *Everson* v. *Board of Education* (1947), the Court began applying the ban on establishments of religion against the states. In the early 1960s, in decisions such as *Engel* v. *Vitale* (1962) and *Abington School District* v. *Schempp* (1963), the Supreme Court struck down school prayer and other state-organized religious practices in public education, resulting in angry public reaction and the proposal of constitutional amendments to reverse these decisions.

The rights of free speech and press granted in the First Amendment have become vital in the twentieth century with the expansion of the federal regulatory state, although these federal guarantees were little used or invoked in the nineteenth century. Even today most of the free-speech battles are fought over state and local restrictions, but since *Gitlow* most of these are confronted by federal suit based on the First Amendment rather than state constitutional guarantees.

The right of the people to "keep and bear Arms" was secured by the Second Amendment. The stated purpose of the amendment was to protect the role of state militias, but the militia should not be confused with the enrolled militia of a state. As the Militia Act of 1792 made clear, the militia was composed of all free, white males from seventeen to

forty-five. Needless to say, the restrictions based on condition of servitude, race, and gender would no longer be appropriate. Despite the fact that this amendment was undoubtedly crafted to protect individual gun ownership rights, it has had little effect and may never provide the basis of any vital court decision. State gun-control statutes would not automatically contravene the Second Amendment, because that amendment has not yet been held to be included within the scope of the incorporation doctrine. In addition, the degree of regulation permissible under the amendment has never been satisfactorily determined judicially.

The Third Amendment, with its ban on the forcible quartering of troops in homes in times of peace, and the Fourth Amendment, with its ban on "unreasonable searches and seizures" and its requirement that warrants be specific and be issued only based on "probable cause," are aimed at protecting the privacy of persons in their homes and in their effects. The Fifth Amendment requires indictment by a grand jury and the due process of law, as well as banning double jeopardy, compulsory self-incrimination, and the uncompensated taking of private property for public purposes. The Sixth Amendment promises a "speedy public trial," an impartial jury, announcement of all charges, a right to confront all hostile witnesses, compulsory power to summon witnesses, and the aid of counsel, while the Seventh Amendment guarantees a jury trial in federal civil suits. The Eighth Amendment forbids excessive bail as well as "cruel and unusual punishment."

The Bill of Rights has gone from a constitutional afterthought, added to placate the objections of Anti-Federalists and of the ratifying states, to the best-known and most widely invoked portion of the Constitution. Taken together with the Fourteenth Amendment, which has applied the Bill of Rights to the states, the first eight amendments to the Constitution were the source for a majority of the most important court decisions of the twentieth century.

[*See also* CONSTITUTION.]

235

BIBLIOGRAPHY

Levy, Leonard W., *Origins of the Bill of Rights* (Yale Univ. Press 1999).

Levy, Leonard W., Kenneth L. Karst, and Dennis J. Mahoney, eds., "Bill of Rights (United States)," in *Encyclopedia of the American Constitution*, 4 vols. (Macmillan 1986).

Peck, Robert S., *The Bill of Rights and the Politics of Interpretation* (West Publishing 1992).

Schwartz, Bernard, *The Great Rights of Mankind: A History of the American Bill of Rights* (Oxford 1977).

Stone, Geoffrey R., Richard A. Epstein, and Cass R. Sunstein, eds., *The Bill of Rights in the Modern State* (Univ. of Chicago Press 1992).

Vile, John R., "Bill of Rights," in *Encyclopedia of Constitutional Amendments, Proposed Amendments, and Amending Issues, 1789–1995* (ABC-CLIO 1996).

PATRICK M. O'NEIL

BIOETHICS

Bioethics is the study of the moral dimensions of medicine and the biological sciences. Beginning in the early 1970s, *bioethics* (the word was first introduced in 1970) both as an academic discipline and as a popular phenomenon superseded an older tradition of medical ethics, a discourse long dominated by physicians. Indeed one of the notable features of the bioethics movement has been the entry of nonphysicians, including lawyers, theologians and clergy, philosophers, and patient advocates, into areas of medical decision-making once the sole province of the medical profession. Members of the National Bioethics Advisory Commission, created by President William Clinton in 1995, reflect the diversity of viewpoints represented in a federally funded organization charged with evaluating such ethical questions as human cloning and research involving persons with mental disorders that affect their reasoning capacity.

Many of the issues considered the province of bioethics at the start of the twenty-first century, such as patients' rights, the rights of research subjects (both animal and human), euthanasia and assisted suicide, truth-telling and confidentiality, disclosure of medical errors, the morality of abortion, and un-

equal access to medical care, existed long before the advent of bioethics commissions and bioethical pundits. (Cloning and the issues raised by the unparalleled expansion of genetic knowledge pose novel moral challenges for the public and the professions.) In the first half of the twentieth century, such ethical issues as consent in medical research and mercy killing appeared both in the popular press and in popular culture. In the 1910s, for example, American newspapers, especially the Hearst newspaper chain, publicized the moral issues in testing vaccines on orphans and other vulnerable populations, as well as decisions by physicians to withhold treatment from "grossly defective" infants. In the 1920s novelist Sinclair Lewis explored some of the ethical challenges in medical research in his Pulitzer Prize–winning book *Arrowsmith* (1925). In the 1930s playwright Sidney Kingsley placed an illegal abortion and its complications at the center of his Pulitzer Prize–winning play *Men in White* (1934). Both *Arrowsmith* and *Men in White* were adapted for the screen in the 1930s, the same decade in which such Hollywood films as *The Crime of Doctor Forbes* (1936) and *The Girl from God's Country* (1940) dramatized for mass audiences the moral dimensions of mercy killing. American mass media popularized some of the ethical issues facing doctors and patients in the first half of the twentieth century, but exercising moral judgment in these decades remained the province of the medical profession, which operated with noteworthy autonomy until the 1960s.

In the 1960s challenges to medical authority and autonomy appeared on several fronts. From within the medical profession itself, for example, came calls for protecting the rights of research subjects, as when Harvard anesthesiologist Henry Beecher called attention to violations of the rights of human subjects in clinical research in an influential 1966 article. From outside the profession, increasing accusations of misuse and mistreatment of research subjects, including retarded children at the Willowbrook State School, black men in the notorious syphilis study conducted by the United States Public Health Service, and elderly patients at the Jewish Chronic Disease Hospital, most notably paved the way for governmental intervention in the conduct of medical research. At the same time the introduction of life-support technologies and the growing importance of organ transplantation prompted widespread discussions about defining death and, perhaps more important, challenging the physician's traditional prerogative to decide such matters at the bedside. In the 1970s the rise of the women's health movement and the anti-psychiatry movements further eroded the social and cultural authority of physicians. Even before the 1973 United States Supreme Court decision *Roe v. Wade* legitimized a woman's right to privacy in the early weeks of pregnancy, legislatures in California and Oregon debated restrictions on the medical use of lobotomy, a psychosurgical procedure highly politicized in such books as Ken Kesey's *One Flew over the Cuckoo's Nest* (1962).

Amid the profoundly changed social and political climate of American medical practice and medical experimentation, bioethics flourished. Such organizations as the Institute of Ethics, Society, and the Life Sciences (founded in 1969 and later known as the Hastings Center) and the Kennedy Institute of Ethics (established in 1971 at Georgetown University with funds from the Kennedy family) provided a new forum for bioethical discussion, as did journals and newly created academic positions within medical schools. In addition to the rapid academic expansion of bioethics, governmental commissions (the National Commission for the Protection of Human Subjects of Biomedical and Behavioral Research, 1974–1978, and in the 1980s, the President's Commission for the Study of Ethical Problems in Medicine) permitted sustained attention to issues related to death and dying, reproductive technologies from in vitro fertilization to surrogate motherhood, and xenotransplantation (cross-species surgery, such as the 1984 transplant of a baboon heart into the infant known in the press as Baby Fae).

Bioethics has been characterized as a "native-grown American product." Historians of the bioethics movement in the United States have cited the tradition of American liberalism, privileging the equality and autonomy of individuals, as critical to the growth of bioethics and its popular reception. Although bioethics originated in the United States and remains dominated by American experts and concerns, interest in bioethics has prospered in other national and international contexts. But reflecting the differing patterns of medical care as well as divergent social, religious, and political traditions, bioethics does not always assume the same form in countries outside the United States. American researchers who conduct clinical trials outside the United States, for example, pursuing tests of acquired immune deficiency syndrome (AIDS) therapies in the developing world, have encountered considerable difficulty and resistance in applying the same ethical standards required for human experimentation in the United States. These problems are likely to intensify in light of changes in transportation, communication, and commerce that foster more tightly connected global networks. Developments in the sciences, especially in molecular biology and the international effort to sequence the human genome, are also likely to create new tensions in both the United States and the world.

[*See also* MEDICINE; PUBLIC HEALTH; HEALTH CARE; ALTERNATIVE MEDICINE; HOSPITALS AND ASYLUMS.]

BIBLIOGRAPHY

Jones, James H., *Bad Blood: The Tuskegee Syphilis Experiment,* new and expanded ed. (Free Press 1993).

Jonsen, Albert R., *The Birth of Bioethics* (Oxford 1998).

Lederer, Susan E., *Subjected to Science: Human Experimentation in America before the Second World War* (Johns Hopkins Univ. Press 1995).

Pernick, Martin S., *The Black Stork: Eugenics and the Death of "Defective" Babies in American Medicine and Motion Pictures since 1915* (Oxford 1996).

Rothman, David J., *Strangers at the Bedside: A History of How Law and Bioethics Have Transformed Medical Decision Making* (Basic Bks. 1991).

SUSAN E. LEDERER

BIRTH CONTROL

Americans, like people in most cultures throughout history, have sought to control reproduction. From the colonial era to the twenty-first century, single men and women, and married couples, for diverse reasons and using diverse methods, have tried to prevent pregnancies and births. The number of contraceptives and abortives in North American folk and medical repertoires has been large, influenced by European, Native American, and African beliefs, practices, and botanicals. Such knowledge has been widespread in American medicine, especially in sectarian and folk medicine. Before the twentieth-century invention of the anovulent contraceptive pill, the intrauterine device, and the controversial abortion drug mifepristone (RU486, the early abortion pill), the contraceptive arsenal included simple methods such as coitus interruptus (withdrawal), prolonged breastfeeding, douching, the use of condoms and diaphragms, and many variants of the rhythm method, as well as many abortion techniques and abortifacient products. Although cultural expectations about effectiveness and safety have varied greatly over time, some of the birth control methods worked. Until the mid-nineteenth century most Americans did not distinguish between contraception and early abortion. It was neither illegal nor considered immoral to induce miscarriage before fetal movement (known as quickening) could be felt. The association of birth control with the practice of contraception, but not abortion, is a product of the deliberate campaign of the early-twentieth-century reformers led by Margaret Sanger.

Throughout recorded history some individuals—adulterers, seducers, fornicaters—used contraceptives and abortives to protect themselves and their partners from illegal and undesired pregnancies. The significant shift in birth control history was its adoption within legitimate marriage. Family size began its steady decline among white, native-born American couples as early as the 1830s. The practice of marital birth control differed by race, class, and ethnicity; but by the twentieth century African Americans and many second- and third-generation immigrants had begun to use reproductive control to space and limit their families.

Although reproductive control has a long history as a private concern in the United States, it also has had a long public and often controversial

UPI/CORBIS-BETTMANN

Birth control pioneer Margaret Sanger (*center*) with supporters at a New York City courthouse in 1917.

role in American public discourse. Effective control over fertility has long held the promise of increased personal liberty for both women and men, as well as the promise of transforming marriage, family, and sexuality. To many Americans such transformative power was not promising but deeply threatening. Birth control has therefore long been a symbol on which opposition to social and cultural change has centered. While reformers across the political spectrum have viewed birth control as a means of achieving their particular goals of social change, others have resisted the powerful challenges to established family, gender, and social relationships contained within the separation of sexuality from reproduction.

Nineteenth-century opponents decried reproductive control because it was first publicized and promoted by freethinkers. Birth control was therefore tainted by free thought's radical class politics (particularly freethinkers' promotion of working-class educational and political power), its challenges to established religion, and its questioning of sexual and gender traditions. In the second half of the nineteenth century, concerted opposition to abortion arose, led by newly professional physicians and social purity reformers and supported by prosecutors and judges in the judicial system.

The resulting state and federal laws (known as Comstock laws, named for Anthony Comstock, the zealous Young Men's Christian Association [YMCA] reformer who helped to secure their passage) limited the availability of abortion and contraception for the next half century. Laws that forbade publicizing information about contraception and abortion remained on the statute books of most states until the 1960s. Laws making abortion a criminal act existed until the Supreme Court's *Roe* v. *Wade* decision in 1973.

In the years just before and after World War I, Margaret Sanger and her fellow advocates of what they had begun to call "birth control" challenged the Comstock laws by founding clinics, dispensing contraceptives, and mounting a public campaign to promote "family planning." These birth control pioneers founded the American Birth Control Association and its later incarnation, Planned Parenthood. From the first, the birth control movement and its organizations such as Planned Parenthood aroused controversy. To some critics, the Sanger-inspired birth control movement in America transformed birth control from a grassroots reform into an elitist one, making the safest and most effective birth control available only to those Americans able to afford private physicians and expensive technologies. Other critics have charged that the birth control movement promoted (white) racial purity by reviving earlier strands in American eugenics thought that focused on fears of "race suicide" and excessive reproduction of the "unfit." Still other critics have publicized the role of birth controllers in creating programs forcing sterilization or forcing hormonal drug implants on poor women and on women of color.

In the last third of the twentieth century, groups coalesced in opposition to the availability of birth control. In the 1970s, for the first time in U.S. history, religious groups worked in concert to oppose birth control. The Roman Catholic Church objected to family limitation in general but in the 1970s or-

ganized the grassroots right-to-life movement to challenge the liberalization of abortion laws. Abortion and contraception also became the focus of the backlash politics of the *New Right*—the umbrella term for the coalition of groups and organizations attempting to undo the framework of the post-1930s governmentally sponsored regulatory state. Fundamentalist Christian groups calling themselves the Moral Majority have sought to turn back the legalization of abortion, the women's rights movement, the sexual revolution, and youth countercultures of the era.

The opposition and the criticism have not gone unchallenged. Supporters argue that because the American birth control movement was moderate and exemplified so sophisticated and pragmatic an understanding of American politics, it succeeded in making birth control part of American mainstream culture. Feminists and other groups mounted their own pro-choice movement to support the availability of safe and legal abortion. Throughout the nineteenth and twentieth centuries, birth control in the United States was a contentious issue over which diverse groups played out struggles over power, world views, gender roles, and social and cultural change.

[See also ABORTION.]

BIBLIOGRAPHY

Brodie, Janet Farrell, *Contraception and Abortion in Nineteenth-Century America,* reprint ed. (Cornell Univ. Press 1997).

Gordon, Linda, *Woman's Body, Woman's Right; Birth Control in America,* rev. and updated (Penguin 1990).

McCann, Carole R., *Birth Control Politics in the United States, 1916–1945* (Cornell Univ. Press 1994).

Reagan, Leslie J., *When Abortion Was a Crime: Women, Medicine, and the Law in the United States, 1967–1973* (Univ. of Calif. Press 1997).

Watkins, Elizabeth Siegel, *On the Pill: A Social History of Oral Contraceptives 1950–1970* (Johns Hopkins Univ. Press 1998).

JANET FARRELL BRODIE

BLACK ARTS MOVEMENT

The black arts movement (BAM), alternately called the black aesthetic movement, was a cultural movement whose generative moments are conventionally placed between 1965 and 1975. BAM allowed black people with and without formal artistic training in theater, poetry, and dance to communicate a growing awareness that the goal of art and culture must be the economic, political, and psychological empowerment of black Americans. The four long, hot, racially charged summers from 1964 to 1968, which smoldered in American cities such as Detroit, Cleveland, and Watts in Los Angeles, support the claim made in Larry Neal's landmark 1968 essay, "The Black Arts Movement," that BAM was "the aesthetic and spiritual sister of the Black Power concept." However, the more profound struggles that BAM expressed burned within the civil rights–era black psyche. Toni Cade's 1970 warning that "[i]t perhaps takes less heart to pick up the gun than to face the task of creating a new identity, a self, . . . via commitment to the struggle" emphasizes that in black people's daily lives, the more trenchant battle is for the souls and minds of black folk so that they may engage in struggle for economic and political justice.

BAM created and proliferated critical journals, publishing venues, community organizations, and theater companies all over the country, institutions that disseminated the works black people sought. Yet, like the Harlem Renaissance and nascent American modernism, BAM had its problems; gender chauvinism and heterosexism are extant in the works of several BAM practitioners. Nonetheless, female artists and critics such as Barbara Ann Teer, Mari Evans, Sonia Sanchez, Carolyn Rodgers, Sarah Webster Fabio, and elder stateswoman Gwendolyn Brooks effectively gave voice to people marginalized by the machismo of some male black arts artists and contributed to the explosion of black female writers in the 1970s, an explosion whose effects reverberate today.

Activist poet Askia Touré (Roland Snellings) in "Conversation: Amiri Baraka and Askia Touré, 1999" considers BAM "the largest cultural upsurge"

UPI/CORBIS-BETTMANN

Poet Gwendolyn Brooks was the first African American to win the Pulitzer Prize.

black people enjoyed in the twentieth century. It brought together people such as LeRoi Jones (Baraka), Larry Neal, and Touré, people whose aesthetic and political practices proved essential to the early flowering of BAM in the metropolitan New York area. Following the assassination of Malcolm X in February 1965, several female and male artists moved to Harlem and established in March the Black Arts Repertory Theatre/School (BARTS). A community teaching and gathering place, BARTS served to, in Touré's words, "organically link writers, activists, musicians, playwrights, et cetera" to their intended audiences. Although short-lived—it closed within a year—BARTS served as a model for more than one hundred similar organizations throughout the United States, and a few survive today. Indeed, inspired by their Harlem peers, playwright Ed Bullins and a pair of young actors with whom he worked in the San Francisco Bay area, Huey Newton and Bobby Seale, founded the Black House Theater and, subsequently, in 1966, established the Black Panther Party for Self Defense with Bullins as its first minister of culture. As funding for Great Society programs dwindled and black power came under the deleterious scrutiny of the Federal Bureau of Investigation and its counterintelligence program, BAM's upsurge waned as theaters and presses closed in the mid-1970s. Yet the spirit of the black arts movement stirs within the art and aesthetic practice of artists such as August Wilson, Adrienne Kennedy, Dudley Randall, Ntozake Shange, and Spike Lee.

[See also AFRICAN AMERICANS, AN OVERVIEW, *and articles on* AFRICAN AMERICAN MUSIC, AFRICAN AMERICANS IN FILM AND THEATER, AFRICAN AMERICAN DANCE, AFRICAN AMERICAN VISUAL ART, AFRICAN AMERICAN FOLKLORE AND HUMOR.]

BIBLIOGRAPHY

Bullins, Ed, ed., *The Drama Review* 12 (Summer 1968).
Cade, Toni, "On the Issues of Roles," *The Black Woman: An Anthology* (New Am. Lib. 1970).
Gabbin, Joanne V., ed., *The Furious Flowering of African American Poetry* (Univ. Press of Va. 1999).
Smith, David Lionel, "The Black Arts Movement and Its Critics," *American Literary History* 3 (Spring 1991):93–110.

YVONNE PASCHAL

BLACK COLLEGES AND UNIVERSITIES

Historically black colleges and universities initially served as the main means for African Americans to pursue higher education. Even as the walls of segregation at majority institutions were broken down by the civil rights movement, black colleges and universities retained their importance as centers of African American heritage and identity.

In 1837 the Institute for Colored Youth (now, Cheyney University) was established by Richard Humphreys, a prominent Quaker. While Humphreys's school originally was for secondary education, in 1854 the all-male Ashmun Institute was founded in Lincoln, Pennsylvania, as the first college to offer degrees solely to African Americans. Two years later, Wilberforce University in Wilberforce, Ohio, became the first coeducational black university. The year 1881 was notable for the establishment of Spelman College in Atlanta, Georgia (the first liberal-arts college for African American women), and Tuskegee University, in Tuskegee, Alabama (founded by Booker T. Washington as the Normal School for Colored Teachers). The first state-supported black college was the North Carolina College for Negroes (later known as North Carolina Central University), which opened in 1925. The establishment of the United Negro College Fund (UNCF) in 1944 greatly enhanced access to black colleges and universities by providing funds for deserving students. The UNCF is a consortium of forty-one historically black institutions of higher education, which has raised over one billion dollars for the private colleges and universities.

The evolution of black institutions of higher education mirrored larger disputes in the African American community. Many schools, such as Tuskegee and Hampton Institute (now, Hampton University), originally emphasized industrial training and integration. The leading proponent of this philosophy was Booker T. Washington, supported by white philanthropists who provided a significant proportion of the funding for the establishment of many black colleges and universities. In the early twentieth century a movement led by W. E. B. Du Bois gained ascendancy. Du Bois emphasized African American culture and history and was much more intellectually and politically militant than Washington and his supporters.

The importance of the historically black colleges and universities to the evolution of the African American community cannot be overemphasized. Many prominent leaders, including Martin Luther King, Jr. (Morehouse College, Atlanta), were graduates of these institutions. In addition, these colleges and universities continue to graduate a vast majority of African American professionals. For instance, Tuskegee University alone has produced more African American military officers than any other college or university, including the U.S. Military Academy, the U.S. Naval Academy, and the U.S. Air Force Academy. By the end of the twentieth century, more than one-third of African American medical doctors and dentists were educated at Meharry Medical College in Nashville, Tennessee. In total, sixty-five percent of African American physicians, fifty percent of African American lawyers, and thirty-five percent of African American engineers are graduates of black colleges and universities.

Today, there are 103 historically black colleges and universities in the United States, divided among the states, the District of Columbia, and the U.S. Virgin Islands (although 14 are in Alabama alone). These institutions include both public and private colleges and both two-year and four-year universities. The importance of black colleges and universities has been recognized by successive presidents, including Carter, Reagan, Bush, and Clinton, who supported programs linking various federal programs to assist historically black colleges and universities.

[See also AFRICAN AMERICANS, AN OVERVIEW.*]*

BIBLIOGRAPHY

Anderson, James D., *The Education of Blacks in the South, 1860–1935* (Univ. of N.C. Press 1988).

Campbell, Clarice, *Civil Rights Chronicle: Letters from the South* (Univ. Press of Miss. 1997).

Schall, Keith L., ed., *Stony the Road: Chapters in the History of Hampton Institute* (Univ. Press of Va. 1977).

TOM M. LANSFORD

BLACK MUSLIMS

Black Muslims is the familiar name for a religious group that attempts to synthesize the principles of Islam with African American experience. Shortly after its founding in the seventh century, the religion of Islam was introduced to Africa by Arab invaders. There is little evidence that slaves carried these traditions with them to America, and Islam did not have a significant impact on the African American community until 1930 when Wallace Fard Muhammad built the first Muslim mosque in Detroit. Elijah Muhammad (born Elijah Poole) established a second mosque in Chicago and later supervised the creation of mosques in other large cities with significant black populations.

The Nation of Islam (NOI), familiarly known as the Black Muslims in the United States, was a leading exponent of black nationalism and separatism. The NOI taught that blacks were racially superior to whites and publicly criticized institutionalized racism and discrimination. Black Muslims believed that Christianity was the white man's chief stratagem for the enslavement of nonwhite people and stressed the significance of establishing a separate black nation in the United States. The descendants of former slaves were encouraged to reject their American surnames and replace them with an X. The movement hoped to create new identities untainted by white racism and control. Under the slogan "Do for Self," Black Muslims pushed for economic development within the black community and advocated a militant sense of black pride. The NOI constructed its own schools, military organization, and a variety of properties and businesses. Members were expected to follow a very strict ascetic lifestyle and refrain from the use of tobacco, alcohol, and drugs.

During the 1950s and 1960s the movement expanded to the Northeast and Mid-Atlantic states and membership reached approximately one hundred thousand. In 1954 Malcolm Little, later known as Malcolm X, became a minister in the Nation of Islam and the organization's most effective recruiter and apologist. He also established the newspaper *Muhammad Speaks*. Malcolm X restated what Fard and other had taught, spoke bitterly about the philosophy of self-protection and white oppression of blacks, and encouraged black Americans to free themselves from their feelings of self-hate. The Black Muslim response to American racism in the 1950s and 1960s stood in stark contrast to the philosophy of the growing civil rights movement led by Martin Luther King, Jr., which preached the doctrine of nonviolence and racial integration. Malcolm X ultimately broke with the Nation of Islam and formed the Organization of Afro-American Unity as a result of his pilgrimage to Mecca, where he encountered various races worshipping together. Malcolm X was assassinated in 1965 by rival factions within the NOI.

When the leader of the Nation of Islam, Elijah Muhammad, died in 1975, his son Wallace D. Muhammad continued the movement under the new name American Muslim Mission. In 1985 the American Muslim Mission disbanded so that its members might become part of the worldwide Islam community. However, a splinter group led by chief minister Louis Farrakhan retained the name Nation of Islam and pursues a black militant agenda in the United States.

[See also ISLAM.]

BIBLIOGRAPHY

Essien-Udom, E. U., *Black Nationalism: A Search for An Identity in America* (Univ. of Chicago Press 1962).

Yvonne Yazbeck Haddad, ed., *The Muslims of America* (Oxford 1991).

Lincoln, C. Eric, *The Black Muslims in America* (Beacon Press 1961).

Marsh, Clifton E., *From Black Muslims to Muslims: The Resurrection, Transformation, and Change of the Lost-Found Nation of Islam in America, 1930–1995,* 2d ed. (Scarecrow 1996).

Marsh, Clifton E., *The Lost-Found Nation of Islam in America* (Scarecrow 2000).

X, Malcolm, and Alex Haley, *The Autobiography of Malcolm X* (Grove 1965).

NATALIE J. RING

BLACK NATIONALISM

The sociologist Max Weber defines a nation as a "community of sentiment," which seeks its own state. Despite being citizens of democratic and pluralist America, most African Americans possess a degree of racial nationalism. In this regard, W. E. B. Du Bois argues that because of white racism, African Americans continually struggle with "two unreconciled strivings," which, according to Mary Frances Berry and John Blassingame, can be expressed in the paradox: Are we American or Negro?

Very early in American history some blacks felt that a separate nation, especially in Africa, was the only means to fulfill black aspirations, and they agitated for this goal. A pioneer in the movement for emigration was Paul Cuffee, a wealthy black New England merchant, who took the first practical step in this direction in 1815 when he settled thirty freed slaves in Sierra Leone at his own expense. Afterward, in 1816, the white-sponsored American Colonization Society (ACS) was formed for the avowed purpose of settling free blacks in Africa. By 1826 the ACS had settled over 1,420 blacks in the colony of Liberia, which it helped to establish in West Africa in 1822. Other sites suggested as homelands were Canada, Central America, and Haiti where, Du Bois notes, two thousand African Americans settled in 1855. The ACS, whose motives ranged from the humanitarian to the racist, continued until the year 1910.

The individual most instrumental in making black nationalism a worldwide movement in the twentieth century was Marcus Garvey (1887–1940). Born in Jamaica and aroused by the racism practiced there and elsewhere against blacks, Garvey formed the Universal Negro Improvement Association (UNIA) in 1914, after returning from studies in England. The UNIA's goals were: to end racism against blacks; to empower blacks in business, industry, and politics; to end colonialism against blacks (especially in Africa); and to make liberated Africa a great power. Arriving in the United States to establish a branch of the UNIA in 1916, ostensibly to consult with the African American educator Booker T. Washington (1856–1915), Garvey remained for eleven years.

Garvey's racial nationalism resonated with both conservative and nationalist segments of the African American community. The conservatives were impressed with his capitalist ethic, organizing ability, business ventures, and his calls for race pride, as in "A race without authority and power, is a race without respect!" The nationalists were inspired by his vow to "Let Africa be a bright star among the constellations of nations!" Unfortunately, Garvey was deported to Jamaica from the United States in 1922 because of a conviction on alleged mail fraud in connection with the sale of stock for the UNIA's shipping line, the Black Star Line. The UNIA soon declined, and American black nationalism suffered an eclipse until the 1960s and the rise of the black power movement.

The black power movement of the 1960s reflected two dominant views. Many African Americans insisted that the community's nationalist aspirations could be achieved by effectively mobilizing the race's economic and political power within the American system. This view was articulated most forcefully by individuals such as Congresswoman Shirley Chisholm. Organizations including the Black Congressional Caucus follow in the Chisholm tradition. Other African American groups, for example, the Republic of New Africa and the Black Muslims, insisted that only a separate nation on U.S. soil could satisfy these aspirations. From the 1960s to the turn of the twenty-first century, the former view dominated.

[See also BLACK POWER; BLACK PANTHERS; AFRICAN AMERICANS, AN OVERVIEW.*]*

BIBLIOGRAPHY

Berry, Mary Frances, and John W. Blassingame, *Long Memory: The Black Experience in America* (Oxford 1982).

Du Bois, W. E. B., *Black Reconstruction in America: An Essay toward a History of the Part Which Black Folk Played in the Attempt to Reconstruct Democracy in America, 1860–1880* (1962; Atheneum 1992).

Garvey, Amy Jacques, ed., *Philosophy and Opinions of Marcus Garvey,* vol. 1 (Atheneum 1969).

Hutchinson, John, and Anthony D. Smith, eds., *Nationalism* (Oxford 1994).

JOHN MCCARTNEY

BLACK PANTHERS

In the wake of the mid-1960s struggle against segregation and disenfranchisement, a new African American political movement emerged that posed a radical challenge to the American status quo. Inspired by the Lowndes County Freedom Organization of Alabama, in October 1966 the Black Panther Party for Self-Defense made Oakland, California, its center. Founded by Huey Newton and Bobby Seale, two students influenced by the revolutionary experience of China, Vietnam, and Cuba, and radicalized by a dialogue of ideas that engaged students at Oakland's Merritt College, the Panthers soon attracted national attention with their advocacy of armed struggle against racial oppression. Along with Seale and Newton the Panthers soon had a group of charismatic figures in its core leadership, including David Hilliard, Elaine Brown,

Eldridge Cleaver, and Fred Hampton. The Black Panther Party, beginning on April 25, 1967, reached a reading audience of thousands through its newspaper, *The Black Panther,* vividly portraying instances of racial oppression and setting forth an agenda geared to the goal of liberation. They also attracted the attention of the public with their distinctive style of dress, which included black leather jackets, blue shirts, and berets.

The Black Panther program called for winning power to enable black communities to determine their own destinies. The program further included demands for full employment, compensation for the historical suffering endured by the African American population, decent housing, education imbued with black history and consciousness, and the exemption of black men from military service. Further points included the release of all blacks held in prison (an issue that drew strength from the reality that blacks were often the victims of unjust law-enforcement and penal institutions) and a demand for black juries in cases involving black defendants (justified by the argument that only such juries could provide trials by one's peers). The Panthers also urged the holding of a United Nations–supervised plebiscite in which black colonial subjects would participate, to voice the will of blacks as to their destiny. Viewing the police in black communities as a hostile force, the Panthers boldly resisted police oppression. They maintained surveillance of the police, provided themselves with guns, and were ready to fire on threatening officers. Their embrace of weaponry was expressed in the phrase "picking up the gun," and they made clear their refusal to be disarmed when, on May 2, 1967, a group of Panthers drove to Sacramento and, carrying their rifles, entered the hall of the state legislature. Their stated purpose was to protest against a proposed legislative bill prohibiting the carrying of loaded firearms into public places. This confrontation garnered much media attention.

The Panther strategy of defying the nation's official institutions was open to question, but their resistance to police oppression won them support. Numerous celebrities endorsed and financially supported the aims of the Panthers and Eldridge Cleav-

Journalist Harry Farrell (*center*) peers out from between Eldridge Cleaver and Bobby Seale in a photo that became a Black Panther poster.

er's book, *Soul on Ice,* was widely read. Policymakers, however, found the Black Panthers intolerable as participants in the marketplace of ideas. The Panthers were committed to a wholesale indictment of American racism and imperialism, and J. Edgar Hoover, director of the Federal Bureau of Investigation (FBI), dismissing them as hoodlum-type revolutionaries, played a key role in assembling a nationwide police assault on the Panthers. The FBI, under its counterintelligence program (COINTEL-PRO), orchestrated a variety of provocative acts to ignite hostility between the Panthers and other black militants. The most notorious assault on the Panthers was the December 4, 1969, police raid on the movement's Chicago headquarters in which officers, guided by information provided by an FBI informer, deliberately shot and killed Panther activists Fred Hampton and Mark Clark.

The Black Panther Party did not have a long-term viable strategy; however, a part of its history is that the U.S. government lawlessly made war on the organization and its leaders, ensuring the group's demise. In the mid-1970s a U.S. Senate investigation committee, headed by Senator Frank Church of Idaho, exposed the government's wrongdoing to the Panthers and during subsequent years lawsuits resulted in some measure of restitution to individuals who had been victimized.

[See also BLACK NATIONALISM; BLACK POWER.*]*

BIBLIOGRAPHY

Brown, Elaine, *A Taste of Power: A Black Woman's Story* (1992; Anchor Bks. 1994).

Cleaver, Eldridge, *Soul on Ice* (McGraw-Hill 1968).

Commission of Inquiry into the Black Panthers and the Police, *Search and Destroy: A Report* (Metropolitan Applied Research Center 1973).

Foner, Philip S., ed., *The Black Panthers Speak,* with a new foreword by Clayborne Carson (1970; DaCapo 1995).

Hilliard, David, and Lewis Cole, *This Side of Glory: The Autobiography of David Hilliard and the Story of the Black Panther Party* (Little, Brown 1993).

Pearson, Hugh, *The Shadow of the Panther: Huey Newton and the Price of Black Power in America* (Addison-Wesley 1994).

Seale, Bobby, *Seize the Time: The Story of the Black Panther Party and Huey P. Newton* (1970; Black Classic Press 1991).

HERBERT SHAPIRO

BLACK POWER

By the mid-1960s the central demands of the early civil rights movement had been answered legislatively with the passage of the Civil Rights Act in 1964 and the Voting Rights Act in 1965. These victories, however, did little to improve the lives of most members of the black poor and working classes. Because the majority of the poor were unable to capitalize on new political and economic opportunities created by the civil rights movement, there were growing divisions within many African American communities, and within the civil rights movement itself.

These divisions became increasingly clear in the wake of the Watts (California) "riots" or social upheaval in 1965, when movement leaders were forced to come to terms with their apparent inability to speak for the economic interests of the urban black poor and working classes. Groups such as the Student Nonviolent Coordinating Committee (SNCC) and the Congress of Racial Equality (CORE) grew increasingly frustrated with the larger movement's liberal rhetoric and ties to the Democratic Party and middle-class interests. They rejected the emphasis on civil rights and nonviolence in favor of what became known as "black power."

While it is not clear who first coined the phrase *black power,* Stokely Carmichael deserves credit for elevating the phrase to the status of a slogan for the later part of the black freedom movement, after uttering it following the March against Fear in Greenwood, Mississippi, in 1966. Carmichael was arrested during the march, and on his release he renounced the traditional rhetoric and position of the civil rights movement, declaring that asking for freedom had not been useful and that what was needed was a demand for "black power!" The crowd responded by chanting the phrase, and it quickly became a slogan around the nation.

There has been debate about whether the black power movement should be seen as a continuation of the civil rights movement, as a separate movement, or as the second phase in the larger "black freedom movement." It is clear, however, that advocates of black power broke ranks with the traditional civil rights movement by rejecting nonviolence and integration in favor of calls for self-defense and economic, political, and cultural self-determination. The black power movement argued that the civil rights movement's focus on formal political rights was insufficient to gain meaningful social equality. The black power movement was itself criticized for defining black liberation in masculinist terms and for its views of women and of homosexuality.

While the black power movement was greatly influenced by Malcolm X, who was assassinated before Carmichael popularized the term, the most visible black power organization was the Black Panther Party for Self-Defense. The Panthers worked for better education and housing as well as for African American control of black communities. They are perhaps best known for their work monitoring police activities while armed, but they also did such things as provide free breakfast for poor children. By the early 1970s the Panthers, and the broader black power movement, had started to fade out, largely as a result of government repression and internal divisions.

[See also BLACK PANTHERS; BLACK NATIONALISM; SLAVERY.*]*

BIBLIOGRAPHY

Barbour, Floyd B., ed., *The Black Power Revolt; A Collection of Essays* (Extending Horizons Bks. 1968).

Carmichael, Stokely, and Charles V. Hamilton, *Black Power: The Politics of Liberation in America* (Random House 1967).

Grant, Joanne, *Ella Baker: Freedom Bound* (Wiley 1998).

Wallace, Michele, *Black Macho and the Myth of the Superwoman* (1978; Verso 1990).

Zinn, Howard, *SNCC, The New Abolitionists,* 2d ed. (1965; Greenwood Press 1985).

JONATHAN MARKOVITZ

BLUES

The blues originated at the crossroads of rural and urban cultures, the spirituals and the music played at such events as plantation corn shuckings. That a distinct musical form arose from the meeting of, for example, eschatological community songs that themselves had the dual purpose of worship and resistance and secular songs sung at communal events where musical virtuosity was paramount should be no surprise given the history of popular culture. But to reduce a music as dynamic and culturally vital as the blues to a musicological schema would simplify the historical record to an untenably singular dimension. It should, however, be noted that the blues as a form is as distinct as most poetic traditions that predate it. For example, the lyrical scheme is reliably built in three-line segments where the opening line is sung, repeated, and answered by a third line. Although the scheme might appear simple, it must be understood in the proper historical context.

The blues borrowed, scholars contend, the theological architecture of the spirituals, with devils and hellhounds ever on the singer's evasive trail. So it is that the blues also introduced a key American cultural trope, the voice that sings only to proclaim it has vacated its spot; the blues singer often professed to have been someplace and then to have gone. This facet of the blues was indulged largely in the Mississippi River Delta and Texas Piedmont

ARCHIVE PHOTOS

Blues and jazz singer Bessie Smith.

regions, where blues singers played guitars, sang, and either tapped vigorous rhythm with their feet or utilized various rhythmic instruments—the triangle, for example—to keep time.

A key element in the evolution of the blues was the creation of what came to be called blue notes, flatted thirds, fifths, and sevenths that recurred throughout a song's progression. The growth of the blue note is vital to the development of all American popular music, for it became central to much jazz in the 1920s, 1930s, and later. Further, blue notes ended up in Broadway stage shows, among the first vehicles to draw in music fans with performance and recordings, rather than with the plainly detailed sheet music that had, in the early twentieth century, enforced a kind of musical correctness to which the blues would never measure up.

Blues musician B. B. King plays at a concert in London, August 13, 1981.

In the twentieth century's first great North American migration, Delta and Piedmont natives, blues musicians among them, traveled in massive numbers upriver and went urban. From the Mississippi River, singers disembarked at St. Louis and took root or headed west to Kansas City or, more often, east for Chicago and New York. It was in the latter city that the first of at least two waves of "urban blues" took what was largely a folk music and translated it into a staple of popular culture. In the 1920s, female singers especially found a vibrant market just as recordings were becoming the backbone of the United States's economy in music. Bessie Smith is merely the most famous of these women, many of whom recorded what were then considered licentiously bawdy songs built from double entendres, songs that seemed related largely to love, both carnal and spiritual.

Meanwhile, the rural blues took root, as well, with folklorists beginning in the 1930s to document the musicians as part of the New Deal's cultural records projects. Robert Johnson (1911–1938), one of the music's most acclaimed progenitors, was, in this way, identified and recorded before dying at the age of 27. Others, however, took the guitar and vocals modus operandi to large cities and began adding two critical elements: drums and amplification. By the 1940s the blues of the Delta and Piedmont had transmogrified into rhythm and blues, only to be followed by another wave of urban blues that relied anew on the rhyme scheme, harmonic properties, and rhythmic formulations of the music's early creators.

Once the presence of electric guitars, drum kits, and amplification became de rigueur for urban blues musicians, their style of the music became preeminent in the national imagination. So popular was the electric, throbbing blues of John Lee Hooker and myriad others that rock and roll began to dovetail with the music, much to the long-term consternation of fans. The "British Invasion" in rock and pop during the 1960s drew much of its inspiration from the blues, a cultural phenomenon reminiscent of the Fisk Jubilee Singers' large-scale popularity abroad. The difference in the 1960s was a much more refined popular-music economy, where youth culture was quickly becoming engrossed in rock and roll at the same time that the struggle for African American civil rights took cultural center stage. Rock and roll won the day, even if the blues remained popular for such artists as B. B. King, John Lee Hooker, Bobby "Blue" Bland, Etta James, Koko Taylor, and others throughout the 1970s.

Scholars have tended to look at the blues as fodder for memoirs and documentation or, on occasion, as elemental to African American literary history. In whatever guise one investigates the music, there are countless matters of historical and cultural interest—from the interchange of musical economies as the blues helped nurture rock as a burgeoning youth movement to the development of rural blues in relation to spirituals and secular music of the nineteenth century to literary and poetic tropes developed by blues singers and picked up later by poets, novelists, and others.

[See also AFRICAN AMERICANS, *article on* AFRICAN AMERICAN MUSIC; JAZZ; POPULAR SONG; ROCK MUSIC.*]*

BIBLIOGRAPHY

Abrahams, Roger D., *Singing the Master: The Emergence of African American Culture in the Plantation South* (Pantheon Bks. 1992).

Baker, Houston, *Blues, Ideology, and Afro-American Literature* (Univ. of Chicago Press 1984).

Cone, James, *The Spirituals and the Blues: An Interpretation* (Orbis Bks. 1991).

Ennis, Philip, *The Seventh Stream: The Emergence of Rock-nroll in American Popular Music* (Wesleyan Univ. Press 1993).

Evans, David, *Big Road Blues: Tradition and Creativity in the Folk Blues* (Da Capo 1987).

Harrison, Daphne Duvall, *Black Pearls: Blues Queens of the 1920s* (Rutgers Univ. Press 1988).

Jones, LeRoi (Amiri Baraka), *Blues People: Negro Music in White America* (1963; Morrow 1999).

Kubik, Gerhard, *Africa and the Blues* (Univ. Press of Miss. 1999).

Lomax, Alan, *Land Where the Blues Began* (Pantheon Bks. 1993).

Neal, Mark Anthony, *What the Music Said: Black Popular Music and Black Public Culture* (Routledge 1999).

Oakley, Giles, *The Devil's Music: A History of the Blues,* 2d ed., updated (Da Capo 1997).

Palmer, Robert, *Deep Blues* (Penguin Bks. 1982).

Spencer, Jon Michael, *Blues and Evil* (Univ. of Tenn. Press 1993).

Ward, Brian, *Just My Soul Responding: Rhythm and Blues, Black Consciousness, and Race Relations* (Univ. of Calif. Press 1998).

ANDREW W. BARTLETT

BOOK CLUBS

Book clubs have been important in America as both voluntary and commercial organizations. Book discussion groups have a long history in the United States, and their contemporary pervasiveness makes them important for investigating class and culture, readers' experiences with print outside of school, and diversity within the cultural mainstream. Commercial book clubs—so-named to invoke the sociability and status of voluntary organizations—locate these same issues within a larger consumer capitalist context, offering opportunities to study the complicated relationship between culture and commerce.

Historically, book discussion groups have been almost invisible to the world of scholarship, because they are leisure-time groups that function within the private sphere. Popular images of reading in the West—the scholarly male in his study surrounded by weighty tomes, the bourgeois woman at home passively consuming frivolous novels—

have elevated private, silent reading and worked to obliterate other (more social and communal) ways of using books. As a result, book clubs have been largely overlooked as important sites for the creation of knowledge and for the dissemination of culture.

Readers excluded from formal institutions of learning—African Americans, the working classes, women from a variety of ethnic, class, and religious backgrounds—have long come together for self-improvement and mutual education. However, the prominence of women's literary societies or study clubs increased dramatically after the Civil War. Colonel Thomas Wentworth Higginson, literary critic and longtime correspondent of Emily Dickinson, wrote in 1880 that "it may fairly be assumed that the women's clubs have become to some extent the popular custodians of literature in America." Turn-of-the-twentieth-century women's clubs, whose most popular topics of study included American or European literature, mythology, the history of classical antiquity, and the Bible, provided many women who lacked access to higher education a means to develop critical literacies as part of supportive communities. Their reading and writing was often communal—reading aloud, dramatic productions, sharing of texts, writing and seeking feedback on position papers, discussion and debate. Although these clubs most often began for the purpose of self-improvement and mutual education, they brought women together for a common purpose, gave them an arena in which to learn leadership and community organizing, and allowed them to practice speaking their minds. This inspired many women to take their skills and ideas into the world as Progressive reformers—founding libraries, kindergartens, and playgrounds and advocating a safer, more humane world in accordance with their domestic roles.

Contemporary book clubs continue to have particular appeal to women, although middle- and upper-middle-class readers of both sexes from a variety of ethnic backgrounds are members. Such book discussion groups typically meet in members' living rooms, although libraries, bookstores, and coffee shops also provide meeting places. Sociologist Elizabeth Long argues that most participants are white professionals who have attended college and are part of the cultural mainstream. However, reading serves a different function in the lives of most book-club readers than it does in the lives of academic readers and literary critics. In book-club discussions readers often speak about characters as if they were real people rather than the constructions of a designing author; they assume that language is a neutral or transparent representation of reality; and they feel a deep allegiance to coherent plots and the conventions of realism. Although their selections of texts are guided by cultural authorities—classics, literary prizes, recommendations of booksellers, reviews in periodicals, syllabi from college literature courses—their interpretations of characters and evaluations of novels often disregard learned opinion. Book-club readers are far less interested than literary critics in creating coherent, unified interpretations of texts, preferring to use the discussion of books for self-understanding and self-revelation, as windows into their own psyches and personal histories. Although this way of reading unproblematically embraces liberal individualism and renders invisible the ways in which language and ideology construct reality, it nonetheless offers readers the opportunity to imaginatively inhabit lives that are not their own. This kind of reading can be crucial for confronting times of individual or social change, allowing readers to consider and reconsider life choices and ways of being in the world.

These ways of reading also characterize the readers who subscribe to the Book-of-the-Month Club (BOMC), the oldest and most influential commercial book club in the United States. Janice Radway argues that the judges at the BOMC are not just offering members a watered-down version of high culture but are embracing a middlebrow aesthetic or ethos that operates according to different principles. Rather than ranking books according to a single hierarchy of value, BOMC judges sort books into a number of categories—serious fiction, popular history, self-help/health, reference, cookbooks, and so on—acknowledging that readers may desire different things from each kind of book. The literary offerings of the BOMC subordinate linguistic artistry and formal experimentation to coherent plots and the subjectivity of central characters, providing members with a "sentimental education," offering suggestions, models, and directions for negotiating their professional, managerial-class lives.

The BOMC was founded in 1926, the brainchild of advertising copywriter Harry Scherman, who imagined the club as a solution to the publishing industry's chronic problems with distribution. The club would connect underserved potential readers with the books they desired through the mail. Scherman assembled a panel of distinguished judges to select the best book of each month, marketing both expert literary advice and the books so selected as commodities. Harold Guinzberg and Samuel Craig founded the Literary Guild, the BOMC's primary competitor, the same year. The Literary Guild created an uproar in the publishing world by selling books at a discount, in special editions released before trade editions reached booksellers. Because of their initial success, numerous imitators followed throughout the 1920s, including the Religious Book Club, Catholic Book Club, Free Thought Book of the Month Club, Crime Club, Detective Story Club, and Children's Book Club, among others.

The clubs operated according to similar principles. They sought to expand the market for books by making it easier for readers—particularly those inconveniently located to bookstores—to purchase them. Members paid a subscription fee to join the club, agreeing to make a certain number of purchases during the year. A panel of judges made the selections, which were automatically sent to all club members. If they did not like a selection, they could return it. The BOMC offered readers advance information about the selections, allowing them to decline before the book was sent or select an alternate. Clubs later added specially priced editions, bonuses for readers making a minimum number of purchases, and a variety of other incentives. The subscriber base insured a large market for each selected title, creating economies of scale. The subscription feature guaranteed repeat customers, although each book was held to be unique. Publicity generated by a book's selection frequently fueled increased purchases from other booksellers as well.

Although some in the publishing world agree that book clubs have benefited the industry as a whole by developing a previously untapped market of new readers, clubs have come under attack from both booksellers and cultural critics. Booksellers were concerned about being undersold by discounted editions offered by some clubs, and they resented the way clubs' early advertising suggested that bookstores were failing to meet readers' needs. Critics asserted that book clubs cheapened or diluted the values traditionally associated with book culture. Clubs were middlebrow institutions—seeking to make the benefits of education and culture more widely available to the general public. As a result they engendered a lot of anxiety about the promiscuous intermingling of commerce and culture, about marketing books as if they were commodities indistinguishable from soap or cornflakes. Book-club critics asserted that clubs interfered with the free exercise of taste, judgment, and intellect, creating passive (often feminized) consumers of a dumbed-down version of elite culture. Club allies insisted that the clubs were not a literary dictatorship but a service for readers whose intellectual lives had languished since leaving school as their careers and families took up more of their time.

Book clubs grew steadily from their inception in the 1920s through the 1970s, with memberships skyrocketing during the economic and educational boom that followed World War II. Because direct mail could reach highly specialized audiences, a number of targeted book clubs appeared in the postwar period—the Playboy Book Club, the Traveler's Book Club, the Limited Editions Club, the Scientific Book Club, to name a few. The appearance of chain superstores offering deep discounts in the 1980s and 1990s cut into clubs' profitability and market share. Buyouts and mergers in the 1980s winnowed the 200-odd book clubs for adult readers to about 150 in 1995. Many book clubs became subsidiaries of multimedia conglomerates, more useful for the database of subscribers than for generating profits. Following the general trend toward more direct involvement of marketing in editorial operations, the BOMC did away with its board of judges in 1994. Although these changes have increased the profitability of clubs, critics lament that the bestseller is being marketed over the best writing and big-name authors have replaced experimental novelists. The tensions between commodity and culture and between uplift and economics continue to shape debate over book clubs into the twenty-first century.

[See also POPULAR CULTURE; PRINT CULTURE.]

BIBLIOGRAPHY

Carvajal, Doreen, "Triumph of the Bottom Line," *New York Times* (April 1, 1996):Sec. D, p. 5.

Gere, Anne Ruggles, *Intimate Practices: Literacy and Cultural Work in U.S. Women's Clubs, 1880–1920* (Univ. of Ill. Press 1997).

Long, Elizabeth, "Women, Reading, and Cultural Authority: Some Implications of the Audience Perspective in Cultural Studies," *American Quarterly* 38, no. 4 (Fall 1986):591–612.

Long, Elizabeth, "Reading Groups and the Postmodern Crisis of Cultural Authority," *Cultural Studies* (1987):306–327.

Long, Elizabeth, "Textual Interpretation as Collective Action," in *The Ethnography of Reading*, ed. by Jonathan Boyarin (Univ. of Calif. Press 1993).

Radway, Janice A., *A Feeling for Books: The Book-of-the-Month Club, Literary Taste, and Middle-Class Desire* (Univ. of N.C. Press 1997).

Rubin, Joan Shelley, *The Making of Middlebrow Culture* (Univ. of N.C. Press 1992).

Tebbel, John, *A History of Book Publishing in the United States*, vols. 3 and 4 (Bowker 1978, 1981).

ERIN A. SMITH

BORDERLANDS

The study of the unique stories of specific regions of the United States has been carried out in one form or another for well over a century. Whether based on reality or myth, histories of New England, the South, and, of course, the West have led simultaneously to a deepened understanding of the diversity of the nation and a further embedding of stereotypes. In the last decade and a half of the twentieth century, scholars focused this same re-

gionalist impulse on contested zones such as borders and coasts. In the United States, an entire area of scholarship has grown to study the regions along the border with Mexico. An aberration in standard American history, and even in the history of the American West, this borderland area has been found to have a unique, hybrid culture and a history of its own.

The U.S.-Mexico border shares some similarity to that between the United States and Canada. In both cases border society is complicated by ideas about the sovereignty of nation-states, the intensification of commerce and social discourse, and strategies of cultural representation. The U.S.-Mexico border is unique, however, in that it is the longest border between a country characterized as "first world," or developed, and a country whose economy is sometimes characterized as "third world," or developing. The growth of a capitalist world economy provided the context for the development not only of U.S.-Mexico border culture but also of other types of cultural processes that incorporate difference (the process of acculturation, the mixing of cultural traits, and the occurrence of various diasporas, or forced movements of specific groups). The North Atlantic Free Trade Agreement (NAFTA) of the 1990s accentuated cultural distinctions while attempting to make trade and commerce the shared medium of border society.

The meeting of cultures along such borders has made them locations of major folk cultural achievements throughout history. A line drawn in various ways, a border marks the place where adjacent cultures and jurisdictions meet. As a reaction, commerce and personal identity attain a higher importance in border society. Just as musical styles come into contact with one another, so do ordinances and laws. This mixing of national laws and customs creates a zone in which movements of people and goods must be carefully regulated, examined, discussed, and hidden. However, these activities are quite futile among such cultural chaos, and greater amounts of illicit activity are also possible. The definition of legal and illegal activity, on a formal and informal basis, contributes to smuggling and legal and illegal immigration. Companies use national differences in labor and environmental regulations to pursue their advantage. Border society thrives on difference, and people and institutions go there to exploit niches in its environment.

One of a border's most absolute characteristics is change. These are dynamic sites, cultural incubators in which contest consistently causes residents to redefine themselves. Borders are artifacts of history that are subject to change over time. When borders shift, lands and peoples are subjected to different sets of rules; this creates opportunities for exploitation, conditions of hardship, and motivations for revolt. With this in mind, scholars who study borderlands do not seek to limit the multiplicity of voices contained in their work. Rather than a central, authoritative perspective, borderland scholars strive for a decentered point of view, one with many representative speakers.

For instance, the history of the southwestern borderlands demands that scholars be willing to hear a particularly disparate multiplicity of stories and voices. The region between the Gulf of Mexico and Baja California has been inhabited by Native Americans, who first settled it, used it, and relocated on it according to the practices and beliefs of their many societies; by Spaniards, who accepted ownership of the lands in grants made by the Spanish crown according to a perceived divine right; by mestizos, whose practices, like their ancestry, combined Indian and Hispanic heritage; and by English-speaking citizens of the United States, whose land acquiring and owning practices were informed by principles of commercial capital and Manifest Destiny. The Mexican and U.S. governments settled the location of the border with the signing of the Treaty of Guadalupe Hidalgo in 1848 and the Gadsden Purchase in 1853. Mexico, of course, had begun from the Native settlements in the areas between the Gulf of Mexico and the Pacific. During the seventeenth century, Spanish settlers established this area as the northern frontier of New Spain and then of Mexico after its War of Independence in 1810. Diversity increased further when Jewish families from central Mexico sought refuge from religious persecution in the eighteenth century. In the latter part of the nineteenth century, a Mexican government concerned about U.S. expansionism encouraged settlement of diverse groups, including Chinese, Mennonite, Molokan Russian, Black Seminole, and Kickapoo.

There were efforts in the twentieth century to regulate the border flow. During the Mexican Revolution, which began in 1910, the border population increased significantly as many Mexicans moved across the border seeking refuge in the United States. When economic recessions hit the United States, efforts mounted to push immigrants back to Mexico. The damming of the Colorado River converted the Imperial Valley along the river into fertile agricultural land. Anglo-American landowners leased this land to Chinese entrepreneurs from California, who smuggled agricultural laborers into Mexico from China. The Bracero Program of 1942–1964, first negotiated by the United States and Mexico as an emergency measure during World War II, encouraged large migrations of Mexican workers to the United States. Under its terms American agricultural enterprises could legally bring Mexican contract laborers for seasonal work. In the off-season many did not return home but settled on the border, often selecting a place where people from their home state were already established. Specific, federally supported development of the border region began in the 1960s. Individuals, groups, and corporate bodies continued to be attracted to the border to exploit niches in an environment created by difference and marginality.

As people from different cultural regions of Mexico have settled on the border, they have evolved a complex layered cultural and social environment that has been created by competition and adaptation for survival. In addition to an active area of scholarship, American society has benefited from borderland culture with, for example, Tex-Mex cuisine, a combination of Mexican, Spanish, and American regional cooking and foods. Commercialized and sold in chain restaurants throughout the nation, Tex-Mex is the perfect illustration of the plurality of a border society.

[See also CHICANOS, AN OVERVIEW, and article on CHICANISMO AND THE CHICANO MOVEMENT.]

BIBLIOGRAPHY

Herzog, Lawrence, *Where North Meets South: Cities, Space, and Politics on the U.S.-Mexico Border* (Univ. of Tex. Press 1990).

Miller, Tom, *On the Border: Portraits of America's Southwestern Frontier* (Harper 1981).

Montejano, David, *Anglos and Mexicans in the Making of Texas, 1836–1986* (Univ. of Tex. Press 1987).

Saldívar, José David, *Border Matters: Remapping American Cultural Studies* (Univ. of Calif. Press 1997).

Suárez-Orozco, Marcelo, ed., *Crossings: Mexican Immigration in Interdisciplinary Perspectives* (Harvard Univ. Press 1998).

BRIAN BLACK

BRACERO

The Bracero Program was established by the U.S. federal government program to import young Mexican men for farm labor in the United States. Farm owners had convinced the government that the need for food during World War II far outweighed any fears about potential danger of importing cheap foreign labor into the country. The federal government increased its role in the economy on behalf of the farm owners, who became so powerful that they were able to keep the program in operation long after the war ended.

Following the Mexican Revolution in 1910, Mexican peasants, despite their skills and habits of hard work, found little opportunity in Mexico and by the end of the 1930s they were hard-pressed to eke out a living. The United States, on the other hand, had a shortage of farm labor because of the needs of the war. On August 4, 1942, the United States and the Mexican government signed an agreement beginning the Bracero Program.

Under the Bracero Program, Mexican migrant workers became the foundation for the rich American agricultural industry. The El Paso–Ciudad Juárez border region, for example, played a major part in this development. At one point, over 80 thousand braceros per year entered the United States through El Paso, Texas. Overall more than 7.5 million Mexican farm laborers went to the United States, mainly to California, to work in agri-culture. It was largely owing to bracero labor that the United States became the most productive farming nation in the world.

The braceros' arrival changed the social and cultural textures as well as the economies of many border towns. Ciudad Juárez, for example, became a recruitment site and gathering point for the Texan agricultural labor force. These workers were routinely exploited. Contracts, for example, were in English and the braceros signed them without the aid of any translator. The bracero contracts were drawn up under the control of independent farmers' associations and the Farm Bureau. At the completion of the contracts, braceros had to return their working permits and go back to Mexico. To return to Mexico at other times, even in emergencies, braceros were required to have written permission from their employers.

Braceros made major contributions to the American economy but their contributions were not always appreciated. They suffered harassment and oppression. Those who wanted to keep America for Americans, forgetting that Texas and California were, for a time, Mexican, derided them. Racist authorities treated them unfairly. In fact, the U.S. Department of Labor officer in charge of the program, Lee G. Williams, described it as a system of "legalized slavery." By the 1960s a ready pool of "illegal" agricultural workers, the development of the mechanical cotton harvester, a growing awareness of the plight of farmworkers, and the rise of leaders such as César Chávez brought an end to the Bracero Program.

[See also IMMIGRATION AND IMMIGRATION LAW.]

BIBLIOGRAPHY

Driscoll, Barbara A., *The Tracks North: The Railroad Bracero Program of World War II* (Univ. of Tex. Press 1998).

Durand, Jorge, Douglas S. Massey, and Fernando Charvet, "The Changing Geography of Mexican Immigration in the United States: 1910–1996," *Social Science Quarterly* 81 (March 2000):1–15.

Herrera-Sobek, María, *Bracero Experience: Elitelore Versus Folklore* (Univ. of Calif. Press).

Weber, Devra, *Dark Sweat, White Gold: California Farm Workers, Cotton, and the New Deal* (Univ. of Calif. Press 1994).

FRANK A. SALAMONE

BREAD AND ROSES

The slogan "bread and roses" captured the goals and dreams of the impoverished, mostly immigrant workers in the dramatic Lawrence textile strike of 1912 led by the Industrial Workers of the World. More than half of the strikers in the prosperous American Woolen Mills in Lawrence, Massachusetts, were women; more than half, young girls between the ages of fourteen and eighteen. Protesting the "sweated" conditions of their work and their lives and pursuing the dream of beauty as well as an adequate standard of living, the men and women of Lawrence pioneered the dramatic strike techniques of singing, mass picketing, and sending their children to safe homes in other cities. The strike appealed to the conscience of the nation to redress the appalling conditions faced by immigrants, women, and child laborers. Their picket-sign slogan of "bread and roses" became a song that inspired their own as well as future generations of working women, participants in movements for social justice, musicians, and artists.

Women have participated in the labor movement and in related social movements since the beginnings of industrialization. They went on strike and organized unions from their first exposure to the long hours and harsh working conditions in the mills. If the predominantly male unions were reluctant to welcome female workers, they continued to organize on their own, sometimes forming all-female unions. As a reserve labor force, women and immigrants made possible the major industrial expansions of the nineteenth and twentieth centuries, as well as the shift from the manufacturing to the service and clerical sectors that began in the 1970s. As the gender of the paid-labor force changed in the twentieth century to include many more female workers and married women, and with the decline of blue-collar jobs and blue-collar unions, and the rise in immigration to the United States, women and immigrants have become increasingly important to the reemerging labor movement of the twenty-first century.

These long-term economic and social changes for both women and unions are creating the opportunity for new relationships. Women are a growing part of the new global workforce at a time when sweated labor is expanding globally. Economically, women in the United States are no longer "secondary workers." The decline in real wages since 1973 and the rise in female-headed families have increased economic pressures on female workers. As wages in the United States fall and as workdays get longer, the competing stresses of work and family life intensify. The conditions that inspired the women in the Lawrence textile strike may inspire a new generation of women workers to revitalize the labor movement and call for "bread and roses."

The evidence from the twentieth century demonstrates that, contrary to the stereotypes, female workers are militant and organizable. In the twentieth century, female department-store workers in Oakland, California, walked out in 1946, sparking a general strike of more than 120 thousand workers. Two-thirds of the 350 thousand telephone workers who went on strike in 1947 were women. In the 1960s and 1970s women accounted for more than two-thirds of teachers, tripling the membership of the teachers' unions to more than two million. The evidence indicates that women are more sympathetic to unions than men and more interested in collective solutions to problems at work.

As women in such female-dominated sectors of the economy as health care, education, federal, state, and city governments, and the clerical and service sectors lead the way into unions, they are pressuring the labor movement to open leadership positions to them and to place issues of work and family squarely in the center of labor's agenda. In 1974, women organized the Coalition of Labor Union Women (CLUW) to press for leadership positions in the labor movement. By the 1990s two in five union members were women. The American Federation of Labor and Congress of Industrial Organizations (AFL-CIO) with its 5.5 million female members became the largest "working women's organization" in the country. In consultation with its members it developed an agenda to place working women's issues center stage and to reach out to both union and nonunion women. Focusing on equal pay, quality child care, voting, organizing new workers into unions, the right to make changes on the job, and a better balance of work and family, the vision of "bread and roses" continues to inspire working women's struggles in the new century.

[See also LABOR MOVEMENT.*]*

BIBLIOGRAPHY

Cobble, Dorothy Sue, ed., *Women and Unions: Forging a Partnership* (ILR Press 1993).

Kornbluh, Joyce, ed., *Rebel Voices, an I.W.W. Anthology* (Univ. of Mich. Press 1964).

Nussbaum, Karen, "Women in Labor: Always the Bridesmaid?," in *Not Your Father's Union Movement: Inside the AFL-CIO,* ed. by Jo-Ann Mort (Verso 1999).

Tax, Meredith, *The Rising of the Women: Feminist Solidarity and Class Conflict, 1880–1917* (Monthly Review Press 1980).

RUTH MEYEROWITZ

BRIDGES

Bridges help define culture. They are among its most visible expressions of public works in a technological age. American bridges of steel and concrete characterize the rise of the United States as a powerful industrial nation, beginning after the Civil War with the completion of the Eads Bridge (1874), a steel-arch bridge designed by James B. Eads that spans the Mississippi River in St. Louis, and the Brooklyn Bridge (1883), a steel-wire-cable suspension bridge designed by John A. Roebling that spans New York City's East River. Each was, at the time it was built, the longest-spanning bridge of its type and the first to use steel. But the Brooklyn Bridge was more than a technical triumph; it also became a cultural symbol demonstrating that engineering designs could be works of structural art as well as a stimulus to other art forms, an idea illustrated in paintings by Joseph Stella and in Hart Crane's great poem *The Bridge* (1930).

National self-confidence created a series of major works in steel during the first half of the twentieth century including the Bayonne Bridge (1931; a steel-arch between New York and New Jersey) and the George Washington Bridge (1931; a suspension bridge over the Hudson River in New York City), again the longest-spanning of their type then and both designed by Othmar Ammann.

Self-confidence was shaken in 1940 with the failure of the recently completed Tacoma Narrows Bridge in Washington in a relatively mild windstorm. This bridge followed the design of the George Washington Bridge by including very little deck stiffness, which led to the Tacoma collapse and to the instability of other bridges built in the 1930s such as the Golden Gate (San Francisco), the Bronx Whitestone (New York City), and the Deer Island (Maine). All of these have been subjected to considerable stiffening since 1940, but none was as narrow as the long-span Tacoma Bridge. This basic design problem was solved by Ammann in his 1964 Verrazano-Narrows Bridge (New York City) and by British designers of the Severn Road Bridge (England) in that same year.

Between 1883 and 1964 America led the world in steel-bridge design, especially with suspension bridges. Roebling's Brooklyn Bridge had diagonal stays to prevent the type of wind oscillations that destroyed the Tacoma Bridge. For the 1903 Williamsburg Bridge (New York City), the engineers did not use diagonal stays and instead designed a deep truss. This ugly design, heavily criticized, led to the lighter design of the Manhattan Bridge (1909; New York City).

In 1926 the Delaware River Bridge connected Philadelphia, Pennsylvania, and Camden, New Jersey, in time for the sesquicentennial celebration in Philadelphia. At the time it was the longest-spanning suspension bridge in the world at 1,750 feet (533 m), which Ammann exactly doubled for his George Washington Bridge.

The early twentieth century brought in reinforced-concrete bridges, of which the most prominent were arches such as the Connecticut Avenue Bridge in Washington, D.C. (1904), and the West-

The gala opening of the Brooklyn Bridge in 1883.

inghouse Bridge in Pittsburgh (1931). The Westinghouse Bridge was at the time the longest-spanning concrete bridge in the United States, with a span of more than 400 feet (122 m), and represents a design that still reflected the imitative forms of ancient bridges in its use of purely historical design elements. The towers are fake and the arcades inessential. Such extraneous effects disappear with the Russian Gulch Bridge (1940; California), America's finest of its type at the time.

In American culture, concrete bridges presented a two-part problem. First, they encouraged owners to seek architectural embellishments because concrete could be cast in the field in custom forms; second, these bridges, when built in profusion after World War II, encouraged cost-conscious engineers to create structurally inarticulate forms in standardized shapes. Thus there arose two ideas about concrete bridges. On the one hand, where owners considered beauty to be crucial, designers sought

The Golden Gate Bridge, which spans San Francisco Bay.

architectural ideas of decoration; on the other hand (and because of costly form work), where designers thought only of economy the results were at best bland. These conditions prevented Americans from drawing on the inspiration of the great European bridge designers Robert Maillart and Eugene Freyssinet, whose ideas focused on economy and elegance. Nevertheless, after World War II the state of California, under bridge engineer Arthur Elliot, completed a series of exceptional designs mostly using the new development, prestressed concrete. Examples of such works are the Adams Avenue overpass, the old Miramar Bridge, and the Lilac Road Bridge all just north of San Diego.

A particularly significant design is the San Mateo Creek Bridge (1970) where Elliot sculpted the high piers into a shape that the local community accepted. Surprisingly the resulting construction bid was lower than the bid on a more conventional and less elegant design. The prestressed concrete cantilever, or segmented-construction technique, developed in Germany the 1950s by Ulrich Finsterwalder, has led to many fine designs in the United States, exemplified by the bridge over the Columbia River near Portland, Oregon, in which the long-beam spans increase in depth near the supports to express the increased internal forces present there, and the vertical piers splay at their bases for the same reason.

In 1976 the state of Washington completed the Pasco-Kennewick Bridge over the Columbia River, the first major cable-stayed bridge in the United States. This European innovation has led to many elegant forms, such as the East Huntington Bridge (1985) over the Ohio River, which, like Pasco-Kennewick, was designed by Arvid Grant and the German Fritz Leonhardt. Two other examples of cable-stay bridges are the Dame Point Bridge located in Jacksonville, Florida, for which Finsterwalder served as consultant to the Howard Needles Tammen and Bergendorf firm, and the Sunshine Skyway Bridge over Tampa Bay, Florida, designed by the French engineer Jean Mueller in collaboration with Eugene Figg.

Two unusual engineering design competitions held out promise of enlivening structural engineering at the start of the twenty-first century. These competitions required strict rules and a juried decision. The state of Maryland, under its bridge engineer Earle Freedman, pioneered this process in 1989 for the U.S. Naval Academy Bridge over the Severn River. The state chose five engineering firms to compete and named a jury consisting mainly of local civic leaders, national engineering experts, and the great Swiss designer Christian Menn. Under Menn's guidance, the process followed the Swiss tradition of such design competitions. The winning bridge was designed by Tom Jenkins of the Greiner Company.

Based on this success, Maryland stimulated a second engineering design competition in collaboration with Virginia and the District of Columbia for the replacement of the rapidly deteriorating and overtaxed Woodrow Wilson Bridge carrying Interstate 95 over the Potomac River. Four designers competed and the winning design by the Parsons Transportation Group, using a form inspired by Menn, once again resulted in an aesthetically superior engineering form.

By 1964 the United States had the four longest-spanning bridges in the world (Verrazano, Golden Gate, Mackinac [Michigan], and George Washington), but by 2000 the five longest-spanning structures in the world were all in other countries. Yet in many states there had appeared smaller bridges showing the promise that engineering refinement can lead to high-quality American bridges. Nevertheless, for Americans bridges have served not only as a means of crossing bodies of water but also as inspirational monuments, evoking feelings of awe and symbolizing the highest achievements of an engineering culture.

[See also ARCHITECTURE, AN OVERVIEW; TECHNOLOGY, AN OVERVIEW.]

BIBLIOGRAPHY

Billington, David P., *The Tower and the Bridge: The New Art of Structural Engineering* (Princeton Univ. Press 1985).
Dupré, Judith, *Bridges: A History of the World's Most Famous and Important Spans* (Black Dog & Leventhal 1997).
Trachtenberg, Alan, *Brooklyn Bridge: Fact and Symbol,* 2d ed. (Univ. of Chicago Press 1979).

DAVID P. BILLINGTON

BROADWAY MUSICALS

The American Broadway musical is arguably the most distinctive and original theatrical form to develop in the United States and one of the most prominent forms of American popular entertainment of the twentieth century. It owes its origin to sources both foreign and domestic, including such diverse European forms as the ballad opera, ballet, extravaganza, operetta (especially the work of Gilbert and Sullivan in the 1880s), pantomime, opera bouffe, and singspiel; native forms helping to create a new hybrid included the blackface minstrel show, vaudeville, Americanized pantomime (in particular those of George L. Fox in the 1860s and 1870s), and burlesque (in the sense of parody

© MARTHA SWOPE/TIME, INC.

The final number of *A Chorus Line*, which ran for fifteen years on Broadway.

or travesty and dating significantly from the success of *The Black Crook* in 1866).

The creators of early musicals were responsible for uniquely American innovations. They included such notables as the teams of Edward Harrigan and David Braham in the 1870s and 1880s with their "Mulligan Guard" musical plays depicting life among New York's working-class Irish, Germans, and African Americans; and Bob Cole and Billy Johnson, creators of early ragtime-inspired African

American musicals at and after the turn of the twentieth century. Prior to the 1920s names such as Reginald De Koven, Victor Herbert, George M. Cohan (who consciously turned to American themes and patriotic sentiment), Jerome Kern, Guy Bolton, P. G. Wodehouse, Rudolf Friml, and Sigmund Romberg (many European-trained or English immigrants) dominated.

However, not until the 1920s did the "book musical," the most prominent form of the Broadway musical, emerge; it subsequently dominated musical theater around the world until the 1970s and the beginning of the so-called British invasion. Among the first true musicals were the jazz-influenced shows by George and Ira Gershwin, who in the 1930s moved into political satire (long a staple ingredient in topical Broadway musicals and revues), most notably with the Pulitzer Prize–winning *Of Thee I Sing* (1931), still a lively satire on elections and the presidency. Joining the Gershwins with a new level of sophistication was the team of Richard Rodgers and Lorenz Hart (*Dearest Enemy* in 1925 and *A Connecticut Yankee* in 1927, among others). However, the form took an especially dramatic turn in 1927 with the Jerome Kern–Oscar Hammerstein II production of *Show Boat*, considered by many the first full American operetta. Certainly its style grew from the earlier European operetta, yet it was American in numerous notable ways: its authors were all native (the story is based on the novel by Edna Ferber); its setting was American and dealt with the American phenomenon of the traveling showboat over a span of several decades; its principals were mostly identifiable, real people; its music, though somewhat derivative, still depended heavily on native patterns; and perhaps most important, its plot was dramatic (in particular its subplot on the subject of miscegenation and family disintegration) and its lyrics and dialogue colloquial. The new serious focus and integrated construction of *Show Boat* set a pattern that would dominate musicals of the 1940s and 1950s, to many the form's heyday.

In 1940 Rodgers and Hart created *Pal Joey*, a musical based on stories by John O'Hara. It was of major historical importance, focusing on an unscrupulous, womanizing Chicago nightclub singer along with other immoral, self-serving characters. The matching of successful lyrics and music with an innovative book led to arguably the most successful team in Broadway history—Rodgers and Hammerstein. From the debut of *Oklahoma!* (1943) to *The Sound of Music* (1959), they were synonymous with the Broadway musical (*Carousel*, 1945; *South Pacific*, 1949; *The King and I*, 1951; *Flower Drum Song*, 1958). Solid stories dominated by serious sentiments were

carefully integrated with melodies, lyrics, and choreographed interludes, all adding to the forward movement of the plot. Rodgers and Hammerstein musicals have been matched for commercial success only by those of the British composer Andrew Lloyd Webber (*Cats, Phantom of the Opera, Sunset Boulevard*). Of subsequent American theatrical composers, only Stephen Sondheim (*Company*, 1970; *Follies*, 1971; *A Little Night Music*, 1973; *Sweeney Todd*, 1979; *Into the Woods*, 1987; *Passion*, 1994, among others) can claim as long a string of artistic successes.

Other successful collaborators (the Broadway musical is invariably the result of partnerships) since the 1930s are Frederick Loewe and Alan Jay Lerner, Richard Adler and Jerry Ross, Jerry Bock and Sheldon Harnick, John Kander and Fred Ebb, Betty Comden and Adolph Green (lyricists/librettists working with numerous composers); and the British team of Tim Rice and Lloyd Webber. Some musical artists have worked with various collaborators, such as Arthur Schwartz, Howard Dietz, Marc Blitzstein, Kurt Weill, Cole Porter, Leonard Bernstein, Vincent Youmans, Otto Harbach, E. Y. Harburg, Frank Loesser, Mitch Leigh, Galt McDermott, and Arthur Freed.

Since as early as the 1600s, musical theater on American shores has responded to cultural changes, though during its heyday (1940s–1960s) the two major threads remained the operatic form and what became known as musical comedy (dating back to such Kern shows of the 1910s as *Very Good Eddie, Oh, Boy!*, and *Sally*), a lightweight, formulaic approach to musical theater creation. Only the 1930s, during the Depression, and the 1960s, during the height of the rock era, witnessed brief moments of notable innovation and timeliness. Though musicals with issue-oriented subjects (such as Paul Green and Weill's *Johnny Johnson*, 1936; the revue *Pins and Needles*, 1937, featuring the music of Harold Rome; and Blitzstein's *The Cradle Will Rock*, 1938) and a limited group of "rock" musicals in the 1960s (most notably McDermott, James Rado, and Germone Ragni's *Hair*, 1967) were of historical importance and reflected paradigms in American culture, their

The cast of *Rent*, Jonathan Larson's Pulitzer Prize–winning Broadway rock musical.

successes were limited, and only a few were produced on Broadway; their lasting influence was minimal.

The dearth of new talent in the 1970s, with the notable exception of Sondheim, led to what became known as the "concept" musical, encouraged most notably by the producer-director Harold Prince. Stressing the director and designers, this approach conceived of all elements (including the work of composer, lyricist, and librettist) in terms of production. Broadway musicals of the 1970s and 1980s were thus frequently dominated by such choreographer-directors as Bob Fosse, Gower Champion, Michael Bennett, Jerome Robbins, and Tommy Tune. When the more talented of this group died or retired, their work gave way to musicals often based on vintage Hollywood films or productions with extraordinary spectacle and technical innovation (such as *Titanic, Les Misérables,* and *Phantom of the Opera*).

The 1970s also experienced a bout of musical nostalgia (propelled by early 1970s revivals of *No, No Nannette* and *Irene*), prompted likely by traditionalists' reactions to both the social-political unrest of the day and the use of "distasteful" subjects and new sounds. Such original musicals as *Grease* (1972) and *Over There* (1974) evoked earlier ages. In truth, nostalgia and tradition have permeated musical theater throughout its history, with interludes in which they seem even more prominent.

Economics has always been a central factor in the development of musicals for Broadway. Rising costs of Broadway production meant that the vehicle had to be a blockbuster in all respects. Producers began to look abroad for possible commercial Broadway musical material. Many hits of the 1990s originated in England or France; others were developed and tested on audiences outside New York or even the United States (especially Toronto and London) or in regional theaters. A majority of the major end-of-the-century Broadway successes were revivals of old standards (*Show Boat, Damn Yankees, Carousel, Chicago, Cabaret, 1776, Annie Get Your Gun, Peter Pan*, and *Kiss Me, Kate,*) or even of the work of Sondheim and others. They were often produced initially or solely by the nonprofit sector of the American theater—for example, the late 1990s *Carousel* by Lincoln Center for the Performing Arts (a staging that began at Britain's Royal National Theater) and *Cabaret* and *1776* by New York's Roundabout Theater Company.

The American musical is undeniably at a crossroads, with too few original products. The enormous cost of staging musicals and the power of theatrical unions force producers to please large audiences and raise ticket prices. As a consequence, small casts and modest productions on Broadway invariably fail, if attempted at all. Frequently the most innovative and original work is seen in Off or Off-Off Broadway productions or outside New York altogether. In the 1990s a new group of musical theater composers did begin to test the waters with some limited success, attempting to create innovative musical scores with often unusual topics (many American in origin), hoping to overcome what many authorities classified as a crisis in the composition of musicals. Among these composers were Jason Robert Brown, Ricky Ian Gordon, Adam Guettel, Michael John LaChiusa, Jeanine Tesori, and Frank Wildhorn.

[*See also* THEATER.]

BIBLIOGRAPHY

Bordman, Gerald, *American Musical Comedy: From Adonis to Dreamgirls* (Oxford 1982).

Bordman, Gerald, *American Musical Theater: A Chronicle,* 2d ed. (Oxford 1992).

Degen, John, "Musical Theater Since World War II," in *The Cambridge History of American Theater, Volume Three,* ed. by Don B. Wilmeth and Christopher Bigsby (Cambridge 2000).

Gottfried, Martin, *Broadway Musicals* (Abrams 1984).

Gottfried, Martin, *More Broadway Musicals: Since 1980* (Abrams 1991).

Green, Stanley, *The World of Musical Comedy,* 4th ed. (Barnes 1980).

DON B. WILMETH

BROWN V. BOARD OF EDUCATION

The Supreme Court's *Brown* v. *Board of Education of Topeka* decision (347 U.S. 483 [1954]; 349 U.S. 294 [1955]) was actually four cases considered under one rubric, with a companion case, *Bolling* v. *Sharpe* (1954). The central question considered was whether legally imposed racial segregation in public primary and secondary education violated the equal protection clause of the Fourteenth Amendment, while *Bolling* took up the segregation issue for the District of Columbia and the due process clause of the Fifth Amendment.

In *Plessy* v. *Ferguson* (1896), the Court had upheld segregation, in a case involving intrastate railway transportation, under the separate but equal doctrine, and most court cases upheld this doctrine until the late 1930s. Then the National Association for the Advancement of Colored People (NAACP) began a successful assault on educational segregation, working downward from graduate and professional higher education in a series of cases including *Missouri ex rel., Gaines* v. *Canada* (1938), *McLaurin* v. *Board of Regents,* and *Sweatt* v. *Painter* (1950).

By 1952, the Supreme Court had heard arguments in *Brown* but had set the cases for reargument. In the meantime, Chief Justice Fred M. Vinson died, and President Dwight D. Eisenhower appointed Earl Warren as chief justice. Under Warren's stewardship, the Court began to wrestle with the potential political impact of *Brown* as well as its legal justification. Segregation had become a way of life in the South, and violent resistance to any order for desegregation was greatly feared.

The chief justice worked hard behind the scenes to insure unanimity in the court decision, with Justice Stanley F. Reid finally agreeing not to oppose the decision and Justice Robert H. Jackson abandoning plans for a concurring opinion. Warren wrote the decision in a bland style, avoiding inflammatory rhetoric and offering no generalized statements about the fate of other aspects of Jim Crow institutions. The decision was based heavily upon the effects on black children of segregated education and resorted to various sociological and psychological studies as evidence.

The following year the Court took up the question of what was to be done about unconstitutionally segregated public schools: were they to be phased out, or must they be ended at once? The Court employed the ambiguous phrase " . . . with all deliberate speed . . . ," leading to much procrastination and necessitating innumerable future suits. In the aftermath of *Brown,* the Court went on in a long series of "per curiam" decisions to eradicate most vestiges of Jim Crow. *Loving* v. *Virginia* (1967), which struck down the laws against interracial marriage, was perhaps the last of the direct legal descendants of *Brown,* but later forced-busing cases, such as *Swann* v. *Charlotte-Mecklenburg Board of Education* (1971), *Keyes* v. *School District No. 1* (1973), and *Columbus Board of Education* v. *Penick* (1979), relied on the *Brown* precedent. In a very real sense, *Brown* lent enormous moral support to nonjudicial aspects of the civil rights movement as well, such as sit-ins and boycotts, and to legislative remedies

for discrimination such as the Civil Rights Act of 1964 and the Voting Rights Act of 1965.

Intellectual opposition to *Brown* did not always originate with prosegregationists. Bitter opponents of segregation such as constitutional scholars Raoul Berger and Alexander Bickel held that the noble outcome of *Brown* should have instead been achieved by constitutional amendment or congressional legislation. Other critics supported the outcome of *Brown* but disputed its rationale as too much based on social science and not grounded firmly enough in legal theory, holding that the Court might have legitimately reached the same conclusion by more cogent legal analysis.

[See also CIVIL RIGHTS AND THE CIVIL RIGHTS MOVEMENT.*]*

BIBLIOGRAPHY

Encyclopedia of the American Constitution, ed. by Leonard W. Levy, Kenneth L. Karst, and Dennis J. Mahoney (Macmillan 1986).

Kluger, Richard, *Simple Justice: The History of Brown v. Board of Education and Black America's Struggle for Equality* (Knopf 1975).

Wilkinson, J. Harvie, III, *From Brown to Bakke: The Supreme Court and School Integration, 1954–1978* (Oxford 1979).

Woodward, C. Vann, *The Strange Career of Jim Crow,* 2d ed. (Oxford 1966).

PATRICK M. O'NEIL

BUDDHISM

Buddhism originated in India in the fifth century B.C. and spread throughout the Asian continent, leaving a lasting impact on the daily lives of the people and making major contributions to high culture—art and architecture, literature and philosophy, theater and music. At the beginning of the twenty-first century, as Buddhism becomes better known worldwide, two historical movements converge to form Buddhism in North America.

First, European scholarship on Buddhism originated in the nineteenth century from the colonizers of India, Burma, Sri Lanka, Cambodia, Vietnam, and China. Their interest focused on philological and historical study of Buddhism. This eventually affected a generation of American intellectuals, such as Ralph Waldo Emerson, Henry David Thoreau, and Irving Babbitt, and stimulated such eclectic religious movements as Theosophy. Second, the stream of Chinese and Japanese immigrants in the late nineteenth century brought their Buddhist faith to Hawaii and the West Coast of the United States. This ended with the Asian Exclusion Act, passed by the U.S. Congress in 1924 (preceded by several partial limits on Asian immigration). The Japanese immigrants, unlike the Chinese, had families and American-born children who maintained their Buddhist faith, primarily in the Pure Land tradition of Jodo Shinshu. The history of their persecution and legal discriminations culminated in the incarceration of 120,000 Japanese Americans, including all Buddhist priests, in ten internment camps from 1942 to 1945.

After World War II, with globalization and rapid methods of communication, more familiarity with Buddhism was developed among the American public. Increasing visits by Buddhist monks and teachers from Japan, Tibet, Vietnam, China, and Southeast Asian countries also gave greater visibility to the religion. Popular literature on Buddhism became common in bookstores across the country, and the number of European American converts increased. Buddhist centers were established all across North America, inspired by a whole array of Asian Buddhist practices from diverse cultural areas, including Japanese and Korean Zen, Tibetan and Vipassana Buddhism, and Nichiren Shoshu. These practices respond to the restless search for spirituality, especially among middle- and upper-middle-class Americans.

The stream of Asian Buddhist immigrants also grew in numbers and complexity with Buddhists from Vietnam, Cambodia, Sri Lanka, Korea, Taiwan, and Thailand establishing their respective Buddhist temples or centers in addition to existing Japanese and Chinese Buddhist temples. These ethnic temples provide a haven for immigrants in a strange land, helping them to maintain their cultural values and customs and forming a community of mutual aid during times of need and crisis.

A tension exists between the so-called ethnic Buddhists and European American Buddhists, the latter stressing individual realization of Buddhist practice and the former emphasizing the sense of community, or *Sangha,* centered on the Buddha and the teaching, or *Dharma.* An American Zen monk who visited Japan summed up the difference: Buddhism in America is therapeutic, whereas Buddhism in Asia is faith-centered. As Buddhism in America evolves, however, these two movements will interact and stimulate each other to form a truly American Buddhism, distinct from its Asian counterparts.

[See also RELIGION AND RELIGIOUS MOVEMENTS.*]*

BIBLIOGRAPHY

Fields, Rick, *How the Swans Came to the Lake: A Narrative History of Buddhism in America* (Shambhala Press 1981).
Imamura, Jane M., *Kaikyo: Opening the Dharma: Memoirs of a Buddhist Priest's Wife in America* (Buddhist Study Center Press 1999).

TAITETSU UNNO

BUFFALO SOLDIERS

The settlement of the American frontier demanded strength, bravery, and military might. When the U.S. government committed to constructing hundreds of forts to help protect settlers from Native Americans and to help provide for settlers' needs, many of the soldiers sent to the frontier appeared different from the traditional model of the American soldier. In fact, this rugged terrain required horseback soldiers willing to move far from families and homes. Nearly one-third of these soldiers were African American, including the famous Buffalo Soldiers.

During the Civil War over 180 thousand African Americans served in the Union Army. While more than 33 thousand died, many of the remaining black soldiers were affected when Congress passed legislation in July 1866 establishing two cavalry and four infantry regiments (later consolidated into two). These were to be units of black soldiers, most of whom had served in all-black units during the war. The mounted regiments were the Ninth and Tenth cavalries, soon nicknamed Buffalo Soldiers by the Cheyenne and Comanche peoples. Until the early 1890s they constituted twenty percent of all cavalry forces on the American frontier.

The Ninth and Tenth cavalries' service in subduing Mexican revolutionaries, hostile Native Americans, outlaws, comancheros, and rustlers was as invaluable as it was unrecognized. It was also accomplished over some of the most rugged and inhospitable country in North America. A list of their adversaries—Geronimo, Sitting Bull, Victorio, Lone Wolf, Billy the Kid, and Pancho Villa—reads like a Who's Who of the American West.

Less well known but equally important, the Buffalo Soldiers aided in such critical aspects of western settlement as exploring and mapping vast areas of the Southwest and stringing hundreds of miles of telegraph lines. They built and repaired frontier outposts around which future towns and cities sprang to life. Without the protection provided by the Ninth and Tenth cavalries, crews building the ever-expanding railroads were at the mercy of outlaws and hostile tribes.

In addition to loneliness and difficult climates, the Buffalo Soldiers consistently received some of the worst assignments the army had to offer. They also faced fierce prejudice (resulting from both their Union uniforms and the color of their skin) by many of the citizens of the postwar frontier towns. Nevertheless, the troopers of the Ninth and Tenth cavalries developed into two of the most distinguished fighting units in the army.

Recruitment of white officers proved to be a serious problem for both the Ninth and Tenth cavalries. Despite enticements of fast promotion, many officers, including George Armstrong Custer and Frederick Benteen, refused commissions with African American units. The following advertisement from the *Army and Navy Journal* illustrates the dilemma: "A first Lieutenant of Infantry (white) stationed at a very desirable post . . . desires a transfer with an officer of the same grade, on equal terms if in a white regiment; but if in a colored regiment, a reasonable bonus would be expected."

The Ninth Cavalry was ordered to Texas in June 1867. There it was charged with protecting stage and mail routes, building and maintaining forts, and establishing law and order in a vast area full of outlaws, Mexican revolutionaries, and raiding Comanches, Cheyennes, Kiowas, and Apaches. In addition to the animosity of these groups, Buffalo Soldiers received harsh criticism from some Texans who wished to control their own fates.

The most ominous job that the Buffalo Soldiers were ordered to participate in came in 1891. Sent to the Pine Ridge Reservation in the Dakotas, the U.S. Cavalry intended to scare the Sioux out of a cultural resurgence that has become known as the Ghost Dance. However, many Sioux, fearing a massacre, fled into the Badlands. The subsequent actions of the army to pacify and return the Sioux to their reservations culminated in the massacre of 146 men, women, and children at Wounded Knee. The Ninth Cavalry played no role in the actual slaughter. This was to be their last campaign on the frontier. With episodes of glory and horror, the Buffalo Soldiers performed as a vital and little appreciated part of the American effort to make western lands inhabitable for settlers.

[*See also* AFRICAN AMERICANS, AN OVERVIEW; SLAVERY; GHOST DANCE.]

BIBLIOGRAPHY

Downey, Fairfax, *The Buffalo Soldiers in the Indian Wars* (McGraw-Hill 1969).

Kenner, Charles L., *Buffalo Soldiers and Officers of the Ninth Cavalry, 1867–1898: Black and White Together* (Univ. of Okla. Press 1999).

O'Connor, Robert, *Buffalo Soldiers* (Vintage 1994).

Schubert, Frank N., *Black Valor: Buffalo Soldiers and the Medal of Honor, 1870–1898* (Scholarly Resources 1997).

BRIAN BLACK

CALIFORNIA

California, as environment and history, represents a dynamic instance of American civilization. For multiple generations in its Native American era, through its existence as a Spanish colony from 1769 to 1822 and a Department of Mexico from 1822 to 1846, then as a military territory of the United States from 1846 to 1850, and, after that, as the ever-growing thirty-first state following its admission to the union on September 9, 1850, California has played an increasingly vital role in each of the societies to which it has been connected. In its current flourishing, moreover, as the most populous (33.5 million by January 2000) and the most ethnically diverse state in the nation, California continues to act out and to probe on behalf of the larger American experiment many significant avenues of social and cultural development.

In the Native American era California was home to one-third (more than 330 thousand) of the indigenous peoples living within the present boundaries of the continental United States. This population was a mosaic of some one hundred different tribes, speaking between sixty-four and eighty languages, representing the five major North American language groups.

As a place, California entered Spanish awareness, first and foremost, as an imaginative construct. In Seville in 1510, Garcí Ordóñez de Montalvo published his romantic narrative *Las Sergas de Esplandián* ("The Deeds of Esplandián"), which described California as an island on the right hand of the Indies, very near the Terrestrial Paradise, inhabited by black Amazons and ruled by Queen Calafía. Similarities between Montalvo's description of the island of California and Baja California led Hernán Cortés in 1535 to name the entire peninsula and its regions to the north after the fabled Amazonian isle. In 1697 the Jesuits established the first permanent Spanish colony. Alta California, however, remained unsettled for the next seventy-two years.

Beginning in 1769 Spain made every effort to colonize Alta California through an interdependent system of missions, presidios, pueblos, and ranchos. While the mission system dotted the landscape of coastal southern and central California with twenty-one picturesque ecclesiastical structures, its effect on Native Americans—mainly from disease and cultural shock—was devastating. Whatever the intent of the Franciscan missionaries, the population of Native Americans decreased by approximately half during the colonial period. In 1834 Mexico, which now controlled California, disestablished the mission system.

Throughout its Spanish and Mexican periods, California remained primarily a cattle-dominated rancho economy. The granting of ranchos, many of them vast in extent, continued through the Spanish era and was accelerated under Mexican rule. Neither Spain nor Mexico, however, could persuade a sufficient number of colonists to settle in California and thereby allow the mother country to achieve a secure foothold in the region.

The concept of Manifest Destiny and the Mexican War brought California into the possession of the United States through a swift series of military movements. In June 1846 American settlers in the Sonoma region north of San Francisco revolted and declared a rump republic, not knowing that the United States had declared war on Mexico the previous month. In July 1846 the United States Navy, under the command of Commodore John Drake Sloat, began a series of naval landings on the coast. A detachment of some one hundred dragoons under the command of Brigadier General Stephen Kearny moved west from New Mexico along the Santa Fe Trail. A battalion of mounted volunteers, meanwhile, under the command of John Charles Frémont and Kit Carson, moved southward from Sonoma. On January 13, 1847, the Mexican governor Pío Pico surrendered to Frémont at the Cahuenga Pass outside Los Angeles.

Because of the slavery question Congress could not come to any agreement regarding the territorial status of the newly acquired region. From 1846 to 1850 the military governed California as a conquered territory. For the first four years of its American existence, California remained a picturesque, sparsely populated American territory of uncertain legal status. The discovery of gold on January 24, 1848, by carpenter James Wilson Marshall on the south fork of the American River in northern California rendered the military administration of California obsolete; for in the following year, 1849, some

Fortune seekers pan for gold in California in 1852.

one hundred thousand gold-seekers arrived in the region, the first of a tide of some three hundred thousand Argonauts, as they called themselves, and permanent settlers.

Recognizing the inadequacies and improprieties of military government over civilians, Brigadier General Bennet Riley, the seventh military governor of California, issued a proclamation on June 3, 1849, calling on the citizens of California to form themselves a government. Elections for delegates were held in August. Between September and November 1849, forty-eight delegates, including seven Hispanic Californians, met in Colton Hall in Monterey and drafted a constitution modeled on the constitutions of Iowa and New York. Bypassing territorial status, the delegates proceeded directly to statehood. On November 13, 1849, the constitution was ratified by popular vote and a full slate of state officials was elected. Not until September 1850, however, could a deeply divided Congress agree on the admission of California to the union as a free state.

In its first one hundred years as an American state, California was developed by technology and population booms. The technology of the gold rush involved, primarily, the movement of water and various arrangements and rearrangements of land. The mining technology of land and water also provided, after some adjustments, the technology of agriculture, especially the way agriculture was practiced in California, on a large, even heroic, scale. This same technology led, beginning in the 1880s, to the irrigation of the Central Valley and following that to the creation of California as the leading agricultural state in the nation.

Once again, through the movement of water and land—this time in great metropolitan aqueduct projects—California urbanized and suburbanized itself at the turn of the century, with the Hetch-Hetchy water project in northern California and the Los Angeles aqueduct and Hoover Dam and Metropolitan Water District projects in the southland. Throughout the middle and late 1860s, meanwhile, the Chinese work crews of the Central Pacific were pushing the California and far western portions of the transcontinental rail project across the Sierra Nevada, through Nevada and into Utah; and on May 10, California became linked to the rest of the nation through rail.

In southern California, at the turn of the century, a system of inter-urban electric railcars unified the vast Los Angeles plain and facilitated its ongoing urbanization. Two new inventions, meanwhile, the airplane and the automobile, were making their first appearance in southern California and would also play an important role in the evolution of southern California as a suburbanized society strongly oriented toward the technologies of aviation and, later, aerospace.

In the rise of California to urban and suburban settlement, northern California led the way in the nineteenth century; southern California, in the twentieth. The gold rush stimulated the creation and rise of numerous townships in the Mother Lode. In 1870 San Francisco was the tenth largest city in the United States. By the turn of the century, more than half of all Californians were living in either the urban or suburban San Francisco Bay Area.

Another characteristic of growth in California was the population boom. The gold rush helped to quickly expand the population; in the first thirty years of the twentieth century, more than 3.5 million newcomers would settle in southern Califor-

nia, with the city of Los Angeles absorbing fully a third of the influx.

Diverse in its population, American California sustained an Anglo-American ascendancy that maintained its strength through the 1960s. During the gold rush American miners demanded a tax on non-American gold seekers. In the frontier period Native Americans, African Americans, and people of Chinese descent were not allowed to vote or to give testimony in court. Serious persecutions of the Chinese population occurred in both Los Angeles and San Francisco during the 1870s. The African American population of California remained small until World War II and was by and large ghettoized, although it did produce a number of outstanding figures.

Toward the Hispanic population Anglo-California had a mixed reaction. In the prestatehood era relations were cordial, despite the recent war, in what remained a mixed Yankee-Latino province. There were numerous instances of intermarriage between Anglo men and Hispanic women (the grandfather of General George S. Patton, Jr., for instance). In the 1860s and 1870s the Hispanic *Californio* population went into demographic decline. At the same time, however, Anglo-Californians, inspired by Helen Hunt Jackson's novel *Ramona* (1884), began to romanticize the Mission era and to re-Hispanicize the imaginative context of southern California. In the 1890s immigration from Mexico recommenced as a source of labor supply for the construction of the inter-urban electric system. Agriculture brought even more Mexicans to California, as well as Japanese, East Asian Indians, Armenians, Yugoslavs and other European groups, and African Americans. When this Mexican immigration population began to urbanize in East Los Angeles in the early twentieth century, it found itself largely restricted to a barrio life.

In terms of the arts and formal culture, California, thanks to the rapid development made possible by the gold rush, soon made the transition from a frontier with cultural interests to what the California-born philosopher Josiah Royce described as the Higher Provincialism. The gold rush itself

A view of downtown Los Angeles.

prompted much good writing; and in the 1860s, especially after the founding of the *Overland Monthly* in 1868, a vigorous regional literary culture exerted itself whose most representative figures were Samuel Clemens, Bret Harte, poet Joaquin Miller, historian Hubert Bancroft, economic commentator Henry George, and naturalists Clarence King and John Muir. At the turn of the century, the San Francisco Bay Area, its intellectual life now augmented by the newly established Leland Stanford Junior University (Stanford) in Palo Alto, witnessed a second efflorescence of literary and artistic talent in such figures as novelists Gertrude Atherton, Frank Norris, and Jack London, essayist Mary Austin, columnist and short story writer Ambrose Bierce, and a half-dozen or more significant painters living and working, after the destruction of San Francisco by the catastrophic earthquake and resultant fire in April 1906, on the Monterey Peninsula at the newly established art colony of Carmel-by-the-Sea.

The twentieth century witnessed the transformation of California from province to ecumenopolis, or world commonwealth, as Arnold Toynbee might describe it. During these decades California increased its population to some thirty-two million, with all that such growth implied for the almost overnight development of the built environment and supportive infrastructure. It served as a garrison state, the Gibraltar of the Pacific, during World War II and was the preferred place for resettlement for hundreds of thousands of returning veterans. California also offered a haven for a larger percent of European émigrés fleeing Nazism, especially writers and musicians who found employment in the motion-picture industry. During the war years, in fact, Los Angeles became a quasi-European city through the creative presence of the émigrés.

The cold war further intensified the development of California as garrison state, or Fortress California, through some forty years of multibillion-dollar spending on defense, research, and manufacture, especially in aerospace. Federal dollars fueled the rise of California as a university-centered technocracy whose infrastructure, especially in and around Stanford University, supported and energized the transistor and microchip-driven electronic industry in nearby Sunnyvale, epicenter of Silicon Valley.

Amid such growth there was the inevitable dissent. From the 1870s California had always nurtured its own distinctive radical tradition, a trait noted by Lord Bryce. The union movement remained strong in the San Francisco Bay Area, as evidenced by the maritime-orientated general strike of 1934. During the 1930s radical activists organized a number of landmark agricultural strikes, and John Steinbeck wrote *The Grapes of Wrath* (1939), the best-known novel to emerge from California. In the 1950s the writers of the beat generation made of California—San Francisco, in particular—a platform for dissent against conformity. In the 1960s, beginning with the free speech movement at the University of California at Berkeley, the state served as one of the centers and formulators of dissent against the Vietnam War and what was perceived as the increasing hold of the military-industrial complex on American society.

Racial tension, meanwhile, erupted into urban violence with the Watts rebellion of August 1965, reprised twenty-seven years later as the Los Angeles Rebellion of April–May 1992. Continuing immigration from Mexico, together with the reform of federal immigration laws in the 1960s, triggered the transformation of California into a minority-dominated state, at least in demographic terms. By the end of the twentieth century, California had become planetary in the diversity of its peoples; and the facilitation of this diversity, or the opposing of it, had become one of the primary objectives of politics and public life.

As the twentieth century became the twenty-first, California found itself struggling with the underside of its success. Its economy was in trillion-dollar overdrive, yet an increasing number of Californians were downwardly mobile or ill prepared for the new economy. The prison population soared, especially among minorities, owing, in significant measure, to gangs and the drug culture. The public school system seemed equally stressed. Defenders of California saw such shortcomings as the inevitable result of what California was being challenged to become in such a short time: a world commonwealth, that is, ground zero of the new technology; a utopia of personal fulfillment; and, through the entertainment industry, the purveyor of myths and dreams to the world at large. By the millennium, California was perceived as both the best and the worst of American places. The experiment remained underway, its outcome hopeful—and uncertain.

[See also REGIONALISM; WEST, THE.*]*

BIBLIOGRAPHY

Davis, Mike, *City of Quartz: Excavating the Future of Los Angeles* (Verso 1990).

Harlow, Neal, *California Conquered: War and Peace on the Pacific, 1846–1850* (Univ. of Calif. Press 1982).

Holliday, J. S., *Rush for Riches: Gold Fever and the Making of California* (Univ. of Calif. Press 1999).

Lotchin, Roger W., *Fortress California, 1910–1961: From Warfare to Welfare* (Oxford 1992).

Starr, Kevin, *Americans and the California Dream, 1850–1915* (Oxford 1973).

Wyatt, David, *Five Fires: Race, Catastrophe, and the Shaping of California* (Addison-Wesley 1997).

KEVIN STARR

CAPITALISM

Capitalism is most properly considered an economic system. It is a system that leaves to private individuals and businesses the economic functions of supply and demand, that is, the production and distribution of goods and services. In capitalism the invisible forces of the market are seen to prevail and competition accounts for the rise and fall of prices. The concepts of free enterprise and the free market are integral to understanding capitalism as Adam Smith formulated it in 1776 in his book *The Wealth of Nations,* an attack on the mercantilist political and economic policies that led to the American Revolution.

For Smith mercantilist economics, in which a state sought to measure its wealth in gold, was wrongheaded. Moreover, mercantilism led to permanent underdevelopment of a state's colonies by forcing them to provide raw material to the mother country and prohibiting the development of manufacturing in those colonies. The mother country in turn would sell finished products to the colonies, forbidding them to trade with other states. The mother country would set prices to suit its needs, thereby killing legal competition and, in Smith's view, stifling initiative and the development of a nation's true wealth.

Capitalism, of course, did not spring full-blown from Smith's head. However, it did reach its peak in nineteenth-century Europe, especially in England. Although capitalism has its roots in antiquity, Karl Marx named it. Marx, a German social scientist and the founder of communism, of course disagreed with Smith's contention that capitalism, through enlightened self-interest, would further the interests of the individual. Smith maintained that the maximum production of those goods and services that people desire would further society's interests. This "invisible hand" of self-interest, private property, and free competition in free markets would lead to the unintended but desirable goal of society's well being.

Classic capitalism of the nineteenth century had certain basic characteristics, foremost among them being private ownership of land and capital. Capital refers to building, machinery, and production equipment as well as services for consumption. Buyers and sellers, left unhampered by government, will coordinate economic activities through the give and take of free markets. There should be no interference, then, with the pursuit of economic self-interest. Workers and employers are free to seek to maximize gains through the use of their resources and labor. Consumers also will spend their money in ways they desire to meet their own self-satisfaction. This "consumer sovereignty" will force producers to use their own resources, then, to best satisfy consumers. Under capitalism government's only appropriate roles are to repel foreign attack, to protect private property, and to safeguard contracts. Government has little role in economic affairs, although Smith did argue that it should regulate child labor and protect the health of workers from exploitation.

A complete understanding of capitalism would require a detailed study of the final days of the feudal period and the manner in which the Crusades (1095–1295) stimulated trade. The Age of Exploration with its discoveries gave a further push to the development of trade. The unearthing of precious metal propelled European economic activity. Mercantilism or a trade-centered economic system emerged. This system contributed, however, a key figure to the growth of capitalism—the entrepreneur, the person who took risks in expectation of future gain.

Other factors involved in the development of capitalism were the forces of the Renaissance and the Reformation, both of which changed society in ways that still are unfolding. The emergence of the modern nation-state, for example, was a major contribution of these movements. The nation-state provided the environment that led to capitalism: essential peace, and consequent law and order. As the sociologist Max Weber (1864–1920) noted, capitalism requires growth based on the accumulation of an economic surplus by private entrepreneurs who then put the surplus back into the economy, thus enabling further expansion. Weber argued that Calvinism, with its stress on strict accounting and ascetic living, fostered the conditions that allowed capitalism to flourish. Weber challenged the Marxist theory of economic determinism through seeking to establish that historical causation was multidimensional. Although one cannot deny economic factors, more than economic factors are involved in any movement, including capitalism. In *The Protestant Ethic and the Spirit of Capitalism* (1904–1905), Weber argued that ethical and religious ideas greatly influenced the development of capitalism. In his *The Religions of the East* series (1920–1921), he put forward the hypothesis that Eastern world views, manifested in its major religions and philosophical ideas, prevented the development of capitalism in these societies, even though favorable economic factors were present.

The surfacing of the Physiocrats in France further advanced the development of capitalist ideology. The Physiocrats were part of the development of Enlightenment thought in eighteenth-century France. Physiocrats held that there existed a natural order in economics, one best served by state noninterference. Indeed, as the economist François Quesnay noted in his *Tableau économique* (*Economic Scene*) (1758), the less interference, the better for the good of the economy. He argued that the flow of money through the economy is both circular and self-sustaining. This flow rests on society's three main classes: the productive class of those engaged in agriculture, fishing, and mining, representing one-half of the population; the proprietary class of landed proprietors and their dependents, about one-quarter of the population; and the artisan, or sterile, class. In sum Quesnay argued that only the agricultural class could produce a surplus. Agriculture alone could produce new wealth; manufacturing could not. Thus, for the Physiocrat and those whom they influenced, such as Thomas Jefferson, a nation's wealth would rest on the farming class, and new taxes would come from them. An interesting aspect of this argument is its contention that mercantilism is a fruitless tenet because it seeks to produce a sterile endeavor, one that cannot produce new wealth but only works on transforming that which farmers produce.

Smith agreed with the Physiocrats that there was a "natural economic order." The search for natural laws was part of the entire Enlightenment movement. However, Smith did not agree with the Physiocrats in regarding industry as unproductive. Smith noted that the division of labor and the expansion of markets offered a means for almost unlimited production of new wealth. He did agree that the role of government should be kept limited. Smith's cogent arguments led to the explosion of an industrialized economy and the materialization of modern capitalism.

With the coming of the Industrial Revolution, capitalism became the predominant economic philosophy in Western Europe, especially in England. The Industrial Revolution, conveniently dated at 1750, witnessed the substitution of mechanical power for human and animal power in the production of goods and services. This substitution of power led to a number of social changes.

First, the specialization of production led to the development of factories. In turn, the development of factories led to the rise of a working class. Small shops with their artisan owners were no longer at the center of production. The new economy pushed them to the margins of economic life. Members of the working class had nothing to exchange but their labor; no longer did they own tools or much, if any, property. Goods, however, became abundant and cheap for those who could afford them. In general, the overall standard of living rose.

Workers, however, often found that their living conditions were appalling. The novels of Charles Dickens, especially *Hard Times*, present a clear indictment of the system, as did the novels of English prime minister Benjamin Disraeli. Child labor, long hours, low pay, dangerous workplaces, pathetic housing, unhealthy environments, and economic exploitation were too often the normal conditions of workers.

Karl Marx was appalled by the abuses of capitalism and he produced two major critiques of the system, *Das Kapital* (1867–1894) and *The Communist Manifesto* (1848). Marx attacked capitalism's very foundations, private ownership of the means of production. Marx held that land and capital belong to society and that society has an obligation to distribute the goods of production according to need.

The United States had become the dominant industrial nation by the end of the nineteenth century. The Civil War (1861–1865) propelled the United States into an era of economic expansion and development. The government saw fit to protect the development of the modern corporation, granting it the status of a "legal person," further aiding its limited liability and tremendous financial power. Industry responded by developing various forms of monopolistic control, which struck at the fundamental principles of capitalism just as surely as Marx's critique did.

The federal government sought to turn the tide through various antitrust legislations. However, although monopoly and its pursuit are illegal, there has been no return to the free and open competition that Adam Smith espoused. At best, such legislation had the function of limiting the monopolistic tendencies of modern corporations. Capitalism did demonstrate its ability to create unprecedented wealth for Americans in general.

The Sherman Anti-Trust Act (1890) was the first antitrust law in the United States. It declared all combination in restraint of trade illegal. The act, however, was not used for its stated purpose for over ten years; when it was first used it was against organized labor. The railroad union that struck against the railroad was declared by the Supreme Court in 1895 to be acting in restraint of trade and contrary to the Sherman Anti-Trust Law.

More than ten years passed before the Sherman Act was used to break up any industrial monopoly. People who believed that the law would restrain trade were greatly disappointed. However, supporters of the bill did send a clear signal that many Americans were eager to use the federal government to halt the spread of monopolies and to open up trade to fair practices. It was a platform on which an eager young president, such as Theodore Roosevelt, could build.

Roosevelt became president in 1901 following the death of William McKinley and at the height of the Progressive movement, which, among other things, sought to control the erosion of what it considered the American way of life. Small businesses were being threatened by the growth of monopolies, which also threatened the power of the consumer.

At the age of forty-two, Roosevelt became the youngest president of the United States and also one of the few who had any sympathy for, or knowledge of, modern urban problems. He had been police commissioner of New York City and governor of New York State before becoming vice president. Roosevelt used the "bully pulpit" of the presidency to fight the trusts and to stir up public opinion to get a reluctant conservative Congress to enact legislation against these industrial combinations in restraint of trade. Although it was difficult to get new legislation from the reactionary Congress he had inherited, Roosevelt could turn to old legislation, the Sherman Anti-Trust Act, which had lain quiet because presidents Grover Cleveland and McKinley refused to enforce it. Additionally, an equally conservative Supreme Court had ruled in 1895 that the law did not apply to manufacturing combinations.

Roosevelt used the law to begin a blitz on trusts. He moved first against the northwestern railroad monopoly in 1902. Then he took on the Beef Trust, oil, tobacco, and other monopolies. Roosevelt's superb use of public relations aided in getting the Supreme Court's backing in every case. Eventually, the Supreme Court, in the oil and tobacco decisions of 1911, reversed its 1895 decision.

In 1903 Roosevelt persuaded a reluctant Congress to establish a Bureau of Corporations. This bureau had great power to investigate business, and its reports helped win decisions against business trusts. Furthermore, Roosevelt intervened on behalf of labor in a strike against mine owners and moved the passage of the Hepburn Act of 1906 to regulate the railroads through Congress. Also in 1906 he was instrumental in moving Congress to pass a Meat Inspection Act and a Pure Food and Drug Act. Upton Sinclair's famous novel *The Jungle* (1906) greatly aided his efforts. Moreover, Roosevelt was a staunch supporter of conservation, and he protected vast areas from economic exploitation.

Woodrow Wilson won the election of 1912, an election marked by a split in the Republican Party. Roosevelt, who had declined to run for president in 1908 when his party wanted him, decided to run for president in 1912 against his hand-picked replacement, William Howard Taft. Roosevelt believed that Taft had betrayed the principles of progressivism. Roosevelt and Taft split the Republican vote, enabling Wilson to be elected president.

Wilson agreed with Roosevelt that the president should lead public opinion, and he also agreed with Roosevelt's progressive principles. He moved such reform measures as the Underwood Tariff Act of 1913, the Federal Reserve Act of 1913 (giving him a flexible currency), and the Federal Trade Commission Act of 1914. The act created the Federal Trade Commission (FTC), and it gave it sweeping authority to prevent business practices that led to monopoly.

The twentieth century brought various other attacks on capitalism. Wars, revolutions, and depressions led people to question its very principles. Russia and China established governments that were in theory based on Marx's ideas. Germany under the Nazis presumably mixed capitalism and socialism in their noxious economic system. Newly independent nations also turned to various mixes of socialism and capitalism or to socialism alone for solutions to their economic problems. However, the end of the cold war left China alone as a major power espousing communism. Other countries turned to a mixture of socialism and capitalism.

These mixed economies in western countries tended to be a reaction to the Great Depression of the 1930s. President Franklin Roosevelt (1933–1945) eloquently stated that one-fourth of the nation went to bed ill clothed, ill housed, and ill fed. Rather than turning to communism, Roosevelt's New Deal sought to attack the worst abuses of capitalism, by, for example, restructuring the financial system and stopping speculative excesses in the stock market. The New Deal also sought to encourage collective bargaining to set up countervailing power against industrial corporations. The welfare state was an attempt to provide a safety net against economic fluctuations. Thus, social security and unemployment insurance, as well as compensation and safety measures, became commonplace.

Many of Roosevelt's actions stemmed from the work of the British economist John Maynard Keynes. His work *General Theory of Employment, Interest and Money* (1936) argues that government—through its power to spend money, to tax, and to control the supply of money—can influence the cycle of "boom and bust." Thus, the appropriate role of government in a depression is to increase spending; in an inflationary period, the government should hold back from spending.

Postwar prosperity aided the spread of capitalism, Keynesian and otherwise, until the late 1960s when both inflation and unemployment rose dramatically. Keynesian solutions no longer worked, basically because of critical failures in supply and shortages in petroleum. Additionally, new social demands put pressure on the economy. Thus, environmentalists, those in favor of ending discrimination against women and other minorities, those lobbying for ending the production of unsafe and hazardous products, and those working to upgrade the workplace put additional costs into the system. Simultaneously, the United States government increased its welfare expenditures as well as its military costs.

However, draconian application of Keynes's ideas, without acknowledgment, led to a deep recession in the early 1980s. Restricting the money supply and reducing spending ended the inflation, but unemployment increased greatly. The United States restricted its use of energy resources, causing energy prices to drop in a demonstration of Adam Smith's notions and the efficacy of President Jimmy Carter's unpopular measures to restrict energy consumption. Late 1980s stock market crashes sent the economy into tailspins that led to the election of President Bill Clinton, who benefited from a strong economy, brought about through good fortune and a judicious use of Keynesian principles.

[See also MERCANTILISM; WALL STREET; GOSPEL OF WEALTH.*]*

BIBLIOGRAPHY

Allen, Larry, *The ABC-CLIO World History Companion to Capitalism* (ABC-CLIO 1998).

Freeman, John R., *Democracy and Markets: The Politics of Mixed Economies* (Cornell Univ. Press 1989).

Galbraith, John Kenneth, *American Capitalism: The Concept of Countervailing Power* (Transaction Pubs. 1993).

Klausen, Jytte, *War and Welfare: Europe and the United States, 1945 to the Present* (St. Martin's 1998).

Kulikoff, Allan, *The Agrarian Origins of American Capitalism* (Univ. Press of Va. 1992).

Marx, Karl, *Capital: A Critique of Political Economy,* tr. by Ben Fowkes (1934; Penguin 1990).

McNally, David, *Against the Market: Political Economy, Market Socialism and the Marxist Critique* (Verso 1993).

Sklar, Martin, *The United States as a Developing Country: Studies in U.S. History in the Progressive Era and the 1920s* (Cambridge 1992).

Weber, Max, *The Protestant Ethic and the Spirit of Capitalism,* tr. by Talcott Parsons (Routledge 1992).

FRANK A. SALAMONE

CARNEGIE, ANDREW

The major problem with evaluating Andrew Carnegie, the richest man in the world before John D. Rockefeller took the title around 1910, is that what he said, wrote, and did was frequently contradictory. Carnegie, who was born on November 25, 1835, in Dunfermline, Scotland, and died on August 11, 1919, in Lenox, Massachusetts, advised emperors and presidents about how to manage their countries, but he used spies to ferret out labor organizers in his own factories, and in 1892 he approved Pinkerton strikebreakers to crush a union in his Homestead, Pennsylvania, plant. An avowed social Darwinist, Carnegie considered Anglo-Americans a superior race, but as an anti-imperialist he bitterly opposed American occupation of the Philippines. The press lauded Carnegie, the philanthropist, for donating 311 million dollars—some ninety percent of his fortune—to finance libraries, provide pensions for teachers, give awards for heroism, and for other estimable works. But he never helped the poor directly, and, without compunction, he sold steel to arms manufacturers. Nonetheless, as a pacifist he considered his Peace Palace at The Hague

THE GRANGER COLLECTION

Andrew Carnegie as he looked in 1905.

to be "the most holy building in the world because it has the holiest end in view." Then there was the Carnegie who had little formal education and helped create the modern corporation and modern philanthropy.

Biographers suggest that Carnegie's ambiguities stem from the grim realities of his early years. Steam-powered looms had driven his father, William, a weaver, from Dunfermline to Pittsburgh and to appalling daily grinds in factories for himself and his eldest son, Andrew. William remained a political radical to the end of his life, but Andrew idolized industrialization and the men who managed it.

Carnegie's ambitious mother, with whom he lived until her death (he was fifty-one), fueled his insatiable need for success, which began early. He took a job delivering telegraphs and then maneuvered himself into the positions of personal assistant and telegrapher for Thomas Scott, a Pennsylvania Railroad executive. Every dollar he could save was invested, but frugality did not make him rich. Nor did buying low and selling high. Coupled with extraordinary intelligence and superb natural gifts as a salesman, it was Carnegie's enormous talent to recruit as aides men who knew more than he did about industrial processes that enriched him.

Additionally, there was his use of the Bessemer process for making steel, his ruthless cutting of labor costs, his reductions in the price of steel, and his understanding of an economic trend that Rockefeller also noticed.

During the Civil War, monopolies had received the federal government's active endorsement because they made possible efficient mass production and thus the Union's victory. After the war the federal government saw monopolies as vital to the national economy. Robber barons who established trusts discovered that they could manipulate government at will and frequently did so.

Adept at irresistible flattery, Carnegie named his first steel plant not for himself but for John Edgar Thomson, president of the Pennsylvania Railroad. This not only implied a close connection to a key figure in American industry but also endeared him to a company that bought his products in volume and was crucial in transporting them to customers throughout the nation.

In 1901 Carnegie Steel was sold to a syndicate headed by J. P. Morgan, in the largest business transaction thus far in world history. Carnegie's price was 303,450,000 dollars in five percent bonds and stock with a market value of some 144 million dollars. The stock had been liberally salted, and Carnegie took most of the bonds together with a mortgage on United States Steel, Morgan's trust replacing Carnegie Steel. This detail very nearly put Carnegie back in possession of the great waterlogged monstrosity when it began to seriously leak a few years later.

As matters stood, however, the deal enabled Carnegie to turn his full attention to philanthropy. Not until he was firmly established as a capitalist was Carnegie much of a giver; his initial ventures in the field were not major donations but two essays published in the *North American Review,* "Wealth" (June 1889) and "The Best Fields for Philanthropy" (December 1889). In both he emphasizes the extent to which charitable funds are "unwisely spent." And, in the second, he offers the salient observation that unless capitalists use their wealth to ease the anger and resentment of growing numbers of the poor, the result might be socialist or communist upheavals.

"Wealth" was reprinted in dozens of periodicals and brought Carnegie immediate and lasting fame as a philosopher. Some historians believe it is arguably the Gilded Age's most cogent defense of laissez-faire economics and philanthropy in an industrialized state.

[*See also* GOSPEL OF WEALTH.]

BIBLIOGRAPHY

Wall, Joseph F., *Andrew Carnegie* (Oxford 1970).
Wall, Joseph F., ed., *The Andrew Carnegie Reader* (Univ. of Pittsburgh Press 1992).
Wheeler, George, *Pierpont Morgan and Friends: The Anatomy of a Myth* (Prentice-Hall 1973).

MILTON GOLDIN

CARNIVALS AND FAIRS

Mardi Gras and other carnivals are celebrations that turn the world upside down, inverting systems of everyday life. In general, those who are on the bottom rungs of society prevail for the period of the carnival. In conformity with what anthropologists describe as rituals of reversal, private spaces become public and areas of commerce become zones of festivity.

Mardi Gras in New Orleans, Louisiana, and Carnaval in Rio de Janeiro, Brazil, are related to the Saturnalia feast of Rome and various Celtic rites, representing the merging of pagan rituals with Roman Catholic feasts. The addition of African elements found in New Orleans, Rio, Trinidad, Angola, and areas of Alabama developed into the carnival as it is known today.

During these festivities a spirit of good fellowship and general unity prevails. Music, which tends to be loud and omnipresent, and dance play a great role in achieving and promoting this feeling. Alcohol and other mind-altering drugs are readily available and add to the general feeling of "flow."

The use of the body is significant: it is a resource available to all, rich and poor. Nudity and near-nudity are common during carnival. Fantastic cos-

© JIM PICKERELL/FOLIO

An elaborate float in the Mardi Gras parade along St. Charles Street in New Orleans.

tumes are worn as well, exaggerating physical features: African Americans in New Orleans, for example, imitate whites who imitate them. Men dress as women and women as men. These all add to the rituals of reversal that are part of Mardi Gras and carnivals in general.

In Louisiana there are at least two versions of Mardi Gras, or Fat Tuesday (the Tuesday before Ash Wednesday, marking the start of the Lenten season; hence the term *carnival* literally means good-

bye to meat). The rural Cajuns, descendants of French settlers from Canada, celebrate a version of Mardi Gras linked to ancient spring fertility rituals and rites of passage. The sexual symbols that pervade New Orleans Mardi Gras are there, including mock abductions, seduction, and ceremonial whips. The Cajuns trace their festivities more directly to a medieval European rite called *fête de la quémande* ("feast of the open hand"), a begging ritual somewhat adapted to frontier conditions. Cajuns donned grotesque costumes and proceeded from place to place, performing for audiences. Ritual begging came into play when the performers asked for contributions for the communal gumbo that was shared later with everyone present.

In the United States the familiar carnival is more closely related to the fair. Consisting of rides, games of skill and chance, and various sideshows, fairs tend to be traveling carnivals, following the pattern of state and county fairs, or presenting their own shows along set routes. Perhaps the classic noir movie based on the novel of the same title, *Nightmare Alley,* best captures the flavor of the traveling carnival with all its tricks and characters. Many other books and movies have been written about carnivals and fairs, some simply using the words *carnival* or *fair* in the title to conjure images of fun, such as James Thurber's *Thurber Carnival* or Kurt Vonnegut's *The Funhouse Carnival.*

Big exhibitions, or world's fairs, are not true fairs, although they incorporate many of the same elements. These increasingly spectacular fairs are used to introduce and display new advances in various industries or to promote national products in an international context.

In the United States the most common type of fair is the county or state agricultural fair, immortalized in numerous movies and plays. Elkanah Watson, a businessman from Albany, New York, organized the first rural fair in Pittsfield, Massachusetts, in 1811, later known as the Berkshire County Fair. In 1819, under Watson's influence, the New York State legislature appropriated ten thousand dollars per year for six years to aid the New York State Fair. The money was set aside for prizes given for agricultural and homemade products, thus establishing the precedent for awarding prizes for, say, best preserves and pies.

Other states followed suit and the state fair became an American institution. Many fairs received government subsidies. County fairs became tremendously popular as well: farmers displayed their livestock and produce; home products and new farm equipment also were on display. The typical two-week fair enabled otherwise isolated farmers not only to socialize but also to keep up on new advances in agriculture and related technology. The Iowa State Fair and the Danbury (Connecticut) Fair became nationally famous.

[See also DISNEYLAND; POPULAR CULTURE; PARADES; CIRCUSES; CONEY ISLAND; MAGIC AND MAGICIANS; TATTOO PARLORS; WORLD'S FAIRS AND EXPOSITIONS.*]*

BIBLIOGRAPHY

Da Matta, Roberto, "Carnival in Multiple Places," in *Rite, Drama, Festival, Spectacle: Rehearsals Toward a Theory of Cultural Performance,* ed. by John J. MacAloon (Inst. for the Study of Human Issues 1984).

Gresham, William Lindsey, *Nightmare Alley* (Rinehart 1946).

Perl, Lila, *America Goes to the Fair: All About State and County Fairs in the United States* (Morrow 1974).

FRANK A. SALAMONE

CATALOGS, MAIL-ORDER

Benjamin Franklin printed America's first catalog to sell academic books, and E. C. Allen ran the first exclusively mail-order business by offering washing powder recipes. But the mail-order catalog truly premiered with Chicago's Montgomery Ward, who created a one-page price list in 1872 to offer goods to farmers at cheaper rates than they could get in their local town stores. Beginning in 1886 Richard Sears sold watches by mail, also from Chicago. Other early mail-order entrepreneurs included the Spiegel, May, Stern Company; Larkin Company; and National Cloak and Suit Company.

Threatened by competition that could put them out of business, small-town shopkeepers raged against the "Chicago millionaires" and held community bonfires to burn catalogs. They harassed mail-order customers and spread rumors that Sears was "a Negro." But the advent of rural free delivery in 1896 and parcel post in 1913 improved the position of mail-order merchants, as did their policy of offering credit.

Catalogs changed greatly over the years. In size, they grew to thousands of pages. In design, pages initially crammed with drawings and customer testimonials yielded to the use of more white space.

Art illustrations evolved into halftones, then to black-and-white and color photographs, and indexes were added. Taboos changed as society did. Pictures of men and women smoking and drinking, and disparaging references to African American models, disappeared. Catalog pages began to feature women in underwear and bikinis. Social upheaval is noticeable as well; prices of goods rose in 1920 because of post–World War I inflation, while electrical appliances disappeared in 1942, the result of World War II shortages. Government laws in 1906 and 1927 chased away patent medicines. The increasing specialization of American mail-order retailing can be seen in the phasing out of merchandise such as handguns, automobiles, prefabricated homes, and groceries, replaced by sewing machines and indoor toilets. Catalogs reflected constant changes in fashions and hairstyles; Walt Disney kept a large collection of Sears catalogs to use as references for period movie costumes.

Mail-order catalogs inspired folklore. Stories spread about Richard Sears's scrupulous honesty, even ranking him next to God. The Sears, Roebuck catalogs themselves were called "the Farmer's Bible" and "the Great American Wish Book," and they were the books most requested by hospitalized soldiers during World War I. Mail-order catalogs even inspired George Milburn's novel of small-town life, *All Over Town* (1936), later reprinted as *Catalog.*

Catalogs, with their set prices for merchandise, are credited with helping to end the bargaining system, establishing the policy of "satisfaction guaranteed or your money back," advancing advertising techniques, and setting standards for clothing sizes and even for language.

By 1995 over one-third of adults had made at least one mail-order purchase a year, with catalog sales accounting for eighteen percent of all retail sales in the United States, adding up to over thirty-eight billion dollars that year. Mail order continues to change with technology, as the Internet becomes an increasingly popular method for shopping. In addition, there are also catalogs targeted to specific racial, ethnic, gender, and income groups, and a new hybrid, called the magalog, combines a catalog and magazine. Though they exist to sell merchandise, catalogs document a changing America.

[*See also* CONSUMERISM; ADVERTISING.]

BIBLIOGRAPHY

Asher, Louis E., and Edith Heal, *Send No Money* (Argus 1942).

Cohn, David L., *The Good Old Days: A History of American Morals and Manners as Seen through the Sears, Roebuck Catalogs 1905 to the Present,* ed. by Sally Zohn (1940; Simon & Schuster 1976).

Emmet, Boris, and John E. Jeuck, *Catalogues and Counters: A History of Sears, Roebuck and Company* (Univ. of Chicago Press 1950).

Latham, Frank B., *1872–1972: A Century of Serving Consumers: The Story of Montgomery Ward,* 2d ed. (Montgomery Ward 1972).

Schroeder, Fred E. H., "Semi-Annual Installment on the American Dream: The Wish Book as Popular Icon," in *Icons of Popular Culture,* ed. by Marshall Fishwick and Ray B. Browne (Bowling Green Univ. Press 1970).

EVELYN BECK

CELEBRATIONS AND HOLIDAYS

Because of its cultural and geographical diversity, the United States has become a festive nation in which holidays and celebrations are important for defining national, regional, group, and personal identities. Nearly every day of the year a holiday is observed and a celebration is in progress somewhere in the country. Some days are legal holidays established by federal and state governments; others are celebrated by religious, ethnic, or social groups; many are birthdays and other rituals of the life cycle that are observed only by individuals and their families. Patriotism, piety, and personality define the various holidays and celebrations of the calendar year.

Holidays are days fixed by law or custom to commemorate some event or person and on which ordinary business is usually suspended. Celebrations often are performances on holidays and other occasions that express the participants' attitudes

© WILLIAM STRODE

The annual Dogwood Trail Celebration is held every April in Paducah, Kentucky.

about the events and their meanings. According to public opinion polls, fifty-five percent of all Americans say they attend religious services regularly, confirming George R. Stewart's observation that: "The most important American holiday is Sunday. In fact, it might be said to be fifty-two times as important as any other holiday." There are only ten annual national holidays in the United States for which employees of the federal government and most other workers receive pay, far fewer than the number of paid holidays in England, France, Germany, or Japan. Typically, Americans have many holidays and celebrations to choose from, but little time to enjoy them.

Major Holidays. The first day of January became New Year's Day with the calendar reforms of the sixteenth century, although the date has no relation to solar, lunar, or seasonal cycles. English Protestant colonists in North America opposed celebration on this day because of its pagan associations. By the time of the Revolution, however, most Americans followed traditional European customs and spent the day visiting, dining, and distributing money and food to roving gangs of drunk and disorderly young men.

As the importance of Christmas grew, New Year's Day declined, although it is one of the ten national legal holidays. New Year's Day often serves as a day of recovery from New Year's Eve parties at which some celebrants overindulge in alcohol while they count the minutes to midnight and the beginning of the new year. Many Americans spend New Year's Day watching televised parades that precede college football games named for various festivals, such as the Rose Bowl, the Cotton Bowl, the Sugar Bowl, and the Orange Bowl. Some Americans eat special foods on New Year's Day, for example, black-eyed peas, which are associated with prosperity in the coming year; others write lists of resolutions for the new year in an attempt to improve their behavior.

Since 1863, when President Lincoln issued his final Emancipation Proclamation, some African Americans have observed January 1 as Emancipation Day, celebrating with parades, speeches, and prayer. The creation in 1983 of a legal holiday on or near January 15 to honor assassinated civil rights leader Martin Luther King, Jr., has diverted attention from the January 1 emancipation celebration. Juneteenth, on June 19, is celebrated as emancipation day in Oklahoma and Texas because it was the day on which slaves received the news that they were free.

An unofficial day of celebration that some might argue dominates other January events is the Super Bowl, a professional football championship that typically attracts the largest television audience of the year. Held on the fourth Sunday of January since 1967, it is heavily promoted by commercial spon-

281

sors who hope to sell their products to viewers. Considering the billions of dollars spent on related tickets, merchandise, and gambling, the Super Bowl and other professional sporting events are significant in the annual cycle of American festivals.

The celebration of Mardi Gras in New Orleans, Louisiana, overshadows all other Shrove Tuesday festivals. Followed by Ash Wednesday, Mardi Gras occurs in February or March and begins a forty-day period of fasting, observed by many Christians, before Easter Sunday. Since the 1850s, social clubs known as krewes, have sponsored parades and dances featuring elaborately costumed and masked participants. Thousands of tourists crowd the city in what has become an annual pilgrimage for some.

St. Valentine's Day, celebrated on February 14, is, like New Year's, St. Patrick's Day, Easter, Halloween, and Christmas, a European festival that has been Americanized. A growing middle class in the 1840s launched a fad for sending cards, flowers, and candy as expressions of love and friendship. By the 1850s the custom was so commercialized that some began to mock it by sending comic and risqué valentines, which remain popular. The exchange of valentines was expanded by schoolteachers who encouraged children to make them as class projects and by the aggressive marketing of the greeting card industry. February 14 is also the birthday of the abolitionist Frederick Douglass and it marks the beginning of Black History Week, observed in most American public schools.

The focus on history and race relations during February is rooted in two holidays, the birthdays of Presidents Abraham Lincoln (February 12) and George Washington (February 22), celebrated separately until 1971 when they were combined into Presidents' Day (called Washington's Birthday in some states and Washington-Lincoln Day in others), a national holiday observed on the third Monday in February. Although some communities still mark the observance with patriotic speeches by public officials, most Americans associate the day with department-store sales.

Easter and Passover, Christian and Jewish religious holidays respectively, occur between the be-

© ROGER RESSMEYER/CORBIS

A Jewish American family at a Passover seder.

ginning of March and the end of April. Easter celebrates the resurrection of Jesus Christ after his crucifixion and death; Passover commemorates the exodus of Jews from Egypt under the leadership of Moses. Easter Sunday remains a holy day for Christians, but since the 1840s it has been increasingly secularized into a spring festival with an emphasis on floral decorations, parades of people in new clothing, and the decorating of eggs. Children are told that Easter eggs are hidden by the Easter Bunny and elaborate hunts for the eggs are organized by parents, churches, and even the staff of the White House. Passover has been less commercialized; instead focus is on the seder, a ceremonial meal that marks the beginning of the holiday and is an occasion for American Jewish families and friends to gather.

Two other days celebrated in April reflect interesting aspects of American culture. April Fool's Day, April 1, is an ancient and global custom involving the playing of pranks on the unwary. This custom is more common among children, although many adults who enjoy practical jokes take advantage of the occasion. College newspapers often use the day as an excuse to lampoon professors and administrators. April 22, Earth Day, has replaced Arbor Day, a holiday that originated in Nebraska in 1872 to encourage the planting of trees for future forests. As the environmental movement expanded its concerns from parks and forests to air and water pollution, endangered species, and global warming, Congress responded by passing new environmental legislation in 1970, which was celebrated by the creation of Earth Day. This day became the occasion for lectures, fairs, community litter clean-ups, and rallies calling attention to the importance of the environment.

May Day, celebrated on May 1, has a long history of conflicting celebrations. Observed in most of the world as a workers' festival, it remains a folk festival celebrating the beginning of summer. In the United States May Day receives little attention, eclipsed by the Kentucky Derby horse race held on the first Sunday in May. The Kentucky Derby has become a national event, drawing tourists and media attention to Louisville from all over the world. A ten-day Derby festival includes public and private parties, popular music concerts, the election of a queen, and parades. For a nation that claims to be a democracy and advocates equality, the Kentucky Derby, which flaunts wealth and social class, is an anomaly, and, like Halloween, an inversion of the normal standards.

Mother's Day, the second Sunday in May, is the invention of Anna Reeves Jarvis of West Virginia. Proclaimed a holiday by President Woodrow Wilson in 1914, it was originally intended to honor the mothers of men who had fought against one another in the Civil War. Florists, the greeting card industry, and long-distance telephone companies seized the opportunity to sell their products and services, however, and Mrs. Jarvis's desire for simple observance was forgotten. At almost the same time a movement for Father's Day was begun, but the idea took much longer to gain support. In the 1920s the toy industry tried to promote the third Sunday in June as Children's Day, but it lost that date to Father's Day, which is now celebrated by some families with cards and presents.

Memorial Day, officially May 30 but celebrated on the nearest Monday, was created at the end of the Civil War to honor those who had died in the war. Some Southern states celebrate on other days, but Memorial Day has grown in significance with each succeeding war. Memorial Day ritual includes the laying of a wreath on the Tomb of the Unknown Soldier (Tomb of the Unknowns since 1958) in Arlington National Cemetery, but there are parades and religious services in almost every American community. Since 1920 the Indianapolis 500 automobile race has become the event most Americans associate with Memorial Day. Like the Kentucky Derby, the race is a ritual that many Americans try to watch either in person or on television. The three-day weekend also marks the unofficial beginning of summer.

Independence Day, July 4, has, since the end of the Revolutionary War, been the premier national holiday. Celebrated for over two hundred years with patriotic speeches, parades, picnics, and pyrotechnics, the day is especially important in presidential election years since the Republican and Democratic Party conventions are held a few weeks later. Groups who feel they have been denied the rights promised in the Declaration of Independence and the Constitution often use the day to protest. In the western states, the Fourth of July is celebrated with rodeos and Native American powwows.

Labor Day, the first Monday in September, was created by union workers in New York City in 1882 to display class solidarity. In 1894 it was made a legal holiday by an act of Congress, a remarkable achievement considering the antilabor attitudes of many politicians. Traditionally celebrated with speeches, parades, and picnics, it marks back-to-school time and the end of summer. With the continuing decline of organized labor, the day has lost some of its distinctive rituals.

Columbus Day, October 12 but celebrated on the second Monday of the month, commemorates the European arrival in the Americas. It was not until the early twentieth century, however, that the day was recognized by federal and state governments as a holiday. Italian Americans were especially active in promoting a day to honor Genoa-born explorer Christopher Columbus, and the creation of this holiday was a tribute to their political strength.

The increase in immigrants from Latin America since the 1960s has resulted in the renaming of Columbus Day to *Día de la Raza* ("Day of the Race") in some parts of the country, and the day is now an occasion to celebrate *mestizos* (people of European and Native American ancestry).

Halloween, October 31, is a relic of pagan harvest festivals celebrated on the eve of All Saints' Day, a Christian holy day, but it has been transformed significantly in the United States since World War II. Halloween is a festival that focuses on symbolic images of death such as skulls, skeletons, and ghosts. Despite episodes of nighttime vandalism, most Americans regard Halloween as a time for youngsters to masquerade as cowboys, princesses, and pirates and walk from door to door in their neighborhoods asking for candy. This "trick-or-treat" ritual reached a peak in the 1960s, but concern for the safety of children has led to stricter adult control. Although not an official holiday, Halloween has become one of the most celebrated days of the year, with elaborate costumes, parades for children and adults, and public and private parties. Since 1987 the gay and lesbian community of Greenwich Village in New York City has led the nation in transforming Halloween into a spectacular parody of American life, featuring an exuberant costume parade.

Election Day, the first Tuesday after the first Monday in November, is not now a national holiday. In the colonial era and early nineteenth century, election days were marked by special sermons, political debate, and feasting, even though only a small percentage of white males could vote. Political reforms, the expansion of the electorate, and the rise of the electronic media have changed the nature of election days, but they remain important, both symbolically and for their political consequences.

Veterans' Day was originally created as Armistice Day on November 11, 1921, the third anniversary of the end of World War I. Celebrated, like Memorial Day, with a wreath-laying at the Tomb of the Unknowns, Armistice Day became Veterans' Day in 1954 after veterans from World War II and the Korean War demanded recognition. Made a federal holiday in 1968, it has gained in importance since the opening of the Vietnam Veterans Memorial on the Mall in Washington, D.C., on Veterans' Day in 1982, which is now the site of an annual service.

Thanksgiving Day, celebrated on the fourth Thursday in November since 1941, commemorates the first Thanksgivings held by English colonists in the early 1600s and is an occasion to give thanks for good health, bountiful food, family, and friends in the preceding year. Schoolchildren are taught about the generosity of the Native people of New England toward the Pilgrims, and many families gather to eat turkey, cranberry sauce, pumpkin pie, and other foods considered typically American. Many Americans make Thanksgiving a four-day holiday, and it has become the busiest travel period in the year. Since it is also considered the beginning of the Christmas season, large department stores in New York and other cities sponsor parades featuring giant balloons representing toys and cartoon characters.

Christmas, December 25, is the traditional celebration of the birth of Christ. Ignored by Puritans, the celebration of Christmas began to take on distinctive American characteristics in 1823 with the publication of Clement Moore's "The Night Before Christmas," which helped to establish Santa Claus as a mythical character who brings gifts to children who have behaved through the year. The myth of Santa proved useful to children, parents, and manufacturers of holiday goods. "Santa" appears in advertisements for toys and soft drinks, on Christmas cards, and in person in department stores, shopping malls, and on street corners, often collecting money for charities.

The American Christmas combines traditional elements such as religious services, caroling, and feasting with innovations including gift certificates, card exchanges, and children's letters to Santa. The latter activities have been studied for what they reveal about class and gender differences. Some scholars argue that Christmas is a more unifying national holiday than Independence Day because most elements in American society can agree on values of generosity and family unity, while many dispute the meaning of the Constitution.

Hanukkah, a Jewish religious holiday in December, is celebrated over an eight-day period by lighting candles (one on the first day, two on the second day, and so on) and exchanging gifts. Kwanza, December 26 through January 1, was created in 1966 by Maulana Karenga, who wanted a celebration for African Americans that emphasized African traditions rather than American materialism. Kwanza is an example of attempts to renew African American family ties and group spirit through celebrations. In the 1990s a new profession, "ritual-makers," emerged to help people plan and find appropriate rituals and symbols for family reunions, birthdays, anniversaries, class reunions, and other life-cycle events. Other American celebrations include annual state and county fairs, holidays commemorating the admission of states to the union, and special religious and civic holidays for various ethnic groups.

Conclusions. Each holiday and celebration in the United States serves many functions and may convey different meanings to individual participants or observers. Every festival has traditions—some ancient—and each has innovations reflecting changing personnel, technology, and social context. Celebrations and holidays are important to American studies because they can be analyzed as microcosms of the larger culture. Celebrations create and maintain group or national identity, while offering playful commentary on the conditions of everyday life. Holidays and celebrations—complex and constantly evolving—reveal attitudes toward the social order, race, gender, and age.

[See also POPULAR CULTURE; RELIGION AND RELIGIOUS MOVEMENTS, and article on RELIGION AND POPULAR CULTURE; FOURTH OF JULY.]

BIBLIOGRAPHY

Barnett, James H., *The American Christmas: A Study in National Culture* (Macmillan 1954).

Cohen, Hennig, and Tristram Potter Coffin, eds., *The Folklore of American Holidays,* 2d ed. (Gale Res. 1991).

Gutièrrez, Ramón A., and Geneviève Fabre, eds., *Feasts and Celebrations in North American Ethnic Communities* (Univ. of N.Mex. Press 1995).

Hatch, Jane M., *The Book of Days,* 3d ed. (Wilson, H. W. 1978).

Lavenda, Robert H., *Corn Fests and Water Carnivals: Celebrating Community in Minnesota* (Smithsonian Inst. Press 1997).

Litwicki, Ellen, *America's Public Holidays 1865–1920* (Smithsonian Inst. Press 2000).

McCrossen, Alexis, *Holy Day, Holiday: The American Sunday* (Cornell Univ. Press 2000).

Santino, Jack, *All around the Year: Holidays and Celebrations in American Life* (Univ. of Ill. Press 1994).

Schmidt, Leigh Eric, *Consumer Rites: The Buying and Selling of American Holidays* (Princeton Univ. Press 1995).

BERNARD MERGEN

CELEBRITY

From the first appearance of "Americans" on the stage of European attention, America was the natural place, unalloyed and uncorrupted by history. The first images of America were the Native tribes, and the first icon the American Indian princess. By the eighteenth century the colonial settlers had absorbed this native newness for themselves, just as the princess was beginning to metamorphose into the goddess Liberty and later Uncle Sam. The American settler, according to Jean de Crèvecoeur in *Letters from an American Farmer* (1782), was the "new man," owing nothing of his nature to family, to wealth, or to the past in general. It was a phrase that both reached back to the Roman republic and looked forward to such latter-day inheritors of American singularity as the heroes of Horatio Alger and Henry James's Christopher Newman in *The American* (1877).

As dynasties collapsed or were threatened across late-eighteenth-century Europe, the first American celebrities were these "natural" men, whose visual presence symbolized the virtues of American freedom. Benjamin Franklin's face appeared on vases, fans, and other memorabilia, while he, along with Washington and Jefferson, were virtually deified on their deaths as embodiments of the democratic spirit. Unlike the crowned heads of Europe sitting

THE KOBAL COLLECTION

Screen star Marilyn Monroe, a popular icon of celebrity.

Davy Crockett who were celebrated in campaign biographies and dime novels, while on the creative side were engineers and inventors including Guglielmo Marconi, Thomas Edison, and Alexander Graham Bell. Already in the nineteenth century, the emblematic quality of American careers was a national preoccupation.

All the aspirants to fame on this new democratic platform relied on something of the inescapable element of performance to convey themselves and, secondarily, what they did to an ever-expanding audience. The invention of photography in the 1830s was immediately seized on as a vehicle particularly suited to extend the long shadow of the depiction of individuals. Already by the mid-1840s Mathew Brady had opened a Gallery of Illustrious Americans in New York City. Unlike the paintings and even the engravings by which visual fame had been broadcast in the past, these rapidly and easily reproducible images of the famous could be inexpensively acquired by virtually anyone who wished. They quickly became a crucial factor in political life. As Abraham Lincoln remarked, he owed his election as president to Brady's Cooper Union photograph, which disseminated the image of an otherwise little-known Illinois politician around the country.

With the advent of film, radio, television, and the whole array of later twentieth-century visual media, the ability to leverage an accomplishment or a mere image into a place in the public eye expanded exponentially. But even the prime exploiters of performance did not immediately understand the power of its allure. It was the pressure of audience fascination that in 1910 induced producer Carl Laemmle to reveal that the name of the otherwise anonymous Biograph Girl was Florence Lawrence, and with that revelation the Hollywood star system was born.

Separated from the past by the barrier of World War I, the 1920s mark what was effectively the first decade of twentieth-century fame. Famous people, those of actual achievement as well as the self-nominated and those anointed by newspapers (such as the Hearst syndicate), magazines (including *Van-*

on ancient thrones or the aristocrats in their ancestral estates, they were models of an individual and national identity that was self-made and self-created. When a painting of Franklin was exhibited in the Paris Salon of 1779, it was considered sufficient to title it simply *Vir,* the Latin for *man* and the root of *virtue.*

Celebrity for such figures mingled the patterns of ancient heroism with the unprecedented American individual in a paradox that reflected the country's own sense of itself as a newcomer to the stage of the world, as well a direct expression of values the monarchies of Europe had either long ago lost or never possessed. Whatever the specifics of their politics, publicity for them was publicity for their country.

For a nation without a native aristocracy or an established religion, celebrities in nineteenth-century America became a pantheon for all occasions. On the political side were politicians such as Andrew Jackson and frontiersmen Daniel Boone and

CULVER PICTURES

Financier J. P. Morgan and his wife.

ity Fair), and movies, became the common coin of the 1920s. Charles A. Lindbergh may have been called the Lone Eagle, the intrepid American hero challenging the elements themselves. But the media context in which Lindbergh flew to fame was the world of celebrity. Drawing on politics, show business, and gangland, this new-fashioned compost of the famous was called café society, to distinguish it from the budding but somewhat more reticent society of wealth that had occupied national attention during the Gilded Age. People had certainly heard of wealthy industrialist J. P. Morgan, Cornelius Vanderbilt, and Andrew Carnegie and had even seen photographs of them; however, it was the 1920s that first put into place the media apparatus that allowed the easy reproduction of such images, along with gossip columns to confirm the feeling that the activities of such public figures constituted a world unto itself and was an appropriate part of the news.

By the end of the twentieth century it seemed as if there could be no aspiration at all in American society that was not structured by the apparatus of media fame, and no fame that meant anything that was not immediate and visual: to say that someone was famous whose face was not recognizable seemed a contradiction in terms. In a

sense, it was the most elaborate fruit yet of the basic American belief in justification for being rather than for doing, the personal equivalent of the "city on the hill," populated only by God's Elect, in whose sight every sin must be confessed and every achievement witnessed, in what has now become an entirely secular benediction.

One result, especially inside the United States, has been the way tabloid magazines and television talk shows, along with the organs of "serious" media, have increasingly vied with each other to help erase the line between public and private. Once again, the motivation appears to be to induce or showcase confession and to make performance the key to character.

In an increasingly populous world, then, the images of famous individuals promulgated by the American media serve the purpose of organizing a complex and incessant array of information and misinformation into the more easily understandable category of biography, replete with scandal and structured by melodrama. It is an attitude toward human experience that is the by-product of American democracy and its theme of individual opportunity but sells even better to the rest of the world. Instead of the physical force necessary to establish the nineteenth-century empires, the modern empire of the celebrated uses methods more benevolent but also more insidious. As a character in Wim Wenders's 1976 film *Kings of the Road* puts it, "The Americans have colonized our unconscious."

[*See also* MEDIA; PUBLIC RELATIONS.]

BIBLIOGRAPHY

Banta, Martha, *Failure and Success in America: A Literary Debate* (Princeton Univ. Press 1978).

Boorstin, Daniel, *The Image: A Guide to Pseudo-Events in America* (1961; Atheneum Pubs. 1987).

Braudy, Leo, *The Frenzy of Renown: Fame and Its History* (Vintage 1997).

Cawelti, John, *Apostles of the Self-Made Man* (Univ. of Chicago Press 1965).

Gabler, Neal, *Life the Movie: How Entertainment Conquered Reality* (Knopf 1998).

Schickel, Richard, *His Picture in the Papers: A Speculation on Celebrity in America Based on the Life of Douglas Fairbanks, Sr.* (Charterhouse 1974).

LEO BRAUDY

CEMETERIES

The cemetery, a Greek word for "sleeping chamber," is a cultural institution reflecting shifting attitudes toward death and nature, changing social relationships, and evolving trends in art, literature, and culture. Early settlers in America had several types of burial places: family-farm graveyards, churchyards, and town or public burying grounds. Most were very small with little landscaping. Graves were either unmarked or marked by a wooden cross or a field stone, with a few carved gravestones of slate, sandstone, or other materials.

Carved gravestones graphically illustrate changing attitudes toward death as well as incidences of epidemics and shifts in marriage and family patterns. As documented by scholars, starting with Harriette Merrifield Forbes in 1927, the first decorated stones appeared in the 1650s and evolved through a series of motifs—death's heads, cherubs, and willow and urns—over the next 150 years.

In the growing cities of the nineteenth century, larger, naturalistic cemeteries supplemented these older styles. The small burial places had become crowded and surrounded by commerce, causing people to question the moral appropriateness of these conditions. Burial places such as the New Haven, Connecticut, Burying Ground (1796) and Père Lachaise in Paris (1804) were experiments in new styles of landscaping, organization, and site planning.

Mount Auburn Cemetery, founded in Cambridge, Massachusetts, in 1831, was the archetype of the new cemetery. This rural cemetery of over one hundred acres (41 ha) was designed along the lines of an English park. Family lots replaced communal or individual graves in a cemetery owned and managed by the lot-holders through a voluntary nonprofit association. Cemeteries in cities and towns from Georgia to Ohio, Virginia to Maine, imitated Mount Auburn.

These cemeteries were typically located in suburban settings and designed in a picturesque manner with serpentine roadways and an abundance of plantings. They were among the first publicly accessible naturalistic landscapes. They predated New York City's Central Park and other urban parks by a generation. Andrew Jackson Downing praised them as proof of the desirability of public parks. They were filled with Egyptian and classical-revival-style monuments as well as naturalistic stones shaped into tree stumps, animals, or flower bouquets. Noted American sculptors such as Horatio Greenough, Ball Hughes, Thomas Crawford, and Augustus Saint-Gaudens placed works of art in them. The combination of setting and art were so popular that the cemeteries became tourist destinations.

Urban parks in turn influenced cemetery design. Starting with European horticulturist Adolph Strauch's redesign of Spring Grove Cemetery in Cincinnati, Ohio, in the late 1850s, the rural cemetery was gradually transformed into the lawn-garden cemetery. These had fewer and wider streets with less dramatic curves. The landscape was opened up by thinning the shrubs for larger lawns and ornamental beds of flowers. Individual markers were lowered so the emphasis was on the family monument.

Cemeteries have always reflected America's diversity. In ethnic cemeteries, large individual gravestones were often crowded into small fields. In urban villages and rural townships, communities established burial places where they could memorialize their dead as they always had. For example, porcelain photographs of the deceased were attached to the gravestone. The grounds might be lavishly decorated, as in Puerto Rican cemeteries, or almost barren save for the grave markers, as in Jewish or some evangelical Christian sects. African burial customs, such as the West African custom of burying food with the dead, were adapted to American conditions. In the cemetery, traditional values brought to America withstood assimilation

Arlington National Cemetery in Virginia, founded in 1864.

© ROB BOUDREAU/STONE

pressures—sometimes for one generation, other times for many.

Cemeteries have also differed regionally. New Orleans cemeteries are almost entirely above-ground interments on sites barren of plantings. In some upland Southern cemeteries survivors carefully scrape bare the graves on a regular basis. In the Southwest, desert climates and the influence of Native American and Southern European cultures have produced burial places with little grass and many personal offerings.

However, in most places the earlier traditions of a person dying at home, the family preparing the body, the relatives overseeing the funeral, and the descendants ensuring that the grave was well kept have gradually been turned over to professionals. American attitudes toward death shifted from the sentimental embrace of the nineteenth-century cemetery to a more distant relationship. Americans are said to deny death, although, more accurately, they avoid it by leaving it to the professionals. Partly, death has become less of a daily presence as death rates have dropped.

Symbolic of this shift is the landscape and organization of Forest Lawn Memorial Park in Glendale, California. Starting in 1917 its managers renamed it a memorial park as a rejection of the

public's perception of the cemetery as a place of death, not renewal; sorrow, not joy; and dreariness, not grandeur. The sweeping lawns hide the burials, which are marked by flush-to-the-ground individual markers and institutional features, such as a copy of Michelangelo's *David* and a stained-glass version of *The Last Supper*. Forest Lawn was derided famously by Evelyn Waugh in *The Loved One* (1948) and attacked by Jessica Mitford in *The American Way of Death* (1963).

The American cemetery is buffeted by many challenges as the new century begins. While fewer than thirty percent of Americans choose cremation over burial interment or entombment, the rate has grown, particularly in the cities, since the first enclosed cremation occurred in 1876 in Lancaster, Pennsylvania. Many Americans no longer have a strong attachment to their family burial lots. Others have had few, if any, personal experiences with death, save for the "celebrity friends" they see in the media. Reformers continue to view the cemetery as a waste of resources and cemetery managers and owners as profiteers of death. Laser engraving of monuments has introduced a more informal style of memorialization, allowing more individuality but, in some people's view, diminishing the sacredness of the cemetery. Millions of Americans continue to rely on the cemetery as a place to mourn their loved ones, as a community repository of memories, and as a place of repose set aside from the hurried activities of daily life.

[*See also* POPULAR CULTURE.]

BIBLIOGRAPHY

Clark, Sandra Russell, *Elysium: A Gathering of Souls: New Orleans Cemeteries*, photographs by Sandra Clark with foreword by Andrei Codrescu (Louisana State Univ. Press 1997).

Jackson, Kenneth T., and Camilo José Vergara, *Silent Cities: The Evolution of the American Cemetery* (Princeton Architectural Press 1989).

Meyer, Richard E., ed., *Cemeteries and Gravemarkers: Voices of American Culture* (Utah State Univ. Press 1992).

Meyer, Richard E., ed., *Ethnicity and the American Cemetery* (Bowling Green State Univ. Pop. Press 1993).

Sloane, David C., *The Last Great Necessity: Cemeteries in American History* (Johns Hopkins Univ. Press 1991).

DAVID SLOANE

CENSORSHIP

In 1735 publisher John Peter Zenger was acquitted of libel for printing complaints about the New York governor in his newspaper. Zenger's victory affirmed the rights to freedom of the press and symbolized the independent voices that protested unfair British taxation and rule in the colonies. After the American Revolution, the U.S. Constitution's writers insured that freedom of speech, both oral and written, was protected by the First Amendment.

Despite this federal legislation many Americans have tried to censor through state courts those materials, statements, and actions they considered offensive. States passed laws to control ideas and information deemed deserving of censorship, such as when antebellum Southerners banned abolitionists' pamphlets. Lacking the systematic national censorship authority of other countries, America's censors freely targeted material and people they believed were indecent, permissive, or dangerous to civilization. They attempted to suppress art, literature, and intellectual and political works.

Numerous obscenity charges were filed during the nineteenth century, mostly regarding the mailing of birth-control devices and related literature and other material considered obscene according to prevailing morals. Early librarians believed that a library's sole purpose was for educational use and refused to purchase books they considered trivial and too sensational for impressionable readers. Books were confined to closed stacks, and patrons had to request permission or provide scholarly credentials to gain access. James M. Hubbard's successful efforts to censor books at the Boston Public Library in the 1880s resulted in the phrase "banned in Boston."

By the turn of the twentieth century, readers reacted to library censorship and demanded access to stacks. Librarians gradually switched from conservative viewpoints denouncing social realism to liberal condemnations of censorship. The American Library Association (ALA) shifted from promoting censorship (by publishing lists of acceptable books, including the Army Index of one hundred books forbidden to soldiers, for example) to advocating the 1939 Library Bill of Rights based on the policy of the Des Moines, Iowa, library. The ALA stated that readers should have the right to choose their reading material, that collections should offer comprehensive coverage of subjects, and that libraries should be open to all Americans regardless of their beliefs.

The legal definition of obscenity has fluctuated over time as judges consider cases. The Hicklin Rule based obscenity criteria on strict nineteenth-century moral standards. By 1913 Supreme Court Justice Learned Hand ruled in *United States* v. *Kennerly,* regarding a book sent through the mail, "to put thought in leash to the average conscience of the time is perhaps tolerable but to fetter it by the necessities of the lowest and least capable seems a fatal policy." In the 1920s the U.S. Supreme Court interpreted the Fourteenth Amendment's due-process clause to mean that states must respect individuals' First Amendment rights to speak freely publicly unless their words posed a threat.

Further legal defeats for censors included the 1934 case *United States* v. *One Book Entitled Ulysses,* in which the justices determined that James Joyce's novel was not obscene because the words that censors considered vulgar were critical to its literary quality and should not be taken out of context. Two years later in *United States* v. *Levine* the court reversed a federal district court's decision accusing the defendant of mailing three obscene books, citing the *Ulysses* standard that an entire book and not specific passages must be deemed obscene. By the 1970s the Supreme Court, in *Miller* v. *California,* clarified that the word *obscene* meant material judged by "contemporary community standards" to appeal primarily to people with a prurient interest in sex.

Wartime and military service have affected censorship. The Committee on Public Information monitored Americans during World War I. After the attack on Pearl Harbor, media cooperated with efforts to prevent revelations of troop locations, casualty statistics, and industrial production in newspapers and radio broadcasts. The Vietnam War, however, created different censorship concerns. Soldiers were court-martialed for criticizing American policies in the war and urging other soldiers to refuse to serve. Because they were noncivilians, soldiers were denied First Amendment rights and forbidden to protest and post any materials that discredited the military and threatened national security. The Supreme Court refused to hear individuals' appeals. The Supreme Court, though, did not stop Daniel Ellsberg from printing the Pentagon Papers, which reported on Vietnam policies, in American periodicals. The court also protected the right of protestors to desecrate the American flag as a form of symbolic speech.

The National Association of Broadcasters' code guides television stations reviewing the content of their programming, including commercials. Censorship of films began when the first newsreels were shown at Atlantic City nickelodeons in 1894. Since then state and local censors have protested movies they consider to be obscene. Most early challenges were successful because judges ruled that films were business ventures and not protected by the First Amendment. Censors stressed that movies should be distributed only if they had educational, entertainment, and ethical values. During the 1950s the Supreme Court reversed its previous decision and said that movies were a form of communication with First Amendment rights, and local censors were less influential in banning movies with realistic themes. In 1968 the movie industry implemented a rating system that assigns letters indicating the age-appropriateness of movies.

Other forms of American entertainment have dealt with censorship. The Federal Communications Commission threatens to strip licenses from radio and television stations that broadcast explicit programs. The music industry labels music recordings with cautions about potentially offensive lyrics. Groups such as the Moral Majority target literature and often succeed in having books removed from public and school libraries. Taxpayers protest

National Endowment for the Arts funding of projects they consider obscene. Two provisions of the Communications Decency Act of 1996, invalidated by the U.S. Supreme Court in *Reno* v. *American Civil Liberties Union* in 1997, attempted to prohibit the transmission and display of "indecent" or "offensive" material on the Internet. Universities have attempted to censor student publications and activities. The American Civil Liberties Union monitors such instances of actual or attempted censorship as these in the United States, defending the rights of individuals. American law stipulates that the only unprotected forms of expression consist of obscenity, child pornography, libel, slander, defamation, fraudulent commercials, and information that endangers public safety.

[*See also* ANTI-INTELLECTUALISM; BILL OF RIGHTS; FREEDOM OF THE PRESS.]

BIBLIOGRAPHY

Amey, Lawrence, ed., *Censorship*, 3 vols.; R. Kent Rasmussen, project ed. (Salem Press 1997).

De Grazia, Edward, *Girls Lean Back Everywhere: The Law of Obscenity and the Assault on Genius* (Random House 1992).

Green, Jonathon, *The Encyclopedia of Censorship* (Facts on File 1990).

Hurwitz, Leon, *Historical Dictionary of Censorship in the United States* (Greenwood Press 1985).

Leff, Leonard J., and Jerold L. Simmons, *The Dame in the Kimono: Hollywood, Censorship, and the Production Code from the 1920s to the 1960s* (Grove Weidenfeld 1990).

ELIZABETH SCHAFER

CENTRAL AMERICAN AND CARIBBEAN IMMIGRANTS

Central American and Caribbean immigrants in the United States encompass a diverse group whose particular identity, linguistic, social, racial, historical, geopolitical, and economic formations challenge any configuration of the Caribbean region as a whole. The sociopolitical notion of the Central American and Caribbean Basin deployed by the Reagan administration to promote U.S. hegemony over the region in the 1980s was highly problematic. With the exception of El Salvador, Central American countries (Belize, Guatemala, Honduras, Nicaragua, Costa Rica, and Panama) share the Caribbean Sea with chains of islands running over 2,500 miles (4,023 km) from the tip of Florida southward to the northern coasts of Venezuela, Suriname, and Guyana. The Caribbean islands are divided into the Greater Antilles (Cuba, Jamaica, Puerto Rico, and the Dominican Republic and Haiti); the Lesser Antilles, an extensive chain of smaller islands, which includes the English-speaking "unincorporated (U.S.) territories" of the Virgin Islands (St. Croix, St. John, and St. Thomas), Barbados, Trinidad and Tobago, the Leeward and Windward Islands nestling St. Kitts–Nevis, Anguilla, Antigua-Barbuda, Montserrat, Dominica, St. Lucia, St. Vincent, and Grenada; the French-speaking overseas departments (DEMs) of Martinique and Guadeloupe; and the Netherland Antilles (St. Eustatius, Saba, and St. Maarten) and the Dutch-speaking islands of Aruba, Bonaire, and Curaçao. The Turks and Caicos, the Cayman Islands, the Bahamas, and others round off the outlying smaller islands.

The Caribbean islands and outlying mainland form distinct cultural, political, economic, and linguistic zones, where English, French, Dutch, Spanish, and many Creole and transculturated African, European, and indigenous languages are spoken. The region comprises independent nations, territories, colonies, departments, associated states (as in the case of Puerto Rico), and former protectorates and current dependencies of Great Britain, France, Spain, the Netherlands, and the United States. Historically tied to Europe and United States, the Central American and Caribbean region sends immigrants to various metropoles. Immigrants from the anglophone islands such as Jamaica have gravitated traditionally toward London, New York, other islands, and Central America, where, during the early twentieth century, labor migrants worked in the construction of railroads, public works, and the Panama Canal, as well as in single-export crop agriculture including banana and sugar production. According to the 1999 Census count of the foreign-born in the United States, Caribbean immigrants

were highly concentrated in the Northeast, including those from hispanophone, anglophone, and francophone points of origin such as Puerto Rico, the Dominican Republic, Cuba, Jamaica, Trinidad, Guyana, Haiti, and other islands. While many of the Caribbean islands lack sufficient employment for their resident populations, others such as Haiti also suffer from great shortages of land, water, and natural resources. At present, according to Anthony Catanese's *Haitians: Migration and Diaspora,* Haiti expels a great number of economic and environmental refugees and labor migrants who generate significant remittances for the island. The 1999 Census reported that of the approximately 26 million foreign-born people living in the United States in 1999, Caribbean immigrants comprised 11 percent, while Central Americans and Mexicans, who lived for the most part in the western United States, made up 34 percent.

According to Raquel Pinderhughes in her study *Our Multicultural Heritage: A Guide to America's Principal Ethnic Groups,* between 1820 and 1993 more than 1 million Central Americans legally immigrated to the United States, with the largest number arriving in the 1980s, as they fled the armed and civil conflicts in the region. Most Central American immigrants are from El Salvador, Guatemala, Nicaragua, and Honduras.

Immigration scholars identify 5 significant waves of Central American immigration to the United States. Beginning in the mid-nineteenth century members of the Central American elite classes, political dissidents in the isthmus, workers of transnational companies (fruit, coffee, railroads, and the Panama Canal), and others resettled in cities such as San Francisco, New Orleans, and New York. In the 1930s and 1940s urban, middle-class Central American immigrants with relatively high levels of education (compared with later immigrants) relocated to cities such as San Francisco, Los Angeles, New York, Houston, and New Orleans, where they filled World War II labor demands in the United States. These immigrants laid the foundation for familial and community networks and enclaves that produced poles of attraction for later immigrants. In the 1960s more than 100 thousand

Central Americans were admitted legally to the United States, backed by the 1965 Immigration Act, which opened new quotas of immigration from Latin American countries in an effort to recruit a skilled and professional labor force to meet the needs of U.S. industries during the years of the wars in Vietnam and Korea. In the 1970s and 1980s many Central Americans, particularly Salvadorans, Nicaraguans, and Guatemalans, were displaced by internal crises and civil wars that induced almost 2 million people to seek refuge throughout the isthmus, Mexico, Europe, Australia, Canada, and the United States.

Scholars anticipate that Central American immigration will not decline in the new millennium, continuing cyclical migration patterns toward the United States. Of the 1.3 million Central American immigrants living in the United States in 1990, almost 75 percent are Salvadoran. About one-sixth to one-fifth of the Salvadoran population were residing in the United States, with the heaviest concentration in Los Angeles.

Half of the current Central American population in the United States arrived seeking refuge and asylum under various immigration laws such as the 1980 Refugee Act, which made provisions for the official classification of refugees and political-asylum seekers, and the 1986 Immigration and Control Reform Act (IRCA), which granted legal-resident status to Salvadoran immigrants showing evidence of having lived in the United States prior to January 1, 1982. Subsequently, with the arrival of a larger number of undocumented immigrants, new legislation such as the Temporary Protected Status (TPS), the Deferred Enforced Departure (DED), and the American Baptist Churches (ABC) program sought to gain permission for temporary and extended stays for immigrants. It is estimated that half of the Central American population currently living in the United States had arrived by 1980s. The 1990 U.S. Census calculated that about 1.3 million Central Americans lived in the United States, without accounting for a large number of undocumented immigrants. The Tomás Rivera Research Center estimates that out of approximately 32 million Latinos in the United States in 1999, about

13 percent were Central and South Americans, making them the largest subgroup after Mexicans (about 64 percent). Puerto Ricans are estimated to compose about 13 percent of the Latino population; Cuban Americans and the other Latino groups accounted for the rest.

Cubans have migrated to the United States since the early nineteenth century, establishing significant settlements in South Florida and New York. The 1959 Cuban Revolution set off the watershed exodus of Cubans who fled Fidel Castro's governance and resettled in the United States. Between 1959 and 1962, the first large wave of immigration of over 200 thousand Cubans arrived in the United States. The "Golden Exiles," comprising ex-government officials, members of the upper class, and other dissidents, were the first to leave Cuba and to arrive in Miami, Florida. For the most part, this group was white and upper class, with some capital or preestablished contacts in the United States. They received much legal, financial, and other material aid to make the transition into the United States and were followed by successive waves of Cuban emigrants "of different politics and more modest wealth," according to María Cristina García. Between 1965 and 1973 "Freedom Flights" were allowed to leave Cuba with families of those who had already departed. Numbering approximately 200 thousand, this group was composed largely of working class and professionals. The Peruvian Embassy take-over (in March 1979) by Cubans wishing to leave Cuba set off the Mariel Boatlift. About 100 thousand Cubans arrived in the United States, including working-class people, people with families already in the United States, political prisoners, and others.

Technically Puerto Ricans are not immigrants in the United States since the island has been under U.S. political jurisdiction since 1898, acquired U.S. citizenship for its citizens with the Jones Act of 1917, and designated itself a "free associated state" tied to the U.S. economy and politics. Since the nineteenth century, Puerto Ricans have migrated to the United States in search of jobs, including those in the fruit plantations of Hawaii and the garment factories of the Northeast. During the "great migration" of 1946–1964, over 2 million rural and urban Puerto Rican dwellers, displaced by the industrialization program "Operation Bootstrap," resettled in New York City. By 1980, about 40 percent of the overall Puerto Rican population lived outside of the island, primarily in the mainland United States. New York City is now home not only to Puerto Ricans but also to Dominicans and other Caribbean immigrants, who claim and develop Boricua, AmeRícan, Nuyorican, Dominicanyorker, and other transnational identities in the United States.

[*See also* IMMIGRATION AND IMMIGRATION LAW; AFRO-CARIBBEAN CULTURE.]

BIBLIOGRAPHY

Catanese, Anthony V., *Haitians: Migration and Diaspora* (Westview Press 1999).

Chamberlain, Mary, ed., *Caribbean Migration: Globalised Identities* (Routledge 1998).

Davis, Mike, *Magical Urbanism: Latinos Reinvent the US City* (Verso 2000).

García, María Cristina, *Havana USA: Cuban Exiles and Cuban Americans in South Florida, 1959–1994* (Univ. of Calif. Press 1996).

Mahler, Sarah J., *America Dreaming: Immigrant Life on the Margins* (Princeton Univ. Press 1995).

Portes, Alejandro, "From South of the Border: Hispanic Minorities in the United States," in *The Immigration Reader: America in a Multidisciplinary Perspective,* ed. by David Jacobson (Blackwell 1998).

Romero, Mary, Pierrette Hondagneu-Sotelo, and Vilma Ortiz, eds., *Challenging Fronteras: Structuring Latina and Latino Lives in the U.S.* (Routledge 1997).

ANA PATRICIA RODRÍGUEZ

CENTRAL PARK

Central Park, in New York City, was the first great urban park constructed in the United States. Extending from Fifty-ninth Street to One Hundred Tenth Street and from Fifth Avenue to Eighth Avenue, the park occupies 843 acres (341 ha), 153 blocks of the city's grid street system, and 9,792 standard 25- by 100-foot (7.6 by 30.5 m) lots. Removing that much land from development, even on what was then the periphery of the developed area of Manhattan, was a visionary response to ur-

banization. So was the park's design, a remarkable collaboration between Frederick Law Olmsted and Calvert Vaux that transformed deforested and scarred acres into a humanly created, naturalistic landscape that stands as a counterpoint to the straight lines and right angles of the city. As architect-in-chief and superintendent, Olmsted oversaw the construction of their plan, "Greensward" (1858), which gave the park its most distinctive landscape features—broad meadows, water courses and ponds, and heavily forested hillsides, all united by an ingenious system of traffic that separated pedestrians from horseback and carriage routes and placed crosstown traffic in sunken transverse roads.

Central Park's seemingly tranquil acres have long been contested space. Prior to its creation the land had been home to more than sixteen hundred residents, including African Americans who lived in Seneca Village on the park's west side. Those people were displaced when the city acquired the land and commenced developing the park. Construction itself became enmeshed in politics in 1857, when the Republican-dominated state legislature gave control of the park to an appointed commission to ensure that it would not be a source of patronage for the city's Democratic administration. In 1870 the state-appointed commission was replaced by a Department of Public Parks whose members were appointed by the mayor, but local control occurred during the ascendancy of "Boss" William M. Tweed and the Democratic political machine, and the park suffered at the hands of administrators who, Olmsted believed, compromised the original design and failed to ensure its proper maintenance and use.

Olmsted envisioned Central Park as the one large expanse of pastoral landscape in Manhattan, and he rejected uses such as sports that would bring the noise, the energy, and the competition of the city into the park. He expected that New York would construct other parks to accommodate different uses, including athletic grounds and small parks in each neighborhood of the city. He fought against the expansion of the menagerie in the park, not because he opposed a zoo and its patrons but because he recognized that a large zoo would require numerous buildings, some of them quite large, and considerable fencing, which would detract from the expanses of landscape he considered essential to residents of the city. Over the years numerous structures, playgrounds, and other facilities have been built to meet the recreational needs of different constituencies, but in some respects these have compromised the breadth of landscape Olmsted considered essential to an urban park.

Central Park inspired the creation of similar large parks in other American cities in the second half of the nineteenth century. Recognition of its importance in the history of landscape architecture and city planning came in 1965, when Central Park and Prospect Park, in Brooklyn, became the first landscapes listed on the National Register of Historic Places. Historian Carl Condit praised Central Park as "perhaps the greatest civic achievement of the United States in the nineteenth century." Throughout its history the park has been, and remains, an incalculable resource for residents of New York City, the one place that welcomes all of the diversity of the city, just as Olmsted had hoped. In Central Park "all classes [are] largely represented," he wrote in 1871, and in their enjoyment of the recreational ground each visitor was "adding by his mere presence to the pleasure of all others, all helping to the greater happiness of each."

[*See also* LAND USE; CITY, *article on* URBAN PLANNING AND DESIGN; OLMSTED, FREDERICK LAW.]

BIBLIOGRAPHY

Beveridge, Charles E., and David Schuyler, *Creating Central Park, 1857–1861*, vol. 3 of *The Papers of Frederick Law Olmsted* (Johns Hopkins Univ. Press 1983).

Reed, Henry Hope, and Sophia Duckworth, *Central Park: A History and a Guide*, rev. ed. (Potter 1972).

Rosenzweig, Roy, and Elizabeth Blackmar, *The Park and the People: A History of Central Park* (Cornell Univ. Press 1992).

DAVID SCHUYLER

CHAPLIN, CHARLES

Charles Spencer Chaplin's roots were in the popular theater of England. Born in London, England,

MOVIE STILL ARCHIVES

Charles Chaplin and child star Jackie Coogan in a scene from *The Kid* (1921).

on April 16, 1889, his parents, who separated when he was less than a year old, were music-hall entertainers. Living in dire circumstances, Chaplin became a professional performer at the age of nine, beginning with the Eight Lancashire Lads. His older half-brother, actor and comedian Sidney Chaplin, helped him get a job with Fred Karno in February 1908. Karno's various theatrical companies specialized in pantomime sketches, providing Chaplin with an ideal opportunity to develop his comic style. During an American tour, Chaplin was spotted by Harry Aiken of the New York Motion Picture Company, who hired him to replace a departing comedian at Mack Sennett's Keystone comedy unit. Chaplin was in Los Angeles, working for Sennett, by early December 1913, the year that Henry Ford inaugurated the endless-chain conveyor for final assembly of the Model T. The Chaplin character's ability to manipulate and mock the workplace (even when focusing on the rich or realms of leisure) played off working-class experiences and resonated with these spectators' fantasies.

Chaplin's comedy was multifaceted. On the one hand he displayed a propensity for crude, even dirty jokes. On the other hand he played a romantic, sentimental, gentleman tramp, a comically unstable construction but one that had many antecedents in popular culture, as well as real life parallels in tramp culture itself. Tramps often prided themselves on their fundamental affinities with the nation's millionaires: both groups were composed of gentlemen who did not work. Of course, tramps often did have to work to survive. Thus Chaplin's gentleman tramp generated an array of jokes about work and "productive" labor that responded to oppressive conditions that his working-class audience experienced on a routine basis. It also became a way to lampoon both the rich and middle-class values.

Chaplin's first film was significantly entitled *Making a Living* (released February 2, 1914), in which he plays an impoverished English fop who cannot even afford a shirt but conceals this lack with a spiffy morning jacket and cuffs. Already Chaplin combined the discerning gentleman and the impoverished opportunist into this character who bums change from a man, then steals the man's girl. With hard work, honesty, and the fundamental values espoused by bourgeois society systematically lampooned, key elements of his comedy were already in place. His next production, according to David Robinson's fine biography, was *Mabel's Strange Predicament*; it was here that he first appeared in that ill-fitting suit and bowler that defined his subsequent costume as a gentleman tramp. He retained the contradictions of the previous costume but reworked these elements to make his character more realistic, more American, and potentially more "ethnic." This refinement of his character is evident in *Kid Auto Races at Venice* (February 1914). Although still working under other directors, the picture's basic idea was Chaplin's, and he was able to improvise on location. A camera crew is trying to film a soap-box derby; but Charlie plays an "innocent" bystander who constantly gets in the way of the camera, making it impossible for the filmmakers to perform their jobs and work productively. Then, after working under several directors in the course of making ten films, Chaplin was thoroughly frustrated by his lack of control and quickly took over the direction his films.

Like his screen persona, Chaplin was peripatetic—never ready to settle down in a regular, long-term relationship with an employer. He made thirty-five films for Mack Sennett and Keystone in 1914, almost half of the approximately eighty films he made in the course of his career. At the end of his Keystone contract, he departed for the Essanay Film Manufacturing Company, for which he produced fourteen films, including *His New Job* (released February 1915), *The Tramp* (released April 1915) and *Work* (June 1915). After another year he was off to the Mutual Film Corporation where he made twelve more films including *The Floorwalker* (May 1916), *The Vagabond* (July 1916), *Easy Street* (January 1917), and *The Immigrant* (June 1917). From there he went to First National where he produced eight films for distribution between 1918 and 1923, including *A Dog's Life* (April 1918), *The Kid* (February 1921), and *The Pilgrim* (February 1923). Ultimately Chaplin turned to independent production as cofounder of United Artists (UA) with Mary Pickford, Douglas Fairbanks, and D. W. Griffith. Although they announced the company's formation in 1919, it would be several years before Chaplin finished his contract with First National and could release films through UA, which totaled eight productions between 1923 and the sale of his interests in UA in 1955. These included *The Gold Rush* (1925), *City Lights* (1931), *The Great Dictator* (1940), and *Monsieur Verdoux* (1947).

Chaplin was politically active on the Left in many ways. As Steve Ross observed, Chaplin was well-known for supporting socialist causes and was hailed by the labor press as one of the "biggest boosters of Organized Labor in Southern California." Right-wing groups and the government would carefully document how he had held a dinner for Communist trade-union organizer William Z. Foster, inviting many progressive industry figures such as William C. DeMille. Effectively forced to leave the United States in 1952 with the rise of anticommunism and the Hollywood blacklist, Chaplin moved with his fourth wife, Oona O'Neill, and his children to Switzerland; he made his last two films in Europe, *A King in New York* (1957) and *A Countess from Hong King* (1967). Chaplin and the establishment reconciled near the end of his life. He received an honorary Academy Award in 1972 and was knighted by Queen Elizabeth in 1975. Chaplin died in Switzerland on December 25, 1979.

[*See also* FILM, *articles on* FILM AND HISTORY, FILM AND THE CONSTRUCTION OF IDENTITY, FILM AND ITS AUDIENCES; INDEPENDENT FILM; STUDIO SYSTEM; MOVIE STARS; HOLLYWOOD.]

BIBLIOGRAPHY

Chaplin, Charles, *My Autobiography* (Simon & Schuster 1964).

Huff, Theodore, *Charlie Chaplin* (Schuman 1951).

Maland, Charles J., *Chaplin and American Culture: The Evolution of a Star Image* (Princeton Univ. Press 1989).

Musser, Charles, and Robert Sklar, eds., "Work, Ideology and Chaplin's Tramp," in *Resisting Images: Essays on Cinema and History* (Temple Univ. Press 1991).

Robinson, David, *Chaplin, His Life and Art* (McGraw-Hill 1985).

Tyler, Parker, *Chaplin: Last of the Clowns* (1948; Horizon Press 1972).

CHARLES MUSSER

CHÁVEZ, CÉSAR

Chicano activist César Estrada Chávez, a third-generation Mexican American, was born on March 31, 1927, near Yuma, Arizona. In 1938 his family moved to Oxnard, California, where they became part of the highly exploited migrant workforce. After serving in the navy during World War II, Chávez met Fred Ross, an important organizer for the Community Service Organization. Chávez eventually became its general director (1958–1962), working to improve living conditions in urban Chicano communities.

By 1962 Chávez's attention turned to the plight of farm laborers. He helped form the National Farm Workers Association, which organized farm workers and fought to improve their dismal working and living conditions. Farm workers suffered harsh indignities; they were paid below the minimum wage, they had no collective bargaining rights, and child labor persisted. For Chávez the Bracero Program—also known as the Emergency Farm Labor Program of 1942–1964 (a guest-worker program agreed on by the U.S. and Mexican governments)—exacerbated the poor treatment of farm workers:

© GLENN WAGGNER/UPI

César Chávez, leader of the United Farm Workers Union.

growers hired Mexican braceros for lower wages and under worse working conditions, thus reducing the availability of jobs, degrading work conditions, and weakening unionizing efforts. Initially Chávez was a strong opponent of any guest-worker program as well as of undocumented immigration, but by the mid-1970s he had changed his position on the latter and had seen the possibilities of solidarity with undocumented Mexican farm workers.

In 1965 Filipino American grape pickers went on strike in California to protest a wage cut. Chávez, as one of the leaders of the newly formed National Farm Workers Association, convinced the labor organization of the importance of the "grape strike." Following the tactics of civil rights leader Martin Luther King, Jr., the association enlarged the strike and began a boycott of California-grown grapes and wine. Chávez also went on hunger strikes to express his deep commitment to the cause. By 1970, when the United Farm Workers (UFW; the new name of the organization) won the labor dispute against California's grape growers, the boycott had garnered national media attention and had become popular among many middle-class Americans. In protest marches held during the five-year strike, the use of the Teatro Campesino, a popular leftist theater group led by Luis Valdez, and the featuring of the image of the Virgin of Guadalupe during the marches, were overt, interreferential acts of resistance and culture.

For the next twenty-three years, until his death, in San Luis, Arizona, on April 23, 1993, Chávez and the United Farm Workers faced a slew of legal, labor (with the support of the growers, the Teamsters also began unionizing farm workers), and political challenges, and their membership numbers fluctuated. Depending on who was in California's governor's office, state laws and policies varied. Republicans generally sided with the growers, while Democrats were friendlier to the UFW. Throughout Chávez's entire public career, Helen Chávez, his wife, facilitated and shaped his activist work with her political acumen.

Perceptions of Chávez vary according to the ideological lens through which his activities are viewed. Mexican Americans usually support his efforts. Many urban ethnic Mexicans had friends and relatives who were farm workers, or they themselves had been farm workers and thus understood that the struggle was necessary to improve wages and working conditions. American liberals and progressives (especially Senators Robert Kennedy, Eugene McCarthy, and George McGovern; California governor Jerry Brown; entertainer Steve Allen; and writer Peter Matthiessen) also were pro-Chávez.

César Chávez generally is remembered as a hero of the Chicano and labor movements who struggled against injustice and for greater democracy. Although Chávez has become an icon, others should be remembered as well, in particular Dolores Huerta, vice president of the UFW, whose work was also integral to the fight in the fields.

[See also CHICANOS, AN OVERVIEW; HUERTA, DOLORES.]

BIBLIOGRAPHY

Ferriss, Susan, et al., *The Fight in the Fields: César Chávez and the Farmworkers Movement* (Harcourt 1997).

Griswold del Castillo, Richard, and Richard A. Garcia, *César Chávez: A Triumph of Spirit* (Univ. of Okla. Press 1995).

Gutiérrez, David G., *Walls and Mirrors: Mexican Americans, Mexican Immigrants, and the Politics of Ethnicity* (Univ. of Calif. Press 1995).

Matthiessen, Peter, *Sal si puedes: César Chávez and the New American Revolution* (Random House 1969).

JAIME CÁRDENAS

CHEROKEE NATION V. GEORGIA

The Cherokee Nation held land in Georgia by virtue of a treaty with the United States. The Cherokee were popularly known as one of the "civilized tribes" because of their embrace of European ways, including a written language, a plantation system of agriculture, and European-style lodgings and dress. In 1824 Georgia passed statutes that purported to deny various American Indian land claims, subject Indian land to state laws, and nullify all Indian laws. The Cherokees brought suit in the U.S. Supreme Court seeking an injunction against Georgia's interfering with Native American sovereignty on tribal lands under the court's original jurisdiction, based on their claim to be a foreign nation.

The Court avoided a confrontation with Georgia or a retreat from its own constitutional principles by ruling 4–2 that the Cherokee Nation was not a foreign nation but a dependent, domestic sovereignty that constituted a "distinct political society." The retreat of the Court was understandable because Georgia was notorious for its violent reactions to what it viewed as federal judicial usurpation of its state sovereignty. An early extra-legal confrontation between the Court and Georgia in the aftermath of *Chisholm* v. *Georgia* (1793) had led to the adoption of the Eleventh Amendment, restoring sovereign immunity to the states.

Preceding the Court's decision in *Cherokee Nation*, Georgia displayed its truculence in the case of Corn Tassel, a Cherokee accused of murdering a fellow tribesman. Georgia tried and convicted Corn Tassel, who sought an injunction on the grounds that a U.S. treaty guaranteed the right of a Cherokee to be tried by Cherokee law, not state law, for crimes committed on Cherokee land. Chief Justice John Marshall issued a writ of error to the Georgia trial court and ordered Georgia to respond to Corn Tassel's application. The Georgia legislature passed a resolution that any attempt to enforce the Court's writ should be met with force, and Corn Tassel was duly hanged. Given the divided opinions in Congress and given President Andrew Jackson's obvious sympathy with Georgia in the *Cherokee Nation* case, the Court had little choice but to avoid confrontation with Georgia.

The central issue that the Court had sidestepped in the *Cherokee Nation* case arose again in *Worcester* v. *Georgia* (1832). Samuel Worcester, a missionary, defied a Georgia statute that required a state license for any white person wishing to live on Indian land, and he was sentenced to four years at hard labor following his conviction. He was subsequently offered a pardon, but he refused it, wishing to raise the issue in the U.S. Supreme Court, which ultimately went on to invalidate the Georgia law as an unconstitutional interference with the exclusive power of the federal government in regard to Indian affairs.

At first President Jackson did nothing to enforce the decision, but in the aftermath of the South Carolina nullification crisis, he persuaded the governor of Georgia to pardon Worcester, thereby defusing the potential confrontation. In 1838, Georgia and the federal government, acting under the Indian Removal Act, forced the Cherokees and several other tribes to remove to the bleak Indian Territory of the West, in what is now Oklahoma. Despite the fact that its decision did not ultimately save the Indians, the Court in *Cherokee Nation* and in *Worcester* was able to take a stand against state usurpation of federal authority.

[*See also* NATIVE AMERICANS, AN OVERVIEW.]

BIBLIOGRAPHY

Burke, Joseph C., "The Cherokee Cases: A Study of Law, Politics, and Morality," *Stanford Law Review* 21:500–531.

Levy, Leonard W., "Cherokee Indian Cases," in *Encyclopedia of the American Constitution*, ed. by Leonard W. Levy, Kenneth L. Karst, and Dennis J. Mahoney (Macmillan 1986).

PATRICK M. O'NEIL

CHICANOS

[The rich heritage of Chicanos in the United States is here surveyed in four distinct articles. The first entry, AN OVERVIEW, *examines the meaning of the term* Chicano/Chicana *and the history of the people it identifies. The remaining three entries cover Chicano contributions to various fields of activity. These articles are as follows:*

CHICANO LITERATURE

CHICANO PERFORMING AND GRAPHIC ARTS

CHICANISMO AND THE CHICANO MOVEMENT.*]*

An Overview

Chicano refers to the communities and individuals of Mexican origin, descent, or emigration in the United States of America. The origins of the word are in some dispute. Some writers have traced it back to indigenous language, while others place its etymology in a linguistic corruption or slur. Regardless of its origins, the association of the term *Chicano* with Mexican Americans arises out of the 1960s social movement for Mexican American civil and social rights (the Chicano movement) and denotes a politically radical, ethnically centered, communal identity. While Mexican American and Chicano are often used synonymously, as they are in this entry, there are subtle yet important differences in political meaning and self-description. In general, a Chicana or Chicano is someone with an articulately political relationship to his or her identity as a Mexican American. It has also come to be expected that the terms *Chicano* and *Chicanos* will be amended with the letter *a* to reflect the importance of gender.

Chicanos are a diverse, multilingual, polyracial population. While increasingly a racial-ethnic group with national presence, the historical area of settlement for Mexican Americans has been the American Southwest. These communities exemplify different urban, suburban, and rural characteristics, as well as represent a plethora of economic, political, and social attitudes and beliefs that make it difficult to identify concretely the parameters of Chicano identity. Chicanos speak Spanish or English or demonstrate varying levels of linguistic ability in either language. While Chicanos can be racially ambiguous, most are *mestizo* ("mixed race"), a combination of Spanish and indigenous lineage that is the legacy of colonization and conquest.

Mexican American and *Chicano* are terms that specifically refer to Mexican-origin populations in the United States that have their literal historical origin within the American experience with the conclusion of the Mexican-American War of 1846–1848. In this sense it is important to note that Chicano identity was forged in this initial conquest, marginalization, and struggle. However, the vast majority of contemporary self-identified Chicanos or Mexican Americans have their origins in post-1900 immigration. In this sense, Mexican Americans are a multigenerational immigrant community, with this important exception: the nascent communities of Mexican settlers present in the Southwest when the United States negotiated an end to the Mexican-American War in 1848.

This schism between immigration and conquest remains a pointed one in debates over Chicano identity, with Mexican Americans often ambiguous over their place in American society. This tension is exemplified in the dyad of ethnicity and race. Some Mexican Americans consider themselves an immigrant group with a traditional, white-ethnic relationship to assimilation and the American nation-state. For others, Chicanos are a racially specific group marked by skin color and the deleterious effects of racism and marginalization. The former opinion largely marks the interwar period of the twentieth century, the latter the Chicano movement of the 1960s and subsequent social formations of Chicanos. It is important to note, however, that these categorizations are conditional and must be understood in a complex manner, dependent as they are on economic class, skin color, lin-

© HAYDEN LIBRARY, ARIZONA HISTORICAL FOUNDATION

Portrait of Estevan Ochoa, who served as the first Mexican mayor of Tucson in 1875.

guistic ability, immigration status, educational privilege, and ideological orientation, as well as subjective experience. This multitiered generational and experiential structure of Mexican Americans has made mass organization historically difficult.

Chicano Sociopolitical Formations: 1848–1965. The Mexican-American War, understood by most Chicano scholars as an imperialist aggression, resulted in the annexation by the United States of a substantial part of Mexican territory, encompassing most of the contemporary American Southwest. Mexican citizens in the annexed territories were offered the choice of emigrating or becoming American citizens. The Treaty of Guadalupe Hidalgo (1848) guaranteed the remaining population substantial civil and social rights within the United States, including rights of language, religion, and property, and Spanish Crown and Mexican land grants of the colonial period. This initial group, numbering at the time no more than one hundred thousand people, forms the kernel of the Mexican American community, the elementary population of Chicanos.

Mexican Americans soon discovered that their treaty rights under Guadalupe Hidalgo had little real value. Historic Crown and Mexican land grants were not recognized by American courts, resulting in massive land grabs by Anglo-American entrepreneurs, ranchers, farmers, and businessmen all over the Southwest. The land-owning classes of the Mexican territories were soon largely dispossessed of capital and economic influence. Increased American migration to the Southwest, especially following the gold rush in California, isolated Mexican communities culturally, socially, and politically. Anglo-Americans derided Mexican Americans because of language, religion, and race. This ethnocentrism, combined with economic disenfranchisement, conspired to transform Chicano communities from stable, economically viable, and socially cohesive groups into Southwestern subalterns. Through the end of the nineteenth century, the community proportionally shrank in the face of Anglo-American immigration to the region; had statistical patterns continued, it might have actually been absorbed within the larger and increasingly dominant Anglo society.

The Mexican Revolution of 1910–1920 spawned a mass migration of political refugees into the United States, reinvigorating and greatly expanding the dwindling communities of Mexican Americans. It was only after these developments with their increases in population into the 1930s and 1940s that a discrete Mexican American identity emerged. The interwar period was a time of transition and activism for Mexican Americans. Many sought to install themselves within reformist social movements or labor activity that spoke directly to their identity as American interlocutors. It is also within this period that the first efforts at the organized academic study of Mexican Americans were undertaken. The interwar period marked the transition from immigrant to American for many Mexican Americans, with an explicit identification with

American social and political mores and values. Implicit in this as well was a developing critique of the inequalities of life in the United States for many Mexican Americans, and a demand for the reform of social and political structures to empower Chicano individuals and communities. The interwar activities of Mexican American activists, largely reformist in character, set the stage for the later radicalism of the Chicano movement of the 1960s.

Contemporary Chicano Sociopolitical Formations: The Chicano Movement. The Chicano movement was a broad-based, multifaceted phenomenon that sought to bring together arts, politics, and activism toward a specific vision of empowerment for Mexicans in the United States. The Chicano movement sought to rectify the historical marginalization of Mexican Americans within the Southwest and to combat the racism and ethnocentrism that had condemned Chicanos to inferior schooling, housing, and economic and social opportunities, which had continued and intensified in the postwar period. Within this struggle was an explicit critique of Anglo-American racism and the limitations of cultural assimilation as a methodology for success. Emerging within the general context of 1960s social agitation, the Chicano movement had by 1969 become a potent force in the social and political development of thousands of Mexican Americans, especially students.

The strike against grape growers in the farm fields of central California by the United Farm Workers (UFW) in 1965 and the 1966 *Plan de Delano* ("Delano Plan") for farm workers' rights figured prominently in a move away from reformist politics toward more radical Left activities. The "Crusade for Justice" in Denver, Colorado, under the aegis of organizer Rodolfo "Corky" Gonzales, addressed civil and labor rights for Mexican Americans. Its most prominent event was the 1969 Chicano Youth Conference, which produced one of the founding documents of the Chicano movement: *El Plan Espiritual de Aztlán* ("Spiritual Plan of Aztlán"). The *plan*, developed by students attending the conference, declared the unity of the student movement with communal and pastoral values and the

Workers in the vineyards of the Baritelli Winery in Napa Valley, California.

goal of the formation of a Chicano nation-state called Aztlán. Aztlán named the desire of 1960s activists to unite the diverse Mexican American population under a singular and largely imaginary nation-state rubric of a homeland. Aztlán literally refers to the American Southwest but spiritually links the contemporary Mexican American to indigenous and activist roots.

The Chicano student movement, developing after a series of 1968 high school strikes, called "blowouts," led the move to cultural nationalism. The Aztlán Chicano Student Movement, *El Movimiento Estudiantíl Chicano de Aztlán* (MEChA), was instrumental in organizing actions on university and high school campuses. MEChA was the driving force behind both the 1969 Denver Youth Conference with its *Plan de Aztlán* (1969) and a later conference in California, from which emerged *El Plan de Santa Barbara* (1969). This later *plan* called for an educational reform of primary and secondary school systems as well as significant changes in access to university-level education. A prime component of university reform was the institution of Chicano studies programs and courses in bilingual and bicultural education. The emergent radical identity

of *Chicano* was specifically opposed to *Mexican American,* presumed by activists to reflect assimilative and "Anglo" values. *Chicano* was a term of affirmation of ethnicity, race, communalism, and a commitment to radical social and political transformation.

The Chicano movement, through its scholarly and literary projects, emphasized this typology by foregrounding an organic Chicano subject rooted in the strength of family, the community, and the cultural nationalism of Aztlán. Chicana feminists at the time issued a harsh critique of the gendered, masculinist elements of this subject position, and Mexican American experiential diversity profoundly limited the effect of this radical subjectivity as a universal rubric for Chicanos and Chicanas. By the mid-1970s, the student movement had dissipated, with student activism nationally in decline after 1971. However, the paradigms of empowerment, community activism, feminist critique, and a negotiated racial-ethnic identity for Mexican Americans continued to resonate as legacies of the Chicano movement.

The tactile successes of the Chicano movement have been felt in growing participation by and representation of Mexican Americans within the political and social processes of American society. Voter registration, political organizing, and the increase in elected Mexican American representatives on the local, state, and national levels are some of the more measurable political results of this period. The presence of Chicano students at the undergraduate and graduate levels in the academy and the formation of a Chicano professorate are directly attributable to the movement's forays into educational reform. The development of a nascent Mexican American middle class and the use of state and federal law to enforce legal standards of nondiscrimination in housing, business, and the civil service are also salient benefits of the movement period. While all of these gains are contingent and incomplete, nevertheless they speak to a transformation in the place of Mexican Americans within the larger American society, both on the level of expectation and on the level of performance.

Contemporary Chicano Sociopolitical Formations: Post-Movement Interpretive Strategies. Clearly, the legacy of the Chicano movement is the most influential factor in contemporary Mexican American life. The benefits resulting from the movement, such as increased access to education and economic opportunity, have been widely embraced by all sectors of Mexican American society. The empowerment mantras of the movement, echoing larger trends in American society, propelled Mexican Americans into government, society, media, capital, and academe in unprecedented numbers. The movement also firmly established Mexican Americans as a historic American minority community and identity with interests, issues, and influence on a national scale.

The United States, and consequently Mexican America, has been deeply affected by socioeconomic changes since the 1970s that have substantially transformed the material and cultural particulars of social formations. Succinctly, some of these factors include the sociopolitical turns toward conservatism and neoliberalism; the rise of a Mexican American middle class; and, perhaps most important, new immigration from Mexico and Latin America, with a subsequent sociocultural implosion of *Chicano* into *Latino*. As Chicanos have benefited from the social and political changes engendered by the social movements of the 1960s, they have suffered serious setbacks as well. The end of programs for redress such as affirmative action have drastically reduced the numbers of Chicano students in professional and degree-granting programs. Class differences within the Mexican American community dilute the possibilities of building political movements based on racial-ethnic unity and empowerment. The persisting presence of racism and the acceleration of these attitudes because of increased immigration from Latin America have continued to present Mexican Americans with the difficult negotiation of identity positions between ethnicity and race, "American" or marginalized outsider.

Chicano intellectuals and cultural producers have responded to this series of crises in varied and promising ways. Borderlands theory emerges from the desire to figure new relationships in light of the decline of racial-ethnic nationalism of the movement period. The borderlands critique differs from earlier efforts in its commitment to complicating the discrete differences between the United States, Mexico, and Aztlán that were such an important aspect of the movement's work. Fomented in the work of cultural producers of the mid- and late 1980s including Gloria Anzaldúa (1987), Guillermo Gómez-Peña (1993; 1996), and Emily Hicks (1991), borderlands theory has proven to be widely popular among postmovement critics.

The popularity of borderlands for postmovement critics and artists is linked to the applicability of the model to different situations and conditions. Succinctly, borderlands theory, as proffered by Anzaldúa, Gómez-Peña, and others, sought to make sense of the interconnected and interdependent nature of Chicano identity (and to a much more limited extent Anglo-American identity) where it overlapped with Mexican culture, language, and politics. Borderlands theories refute the interpretation of the Mexican-U.S. frontier as a solid and implacable distinction between peoples, culture, societies, and bodies politic. It rejects "either/or" choices of identity in favor of a holistic and, in Anzaldúa's case, a decidedly feminist imagination of shared conditions.

Within the borderlands paradigm critics have found a powerful tool not only for articulating Chicano cultural politics but also for challenging and potentially overturning Anglo-American hegemonic discourses. As such, one of the appeals of borderlands theories is that they can potentially fill the political vacuum caused by the decline of movement ideologies. The political value of borderlands theories is that it seeks to resolve earlier ideological contradictions within new paradigms that promise, on some level, a greater degree of success on political and interpretive levels. This success is seemingly predicated on a more realistic and less ideological relationship to cultural practice and social formation. Another aspect of this theoretical success is the verisimilitude in which borderlands theories capture the specific cross-cultural and multilinguistic vernacular forms of popular culture (television, media technologies, music, art, and cultural sensibility) that compose quotidian Chicano life. Linguistic code switching between Spanish and English and a fundamental ambivalence of place (politically, socially, and culturally) in American society are some aspects of Mexican American sociocultural attitudes encompassed within borderlands models.

Although emergent, the new discourses of this era are grounded in a dialectical relationship with movement discourses. They also coexist within the debates engendered by poststructuralism, feminism, neomovement scholars, neoliberals, and lesbian and gay critics. However, to a large extent and aside from residual or strategic essentialisms, the new discourses of borderlands and the potential value of others, such as diaspora, are representative of the move away from strict positivist comprehension of identity by Chicano thinkers, academics, and activists. These new critical strategies offer, at the very least, new tools with which to engage the comprehensive intellectual study of Mexican America.

[See also MESTIZA CONSCIOUSNESS; CHÁVEZ, CÉSAR; BORDERLANDS.]

BIBLIOGRAPHY

Acuña, Rodolfo F., *Occupied America: A History of the Chicanos,* 4th ed. (Longman 1999).

Anzaldúa, Gloria, *Borderlands/La Frontera: The New Mestiza* (Aunt Lute 1987).

Camarillo, Albert, *Chicanos in a Changing Society: From Mexican Pueblos to American Barrios in Santa Barbara and Southern California, 1848–1930* (Harvard Univ. Press 1979).

García, Mario T., *Mexican Americans: Leadership, Ideology, Identity, 1930–1960* (Yale Univ. Press 1989).

Gómez-Quiñones, Juan, *Chicano Politics: Reality and Promise, 1940–1990* (Univ. of N.Mex. Press 1990).

Muñoz, Carlos, Jr., *Youth, Identity, Power: The Chicano Movement* (Verso 1989).

Rendon, Armando B., *Chicano Manifesto* (Macmillan 1971).

AURELIANO MARIA DESOTO

Chicano Literature

Historically, "Chicano" literature has been defined in a variety of ways. Some critics have limited the scope of Chicano literature to that written at least partially in the Spanish language. Others have stressed the ethnicity of the writer, insisting that Chicano literature can be produced only by Chicanos. Still others have focused on content, defining as "Chicano" only that subject matter representing a politicized identity and an oppositional consciousness. What has come to be understood as Chicano literature, however, includes the above criteria but is not limited to a single definition. Chicano literature may be defined as writing produced by Chicano and Chicano-identified authors and narratives that depict Chicano perspectives, experiences, realities, and culture.

The History of Chicano Literature. Chicano literature has its origins in the late-nineteenth- and early-twentieth-century literary and oral discourses of Mexican Americans. A generation after the Treaty of Guadalupe Hidalgo (1848), through which the United States annexed a large part of Mexico's territory, Mexican Americans began to define themselves as a collective identity against the racist stereotypes disseminated by mainstream Anglo-America. Chicano literature thus originated in a frontier context informed by the Spanish, Indian, and Anglo-American cultures.

It was in this context that the *corrido* (a form of oral epic or ballad) evolved, becoming a definitive feature of Mexican American cultural expression. The *corrido* expressed and continues to embody themes present in much of contemporary Chicano fiction. These include the affirmation of Mexican American ethnocultural identity, challenges to the negative stereotyping of Mexican Americans, and pride in Southwestern origins. For the first few decades of the post-Treaty era, the Spanish language, Roman Catholicism, and a strong association with Spain and a Caucasian ancestry characterized Mexican American literature. Until the mid-1900s Mexican American literature often depicted nature and folk life, nostalgia for a simple past, and loyalty to both the United States and Mexico.

The 1960s marked a radical change in the self-definition of Mexican Americans and the content of Mexican American writing. Some Mexican

© CHRIS FELVER/ARCHIVE PHOTOS

Author Richard Rodriguez, whose autobiography details his education and assimilation into American culture.

Americans began to self-consciously call themselves "Chicanos," a label that to them represented the oppositional nature of their collective identity. This politicization of Mexican American identity grew out of the sociopolitical climate of the 1960s: the Chicano movement followed and paralleled the civil rights and the women's liberation movements. Chicanos saw themselves as a negatively racialized group, denigrated by a dominant Anglo-American culture. From this awareness of a subordinated collective status evolved the Chicano Literary Renaissance (1968–1974). Although sharing certain themes and stylistic techniques with its Mexican American predecessors, it is the literature produced at this time that first may be accurately called Chi-

cano because of the self-association of its authors with a politicized ethnoracial identity.

Also emerging at this time, the Teatro Campesino was an influential presence in Mexican American artistic and political circles. Established by Luis Valdez in 1965, the Teatro Campesino inspired the creation of clearly oppositional Chicano art. This theatrical company was unique in its representation of the concerns and identities of the formerly "invisible" working-class Mexican Americans. Its writing and dramatic productions were highly political and represented radical critiques of the ways in which Mexican Americans were treated as a racialized minority.

The Teatro Campesino influenced the Mexican American literary world by motivating the establishment in 1967 of Quinto Sol Publications. This publishing house, in turn, greatly influenced the nature and evolution of Chicano writing. It facilitated the publication of Mexican American and Chicano authors who previously had not been recognized by mainstream publishing houses. It furthermore represented an overtly political agenda. Like the Teatro Campesino, Quinto Sol promoted literature as an art form with the potential to critique the sociopolitical status quo, and to redefine and validate the Chicano ethnoracial and cultural identity.

In addition to its overtly oppositional nature, the Chicano writing associated with the Quinto Sol period was characterized by experimental techniques. Quinto Sol writers often used multiple narrators, adapted genres, mixed poetry and prose, and "code-switched" or wrote bilingually. These experimental techniques not only distinguished a Chicano literary style from canonical Anglo-American literature but also helped define and ultimately represent a particularly Chicano culture and identity. The deployment of code-switching as well as the depiction of Chicano dialects especially marked the writing of the Chicano Renaissance as distinctly Chicano. Chicano authors of the 1960s and 1970s also recuperated a corrupted sense of collective history by conceptualizing "Aztlán," which represents both the legendary origins of the Aztecs and the Southwestern U.S. geography once belonging to Mexico. Thematizing Aztlán in their literature enabled Chicanos to validate a subordinated identity and an effaced history. Representing the Chicano homeland, Aztlán became a national, cultural, historical, and political symbol for many Chicano writers. (Much of the information on the development of a Chicano literary discourse may be found in Raymund Paredes's "Mexican-American Literature: An Overview," published in 1993. His essay is an excellent source for a detailed chronological history of Mexican American and Chicano literature.)

The Evolution of a Chicana Literary Tradition. The history of Chicana writing is a relatively recent one. Although extant in the nineteenth and early twentieth centuries, much of early Chicana writing was not published. Owing in large part to the combined influences of the Chicano, the civil rights, and the women's liberation movements, increasing numbers of Chicanas began writing and publishing in the 1970s. Because of the proliferation of their writing in the decades since, Chicanas have become an influential presence in a contemporary literary discourse.

As women of color, Chicanas are negatively gendered and raced through both invisibility and coerced silence: historically, Chicanas have been excluded as the "exotic other" by white feminists and silenced within the gendered and politicized Chicano movement. Chicana critic Tey Diana Rebolledo has pointed to the necessity in the last decades for Chicanas to "seize their subjectivity" through the development of their own gendered and racial discourse. By working directly against oppressive cultural values and norms, much of contemporary Chicana writing signifies active authorial participation in oppositional forms of cultural expression. Chicana writers create self-determined characters against pejorative images of the gendered, raced identity disseminated by, and perpetuated within, both the dominant and the mother cultures.

Many contemporary Chicana texts portray a heroine's progression from powerless victim to self-empowered agent. Although the specific trajectory in Chicana fiction varies from text to text, on comparison a distinct pattern emerges. Common stages within this pattern include a conscious awareness on the part of the heroine of her oppressed position, attempts at resistance (from reactive to creative, exhibiting varying degrees of agency), the envisioning of alternatives (alternative definitions of self, family, and community), and, ultimately, the development of a more self-empowered subjectivity.

One of the primary ways in which contemporary Chicana authors create their own gendered and racial discourse is through redefinition. In the process of revisioning, Chicana narratives create positive images of Chicana identities with the portrayal of viably agentive female protagonists. Redefinition enables transformation, which, in turn, allows for the more empowering alternatives to the subordinate social positions and inferior definitions of self offered the Chicana by both the dominant culture and her ethnic community.

In contemporary Chicana writing, strategies of redefinition include the adaptation of traditional literary conventions for the representation of the specifically Chicana experience; the translation of two or more languages and sets of cultural values to the creation of a third, hybrid discourse; the rewriting of patriarchal (mainly Catholic) religious narratives and the re-imagining of religious symbols and figures; the rewriting of cultural myths and legends; the restructuring of family (including the reconceptualization of motherhood) and the repositioning of the Chicana within her community(ies); the redefinition of patriarchal traditions through the portrayal of resistive practices and the establishment of more feminocentric traditions; the recuperation and recasting of histories through analysis and revisioning; and, finally, the metaphorized remapping of geopolitical boundaries through parallels between national narratives and personal narratives.

A later shift in contemporary Chicana writing places Chicana subjectivity in a transnational context by thematizing movement across borders (national, cultural, and geographical) and the transgression of boundaries (political, social, and psychological). This trend marks a move away from traditional generic formats within American literature. Both ethnic bildungsroman and early-twentieth-century immigrant writing, for example, primarily narrated processes of assimilation. The works of the Chicano Renaissance tended to focus on sociopolitical resistance in a domestic context. Contemporary Chicana writing of the last two decades of the twentieth century, however, increasingly negotiated national identities within a transnational imaginary. The thematization of transnational identities, experiences, and connections contributed to the shape of a continuously developing Chicana discourse that resisted either subordination to, or assimilation into, a dominant canon defined by opposing white, masculinist, and nationalist ideologies. Chicana authors have used their writing as a thematic space in and through which to create often mutually defining alternatives: alternative definitions of self, family, and community; alternative histories and mythologies; alternative paradigms for international relations; and alternative visions of empowered futures.

Representative Chicano Authors. The literary *antepasados* ("ancestors") of contemporary Chicano writers include Nina Otero Warren, Josephina Niggli, María Amparo Ruiz de Burton, Fabiola Cabeza de Baca, Jovita González, Cleofas Jaramillo, Fray Angélico Chávez, Eusebio Chacón, José Antonio Villarreal, and Mario Suárez. Of these, Suárez's short stories, serialized in the *Arizona Quarterly*, are representative in the way they prefigure portrayals of a distinct and viable Chicano identity found in later Chicano texts. First published in 1947, Suárez's stories are complex depictions of whole Chicano characters, who serve to contest the negative stereotypes of Mexican Americans prevalent in the midcentury United States. Suárez uses both standard English and Chicano dialect, self-consciously writing about a collective Chicano identity with its own history, customs, values, and language.

Quinto Sol produced three major Chicano writers—Tomás Rivera, Rolando Hinojosa-Smith, and Rudolfo Anaya. Although distinct in style and genre, their texts each thematized Chicano experience and culture. Rivera is best known for his 1971 work entitled *. . . y no se lo trago la tierra* ("And the Earth Did Not Devour Him"), a series of related vignettes written in Spanish about the poverty and discrimination experienced by Mexican American migrant farm workers and the personal and cultural resistance they develop against racial oppression. In *The Klail City Death Trip* series of novels, beginning in 1973, Hinojosa-Smith employs a style similar to the *criollismo* ("creole") movement of Latin America to portray the daily reality and cultural values of a Chicano community in Texas without idealization or romanticization. Published in 1972, Anaya's best-known work, *Bless Me, Ultima,* depicts the rural Mexican American context in which a young boy must negotiate the conflicting influences of the Spanish, Indian, and Anglo cultures. This bildungsroman defines Mexican American culture as essentially hybrid.

Since Quinto Sol, the Chicano literary tradition has demonstrated its maturation with the publication of two very different narratives, Oscar Zeta Acosta's *Autobiography of a Brown Buffalo* (1972) and Richard Rodriguez's *Hunger of Memory* (1981). Dramatically opposed in style, technique, and content, these texts represent two extremes in Chicano identity and philosophy. In *Autobiography* and its sequel, *The Revolt of the Cockroach People* (1973), Acosta writes about his experiences with 1960s counterculture, drugs, and Chicano militancy. Against both affirmative-action and bilingual-education programs, Rodriguez delineates in his memoir a conservative philosophy and an assimilationist ideal for Chicano identity. Together these narratives demonstrate the breadth of intellectual thought within Chicano culture and the complexity of Chicano identity.

Influential Chicana authors include Lorna Dee Cervantes, whose 1981 collection of poems, *Emplumada,* focused on Chicanas' experiences and a gendered identity. In 1983, Cherríe Moraga published *Loving in the War Years,* an autobiographical narrative that simultaneously critiques the patriarchal values of the Chicano culture, the racism of Anglo-American society, and the discriminatory heterosexism of both. Moraga defines herself as a *mestiza* (a woman of mixed racial and cultural ancestry) who experiences the intersected nature of race and gender oppression and a raced and gendered identity. Her narrative is experimental in its code-switching and use of various genres and styles.

Sandra Cisneros is a widely read Chicana author who is best known for *The House on Mango Street*, published in 1984. This bildungsroman consists of a series of vignettes depicting the maturation of a young Mexican American girl; in it Cisneros tackles the themes of female sexuality, ethnic American identity, patriarchy, and self-empowerment through creativity and voice. In 1987 Gloria Anzaldúa published *Borderlands/La Frontera*, a creative and theoretical work detailing her theory of Chicana identity and *mestiza* consciousness. *Borderlands* fundamentally influenced the Chicana literary tradition, theorizing the interrelated nature of race, class, gender, and sexual identities and articulating alternative paradigms not only for Chicana but also Chicano, Anglo-American, and other ethnic American subjectivities.

Today's Chicano literature has a diverse tradition. Chicana and Chicano authors address a variety of issues, both those associated with Chicano culture and those less overtly related to Chicano experience. Many Chicano texts are *mestizo* or hybrid narratives that use Spanish, English, and "Spanglish," include both poetry and prose, and embody different genres and styles. Many Chicano texts share common themes in representing Chicano experience and identity. These include explorations of sexuality, familial relationships, folklore and mythology, gang subculture and violence, racial passing, migration and migrant labor, urban life, assimilation and resistance to assimilation, the American Dream and its evolution within a Chicano collective imagination, machismo and its role in contemporary society, and religion. Diversified in technique and subject matter, Chicano literature nonetheless shares a history and a cultural identity. It offers the American literary canon a rich and varied tradition.

[See also MESTIZA CONSCIOUSNESS; BILINGUALISM.*]*

BIBLIOGRAPHY

Calderón, Héctor, and José David Saldívar, eds., *Criticism in the Borderlands: Studies in Chicano Literature, Culture, and Ideology* (Duke Univ. Press 1991).

Gutiérrez, Ramón, and Genaro Padilla, eds., *Recovering the U.S. Hispanic Literary Heritage*, 2 vols. (Arte Público Press 1993).

Jiménez, Francisco, ed., *The Identification and Analysis of Chicano Literature* (Bilingual Press 1979).

Lattin, Vernon E., ed., *Contemporary Chicano Fiction: A Critical Survey* (Bilingual Press 1986).

Paredes, Raymund A., "Mexican-American Literature: An Overview," in *Recovering the U.S. Hispanic Literary Heritage*, ed. by Ramón Gutiérrez and Genaro Padilla, 2 vols. (Arte Público Press 1993).

Rebolledo, Tey Diana, *Women Singing in the Snow: A Cultural Analysis of Chicana Literature* (Univ. of Ariz. Press 1995).

Saldívar, Ramón, *Chicano Narrative: The Dialectics of Difference* (Univ. of Wis. Press 1990).

MARY JANE SUERO ELLIOTT

Chicano Performing and Graphic Arts

The beginning of the twenty-first century marks the third decade of Chicano and Chicana performing and graphic arts production. The creation of a Chicano arts movement in the 1960s emerged with the Chicano movement for social equality. The aesthetics and themes of this movement have multiplied and transformed tremendously over the last thirty years: it both helped to create and responded to new conditions and possibilities in aesthetic representation. The "third wave" of Chicano art retains a critical stance toward lingering institutional structures that reproduce social inequality; at the same time it registers a relentless self-critique of the changing social dynamics of Chicano culture.

The history of Spanish-language professional performing and graphic arts in the United States began in the late nineteenth century; however, the late 1960s initiated the development of bilingual Chicano theater and graphic arts. The Chicano movement overlapped with the women's and other developing-world movements for social justice, but the crusade by the United Farm Workers (UFW)

Felipe Cantu, Lou Diamond Phillips and Esai Morales in a scene from *La Bamba,* the story of Richie Valens, which was directed by Luis Valdez.

for safe working conditions brought national attention to it. Students and artists flocked to support the farm workers' struggle. Early Chicano art themes expressed the need to uncover the suppressed history of people of Mexican descent in the United States; to counter the myth that Mexican American culture and people were inferior to the dominant culture; to fight for adequate and fair public schooling and higher education, better job opportunities, housing, and health-care; to fight against police brutality and the biased penal system; and to embrace the indigenous past of Mexican history. During this first wave, barrio iconography blended with indigenous iconography of *Aztlán* (an imagined homeland located in the Southwest that predated Spanish, Mexican, and U.S. colonization). By the 1990s Chicano and Chicana art-

ists began questioning the utility of uncritically recycling that imagery. At the turn of the twenty-first century, many Chicano and Chicana artists employed syncretic spiritualities to address global social inequities. Because Chicano and Chicana performing and graphic arts emerged in relation to the movement, strong links continued between the two art forms. Equally important, Chicano and Chicana imagery continues to inspire youth culture around the world through cyberspace.

Performing Arts. The performing arts in which Chicanas and Chicanos participate include but are not limited to *teatro* ("theater"), playwriting, performance art, comedy, and dance. From the agricultural fields of California's Central Valley to the Broadway stage, the Obie Award–winning Teatro

Campesino ("Farmworkers Theater") is the most widely acclaimed of the teatro movement. UFW union organizers César Chávez and Dolores Huerta understood the power of art to illustrate the struggles for social justice and supported Teatro Campesino's development. Founded in 1965 by Luis Valdez and Augustin Lira, early *actos* ("actions") consisted of compact agitprop-like productions influenced by working-class Mexican performance traditions. Performed on flatbed trucks for *campesinos* ("farmworkers"), *actos* such as *Las dos caras del Patroncino* ("The Two Faces of the Boss") and *Huelga* ("Strike") included migrant workers as performers in short skits illuminating how unequal power-relations might be transformed. Teatro Campesino separated from the UFW to explore such themes as high school blowouts (student strikes), police brutality, the Vietnam War, and indigenous spirituality. During the 1980s Valdez enjoyed much success transferring historical themes, developed with Teatro Campesino, to Broadway and film production with *Zoot Suit*(based on the 1945 Zoot Suit riots). Valdez's 1987 hit film *La Bamba* memorialized the life of rock and roller Ritchie Valenz and employed Teatro Campesino actors. TENAZ, a national network, nurtured East and West Coast teatro, festivals, and playwrights, including productive playwright and director Carlos Morton and Jorge Huerta. Contemporary teatros are linked by a cyber-network.

Scholars acknowledge that Chicana writers and directors propelled Chicano theater's dynamism during the 1980s and 1990s. Groundbreaking plays launched critiques of sexist practices enacted by both mainstream and Chicano culture and explored the violence and homophobia inherent in the traditional patriarchal family structure. Cherríe Moraga, one of the best-known Chicana playwrights, gained recognition for such plays as *Heroes and Saints* that highlight the experiences of Chicanas and openly explore issues of religion, sexuality and social injustice. Plays by Josefina López (cofounder of the Pinche Mentirosa Sisters, or P.M.S.) and Silvia Gonzalez-S demonstrate Chicana theater's continuing transformation. Diane Rodríguez, former Teatro Campesino player, cofounded Teatro Esperanza and the comedy troupe Latins Anonymous. In 1994 Rodríguez utilized her vast experience to begin the invaluable work of codirecting the Latino Theatre Initiative (LTI).

The LTI provides advocacy and access for Latino artists and audiences at Los Angeles's Mark Taper Forum and has produced over 236 plays seen by 140 thousand people. The Guadalupe Cultural Arts Center in San Antonio, along with the Esperanza Theater, also provide dynamic spaces for Texas-based Chicana and Chicano theater.

Emerging during the same period as the teatro movement, Chicano performance art developed in urban East Los Angeles. In the late 1970s Asco (Nausea), an important art-making collective, deployed "guerrilla" performances and installations on city streets. Like teatro, founding members Patssi Valdez, Harry Gamboa, Gronk, and Willie Herron thematized social exploitation and inequality, yet invented completely different treatments. Lack of access to funding institutions forced them to blur ingeniously the line between performance and visual art. Asco's "No-Movies" juxtaposed punk and new-wave aesthetics, Hollywood imagery, high fashion, and postmodern alienation to comment on the exclusion of Latinos from Hollywood and the art world. In the mid-1980s, inclusion of spoken-word artist Marisela Norte and visual artist Diane Gamboa reinvigorated the group. Ironically, Asco broke up over arguments catalyzed by the very themes it engaged: the desperation and dysfunction bred by individualism. In 1992 Norte impressed critics with *Norte/Word* (New Alliance Records), the first collection of Chicana spoken word recorded on compact disc.

The MacArthur Foundation recognized the history of Chicano performance art, including the Border Arts Workshop, when it granted Genuis Awards to Guillermo Gomez-Peña in 1991 and Luis Alfaro in 1997. When Alfaro won the award, the artistic sensibility and point of view of working-class Los Angeles Chicanos were nationally praised. A prolific American writer, Alfaro thematizes urgent social issues. From staging guerrilla education on acquired immune deficiency syndrome (AIDS) in

Latino immigrant gay bars with Teatro Viva! to developing collaborative works such as *Black Butterfly, Super Chela, Piñata Woman and Other Super Hero Girls, Like Me* written by Marisela Norte, Alma Cervantes, and Sancha C. Muñoz for the Kennedy Center, Alfaro seriously engages issues of queer sexuality. His acclaimed solo performance *Downtown* registers Los Angeles's demographic and cultural changes. As codirector of LTI, Alfaro tirelessly promotes Chicano theater and performers, including the provocative gender-critiquing solo performances of Nao Bustamante.

Teatro, in part, paved the way for Chicano and Chicana comedians and choreographers. In the early 1980s Monica Palacios and Marga Gómez formed the first Chicana-Nuyorican-Cubana comedy duo, before forming and splitting from the first Chicano and Latino comedy troupe, Culture Clash (composed by José Burciaga, Richard Montoya, Ric Salinas, and Herbert Siguenza). In 1995 *Culture Clash* produced the first televised Chicano comedy series, recruiting comedy writers from the *Chicano Secret Service* troupe. As solo comedians, Palacio and Gómez continue to make biting social critiques through humor.

Los Angeles's Plaza de la Raza has supported choreographers including Gema Sandoval (director of Danza Floricanto/USA), Francisco Martinez, Miguel Delgado, and Frank Guevara (founder of the Dance Theater of East L.A., best known for developing Hyper Dance). During his short life, Guevera's choreography forever transformed postmodern dance. Performer and musician Robert Lopez, also known as El Vez, the Elvis translator, combines the energy of teatro, comedy, dance, and pop music to create energetic, cabaret-like shows that promote cross-cultural understanding.

Graphic Arts. The graphic arts include but are not limited to silk-screen prints, etchings, monoprints, plate prints, poster art, photography, comics, and digital graphics. The creation of Chicano cultural centers throughout the United States during the 1970s significantly boosted the development of Chicano graphic arts. Self-help Graphics, Los Angeles; San Francisco's Mission Cultural Center; Centro de la Raza, San Diego; and Plaza de la Raza, Los Angeles, among others across the nation, held art workshops geared toward youth. Royal Chicano Airforce was one of the first Chicano collectives to make prints and posters supporting the UFW.

The best of Chicano and Chicana graphic arts circulates in museums, on album-cover art, film festival programs, play broadsides, and in cyberspace. By 1990 enough art had been collected to launch the seminal Chicano Art: Resistance and Affirmation (CARA) exhibit. CARA included compelling graphics by Ester Hernández, Barbara Carasco, and Yolanda López. Diane Gamboa stands out as one of the most prolific graphic and visual artists included in CARA. Over the course of twenty years, Gamboa's critically acclaimed work extends into paper fashions, photography, and lithographs.

From the late 1980s into the 1990s, fotonovelas (graphic novels) and comics came into their own. *Love and Rockets* and *Heartbreak Soup* by Jaime and Gilbert Hernández combined the imagery of science fiction with the imagery of Frida Kahlo to project the Chicano future. Depicting lives of Chicano community outcasts with extraordinary storytelling abilities, they garnered a devoted international audience. The most circulated Chicano political cartoon, "La Cucuracha" by Lalo Alcaraz, also known as Lalo López (founder of Pocho Productions, a multimedia Chicano comedy company), documents issues affecting "Generation Mex."

Internet and digital technology transformed the context of Chicano graphic art archival collection and production. In 1995 Professor Yvonne Yarbro Bejarano initiated the Stanford University Chicana Arts Data Project to collect and disseminate Chicana art on-line. The University of California at Santa Barbara manages an excellent cyber-archive that displays Chicano graphic arts. A new generation of Chicano graphic cyberart is disbursed on a multitude of Web sites. The digital art of Alma López utilizes state-of-the art technology to create images of American life that point to the promise of a more just future.

BIBLIOGRAPHY

Broyles-González, Yolanda, *El Teatro Campesino: Theater in the Chicano Movement* (Univ. of Tex. Press 1994).

Chavoya, Ondine C., "Pseudographic Cinema: Asco's No-Movies," *Performance Research* 3, no. 1 (1998):1–14.

Griswold del Castillo, Richard, et al., *Chicano Art: Resistance and Affirmation, 1965–1985* (Wight Art Gallery/Univ. of Calif. 1991).

Habell-Pallán, Michelle, "El Vez Is 'Taking Care of Business': The Inter/National Appeal of Chicana/o Popular Music," *Cultural Studies* 13, no. 2 (April 1999):195–210.

Huerta, Jorge A., *Chicano Theater: Themes and Forms* (Bilingual Press 1982).

Pérez, Laura E., "Spirit Glyphs: Reimagining Art and Artist in the Work of Chicana Tlamatinime," *Modern Fiction Studies* 44, no. 1 (Spring 1998):36–46.

Román, David, *Acts of Intervention: Performance, Gay Culture, and AIDS* (Ind. Univ. Press 1998).

MICHELLE HABELL-PALLÁN

Chicanismo and the Chicano Movement

The origins of the word *Chicano* are obscure. Since the nineteenth century ethnic Mexicans have used it among themselves to denote those of lower social standing. However, it was not until the twentieth century that the phrase was used in public discourse; Mario Suárez's 1947 short story "El Hoyo" marks the first time the word *Chicano* appeared in print, yet twenty years would pass before it would gain a wide usage.

Between 1950 and 1960 a high birthrate and continuous immigration guaranteed the growth of the ethnic Mexican population in the United States and planted the seeds of the Chicano movement in the following two decades. Believing in the American dream, Mexican Americans born during the cold-war era confronted social, economic, and political conditions that prevented its attainment. This reality, combined with the civil rights movement of the 1960s, generated the Chicano movement. Young people rejected the label *Mexican American*, deeming it assimilationist and indicative of their second-class status as "hyphenated Americans," and instead transformed the pejorative term *Chicano* into

a positive self-identifier that made clear their critique of prevailing institutions. Chicano often came to signify a monolithic activist within a homogeneous community. In their quest for empowerment, Chicano activists essentialized the term and by so doing imagined a universal male subject. However, recent scholarship has clearly shown that the Chicano and the Chicano community are best viewed as dynamic entities, and that gender and region played a part in the formation of these identities.

In the 1960s and 1970s Chicano activists voiced demands for change and recognition in the common anti-American language of *Chicanismo* (used to express Chicano nationalism) that emphasized *la raza* ("the people"), *huelga* ("strike"), *carnalismo* ("brotherhood"), *Chicano,* and *Aztlán* (the recreation of the Aztec homeland that some believed had existed in the Southwest). Beneath that common language, however, was great diversity in the goals and strategies. Thus, the Chicano movement is best viewed not as a unified entity but as an amalgamation of organizations pressing for ethnic Mexican empowerment in various localities. These groups had a Chicano cultural nationalism in common but sometimes augmented this ideology with other beliefs.

Among the groups subscribing to a narrow cultural nationalism was Denver's Crusade for Justice, formed in 1966 by Rodolfo "Corky" Gonzales and others. The Crusade for Justice espoused a Chicano nationalism based on strengthening the Mexican American family and promoting cultural awareness. It protested police brutality and the Vietnam War, called for better education for Mexican Americans and eventually created its own school, and ran a social center. Perhaps the Crusade's greatest accomplishment was organizing the Chicano Youth Liberation Conference in March 1968. The three hundred activists in attendance approved the *Plan de Aztlán,* the quintessential expression of Chicano nationalism, which declared that Chicanos constituted a nation within the nation, and sought to bring about a more unified Chicano student movement with the creation of the *Movimiento Estudiantíl Chicano de Aztlán* (Chicano Student Movement of Aztlán) on college campuses. The Brown Berets, a paramilitary organization founded in Los Angeles in 1967, also used Chicano nationalism as its lodestar. The Berets, under the leadership of David Sánchez, were present in March 1968 at the East Los Angeles "blowouts," offering support and protection against law-enforcement officials to the three thousand students who walked out of their classes to protest an unequal educational system. The Berets also founded a free clinic, and by the time of their demise in 1972 boasted thirty-six chapters throughout the Southwest. Yet another highly nationalist group was the Chicano Moratorium Committee, which came to the fore in 1969 to protest the disproportionate numbers of Mexican Americans who were dying in Vietnam. Led by Rosalio Muñoz and Ramces Noriega, the committee organized the August 29, 1970, Chicano Moratorium, which featured twenty thousand protesters marching through the streets of East Los Angeles to demand an end to the war.

The Chicano insurgency also included organizations that sought to blend other ideologies with Chicano nationalism. In Texas, José Angel, Luz Gutiérrez, Mario Compean, and others mixed Chicano nationalism with liberalism to create a Chicano third party, *La Raza Unida* (The People's Party), in 1969. La Raza Unida Party (LRUP) sought to give power to Chicanos through the ballot box, and the idea soon spread to California, Colorado, and New Mexico. Given the multifaceted nature of Chicanos, the LRUP was far from being a unified party. This was most evident at their only national conference held in El Paso, Texas, in September 1972.

Still others synthesized Marxism with Chicano nationalism as did the *Centro de Acción Social Autónomo* (Center for Autonomous Social Action), commonly known as CASA. In 1969 Bert Corona, Soledad Alatorre, and other labor organizers constituted CASA as a mutual-aid association. Five years later a cadre of younger activists, among them Antonio Rodríguez, Isabel Rodríguez, and Carlos Chávez, assumed its reins and transformed CASA into a Marxist-Leninist organization that stressed the organic link between ethnic Mexicans north and south of the border and sought to empower Mexican immigrants by dismantling capitalism. At its

height in 1975 CASA had centers in Los Angeles, San José, San Diego, and Santa Barbara, California; Greeley, Colorado; Chicago, Illinois; and San Antonio, Texas. It soon fizzled when members could not agree on its direction, and by 1978 it no longer existed. Similar to CASA's vision for Chicano power was the August Twenty-ninth Movement (ATM) founded by Cruz Becerra, William Flores, and James Franco. Guided by Joseph Stalin's ideas, the organization argued that Chicanos constituted a separate nation.

Though radicalism was at its core, the Chicano movement also sought to reform existing institutions. This streak was most evident in *Catolicos por la Raza* (Catholics for the People), a Los Angeles group formed by Ricardo Cruz in 1969, which concentrated on making the Catholic Church more responsive to its Mexican American parishioners. Another reformist group was New Mexico's *La Alianza Federal de Mercedes*. With the fiery Reies López Tijerina at its helm, La Alianza (The Federal Alliance of Land Grants) called for the U.S. government to return communal lands taken from New Mexicans following the American conquest. Perhaps the best-known of these reform groups was the United Farm Workers (UFW), which was fundamentally a multiethnic labor organization, with ties to the Democratic Party, that sought better working conditions for its members. However, the inspiration of its leaders, César Chávez and Dolores Huerta, ensured that the UFW would be viewed by many as part of the Chicano movement.

The Chicano movement was part and parcel of Vietnam-era America. Like other young people in that period, Chicano insurgents fundamentally sought to fulfill the republic's promise. Among the Chicano movement's long-lasting effects was the transformation of the academy through the development of Chicano studies programs, the greater number of Mexican Americans at colleges and universities, and the higher visibility (though there is still a long way to go) of Chicanos, and other Latinos, in popular culture, politics, and the life of the nation in general.

BIBLIOGRAPHY

Acuña, Rodolfo, *Occupied America: A History of Chicanos,* 3d ed. (Harper 1988).

Chávez, Ernesto, "Birth of a New Symbol: The Brown Berets' Gendered Chicano National Imaginary," in *Generations of Youth: Youth Cultures and History in Twentieth Century America,* ed. by Joe Austin and Michael Willard (N.Y. Univ. Press 1998).

García, Ignacio M., *Chicanismo: The Forging of a Militant Ethos among Mexican Americans* (Univ. of Ariz. Press 1997).

Gómez-Quiñones, Juan, *Chicano Politics: Reality and Promise, 1940–1990* (Univ. of N.Mex Press 1990).

Muñoz, Carlos, *Youth, Identity, Power: The Chicano Movement* (Verso 1989).

ERNESTO CHÁVEZ

CHILDHOOD

"Childhood," wrote Ambrose Bierce in his *Devil's Dictionary* (1906), is "the period of human life intermediate between the idiocy of infancy and the folly of youth—two removes from the sin of manhood and three from the remorse of old age." This may be as clear a definition as one is likely to find, since it incorporates the idea of a recognizable period in the life cycle, while making a caustic comment about the characteristics of the ages with which (male) childhood is contrasted in American culture.

Childhood has been defined in different ways at various times in American history depending on who is doing the defining and what biological or behavioral characteristics they are using. Historians have wisely noted that there is no such thing as childhood in the abstract, only children. Yet they usually go on to use definitions based on a child's relative autonomy. Thus, a child is a person who has grown beyond the helplessness (idiocy) of infancy, able to speak and begin to think, but who has not achieved sufficient independence from adults to function without extensive economic and psychological support. Childhood is defined as the process of growing up and leaving it.

Any definition of childhood must take into account both the external environment and internal development of children. The external environment includes but is not limited to the physical spaces in which a child lives (home, neighborhood, playgrounds, schools) and the social environment (family, friends, strangers, teachers, health-care workers, media). Internal development includes the mental and physical changes from birth to that point at which the child is considered a young adult, youth, or adolescent. The years three through twelve are especially important, because children experiment with the knowledge they are acquiring by creating what may be called a distinct culture.

The principal characteristics of children's culture are as follows: a dependence on oral communication before the acquisition of literacy, a resistance to at least part of the restrictions imposed by adult cultures, and the relative brevity of childhood in the larger life course. These three characteristics may also vary in relation to adult-defined factors such as gender, ethnicity, and social class.

The dependence on oral communication has many important consequences, not the least of which is that it is confined to the nature, frequency, and duration of face-to-face contacts. The preservation of children's lore requires opportunities for children to learn from others. The historical trend toward smaller families, more structured education, and electronic entertainment limits the possibilities for the transmission of such lore. On the other hand, these new factors seem to encourage innovation in play and opposition to adult supervision. Finally, as Iona and Peter Opie, British students of children's lore, have suggested, there is a new generation of children in playgrounds every six years. Even within a family, childhood appears and vanishes in a few years, but its influence, as measured by the attention given it by novelists, poets, politicians, and psychologists, is profound.

Children in colonial America were not usually accorded a special status, but differences among infants, children, youth, and adults were observed in various ways. In the Puritan settlements of New England, the distinction between child and youth was often marked by admission into a congregation. By the age of thirteen or fourteen children were expected to have the ability to understand the Bible.

Children were given chores and expected to learn useful skills as soon as they were physically able, but they also participated in a variety of activities appropriate to their age including ball games, ring games, hopscotch, blind man's buff, and hide-and-seek. Since most lived on farms or in villages, children were able to escape adult scrutiny by spending much of their time out-of-doors. Even Boston, with a population of about ten thousand in 1716, provided ample space for children to experiment with juvenile variations on adult life. Benjamin Franklin recalled in his autobiography that when he was ten he and his friends took a pile of stones intended for building a house and constructed a wharf in a salt marsh so they could fish during high tide. Franklin's anecdote provides a glimpse into the culture of childhood before compulsory education made schools the principal site of children's activities.

Childhood was a brief, inchoate period of life in the seventeenth and eighteenth centuries, but beginning in the 1800s a series of reform movements began that sharply defined the meanings of infancy, childhood, and youth. The creation of free schools, orphan asylums, and infant schools in the first three decades of the nineteenth century provided institutions in which poor children were taught to read, on the assumption that literacy would separate them from the negative influences of their families and neighborhoods. Children as young as three received formal education but left school for work after five or six years. Children from middle-class families, on the other hand, were entrusted to their mothers until the age of six or seven and then went to school until the age of fifteen or sixteen. Thus, childhood for the working class lasted from ages three through ten, while middle-class children enjoyed more years at home and a six-year transition from childhood to youth.

In all cases, a child's world begins with adults, usually parents, and grows to include siblings, relatives, neighbors, schoolmates, and strangers. In the nineteenth century the majority of Americans lived on farms or in rural villages; families were isolated and schools were small. Children of all ages shared classrooms and schoolyards. Although they might

THE GRANGER COLLECTION

Author Laura Ingalls Wilder (*right*) as a young girl, with her sisters Carrie (*left*) and Mary.

be excluded from some activities because of size or strength, younger children had ample occasions to observe and imitate older children. Although forced to work with their families, most children had time and opportunity to learn the distinctive lore of childhood, the songs, games, rituals, and pranks that were recognized by both adults and children as defining a happy childhood.

Childhood in the years between the 1820s and the 1880s has been immortalized in the autobiographies of Edward Everett Hale, Lucy Larcom, William Dean Howells, Lincoln Steffens, and William Allen White; in the novels of Louisa May Alcott, Thomas Bailey Aldrich, Mark Twain, Hamlin Garland, and Laura Ingalls Wilder; and in the paintings of Lilly Martin Spencer, Eastman Johnson, John George Brown, Winslow Homer, Mary Cassatt, and others. By ignoring the misfortunes of Huck's life (in Twain) or Garland's, commentators have turned these years into a "golden age" of childhood against which modern childhood is measured and frequently found wanting. The stereotypes of the innocent child, the naughty child, the barefoot boy, the plucky girl, while based on personal experience, obscure some of the brutal realities.

The lives of slave children, as glimpsed through autobiographies and reminiscences, were stunted in many ways. Even when they played with white children on plantations and in cities, their chattel status denied them the opportunity to challenge authority and mock adult behavior, essential elements of children's culture. Freed by the Civil War, most African American children were, like other poor children, forced to sacrifice much of their childhood to wage labor in agriculture or street trades such as shoe shining. Nevertheless, fields and streets provided places where children could assert their own authority and could socialize without adult supervision.

One can confidently assume that a rich and varied culture of childhood was flourishing in the last decades of the nineteenth century because in 1883 it was suddenly "discovered" by adults. Ironically, the children's world that the psychologists, folklorists, and anthropologists found was at least partially created by other adults, who had succeeded in bringing children together in schools and settlement houses and teaching them songs, games, and stories that were thought to instill a sense of fair play, self-reliance, and patriotism. Nor were the discoveries surprising.

G. Stanley Hall, an early psychologist, collected responses from children entering the first grade to questions about food production, parts of the body, and geographic and atmospheric conditions, finding that those who had attended kindergarten generally knew more than those who had not. William Wells Newell, one of the founders of the American Folklore Society and author of *Games and Songs of American Children* (1884), was impressed by the ability of children to preserve ancient rhymes and games, but he was equally fascinated by their inventiveness. He reconciled this paradox by arguing that pastimes that survive from generation to generation are those that best serve the needs of children themselves, not adults who "remodeled [children's games], professedly for their amusement, but with the secret purpose of moral direction."

While relatively little is known about childhood as experienced by children, it is clear that since the 1880s a number of important changes have taken place that profoundly affect children. These changes may be grouped into four categories: (1) demographic: families have shrunk in size; children have fewer siblings; (2) psychological: professional child-rearing experts have attempted to guide parental attitudes and behavior and to influence laws regulating the care and welfare of children; (3) environmental: children increasingly live in cities and adjacent suburbs; their lives are organized by schools and adult-supervised activities; and (4) communication: motion pictures, radio, television, and personal computers allow children to observe aspects of adult life previously denied them.

Changes in family size and structure are, of course, part of the multiple changes in society brought about by science, technology, and urbanization. Although children were employed in industry, their labor was less valuable than on a farm. As Viviana Zelizer argues, children became economically worthless but emotionally priceless. In settling suits over the death of a child, American courts have evolved from calculating the potential earnings of the victim (minus expenses) to estimating the dollar value of emotional loss and the value of companionship to parents in their old age. The meaning of work was also redefined. As more and more jobs were deemed unsafe or unhealthy for children, other occupations such as newspaper delivery and shoe shining were sanctioned and "little merchants" encouraged. Many parents began to pay their children an allowance, wages not for household tasks but for being good sons and daughters. The allowance also provided the child a measure of independence, making him or her a full citizen of the pecuniary society.

The rise in divorce has also had an impact on children and childhood. The children of single parents may gain additional value, both economic and emotional. The only child achieves a numerical equality; siblings outnumber the single parent. Peer groups take on additional significance in socialization. Even in a majority of two-parent families both parents are working outside the home. Like single parents, they depend on day care, schools, and organized after-school activities to supervise their children. As children become even more of a financial burden, they may be expected to assume responsibility for shopping, cleaning, and cooking, their childhood truncated in a way similar to the working class a century ago.

As children have adapted to changes in the domestic situation, they have also had to cope with changes in attitudes toward them in the medical, legal, and social science professions. Since the founding of the American Pediatric Society in 1889, children's health has been a public concern and infant mortality has declined, nutrition has improved, and many diseases have been eradicated. Better health has meant a more active and happy childhood for a larger percentage of children. Children acquired more legal rights in the twentieth century as well, although the courts were not always consistent in their interpretations. Public concern over juvenile delinquency periodically resulted in attempts to enact and enforce curfews and censorship of minors. Although fewer than half the states allowed corporal punishment as discipline in schools, the U.S. Supreme Court refused in 1977 to rule that such punishment was "cruel and unusual."

Indeed, some analysts believe that anxiety over child abuse, which focuses on cases of individual physical and sexual abuse, is a mask for Americans' ambivalence toward children. In 1998 children constituted forty percent of Americans living below the poverty line and twenty-five percent of the homeless population. Parental unemployment and low wages clearly harm more children than does individual assault. Impoverished, neglected children, if not "abused" by legal definitions, are suffering. The causes of that suffering may be parental or societal. Blaming parents raises questions of parental rights and responsibilities. The courts have not been consistent on this matter. Policymakers and legislators have failed to solve the problem of children's poverty, but professional advice givers have not been reluctant to challenge parental authority.

From the Playground Association of 1906 to *Parents* magazine in 1927 to Dr. Benjamin Spock's *Baby and Child Care* in 1946 and the Dick and Jane school

© BERNARD BOUTRIT/WOODFIN CAMP/PICTUREQUEST

A boy and a girl climb on an "Alice in Wonderland" sculpture in New York City's Central Park.

books of the 1940s and 1950s, the message from "child savers" was increasingly what one scholar called "the fun morality." By focusing on the child's inclination to play—defined by adults as contributing to identity formation, learning, socialization, creativity, and other desired ends—child-development experts have attempted, with varying degrees of success, to accomplish what Newell thought impossible, that is, to steer children's culture in a moral direction. A vast toy industry grew in the twentieth century in the belief that the objects children play with can improve their social, motor, and intellectual skills. Christmas as a religious celebration has become largely a ritual of gift-giving dominated by Santa Claus, an imaginary figure who helps maintain parental control over the emotional lives of their children. To make the ritual a success, children must pretend to be asleep, pretend to be good, and agree to believe. A shared suspension of disbelief characterized parent-child relations in the late twentieth century.

Childhood in the years 1940 to 2000, as depicted in literature and the arts, looks quite different than it did a century earlier. Although some autobiographers continue to depict childhood as a "golden age," those born since the late 1930s (Caryl Rivers, Annie Dillard, Tobias Wolff, Joyce Maynard, Gary Soto) are more inclined to emphasize the traumas and violence of those years. Novelists have been even more emphatic in their examinations of the psychological and physical abuse suffered by children in the late twentieth century. J. D. Salinger's *Catcher in the Rye*, Toni Morrison's *Bluest Eye*, Marilynne Robinson's *Housekeeping*, Gish Jen's *Typical American*, and Russell Banks's *Rule of the Bone* (a contemporary version of *Huck Finn*) all subject their protagonists to torment by adults. In movies and on television the image of childhood has swung from innocence to malevolence, from *Meet Me in St. Louis* (1944) and *The Yearling* (1946) to *The Bad Seed* (1956) and *Home Alone* (1990).

Children and childhood endure despite adversity. Given their relative helplessness, children are remarkably resourceful in resisting and refashioning the many strictures imposed by adults. As in previous periods of history, children watch and judge those who are working hard to get them to "grow up," to exchange childhood for adult culture. Whether the judgments lead to the kind of behavior adults desire will depend, as it always has, on the degree of mutual respect that the two cultures have for each other.

[See also FAMILY.*]*

BIBLIOGRAPHY

Clark, Cindy Dell, *Flights of Fancy, Leaps of Faith: Children's Myths in Contemporary America* (Univ. of Chicago Press 1995).

Elder, Glen H., Jr., et al., eds., *Children in Time and Place: Developmental and Historical Insights* (Cambridge 1993).

Hiner, N. Ray, and Joseph M. Hawes, eds., *Growing Up in America: Children in Historical Perspective* (Univ. of Ill. Press 1985).

Howard, Dorothy, *Dorothy's World: Childhood in Sabine Bottom 1902–1910* (Prentice-Hall 1977).

Sutton-Smith, Brian, et al., eds., *Children's Folklore: A Source Book* (Garland Pub. 1995; reprint, Utah State Univ. Press 1999).

West, Elliott, and Paula Petrik, eds., *Small Worlds: Children and Adolescents in America, 1850–1950* (Univ. Press of Kans. 1992).

West, Elliott, *Growing Up in Twentieth-Century America: A History and Reference Guide* (Greenwood Press 1996).

Zelizer, Viviana, *Pricing the Priceless Child: The Changing Social Value of Children* (Basic Bks. 1985).

BERNARD MERGEN

Cover illustration from *Rapunzel* (1998) by Paul O. Zelinsky.

CHILDREN'S LITERATURE

It is a commonplace that society sees the future in its children; it is equally commonplace for adults to believe that children's literature holds no interest for anyone much over the age of twelve. Read in cultural context, however, children's literature is full of meaning. At least as much as any other literature, what is written for children reveals a society's attitudes toward the future. Hope and fear, optimism or despair, social assumptions, anxieties and complacencies, all speak through the models and morals of children's stories.

Except for Puritan catechisms and schoolbooks, most books for American children before 1820 were imported. But the nationalistic fervor that followed the War of 1812 brought about a home-grown juvenile literature, written to cultivate in American children the qualities necessary to serve and preserve the young republic. Unselfishness, self-control, industriousness, and a keen sense of duty planted early in the growing child ensured responsible citizens in the future.

Moralistic fiction dominated children's fare. The American Sunday School Union produced and distributed hundreds of nonsectarian, morally didactic books for children. Secular publishers also found profit in children's books, just as didactic, although occasionally more interesting. Jacob Abbott's *Rollo* and *Franconia* stories are perhaps best known. Many periodicals thrived while some failed. *Youth's Companion,* one of the hardiest, began publication in 1826 and lasted, remarkably, until the early years of the twentieth century. Its strongly evangelical content was aimed at adults as well as children.

By the 1860s better distribution, wider literacy, and cheaper printing methods had created a mass market. Publishing began to divide its wares into categories, which can be roughly labeled mainstream and popular. Popular "pulp" fiction, sensational, exciting, and badly written, appeared in both periodical and book form, aimed at consumers of lowbrow materials. To the dismay of middle-class adults, however, it was eagerly read by boys of all classes, challenging mainstream publishers to compete with equally engaging but more respectable stories for the young. Formula fiction by such authors as William Taylor Adams, Horatio Alger, and Sophie May was somewhat better tolerated, but the time was ripe for a new, "good" literature for children, neither sensational nor overly preachy, a literature acceptable to the educated middle classes in the late nineteenth century.

Changing attitudes toward childhood also fostered a new approach to children as readers. By the second half of the nineteenth century, childhood had acquired a value in itself, apart from its role as preparation for adulthood. Authors as dissimilar

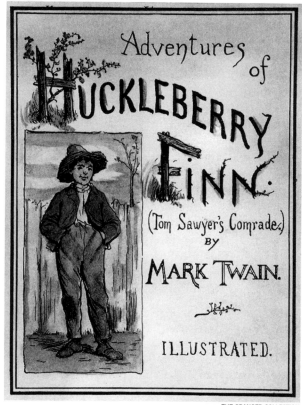

THE GRANGER COLLECTION

The cover from the 1885 edition of Mark Twain's *Adventures of Huckleberry Finn*.

as Sarah Woolsey, Louisa May Alcott, Thomas Bailey Aldrich, and Mark Twain wrote for children in new ways, with resounding success. Although Woolsey's and Alcott's stories retained a good deal of open moralizing, the messages were offset by lively, believable characterization. Aldrich and Twain, with their "boys will be boys" philosophy, more frankly jettisoned morals for entertaining narratives. Instructed by storypapers and dime novels, publishers and writers came to understand that, whatever else they were, stories for the young must be fun to read.

In the last quarter of the nineteenth century, mainstream children's literature attained at least a junior partnership with the larger literary culture. It was reviewed in such respected journals as *Atlantic Monthly, Harper's* and *Century* magazines. It joined the periodical scene in 1873 with *St. Nicholas* magazine, the most successful children's magazine ever produced. And adults read children's fare: many Americans admired Alcott, Rudyard Kipling, Twain, Frances Hodgson Burnett, and Sarah Orne Jewett as much for their children's stories as for their adult works. *Peter Pan* and *Little Lord Fauntleroy* charmed sentimental adults, perhaps more than they did children. Adults and children often read together the romantic histories, legends, and hero tales produced for the young: Robin Hood, Roland, King Arthur, and William Wallace. Major publishers issued these with handsome illustrations, as idealized as the texts. With improved technologies for art reproduction, children's books were a market for some of the best illustrative artists of the time, including Winslow Homer, A. B. Frost, Howard Pyle, N. C. Wyeth, Jessie Wilcox Smith, and Maxfield Parrish.

By the early decades of the twentieth century, however, when adult taste in literature shifted from romanticism toward realism, children's literature, still romanticized, fell away from adult literary culture. Yet the children's book field prospered. Children's literature became a recognized professional specialty for librarians, editors, and reviewers; public libraries expanded their services to children and chose their books with care. Publishing houses created separate departments, with specialists in charge, to produce children's books. The women (they were all women) who ran these departments were well educated, artistically savvy, and prepared to compete for the best authors and illustrators. In 1924 *Hornbook* magazine, the first reviewing journal devoted entirely to children's books, began publication. The Newbery Award, established in 1922 to honor the year's "most distinguished children's book," became every children's book editor's goal.

The prosperous 1920s also supported a revolution in children's picture books. Progressive-era educational research combined with imaginative publishing to create a fresh approach to books for the very young. A new group of illustrators, modern in taste and training, supported by knowledgeable editors and book designers, revitalized the American picture book. The 1920s and 1930s stand out in the annals of graphic art production, not least for the art in children's picture books. Oddly, 1920s fiction for older children was pedestrian, romanticism having worn down to conventional sentimentality.

Children's literature weathered the Depression years surprisingly well. Although the rate of new book production slowed, public library use increased and the institutional market for children's books was strong. Not surprisingly, realism finally overtook the idealized stories so popular for so long. In a grim economy, "light historical fiction, gay stories of girls at a boarding school, and good, clean accounts of young adventure are not enough," wrote one author in a 1930s *Hornbook* article. Editors and publishers apparently agreed. If the realism in children's books of the 1930s was not very gritty, if it screened out the harshest aspects of a society in crisis, still, it acknowledged a changed world. The focus broadened; family and community mattered more than personal success and material achievement.

Social cataclysms, even including a popular war, tend to enter children's literature slowly; it was years before World War II got more than indirect attention. Yet the teen novel, a major genre of postwar literature, was itself an artifact of social and economic changes after 1945. Postwar prosperity allowed more American children to stay in school longer; by 1960, ninety percent attended high school. If adolescents worked, it was part-time and their wages were theirs to spend. Teenagers were a new market for everything from raincoats to records, and the teen novel became an established genre.

Socially conservative, white, middle class, restrictive toward girls, anxious toward boys, teen literature was at once insular and representative. The novels registered the change in adolescent experience: a longer economic dependence on the one hand, and an unprecedented freedom, conferred by old cars and new money, on the other. Girls' novels, mild romances written to fit their readers' interests, also fit the demographic reality of early marriage in the 1950s. Children's book professionals and publishers were enclosed in a comfortable, self-contained world.

The tumultuous 1960s changed everything about that world, shattering its isolation and politicizing its discourse. Where, after all, were minorities in what Nancy Larrick called "The All-White World of Children's Literature"? Why did children's literature stereotype girls and women as passive and dependent? The National Organization for Women raised popular consciousness with a traveling slide show of picture-book illustrations: mother in an apron, father reading the newspaper, boys climbing trees, girls watching—over and over again. Reviewers outside the children's book field began to read children's books for what they said about equality, racism, sexism, and justice overdue. The old confidence in the American family—indeed, in American society—dissolved as the literature confronted realities long ignored.

Once opened, the door to the outside world stayed open. In the decades that followed, children's books explored such subjects as alcoholism, drug addition, homosexuality, premarital sex, and child abuse. Predictably, early excursions into controversial subjects were heavily message-laden—witness the monotonously downbeat "problem novels" of the 1970s and 1980s. But while release from old taboos produced some very bad writing, overall freedom has expanded children's literature at every level. Contemporary picture books, which reach far beyond a preschool audience, are experimental and artistically adventurous. In a visually oriented society, authors of nonfiction have learned to use techniques adapted from television, film, and video to convey information in new ways.

At the beginning of a new century, questions arise about a literature that is defined by its audience and whose audience is in turn defined by the social conceptions of childhood. With competition on every side for a child's time and attention, with adults less willing—or less able—to protect children in a world saturated with information, why and how will a children's literature survive? It is a reasonable question, yet the fact is that publication of children's literature goes on apace and so does the discussion of the meaning and influence of such literature on children and, by extension, on American society.

[See also POPULAR LITERATURE; POPULAR CULTURE; PRINT CULTURE; YOUTH CULTURE; CHILDHOOD.*]*

BIBLIOGRAPHY

Estes, Sally, ed., *Growing Up Is Hard to Do: A Collection of "Booklist" Columns* (A.L.A. 1994).

Lindgren, Merri V., *The Multicultural Mirror: Cultural Substance in Literature for Children and Young Adults* (Highsmith Press 1991).

Nodelman, Perry, *The Pleasures of Children's Literature,* 2d ed. (Longman 1996).

Rochman, Hazel, *Against Borders: Promoting Books for a Multicultural World* (A.L.A. 1993).

Sutherland, Zena, *Children and Books,* 9th ed. (Longman 1997).

ANNE SCOTT MACLEOD

CHINESE AMERICANS

The first Chinese to arrive in the Americas were crew members on Spanish ships involved in the trade between the Philippines and Mexico in the sixteenth century. Later, Chinese sailors and small merchants involved in the trade between North America and China settled in the port cities of New York, Boston, and Philadelphia. Appreciable numbers of Chinese, however, did not emigrate to the United States until the California gold rush of 1849. From this date until 1882, approximately four hundred thousand Chinese arrived in Hawaii and the United States. Pushed out of China by internal disorder and foreign imperialism, the Chinese were initially drawn to America by the possibility of striking it rich in the gold fields. Later they were recruited to build the first transcontinental railroad, and they played a major role in shaping the economy of the American West. They worked on sugar plantations in Hawaii, in the fishing and agricultural industries in California, and in light manufacturing, domestic service, and other forms of crafts and labor.

Despite the Chinese contribution to the economic development of the western United States, an anti-Chinese movement developed, which eventually became national in scale. The Chinese presence in the United States was met by many with great hostility, which was expressed on a variety of levels:

violence, legal restrictions, anti-Chinese publications, and ultimately the denial of naturalization and a ban on immigration. The violence against Chinese took the form of lynchings, massacres, expulsion from various cities, and other forms of physical abuse. The Chinese had little recourse in these matters because of the legal restrictions under which they lived. In many states they were not allowed to testify for or against a white person in a court of law. Denied the right of naturalization, Chinese immigrants could not vote and thus had little political power to change their situation. In turn, few politicians came to their aid since they offered little in return in terms of votes. In fact, taking an anti-Chinese position often won many votes for some politicians.

Anti-Chinese propaganda and its rhetoric revolved around two main points, economics and race, both of which were usually framed as critiques of Chinese culture. European American politicians, labor leaders, missionaries, and journalists argued that the Chinese degraded American labor by working under conditions and accepting wages well below the standard. These economic issues were entwined with American racial antipathy toward the Chinese, who were considered immoral and unclean, biologically inferior, and perhaps most important, unassimilable. Chinese immigrant presence in the United States was thought to be a threat to American institutions and "civilization." Coming at a time when much of the country was embroiled in the debate over slavery, Chinese immigrants were accused of fostering in the United States a new system of slavery known as coolieism.

Chinese immigrants were kept from entering the American sociopolitical mainstream through legal restrictions. Various local and state laws regulated Chinese immigrant life. In many states Chinese could not marry Caucasians, own land, or work in certain occupations or during certain hours, and they often paid special taxes and fees. In 1875 Congress passed the Page Law, banning the entry of Asian contract laborers and women who were thought likely to become prostitutes. Because many Americans suspected that most, if not all, Chinese women were probably prostitutes, they were sub-

jected to humiliating insinuations by immigration officials that they were coming to America for illicit reasons. As a result many Chinese women did not even attempt to emigrate to America. This contributed to an unequal gender ratio in the Chinese immigrant community, and the development of Chinese American families was extremely slow. The most damaging legislation was the passage of the first Chinese Exclusion Act in 1882, prohibiting the immigration of Chinese laborers for ten years; it was the first American immigration law to exclude a single group based on race and class. It also reaffirmed the ban on Chinese immigrants becoming citizens. Strengthened and renewed in 1888, 1892, 1902, and made permanent in 1904, this legislation was not repealed until 1943 when China and the United States were allies during World War II. Even at that point the Chinese were assigned the minimal quota of 105 persons eligible to immigrate a year. World War II proved to be a turning point for Chinese Americans. Because of their participation in the military and defense industries, Chinese Americans served their country alongside their fellow Americans, often for the first time. The American image of the Chinese improved and Chinese Americans themselves began to feel a part of American society.

The Chinese were not passive victims of legal discrimination. They wrote articles to counter anti-Chinese propaganda and frequently challenged local, state, and federal restrictions in court. The Chinese also developed various means of circumventing what they viewed as unfair emigration laws. The most well-known plan was that of the "paper son" system, whereby an aspiring emigrant would purchase the papers, often fraudulent, of a Chinese American citizen or someone else eligible to immigrate. He would then have to pose as that person in order to gain entry into the United States. The lasting legacy of this, however, was that many Chinese immigrants lost their true identities when they were forced to maintain their fictional identities for fear of deportation.

Since the passage of the Immigration Act of 1965, which did away with quotas based on nationality, Chinese immigrants have continued to settle in

America, contributing to the ongoing evolution of American culture. Through their continued struggle for civil rights, artistic expression, labor, business activities, and social and political involvement, Chinese Americans have come to claim an important and visible role in American society.

[See also ASIAN AMERICANS, AN OVERVIEW, *and articles on* ASIAN AMERICAN ART AND LITERATURE, ASIAN AMERICANS IN FILM AND THEATER.*]*

BIBLIOGRAPHY

Lee, Robert G., *Orientals: Asian Americans in Popular Culture* (Temple Univ. Press 1999).

McClain, Charles J., *In Search of Equality: The Chinese Struggle against Discrimination in Nineteenth-Century America* (Univ. of Calif. Press 1994).

Salyer, Lucy E., *Laws Harsh as Tigers: Chinese Immigrants and the Shaping of Modern Immigration Law* (Univ. of N.C. Press 1995).

Wong, K. Scott, and Sucheng Chan, eds., *Claiming America: Constructing Chinese American Identities during the Exclusion Era* (Temple Univ. Press 1998).

Yung, Judy, *Unbound Feet: A Social History of Chinese Women in America* (Univ. of Calif. Press 1995).

K. SCOTT WONG

CHISHOLM, SHIRLEY

The first African American woman elected to the United States Congress, Shirley Chisholm was a forceful advocate throughout her career on behalf of children, the economically disadvantaged, and Americans of color. A tireless and courageous proponent of progressive causes, including federally financed social programs, Chisholm served as a role model to many Americans and as a symbol of big-spending, liberal interventionism to others.

Born Shirley Anita St. Hill in Brooklyn, New York, on November 30, 1924, Chisholm spent her early childhood in Barbados, her parents' country of origin, returning to Brooklyn when she was ten. Chisholm earned a bachelor of arts degree in sociology from Brooklyn College and a master's degree in early childhood education from Columbia University. She married Conrad Chisholm in 1949. They divorced in 1977, and she married businessman

Arthur Hardwick, Jr., later that year. While serving as a teacher and school administrator in New York City, she organized and campaigned on behalf of black political candidates in the Democratic Party. In 1964 Chisholm ran for the New York State Assembly, winning by a significant margin. Her adherence to principle rather than party lines contributed to her growing reputation as an effective and independent legislator. Running for Congress in New York's Twelfth District in 1968, Chisholm overcame racist and sexist opposition to win her party's nomination and ultimately the election to the Ninety-first Congress, where she served on the powerful Ways and Means Committee and the Committee on Agriculture.

Known primarily for her stands on increased funding for education and anti-poverty programs and against military spending and South African apartheid, Chisholm served in Congress for fourteen years. She eventually served on the Veterans Affairs Committee, the Committee on Education and Labor, the Rules Committee, and the Committee on Organization and Review.

In 1972 Chisholm again made history by seeking the Democratic nomination for president. Despite a poorly financed campaign and opposition from the party establishment, Chisholm refused to abandon the race. She garnered 150 votes from convention delegates on the first ballot. Although she failed to win the nomination, she characteristically influenced the party's platform and debates beyond others' expectations, although she was stung by the lack of support from organizations primarily led by African American men and white women.

After retiring from the House in 1983, Chisholm moved to upstate New York with her husband. Although she lectured periodically, and spoke for Jesse Jackson's presidential campaigns, she considered herself withdrawn from politics. President Bill Clinton nominated her as United States Ambassador to Jamaica in 1992. Citing failing eyesight, she declined.

Although her liberal leanings eventually fell out of favor in Congress and in America during the Nixon, Ford, and early Reagan administrations,

Chisholm was praised, even by her critics, for her tenacity and integrity. Her fearless advocacy for unpopular stands and on behalf of disenfranchised individuals with little clout has led many, especially African Americans and women, to consider her a catalyst for change and a heroic maverick.

[See also AFRICAN AMERICANS, AN OVERVIEW.*]*

BIBLIOGRAPHY

Brownmiller, Susan, *Shirley Chisholm: A Biography* (Doubleday 1970).

Chisholm, Shirley, *Unbought and Unbossed* (Houghton 1970) [Chisholm's first autobiography, titled after her campaign slogan].

Chisholm, Shirley, *The Good Fight* (Harper 1973) [focuses primarily on her bid for the presidency].

Duffy, Susan, comp., *Shirley Chisholm: A Bibliography of Writings by and about Her* (Scarecrow 1988).

DAVID GOLDSTEIN-SHIRLEY

CHURCH AND STATE

While many who came to America from Europe were seeking religious liberty, they often sought it for themselves and their coreligionists alone. As a result, most colonies had established churches (most often the Church of England) and a legal code that enforced biblical and ecclesiastic moral codes.

In 1636, however, Roger Williams founded Providence Plantations (Rhode Island) on the principles of firm separation of church and state and tolerance for all religions. The Maryland Toleration Act (1649) extended religious liberty to all believers in Jesus Christ, although the Anglican Church eventually became the established church of this proprietary colony, which Lord Baltimore had founded as a refuge for Catholics. In the aftermath of the Glorious Revolution, however, Catholics were excluded from public office and were eventually disenfranchised.

Pennsylvania, with the Quaker William Penn as its proprietor, adopted "The Great Law" (1682), which established religious toleration and enforced Christian morality. The population of New York, on the other hand, was so religiously diverse that the Duke's Laws (1665) and the Ministry Act of 1693 (as interpreted) allowed dissenting Protestant clergy as well as Anglicans to be selected for the locally tax-supported ministries.

In the aftermath of the American Revolution, the Virginia Assembly passed Thomas Jefferson's Statute of Religious Liberty (1786), which disestablished the Episcopalian Church and forbade the punishment of religious expression or belief. The Northwest Ordinance (1787), passed by the Confederation Congress, guaranteed religious liberty to the inhabitants of the territories and set aside public lands for the support of schools.

The Constitution of the United States, proposed in 1787 and ratified in 1789, had little to say on the subject of religion, but it did contain a prohibition on religious tests for public office [Article VI, paragraph iii]. The absence of a bill of rights proved a major obstacle to acceptance of the Constitution, and several states made their ratifications conditional on the creation of one. When, under the stewardship of James Madison, Congress proposed a Bill of Rights, the First Amendment (as ratified) contained the clause, "Congress shall make no law respecting an establishment of religion, nor interfering with the free exercise thereof. . . . "

Throughout much of the nineteenth century, most interaction of church and state occurred on the state level, where the U.S. Bill of Rights did not apply. In 1833 the last state-supported church, the Congregationalist Church, was disestablished in Massachusetts. From the 1830s through the 1850s, Catholics and then Mormons were subjected in many areas to discriminatory legislation and hostile mob action. In 1854 the Maine Supreme Court in *Donahoe* v. *Richards* upheld the expulsion of a Catholic public-school student who declined to participate in a Protestant religious exercise, and officeholding by Catholics was not permitted in New Hampshire until the 1870s. Despite these exceptions, however, the nation did seem to move toward greater religious toleration. Federal involvement in religious affairs was generally limited to things such as appointing chaplains for the military and for the houses of Congress, but the Congress also had municipal authority in the territories, so there arose a series of antipolygamy statutes aimed against Mormon practice in the Utah Territory.

Early church-state judicial battles in the twentieth century were often fought on grounds other than religious freedom. In *Pierce* v. *Society of Sisters* (1925), the Court struck down an Oregon statute requiring children to attend public schools on the grounds of "substantive due process" involving the rights of parents over the raising of their children. In *West Virginia State Board of Education* v. *Barnette* (1943), which reversed the holding in *Minersville School District* v. *Gobitis* (1940), the Court used the First Amendment's guarantee of freedom of speech to invalidate the expulsion of Jehovah's Witness children from public school for refusing to pledge allegiance.

In *Cantwell* v. *Connecticut* (1940), the Court first applied free exercise of religion against the states, overturning a conviction for soliciting without a license and incitement of a breach of the peace against a Jehovah's Witness and his two sons who had been proselytizing in a heavily Catholic area with an anti-Catholic recording. In *Everson* v. *Board of Education* (1947), the Court applied the establishment clause to the states in line with its adoption of the incorporation doctrine in *Gitlow* v. *New York* (1925). In *Everson,* the issue was whether New Jersey's busing of parochial school students violated the Constitution. The Court held that it did not, but the phrase "wall of separation" (quoted from a letter of Thomas Jefferson) appears in a Supreme Court decision for the first time.

Education would remain a vital battleground in church-state relations. In *Engel* v. *Vitale* and *Murray* v. *Baltimore City Schools* (1962) mandatory prayer in public schools was banned, and in *School District of Abbington Township* v. *Schempp* (1963) the reservation of time for prayer and biblical recitation was likewise ruled out. In *Lemon* v. *Kurtzman* (1973), the Court, in striking down some programs of aid for parochial schools, set up a tripartite test for constitutionality: the program must (1) not further religion, (2) have a secular legislative purpose, and (3) avoid excessive church-state entanglements.

The situation in education has remained complicated, and each year brings new rulings without any predictable procedures for determining the constitutionality of religious practices within the schools or of particular instances of aid to parochial schools. In *Yoder* v. *Wisconsin* (1972), the Court rejected the application of state truancy laws to Amish children withdrawn by their parents from school at age fourteen in compliance with long-held Amish practice.

In cases such as *Epperson* v. *Arkansas* (1968) and *Edwards* v. *Aquillard* (1987), the Court struck down respectively an antievolution statute and a law requiring the teaching of "creation science" on an equal footing with evolutionary theory. In *Sante Fe Independent School District* v. *Doe* (2000), furthermore, the Court ruled that organized, student-led public prayer at a high school sporting event was unconstitutional.

In employment law, the Court has also vacillated. In *Sherbert* v. *Verner* (1963), it was held that South Carolina could not refuse unemployment benefits to a Seventh-Day Adventist fired for refusing to work on Saturday (his sabbath), setting the standard that interference with religious practices is permitted only if the state has a compelling interest of the highest order and no other way of achieving its purposes.

Displays of religious symbols on public land have presented a recurring problem, and in *Marsh* v. *Chambers* (1983), *Lynch* v. *Donnelly* (1984), and *County of Alleghany* v. *American Civil Liberties Union* (1989), the Court abandoned the three-fold standard of *Lemon* and permitted such displays if they occurred within a secular context; thus a manger scene could be displayed if it appeared with a display of nonreligious symbols of the Christmas season, such as Santa Claus, elves, and so forth.

Another area of church-state tensions has come in the area of Native American religious rights. In *People* v. *Woody* (1964), the California Supreme Court reversed the conviction of several Navajos charged with using peyote in a religious ceremony, applying the "compelling state interest" standard from *Sherbert.* By Public Law 280 (1953), Congress placed

American Indian reservations in several states under the civil and criminal jurisdiction of the states, which greatly increased the conflicts between state laws and Native American religious practices. Some of the problems arising therefrom were eliminated by the Indian Civil Rights Act of 1968, which required tribal consent for the implementation of state jurisdiction. The 1968 act also applied portions of the Bill of Rights to the tribal governments (which were separate but "dependent, domestic sovereignties"), including the guarantee of religious liberty, but the establishment clause was not applied since that would have crippled the functioning of many Indian religious practices that were tied to tribal structures.

In *O'Lone* v. *Estate of Shabazz* (1987), the Supreme Court adopted a "reasonableness" standard in regard to religious observations by prisoners. Many such suits have been pursued by incarcerated Native Americans whose practices were not generally accommodated in the state and federal penal systems. Similar difficulties have arisen for Native American students in the public schools where dress codes and other regulations often interfere with their religious practices.

Hunting regulations have been judicially examined in light of American Indian religious practices, as in *Frank* v. *State* (1979), in which the Alaskan Supreme Court upheld the right of Natives to hunt moose out of season for the purposes of a religious feast, and in Congress's 1962 amendment to the Eagle Protection Act, allowing the Department of the Interior to license the taking of eagles for legitimate religious ceremonies.

In 1978 Congress passed the American Indian Religious Freedom Act (AIRFA), which declared that government agencies should attempt to carry out their operations in such a way as to respect Indian religious practice and belief. In *Lyng* v. *Northwest Indian Cemetery Protection Association* (1988), the U.S. Supreme Court recognized that AIRFA had created no judicially enforceable rights. By the Indian Child Welfare Act (1978), however, Congress provided that adoptions be done in such a fashion as to preserve the cultural and religious heritage of

Indian children. By the National Museum of the American Indian Act (1989) and the Native American Graves Protection and Repatriation Act (1990), Congress attempted to solve the problem of the desecration of graves by anthropologists and other scholars.

Congress has begun to attempt to play a greater role in the defining and protecting of religious liberty. In the Religious Freedom Restoration Act (1993), Congress attempted to require the courts to utilize a "compelling state interest" standard in evaluation laws that interfere with religious practices, but in *City of Boerne* v. *P. F. Flores, Archbishop of San Antonio, and the United States* (1997), the Court declared the act unconstitutional on federalism grounds, because of an impermissible interference with state exercise of police powers.

Finally, although they were not decided on religious grounds, many Supreme Court decisions in regard to morals legislation have provoked angry reactions from religious leaders and laity alike. Many of the pornography decisions, beginning in the late 1950s, which severely restricted the ability of the state and federal governments to punish the producers and distributors of obscene material, outraged the religiously conservative, as did *Roe* v. *Wade* (1973) legalizing abortion throughout the country. These and similar Court decisions have mobilized a Religious Right committed to banning or restricting abortion, outlawing pornography, and restoring school prayer, and numerous constitutional amendments have been submitted on these matters, but Congress has not acted to propose one for ratification by the states.

[*See also* CIVIL RELIGION; BILL OF RIGHTS.]

BIBLIOGRAPHY

Finkelman, Paul, ed., *Religion and American Law: An Encyclopedia* (Garland 2000) [see especially the essays by Philip Presby and Donald G. Nieman on *Lemon* v. *Kurtzman,* by Melvin I. Urofsky on *Cantwell* v. *Cantwell,* and by Brian H. Wildenthal and Patrick M. O'Neil on *Native American Religious Rights*].

Kauper, Paul G., *Religion and the Constitution* (La. State Univ. Press 1964).

A circus poster from the early twentieth century.

Levy, Leonard W., *The Establishment Clause: Religion and the First Amendment* (Macmillan 1989).

Levy, Leonard W., Kenneth L. Karst, and Dennis J. Mahoney, eds., *Encyclopedia of the American Constitution,* 4 vols. (Macmillan 1986) [see especially the essays on the "First Amendment" by Archibald Cox, on "The Establishment of Religion" by Leonard W. Levy, and on "Religion in Public Schools" and "Religious Liberty" by Leo Pfeffer].

Morgan, Richard E., *The Supreme Court and Religion* (Free Press 1972).

Pfeffer, Leo, *Church, State, and Freedom,* rev. ed. (Beacon Press 1967).

Stokes, Anson Phelps, and Leo Pfeffer, *Church and State in the United States* , rev. ed. (Harper 1964).

PATRICK M. O'NEIL

CIRCUSES

With an unbroken history of over two hundred years, the American circus, originally transported from England to Philadelphia by the equestrian John Bill Ricketts in 1793, is experiencing a new golden age at the dawn of the twenty-first century. A hybrid form of entertainment, the American circus has survived changing times and tastes and has done so with some noticeable recent alterations. For example, in 1998 the largest circus operation in North America was the new-wave Cirque du Soleil founded in Montreal, Canada, in 1984, featuring six discrete shows, including touring and permanent venues (two in Las Vegas and one at Disney World). Other circuses have attempted to capitalize on Cirque du Soleil's nonanimal, theatricalized production concept (such as the more modest Cirque Ingenieux). Yet more traditional American circuses—diminished in number from ninety-eight in the peak year of 1903—have prevailed, with several dozen in existence at the end of the twentieth century. Ringling Brothers Barnum & Bailey (a merger of several circuses in 1919), the best known, continues to flourish with two traveling three-ring units and, in 1999, a one-ring under canvas circus (the first from this organization since 1956), named Barnum's Kaleidoscape.

The late-twentieth-century movement in North America toward more focused circuses, frequently with one ring, was a reversal of the American circus's early trend toward ever-increasing size and mobility. Unlike its European forebears dating from the eighteenth century, which most frequently remained in fixed locations with one-ring configurations, the American circus, especially during its first golden age, 1871–1917, incorporated the once autonomous traveling animal menagerie, the concert, the *sideshow* (a term for any auxiliary show), and the street parade, all integral components surrounding the display of animals, clowns, and skilled daredevils and performers in three or more rings. For most of the American circus's history, circus entrepreneurs believed that bigger and more spectacular was somehow better, thus setting its development apart from circuses in other parts of the world. The size of the United States and its largely rural landscape during much of the nineteenth century encouraged mobility, so the nomadic nature of the circus evolved out of necessity. Initially, enterprising showpeople turned to water transportation via the Ohio and Mississippi rivers, but by the mid-nineteenth century they traveled on the expanding railroad system.

Throughout its history the American circus has reflected changes in American society. For many adults the circus recaptures the fun and romance of youth, a way to cling to something enduring. For children the circus is a live exposure to amazing feats and wonders. And, although survival is not guaranteed, the circus in America continues to be surprisingly resilient. Despite the rising expenses of insurance, salaries, transportation, and tents for those shows under canvas; other factors including competition from home-based entertainment, such as television and computers; and, in particular, the negative press of a prolonged dispute with animal rights activists, the modern American circus continues to bring people together to celebrate the daring and indomitable human spirit.

[See also CARNIVALS AND FAIRS; DISNEYLAND; PARADES; CONEY ISLAND; MAGIC AND MAGICIANS.*]*

BIBLIOGRAPHY

Albrecht, Ernest J., *The New American Circus* (Univ. Press of Fl. 1995).

Culhane, John, *The American Circus: An Illustrated History* (H. Holt 1990).

Eckley, Wilton, *The American Circus* (Twayne 1984).

Hoh, LaVahn G., and William H. Rough, *Step Right Up! The Adventure of Circus in America* (Betterway Pub. 1990).

Wilmeth, Don B., *Variety Entertainment and Outdoor Amusements: A Reference Guide* (Greenwood Press 1982).

DON B. WILMETH

CITIZENSHIP

The Fourteenth Amendment (1866) to the United States Constitution, one of the Civil War amendments, provides the first constitutional definition of American citizenship. It states that everyone born or naturalized in the United States is a citizen and is therefore entitled to equal protection of the laws. This equal protection extends to both federal and state governments. The Fourteenth Amendment states, further, that no additional requirements can be demanded for citizenship. Penalties are listed to which states attempting to circumvent the amendment's provision are liable. These include reduction of representation in Congress and the Electoral College. The amendment restricted its definition—and, therefore, its protection of citizens—to males only.

Requirements for naturalization, the process of becoming a citizen other than by birth, have varied from time to time. The requirements of the McCarran-Walter Act (1952; amended, 1965), the immigration act under which the United States currently operates, are lawful entry, a five-year residency, petition for citizenship, ability to read and speak English, good moral character, and the swearing of allegiance to the United States Constitution. The United States by law makes no distinction among naturalized citizens and those who are citizens by birth.

A person must be eighteen or older to apply for naturalization. In addition a person must be a lawful permanent resident of the United States. The five-year residence period is waived for someone married to and living with a United States citizen for three years. The applicant needs to complete a fingerprint chart and submit three photographs. On approval by the appropriate Immigration and Naturalization Service office, the applicant will be notified to appear for an interview. A person seeking naturalization must read and write simple English, and the applicant must have a basic knowledge of American history and government.

The rights of citizenship have been illegally denied on a number of occasions. During World War II, the United States government placed more than one hundred thousand Japanese Americans living in the western states in ten internment camps. The relocation took place in 1942. Forty years later the Supreme Court declared the action unconstitutional and ordered compensation. The racism and hysteria brought about by the Japanese attack on Pearl Harbor is part of the explanation for the deviance from legal principles and protections.

THE GRANGER COLLECTION

European immigrants at Ellis Island, in view of the Statue of Liberty, in the early 1900s.

The struggle of African Americans for civil rights illustrates both the manner in which the rights of citizens have been abused and the constitutional means for redressing these grievances. The American Civil War (1861–1865) led, among other things, to the abolition of slavery in the United States. Immediately following the war, the Thirteenth, Fourteenth, and Fifteenth amendments ended slavery in the United States, defined citizens, and provided legal means to enforce those guarantees, including the right to vote. Unfortunately, it took another century to put many of the amendments' provisions into place.

In 1896 the Supreme Court's infamous *Plessy* v. *Ferguson* decision approved of separate but equal facilities for whites and blacks. The National Association for the Advancement of Colored People

(NAACP) gained support in the early years of the twentieth century and opposed this legal segregation. The *Brown v. Board of Education* decision of the Supreme Court, May 17, 1954, reversed *Plessy*.

The 1950s witnessed the blossoming of the civil rights movement, especially under the leadership of Martin Luther King, Jr. King came to prominence in 1955 as leader of the Montgomery, Alabama, bus boycott. The 1950s also saw the first civil rights bill passed in Congress since Reconstruction. In the 1950s and 1960s other court decisions outlawed segregation in interstate commerce, housing, restaurants, and other public places. The movement continued into the 1960s when the Voting Rights Act and other civil rights bills were passed. Violence accompanied the struggle by African Americans to obtain the rights of full citizenship.

Traditionally, Americans expected naturalized citizens to become "Americanized." The concept of the melting pot meant that naturalized citizens were to keep some of their ethnic ways but adopt American civic values. As this "consensus" view gave way in the 1960s to a "conflict" view of American culture, many came to expect that naturalized citizens would be able to maintain their ethnic traditions, including home languages, foodways, and dress. The late-twentieth-century idea of multiculturalism valued the ability of the naturalized citizen to maintain a sort of biculturalism, moving comfortably between a home culture and the more generalized "American" culture.

In the United States citizens are guaranteed the right to participate in all aspects of civic life. Race, creed, color, religion, sex, and other similar characteristics should not interfere with that right. The Bill of Rights, the first ten amendments to the Constitution, guarantees civil liberties, while court decisions and other amendments have extended protection to other civil rights and liberties.

Times of national crisis often threaten American civil liberties. The rise of the Nazi and other fascist powers, the perceived threat of communism, and other problems have been occasions for the United States government to suspend certain rights.

[See also NATURALIZATION; BICULTURALISM.*]*

BIBLIOGRAPHY

Glenn, Evelyn, "Citizenship and Inequality: Historical and Global Perspectives," *Social Problems* 47 (2000):1–20.

Kerber, Linda K., "The Meanings of Citizenship," *Journal of American History* 84 (1997):833–854.

Kettner, James H., *The Development of American Citizenship, 1608–1870* (Univ. of N.C. Press 1978).

Schudson, Michael, *The Good Citizen: A History of American Civic Life* (Martin Kessler Bks. 1998).

Tobey, Ronald, Charles Wetherell, and Jay Brigham, "Moving Out and Settling In: Residential Mobility, Home Owning, and the Public Enframing of Citizenship, 1921–1950," *American Historical Review* 95 (1990):1395–1422.

VIRGINIA SALAMONE

CITY

[Under the present heading are collected two separate but related articles dealing with the place of cities in the United States. THE IDEA OF THE CITY *presents a summary of the differing views and expectations regarding concepts of the city as put forth by observers and commentators throughout the nation's history.* URBAN PLANNING AND DESIGN *centers more specifically on the work of professional planners and the urban spaces they helped to create.]*

The Idea of the City

As centers of cultural, social, and economic innovation, cities are simultaneously seductive, sublime, dangerous, alienating, and liberating. "In the city," wrote sociologist Robert E. Park, "every type of individual—the criminal and beggar, as well as the man of genius—may find congenial company" in which his particular vice or talent may flourish. Park spoke in praise of cities, but others decried their effect on how people shape their identities, experience space and time, and value tradition. Thomas Jefferson warned that "corruption of morals . . . is the mark set on those, who . . . depend . . . on the casualties and caprice of customers," omitting his agrarian republic's dependence on slavery. Foreseeing industrialization (Paterson, New Jersey, was founded as a national manufacturing center in 1791), he protested in *Notes on the State of Virginia* that urban laborers "add just so much to the support of pure government, as sores do to the strength of the human body." The corrupting influence of urban life is a recurring theme in American literature, from the first American drama, Royall Tyler's *The Contrast,* through Nathaniel Hawthorne's "My Kinsman, Major Molyneux," an entire subgenre of nineteenth-century tales about the evil awaiting young women alone in the city, to F. Scott Fitzgerald's *The Great Gatsby* and John Dos Passos's *Manhattan Transfer.* Much antiurbanism manifests anxiety over the fading of a once-dominant cultural and moral order.

Paradigms of Urban Form: Pluralism and Progressivism. Concepts of the American industrial city may be distinguished by their orientation as pluralist or progressivist. Both acknowledge that disorientation is fundamental to urban experience: it arises from the close coexistence of people whose cultures and beliefs differ significantly; the separation of urban space into workplaces, residences, and leisure spaces; the specialization of urban roles; and the loosening of traditional social controls. Both conceive of individuals and groups as connected by overlapping matrices of political, economic, social, and cultural power that operate on scales ranging from the city to the neighborhood to the individual. They differ in their emphases. Pluralists study the experience of difference and seek to define its value. Progressives seek to understand and to optimize the functioning of the city's economic, social, and political institutions and infrastructures. These orientations are neither mutually exclusive (progressives and pluralists advocate economic and social justice) nor mutually congruent (the premium on efficiency and the "general good" leads progressives to regard differences as obstacles to improvement). In "The Metropolis and Mental Life," German sociologist Georg Simmel usefully defined the city as "the arena for [the] struggle and reconciliation" of two goals: liberation of "the general man" and the realization of each person's "qualitative uniqueness."

Such early urban pluralists as Park and his University of Chicago colleagues understood that without the common institutions and history that define the boundaries of life in small communities, the city-dweller experiences new modalities of freedom and social control. Their insight was that the new conditions are not merely disruptive. The lighter attachments, the many options for elective affiliation among groups organized by heritage, belief, occupation, or interest—indeed, the very cover of anonymity itself—present opportunities for self-creation and expression unthinkable elsewhere. Participation in several such groups, which admit to neither concentric nor hierarchic organization, develops capacities that go untested in less diverse environments. In "Urbanism as a Way of Life," Lewis Wirth, Park's student and colleague, proposed that urban complexity and unpredictability lead the city-dweller beyond parochialism "toward the acceptance of instability and insecurity in the world at large as a norm," and that decentered subjectivity and heightened interest in other ways of being produce a stronger collective life as recognition, rights, and respect are extended across the social field. Richard Sennett revisits these postulates in his studies of urban experience, *The Uses of Disorder, The Fall of Public Man,* and *The Conscience of the Eye.*

All of these theorists recognize, however, that the ideal of urbanity is also threatened by otherness. The urban round of transient, often instrumental encounters among strangers may elicit affective distance and indifference as psychic defenses. In his *Autobiography,* Benjamin Franklin records with humor how as a youth he found Philadelphian ways mysterious. The crossings made by immigrant and ethnic Americans are far more perilous and far more important to understanding the role of cities in the creation of American identities. From Abraham Cahan's *The Rise of David Levinsky* and James Weldon Johnson's *Autobiography of an Ex-Colored Man* onward, narratives of ethnic and immigrant education seldom end otherwise than in ambivalence. As art and as cultural documents they succeed by portraying the conflicts engendered by the desires to succeed in the wider world and to remain true to a natal identity, and by turning these conflicts into windows on the relation of hegemonic and minority cultures.

A distinctively urban psyche appears in literature as early as Edgar Allan Poe's "The Man of the Crowd" as something foreign to American experience. The urban masses are the very oxygen of life for the mysterious Londoner who is the title character, but the man and the crowd prove inscrutable to the narrator, whose moral surmises ring hollow. Walt Whitman's poetry of the seductive urban spectacle, from "Crossing Brooklyn Ferry" to "Broadway" and "Manhatta," launches an American literature of urban experience. East Coast realism explores the social semiotics that preserve order in what Edith Wharton in *The Age of Innocence* called the "hieroglyphic world" of the upper classes, where what one did or refrained from doing, how one dressed, where and when one allowed oneself to be seen all conveyed messages about one's character and status. The grittier realism of Chicago writers Theodore Dreiser, Upton Sinclair, James T. Farrell, and Nelson Algren chronicles working-class life and ethnic neighborhoods.

The most distinctive urban figure is the *flâneur*, the stroller in the city who visually consumes its spectacle. Dependent for his existence (the *flâneur* is, historically, male) on the world of objects on display and himself one of those objects, he cultivates an appearance that marks his exclusion from the world of productive labor and the norms of leisure-class life. Feeding on, yet often bored by, urban novelty (the vagaries of fashion and fashionable entertainment, unfathomable otherness) the *flâneur* combines the antithetical experiences of desire and ironic distance. Tracing an arc from *flânerie* to disaffection in American urban literature, we move through Nick Carraway, who prowls New York City's twilit streets in *The Great Gatsby* but fears what their mysteries may reveal about himself, to the jaded film-noir detective who has peered into the heart of urban darkness in Otto Preminger's *Where the Sidewalk Ends;* Roman Polanski's *Chinatown,* in a retro mode; or, futuristically, Ridley Scott's *Blade Runner.* The knight-errant of Martin Scorcese's *Taxi Driver* is infected with the city's own disease;

in Terry Gilliam's *Fisher King,* for a change, the city unlocks its benevolent secrets only to the "insane."

Progressives include proponents of moral and structural reform. Through institutions dedicated to Americanization, moral reformers sought to instill Anglo-Protestant norms of conduct among immigrants and the poor; one of their initiatives was redefining ghetto space to promote domesticity over communal life. Progressive social scientists regarded the city as an evolving organism or field of forces; either way, it required administration by scientifically trained professionals. They attributed political disagreements to flawed comprehension of the issue, although occasionally, such as with machine politics, they agreed with moral reformers that dissension was rooted in vice. Confident of their authority and failing to see how urban machines mediated interethnic conflict (or perhaps seeing only their own exclusion), reformers of both stripes advocated government by nonpartisan city managers and commissioners.

The progressives' characteristic literary forms are tracts and utopias. Notable among reform tracts are Charles Loring Brace's moralizing *Life among the Dangerous Classes of New York* and Jacob Riis's muckraking classic, *How the Other Half Lives,* a cry for housing and health reforms whose manifest distaste for ethnic ways distinguishes it from Jane Addams's salutary combination of pluralism and progressivism, *Twenty Years at Hull-House.* The most influential literary utopia of its time, Edward Bellamy's *Looking Backward* represents Boston in the year 2000 as a marvel of convenience created by efficient management and cultural consensus; influenced by *Looking Backward* but taking a far dimmer view of cities, William Dean Howells quarantined them in his Christian socialist utopia, *A Traveler from Altruria.* If it is difficult to imagine diversity of interests and beliefs in a world as regimented as gentility and consensus require, the world that Bellamy and Howells represent, many progressives were willing to pay that price, particularly as they were certain of their rightness. What makes *Sister Carrie* the exemplary urban novel is Dreiser's ability to form a rich panorama of urban life into a representation of Chicago and New York as evolving organisms, and to leave in play the contrast between the naively desiring woman of the crowd and his figure of the progressive engineer and social critic Robert Ames.

Howells's condemnation of the city built by speculative capitalism foreshadows the writing of Lewis Mumford (1895–1990), a public intellectual whose books and essays on cities and technology are still widely read. Adopting the garden city concept developed independently by Ebenezer Howard and Patrick Geddes, Mumford and the Regional Planning Association of America (RPAA) advocated planned communities built around greenspaces and ringed by greenbelts to prevent sprawl. Wedding Geddes's biological theories of urban growth to a Jeffersonian ethos, Mumford advocated towns of thirty thousand inhabitants, which he believed would be large enough to sustain themselves but small enough to permit full participation in political and social life. The visual contrast between the garden city and contemporary plans for skyscraper utopias, such as Le Corbusier's *Ville radieuse* ("Radiant City") and Hugh Ferris's *Imaginary Metropolis*, is striking, yet the informing ideas are far more similar than not. Both cities are offered as aesthetic solutions to social and economic crises; they pursue a unity of design and detail intended to foster the higher human development, which they tacitly assume has but one proper end. It was not to the advantage of the RPAA that its one garden city, Radburn, New Jersey, opened in 1929 and was governed by restrictive covenants, but even in 1980 this "Town for the Motor Age" was inhabited overwhelmingly by white Protestant professionals. While the garden city ideal continues to influence planners, it speaks compellingly only to people who find their values and practices reflected in its institutions and built landscapes; the aura of stability in the garden city and the skyscraper utopia rests on suppression of the unanticipated or unknown—anything capable of sparking interest or curiosity. The failure to build utopia returns us to the dialectic of progressivism and pluralism implicit in Simmel's description of the city: the political project of pursuing social and economic justice while maintaining due respect for the value of difference.

The Material City. The same dialectic is expressed in the built urban landscape, which typically is an aggregation of planned and unplanned elements that support modes of collective life. Variations among neighborhoods whose basic elements of construction are similar reveal them as artifacts of particular cultures. Moreover, as populations change, built landscapes become palimpsests in which traces of other times, ideologies, and communities survive in the architecture, decoration, and signage.

Painters and photographers have long found subjects in this visual richness. Ashcan school painters recorded the technological transformation of the built landscape—elevated railroads, bridges, skyscrapers—but their true subject was the public life of saloons, sporting events, and other popular entertainments. Their canvases were a means of embracing the crowd. In contrast Edward Hopper manipulated light and architectural detail as framing devices to depict the alienation and anonymity of urban life. Photography, a product of the industrial age, was particularly well suited to capture the characters and characteristic juxtapositions of the urban scene. Alfred Stieglitz's urban scenes are at once documents of realism and exquisitely balanced compositions. The title of Berenice Abbott's 1939 collection, *Changing New York,* suggests her eye for juxtapositions of the old and new, and the random conjunctions of people or objects that the city affords; it does not begin to do justice to the aesthetic qualities of this photographic suite. Turning to the everyday landscape and its "leftovers"—outdated or no longer functional objects—pop artists use collage as an art of reclamation. Robert Rauschenberg's combines, especially the ongoing *¼ Mile or 2 Furlong Piece* (begun in 1981), are visual and aural records of *flânerie;* their amalgamation of material that defies hierarchical integration suggests a visual equivalent of the decentered urban identity theorized by Wirth.

Speculative development decentered the physical city, but with undesirable results when developers disregard the place of individual projects in the built landscape, their effects on traffic, crowding, or other quality-of-life measures. Against the backdrop of perceived spatial and social disorder, the White City that formed the ceremonial center of Chicago's 1893 Columbian Exposition was hailed by many commentators as a harbinger of urban order and stability. Inspired by this ensemble of neo-classical buildings and plazas, the City Beautiful movement sought to enhance civic identity by creating spaces in which individuals might come together as a public: civic centers, boulevards, and parkland that would become sites for performing and contesting the rituals of recognition on which social order rests. Its members included Daniel Burnham, who oversaw design of the White City and later produced an influential plan for Chicago (1909) and largely unrealized plans for Cleveland (1903) and San Francisco (1906).

Like the earlier parks movement, City Beautiful has been criticized for its class-specific values and disregard for cities' most crowded, unhealthy districts. At the other end of the twentieth century, however, numerous critics attributed the decline of civic culture to the dearth of genuinely public spaces, an oversight in which modernist urban development was complicit. Among modernist architects and planning theorists, a common desire was to liberate the city from its past by remaking it as an ideal form free from the determinations of history, whether as a skyscraper or garden city. There is scant attraction to the plazas of mid-twentieth-century skyscrapers that exist in autotelic isolation. Late-modern megastructures (offices on top, parking underground, and shops oriented around indoor plazas) often turn a blank wall to the streets and rely on private security forces to run off "undesirables" (that is, anyone behaving other than as a consumer). Postwar government-sponsored urban renewal adapted the modernist program to produce a more legible city, one easier to administer and to police. Older neighborhoods became symbols of intrigue and danger in the popular imagination, until it became clear that the built landscape, communal identity, and local structures of social control were intertwined, and by disrupting them urban renewal often worsened the problems it promised to solve.

Lambasting planners' infatuation with what she called the "Radiant Garden City Beautiful" and their failure to understand how actual neighborhoods work, Jane Jacobs's *The Death and Life of Great American Cities* hastened a critical reassessment of planning practice. An aesthetic of collage emerged as an alternative practice that respects and incorporates existing neighborhoods' patterns of order. Whether the result is a socially committed or merely scenographic architecture is debated. Regardless, public housing and other civic projects are of particular interest because they embody aesthetic judgments about urban form and political decisions about the relative importance of various constituencies and interests.

In the last quarter of the twentieth century, a popular urban revival strategy focused on development of what are in effect urban theme parks. Appealing to the desire of a suburbanized populace for controlled doses of city life (more than half of Americans lived in cities by 1920, more than half in suburbs by 1990), so-called festival marketplaces dress upscale malls in historicist décor. Notable examples of the practice include Baltimore's Harborplace; New York City's South Street Seaport, and similarly retrofitted waterfronts, factories, mills, and warehouses; and more ambitiously, Universal Studios' CityWalk, a fantasy Los Angeles on the city's fringe. Trafficking in popular "memories" of a more coherent city that never existed, these sites of simulated *flânerie* are negations of urbanity; they draw consumers stimulated by the goods for sale, not citizens engaged with each other. As in suburban malls, the right of free speech may be curtailed, and the economic barriers to entry ensure a level of cultural homogeneity. Outside these controlled environments, the postindustrial urban cores are dividing into areas of intensive development; luxury residences and centers of global finance and information management; and inner-city neighborhoods inhabited by racial minorities, recent immigrants, the unemployed, and low-wage service workers, a trajectory whose dystopian terminus would be *Blade Runner*'s Los Angeles. Yet cities may again become the hope of democracy if Americans can recognize conflict as a form of engagement and build on it a politics that negotiates the values of pluralism and progressivism.

[See also ARCHITECTURE, *article on* URBAN ARCHITECTURE; LAND USE; PUBLIC SPACE; SUBURBS.*]*

BIBLIOGRAPHY

Boyer, M. Christine, *The City of Collective Memory: Its Historical Imagery and Architectural Entertainments* (MIT Press 1994).

Conrad, Peter, *The Art of the City: Views and Versions of New York* (Oxford 1984).

Dear, Michael, and Steven Flusty, "Postmodern Urbanism," *Annals of the American Association of Geographers* 88, no. 1 (May 1998):50–72.

Erenberg, Lewis A., *Steppin' Out: New York Nightlife and the Transformation of American Culture, 1890–1930* (1981; Univ. of Chicago Press 1984).

Jacobs, Jane, *The Death and Life of Great American Cities* with a new foreword by the author (1961; Modern Library 1993).

McNamara, Kevin R., *Urban Verbs: Arts and Discourses of American Cities* (Stanford Univ. Press 1996).

Mumford, Lewis, *The Urban Prospect* (Harcourt 1968).

Sennett, Richard, *The Conscience of the Eye: The Design and Social Life of Cities* (Knopf 1990).

Whyte, William H., *The City: Rediscovering the Center* (Doubleday 1988).

Zukin, Sharon, *The Cultures of Cities* (Blackwell 1995).

KEVIN MCNAMARA

Urban Planning and Design

In less than four hundred years, the North American continent has undergone massive transformation from a diverse natural geography inhabited by small tribal populations to the broadly settled landscape familiar today. Now 281 million inhabit the continent's midsection. The particular patterns of settlement and city form that define this landscape are a unique expression of American culture. They reflect in hybrid form the ideas of individualism, democracy, pragmatism, and capitalism that have been driven forward since the eighteenth century by ever-advancing techniques of production, communication, and transportation. Born of the social and scientific thought of the Enlightenment and Industrial Revolution in Europe, the remarkable de-

Small replicas of buildings rise from an architectural model of a section of a city.

velopment of the nation was nevertheless a product of opportunities presented in the New World, a grand experiment undertaken in a context free from existing traditions and hierarchies and unconstrained by the limitations of space.

Early Colonial Settlements. What is now the United States was colonized by the Dutch, Spanish, and English in the sixteenth and seventeenth centuries. The first civil settlements were dangerous experiments in creating enduring communities in a vast terra incognita. Unlike the exploratory forays of the sixteenth century, seventeenth-century settlements served agricultural, commercial, and religious ends. Although not military in function, they were frequently formed in a defensive mode, since they were vulnerable to attack from both Native Americans and competing colonial interests.

English and Dutch settlements drew their formal organization from their contemporary town planning practices in their places of origin in the Old World. These were still fundamentally medieval, with towns and cities favoring a strong, fortified nucleus focused on the church and marketplace, with an organic street pattern spiraling outward to surrounding agricultural lands. Puritan towns of colonial New England were formed from this spatial and spiritual concentricity with the church and village green as the framework for a strict social order. Individual dwellings, with their home-based cottage industries, were situated in close proximity to the center, and garden lots occupied an outer ring.

In contrast, the original tidewater colonies of Virginia and North Carolina had no such underlying social intent; they were settled to develop and organize an English colonial economy based on agricultural trade. Jamestown, a crude fortified town, was meant to function as the region's central locus of defense, taxation, and export for various tobacco farms, but owing to the decentering nature of agriculture and the lack of a sustaining social framework, the experiment failed.

The Dutch settlement on the tip of what is now Manhattan was ideally situated for trade in the New World. Like Amsterdam itself, New Amsterdam's geography provided the auspicious conditions for a city of commerce. It was located midway between the Virginias and New England, on a protected peninsula downstream from Hudson River agricultural estates and the Dutch fur-trading outpost at Fort Orange (later, Albany). The internal town organization reflected the pragmatic response to the demands of defense, trade, and dwelling, importing urban patterns and features from the Dutch landscape. The city was densely built with gabled structures and streets and canals shaped by the city's natural form, serving its commercial ends. Broadway, a major internal street stretching north from a fort at the southern tip of the peninsula, provided a connection with other Dutch settlements on Manhattan, forming a spine that would organize the city's continued growth as it passed into English and American rule during the eighteenth century.

Classical Planning in America. Whereas the English and Dutch colonists of the early seventeenth century drew on medieval precedents, continental Europe had been steeped for over a century in the rational artistic theory of the Renaissance. In this classical paradigm, streets and squares were conceived in a coherent overall plan, primarily relying on rectangular and radial geometries. Seventeenth-century French urban design was typified by the regularly shaped, architecturally defined *place* (city square) and by broad, orthogonally organized streets with axes connecting one important palace or monument to another. This idiom, promoting royal and military display, was most extravagantly realized in Paris and Versailles.

These modern concepts did not reach the English colonies until the turn of the eighteenth century. During the Restoration, Charles II had brought home to England ideas he had absorbed while in exile in France, and he was able to explore and realize them on a large scale in the rebuilding of London after the Great Fire in 1666. A majority of the proposals for London's reconstruction used a gridiron plan, punctuated regularly with squares and grand plazas for important public buildings.

The design of two colonial American cities, Philadelphia and Savannah, owe much to the ferment of new ideas following London's disaster. The 1682 plan for Philadelphia reflected not only this new formal sensibility but was infused with the philosophy of the Quaker settlers—a religious sect seeking to establish a colony where it would be free to worship. Land comprising much of today's southeastern Pennsylvania was granted in 1674 to Quaker gentleman William Penn. Of this, a square mile between the Delaware and Schuylkill rivers was to be a new capital city, Philadelphia, "a faire and greene countrie towne" laid out in generous lots so as to avoid the perils of fire and disease so recently experienced in London. A shared vision of Penn and surveyor Thomas Holme, the Philadelphia city plan consisted of a front street on each river with two major cross-axial streets defining a city center and four quadrants. At the center was a large, ten-acre (4-ha) square to be surrounded by religious, commercial, and public buildings. The four quadrants were laid out in a gridiron of smaller-scale streets for individual house and garden lots. At the center of each of the residential quadrants was an eight-acre (3-ha) square to be used for more informal collective purposes "as the Moore-fields in London."

The city plan of 1682 was an act of intentional long-term planning, an optimistic vision of organized growth, river to river, that in Penn's words "might have Room for present and after Commers.

. . ." Penn's vision for Philadelphia was grounded in a religious faith that was pacifist, fundamentally nonhierarchical, recognizing "that of God in all men." Such a balanced, humanistic dwelling paradigm was remarkably self-sustaining. In its early decades the city developed first along the Delaware, expanding in substantial accordance with the plan, to become the most important urban center in colonial America.

Like Penn's "holy experiment," the new city of Savannah also provided a haven for the oppressed. Those who migrated with reformer James Oglethorpe to the new colony in Georgia were debtors and persons of modest means who took advantage of the unique opportunity to start afresh in the New World. The city charter of Savannah employed a system of town and country land allotment similar to Philadelphia's and thereby established the beginning of a broad regional plan.

The city was sited on a plateau above the Savannah River ten miles (16 km) from its mouth. The city and its outlying garden plots and farm lands were laid out using the gridiron organization. Within the city, the grid became highly differentiated in a pattern of smaller autonomous units called wards, each of which contained at its center a formal square with trustee lots for grand homes or public buildings. A hierarchy of streets and building lots completed the inner and outer perimeters of each ward. When aggregated, the wards created a unique fabric of alternating built and open space and a series of internal visual axes, which would provide the urban structure to support the city's incremental expansion.

Eighteenth-century colonial towns and cities employed the pattern of orthogonal streets and central public square as much as geography would permit. Boston was a notable exception, using instead a loosely radial geometry in response to the contours of the neck of land on which it was situated. When the new nation emerged as an independent state, a full palette of neoclassical, indeed baroque, planning devices was brought to bear on the new capital, Washington, D.C. In 1791, Frenchman Pierre Charles L'Enfant created a plan for the city that drew heavily on the examples of André Le Nôtre's Versailles and Christopher Wren's well-known plan for London. Overlaid on a regular gridiron of streets was a grand web of axial avenues that emanated from the two major seats of power: the "Federal House" (the Capitol) and the "President's Palace" (the White House). The plan provided for a "Grand Avenue" (the Mall), expansive public gardens, water features, many squares and plazas with monuments, and elegant neoclassical buildings with areas of commerce at some remove from the places of visual grandeur. Unlike other American cities of that time, Washington, D.C., was unabashedly designed as a place of beauty; it was meant to inspire awe and to invoke the power of a new democracy derived from an ancient model.

Gridiron Planning. With the struggle for independence successfully resolved, the nation was able to grow and develop. Expansion on all civil fronts took place: population increased, trade and industry flourished, and people became educated and owned land at an unprecedented rate. Established cities grew and planned for future growth, using the simple gridiron street plan and row-house typology as the primary urban pattern. The 1811 Commissioner's Plan for New York City, the landfill reclamation of the Back Bay in Boston, and the expansion of Philadelphia and Savannah in the early decades of the nineteenth century reflect an attitude toward urban growth that was chiefly concerned with expediency. Rejecting the richer patterns of space inherent in the early city design, the city planners adopted the simple grid as a convenient tool for land transactions.

On a large scale, the same device was used to claim and lay out the vast western territories acquired in the Louisiana Purchase. Thomas Jefferson, under whose auspices the meting out of western territories began, held a belief in the moral superiority of the agrarian life. His democratic ideal seemed to conflate well with the dispersion of population across the landscape rather than in dense urban settings, a bias that remains part of the national idiom. Jefferson's influence on the shape of the American landscape and way of life reflects a combination of two paradoxical tendencies that are deeply American: the romantic Rousseauistic view that man is in his most pure state when at one with nature, and the Cartesian view of the universe in which all things are knowable through objective and rational delineation.

The western states were settled amid the rush and profit of land speculation with the efficient, familiar, and uniform gridiron plan as its parceling tool. Like the military encampments from which the gridiron derived, it could be applied universally and without intimate knowledge of the land on which it was projected. Railroads forged westward along orthogonally platted terrain, spawning towns and cities. The grid was most plausible in the flat prairie states, but it was used even in such places as San Francisco despite challenges presented by natural topography. Conceptual plans for new state capitals often included some baroque design elements, but most elaborate plans were not realized, in the flurry of private profit-taking.

The development of Chicago reflects nineteenth-century opportunism. In 1833 it was a rough town clinging to the swampy shores of Lake Michigan, driven by the prospect of a proposed canal that would provide a vital transportation link with the East, doing for the Midwest what the Erie Canal had done for the cities in upstate New York. Chicago's hastily erected wood buildings and unpaved streets gave it the appearance of a temporary encampment, and its population—mostly male—hovered at about 400. On the strength of canal speculation, population grew to 1,800 by 1834 and to 4,000 in 1836. It recovered from the crash of land values in 1837, and by 1848 the canal was built and the city had a population of 20,000. But the importance of navigation was soon outstripped by railroads, and by 1865 the fabric of Chicago's rail system had been laid down. Railroads feeding through the city made Chicago the nation's central hub, which profited from westward expansion.

The Growth in the Industrial East. While the West was being settled, the eastern seaboard continued to flourish. Mill towns sprang up along rivers taking advantage of water power to manu-

facture their goods, such as textiles, shoes, guns, and so forth. These were in turn transported via canal or the burgeoning rail system to the large seaboard cities for distribution. New York, Philadelphia, Boston, and Baltimore became great centers of commercial activity, with shipping industry in its heyday at midcentury and railroads gaining as the great mode of transport. The economy of the Southern states was still based on the neofeudal plantation system. The production of tobacco, rice, and especially cotton relied on slave labor to flourish on a grand scale. Raw materials were shipped by sea from New Orleans, Charleston, and Savannah, and by rail from the new city of Atlanta, Georgia to the industrial centers of the northeastern United States and England for processing and further distribution.

The Civil War had a devastating impact on the landscape and the economy of the South but had quite the opposite effect in the Northeast, where a heavy industry was propelled forward by military exigencies. The creation of a complex and extensive rail system, the mining and transport of anthracite and other minerals, the production of steel, and the construction of heavy machinery, weapons, locomotives, and ships were all results of an accelerated industrial economy that would continue to boom well into the next century. Moreover, waves of immigrants from Europe fleeing political oppression, poverty, and famine began to arrive in the port cities of the eastern seaboard seeking opportunity promised by the phenomenal economic and geographic expansion of the United States. Soon to be followed by former slaves from the South, these immigrant populations were indispensable to the creation of the great industrial cities and to the settling of towns and the cultivation of farms in the American West.

The post–Civil War period was a time of extraordinary urban growth and prosperity for capitalists in the North. Industrial Philadelphia became the "workshop of the world," with great factories lining the rail corridors that crisscrossed the northern districts of the city. Block after block of brick row houses sprung up for the workers and their families. In three decades what had been a landscape of stream-laced woodlands had become completely built up; a uniform gridiron had replaced the humanizing influence of William Penn's plan for intermittent city squares. New York City likewise expanded northward into its previously platted grid of streets.

Arcadia and the City Beautiful. Denser still than Philadelphia, a built-out Manhattan would have become one of the most suffocating places in urban America had it not been for the incredible foresight of the planners of Central Park. In 1857 landscape architect Frederic Law Olmsted and his colleague Calvert Vaux began work on the 500-acre (200-ha) public park, stretching almost fifty blocks to the as-yet-undeveloped districts uptown. Using the existing character of the site as their guide, they created a naturalistic composition of lakes, meadows, cliffs, and woodlands for the enjoyment of all the people of New York City.

The concept of this great urban oasis was neither without precedent nor disconnected from a larger current of thought. Indeed, the great urban parks of continental Europe and the work of landscape designers Humphrey Repton and Capability Brown were well known. Moreover, the Romantic ideal that proclaimed the purifying influence of nature on man—already deeply rooted in European arts and culture—began to have greater currency and meaning in urban America. As more and more land was consumed by the rapacious forces of industry and land speculation, a nostalgia for the lost innocence of the Arcadian world gripped the American sensibility.

The development of park systems within the cities and of suburban enclaves at their perimeter would profoundly influence the shape of the American landscape. It reflects as well the strong cultural proclivity to escape from harsh urban life into a bucolic environment, artificial or not. Indeed, these "natural" landscapes were as self-consciously designed as were the geometric compositions of classical urban design. Both park and suburb employed informal curving roads, rough-hewn materials that evoked a preindustrial past, and patterns of planting and land contour that manipulated spatial sequence and experience to conceal, reveal, and delight. Boston, Philadelphia, and Baltimore soon had major city parks. And these cities as well as Chicago, Cincinnati, and Detroit had developed picturesque, bucolic suburbs for the upper-middle class.

Toward the end of the century, a further antidote to the dreariness of the monotonous grid of American cities was introduced through the City Beautiful movement. This aesthetic movement was born of the first generation of American architects to be professionally educated in Europe, who had experienced Hausman's Paris firsthand. In pictorially classicizing forms, the City Beautiful movement reintroduced the baroque city design that had been left waiting in the wings for almost a century since L'Enfant's design of Washington, D.C.

The Chicago World's Columbian Exposition of 1893, a temporary installation featuring monumental white structures in cross-axial spatial composition, captured the imagination of planners and leaders who sought a greater sense of grandeur for their cities. Daniel Burnham and other architects from the École des Beaux-Arts in Paris drew up proposals for Chicago, Washington, D.C., San Francisco, Philadelphia, and New York. Most were only partially realized, but the legacy of grand avenues and vistas terminating in monumental compositions of building and sculpture are a defining aspect of the American city today.

Reforms, Regulations, and Utopian Visions. A crisis of overcrowding, pollution, and the deterioration of already aging physical infrastructure began to plague the large "gateway cities." During the Progressive Era at the beginning of the twentieth century, housing reform was enacted in many cities in order to protect the health, safety, and welfare of the citizenry. In the 1910s and 1920s, zoning legislation was introduced as an aesthetic device protecting the interests of the wealthy from the intrusion into fashionable areas by unwelcome industry and unsavory populations. A powerful, although crude, tool in planning the American city, zoning laws grew to regulate land uses and their adjacencies, building height and lot coverage, and dwelling densities.

In the face of the continued population growth and the imposition of zoning controls, new strategies for residential development outside the urban core were needed. Of the many social utopian models cultivated in Europe, Ebenezer Howard's Garden City concept of 1898 was the most influential. The Garden Cities were cooperative satellite villages linked by rail to large urban centers, providing their inhabitants with the best aspects of town and country. Each was formed in concentric rings, with the formal civic center ringed by clustered housing, industries, and workplaces and by an agricultural greenbelt. Garden City design principles were applied to such places as Yorkship near Philadelphia; Sunnyside in Queens, New York; and Morgan Park near Duluth, Minnesota. Yet they lacked the vital social ingredient of a shared economy and self-government, and the American Garden Cities became expressions more of proto-suburbanism than the vision of a new social order.

The modernist design revolution that had erupted in Europe following World War I did not affect American urban planning and development until the mid-1930s. The Depression-era economy could no longer afford the lavish forms of Beaux-Arts architecture, and the public sector became, by necessity, the benefactor of most urban projects, notably those having to do with housing the newly destitute. Early public-housing schemes were of a scale and formal language amenable to the existing neighborhood contexts. However, by the late 1940s the economies of scale and the lure of minimalism conspired to encourage the construction of new mass-housing schemes that broke with even the humblest traditions in urban dwelling form. The shining modern towers that took the place of acres of substandard row housing would soon become decrepit, dangerous, and obsolete, occupied by only the poorest, most dependent segment of society.

Another utopian proposal for American dwelling was Frank Lloyd Wright's Broadacre City, a twentieth-century iteration of romantic, Jeffersonian agrarianism. Born of the Midwestern prairie, Wright was a committed antiurbanist, claiming that democracy could only be realized through the individualism and self-sufficiency that could thrive in a planned physical structure of decentralization. In Broadacre City the single-family house, sited at the center of its own one-acre farm lot, reflected Wright's belief in the organic supremacy of the nuclear family. Private automobiles (and even helicopters) provided transportation, and the regional centers of commerce where farm products could be exchanged were located at the freeway interchanges. This was a regional concept, and the "city" was itself multicentered and dispersed. In a stroke of frightening misinterpretation, Wright's vision helped to inspire the mass suburbanization that would take place following World War II.

Post–World War II Development. World War II brought the United States out of the Great Depression. Economic development naturally focused on industries related to the military, but despite the public sector's involvement, housing production and maintenance of the existing urban fabric had fallen dangerously behind. When the soldiers returned, the United States was facing a monumental housing crisis. As a means of stimulating the private building industry, business loans and home mortgages were made broadly available for the construction and purchase of new, single-family homes. Simultaneously, the federal government financed construction of a vast highway system that provided access to lands for suburban development, making the private automobile a necessity. As suburban real-estate development exploded during the 1950s, massive schemes such as Levittown (planned communities in New York and Pennsylvania) transformed agricultural lands at the outer reaches of the large urban centers.

Like the satellite village of the Garden City and the gleaming tower of the modernist city, the decentralized vision of Broadacre City was adopted in superficial form only. Indeed the family farm that was at the heart of Wright's democracy was virtually eradicated in the mass suburbanization of the postwar period. The relentless subdivision of open lands into a dense but decentered suburban landscape radically transformed the national geography in the second half of the twentieth century.

Nowhere is this trend more purely manifest than in Los Angeles and Orange counties in southern California where formless "cities" sprawl across the landscape. Homes, workplaces, and schools are dispersed. The automobile is required for daily commutation to the workplace and all other activities, creating a dense web of roadways, private driveways, and parking lots. Where pedestrian circulation and public-transportation systems once brought strangers into regular contact, car culture has had an isolating effect. Moreover, built expressions of a civic culture have devolved from the realm of public city centers to the privately owned, internalized world of shopping malls. These are often located—as Wright would have had it—at a freeway interchange, but consumption of goods rather than their exchange has placed the citizen in a passive rather than an interactive role.

The mirror effect of mass suburbanization was felt acutely in the cities, where deteriorating working-class neighborhoods were abandoned by those who could pursue the "American Dream." Those left behind were disproportionately African American, Latino, or other economically disadvantaged groups. Moreover, the industrial economy had collapsed, unskilled jobs were no longer available, and banks excluded whole areas from home-mortgage and small-business loans, making inner cities places of desperation. The riots of the mid-1960s brought the issue to crisis but also sealed the fate of the inner city. Federal investment in core urban redevelopment, meager as it had been, was drastically reduced in the 1970s, and American cities continued to depopulate.

New Directions. New directions in planning and urban design have emerged since the 1960s in response to pragmatic needs and a critical assessment of American culture. Slowly Americans have recognized that in the fury to fulfill their "Manifest Destiny," they have occupied territory rather than created places. As densely populated as the nation has become, Americans have yet to develop a nuanced language of collective form that sets a stage for civil and democratic public life. A sense of the limits of resources, including geographic

space—first an environmental issue—now defines the movement for "sustainable" cities.

The sprawling development practices that plague the American landscape with traffic, pollution, and spatial fragmentation are slowly being challenged and reversed. Inheritors of the Garden City tradition, "new urbanist" developers and designers have proposed models of towns formed to promote the sense of community missing from typical suburban development. New towns such as Seaside and Celebration in Florida emphasize a strong, well-defined town center, increased housing density, and a hierarchy of streets that encourage pedestrian contact. This formula has had significant success in supplanting the older suburban model, but in a fundamental respect it is the same. It is most attractive to the private developer where a clear "greenfield" site is used and a fairly homogeneous middle-class population is to be served.

The great challenge for the paradigm of sustainability is in confronting the American obsession with newness, uniformity, and privatization in existing contexts. It requires a fundamental recognition that urban text is a constantly evolving organism that must be maintained, rewoven, and periodically reinvented. Having begun a reflective course with the historic preservation movement of the 1960s, urban designers now must embrace and reinvent difficult sites: residual spaces between and below highways, decaying waterfronts, crumbling neighborhoods, abandoned industrial "brownfields," and postindustrial shopping centers.

As urbanists bring twenty-first-century land uses and patterns of inhabitation to these sites, they do so recognizing the strength that multiple layers of formal expression confer on a place. Similarly, by reintroducing natural ecological systems suppressed during the rapid growth of gridiron cities, a dialogue can be reestablished between nature and urban form. This approach is contrary to the practices of mass culture that have defined so much of the American landscape. Fashioning unique, meaningful space from existing contexts is labor-intensive, and it requires the participation of already invested constituencies. But in the careful process of reweaving an urban fabric, new public space that reflects its diverse texture can emerge, bringing with it a more democratic interpretation of American civic life.

BIBLIOGRAPHY

Fishman, Robert, *Urban Utopias in the Twentieth Century: Ebenezer Howard, Frank Lloyd Wright, and Le Corbusier* (Basic Bks. 1977).

Katz, Peter, *The New Urbanism: Toward an Architecture of Community* (McGraw-Hill 1994).

Lang, Jon, *Urban Design: The American Experience* (Van Nostrand Reinhold 1994).

Mumford, Lewis, *The City in History: Its Origins, Its Transformations, and Its Prospects* (Harcourt 1961).

Peirce, Neal R., and Robert Guskind, *Breakthroughs: Re-Creating the American City* (Ctr. for Urban Policy Research, Rutgers, State Univ. of N.J. 1993).

Reps, John W., *The Making of Urban America: A History of City Planning in the United States* (Princeton Univ. Press 1965).

Scully, Vincent, *American Architecture and Urbanism* (Praeger 1969).

Sorkin, Michael, ed., *Variations on a Theme Park: The New American City and the End of Public Space* (Hill & Wang 1992).

Stern, Robert A. M., Gregory Gilmartin, and Thomas Mellins, *New York 1930: Architecture and Urbanism between the Two World Wars* (Rizzoli Intl. Pubns. 1987).

Wright, Gwendolyn, *Building the Dream: A Social History of Housing in America* (Pantheon Bks. 1981).

SALLY HARRISON

CIVIL RELIGION

Civil religion is a nearly simultaneous outgrowth and synthesis of secularism and the ideology of nationalism. As a traditional religion went into decline, the state would co-opt its functions, thereby increasing the state's power and conferring a pseudo-sacredness upon itself. Among Western European peoples generally this pattern has been increasingly visible since the Renaissance and Reformation. But it is not unique to the West. In Japan, state Shinto flowered from the Meiji Restoration of 1868 C.E. until 1945, to be replaced by a secular nationalism. The *Panca Sila* ("Five Foundations") of secular Indonesian nationalism, unashamedly echoing the Five Pillars of Islam, flowered after the islands' independence from Holland in 1949. Around the world, parallel with the decline of state or established churches, the state itself has come to occupy the place of a church. This transformation is especially clear in the case of the United States.

Civil religion first involves a progressive replacement of the forms and structures, privileges, and responsibilities of religions within society by institutions of government. One of the earliest instances resulted from the dispute over Roman Catholicism's authority in matters of divorce, which led to the establishment of the Church of England and expansion of the state's power in that area. Similarly, marriage, the recording of births and deaths, and rules of inheritance came to be concerns of emerging secular governments, replacing traditional religious roles and authority. Works of charity, from building and staffing hospitals to care of the poor, became national concerns. At the same time that religion's social roles were absorbed by the state, so were its outward forms. As divisively sectarian holy days were no longer observed, nationalistic holidays entered the calendar, celebrating victory in a war or whatever else the state wanted to emphasize in building fervent nationalism. These paralleled the quasi-cultic celebration of popular heroes whose birthdays replaced saints' days, while everything from birthplaces and battlefields to such monuments as Mount Rushmore became places of pilgrimage. Rituals such as the recitation of creeds and singing of hymns were replaced by pledges of allegiance and national anthems, again attuned to the ideology of nationalism. But these were only the external trappings of religion. The more important dimension of civil religion came in the creation of an ideology, defining various peoples as an imagined community, and in essentially transcendent terms.

Once states came to define themselves as *über alles* ("superior to all others"), their need to control how people thought became of primary concern. The role of religion in defining the nature and purpose of life and society was replaced by the ideology of nationalism itself. With the concept of citizenship in the state being the highest good came

© CORBIS-BETTMANN

The Pledge of Allegiance became the nation's official flag pledge in 1943.

logical arguments for forced conscription into the military, along with a concept of obligation on the part of the citizen-soldier to die for the well-being of the nation rather than the state existing to benefit the individual. In law, the survival of the country became paramount, often overriding individual rights. The right of the individual to refuse conscription or a draft, an obligation of involuntary servitude to the state, became highly controversial. While the original colonies that made up the United States had respected the individual's right to refuse to fight or render militia service, national conscription was not nearly so flexible. After more than a century of battles, the United States finally accepted a relatively few circumstances in which an individual's conscience might take precedence over the state. Religious or even philosophically based conscientious objection to participation in war in any form came to be tolerated because it was absolute and did not challenge the wisdom of the state. But the individual who disputed the state's judgment in a particular war, claiming as a right selective conscientious objection, was punished without exception. The courts could not allow the individual's claim to a greater moral knowledge than that of

the seemingly omniscient state. Further challenging the ideology and content of nationalism became heresy, with ideological crime becoming the ultimate sin. In the United States, President Harry S. Truman began a pattern after World War II of describing the cold war as a struggle against "godless communism," and "communist sympathizers" were subjected to ideological inquisitions. Few dared to question allegiance to the bizarrely implicit ideological alternative: a holy or perhaps godly capitalism. American civil religion reached a peak in America with the Vietnam War, which became a watershed separating those who were devoted to it and those who had lost faith.

In the United States the substitution of a secular, nationalistic civil religion for traditional theistic creeds was accelerated ahead of other nation-states. The early migrants to British North America saw it as a new Eden, needing only to be redeemed from the pagan indigenous populations. Politicians later would not blush at describing an independent United States as humanity's last, best hope, but by then it was to be a secular paradise on earth. In the beginning, they were sensitive to the religious persecutions that had prompted much of the migration from England. Most were aware of the English Civil War (1641–1660), the later passage of the Bill of Rights (1689), and of the stresses that resulted from the superimposition of modern nationalism over traditional religious views.

Most of the British colonies along the Atlantic seaboard of North America had supported their own established or state church, built into their original compact, charter, or constitution. In attempting to create an overarching federal system in America, it became obvious that states with different denominational commitments or preference would never agree to anyone's but their own state church being established on the national level. In Thomas Jefferson's *Notes on the State of Virginia*, he affirmed in consequence the necessity of creating a "wall between church and state." Creating this *novus ordo seclorum* ("new order of the ages"), the state would thereby survive, while an attempt to enforce any of the particular creeds would have shattered the nascent Union in civil war. The Constitution affirmed this necessary government neutrality toward conventional religions by affirming that "no religious test shall ever be required as a qualification to any office or public trust under the United States" (Article VI, section 3). The First Amendment of the Bill of Rights only strengthened and raised this wall in prohibiting Congress from making any "law respecting an establishment of religion, or prohibiting the free exercise thereof." Nothing in those texts, however, recognized or challenged the emergence of the secular nationalism of the civil religion. Whatever disputes there were about the means, there was little question that the role of the state was to "form a more perfect union, establish justice, insure domestic tranquility . . . and secure the blessings of liberty," while no mention was made of personal piety.

Beginning early in the republic's history, tension in the civil religion centered on questions of social class, complicated by gender and ethnicity, which would continue and expand into the present day. While George Washington and John Adams believed in an essentially elitist ideology of government, Thomas Jefferson, continuing with the theme that "all men are created equal," pushed for a more democratic understanding. The Jeffersonian dogma, strengthened in the populist presidency of Andrew Jackson, gave place to the lower class in the civil religion. But this left a paradox based in the continuing gaps between social classes. It also left unanswered whether religious peoples such as the Mormons, who affirmed obedience to a higher law than that of the nation-state, could coexist within it. Generally speaking, the courts rejected such religious grounding. Subsequently, there began to develop as part of the civil religion an idea that came to be known by the label "the melting pot." This new doctrine held as a higher good the effective abolition of differences, as epitomized by traditional ethnic and faith communities, which might upset the national equilibrium. These tensions never have been resolved, and the twenty-first century in America begins with a Religious Right asserting a view of the purpose and meaning of the nation in poli-

tics that challenges the traditional civil religion and its secular faith in liberal democracy in many particulars.

[See also CHURCH AND STATE.]

BIBLIOGRAPHY

Anderson, Benedict, *Imagined Communities: Reflections on the Origin and Spread of Nationalism,* rev. ed. (Verso 1991).

Bellah, Robert Neely, *The Broken Covenant: American Civil Religion in Time of Trial,* 2d ed. (Univ. of Chicago Press 1992).

Bellah, Robert Neely, and Phillip E. Hammond, eds., *Varieties of Civil Religion* (Harper 1980).

Marty, Martin E., ed., *Civil Religion, Church and State* (K. G. Saur 1992).

Marty, Martin E., and R. Scott Appleby, eds., *Religion, Ethnicity, and Self-Identity: Nations in Turmoil* (Univ. Press of New England 1997).

Mead, Sidney Earl, *The Nation with the Soul of a Church* (Mercer Univ. Press 1985).

Rouner, Leroy S., ed., *Civil Religion and Political Theology* (Univ. of Notre Dame Press 1986).

GORDON C. THOMASSON

CIVIL RIGHTS AND THE CIVIL RIGHTS MOVEMENT

[The long, arduous road to achieving some measure of political and socioeconomic equality for African American citizens in the United States is here discussed in two topically related but thematically distinct articles. The first, AN OVERVIEW, *provides a discussion of the historical context in which the civil rights movement unfolded, culminating in a review of major civil rights legislation in the 1960s. The second entry,* THE AFTERMATH OF THE CIVIL RIGHTS MOVEMENT, *examines the outcome of that legislation and continuing problems regarding civil rights for African Americans. For related articles in the encyclopedia, see also* AFRICAN AMERICANS, AN OVERVIEW.]

An Overview

The civil rights movement was a struggle to fulfill the promise, made in the Thirteenth, Fourteenth, and Fifteenth Amendments to the U.S. Constitution, of full citizenship and equal opportunity for African Americans. It originated with those amendments (in fact, one could say, with the earliest African Americans) and more particularly with the decline in commitment to those amendments that the rise of segregation and disfranchisement embodied by the early twentieth century. Thus, though it came to a climax in the first half of the 1960s, it began long before the 1950s. The civil rights movement was a response to the Jim Crow era—the era of state-sponsored segregation, disfranchisement, and discrimination—which it sought to eradicate.

Something of a canon of actions has been established by historians to trace the trajectory of the civil rights movement, particularly between, on the one hand, the Supreme Court decisions in *Brown v. Board of Education* (1954 and 1955) and the Montgomery bus boycott of 1955–1956 and, on the other hand, the Civil Rights Act of 1964 and the Voting Rights Act of 1965, with the sit-ins that began in February 1960 a key development in between. Though that chronology will largely be followed here, the fact is that the civil rights movement can also be understood as a myriad of actions, throughout the South (or even the nation) and across the twentieth century, a broader definition that reflects the universality not only of racial discrimination but of resistance to it.

Precursors, Premonitions, Parallels. Among the premonitions and reflections of the civil rights movement, many forces converged to nurture it and bring it to fruition in the 1960s. The work of Franz Boas and other anthropologists called into question the very concept of race as a biological reality. Hitler's Germany, together with the tremendous U.S. effort in World War II required to defeat it, demonstrated the utter ugliness of race-based policies. Jackie Robinson's baseball exploits with the Brooklyn Dodgers beginning in 1947 led to an easing of segregationist attitudes and practices across the nation; mixed-race audiences were soon attending spring-training games in the South. Racial styles of American music converged in the mid- to late 1950s, as "Little Richard" Penniman, a black singer, and Elvis Presley, a white one, alike reached mass

biracial audiences. Writers found receptive audiences with such varied works as Gunnar Myrdal's *An American Dilemma* (1944), Lillian Smith's *Killers of the Dream* (1949), Ralph Ellison's *Invisible Man* (1952), and Harper Lee's Pulitzer–Prize-winning *To Kill a Mockingbird* (1960), as well as *The Family of Man: The Photographic Exhibition created by Edward Steichen for the Museum of Modern Art* (1955) and "Letter from the Birmingham Jail" (1963) by Martin Luther King, Jr.

Comparisons of the 1920s and 1930s with the 1950s and 1960s suggest some of the changes as well as continuities. A successful campaign to end the white Democratic primary resulted in a series of decisions by the U.S. Supreme Court between 1927 and 1944, yet African Americans were still prevented from voting at all in many places in the Deep South into the 1960s. In the Great Depression years of the 1930s, African Americans in such cities as Chicago and New York campaigned for "don't shop where you can't work." At Southern lunch counters during the sit-in movement in the early 1960s, the campaign was more like "don't shop where you can't eat."

A successful struggle to begin desegregating schools at every level in the 1960s originated many years earlier. Litigation began in the 1930s to target black exclusion from public universities' graduate and professional programs. Little changed during the first decade, but all seventeen segregated states ended black exclusion from "white" universities by 1965. At some schools, such as the University of Arkansas in 1948, the desegregation of professional programs proceeded with little difficulty, but at others, notably the University of Mississippi in 1962 and the University of Alabama in 1963, tension was enormous and violence considerable. Most of the segregated states and schools fell somewhere in between, in both timing and tension.

Throughout the campaign to end black exclusion from segregated universities and other schools, white parents and politicians conjured up images of interracial sex and the threat of racial "mongrelization." Whatever the fears or tactics of those who resisted integration, the African American campaign

AP/WIDE WORLD PHOTOS

James Meredith, the first African American to attend the University of Mississippi, with fellow graduates.

to desegregate higher education had two main objectives. One was to open up opportunities for African Americans to obtain the formal training to enter such professions as law, engineering, medicine, and pharmacy. The other, largely successful by 1950, was to establish precedents that would permit an assault on segregation in public elementary and secondary schools.

In the 1930s and 1940s the main effort regarding racial change in the nation's elementary and secondary schools was to obtain a greater measure of the "equal" within the old framework of "separate but equal." Black lawyers, educators, and entire communities worked to obtain more nearly equal school facilities, high school curricula, and teachers' salaries. In the early 1950s the strategy was redirected to achieving desegregation and an end to dual school systems, one white, one black. After a major Supreme Court victory in 1954, schools began to desegregate in some states but not at all in various other states, and efforts continued

through the 1960s to force the implementation of the 1954 victory and bring an end to segregation in the schools.

The civil rights movement necessarily involved private actions as well as efforts in conventional politics. Threats of direct-action protest in the 1940s were instrumental in obtaining presidential decisions to open jobs in defense plants to black workers and to desegregate the U.S. military. After the Supreme Court ruled against segregated interstate bus travel in *Morgan* v. *Virginia* (1946), a biracial group of freedom riders from the Congress of Racial Equality went on a bus ride into the South to highlight that decision and test its effectiveness. Protests in Birmingham, Alabama, in 1963 spurred passage of the Civil Rights Act of 1964. Similarly, protest activity in Selma, Alabama, in early 1965 had much to do with passage of the Voting Rights Act later that year.

Groups and Leaders. Various groups and organizations marshaled commitment, creativity, and energy to bring racial segregation and disfranchisement under siege. The National Association for the Advancement of Colored People (NAACP) began in the 1910s to bring cases in the federal courts to undo the laws that curtailed African Americans' rights regarding voting, housing, schooling, transportation, and criminal justice. During World War II, the all-black March on Washington movement attacked discrimination in employment and segregation in the military. At the same time, and for many years afterward, the biracial Congress of Racial Equality (CORE) took direct action against segregation in public accommodations as well as transportation. The Southern Christian Leadership Conference (SCLC) grew out of the Montgomery Bus Boycott of 1955–1956, and the Student Nonviolent Coordinating Committee (SNCC) grew out of the sit-ins of 1960.

A. Philip Randolph (1889–1979), "Mr. Labor" as well as "Mr. Civil Rights," spanned the civil rights movement and was one of its towering figures. His March on Washington movement called for equal access to jobs in the federal government and in defense plants and an end to segregation in the United

A student sit-in conducted by the New York Youth Committee at a Woolworth's lunch counter in the South, in the early 1960s.

States military. Randolph postponed the march when President Franklin D. Roosevelt agreed to issue Executive Order 8802 and ordered establishment of the President's Committee on Fair Employment Practices. Seven years later, Randolph's opposition to a cold war peacetime draft for a segregated military provoked President Harry S. Truman into issuing Executive Order 9981, which inaugurated an integration of all the armed forces in the United States.

Thurgood Marshall (1908–1993), barred from admission to the (white) University of Maryland law school in his hometown, Baltimore, had to commute to Washington, D.C., to attend law school at (black) Howard University, from which he graduated in 1933. From the 1930s until the 1960s, Marshall applied his formidable legal skills to the NAACP's efforts to break down segregation in schools at every level, and the NAACP won *Brown v. Board of Education* in 1954, when the U.S. Supreme

© KEVIN GLACKMEYER/AP/WIDE WORLD PHOTOS

Actress Cicely Tyson reacts upon seeing a life-size bronze sculpture of Rosa Parks in the Rosa Parks Library and Museum in Montgomery, Alabama, following a dedication ceremony in December 2000.

Court declared school segregation a violation of the equal protection clause of the Fourteenth Amendment. Though not until the late 1950s or the 1960s did desegregation even begin in some states, that decision proved the basis for subsequent victories in federal court against segregation in public facilities ranging from parks to colleges to eating establishments. Moreover, it symbolized the possibility of dismantling American apartheid in all dimensions of life and helped energize the further development of the civil rights movement.

Adam Clayton Powell (1908–1972) represented the Harlem area of New York City in the U.S. House of Representatives from 1945 to 1971. He repeatedly introduced what became known as the Powell Amendment to spending bills, insisting that federal programs not support segregation. The gesture proved symbolic before the 1960s, but later, as chairman of the House Committee on Education and Labor for six years, Powell played a sometimes important role in shaping Great Society legislation, and Title VI of the Civil Rights Act of 1964 embodied the Powell Amendment. During his quarter-century in the House, Powell represented more than his New York constituents. He served as unofficial

congressman for millions of African Americans who, especially in the South, had no other voice in national politics. Moreover, he symbolized the rise of black political power in the North, a force that had a tremendous influence in shifting the opinions of white politicians toward curtailing the pervasive power of Jim Crow policies in American life.

King (1929–1968) emerged on the national stage with his involvement in the Montgomery bus boycott after Rosa Parks refused to obey an order to give a white man her seat on an Alabama bus. Following the success of the Montgomery Improvement Association, King organized the Southern Christian Leadership Conference in 1957 to coordinate antisegregation activities throughout the South, and he published *Stride toward Freedom: The Montgomery Story* in 1958. His application of Gandhian strategy and tactics, fused with the rhetoric of a Baptist preacher, played a critical role in his leadership. He applied that approach to segregation, especially in the massive protests in Birmingham in 1963, and to disfranchisement, particularly in Selma in 1965. In between those events came the March on Washington in August 1963, at which Randolph introduced several speakers, including the final one, King, who gave his now famous "I Have a Dream" address.

Apex and Legacy of the Civil Rights Movement. The Civil Rights Act of 1964 followed by the Voting Rights Act of 1965 brought formal recognition that federal policy would no longer permit public policies of segregation and disfranchisement. The Civil Rights Act mobilized federal power to curtail racial discrimination in employment, education, and public accommodations. The Voting Rights Act attacked the panoply of screens that various Southern states continued to employ to hold black voter registration to as near zero as possible. Those two federal acts hardly brought about full integration of American society, nor did they even bring a complete end to the old Jim Crow laws, but they signified tremendous change in American social and political life. A Supreme Court decision in 1967, *Loving* v. *Virginia*, invalidated laws in sixteen states that still banned interracial marriage.

UPI/CORBIS-BETTMANN

President Lyndon B. Johnson shakes hands with Martin Luther King, Jr., after handing him a pen for the signing of the Civil Rights Bill of 1964.

The Civil Rights Act of 1968 attacked persistent segregation in the nation's housing markets.

Among the explanations for the accomplishments of the civil rights movement was the technology of communications media that vividly portrayed stark images of violent actions taken toward black Southerners. Television, in particular, brought viewers direct visual and audio access to the scenes in Birmingham in 1963, for example, where cattle prods, fire hoses, billy clubs, and police dogs savaged peaceful protesters. Americans responded by becoming more supportive of change, even by participating in the change themselves, as so many Northern college students chose to do, for example, in Mississippi in summer 1965. Meantime, people outside the United States saw what was happening and made their own perspectives known, and U.S. leaders had to consider the role of domestic race relations in shaping perceptions of the United States in nonwhite nations during the cold war with the Soviet Union.

By a host of measures American society was markedly less segregated by the late 1960s and early 1970s than it had been before, or even just after, World War II. Beginning in 1967 Marshall served

as one of nine justices on the U.S. Supreme Court. *Guess Who's Coming to Dinner,* a 1967 movie starring Sidney Poitier, portrayed an interracial couple, a black man and a white woman. Diana Ross was one among a number of African American superstar performers whose fans included millions of whites as well as blacks. Historically nonblack institutions of higher education throughout the South enrolled black students and recruited black athletes. World heavyweight boxing champion Muhammad Ali, who elicited hostility among white Americans in the 1960s reminiscent of Joe Louis some thirty years earlier, became hugely popular in the 1970s with a mass following among whites as well as blacks. In music, dance, literature, sports, politics, law, and movies the change was stunning, although a clear eye could discern that it remained sharply limited as well, such as in schools and housing.

In the 1990s basketball player Michael Jordan became an international icon; a half century earlier he could have neither attended the University of North Carolina nor played in the National Basketball Association. Yet changes in policy and culture went far beyond an end to laws regarding African Americans that restricted behavior on the basis of racial identity. The civil rights movement spilled over into efforts by Mexican Americans, Asian Americans, and Native Americans to secure greater opportunity and to curtail prejudicial attitudes and discriminatory practices directed against them. Deaf and disabled Americans adapted the ideas and tactics of the civil rights movement to achieve more of the promise of equal access for their groups. Female Americans benefited from such legislative initiatives as Title VII of the 1964 Civil Rights Act (regarding employment) and Title IX of the Educational Amendments of 1972 (regarding athletics and education). The civil rights movement reverberated long after the 1950s and 1960s.

BIBLIOGRAPHY

Branch, Taylor, *Parting the Waters: America in the King Years, 1954–63* (Simon & Schuster 1988).

Burns, Stewart, ed., *Daybreak of Freedom: The Montgomery Bus Boycott* (Univ. of N.C. Press 1997).

Halberstam, David, *The Children* (Random House 1998).

Kluger, Richard, *Simple Justice: The History of Brown v. Board of Education and Black America's Struggle for Equality* (Knopf 1976).

Powledge, Fred, *Free at Last? The Civil Rights Movement and the People Who Made It* (Little, Brown 1991).

Sitkoff, Harvard, *The Struggle for Black Equality, 1954–1992,* rev. ed. (Hill & Wang 1993).

Van Deburg, William L., *New Day in Babylon: The Black Power Movement and American Culture, 1965–1975* (Univ. of Chicago Press 1992).

PETER WALLENSTEIN

The Aftermath of the Civil Rights Movement

During the civil rights movement of the 1950s and early 1960s, there emerged considerable optimism over the potential for true social and economic integration of racial and ethnic minority groups within the United States. In spite of the considerable opposition to integration, especially in the Deep South, the passage of major civil rights legislation and the intervention of the Supreme Court in overturning segregationist laws and policies seemed to foreshadow the eventual breakdown of racial and ethnic barriers. However, in the aftermath of the civil rights movement, beginning with the assassination of Martin Luther King, Jr., in 1968, progress toward true integration slowed and has been marred by lingering problems of racism and a backlash against programs designed to promote racial equality.

By the late 1960s significant legal protections had been established to ensure racial equality and promote civil rights. The landmark Supreme Court Case *Brown* v. *Board of Education of Topeka* (1954) had overturned *Plessy* v. *Ferguson* and the segregationist doctrine of "separate but equal." The Civil Rights Act of 1957, the first such legislation since 1875, established a Civil Rights Commission and was followed by major legislation in 1960 and 1964. The implementation of the Supreme Court decisions and new laws was opposed by many in the South, and it fell to groups such as the National Association for the Advancement of Colored People (NAACP) and the Congress of Racial Equality (CORE) to force

federal intervention and the application of these measures through boycotts, sit-ins, and the famous "freedom rides" of the early 1960s. President Lyndon B. Johnson included civil rights among his priorities in his Great Society programs and skillfully maneuvered the Voting Rights Act of 1965 and the Civil Rights Act of 1968 through Congress. Johnson's War on Poverty was also designed to alleviate the economic disparities among the races and provide increased educational opportunities for African Americans. However, the escalating conflict in Vietnam translated into decreased funding for the president's social programs, and by 1967 many of the reform efforts were stalled.

The civil rights movement seemed to peak in 1965 with the Voting Rights Act and King's Selma march. The slow pace of integration in the South, and the seemingly unnoticed or underreported racial divisions in northern and western states, culminated in a backlash against the nonviolent tactics used by the mainstream civil rights groups. The failure of King and the NAACP to integrate Chicago was seen by many as a repudiation of the peaceful tactics used in the South. Between 1965 and 1968, a series of violent riots swept through several major urban areas of the nation during what were described as the "long, hot summers." In the Watts area of Los Angeles, 34 people were killed and 40 million dollars in property damage resulted from violence in 1965. In 1967 violence in Detroit claimed the lives of 43 people and led to fires that essentially destroyed the core of the city. Within a week of the Detroit riots, Newark, New Jersey, erupted and 26 people were killed and over 1,200 were injured.

The violence of the urban riots came as a surprise to many leaders in the civil rights movement since African Americans in urban areas generally had much better economic conditions and were more integrated than those in the Deep South. Los Angeles also had a high level of political integration and had three African Americans on the city council, two in the state assembly, and the Watts section of the city was represented in Congress by an African American. However, the urban riots throughout the nation revealed an intense anger and resentment at the disparities remaining in American society. The promises of the Great Society programs had not been realized and the rising expectations of African Americans remained unmet. Chronic unemployment had not been alleviated by the War on Poverty and the combination of economic and racial segregation had created a ghetto system that provided little opportunity for the urban poor. Conditions were exacerbated by long-standing tensions between mostly white police forces and the minority communities. Perceived and real police abuses often provided the spark that ignited these riots.

In the background, the ongoing war in Vietnam further eroded race relations as many upper- and middle-class whites were able to gain exemptions from military service through, for instance, continuing their college educations. As a result, a disproportionate number of African Americans served in the war. Vietnam came to be seen as a conflict fought with the bodies of the poor and minorities.

The continuing violence of anti-integration forces in the South, the riots of the late 1960s, and the assassination of King all combined to create a fissure within the civil rights movement. While mainstream groups continued to emphasize nonviolence and political activism, organizations such as the Student Nonviolent Coordinating Committee (SNCC) and ultimately the Black Panthers began pressing for a more confrontational approach. SNCC leader Stokely Carmichael rejected white allies and called for African Americans to build their own political power base. Groups such as the Black Muslims asserted a version of black power that included separation from whites under the concept of black nationalism. One of the leaders of this movement was Malcolm Little, or Malcolm X, a Black Muslim who initially rejected the integrationist approach of King and endorsed black separatism. After his assassination in 1965 his memoir *The Autobiography of Malcolm X,* written by Alex Haley, became a national bestseller.

While the emphasis on black power created a schism in the civil rights movement, it also led to a greater appreciation and understanding of the Af-

rican American experience, inspiring many to take greater pride in their heritage. Black power encouraged the adoption of African American role models, instead of the traditional white figures, and a renewed interest in African history, culture, and society. After numerous student protests, many white universities and colleges began to hire larger numbers of African American professors and establish black studies programs.

In his presidential campaigns in 1968 and 1972, Richard M. Nixon adopted a strategy that emphasized law and order. This "Southern strategy," designed to appeal to conservative white Southerners, was manifested in the Nixon administration's opposition to school busing as a means to desegregation. However, in 1971, the Supreme Court ordered North Carolina to use busing and later extended similar rulings across the nation. When the High Court ordered Boston to begin busing, the white community reacted violently and there began a "white flight" of students from the public school system that would be repeated in other urban areas. Concurrently, affirmative action programs were established, which some interpreted as mandating minimum quotas for minority employment in private business and government service and enrollment in higher education. However, the Supreme Court rejected the concept of rigid quotas in the 1978 case *University of California Board of Regents* v. *Bakke.*

Affirmative action continues to be a controversial issue. In 1989 the Supreme Court in *City of Richmond* v. *J. A. Croson Company* ruled a government set-aside program as unconstitutional. In the 1990s, court cases in Texas and statewide ballot initiatives in California and Washington overturned affirmative action programs in higher education.

Meanwhile, the decades of the 1970s and the 1980s witnessed a marked decline in the economic fortunes of many African Americans. While the overall poverty rate of African Americans declined, there was also a sharp decrease in employment among African American males, much of which was the result of the loss of high-wage factory jobs. The rise in unemployment and the continuing deterioration of urban centers led to the formation of what many sociologists termed an urban underclass. This trend was exacerbated during the 1980s by an elimination of federal revenue-sharing programs that translated into a further erosion of urban services. Immigration also brought waves of new competitors with the African American community for entry-level jobs.

The election of Ronald Reagan revealed a significant racial gap in the electorate. For instance, although the overwhelming majority of whites voted for Reagan, 90 percent of African Americans voted for his opponent, Walter Mondale. This racial divide continued in the 1988 election, when, in an attempt to show his opponent as "soft on crime," the campaign of Republican George H. Bush publicized the image of Willie Horton, an African American criminal who had committed murder while on parole. Economic problems and continuing tensions with local police forces exploded in the 1990s with renewed rioting following the 1992 innocent verdicts in the trials of white police officers accused of beating African American motorist Rodney King. Conversely, the innocent verdict in the 1995 O. J. Simpson trial angered many in the white community (polls showed that 65 percent of whites believed Simpson to be guilty, while 87 percent of African Americans believed him innocent). There also emerged a cultural backlash against the multicultural programs at many colleges and universities. Poverty continued to have an impact on African Americans at a higher rate than on society in general, and there also emerged a growing gap between affluent and impoverished African Americans. Despite the many gains made by African Americans, at the start of the twenty-first century racial divisions persisted in the United States and many of the goals of the civil rights movement remained unfilled.

BIBLIOGRAPHY

Cashman, Sean Dennis, *African-Americans and the Quest for Civil Rights, 1900–1990* (N.Y. Univ. Press 1991).

Foreman, Christopher, Jr., ed., *The African-American Predicament* (Brookings Inst. Press 1999).

Hanes, Walton, Jr., and Robert C. Smith, *American Politics and the African American Quest for Universal Freedom* (Longman 2000).

Lowe, Eugene, ed., *Promise and Dilemma: Perspectives on Racial Diversity and Higher Education* (Princeton Univ. Press 1999).

Massey, Douglas S., and Nancy A. Denton, *American Apartheid: Segregation and the Making of the Underclass* (Harvard Univ. Press 1993).

Smith, Jennifer B., *An International History of the Black Panther Party,* in the series *Studies in African American History and Culture* (Garland 1999).

Weiss, Robert, *"We Want Jobs," A History of Affirmative Action* (Garland 1997).

TOM M. LANSFORD

CIVIL SERVICE

The U.S. civil service has grown from a minuscule organization to the largest single group of employees in the nation. When the present government, based on the Constitution, was established in 1789, there were only three departments—State, War, and Treasury—with a total of 50 employees. Although the bureaucracy steadily grew through the nineteenth century, even during the Civil War it had only 36,672 personnel. The dramatic growth of the civil service is predominately a twentieth-century trend, which accelerated after World War II. By 1999, excluding the military, there were 2.7 million fed-

© JOHN HAYES/AP/WIDE WORLD PHOTOS

In 2000, the Census Bureau set up outreach centers staffed by civil service workers to help people fill out questionnaires.

eral employees in fourteen departments and hundreds of other agencies and bureaus.

The first federal employees were political appointees who owed their allegiance to the Federalist Party. When Thomas Jefferson was elected president in 1800, he fired more than one hundred federal workers and replaced them with members of the Democratic-Republican Party. The continuous control of the White House by the Democrats over the next twenty-eight years allowed a core group of professional bureaucrats to dominate the civil service and to retain their positions no matter the results of presidential elections. However, in 1828, the election of Andrew Jackson marked the reemergence of the spoils system of political patronage whereby the victor replaced civil servants with those loyal to him. The spoils system, when combined with the growth of the government, led to widespread and flagrant corruption.

Calls for reform were initially resisted as the major political parties had vested interests in retaining patronage as a tool to secure political support. Nevertheless, under President Ulysses S. Grant, a Civil Service Commission was established that advocated the adoption of European-style reforms including merit promotion and appointments based on entrance exams. These ideals were codified in the 1883 Pendleton Act (Civil Service Reform Act), which ultimately ended the spoils system for all but a few hundred federal positions.

The Pendleton Act was followed by a number of other reform efforts designed to increase the efficiency of the civil service and to combat corruption. In 1923 the Classification Act established the concept of equal pay for equal work for federal employees. Meanwhile, in 1939, in response to federal employees using their positions to campaign for President Franklin D. Roosevelt, Congress passed the Hatch Act (Political Activities Act), which prohibited civil servants from engaging in political activities while on the job. It also forbade officials from using their position to force their workers to make political contributions.

Since the 1960s, there has been a significant effort to make federal agencies more responsive to the needs of their workers and the public. In 1976 Congress passed legislation requiring most federal agencies to hold their meetings in public sessions, and in 1978 the Civil Service Reform Act created the Office of Personnel Management (OPM) to oversee promotions and hiring. Concurrently, the Merit Systems Protection Board (MSPB) was established to hear employee complaints and evaluate charges of wrongdoing. The 1978 act also established protections for whistle-blowers who alert the government or public to gross inefficiency or illegal actions by bureaucratic entities. The successful unionization efforts also increased protections for federal workers.

[See also FEDERAL GOVERNMENT.]

BIBLIOGRAPHY

Cook, Brian, *Bureaucracy and Self-Government: Reconsidering the Role of Public Administration in American Politics* (Johns Hopkins Univ. Press 1996).

Crenson, Matthew, *The Federal Machine: Beginnings of Bureaucracy in Jacksonian America* (Johns Hopkins Univ. Press 1975).

Ingraham, Patricia W., *The Foundation of Merit: Public Service in American Democracy* (Johns Hopkins Univ. Press 1995).

Johnson, Ronald D., and Gary D. Libecap, *The Federal Civil Service System and the Problem of Bureaucracy: The Economics and Politics of Institutional Change* (Univ. of Chicago Press 1994).

Wilson, James Q., *Bureaucracy: What Government Agencies Do and Why They Do It* (Basic Bks. 1989).

TOM M. LANSFORD

CIVIL WAR

The American Civil War began in April 1861 and ended in April 1865. Those four years transformed American society. Over six hundred thousand men died, and hundreds of thousands more bore the scars of war. The institution of slavery was abolished, and the society built around it was destroyed. The national government was strengthened tremendously, altering federal relations permanently. The Southern states were wrecked physically and condemned to over a century of economic underdevelopment, while Northern wartime financial and in-

A battle between North and South at Corinth, Mississippi, in October 1862.

dustrial consolidation have influenced the course of American development to the present day.

Origins of the War. The mid-nineteenth-century United States was notable for its rapid expansion, especially in the areas of geography, population, and economy. Yet despite a common language, religious faith, and history, two distinct economic and cultural regions (North and South) were coming to see each other as threatening to their own ways of life and visions of the American republic.

Economically the American South relied almost entirely on crops grown by slave labor, particularly cotton. Although most Southerners did not own slaves personally, this dependence on slavery had a profound impact on Southern culture, making white Southerners extremely defensive about their "peculiar institution." Their sensitivity was heightened by fear of slave insurrection, for slavery was as much a system of race control as of labor. Thus Southerners reacted sharply to any possible threats to slavery. They defended themselves from attacks on the slave system and masked internal dissension by emphasizing the purity of what they saw as a chivalrous society. Southerners came to perceive the North as a region dominated by avaricious, exploitative industrialists whose values were

354

subverting the virtuous agricultural republic envisioned by America's founding generation.

Most Northerners did not favor interfering with slavery in the Southern states. Whatever moral aversion to the concept of slavery many of them may have felt was less important than maintaining a harmonious union of states. Yet, rocked by massive social change arising from burgeoning industrialization, increasing materialism, and large-scale immigration, Northerners veiled doubts about their society by focusing on their industriousness and self-reliance and praising free-labor ideals by which any man could earn economic and social respectability. They saw the South as the antithesis of that ideal, a place where slaveholding degraded the status of labor and aristocratic planters dominated society and government, in short, a society opposed to the ideals of the republic's founders.

Southerners, anxious to protect the viability of slavery, worked to promote their institution's spread into the western territories. Northerners, however, saw the territories as the basis of an "Empire of Liberty," where equal opportunity and free-labor values would reign, and they feared having western emigrants exposed to the competition of slave labor. These opposing perspectives led both sides to interpret each other's actions as aggressive and threatening. The more Southerners fought to keep the territories open to slavery, the more Northerners embraced the idea of a mighty oligarchy of slave owners—the "slave power"—conspiring to control the federal government and open all America to slavery. In the mid-1850s many Northerners joined the new Republican Party, with the exclusion of slavery from all federal territories as its primary goal. Southerners viewed this party as a blatant attempt by Northern antislavery forces to control the national government and attack slavery.

When Republican Abraham Lincoln was elected president in 1860 without a single Southern vote, the seven states of the Deep South decided that the federal Union could no longer protect slavery. They seceded and formed their own government, the Confederate States of America. When armed conflict erupted over federal occupation of Fort Sumter in Charleston, South Carolina, Lincoln called for volunteers to maintain the Union by force. Four more slave states seceded, afraid to remain in a Union held together by armed coercion. The war began.

Both sides drew on a powerful devotion to the legacy of the Revolution. Southerners associated themselves with the American colonists' defense of their homeland from a distant, power-hungry invader and fought for a purified version of the republic they believed Northern values had corrupted. Northerners struggled to save the Union of the founders—the grand experiment in republican government—from those who would corrupt and destroy it.

The Soldiers' Experience. Hundreds of thousands of Northerners and Southerners sprang to volunteer, as parades and banquets across the country stirred patriotic fervor and pressured young men to enlist. Almost everyone expected a short war— one brief campaign or even a single, all-out battle. Volunteers soon found that their visions of glory did not match the reality of life in camp, where they spent most of their time. They drilled for a part of every day and spent the remainder fighting profound boredom by reading, writing letters, playing pranks, performing plays and concerts, and other activities. Religion was popular among many soldiers, and camp revivals were common. But perhaps the most significant factor in camp life was disease, which killed far more men than battle did.

Since volunteer regiments were drawn from single towns or regions, home community life carried over into the armies. That carryover was crucial to the courage displayed by soldiers in the terror and confusion of battle: for many, what kept them in the lines was knowing that their families and communities would find out should they run. Loyalty to one's companions, what sociologists call "small-group cohesion," was another important factor in the steadfastness-under-fire displayed by most Civil War soldiers. Such courage prevailed despite staggering carnage: it was common for a unit to suffer twenty-five to fifty percent casualty rates in

General Robert E. Lee in an 1865 photograph.

battle. In all, disease and battle killed over 620 thousand men in the Civil War.

The Southern Home Front. With America's capital and industry concentrated in the Northern states, the Confederacy faced tremendous challenges in running a war. The government tried numerous means of financing the war, including borrowing and taxation. A ten percent "tax in kind," payable in agricultural products owing to the region's money scarcity, was particularly odious to Southerners because of the harsh measures employed by government collectors. Yet these sources proved inadequate, and the Confederate war effort was funded primarily by the printing of over a billion dollars of unsupported paper money. Inflation stemming from this policy and from widespread shortages shattered the economy, resulting in massive deprivation and food riots.

The dearth of Southern industries forced the government to direct war production itself, building foundries, shipyards, and other necessary works, and, by the end of the war, seizing all railroads and telegraph lines and strictly regulating all imports and exports. A bureaucracy over seventy thousand strong controlled this far-reaching apparatus.

In the spring of 1862 the Confederacy instituted America's first centrally directed draft. Conscription sparked a great deal of resistance, but the most bitterly resented aspect of it was what was called "the twenty-nigger law," which exempted one white man on every plantation with twenty or more slaves. Small farmers felt that they were unfairly bearing the brunt of the war's hardships.

Inflation, shortages, the tax-in-kind, conscription, and the "impressment" of produce and livestock by Confederate armies all produced resentment and dissension. Women were hit especially hard by the demands of war, frequently left alone to perform work for which they were ill-prepared. Many upper-class women felt betrayed by a society that had led them to expect to be cared for and protected, while lower-class women struggled to keep their families and farms intact. As the war progressed many wrote desperate letters begging their men to come home. These letters were no doubt a primary cause for high Confederate desertion rates late in the war.

Despite such intense war weariness, most white Southerners remained devoted to the cause. Through four brutal years of war white men continued to fight and white women continued to run farms and plantations. In fact, mounting casualty lists added to their determination, forcing them to find some meaning behind the destruction and increasing their hatred of Yankee armies. Not until April 1865, when the surrender of Robert E. Lee's seemingly invincible Army of Northern Virginia broke the spirit of the Confederacy, did the underlying will to fight cease.

The Northern Home Front. Although the nation's rate of economic growth slowed during the war, largely owing to the expense of maintaining a military totaling 2.2 million men, virtually every aspect of the Northern economy flourished. Directing this boom were activist Republican policies. The

A burned district of Richmond, Virginia, after the Confederate capital fell to the North in April 1865.

Republican Congress instituted such dramatic reforms as a national banking system, income and excise taxes, and the granting of millions of acres of public lands for the support of railroads, colleges, and western emigrants. Although their aim was to fuel the economy and advance the public good, the unforeseen consequences of these policies were the concentration of economic power in the hands of northeastern bankers, the strengthening of industrialists at the expense of laborers, and the laying of a general groundwork for the massive economic consolidation of the Gilded Age.

Although farmers, the majority of the Northern population, flourished during the war, not all segments of the population thrived. Wartime inflation outran industrial wages, provoking labor unrest. The Lincoln administration's use of federal troops against strikers and its restriction of critics' civil liberties aroused opposition among workers. When, in the spring of 1863, the government announced a new conscription policy that allowed exemptions for those who could provide a substitute or pay a three-hundred-dollar commutation fee, resistance broke out in cities across the North. For four days in July, the worst riot in U.S. history raged in New York, killing over one hundred people. Much of the violence there consisted of Irish laborers' attacking free blacks, blaming them, in the wake of the government's new emancipation policy, for the war.

Emancipation. Most Northerners went to war not to attack slavery but to preserve the Union, which had come to symbolize individual liberty, self-government, and law and order. But as the contest wore on more and more Northerners became convinced that victory would require striking at the heart of Southern society, abolishing slavery and remodeling the South in the Northern image.

The institution of slavery began to disintegrate as soon as Southern men left farms and plantations for the army, leaving behind them a strange new society composed of white women and slaves. From the beginning the slaves viewed the conflict as a divinely directed war for their deliverance, and they acted on this idea by escaping by the thousands to Union encampments whenever Northern armies came near. In addition to undermining the slave system, these refugees forced the Northern people to consider the moral aspects of slavery and convinced increasing numbers of Northerners that the slaves should be freed.

Lincoln himself came to this conclusion by the summer of 1862. Following the Union victory at Antietam in September, he announced his intention, as commander-in-chief, to abolish slavery and to utilize African Americans as soldiers. On January 1, 1863, Lincoln signed the Emancipation Proclamation, and the Civil War became a war to end slavery as well as to save the Union. Many Northerners opposed this radical move, but the dragging on of the war convinced more and more people of the need for it. Moreover, the distinguished service of almost 180 thousand black troops—most of them former slaves, and all facing segregation, inferior pay, and other forms of discrimination—convinced many whites of the utility of arming African Americans and created a climate of sympathy for blacks, which had a great influence on the course of postwar Reconstruction.

The War's Legacy. The Civil War was a watershed event in American history. It resolved constitutional ambiguities concerning federal supremacy and the legal right of secession, and, by the end of the nineteenth century, resulted in a truly unified nation. Perhaps more important, it freed over three million slaves and wrote into the Constitution full citizenship rights for African Americans.

White Southerners did not adapt easily to the new racial order. As soon as possible they turned to blatant racist appeals and terrorist campaigns to reverse black political and social advances. By the 1890s the Jim Crow system was replacing the institutionalized race control lost with slavery. This system would dictate race relations into the 1960s. In the meantime the economic and social devastation of the South was terrific, and the region would remain an economic backwater for decades.

In the North the wartime economy initiated the massive economic consolidation that occurred during the last decades of the nineteenth century, setting the stage for the modern American economy. Moreover, by bringing to fruition the most radical of the antebellum reform movements—abolitionism—and by subjecting a generation of young men to military discipline, the war marked the climax of the idealistic reform impulse. Thenceforth, a more conservative intellectual climate prevailed, which emphasized organization and professionalism.

The Civil War in Popular Memory. The Southern myth of the Lost Cause arose quickly, positing that the North won not because of superior skill or courage but through sheer force of numbers and industrial might, thus bringing no dishonor to Southerners, who had been doomed to fail despite the most valiant resistance. This myth recalled for Southerners the Old South for which they had fought as a land of idyllic plantations and contented slaves. These images have been propagated by such influential films as *Birth of a Nation* (1915) and *Gone with the Wind* (1939) and are popular today among legions of Civil War buffs and reenactors.

Meanwhile the North created its own romanticized mythology, portraying the war as a moral crusade to erase the stain of slavery. It found its hero in Abraham Lincoln, whose image as a humble, honest frontier rail-splitter who rose to the highest office, stood up to the aristocratic slave power, and became the "Great Emancipator" captured perfectly the image of war Northerners wished to cherish. This image of the war has been maintained through Carl Sandburg's monumental popular biography of Lincoln (1926; 1939) as well as later novels such as *The Killer Angels* (Michael Shaara, 1974) and films such as *Gettysburg* (1993).

[See also LINCOLN, ABRAHAM; SOUTH, THE; STATES' RIGHTS.*]*

BIBLIOGRAPHY

Clinton, Catherine, and Nina Silber, eds., *Divided Houses: Gender and the Civil War* (Oxford 1992).

Cullen, Jim, *The Civil War in Popular Culture: A Reusable Past* (Smithsonian Inst. Press 1995).

Gallagher, Gary W., *The Confederate War* (Harvard Univ. Press 1997).

Hummel, Jeffrey Rogers, *Emancipating Slaves, Enslaving Free Men: A History of the American Civil War* (Open Court 1996) [an insightful, brief account with useful and stimulating bibliographical discussions].

Jimerson, Randall C., *The Private Civil War: Popular Thought during the Sectional Conflict* (La. State Univ. Press 1988) [looks at both soldiers and civilians].

McPherson, James M., *Battle Cry of Freedom: The Civil War Era* (Oxford 1988).

Paludan, Phillip Shaw, *A People's Contest: The Union and Civil War, 1861–1865* (Harper 1988)[an outstanding integration of social, cultural, economic, and political perspectives].

RUSSELL McCLINTOCK

CLASS AND CULTURE

Perhaps the most definitive thing one can say about "class" and "culture" in America is that, as long as there has been an American culture, Americans have been confused about class. At its most extreme this has led to the claim that class does not exist, or at least does not matter, in the United States. This idea makes little sense, but its persistence is itself part of the reality of class in U.S. culture. From the sumptuary laws of colonial New England, which dictated that clothing must be class-coded, to arguments about the nature of the "underclass" in late twentieth-century cities, consciousness of class has been quite intense, and it has shaped colonial and U.S. culture from top to bottom, bottom to top. But the precise nature of that shaping has always been hotly contested.

Two main schools of class analysis have influenced American studies, one derived from Karl Marx, the other from Max Weber. For Marx class was above all an economic category, one tied directly, deeply but complexly, to one's position in the production process. While he showed in such works as *The Eighteenth Brumaire* the importance of analyzing multiple classes and class-fractions, for Marx, in capitalist society, these classes ultimately align into two grand ones: capitalists (who own the means of production and profit immensely from that ownership) and workers (who own only their own labor power while most of their wealth is expropriated by capitalists). German sociologist Max Weber preferred always to work with multiple classes and to define class itself in relation to multiple variables: in addition to economic status, Weber included education, status of occupation, and a number of other factors as contributing to class stratification.

Both Marx and Weber understood that "class" is always both an objective phenomenon and a subjective one. For Marx this insight took the form of a distinction between a "class-in-itself" (the objective fact of its place in the economy), and a "class-for-itself" (the subjective awareness of one's class positioning). For Marx these two sides were never separate, always interacting. Similarly, Weber demonstrated that the relatively solid economic facts of class were always mediated through more culturally variable dimensions (a viewpoint developed in a somewhat different direction by America's most original theorist of class, Thorstein Veblen).

Unfortunately, the subtlety of class analysis as practiced by these theorists was not always passed on to their disciples. Marxists sometimes reductively treated class in America as nothing but economic struggle, while Weberians often reductively treated it as nothing but multiply-layered stability. Many

later scholars would probably share a position articulated by Anthony Giddens that class is neither economically determined nor culturally amorphous but is one of the key "mediating structures" through which economic realities are given particular cultural meanings. In the course of U.S. history, those structures have been made and remade in a variety of ways that have shaped cultural forms and practices.

Two factors have contributed greatly to the difficulty of establishing a clear and nuanced study of class in U.S. culture. The first factor is the doctrine known as American exceptionalism. This doctrine includes the claim that consciousness of class, let alone class consciousness in a Marxist sense, has been relatively absent in America. This claim makes sense only against some very rigid notion of what form such consciousness should take, and it is has hindered discussions of class and culture in the United States by begging the question: "Exceptional" compared to what? The implicit model of contrast is usually England and western Europe where, in a kind of backhanded tribute to Marx, it is acknowledged that class struggle has existed historically. Yet if one looks closely, there are certainly some parallels to the evolution of class in Europe and America (and more and more so in recent years), while other cultures, particularly "colonial-settler" societies such as Brazil, Australia, and South Africa, show even more similarities in class evolution. The point is that all cultures are "exceptional" at some levels of analytic specificity and "unexceptional," or comparable, at other levels of analysis. Patterns of class structure and consciousness should always be analyzed in their culture-specific dimensions, but this need not preclude comparing American patterns to those of other cultures; indeed it cannot since only comparison can determine what is specific and what is not.

The second related factor that has inhibited clear thinking about class in the United States stems from differing interpretations of that key value in American political life, "equality." Throughout U.S. history citizens have argued about how much equality of rights, which everyone seems to agree is desirable, requires equality of economic condition.

A society dinner party at New York's fashionable Sherry's Restaurant in 1901.

People have argued both about the extent of economic class differences and the importance of those differences in assuring political equality. The dominant voices have tended to argue that class is not really important because it is a changeable rather than a permanent condition, given an allegedly high degree of economic mobility in the country. Or they have argued that people treat each other equally and are treated equally under the law despite differences of wealth. Opposing voices have argued that class matters a great deal in America, that po-

litical, social, educational, and other opportunities have always been closely tied to economic conditions, which have never been as easily changed as those already well off have claimed. American-studies scholars, like other Americans, have been in the middle of these debates.

Much confusion about class stems from the fact that compared to the mother country (England) colonial America was relatively less hierarchical (though still very much so) and that, later, the American Revolution put in place a ruling class that felt itself to be a middle class in comparison to the British aristocracy. Ever since, upper classes in the United States have tended to assimilate themselves, rhetorically at least, to the middle class. At the same time, the myth of class mobility (the American dream, rags to riches) has tended to obscure the fact that crossing class lines has been tremendously difficult and therefore rare. Compared to the Old World of Europe, America often did have greater class mobility. But *greater* is a relative term, and that comparison has hardly comforted the masses of people trapped in the lower classes. Undoubtedly, the particularities of U.S. culture shape class patterns in ways not found elsewhere. Sean Wilentz argues, for example, in *Chants Democratic* (1984), that an ideology of radical republicanism stemming from the Revolutionary era led to a rhetoric of class struggle that was more political, less economic, than was typical in Europe. But such complications do not undermine the importance of class in analyzing U.S. culture.

Increasingly, in searching out the particularities of class in U.S. culture, scholars have found it limiting to isolate class from other social forces. In particular, they have looked to intersections of class with race and gender as crucial to a full understanding of American social life. Michael Rogin, for example, argues in his book *Subversive Genealogies* (1983) that novelist and poet Herman Melville was a kind of American Marx who understood that in U.S. culture race was class and vice versa, and that little sense could be made of these in isolation from one another. Marx himself observed that white labor in the United States would never be free so long as black labor was enslaved, and this analysis still seems accurate in the twenty-first century where differences of race, ethnicity, gender, and region continue to complicate any notion of a single U.S. working class.

Race has complicated class identity in America from the time of the first white settlers, whose own class differences were moderated when they formed themselves as "white" people putatively different from Native Americans and black slaves. Later, as David Roediger has shown in *Wages of Whiteness* (1991), the ethnically diverse, European American

working class used the rhetoric of antislavery ("No wage slavery!") to shape their early labor movements, while simultaneously forming their identity around "whiteness" in racist contrast to African Americans.

The course of America's empire as it spread from east to west also clearly shaped and was shaped by intersections of class and race. At least since Frederick Jackson Turner offered his famous "frontier thesis" in 1892, scholars have argued that the racial conflict with Native Americans that created supposedly "open" land in the West damped down class conflict by serving as a kind of "safety valve" for impoverished workers who could move west rather than remaining trapped in eastern cities. This vision, however, has been considerably complicated by Richard Slotkin who, in *The Fatal Environment* (1985), elaborately documents how the West was developed not primarily by free frontier labor but by government-subsidized railroad corporations, backed by the U.S. Army, using nearly enslaved Chinese and Irish workers to expropriate vast wealth that accrued to only a few.

Tomás Almaguer's intricate history of race and class in California, *Racial Fault Lines* (1994), likewise demonstrates how differing racialization processes for Mexican Americans, African Americans, Native Americans, and Asian Americans created and recreated class divisions. Almaguer shows that shifting racial categories were used by Anglo-Americans to fit their shifting economic and political needs. American Indians and Chinese immigrants, for example, were at times seen as one race, at other times as separate races, when it became convenient to play one off against the other. Again and again in U.S. history, racial tensions have been used to undermine attempts to form class coalitions. This is perhaps clearest during the latter half of the nineteenth century, when the efforts of populists and labor leaders to unite the producing classes (farmers and industrial workers) were severely undermined by racist appeals across class lines.

Gender has similarly played a crucial role in shaping the history of class formation in the United States. Mary P. Ryan argues in *Cradle of the Middle*

Class (1981), for example, that American middle-class politics in the late eighteenth and nineteenth centuries were deeply shaped by a domestic ideology in which family became the center of class identity. Christine Stansell, in *City of Women* (1986), covering much the same time period as Ryan, elucidates how a class struggle between working- and middle-class women over "proper" feminine behavior profoundly shaped class relations for both genders. In *Cheap Amusements* (1982), Kathy Peiss examines the rise of modern "popular culture" at the turn of the twentieth century, arguing that American Victorian culture and class structures were deeply transformed by the leisure habits of young immigrant working women. The current scholarly ideal of showing the intersection of gender, race, and class is perhaps most brilliantly illustrated in Jacqueline Jones's *Labor of Love, Labor of Sorrow* (1995), which in tracing the lives of African American women across several centuries demonstrates clearly how these three dimensions combined and recombined to shape those lives.

Scholars seeking to understand these complex interweavings of class, race, gender, and related factors in America have found the concept of cultural hegemony a very useful synthesizing tool. Derived from Italian theorist Antonio Gramsci, "cultural" or "class hegemony" is the ability of a ruling coalition to insinuate a sense that its interests are the interests of all, thus achieving domination largely by consent of the populace rather than by force. Alan Trachtenberg's survey text *The Incorporation of America* (1982) illustrates this concept aptly. Trachtenberg shows on a grand scale and in detail how the needs of a small group of industrial capitalists in the latter half of the nineteenth century utterly transformed American culture in the image of their new creation, the "corporation." He argues that every level of American culture was profoundly reshaped as this strange new economic and cultural form was made to seem an inevitable and natural center for the culture. He shows how from the decision-making of the Supreme Court, which made the corporation an "individual" with rights, to the evolution of literary genres to the physical layout of the World's Fair of 1892 U.S. culture was

transformed in ways that worked to the benefit of, or by analogy with, the corporation. The logic of giving corporations rights as persons was no doubt fueled in turn by the ways in which the rags-to-riches storytelling genre, with deep roots in U.S. culture and popularized by Horatio Alger, was rewritten in this Gilded Age in highly mythologized biographies of such atypical capitalists as Andrew Carnegie.

In addition to looking at broad patterns of culture as they have shaped and been reshaped by class relations, scholars have looked at specific aesthetic and cultural forms as factors in mediating and even helping to form class structures. Excellent American-studies work has been done over the years, for example, on the meanings of blackface minstrelsy (white folks dressing up as caricatured black folks), one of the most popular forms of American entertainment from the mid-nineteenth to the mid-twentieth century. Alexander Saxon, William Toll, David Roediger, and Eric Lott have shown in various ways how playing at blackness helped solidify whiteness in a way that increased the racial divide between blacks and whites and had a deep impact on the evolution of the class cultures in the United States generally. In a different vein, Lawrence Levine shows how in the late nineteenth and early twentieth century the distinctions between lower, middle, and upper classes were made stronger by inventing distinctions between supposedly "higher" and "lower" forms of culture. Levine shows that in the mid-nineteenth century, productions of Shakespeare's plays were often very popular occasions in America, in which people from all walks of life would mingle in a lively, almost circus-like atmosphere. But as the nineteenth century wore on, increasing efforts were made to segregate Shakespeare as "high culture" unsuitable for the working classes, something to be performed in quiet temples of theatrical observance. Levine shows a similar process at work with music, as the varieties of musical theater became separated out so that a certain type of music eventually called classical could be set off from lower-class musical forms. These new forms and institutions alone did not (re)create America's classes, but as part of the incorporation process traced by Trachtenberg they did reinforce, rationalize, and strengthen those lines, while deeply reshaping the nature of American culture itself.

Thus, by the early twentieth century the introduction of the terms *highbrow, middlebrow,* and *lowbrow* culture made sense to many Americans. The terms themselves were derived from the prominent nineteenth-century "science" of phrenology (the reading of intelligence and other characteristics from the shape of a person's head). What now seems ludicrous was serious science in the nineteenth century, accepted by many of the most prominent intellectuals of the day. Not surprising, perhaps, given the race, gender, and class of the practitioners of this science, signs of greatest intelligence turned out to match perfectly the physical features of white Anglo-Saxon men. These men had prominently "high" brows, while the supposedly less intelligent working-class specimens exhibited "low" brows. These questionable origins suggest a good deal about the limits of these categories of culture. They had their greatest impact in the mid-twentieth century and had fallen somewhat out of fashion by the late twentieth century, when a putatively postmodern culture was said to be blurring the lines between higher and lower forms of culture.

But even as the terms fell into disuse, the basic categories continued to mark the way that many Americans think about culture. Does anyone doubt that opera is "high" culture, while rap music is merely "popular" culture? And does not the presence in a home of the *Reader's Digest* still mark it as middle class, if not middlebrow? One of the most significant and influential American studies of this mid-level taste culture is Janice Radway's insightful work *A Feeling for Books* (1997), on the Book-of-the-Month Club (BOMC). Like *Reader's Digest,* BOMC has long been coded as an indicator of middlebrow tastes, as part of a desire to have "classy" literary tastes without putting in the effort required to find and read "difficult" ("highbrow") fiction. Radway's careful study of the creators of and audience for the book club illuminates the anti-middle-class prejudices that shape the people who disparage it. In so doing she also reveals the strange

fact that while U.S. culture is often thought to be predominantly middle class, too little scholarly work has actually explored the middle (brow) category of culture.

Struggles over these categories of culture and class were never more intense than in the 1930s, 1940s, and 1950s. Indeed, Warren Susman has suggested that the rise of American studies in its later, institutionalized form owes much to the economic crisis of the 1930s. Susman argues that the Depression dealt a severe blow to America's mythology of mobility and that in the face of economic hardship and much class struggle the search for a common American culture deepened. He saw this primarily as a conservative move to deflect class, racial, and other differences into a common Americanness rooted in a new, anthropological sense of U.S. culture, represented especially in America's folklore and folkways. This in turn led to a conservative current in American studies used during the cold war to distinguish Americanness from the scourge of communism.

In contrast, Michael Denning argues that this same time period also gave rise to a different, more radical current in American studies. Denning analyzes *The Cultural Front* (1996) that began in the 1930s and continued to be a prominent force in American life until the (Senator Joseph) McCarthy era of the late 1950s. He sees this social and cultural movement as a major source for the American-studies tradition and a precursor of the radically multicultural American studies that emerged in the last decades of the twentieth century. By "the cultural front" Denning means a broad-based attempt to place the experiences, needs, desires, and tastes of the ethnically and racially diverse American working classes at the heart of the culture then dominated by the styles, tastes, and economic interests of middle-class, white, Anglo-Saxon Protestants. Building on earlier work by Alan Wald, Paul Lauter, and others, Denning shows how a host of prominent writers, musicians, artists, and intellectuals including John Dos Passos, Richard Wright, Billie Holiday, Orson Welles, and Carey McWilliams were shaped by this "counter-hegemonic" movement. George Lipsitz, in *Rainbow at Midnight:*

Unemployed workers line up for a free meal at a "soup kitchen" during the Great Depression.

Labor and Culture in the 1940s (1994), offers a parallel analysis using cultural forms, especially music, to trace the attempt by the American working class to maintain independence in the face of conservative forces unleashed after World War II. In looking at such phenomena as the working-class roots of rock and roll, Lipsitz carefully interweaves analyses of the role played by race and gender in addition to class. Lipsitz, Denning, Alan Wald, Paul Lauter, Paula Rabinowitz, and a host of other scholars have done much to give modes of class analysis a central place in American studies along with race, gender, and sexuality. This trend is likely to deepen if the gulf between rich and poor within the United States continues to widen. (The last decade of the

twentieth century saw the top one percent of wealthy families in the United States in control of forty percent of the wealth.)

But as should be clear from the examples cited above, questions of class and culture have never been a purely domestic issue. From the colonial slave trade to the Persian Gulf War, international and transnational currents have shaped and been shaped by American class structures. In particular, U.S. class relations have been deeply affected by the fact that political, economic, and cultural imperialism have made even the lowest-paid American workers often better off than their peers elsewhere. Scholarship on these long-standing questions has been collected by Amy Kaplan and Donald Pease in a volume entitled *Cultures of United States Imperialism* (1993). Various essayists show how American imperialism, beginning ironically when America itself was a set of colonies, created cultural objects that have influenced global cultures and altered class and culture domestically. The essays analyze how, from American Indians placed on display in seventeenth-century Europe to nineteenth-century Wild West Shows to late-twentieth-century Japan's version of Disneyland, class culture on a world scale has been shaped and reshaped by U.S. economic power and its political formations, while in turn U.S. imperial imperatives have shaped and reshaped internal class, racial, and gender relations.

At the beginning of the twenty-first century, with the income gap between the "underdeveloped" world and the "overdeveloped" world (headed by the United States) remaining enormous, evidence abounded that issues of class and culture in America would increasingly be written not only in relation to gender, ethnicity, and race but in transnational, if not global, terms as well. Whether a conservative Americanism that minimizes or justifies class differences, internally and internationally, or a progressive perspective that argues the injustice of those differences will prevail in America or in American studies in the twenty-first century remains to be seen.

[See also POPULAR CULTURE; AMERICAN STUDIES, AN OVERVIEW; BOOK CLUBS.*]*

BIBLIOGRAPHY

Compton, Rosemary, *Class and Stratification: An Introduction to Contemporary Debates* (Blackwell 1998).

Denning, Michael, *Mechanic Accents: Dime Novels and Working-Class Culture in America* (Verso 1987) [examines the complicated negotiations of meaning between, on the one hand, middle-class writers and editors and, on the other, the working-class readers of popular fiction in nineteenth-century America].

Dimock, Wai-chee, and Michael T. Gilmore, eds., *Rethinking Class: Literary Studies and Social Formations* (Columbia Univ. Press 1994) [surveys approaches to class and culture in the wake of postmodern critiques of "class" as an objective category].

Ehrenreich, Barbara, *Fear of Falling: The Inner Life of the Middle Class* (Pantheon Bks. 1989).

Gilmore, Michael T., *American Romanticism and the Marketplace* (Univ. of Chicago Press 1985) [an important examination of mid-nineteenth-century American literature in relation to social class and the political economy of the writing trade].

Gutman, Herbert, *Power and Culture: Essays on the American Working Class,* ed. by Ira Berlin (Pantheon Bks. 1987) [influential essays on the evolution of the American working class cultures in the nineteenth and twentieth centuries].

Joyce, Patrick, ed., *Class* (Oxford 1995) [solid collection of writings in classic and contemporary approaches to class analysis].

Kelley, Robin D. G., *Race Rebels: Culture, Politics, and the Black Working Class* (Free Press 1994).

Linkon, Sherry, ed., *Teaching Working Class* (Univ. of Mass. Press 1999).

Lipsitz, George, *The Possessive Investment in Whiteness: How White People Profit from Identity Politics* (Temple Univ. Press 1998) [important study of how race continued to shape class experience on the cusp of the twenty-first century].

The Marx-Engels Reader, ed. by Robert C. Tucker (Norton 1972) [best way to get a sense of Marx's approach to class analysis is to read him directly].

McNall, Scott G., Rhonda F. Levine, and Rick Fantasia, eds., *Bringing Class Back in Contemporary and Historical Perspectives* (Westview Press 1991).

Nelson, Cary, and Lawrence Grossberg, eds., *Marxism and the Interpretation of Culture* (Univ. of Ill. Press 1988) [a wide-ranging collection of sophisticated cultural studies examining class in relation to race, gender, and colonialism and other social forces].

Rothenberg, Paula S., ed., *Race, Class, and Gender in the United States: An Integrated Study,* 5th ed. (Freeman Press 2000) [excellent introductory reader].

Vanneman, Reeve, and Lynn Weber Cannon, *The American Perception of Class* (Temple Univ. Press 1987).

Weber, Max, *The Protestant Ethnic and the Spirit of Capitalism,* tr. by Talcott Parsons (Routledge 1992).

Williams, Raymond, *The Sociology of Culture* (Schocken Bks. 1981) [offers a rich set of concepts for thinking about culture in class terms].

T. V. REED

CLEMENS, SAMUEL LANGHORNE

There are few writers in American literary history who have become cultural icons. Yet Samuel Langhorne Clemens, born in Florida, Missouri, on November 30, 1835, and later known as Mark Twain (a nom de plume taken from his riverboat piloting days meaning two fathoms deep, or safe water), has clearly staked a place for himself in the larger American collective conscience, leaving a legacy not only as a fountainhead of American literature itself but also as a resilient and persistent figure in American popular culture. Ernest Hemingway famously remarked that "all American literature comes from one book by Mark Twain called *Huckleberry Finn*." William Faulkner echoed Hemingway's canonizing praise, acclaiming Twain "the father of American literature." At the same time, Twain's image, humorous quips, and aphorisms have been a constant of the popular media. His novels and stories have been remade into comic strips, children's films, and cartoons; his image and his words regularly figure in commercial advertising campaigns; and his likeness even appeared in a 1990 segment of the television program *Star Trek*. That he continues to predominate and to be celebrated in circles of both high and low culture is only fitting, for in his life as in his art, Twain played with and on the distinction between high art and popular culture and in doing so fashioned a literature grounded in the American vernacular. In this light, he joins Walt Whitman in fulfilling Ralph Waldo Emerson's call for a truly American voice and literature.

The tension between serious art and popular culture in Twain's work and career can be traced to his earliest writing. In 1866 he published "The Celebrated Jumping Frog of Calaveras County," a Western tall tale that earned him a national reputation. This story resonates with the influence of his literary forerunners: Augustus Baldwin Longstreet, Artemus Ward, Josh Billings, Bret Harte, and Joaquin Miller, writers who established the tall-tale tradition and dialect humor that would become the staple and hallmark of Twain's literary style and success. Capitalizing on his popularity, Twain then moved East in order to fulfill, as he said, "a 'call' to literature of a low order—i.e. humorous." Twain's relocation signaled an attack on the aesthetic stronghold exercised by New England literary culture and the genteel tradition. Along with his contemporary

THE GRANGER COLLECTION

A 1906 photograph of Samuel Clemens, known to generations of readers as Mark Twain.

realist and naturalist writers, he undertook to democratize American literature, linking local-color and the Western tradition with the social, economic, and intellectual concerns of the *Gilded Age,* a term coined by Twain (and coauthor Charles Dudley Warner). A self-fashioned cultural weathervane and critic, Twain employed his homespun materials and lowbrow style in the service of biting social commentary and satire and in doing so became a far reaching and influential writer. Twain died on April 21, 1910, in Redding, Connecticut.

Yet, although an insightful critic of late-nineteenth-century American culture, Twain was also at one with his time. The Gilded Age saw America become a culture of exchange and speculation, a world generated by claim-holders, imaginative schemers, and confidence men. Twain not only recognized and lampooned this aspect of American culture but was himself representative of this particular zeitgeist, a fact perhaps best borne out by his disastrous and bankrupting speculation in the Paige automatic typesetting machine, an invention that Twain hoped would make him a fortune. His sense of the market and his awareness of his audience's taste to a certain extent informs the generic and formal composition of many of his novels. He paid close attention to the bestseller market and incorporated in his fiction such popular forms as children's books, European romance fantasies, the detective story, and historical costume romances. He was highly aware of the late-nineteenth-century craze for dialect writing as well. Dialect itself became the linguistic force behind his vernacular aesthetic, and through the voice and point of view of the young, unsophisticated, and vulgar Huck Finn, Twain was able to reveal that the real tyrant in the world was the sensibility—be it adult, Northern, Southern, or highbrow—that enabled individuals to tolerate and approve acts of violence, brutality, and oppression. Significantly, Twain's vernacular aesthetic also freed American literature from the traditional artistic and formal criteria to which, in large part, it had been bound.

As critics have observed, Twain also resorted to racial stereotypes, perhaps most crudely with Injun Joe in *The Adventures of Tom Sawyer*. Elsewhere he appropriated and exploited blackface minstrelsy, what he himself revealingly referred to later in his autobiography as "the genuine nigger show, the extravagant nigger show." According to Eric Lott the forms and rhetorical strategies of blackface minstrelsy in large part underwrote *The Adventures of Huckleberry Finn*, Twain's most popular novel, which is considered by many to be one of the nineteenth century's most powerfully antiracist texts. But if the minstrelsy tradition enabled Twain to convey the brutality, envy, condescension, jealousy, and fascination that characterized popular white responses to black people during Twain's time, it also revealed what George Frederickson has termed the *romantic racialism* underlying Twain's racial sensibility. For within Twain's ostensible indictment of white on black oppression in Reconstruction America, one also finds traces of a sensibility that simultaneously, if unconsciously, privileges "whiteness" and in doing so projects a sense of the inferiority of African Americans. Racism continues to inform debates over the cultural and pedagogical merits of Twain in general and *Huckleberry Finn* particularly. Having been banned in Concord, Massachusetts, on its publication for being "rough, course, and inelegant,"

and hence because it would undermine the morals of young and genteel readers, *Huckleberry Finn* continues to generate charged debate. A public school administrator campaigned at the end of the twentieth century against teaching the novel in primary and secondary schools, denouncing it as "the most grotesque example of racist trash ever written."

But such virulent attacks have not left Twain without his defenders: in his own time he was championed by William Dean Howells, who challenged *Huckleberry Finn*'s genteel detractors by esteeming Twain "the Lincoln of American literature." Ironically, Bernard DeVoto would later have to defend Twain from the opposite edge of the same critical sword. For in *The Ordeal of Mark Twain*, Van Wyck Brooks disparaged Twain for what he considered his arrested development, a condition that he saw as resulting from the fact that Twain was "captured" by the genteel tradition represented by his wife. While later critics have been less interested in salvaging Twain's reputation itself, their scholarship has pointed to aspects of his writing that problematize his presumed racial politics and sensibility. Such critics as Eric Sundquist read *Pudd'nhead Wilson* as a critique of the segregationist Supreme Court decision, *Plessy* v. *Ferguson* (1896). Ralph Ellison has reassessed Twain's understanding of the moral dilemmas posed by race by focusing on the characterization of Jim, noting "Jim's dignity and human capacity—and Twain's complexity." In *Was Huck Black? Mark Twain and African-American Voices*, Shelley Fisher Fishkin further explores the complexity that Ellison identified, arguing that Huck's voice was modeled on that of a black child whom Twain knew in his youth. Given the historical and cultural significance of *Huckleberry Finn*, Fishkin's thesis thus illuminates the seminal role that the African American vernacular has played in the development of American literature. It also points toward Twain's stylistic versatility and range, a universality that is perhaps best summed up by his own Whitmanesque self-assessment: "I am the entire human race compacted together. I have found that there is no ingredient of the race which I do not possess in either a small way or a large way."

[See also LITERATURE, AN OVERVIEW; REALISM AND NATURALISM IN LITERATURE.]

BIBLIOGRAPHY

Cox, James, *Mark Twain: The Fate of Humor* (Princeton Univ. Press 1966).

DeVoto, Bernard, *Mark Twain's America* (1932; Univ. of Nebr. Press 1997).

Ellison, Ralph, *Shadow and Act* (Vintage Books 1995).

Fishkin, Shelley Fisher, *Was Huck Black? Mark Twain and African-American Voices* (Oxford 1993).

Kaplan, Justin, *Mr. Clemens and Mark Twain: A Biography* (Simon & Schuster 1966).

Lott, Eric, *Love and Theft: Blackface Minstrelsy and the American Working Class* (Oxford 1993).

Smith, Henry Nash, *Mark Twain: The Development of a Writer* (Belknap Press 1962).

Sundquist, Eric J., *To Wake the Nations: Race in the Making of American Literature* (Belknap Press 1993).

GEOFFREY PITCHER

CLOTHING

In an *Atlantic* magazine essay published in 1899, Jane Addams questioned: "Have we worked out our democracy in regard to clothes farther than in regard to anything else?" Indeed, in some ways, the cultural history of clothing styles in the United States has involved "working out democracy." Patricia Cunningham and Susan Voso Lab note in *Dress in American Culture* (1993) that Americans have used clothes as a mediating factor to adapt to new situations. The process of negotiating American identities has also included contradictions such as the simultaneous elimination and appropriation of difference. Anxieties posed by diverse appearances and cultural politics underlie the somewhat casually democratic style often characterized as "American." By the late twentieth century the American apparel industry was most commonly known for sportswear and other separates (for example blue jeans, athletic shoes, and baseball caps) that, on the surface at least, blurred the boundaries among classes, races, genders, ages, and indeed nations. Increasingly throughout the nation's history "American style" has become defined as the mixing and matching of separates, to the extent that it is not

© CULVER PICTURES/PICTUREQUEST

Two women and a man are dressed for a tennis match in the late 1800s. Sports attire later was simplified.

only what one wears that matters but also how one wears it. Together, three themes summarize the construction of an American style: (1) casual simplicity; (2) anxieties and ambiguities regarding social difference; and (3) aggressive capitalization and commodification.

Casual Simplicity. There was little focus on creating New World styles during the early colonial years; clothing delineated social station and occupation, much as it had in England, according to Lois Banner, author of *American Beauty* (1983). However, republican simplicity had become a dominant ideology by the post-Revolutionary period. Homespun fabrics symbolized independence from British hierarchy and formality; Benjamin Franklin, Thomas Jefferson, and John Adams wore homespun on occasion to convey republican ideals. Still, many affluent Americans continued to wear European fashions, and a tension between fashion and republican simplicity carried into the nineteenth century.

Social observers in the 1830s remarked on the fashion obsession among American women, including rural, working-class, frontier, and immigrant women. They also noted a relative absence of national dress or class symbolism, which were so characteristic of European societies. Bourgeois men wore

Men and women clad in fashionable clothing parade along Fifth Avenue, New York City, on Easter Sunday.

© CULVER PICTURES/PICTUREQUEST

simple black suits that came to symbolize American democracy in the nineteenth century, while women of various classes used fashion as a vehicle for influence in a nation that denied them access to a political voice. Images of working-class masculinity included rugged Western attire; during the Gold Rush, Levi Strauss, a Bavarian Jewish merchant, produced durable work pants (jeans) for miners and other laborers. Denim jeans were to assume global significance as an American symbol in the next century.

Menswear and women's cloaks were mass-produced by the middle of the nineteenth century. Otherwise, women either made their clothes or had them custom-made by dressmakers who often affected French names. The simplicity of menswear, along with industrialization and the health, sports, and dress reform movements, contributed to the eventual simplification of women's clothing by the end of the nineteenth century. By the 1890s apparel manufacturers were making women's suits and shirtwaists modeled after menswear, and after World War I ready-to-wear dresses were cut along

simple lines in a modern "flapper" style popularized by Parisian designers as well as Hollywood film stars. In the 1930s American designers such as Claire McCardell were developing functional, comfortable clothes for everyday occasions, helping to put New York's Seventh Avenue on the fashion map. While the Nazis occupied Paris in the 1940s, "the American look" became a tool to promote pride in U.S.-made fashions. The French again dominated the American fashion scene after the war, but McCardell brought American sportswear and practical everyday wear to prominence. McCardell was deeply committed to the democratization of fashion; she believed that it was possible to make fashion affordable to all Americans. She adopted features from menswear (such as denim, double rows of stitching, metal fasteners) and developed a system of interchangeable separates that became associated with later American designers such as Anne Klein and Donna Karan.

The 1960s marked the decline of Parisian fashion dominance, as the youth, civil rights, and feminist movements began to influence clothing styles worn by American women and men alike. "Hip," "ethnic," and "natural" looks, respectively, emerged from these movements and were appropriated by fashion designers. For example, in the 1970s Calvin Klein and Gloria Vanderbilt transformed blue jeans from symbols of the working-class and youth cultures to sexy, designer-branded commodities. And for the rest of the twentieth century, designer labels "legitimated" American styles emerging from youth, working-class, minority, and gay and lesbian cultures.

Anxieties and Ambiguities regarding Social Difference. During the nineteenth century a general democratization of clothing occurred in the United States. Despite an ideology of egalitarianism, however, sartorial signs of social status endured. Moreover, the young nation's "melting pot" ideology largely excluded those who did not look white. Physical features (such as skin color, hair texture, and facial features) marked sharp divisions and tensions within U.S. society, despite dominant discourse regarding the democratization of clothing and the promise of assimilation. These divisions and tensions can be identified as early as the initial colonial contacts with Native Americans in the New World. Although Europeans were intrigued with the painted bodies and hair styles of Native Americans, themes of cultural superiority and anxiety pervade their accounts of the "savage and uncivilized" indigenous peoples.

African slaves were involuntary immigrants who were brought to the New World without any material possessions. However, they brought West African aesthetics, including an ability to embrace newness while retaining a sense of cultural expression, to the extent that resources allowed. During slavery both men and women strove to look their best, especially on Sundays, and they managed to improvise in their use of European cloth and clothing in ways that were culturally unique. For example, they contributed technical knowledge such as methods for dyeing fabrics with indigo (used in blue denim). They also adapted materials and garments in ways that European Americans often found unsettling, because the resulting looks often either resisted or surpassed European American style in their distinctiveness. For example, the zoot suits worn by some African American and Mexican American (*pachuco*) men in the 1940s generated anxiety, if not hostility, and riots ensued in Los Angeles and other cities when white servicemen attacked nonwhite men who overtly signified their difference. A late-twentieth-century example of improvisation could be seen in hip-hop style, which appropriated elements of a white Anglo-Saxon Protestant (WASP), preppy aesthetic (such as khaki trousers, polo shirts, and name-brand sneakers) but adapted the way these elements were worn in a manner that both resisted and influenced the mainstream style.

Dominant cultural discourse has also historically expressed anxiety and ambivalence about the blurring of class lines and about women's absorption with fashion and consumerism. In the 1850s women from modest backgrounds wore colorful garments on city streets, moving away from the dark colors signifying working-class culture. Nineteenth-century style innovations emerged not only from the

elite, as writers at the end of the century such as Thorstein Veblen and Georg Simmel suggested. Lois Banner notes that styles were also influenced by actresses and chorus girls from working-class backgrounds.

Immigrant women striving to "look American" recognized that their new lives were intertwined with American capitalism. As department stores added bargain basements, women could study the latest fashions and imagine making, if not purchasing, them. Barbara Schreier describes in *Becoming American Women: Clothing and the Jewish Immigrant Experience, 1880–1920* (1994) how Jewish immigrants, who dominated the garment industry, scrimped and saved in order to look more American themselves. More generally, waves of immigrants from eastern and southern Europe came into the United States at the end of the nineteenth century. Immigrant and African American publications defended the rights of their communities to American life and fashion, while some popular etiquette books were questioning whether such communities should spend their resources accordingly. The 1950s and early 1960s probably marked the end of dominant culture's ability to ignore or to deny the place of minority cultures in constructing American looks.

Aggressive Capitalization and Commodification. Tensions between aggressive capitalization and republican virtue, as well as between assimilation and differentiation, have largely played out in mass marketing. Branded, casual separates seem to represent a way of negotiating these tensions; they also represent a point of articulation between working and elite classes, appropriating elements of both. Separates enable the stylistic improvisation (for example mixing and matching, modifying standards of fit, and altering how clothes are worn) that often characterizes specific cultural groups. Much of this can be accomplished in such a way that simultaneously communicates and resists mainstream values.

Typically "American" branded separates have often been promoted as nationalist icons. During the Spanish-American War in the 1890s, the Amer-

VERNON MERRITT III/LIFE MAGAZINE, © TIME, INC.

A young woman wearing a miniskirt characterized the youth culture of the 1960s.

ican flag was overtly used on clothes and accessories to sell nationalist pride. The ideology of Manifest Destiny, or the idea that the United States was fated to become a dominant world power, was used to justify nationalist fervor. Although some commentators worried that it was disrespectful to use the flag in such a way, capitalism won out. The 1890s marked the beginning of an intense period of capitalization and rationalization of the apparel, cosmetic, and retail industries. A century later Teri Agins in *The End of Fashion: The Mass Marketing of the Clothing Business* (1999) reported that clothing designer Ralph Lauren had taken "ownership of the American flag for a cool 13 million dollars."

Lauren, who frequently used the American flag as a marketing tool in his clothing and advertisements, made a substantial contribution to the renovation of Old Glory in the Smithsonian's National Museum. In a speech expressing gratitude, President Bill Clinton remarked that both he and his wife, Hillary, had those "great Polo sweaters with the American flag" on them.

In the late 1970s Lauren, the son of Russian Jewish immigrants, had appropriated symbols of the established American elite (including traditional WASP old-money and English-country looks and Ivy League imagery) to create his successful lines of casual clothing separates. As he described it, he "elevated the taste level of America," and "the American sensibility has become a very important international sensibility. We created sportswear . . . Americans are the leaders because we know how to do sportswear better here than anywhere else." In the 1990s Tommy Hilfiger took Lauren's elite look a step further, connecting it consciously with inner-city street style. Agins argues that both Hilfiger and Lauren used their clothing lines as expressions of their personalities, which were licensed for others to buy. They both made use of the flag to symbolize their manipulation of fashion in an "American" way, appealing to consumers' desire to belong and to be distinctive simultaneously. Hilfiger also linked his incorporation of African American hip-hop style to a multicultural mission: "By respecting one another, we can reach all cultures and communities." He explained, "I like things to be mixed-up—not confused, but diverse. There are all different types of people in this American melting pot: gay, straight, black, white, Hispanic, Asian—all making up a whole that gives American life its incredible vibrancy." Hilfiger successfully appropriated multicultural discourse. At the same time, labels such as FUBU (For Us, By Us) emerged from the African American community to foster ways of keeping profits within that community.

Lauren, Hilfiger, and others (The Gap Incorporated, Liz Claiborne, and Calvin Klein) built on the trend in the 1970s toward intense commodification of casual separates. Beginning with designer jeans, this commodification eventually broadened to include bourgeois and elite separates and elements from African American culture. The melding and manipulation of symbols by individuals of various ages, genders, sexualities, races, and ethnicities demonstrate how fashion thrives on continuing resistance to dominant norms, albeit with some complicity to these same norms. At the dawn of the twenty-first century, looks such as "business casual" and youth street styles continued to negotiate contradictions and diversity through a range of looks constructed with branded separates. For those individuals who purchase them, these separates can simultaneously signify status, casual simplicity, and perhaps even American democracy as it manifests itself materially in the context of global, advanced capitalism.

BIBLIOGRAPHY

Agins, Teri, *The End of Fashion: The Mass Marketing of the Clothing Business* (Morrow 1999).

Banner, Lois W., *American Beauty* (Knopf 1983).

Cunningham, Patricia A., and Susan Voso Lab, eds., *Dress in American Culture* (Bowling Green State Univ. Pop. Press 1993).

Foster, Helen Bradley, *New Raiments of Self: African American Clothing in the Antebellum South* (Berg 1997).

Kaiser, Susan B., *The Social Psychology of Clothing: Symbolic Appearances in Context,* 2d ed. revised (Fairchild 1997).

Schreier, Barbara A., *Becoming American Women: Clothing and the Jewish Immigrant Experience, 1880–1920* (Chicago Historical Soc. 1994).

Schorman, Rob, "Remember the Maine, Boys, and the Price of This Suit," *Historian* 61, no. 1 (Fall 1998):119–134.

SUSAN B. KAISER

COCA-COLA

Invented May 8, 1886, by Atlanta, Georgia, chemist John Pemberton, Coca-Cola has become both an American institution and a world-recognized symbol of the United States. Pemberton developed Coca-Cola as a nonalcoholic alternative to patent medicines, such as Vin Mariani, and at first it was marketed as a delicious and refreshing nerve tonic available at the soda counters of Atlanta drug stores.

UPI/CORBIS-BETTMANN

Coca-Cola has been served at soda fountains throughout America since the 1890s.

In this respect it was but one of a number of carbonated drinks, including Dr Pepper, developed across the United States in the period. What made Coca-Cola more successful, according to business historian Richard Tedlow, was the entrepreneurship of Asa Candler, who took control of the Coca-Cola Company in 1888 and ran it until 1918, and Robert Woodruff, the chief executive officer (CEO) from 1923 to 1981.

Aided by Frank Robinson, who had earlier named the drink and developed the trademark script logo, Candler took Coca-Cola to the nation. By 1892 the drink was being sold in New England, and the company's advertisements appeared in the national press by 1904. The company also authorized Coca-Cola bottlers as early as 1894, which expanded the drink's availability beyond soda-counter customers.

Candler believed in marketing. Coca-Cola salesmen received a thorough briefing on the product and its benefits. In 1905 the company began holding sales conventions in Atlanta, which imbued the attendees with almost religious faith in the product and company. Furthermore, Coca-Cola poured money into advertising and promotion. In 1892 the company spent 11 thousand dollars on promotion;

twenty years later in 1912 it spent some 1.2 million dollars. Of this sum less than a third was spent on newspaper and magazine advertising with the bulk of the budget spent on promotional material. For instance, in 1913 the company produced a million Japanese fans, two million soda-fountain trays, five million metal lithograph signs, and ten million matchbooks. The images in much of this material featured young women enjoying healthful leisure activities, such as golf and swimming.

Coca-Cola was one of the products that helped shape the developing culture of consumption in the early years of the twentieth century. The marketing of the company created national demand for a product, established a brand name, and created an image of youthful good health and vitality associated with that brand name. Equally Candler and Woodruff established a corporate culture where employees had absolute faith in their product. The company's early success can be measured by the sales growth from forty-seven thousand dollars in 1892 to almost nine million dollars in 1913.

In 1919 Candler's children, to whom he had given the majority of the stock, sold Coca-Cola to a syndicate led by Atlanta banker Ernest Woodruff. In 1923 Woodruff's son Robert became the CEO of the company. Robert Woodruff revitalized the somewhat stagnant company. Neither the product nor the advertising style changed, but the company did expand its range of merchandising efforts, making Coca-Cola more widely available in six-pack cartons, in new dispensing machines, and at grocery stores. Woodruff also increased the international operations of the company. By 1930 sales had almost doubled over those of 1923, and profits had tripled. Artists such as Norman Rockwell and N. C. Wyeth created folksy images for Coca-Cola advertising and another artist, Haddon Sundblom, transformed the image of Santa Claus into the chubby jolly fellow in the red suit, in his advertisements for Coke.

Coca-Cola was so ubiquitous in American culture by World War II that an advertisement for United States Rubber Company in *Newsweek* (September 7, 1942) suggested that servicemen were motivated to fight the war in part for the right to drink Coke in the corner drug store. During the war Coca-Cola both cemented its place in American culture and expanded to the global stage. General Dwight Eisenhower thought Coca-Cola so important to troop morale that he ordered ten bottling plants to accompany troops in the various theaters of the war. This gave many non-Americans their first taste of the drink. Resistance to American cultural influence in the postwar era often referred to *Coca-Colanization*.

In 1985 a public outcry followed Coca-Cola's introduction of a new-formula Coke, demonstrating how far it had moved beyond being simply a carbonated beverage to being a national symbol. Coke lost market share to competitor Pepsi-Cola, produced by PepsiCo, which for the first time topped Coca-Cola in sales. The result was the reintroduction of classic Coca-Cola, which quickly regained the lost ground.

[*See also* FOODWAYS.]

BIBLIOGRAPHY

Allen, Frederick, *Secret Formula: How Brilliant Marketing and Relentless Salesmanship Made Coca-Cola the Best-Known Product in the World* (Harper Business 1994).

Goodrum, Charles, and Helen Dalrymple, *Advertising in America: The First 200 years* (Abrams 1990).

Pendergrast, Mark, *For God, Country, and Coca-Cola: The Unauthorized History of the Great American Soft Drink and the Company That Makes It* (Scribner 1993).

Tedlow, Richard S., *New and Improved: The Story of Mass Marketing in America* (Basic Bks. 1990).

IAN GORDON

COINS, CURRENCY, STAMPS, AND COMMEMORATIVE MEDALS

At first glance, the coins and currency with which we buy and sell, the postage stamps with which we mail our letters, and the medals with which we celebrate and commemorate important events and people have little in common. True, coins and currency are used in the same general fashion, but coins are intended specifically for small purchases and notes are designed for large purchases. The postage stamp lacks the monetary function of coinage

President Franklin D. Roosevelt uses a magnifying glass to study new additions to his stamp collection.

and currency (except in very limited and short-lived circumstances), while the medal appears to be related to coinage only in its physical form, and it is completely unrelated to currency or stamps. However, these four disparate objects do indeed share a common basis and correspond to a unifying theme: coins, currency, stamps, and medals have helped to create an American identity through the common motif of the patriotic image.

When the first coins were struck in New England in the mid-seventeenth century, they were denominated in the money of England; but one of the earliest images imprinted on coins was a pine tree, symbol of the lush forests of the New World, suggesting a separate identity from Britain. A three-penny piece struck in Connecticut some eighty years later displayed another denizen of the North American forests, a deer, as well as proudly proclaiming the American origin of the metal used to create the token. These modest first efforts established an idea that would soon be acted on in a bolder, more consistent way.

As the colonies revolted against Great Britain and ultimately claimed their independence, it became necessary to get the insurgent point of view across to audiences on both sides of the Atlantic.

Those in America had to be persuaded that they were a new people, with a splendid destiny. Those in England had to be persuaded that their American cousins had the right to a separate existence and, in any case, could not be kept from it.

The colonial and Revolutionary economies saw very little coinage in circulation, so an American identity promoted through money had to use paper for the purpose. Many now-familiar national images, such as the thirteen arrows, the eagle, the virtuous patriot, and the evil George III were initially disseminated by means of notes. Engravers and printers used what they had to bolster insurgent morale. The process continued after independence in 1776, and soon after the war's end a distinctive coinage helped inculcate the American idea.

Within the legal framework of the Articles of Confederation, states enjoyed the right to coin money during the years after the battle of Yorktown. Not all states took advantage of this right, but those that did added to the growing store of national images, with renditions of American eagles, the national shield with the motto *E Pluribus Unum* ("From Many, One"), and seated personifications of Liberty.

With the adoption of the Constitution in 1787, the national government took over from the states the obligation of producing and providing money. The United States Mint was established in 1793. While the U.S. Mint tried to convey an American identity on its coins, it was not particularly efficient, and it had difficulty securing metal for the creation of a national money.

The first American coin to display a representation of Liberty on one side and an eagle on the other side went into commerce. The images lacked artistry but had a certain crude vitality, not unlike the country and the people whom they served. The coins played a role in the creation of an American sense of identity that was out of proportion to their commercial success, for they were outnumbered by other coins, especially the ubiquitous golden *onzas* (Spanish coin, approximately one ounce of gold) and silver pieces of eight of Spanish America, until the 1850s. All the same, more American paper

The coins in a series of quarters honoring the fifty states were released in 1999.

money than American coinage was used during the first few decades of the nation's existence, simply because paper was an infinitely expandable commodity, while coinage (which had to be either made from precious metal or based on precious metal) was not.

The images on paper notes celebrated national heroes who had been instrumental in creating the identity of the new country. But the notes also celebrated everyday life and ordinary people in a way

never attempted before or since in America. The images that the notes displayed, created, and disseminated at the behest of predominantly male bankers, artists, printers, and businesspeople tell what opinion-leaders thought the country was all about during a formative phase in its story. These individuals' musings, distributed to a willing audience across the expanding republic, played an incalculable role in the formation of the American ideal and idea.

A sheet of redesigned hundred dollar bills, which were first released into circulation in 1996.

When postage stamps and medals appeared, they strengthened the patriotic effects of coinage and currency. Postage stamps, invented in Great Britain, were introduced in the United States in 1847 during the Mexican War. The first two subjects to adorn stamps were, appropriately enough, the first president, George Washington, and the first postmaster, Benjamin Franklin. Other national leaders were featured as time went on and then, with a definitive issue of 1869, stamps began to mirror images seen earlier on currency, portraying the American scene itself. This shift was modest at first, but it was eventually strengthened by the discovery and exploitation of a commemorative function promoted during the celebration of the centennial in 1876, and it was firmly established by a series of stamps printed in connection with the World's Columbian Exposition of 1893. By the opening years of the twentieth century, the postage stamp was coming into its own as a vehicle for disseminating an American identity.

The earliest American medals generally paralleled the trends established by the designers of money and stamps. Medals were used to celebrate American heroes and anniversaries, while medalists and minters gained artistic confidence and be-

came more comfortable with their crafts. By the late nineteenth century American medalists were producing work of a high technical excellence, and by the beginning of the twentieth century medalists' work reflected artistic trends in Europe and elsewhere but always with a desire to celebrate American themes and to create a distinctly American medal. The work of Augustus Saint-Gaudens for the World's Columbian Exposition is a good example of this trend.

The twentieth century saw a number of interesting variants on long-established practices and themes. On coinage images of Liberty were generally replaced by depictions of actual, eminent (usually male) Americans including Abraham Lincoln, Thomas Jefferson, Franklin Delano Roosevelt, Benjamin Franklin, and John Fitzgerald Kennedy. Occasionally females were represented, such as Susan B. Anthony and later Sacajawea, both of whom graced a dollar coin. The images on coins for circulation have changed infrequently; Lincoln has been on the cent since around 1910 and Washington has been on the quarter since around 1930. The story of commemorative coinage is much different, and many persons, places, and events, all with an inherently American content, have received their due. An exciting trend, a series of celebratory quarter dollars paying honor to each state in the order in which it entered the Union, was introduced in 1999. Unlike earlier commemoratives, these quarters were released directly into circulation, inspiring discussion and collecting among a wide segment of the public.

The same cannot be said for American currency. As a consequence of the Civil War, the private banks' issues came to an end, and with them the marvelous variety of images that had previously distinguished paper currency. Federal notes took their place and, while many of them continued to have commemorative and genre content for some years, in time they descended to a dull consistency, with the image of a famous deceased American on the faces, and, on the back, a building or monument. It is possible that American paper money will eventually begin to explore the potential for nation-building established by American coinage and American postage stamps and medals.

Postage stamps are decorated with a rainbow of colors, images of people (some long overdue for recognition) and of places. Events are also commemorated, but they tend to be less epochal, more local in nature.

Medals reflect wider artistic trends, paying homage and celebrating the national and the local. In one sense, the medallic medium lost ground because long-established firms that specialized in their creation and distribution have ceased production. But on another level, new generations of talent have discovered and exploited this branch of numismatics, utilizing emerging technologies in the process.

[See also DESIGN, COMMERCIAL AND INDUSTRIAL; PUBLIC MEMORY.]

BIBLIOGRAPHY

Doty, Richard G., *America's Money—America's Story* (Krause Pubs. 1998).

Hessler, Gene, *The Comprehensive Catalog of U.S. Paper Money,* 4th ed. (BNR Press 1983).

Hessler, Gene, *The Engraver's Line: An Encyclopedia of Paper Money and Postage Stamp Art* (BNR Press 1993).

Newman, Eric P., and Richard G. Doty, eds., *Studies on Money in Early America* (American Numismatic Society 1976).

Scott Specialized Catalogue of United States Stamps (Scott Publishing Co. 1999).

Stahl, Alan M., ed., *The Medal in America* (American Numismatic Society 1988) [proceedings of the Coinage of the Americas Conference at the N.Y. Numismatics Society].

Vermeule, Cornelius C., III, *Numismatic Art in America: Aesthetics of the United States Coinage* (Belknap Press 1971).

RICHARD G. DOTY

COLD WAR

George Orwell first used the term *cold war* in a 1945 article entitled "You and the Atom Bomb," which described the United States, Russia, and China as postwar "superstates" whose nuclear arsenals would involve them in a "permanent state of cold war." Orwell borrowed this phrase from the French

CORBIS

Americans were advised to use bomb shelters in the event that the cold war became a nuclear war.

la guerre froide ("the cold war"), which he translated as a state of war that lacked the overt conditions of war. The term entered the American lexicon in 1947 following the publication of the political commentator Walter Lippmann's *The Cold War.* Lippmann had written the book in response to "The Sources of Soviet Conduct," an essay that the diplomat George Kennan had published that year in the journal *Foreign Affairs* under the signature Mr. X. It was in this essay that Kennan recommended that the United States adopt a policy of containment to curb the threat of Russian expansionism.

Lippmann invoked historical evidence to disagree with Kennan's contention that Russia posed a danger to the international order. Arguing that Russian nationalism was far more important to Soviet policymakers than international communism, Lippmann concluded that the United States could not afford to police the world. But the atmosphere of mutual suspicion and fear then enveloping the globe favored Kennan's recommendations over

Lippmann's refutations of them, and for the next half century the world's geography was separated along a symbolic East-West divide, which transformed the West into an imaginary community of democratic states united in their defense of "universal" values against the incursions of world communism.

The policy of containment tacitly empowered the United States and Russia to remap the borderlines of territories according to ideological rather than spatial coordinates. Throughout the cold war, developing countries acquired significance through their alignment on one or the other side of these opposed ideological systems. The global hegemons thereafter supplanted the political arrangements of the complex societies they occupied with the systems of representation through which they administered and controlled their territories. As evidenced by their placement of the Asian nations of Japan, Korea, and Vietnam within the symbolic geography of the West and the Central and South American nations of Cuba, Nicaragua, and Chile within that of the East, however, the efforts of cold war cartographers to redraw the world map at times produced highly disorienting effects.

In addition to establishing the coordinates of U.S. foreign policy, the cold war also dramatically reorganized U.S. domestic life. When President Harry Truman signed National Security Council (NSC) document number sixty-eight (NSC68) into law in 1950, he invoked the need for the containment of communism at home as well as abroad as the official rationale for a national security state. With NSC68 Truman inaugurated a cold war nation-state that correlated domestic policies and national security interests and transformed the foreign policy of Americanization abroad into an instrument for securing domestic solidarity. "There is a basic conflict," said Truman, "between the idea of freedom under a government of laws and the idea of slavery under the grim oligarchy of the Kremlin."

Truman intended that this declaration of an imaginary war with the Kremlin would solicit from American citizens the willingness in peacetime to subordinate themselves to wartime emergency measures. When it shifted its area of concern to the sphere of culture, however, the discourse of containment did not restrict its operations to the regulation of domestic communists. After President Truman signed an executive order banishing gays and lesbians from federal employment in 1950, the cultural terrain over which containment exercised its policing powers expanded to include the regulation of sexual norms, race relations, social movements, civil rights, artistic expression, and gendered hierarchies.

According to Stephen Whitfield, cold-war culture was the agent as well as the outcome of the interaction of domestic fears and foreign threats. Literature, movies, television, and the media collaborated with organized religion, the inquisitorial tactics of the House Un-American Activities Committee, and McCarthyism in the "holy war" they jointly waged against domestic communism. The public trials of Alger Hiss, Julius and Ethel Rosenberg, and the Hollywood Ten solidified the citizenry's belief that an enemy within was working hand in glove with the Kremlin to subvert the "American way of life."

The alarm with which the nation's writers and artists responded to McCarthyism, and their disaffection with the radical politics of the Popular Front, precipitated a massive shift in political loyalties. Flannery O'Connor, Norman Mailer, Jackson Pollock, James Baldwin, Arthur Miller, and Ralph Ellison abandoned the New Deal's ethos of populist sentimentality and embraced what Lionel Trilling described as the tragic ambiguity of political and moral decisions. The "consensus school" of historians that emerged in the 1950s fostered a political attitude that tempered the worst excesses of the strategy of containment. Arthur Schlesinger, Daniel Boorstin, and Louis Hartz described McCarthyism and communism as related forms of ideological reasoning that were antithetical to the "practical genius" of American liberalism.

In 1957 Daniel Bell introduced the slogan "the end of ideology" to distinguish America's tolerance of dissent, embrace of multiple points of view, and willingness to compromise from Russia's commitment to the infallibility of the Marxist dialectic and its equation of dissent with treason. But the consensus school of history might itself be described as having provided an ideological cover for the policy of containment. When consensus historians proposed that their historical analyses be submitted to the tenets of pragmatic thought, they frequently confused pragmatism's tenets with the reason of state.

The consensus and the cold-war mentality both underwent severe changes in the period between 1963 and 1974. Their breakdown was precipitated by such enormous political events as the Cuban missile crisis; the assassinations of John and Robert Kennedy, Malcolm X, and Martin Luther King, Jr.; détente; President Nixon's China visit; the Watergate trial; and Nixon's resignation from office. But when the free speech movement joined forces with the opposition to the war in Vietnam, the resultant coalition of oppositional forces produced profound challenges to the foundational assumptions of the cold-war mentality.

In place of ratifying basic Americanist values, the counterculture struggled for liberation from them. Including the perspectives of women, as well as the racial and sexual minorities who had been the victims of the state's repressive policies during the cold war, such revisionist historians as William Appleman Williams and Howard Zinn challenged the official explanations of the consensus school of United States history. Noam Chomsky resurrected Walter Lippmann's argument that America's motives for entering into a cold war had more to do with control of foreign markets and the control of global resources than the defense of democratic freedoms. Chomsky discerned a congruence between the repressive regimes that the United States had established throughout the developing world and its policing of domestic minorities. In 1979 E. L. Doctorow retold the history of the cold war epoch from the revisionists' perspective in *The Book of Daniel*.

The political upheavals of the 1960s and 1970s left the cold war in a moribund condition. But the cold war would undergo an eight-year revival dur-

ing Ronald Reagan's presidency and just before the dismantling of the Berlin wall in November 1989. Recalling eschatological themes from the Book of the Apocalypse, Reagan claimed the Bible as the ultimate authority for the United States's possible use of nuclear weapons against the Soviet Union. "We are about to undergo a dreadful period of suffering," Reagan confided to some visiting theologians, "in connection with the extraordinarily violent struggle between the forces of good and evil that is to precede the return of Jesus and the millennium of his rule."

But in place of the global nuclear Armageddon that Reagan, along with many other authorities, had foreordained, the "evil empire" collapsed as a consequence of the loss of totalitarian communist control. This terminal event dismantled the narrative of containment on which the cold war had been founded. Among several other consequences this ending posed a problem of historical closure. The nation's subsequent entry into a global economic order displaced the grounding assumptions that had constituted its coherence. Entry into the new world order did not conclusively sum up the historical purpose of the preceding fifty years. The events that had taken place during the cold war simply ceased happening, and the narratives that had endowed historical events with their intelligibility simply broke off.

At the end of the cold war, the provision of an appropriate formal closure would have performed the essential political function of providing a model of order capable of bringing its end into concordance with its beginning. The absence of an ending consonant with the nation's official account of its beginning has animated the fear of a disintegrating state. United States citizens have responded variously to the disappearance of the symbolic structures in which they had constituted their national identities.

In an effort to supply a conclusion, Francis Fukuyama has proposed the phrase "the end of history" as a way to conceptualize the cold war as the accomplishment of the historical destiny of the West through the realization of the "universal truths of

A U.S. destroyer and patrol plane observe a Soviet freighter removing missiles from Cuba in November 1962.

equality." But like the consensus historians' term *the end of ideology*, Fukuyama's *the end of history* has only reassembled capitalism versus totalitarianism into a new cognitive map that would oppose free market ideologies of vanguard Western states to the socioeconomic arrangements of the rest of the globe. Whether the cold war has in fact ended or has simply been refunctioned as the core discourse of globalization remains to be seen.

[See also SOCIALISM.*]*

BIBLIOGRAPHY

Boyer, Paul, *When Time Shall Be No More: Prophecy Belief in Modern American Culture* (Harvard Univ. Press 1992).

Hogan, Michael, ed., *The End of the Cold War: Its Meaning and Implications* (Cambridge 1992).

Kennan, George, "The Sources of Soviet Conduct," *Foreign Affairs* 25 (1947):568–582.

Lippmann, Walter, *The Cold War: A Study in U.S. Foreign Policy* (Harper 1947).

Nadel, Alan, *Containment Culture: American Narrative, Postmodernism, and the Atomic Age* (Duke Univ. Press 1995).

Schaub, Thomas, *American Fiction in the Cold War* (Univ. of Wis. Press 1991).

Schrecker, Ellen W., *No Ivory Tower: McCarthyism and the Universities* (Oxford 1986).

Whitfield, Stephen J., *The Culture of the Cold War* (Johns Hopkins Univ. Press 1991).

Yergin, Daniel, *Shattered Peace: The Origins of the Cold War and the National Security State* (Deutsch 1978).

DONALD E. PEASE

COLONIALISM

A century after Columbus, Cortés, and the rapid colonization of Mexico and the Caribbean and South American territories, the first Europeans began settling the part of North America that would become the United States. The exploration and charting of the New World constituted "discoveries" for Europeans. They were not the first here, of course: the Americas had been inhabited for at least eleven thousand years prior to the arrival of the Europeans, and it is also thought that various wanderers—from Ireland, Scandinavia, perhaps even Africa—had reached the Americas centuries before the Spanish or English. Of these, the Vikings may have stayed a couple of winters but no permanent colonies took root until the arrival of Columbus and his followers. To Columbus's triple motivation of "God, gold, and glory" and the subsequent Spanish plunder of the great Aztec and Inca civilizations would be added the more mundane colonial objectives of land, liberty, and livelihood.

The terms *colony* and *colonization* originate not in military conquest but in agriculture. Their Latin root *colere* means to cultivate, to put to use, and to make of value. A colony was planted and thereafter referred to as a plantation. Because prior to their arrival this land, from the European perspective, was a desert or wilderness, inhabited only by savages who did not make proper use of it, its occupation by the English made sense to them—was in fact ordained by divine providence. To the English colonists on the *Mayflower* or the *Arbella*, God's injunction to "replenish the earth, and to subdue it" (Genesis 1:28) justified their dominion over the new lands and peoples. If the English (or Dutch, or French) colonists did not mine gold on their new lands, they eventually harvested other enormously profitable treasures, including tobacco, sugar, coffee, timber, codfish, and cotton. This transformation of the wilderness meant seizing it from its aboriginal inhabitants, a process assisted by war, imported diseases such as smallpox, and forced or negotiated relocation. The mandate to Christianize indigenous people implicitly meant conversion to the European view of property and industry. Not all were convertible: *cannibals,* a word mistaken by Columbus to signify the fierce Caribs, came to be used to translate into moral and spiritual unredeemability any resistance to European colonization.

Of course, colonialism is viewed from the historical vantage of the modern consciousness of decolonization movements and the resulting so-called third world, and of the legacy of slavery and Indian "removal." In the realm of historical and cultural criticism, the development of colonial discourse theory and, subsequently, postcolonial theory has provided intellectual tools with which to reassess colonialism. Edward W. Said's landmark study of Europe's invention of "the East," *Orientalism* (1978), remains a founding text of colonial discourse analysis. A reader might next turn to *The Empire Writes Back: Theory and Practice in Post-Colonial Literatures* (1989), by Bill Ashcroft, Gareth Griffiths, and Helen Tiffin, for an introductory overview of postcolonialism, a field that grew explosively during the latter part of the twentieth century. Many scholars and students of American studies adopted these critical approaches, which help to illuminate the ways that power and knowledge shape language (discourse) and therefore historical accounts.

For example, Captain John Smith's descriptions of the earliest permanent English settlement, built at the mouth of the James River in Virginia in 1607, make fascinating reading. In successive self-aggrandizing books, Smith told and retold stories such as his "rescue" by the eleven-year-old "princess," Pocahontas. Although the tale got very little attention in his first book, *A True Relation of Such Occurences*

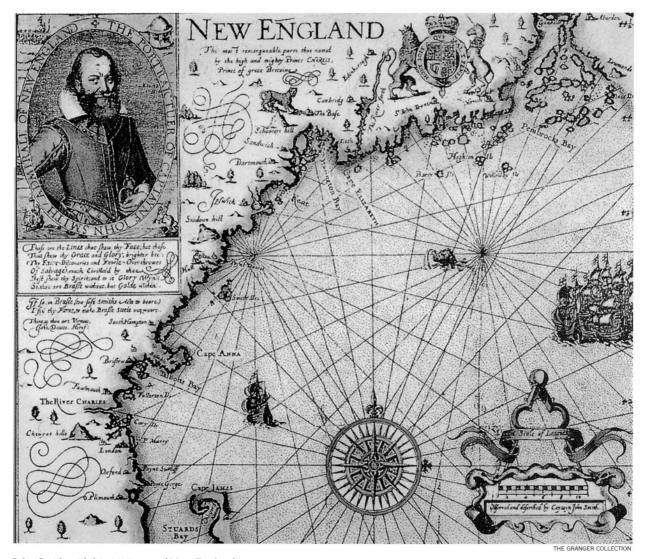

John Smith with his 1616 map of New England.

and Accidents of Noate as Hath Hapned in Virginia (1608), in subsequent versions it became increasingly more elaborate as Smith realized its symbolic power. His description of a European-inflected nobility in such "savages" as Powhatan and his young daughter helped to attract nervous would-be settlers to the new colonies by reassuring them that good Christian virtues could be found—or nurtured through the missionary efforts of the faithful—in the wilderness. Pocahontas herself converted and

later married a Virginia colonist, John Rolfe, and with her husband and child traveled to England, where she died, not yet twenty-one.

The Pocahontas story inspired a long (still vital) tradition of Romantic poetry, fiction, and allegorical art (including *Baptism of Pocahontas,* John Chapman's famous painting in the rotunda of the U.S. Capitol), amplifying the romantic and moral implications of the incident so as to legitimate the colonial and national project. Like the similar legend of the first Thanksgiving in the Plymouth colony, the Pocahontas story has come to represent the harmonious if ultimately tragic encounter between Europeans and Native Americans.

Yet a reading of Smith's writings supported by colonial discourse theory and anthropology shows that often he misunderstood or willfully misinterpreted the Indians he met. Probably the incident of his near-execution by Powhatan and daring rescue by Pocahontas was in reality an adoption ceremony in which the girl played an honorary symbolic role. The story also belongs to the important genre of Indian captivity narratives that might be said to constitute America's most distinctive foundation texts and form for the field of American studies the richest documentary source of early colonial cultural psychology. As one-sided and lurid as they often were, these captivity narratives depict the brutalities committed by both colonists and natives as well as reveal the possibilities for cultural exchange. An incident even more vicious than the fraught relations between Virginian settlers and Powhatan's people was "King Philip's War" in New England during the years 1675–1676. "King Philip" was the name the English settlers gave Metacom, a *sachem* (leader) of the Wampanoags. Recent historians and Americanists, influenced by colonial discourse and postcolonial theory, have reexamined how this perhaps less-than-necessary evil informed colonial cultural politics and its legacy for the United States.

The thirteen colonies that united to declare independence from Great Britain comprise only a part of the colonial story in America, of course. France (before the Seven Years' War of the 1750s) and Spain (before the Louisiana Purchase and the Mexican War) each possessed a comparably large portion of the continent. Although in much U.S. national history the English colonies of the Atlantic coast get pride of place, all of these other settler cultures and the Native American societies with which they interacted must be taken into account in studying the development of an American culture or identity.

[See also IMPERIALISM; NATIONALISM; IDEOLOGY; MANIFEST DESTINY.*]*

BIBLIOGRAPHY

Derounian-Stodola, Kathryn Zabelle, ed., *Women's Indian Captivity Narratives* (Penguin 1998).

Hulme, Peter, *Colonial Encounters: Europe and the Native Caribbean, 1492–1797* (1986; Routledge 1992).

Jehlen, Myra, "Why Did the Europeans Cross the Ocean? A Seventeenth-Century Riddle," *Cultures of United States Imperialism,* ed. by Amy Kaplan and Donald E. Pease (Duke Univ. Press 1993).

Lepore, Jill, *The Name of War: King Philip's War and the Origins of American Identity* (Knopf 1998).

Morgan, Edmund S., *American Slavery, American Freedom: The Ordeal of Colonial Virginia* (Norton 1975).

MARK KEMP

COLUMBIA

The development of Columbia—the symbolic, female personification of the United States—traces the history and evolution of the American self-image. The first graphic representations of the Americas appeared in Europe immediately following Christopher Columbus's explorations. These images usually included the figure of an Indian princess, who represented both the rugged landscape and the indigenous peoples of the New World. Young, fertile, and alluring in her partial or full nakedness, the Indian princess was often depicted as a passive figure awaiting the vitalizing influence of the European man of action.

The Indian princess was the dominant personification of the New World until after the American Revolution. The United States, seeking cultural legitimacy to coincide with its hard-won political legitimacy, sought new, democratic symbols. As the nation turned to ancient Greece and Rome for cultural models, the Indian princess evolved into a Greek goddess of European ethnicity. Wrapped in Grecian robes rather than a feather skirt, wearing ostrich plumes in her hair (reflecting European fashion) rather than a Native American feathered headdress, the Greek goddess was the embodiment of such neoclassical ideals as honor and chastity. Unlike the Indian princess, she represented the United

States specifically, to the exclusion of other New World nations and peoples.

Thomas Crawford's *Statue of Freedom*, placed at the top of the U.S. Capitol dome in 1863, united the rugged spirit of the Indian princess with a neoclassical representation of democratic virtue. Crawford's statue was a variation of the most popular version of the Greek goddess—Liberty. An explicitly allegorical figure, Liberty was often depicted holding a liberty pole and cap and sometimes a copy of the U.S. Constitution or the Bill of Rights. Typically, she was shown breaking the chains of slavery (a glaring contradiction in the United States before emancipation). She assumed her most recognizable form in Frédéric August Bartholdi's 1886 creation, *Liberty Enlightening the World,* or the Statue of Liberty.

All of these representations—the Indian princess, the Greek goddess, and Liberty—unite in the figure of Columbia. Appearing first in the mid-eighteenth century, she is the New World bride of Columbus, taking his name and, implicitly, bearing his children. Like the Greek goddess, Columbia is European in appearance. She was the favored figure in a wide range of cultural productions, from Revolutionary War songs to belletristic poem cycles. She also became the symbolic patron of public institutions: Kings College in New York City was renamed Columbia College in 1784; the nation's capital was renamed the District of Columbia in 1871. As a visual representation, she was most prominent at the 1893 World's Columbian Exposition in Chicago, a celebration of North American progress marking the quatercentenary of Columbus's arrival in the New World.

Columbia and her forebears survive as civic emblems adorning money, state seals, and awards, as well as corporate logos. But Columbia's cultural impact, as a European and female personification of the nation, has steadily diminished as U.S. society increasingly celebrates ethnic and cultural diversity.

[See also PUBLIC MEMORY; PATRIOTISM; AMERICA, *article on* THE IDEA OF AMERICA.*]*

BIBLIOGRAPHY

Blanchet, Christian, and Bertrand Dard, *Statue of Liberty: The First Hundred Years,* English language version by Bernard A. Weisberger (American Heritage 1985).

Fleming, E. McClung, "From Indian Princess to Greek Goddess: The American Image, 1783–1815," *Winterthur Portfolio* (1967):37–66.

Honour, Hugh, *The New Golden Land: European Images of America from the Discoveries to the Present Time* (Pantheon Bks. 1975).

Sund, Judy, "Columbus and Columbia in Chicago, 1893: Man of Genius Meets Generic Woman," *Arts Bulletin,* 75, no. 3 (September 1993):443–466.

Trachtenberg, Alan, *The Incorporation of America: Culture and Society in the Gilded Age* (Hill & Wang 1982).

JOHN TESSITORE

COMIC STRIPS AND COMIC BOOKS

Telling stories through a combination of pictures and words has been a part of the culture of nearly all nations, but it was not until the development of European graphic satire, pictorial broadsheets, illustrated books, and cartoons in humorous periodicals that the formal elements of the comics began to fall into place. While comic art has much in common with fiction, drama, and film, it differs in specific ways and provides a form of amusement and communication that is quite distinct.

For example, the comics require a balanced combination of words and pictures, one depending on the presence of the other for maximum effect and full understanding. Comic strips appear in newspapers on a daily basis, while comic books are monthly serial publications mainly sold in comic-book shops, newsstands, and bookstores. Both usually are printed on inexpensive paper (comic strips in black and white but in color on Sundays, and comic books generally in color), although the longer graphic novels are printed on high-quality paper stock. Both comic strips and comic books feature a set of recurring characters whom readers come to know over a period of time and for whom time generally stands still in that they do not age chronologically. The dramatic narrations or the series of comic situations and jokes are open-ended and

Comic strip characters Daisy Mae and Li'l Abner.

have no conclusions or beginnings, except in the case of the stories about the origins of comic-book superheroes. Comics seldom reflect contemporary events or personalities, except for such specifically satiric strips as *Li'l Abner* by Al Capp, *Pogo* by Walt Kelly, or *Doonesbury* by Garry Trudeau. Given the restrictions of the printed page, comic artists have developed a set of pictorial conventions with which to convey motion and sound: dialogue appears in floating balloons; onomatopoeia is used to convey sounds (*slam, bang, sock,* for example); and emotions are expressed through the use of symbols (stars to show pain, drops of water to express worry or exertion, and so on). The final impression is of an energetic and noisy medium.

The development of the comics in America has witnessed a continuing series of trends in subject matter and innovations in style. The 1890s were a time of great adjustment in the United States as immigrants from all over the world arrived to experience crowded tenements and impoverished living circumstances. Reformers such as Jacob Riis and novelists including Stephen Crane, Frank Norris, and Theodore Dreiser were portraying the squalor of city life from a naturalistic perspective, when Richard Felton Outcault, a cartoonist for the New York *World*, decided to address the situation from a comic perspective. In the spring of 1895 he began publishing a series of panel cartoons set in fictional

Hogan's Alley about an ethnically mixed group of slum children playing dangerous games and causing riots in the back alleys of New York City. A big-eared, large-headed child of apparent Irish descent would emerge from the crowd as a central figure who would communicate with the reader through dialect words printed on his long shift. When the shift was printed in yellow early in 1896, he became known as the Yellow Kid, soon a widely popular figure among readers, star of his own comic strip, subject of extensive merchandising, and center of a newspaper war between Outcault and Joseph Pulitzer over ownership of the character when the cartoonist moved to William Randolph Hearst's New York *Journal*.

The emphases on ethnicity and urban life continued into the twentieth century as new features were created to fill the pages of the comic Sunday supplements, soon known as funny papers, generated by Outcault's success. The Germans were treated humorously in *The Katzenjammer Kids* by Rudolph Dirks and *The Kin-der-Kids* by Lyonel Feininger; the Irish in *Bringing Up Father* with Maggie and Jiggs by George McManus and *Happy Hooligan* by Frederick Burr Opper; and the Jews in *Abie the Agent* by Harry Hershfield. The gamblers and ne'er-do-wells of city life would find their place in Bud Fisher's *Mutt and Jeff,* the first daily comic strip, and Billy DeBeck's *Barney Google* (before being displaced later by a comic mountaineer named Snuffy Smith). Middle-class values would also assert themselves as popular subject matter in such family-oriented features as *The Gumps* by Sidney Smith, *Gasoline Alley* by Frank King, and *Blondie* by Chic Young.

Several examples of comic art at its aesthetic best also appeared during the beginning decades of the century: the distinctive artistic stylings and designs of Cliff Sterret in *Polly and Her Pals;* the moody narrative thrills of Elzie C. Segar in *Thimble Theater,* after Popeye joined the cast of characters as the first comic superhero; the exquisite line drawings and striking use of perspective by Winsor McCay in *Little Nemo in Slumberland;* and the pure lyric whimsy and surrealist fantasy of George Herriman in his masterpiece, *Krazy Kat.* While the paper on which these works of art were printed was ephem-

Dagwood and Blondie are popular characters in a family-oriented comic strip, *Blondie*.

eral, the power and influence of their example would prove unlimited.

As was true with popular fiction and film, adventure and romance moved strongly into comics in the 1920s and later with *Little Orphan Annie* by Harold Gray, *Captain Easy* (and later *Buzz Sawyer*) by Roy Crane, *Tarzan* and *Prince Valiant* by Harold Foster, *Buck Rogers* by Richard W. Calkins and Phil Nowlan, *Dick Tracy* by Chester Gould, *Terry and the Pirates* (and later *Steve Canyon*) by Milton Caniff, *Flash Gordon* by Alex Raymond, and *The Spirit* by Will Eisner, to mention only a few of the most popular. By midcentury and after, satiric humor gained ground against the adventure strips in features such as *Peanuts* by Charles Schulz, *Beetle Bailey* and *Hi and Lois* by Mort Walker, *B.C.* by Johnny Hart, *Garfield* by Jim Davis, *The Far Side* by Gary Larson, *Mutts* by Patrick McDonnell, and that splendid commentary on life, the imagination, and the human condition, *Calvin and Hobbes* by Bill Watterson.

The comic book came into being in 1933 as a place to reprint popular comic strips, but its independent success led to the creation of new material for its full-color pages. When Jerry Siegel and Joe Shuster, two teenagers in Cleveland, Ohio, introduced Superman in the first issue of *Action Comics* in 1938, sales skyrocketed, and they established a pattern for many other superheroes to follow, among the most popular of whom are Batman, Captain Marvel, Wonder Woman, Captain America, the

Fantastic Four, and Spider-Man. Other comic-book titles were devoted to Western stories, romance, teenage humor, funny animals, science fiction, crime, and horror. It was the last two, especially the tales of terror masterfully produced by the Entertaining Comics (EC) firm owned by William M. Gaines, that attracted the attention of politicians and moral reformers to comic books in the 1950s and led to the development of the restrictive Comics Code Authority, a self-policing system. Gaines discontinued his horror series and turned his comic book *Mad* (created by Harvey Kurtzman) into a powerful magazine of satiric subversion.

It was the influence of Kurtzman and *Mad*, as well as the freedom to violate the Comics Code Authority's guidelines, that inspired the underground comix movement of the 1960s, out of which came such original talents as Robert (R.) Crumb, Bill Griffith, Harvey Pekar, and Art Spiegelman. This same cultural ferment encouraged the development in the 1980s of book-length comic narratives called graphic novels, including such notable examples as *A Contract with God* by Will Eisner, *Watchmen* by Alan Moore and Dave Gibbons, and Art Spiegelman's *Maus*, which won a Pulitzer Prize.

In an era that is largely dominated by visual culture—film, television, and the computer screen—the comics appropriately provided not only alternative entertainment but intellectual and educational experiences of a high order. Although many academics continue to resist acknowledging the social and aesthetic value of comic strips and comic books, an increasing number of scholars began to see them as enduring and important parts of America's cultural heritage and a viable literary form of the future.

[*See also* DISNEY, WALT; CHILDREN'S LITERATURE; POPULAR LITERATURE; POPULAR CULTURE; SUPERHEROES.]

BIBLIOGRAPHY

Harvey, Robert C., *The Art of the Funnies: An Aesthetic History* (Univ. Press of Miss. 1994).

Inge, M. Thomas, *Comics as Culture* (Univ. Press of Miss. 1990).

McCloud, Scott, *Understanding Comics* (Kitchen Sink Press 1993).

Coulton, Waugh, *The Comics* (1947; Univ. Press of Miss. 1991).

Witek, Joseph, *Comic Books as History: The Narrative Art of Jack Jackson, Art Spiegelman, and Harvey Pekar* (Univ. Press of Miss. 1989).

M. THOMAS INGE

COMMUNITARIANISM

Beginning in the eighteenth century, individualism gained ground as the defining organizational principle of society and as its underlying social philosophy. At the same time, various collectivistic social and political philosophies, including communism and a variety of socialisms, evolved into a counter-tradition to the prevailing social ideology. Throughout U.S. history, however, a small but significant intellectual tradition has rejected both excessive individualism and extreme collectivism.

Its adherents would insist that throughout much of history a tacit communitarian philosophy governed much of human social thought, if not always the actions of rulers. What marks the rise of modern communitarianism has been its self-conscious evocation of community and "moral ecology." Modern communitarians trace their strain of thought back to Socrates, Plato, and Aristotle, on through the Stoics and Cicero, and into the writings of the patristic and Scholastic theologians—the philosophers of early Christianity and of medieval Catholicism.

When self-conscious communitarianism arose in the latter days of the eighteenth century, it traced the decline of traditional community to the rise of capitalism, ultra-Protestantism, and radical empiricism. Protocapitalism and capitalism emphasized the competition of the individual in the marketplace, which is itself seen as merely a conglomeration of individuals assembled for their productive capacities. In ultra-Protestantism, it could be argued, true spiritual community declines, since the congregation becomes a common, but not a necessary, part of spiritual life. Radical empiricism further eroded the concepts of community because it could only deal with the individual or with groups seen as individuals acting together for various purposes. The mystical qualities that adhere in concepts and institutions such as the family, church, and nation do not easily yield to empirical analysis.

In their historical and philosophical analysis, communitarian commentators have seen the ultra-collectivism of certain modern political philosophies springing up in reaction to the rise of radical individualism and from radical individualism's assault on the traditional notions of society. From the eighteenth century onward, the extended family was slowly reduced to the nuclear family. The nation-state reached its zenith as a result of the atrophy and decay of the smaller, more intimate communities that tended to block the power of the impersonal nation-state.

In the nineteenth and early twentieth centuries, the communitarian impulse revealed itself primarily in the establishment of utopian and quasi-utopian communities, some of a decidedly religious character and some of a secular or even an antireligious character. The religious communities often used as a model the early days of the Apostolic Church in the New Testament with its community of property, while still others saw themselves as entering the perfectionistic preparations of the end-time, when the blessed will be saved by the Lamb of God and the followers of the beast (Antichrist) will perish. Such groups often adopted unique lifestyles, family arrangements, sexual practices, and religious ceremonies, which tended to separate them from the communities of the ordinary world order.

The Shakers, also known as the United Society of Believers in Christ's Second Appearing, followed the teachings of Ann Lee, an Englishwoman who emigrated to the United States. They believed that the millennium was accomplished in the perfection of their communities, which were extended families of males and females, housed in one building and holding their goods in common. They practiced absolute celibacy and engaged in a kind of auricular confession. They became famous for their excellent handiwork, including furniture, woven and sewed items, and metalwork.

The Amana Society, also known as the Society of True Inspiration, was a German separatist sect whose early leaders included Christian Metz and Barbara Heynemann. They settled outside of Buffalo, New York, in 1843 and later removed to Iowa. The Hutterian Brethren, or Hutterites, were a Mennonite sect from Germany, dating back to Jacob Hutter in the sixteenth century. They settled in southern Dakota in 1874 and were so completely communistic that they did not regard clothing as individually owned.

Harmonists (or Rappites), a German separatist, millennialist movement led by George Rapp, settled in Economy, Pennsylvania, in 1824, establishing a celibate, communistic community. The Zoarites (1817–1898), or Separatist Society of Zoar, established a colony in Zoar, Ohio, practicing nonresistance, community of goods, and the community care of children. Russian religious communists, known as Doukhobors, settled in western Canada in 1897. Jansonites, a Swedish separatist sect led by Eric Janson, set up a community at Bishop Hill, Illinois, in 1848. Dr. Keil, a German immigrant, set up communistic religious communities at Bethel, Missouri (1844–1880), and at Aurora, Oregon (1852–1881).

John Humphrey Noyes began his Perfectionist movement in Putney, Vermont, featuring a direct communion with God, communism in property, and a system of "complex marriage" with a kind of free love and the practice of coitus reservatus. They eventually resettled in Oneida, New York, becoming known as the Oneida Community. Women enjoyed full equality, and children were raised in communal nurseries. In Hopedale, Massachusetts, Adin Ballou, a Universalist minister, established a socialistic community in 1842, which, although religious, resembled the secular utopian communities. Finally, early Mormonism tended to be collectivistic. Under Joseph Smith the church established the United Order plan, which had members consecrate their belongings to the church, receiving back a stewardship over the goods, with the requirement that they make an annual accounting to the church.

On the secular front, Owenites, the followers of Robert Owen, a British industrialist and philanthropic social reformer, established several communities in America such as the one at New Harmony in Indiana from 1824 to 1827, where all labor was regarded as equal and where goods were distributed by need. The Fourierists, disciples of the French writer-philosopher Charles Fourier, established several socialistic communities, or "phalanxes." Brook Farm, near Roxbury, Massachusetts (1841–1846), and Fruitlands (1843) in Harvard Township, Massachusetts, were originally nonideological experiments in limited communal socialism that eventually became Fourierist phalanxes. The Icaria movement started in 1848 with absolute communism of goods.

An unusual experiment was undertaken in a series of anarchistic villages founded by Josiah Warren in such places as Equality and Utopia, Ohio; and Modern Times, New York (Long Island). The Ruskin Commonwealth, a semianarchistic settlement, was set up in Tennessee and later removed to Georgia. Also, American land-reform colonies, committed to the single-tax idea, were established in Topolobampo, Mexico, and Fairhope, Alabama.

In the 1960s and 1970s experiments in radical community living, often including degrees of unorthodox sexual arrangements, again arose in the arrangements of certain secular groups, for example, hippie communes and numerous religious sects. At the same time, in the academy, various philosophers and social theorists began to search for a middle way between state socialism and capitalist individualism. The repressiveness and economic stagnation of ultracollectivistic states, on the one hand, and the anomie and alienation of the liberal capitalist states, on the other, have caused such communitarian thinkers as Henry Tam, Michael Walzer, and Amitai Etzioni, among others, to seek new solutions to current and recurring social and economic problems by a return to true community.

[See also COMMUNITY; INDIVIDUALISM.*]*

BIBLIOGRAPHY

Douglas, Dorothy W., and Katharine Du Pre Lumpkin, "Communistic Settlements," in *Encyclopedia of the Social Sciences,* ed. by Edwin R. A. Seligman and Alvin Johnson, 15 vols. (Macmillan 1935).

Foster, Joann McDonald, *The Communitarian Organization: Preserving Cultural Integrity in the Transnational Economy* (Garland 1998).

Kramer, Matthew H., *John Locke and the Origins of Private Property: Philosophical Explorations of Individualism, Community, and Equality* (Cambridge 1997).

Lawler, Peter Augustine, and Dale McConkey, eds., *Community and Political Thought Today* (Praeger 1998).

Phillips, Derek L., *Looking Backward: A Critical Appraisal of Communitarian Thought* (Princeton Univ. Press 1993).

PATRICK M. O'NEIL

COMMUNITY

The most lasting images of popular culture and life ordinarily resonate with at least one of the basic ideals that compose American identity. While individual strength and fortitude are often part of these images, one often finds a contradictory American impulse: the desire for community—the need to fit into a whole.

Despite many contradictory forces, a sense of community has endured as a unique American priority in society and a clear icon in terms of cultural imagery. One of the first observers to note the basic characteristics of American democracy was the French writer Alexis de Tocqueville. Most intrigued by the experimental status of such a democracy, Tocqueville carefully scrutinized the status of what he viewed as the most essential cultural mechanisms for constructing a nation on ideas. While entirely enamored with the ideal of democracy, Tocqueville could not bring himself to believe

in its long-term success. Most problematic, he wrote, "the moral power of the majority is founded upon yet another principle, which is, that the interest of the many are to be preferred to those of the few." He goes on to say that "if equality of conditions gives some resources to all members of the community, it also prevents any of them from having resources of great extent." In these and other ways, Tocqueville noted that the sense of community acted to reassure many of the basic democratic principles for founding the United States. While he doubted its ability to endure, the American experiment dazzled the philosopher from France. The importance of community was at the heart of the original experiment and it remains a primary ideal in American society.

While the idea of community clearly endures, it has changed greatly since the time of Tocqueville. It has even changed a great deal since 1956, when Walt Disney constructed Disneyland, a theme park structured around ideals of American life. Designers intentionally structured the park around the most ubiquitous symbol of American community: Main Street U.S.A. Despite changes in this idealization, Americans still prioritize a sense of community on many levels of society—even the Disney corporation replaced Main Street with shopping malls and megastores. *Community* is at once a sociological and a cultural term, carrying with it many different conceptualizations and forms. Disney attempts to interpret only the simplest level of America's communities. Sociologists, historians, and others have used analysis of this cultural structure to significantly deepen the understanding of the United States.

Community as an academic construct is one of the most important units of historical and sociological analysis, as well as one of the most diffuse. In academic and popular discourse, community usually implies a common-sense bonding, a deeper sense of belonging that carries harmonious values of family outward to a broader society. Although *community,* as a collective term, can refer to either a social unit or a set of social relationships, it is most widely used to describe a combination of the two in which territoriality shapes social interaction

A community band performs at the Groton Fall Foliage Festival in St. Johnsbury, Vermont.

and organization. Often these dynamics vary with geographic locations, typically with the region influencing cultural nuances or details.

In sociology, the community concept is often traced to the German sociologist Ferdinand Tönnies, who in 1887 traced the evolution of community from a traditional village-like society built on interlocking bonds to a less personal, modern world of segmented social roles. Despite such a critical perspective, Tönnies felt traditional aspects of community could coexist with those of modern society and the city. The transitional stages included *gemeinschaft* (society characterized by strong reciprocal bonds of sentiment and kinship) to *gesellschaft* (society characterized by impersonal relationships). Tönnies first proposed that these stages depicted a process of community decline. Sociologists were fairly accepting of this declinist model, which cul-

minated with Louis Wirth's classic article of 1937 "Urbanism as a Way of Life."

The idea that modernization inherently resulted in community decline began to be attacked in the early 1960s when Herbert Gans, in *Urban Villagers*, reported the persistence of strong communal ties within urban ethnic village communities. In *The Levittowners* as well as in other studies, Gans and his followers began to unearth the existence of community within prefabricated suburbs such as Levittown. The idea of telling larger history through the experiences of a single community was pioneered by *Middletown*, written by Robert Lynd and Helen Merrell Lynd in 1929. Nine years later, the Lynds returned to restudy the same community, eventually identified as Muncie, Indiana, and described a community and its leaders in the throes of the Great Depression, thus providing a second reference point on community values in the midst of crisis. Achieving the status of cultural benchmarks, these two books became the subject of an enormous secondary literature on Muncie-Middletown, including hundreds of essays, articles, dissertations, and documentary films. (Inspired by the Lynds, the sociological and historical documentation of life in Muncie is now collected and housed in the Center for Middletown Studies at Ball State University, allowing scholars to carefully chart the community's change over seventy-five years.) The lessons of Middletown are clear: changes in the nation's identity can be revealed through the stories of specific American communities.

Most scholars now agree that the community ideal did survive urbanization, although many still debate the extent to which social interaction was limited by territory. Increasingly, sociologists have come to view community in terms of its constituent interpersonal ties. Social network analysis is widely used to study the whole constellation of primary social ties that extend beyond the household to encompass neighbors, the workplace, relatives, and even the distant linkages among telephone and e-mail contacts.

Historical studies of community often reflect broader sociological debates. Towns and cities have long served as territorial units of analysis in historical community studies, as scholars sought places through which to study social processes in microcosm. But not until the 1970s did historians such as Thomas Bender and Gary Nash begin to challenge a wide range of historical studies that traced the decline of community in numerous locales over various periods. Subsequent historical studies of Italian, German, Canadian, and eastern European immigrants have shown how city dwellers preserved strong family and communal bonds despite increased crowding and the ordeal of immigration. Labor historians have likewise shown how displaced artisans and factory workers clung to institutions of mutual support and cooperation in the midst of industrial upheaval.

Planners and politicians have also used the community concept to define social policy since the

1960s. Trial and error has defined this process, with its most common application being on urban areas. Community Action Programs (CAP) grew out of the Economic Opportunity Act of 1964 and President Lyndon Johnson's War on Poverty. These, in turn, grew out of the community development ideas begun under the Kennedy administration. CAP as a program ended in 1967, but the idea has continued in economic and social planning. One aspect of this is community-based corrections, which are social welfare projects designed to avoid incarcerating criminals. Probation and work release as well as various sorts of half-way houses are only a few examples. The proliferation of community-based corrections in the 1960s and 1970s has had a profound influence on America's "criminal class." In particular, the spread of community corrections, coupled with the Reagan administration's "get tough on crime" strategy, greatly expanded the state's social-control network, particularly over the urban poor community. Many critics now look on such community-based projects as an unnecessary drain on tax dollars.

The 1990s saw such developments in socially constructing communities as Community Development Block Grants (CDBG). The CDBG program addresses problems that are national in scope, such as affordable housing, neighborhood revitalization, and declining business districts. It awards funds to cities and counties designated as entitlement communities. By statute, seventy percent of the funds appropriated for CDBG activities are designated for use by these areas and thirty percent to states for distribution to nonentitlement communities and other ancillary activities. Also, the statute requires that communities and states spend seventy percent of the funding on activities that principally benefit low- and moderate-income persons. As intended by Congress, block-grant funding gives the recipient discretion to use the money to solve problems in a broad area. Many critics believe that such programs have weakened the connection between urban and suburban areas as suburban areas lose their connections with and concerns for urban areas.

While academicians and politicians struggle to utilize and define the community concept, participants in American culture have only recently begun to realize that such a sense of inclusion needs to be maintained and developed. While conscious of community ideals in the nation's first two hundred years, Americans by and large simply assumed the existence of ideas and common feelings that united its disparate population. It proves instructive to trace the cultural use of the community ideal through a number of specific examples.

Even during the colonial era Puritan New England constructed itself as a social fortress based on common ideals. This was evident in John Winthrop's call for New England to serve as a "city on a hill" to provide a model to Puritans everywhere. Being a member of the community could clearly be the difference between life and death in the wilderness of North America. This realization was at the root of the first official act carried out by William Bradford and the other founders of New England when they accepted the Mayflower Compact even before disembarking the vessels that had carried them across the Atlantic Ocean. The text of the compact had each member promise to "solemnly and mutually in the presence of God and one of another, Covenant and Combine ourselves together into a Civil Body Politic, for our better ordering and preservation."

Although community membership remained a priority, the type of ideals knitting the people together often contradicted other American ideals, such as tolerance of others. When Roger Williams prioritized tolerance of diversity over Puritan doctrine, he was banished. Ultimately, he established his own community, Providence (later, Rhode Island). The ideals pursued by Williams were included in the founding fathers' structuring the United States with the motto *E Pluribus Unum* ("From Many, One").

From this intellectual level the construction of communities also took literal form. The necessity for dispersing open land created a unique American need to devise methods for planning communities. A system was required to divide land for sale while maintaining some structural mechanism devoted to community connection. The answer was the national grid. The grid was a product of the era's neoclassical spirit, at once practical and idealistic. It was rational, mathematical, and democratic. The federal survey, begun through the influence of Thomas Jefferson, platted the raw land of the Middle West into square township units measuring 6 miles (10 km) on each side. These were divided into 36 square-mile (93 sq-km) "sections" of 640 acres (259 ha) each. At first, only full sections were sold, but eventually the quarter section (160 acres, or 65 ha) became the standard, since it was considered the ideal size for a family farm. Over 5 million farms were platted on public lands between 1800 and 1900. Somehow, these rural grids still needed to construct a spirit of community.

The grid was primarily concerned with the squares of private property that lay within the gradients, not with the gradients themselves, or how the two related to one another. This dictated a way of thinking about the community in which private property was everything and the public realm—namely, the streets that connected all the separate pieces of private property—counted for little. This spawned towns composed of blocks unmodified by devices of civic art, checkerboard towns without visible centers, open spaces, odd little corners, or places set aside for the public's enjoyment.

While it could be argued that the grid composed a utopian community in its own right, many groups of people sought to construct ideal structures apart from the national models. Shakers and Mormons, of course, pursued utopianism in their settlements. Another group, Quakers, created a model that grew well beyond its original mandate. Philadelphia began as an experiment in town planning to create a city out of individual houses on large lots. William Penn's initial idea for a utopian metropolis called for 10 thousand acres (4 thousand ha) divided into 10 thousand 1-acre (0.405-ha) lots, on which were to sit 10 thousand single-family dwellings, each one to be surrounded by its own gardens and orchards. The transportation problems presented by such a sprawling pattern seem not to have occurred to Penn.

Penn's "holy experiment" quickly proved too fanciful and abstract. No sooner had Penn doled out the first parcels of his utopian community than their owners subdivided and sold them off. Blocks of row houses and warehouses quickly went up, and Penn was forced to revise his design to have a central square and city center that connected the outlying residents to the marketplace. In general, Philadelphia and most American cities flourished as centers for business. This would grow even more complicated by the concentration of industry and factory work within cities.

There were other methods for constructing community ideals. Many times the mechanisms of culture paved the way, physically and literally, for political and social ideals. An early example was put into practice in Penn's Philadelphia: Benjamin Franklin's *Poor Richard's Almanack,* first published in 1732, which quickly knit the reading public into a common network. Franklin used this publication, which mixed fact and humor, to help idealize the traits of common American life at a time when nearly every American seemed an outsider to the European community. Community, and particularly the consideration of others, would be an ideal marketed through American cultural channels until the end of the twentieth century. The suburban models of 1950s television, for instance, including *Leave It to Beaver, Father Knows Best,* and *My Three Sons,* were, at some level, morality plays regarding the need for Americans to respect the order of society, particularly based on a confidence in the federal government during the cold war. Many cultural critics argue that images of the 1990s (such as the animated television program *The Simpsons*) suggest that these American ideals have eroded under the weight of modern technology.

The technology that is most singularly responsible for this change is the automobile. Ultimately, the automobile created individual space apart from the larger community. Enabling the population to spread itself widely, the auto also cleared the path for new residential patterns. Most important, the American middle class of the post–World War II era would take up residence in a new form called the suburb. From their start in the 1850s, suburbs

offered residents the ability to live outside of structured communities. The newer form of the post-1945 era created entire satellite communities beyond the reach of cities and other social structures. It was thought that such places would create their own sense of community.

Many critics argue that the suburbs that developed after 1950 could never be communities based on traditional American ideals. James Kunstler and others argue that community values cannot be constructed in a form such as the Levittown model that started on New York's Long Island in 1947. The priority for Levittown-type suburbs belonged to their developers: namely, speed of construction and low cost of homes. Developments replaced planned communities and urban populations spread farther and farther from community centers. Most important to Kunstler and Jane Jacobs is the American reliance on the automobile. The deconcentration of populations contributed to sprawl, which connects urban and suburban areas with goods and services but not community in the traditional sense. Instead of interacting with other humans, these critics argue, Americans sit in their automobiles. Everyday life in this America, they argue, is nearly absent of civic interactions.

Technological substitutes seek to redefine ideas of time and place and, by association, of community. Most important, the use of computers and the Internet have altered such ideals in America. While such technologies contribute to the detraction of face-to-face human interaction, they also create a new forum for constructing communities. Cyberspace offers an intellectual community that is available to users from any location; it is truly unbound by time and space. Chat rooms and discussion lists offer a modern version of the city street or the local coffee houses where one could exchange thoughts and ideas. They are, on a basic level, an electronic version of Franklin's *Almanack,* providing information and assistance on any topic. But many critics of the status of community in contemporary America refuse to rely on such new modes of exchange. They want to change the very ways that Americans live.

Utopian town planning is alive and well among those attempting to maintain traditional ideals of community in a postmodern world of new technologies. New urbanists reject much of what modernism brought to town planning—namely, the prefabricated suburb—and argue that communities need to be designed much as they were 150 years ago. Most important, new urbanists accept a higher density in order to design communities around human walking patterns, not around the automobile. In order to combat sprawl, new urbanists include multiple-use areas within communities: stores, parks, libraries, and schools are included within the accessible design. In such designs, residences would not be limited to specific areas, in hopes that there could once again be a constant civic interaction with other members of the community. The first great example of new urbanism is Seaside, Florida, an affluent community constructed in the 1980s. Refusing to be left out, Disney planned its own ideal community in the 1990s. Celebration, Florida, is based on new urbanist ideals but adds the complicating involvement of a major corporation.

Clearly, Celebration demonstrates that the ideal of community continues to be important to Americans. Despite an era when many argue that the basic characteristics of community are under attack by social and technological forces, American priorities remain very similar to those of the nation's early days. While gated communities and corporate-financed suburbs appear incongruent with American ideals of democracy, they still maintain a basic hope for equal interactions with others. The change over time has been to choose exactly with whom one wishes to interact.

[See also COMMUNITARIANISM; MIDDLETOWN.]

BIBLIOGRAPHY

Bender, Thomas, *Community and Social Change in America* (Rutgers Univ. Press 1978).

Boyte, Harry, *The Backyard Revolution: Understanding the New Citizen Movement* (Temple Univ. Press 1980).

Fisher, Robert, *Let the People Decide: Neighborhood Organizing in America,* updated ed. (Twayne 1994).

Gans, Herbert J., *Urban Villagers: Group and Class in the Life of Italian Americans* (Free Press 1982).

Jackson, Kenneth T., *Crabgrass Frontier: The Suburbanization of the United States* (Oxford 1985).

Kunstler, James H., *Home from Nowhere: Remaking Our Everyday World for the Twenty-First Century* (Simon & Schuster 1998).

Mohl, Raymond, ed., *The Making of Urban America* (Scholarly Resources 1988).

Wilson, William Julius, *The Truly Disadvantaged* (Univ. of Chicago Press 1987).

Wright, Gwendolyn, *Building the Dream: A Social History of Housing in America* (Pantheon Bks. 1981).

BRIAN BLACK

COMPUTERS

Perhaps more than any other modern technology, computers have changed the way Americans live, play, and think. Computers are everywhere: in the workplace, the home, the car, and the school. Computers are used for entertainment, healthcare, and banking. There are desktop computers, laptops, and handheld computers. They are wired and wireless; computers can be used anywhere at any time.

The introduction of computers into daily life can be said to have started with the Electronic Numerical Integrator and Calculator (ENIAC), used in World War II for calculations of missile trajectory and later for federal income taxes. By the start of the twenty-first century, intelligent computer systems diagnosed diseases and designed complex computer networks, tasks that once were performed by human experts and that took a great deal of time to complete.

Although such terms as the *New Economy* or the *Digital Age* are associated with the dawn of the new millennium, these concepts were born nearly four decades earlier. In 1962 the economist Fritz Machlup coined the term *knowledge industries* to describe a new kind of work not based in the traditional industrial or agricultural sectors. In 1977 Marc Porat confirmed Machlup's thesis with his concept of the information economy, noting that overall information activities accounted for forty-six percent of the Gross National Product (GNP) in 1967.

Most relevant here, however, may be Marshall McLuhan's notion in 1964 that media are extensions

ENIAC, the computer developed at the University of Pennsylvania in the 1940s.

THE GRANGER COLLECTION

of man. Computers have evolved from being massive devices that were external and even remote from humans (as in the early days of mainframe computing) to becoming part of everyday life. The popular 1970s television series *Bionic Man* even foresaw computer chips in humans, whereupon persons become computers.

The pervasiveness and power of computers today allow multitasking at incredible rates. Any number of activities can be performed simultaneously; one can chat, e-mail, word process, build spreadsheets, often integrating one with the other. As a result of computers, work is done differently—but it is also different work.

The pace of change is rapid and the industry mantra is "faster, cheaper, better." According to Moore's Law, the capacity of computer chips doubles every eighteen months. Bill Gates, founder of software giant Microsoft, reportedly once compared the computer industry with the automobile industry and stated that if the auto industry had kept up with technology as the computer industry has, everyone would be driving twenty-five dollar cars that get one thousand miles to the gallon. But

such rapid changes lead to disposability and obsolescence. The average life-span of a computer or computerized device is two years and shrinking. This state of affairs leaves one wondering: how can one keep up with all of these new technologies? What does one do with the trappings of the old technologies?

Microprocessor technology is also driving the miniaturization of all types of devices: desktop-size adding machines have become credit-card-size calculators with more feature functionality and at a fraction of the former cost. There are programmable microwave ovens in the kitchen; global positioning satellite systems in the car; smart homes in which one can control the lights, heating, and security systems remotely; and e-books that can be read from handheld computers.

Digitalization of information has made the computer a distribution mechanism for mail, music, and video. Convergence of content is also occurring. It is not uncommon for a teenager to be watching his or her favorite television program while simultaneously chatting with friends or a fan group on the Internet. Digitalization has also turned computer users into potential producers; the average user can produce professional quality newsletters and mailings, create compact discs (CDs), edit videos, and share photos via the World Wide Web.

At the turn of the twenty-first century, thirty percent of U.S. workers were in information-related careers; 136.9 million people in the United States had access to the Internet from home, with over 51 million households connected. Shopping online generated 10.5 billion dollars in revenue in 1999. The computer literate are making travel reservations by computer, sampling music from new CDs before actually buying them, and getting "second opinions" from computer-based medical resources. By 2004, 210 million U.S. residents are expected to be online, including more low-income and older people. These changing demographics will change the face of e-commerce as well.

There are sources of concern, however. For example, eighty-three percent of U.S. workers polled reported that they were in touch with the office on a typical seven-day vacation, increasingly through e-mail. Remedies are needed for this information overload and the resulting blurring of work and home spaces. Computer users are increasingly turning to computer-based intermediaries or "bots" to help them with this seemingly implacable situation. These new digital intermediaries filter and find information for them the way they once relied on publishers and librarians.

Access to computers has moved from being a luxury to a necessity in the new economy, and computer-related skills are now a ticket for entry into it. Computer knowledge has become a prerequisite for participation in the workplace, the classroom, and the marketplace. Automation of many activities of daily life has replaced human interaction. In fact, interactions with others are increasingly mediated, too; that is, there is a computer between the person at the keyboard and the person on the other end of the transaction. There are also now ailments caused by spending too much time on computers, including repetitive stress injuries and eyestrain.

Consumers now care about how computers look (for example, color-coded Macintosh computers) and how they look with them; the Palm Pilot became a status symbol among the *digerati* (a term *Wired* magazine used to describe the new digital generation). Computers have also changed human sensibilities and perceptions of fundamental concepts such as distance, time, and speed. Computer users expect nanosecond responses to queries and in daily business and personal transactions. Distance and time have almost become irrelevant because one can communicate and transact anytime from anywhere.

People, especially young people, spend more and more time on the computer, listening to and sharing music, playing games, and surfing the Internet. But not all of these activities should be thought of as solitary or isolating. While playing games and surfing the Net, they are also "doing e-mail" or chatting with their friends. This is truly a "plugged-in" generation at one with their computers that does not know life without computers.

[*See also* TECHNOLOGY, AN OVERVIEW, *and article on* CONSUMER TECHNOLOGY; INTERNET.]

BIBLIOGRAPHY

Gates, Bill, *The Road Ahead* (Penguin 1996).
McLuhan, Marshall, *Understanding Media: The Extensions of Man* (McGraw-Hill 1964).
Turkel, Sherry, *The Second Self: Computers and the Human Spirit* (Simon & Schuster 1984).

CONCETTA M. STEWART

CONEY ISLAND

When first seen by Henry Hudson in 1609, the site later known as Coney Island was a five-mile- (8-km-) long, quarter-mile- (.40-km-) wide tract consisting of sand dunes, clam beds, and scrub offshore of what is now the borough of Brooklyn, New York City. No one knows for certain how Coney Island acquired its name; however, it became a peninsula when the tidal creek separating it from the mainland was silted over. Beginning in the 1840s successive waves of visitors would make Coney Island America's best-known amusement area, until the advent, in the mid-1950s, of the first Disneyland theme park.

Brooklyn's playground leapt to significance in popular culture because New York's businesspeople, politicians, and socialites discovered a beach hideaway five miles from Manhattan and convenient by boat. The working class quickly followed suit, and early in its history the island attracted the weird population mixture that would later characterize it. West Brighton, Brighton Beach, and Manhattan Beach (which featured Corbin's Manhattan Beach Hotel, the most fashionable hostelry in the nation) attracted affluent patrons. Nearby, shacks and saloons of the Gut (an area of saloons and brothels) offered every conceivable vice associated with alcohol, sex, and gambling. Between and around Corbin's and the Gut, the creator of the hot dog became a wealthy restaurant owner and exclusive New York social clubs leased hotels in whose restaurants dinner could cost as much as three dol-

UPI/BETTMANN

A 1928 view of Coney Island, New York's famous seaside amusement area.

lars and fifty cents, a worker's weekly salary. Among the popular stall amusements for visitors was hitting black men on their heads with baseballs.

Reformers described Coney Island as Sodom-by-the-Sea, but they were able to change nothing. Powerful Brooklyn and Manhattan business and political establishments argued that thousands of immigrants depended for employment on Coney Island's bars, brothels, gambling dens, restaurants,

and rides—the latter eventually evolving to include such innovations as roller coasters and a parachute jump.

From the 1920s through the 1940s, what brought a million visitors a day to a location where working classes could throw off almost all inhibitions—and where armies of sham artists and pickpockets thrived—was New York's Rapid Transit System. For a nickel fare, from anywhere in city's five boroughs, anyone could sun on Coney Island's beaches, walk

The first Coney Island roller coaster, built in 1884, gave passengers a one-minute ride for a nickel.

© THE GRANGER COLLECTION

along its three-mile- (4.8-km-) long boardwalk, enjoy its rides and fast-food stands, and ogle contestants at beauty pageants. The latest visitors had little need for hotels and elegant restaurants; they brought their own food and wore bathing suits under their street clothing.

Ironically what doomed Coney Island as an amusement and resort area was what had made it possible in the first place: convenient, fast transportation. Trains, highways, and then aircraft would make it possible for New York's masses to reach such varied locations as Catskill Mountain resorts, Atlantic City, Disney parks, and Las Vegas. By the end of the twentieth century, Coney Island's most prominent feature was a housing development, albeit hundreds of thousands of visitors still came daily during the summers to sun themselves.

Although Coney Island's glory days are long gone, it remains celebrated in collective memory. Such poems as Lawrence Ferlinghetti's satiric *A Coney Island of the Mind* (1958) and the con-man character immortalized by Phil Silvers in the movie *Coney Island* recall the unique tone of the place.

[*See also* DISNEYLAND; CARNIVALS AND FAIRS; POPULAR CULTURE; CIRCUSES.]

BIBLIOGRAPHY

Burrows, Edwin G., and Mike Wallace, *Gotham: A History of New York City to 1898* (Oxford 1999).
McCullough, Edo, *Good Old Coney Island* (Scribner 1957).
Snyder-Grenier, Ellen M., *Brooklyn!: An Illustrated History* (Temple Univ. Press 1996).

MILTON GOLDIN

CONGRESS

The U.S. Congress was created as a result of the compromises reached during the Constitutional Convention in Philadelphia in 1787. It replaced an existing unicameral chamber with a bicameral system and greatly expanded the powers of the legislature. During the course of American history, the power of Congress has waxed and waned, often dependent on the personalities in the White House and in leadership positions in the House of Representatives and the Senate.

Under the Articles of Confederation, which governed the United States from 1777 to 1787, there was a weak central government. Each of the original thirteen states was recognized as a sovereign entity. The Congress did not have the ability to impose taxes, all decisions had to be passed by a two-thirds majority, and any changes to the Articles had to have unanimous consent. The inability of the Congress to raise funds for troops to put down Shay's Rebellion in 1786 led to calls for a constitutional convention in 1787.

At the Philadelphia convention in May 1787 there were two main problems that the attendees had to address: how to preserve the autonomy of the states but strengthen the central government, and how to establish an equilibrium allowing the small states to retain influence but giving greater representation to the bigger states in order to account for their larger populations. A compromise was reached that created a bicameral chamber. The upper chamber, or Senate, would consist of two representatives from each state and, hence, ensure the equality of the states. Originally, the two senators from each state were elected by the individual state legislatures for six-year terms. In 1913 the passage of the Seventeenth Amendment changed the electoral process to direct election by the people. The framers of the Constitution thought that the Senate should be the more "mature" of the two bodies and therefore candidates for the Senate had to be thirty years old, compared to twenty-five for the House. The lower chamber, or House of Representatives, is apportioned on the basis of population so that the more populous states have greater representation. Members of the House are directly elected by the people for two-year terms (Senate terms are six years). The first Congress had sixty-five members. In 1911 the House had 435 members, at which point the Congress capped the number of representatives. Hence, the Senate may expand, but the House will simply continue to re-apportion its seats.

The Constitution also established two other branches of government, the executive and the judicial. An intricate system of checks and balances keeps any single branch from completely dominating the others. Hence, although the legislature has sole authority to pass legislation, it is dependent on the executive for enforcement of laws and the executive has the power to veto bills (Congress can override vetoes with a two-thirds majority vote in both chambers). Congress also has the responsibility to confirm presidential appointments, including those to the judiciary. The judicial branch is responsible for interpreting federal law.

Under the Constitution the Senate has the responsibility for confirming presidential appointees, including federal judges and Supreme Court justices, ambassadors, and senior members of the executive branch. The Senate must also approve all treaties by a two-thirds majority. The House has authority to initiate budgetary matters and can launch the process of removing the president or federal judges through impeachment (for removal of the president, the House must vote for impeachment, which, if approved, leads to a trial in the Sen-

ate in which two-thirds of the members must register votes of guilty to remove the official). Members of the Senate also have the right of filibuster or unlimited debate. Members may use this right to prevent action on a particular bill by literally talking it to death. A filibuster may only be halted by a vote of cloture, which requires a three-fifths majority vote. The House initially had a similar tradition, but it was abandoned in 1811.

The House has the power to decide presidential elections in the case of a tie or if no candidate is able to win an outright majority of the electoral vote. This has happened twice in American history: in the 1800 presidential election between Aaron Burr and Thomas Jefferson, and in the 1824 election in which there were four candidates. This power of the House takes on heightened importance during elections in which there is a strong third party. Congress also has oversight responsibilities and can conduct investigations through its subpoena power.

In drafting the Constitution, James Madison and the other framers felt that the legislature should be supreme since it was the embodiment of the will of the people. Throughout the early history of the nation, Congress was the dominant force in American politics. For instance, the framers left it up to the Congress to establish the structures of the other two branches. The executive consisted of an elected president who would oversee the various agencies of the federal government. Initially Congress passed legislation that created three cabinets: War, State, and Treasury. However, over time, the executive branch greatly expanded so that there are now fourteen cabinets and hundreds of other government agencies.

The judicial branch consisted of the federal court system and the Supreme Court as detailed by the Judiciary Act of 1789. One of the first and most significant limitations on Congress's legislative authority is the power of judicial review. This gives the judiciary the ability to review and, if necessary, overturn federal legislation. The right of judicial review was established by the Supreme Court in the 1803 case *Marbury* v. *Madison*. Since this point, there has been a tension between Congress and the judicial

Patrick Henry speaks to the First Continental Congress in Philadelphia in 1774. Thirteen years later the U.S. Congress was created.

branch as some 159 federal laws have been struck down by the courts. In response, Congress has utilized both the amendment process and its ability to shape legislation to conform to court decisions. For instance, the repeated rejections of the federal income tax by the Supreme Court led to the Sixteenth Amendment in 1913, and rulings on the Fourteenth Amendment and equal rights led to the passage of statutes such as the Civil Rights Act of 1964. One of the most significant demonstrations of the power of Congress has been evidenced in battles over the confirmation of federal judges. While judicial appointments used to be the sole domain of the president with little interference from the Senate, in the 1980s the upper legislative chamber took an increasingly visible role in determining Supreme Court appointments. This was most dramatically illustrated in the 1987 nomination of Judge Robert Bork (in which the Senate rejected the nomination 58–42) and the 1991 televised nomination hearings of Judge Clarence Thomas (whom the Senate confirmed 52–48).

Many of the powers of Congress are expressly stated in the Constitution, including the right to impose taxes, borrow money, raise an army, print money, and so forth. However, most of the power of the legislative branch has been acquired through the commerce clause, which gives Congress the power to regulate interstate commerce and international trade (Article I, section 8), and the necessary and proper clause or elastic clause (Article I, section 8), which gives Congress the ability to pass laws required to carry out its other functions.

The overall power and influence of Congress has been historically in direct proportion to the power and prestige of the president. Many presidents, ranging from George Washington to Calvin Coolidge, perceived Congress as the embodiment of the people's will and saw their primary function as president to enact legislation. These presidents were content to allow Congress to establish and implement agendas. Other occupants of the White House, especially in the twentieth century, took a much more activist role and endeavored to control or shape the legislative agenda. This trend began with the presidency of Theodore Roosevelt, who battled with the enormously powerful speaker of the House, Republican Joseph G. Cannon. Later presidents such as Franklin Delano Roosevelt and Ronald Reagan were able to use their popular appeal to take the legislative initiative away from Congress.

One feature of late-twentieth-century American politics that constrained the power of Congress was a divided government in which the political party controlling the White House was different from the party controlling Congress. From 1897 to 1954 divided government occurred in eight of the fifty-eight years; however, in the next forty-six years this circumstance existed for thirty-two of the years. Initially the Democrat-controlled Congress often found itself at odds with a Republican (GOP) president in the White House. From 1994 to 2000 the situation was reversed and the administration of Democratic President Bill Clinton faced a GOP-controlled Congress, which impeached the president over allegations of perjury and obstruction of justice. Throughout the post–World War II era, various presidents liberally used their veto powers to stem the agendas of partisan Congresses with a resultant legislative gridlock. This occurred simultaneously with a rise in partisan politics within Congress, which further eroded the potential for compromise and consensus legislation.

[See also PRESIDENCY, THE; SUPREME COURT; FEDERAL GOVERNMENT; CONSTITUTION.]

BIBLIOGRAPHY

Barone, Michael, and Grant Ujifusa, *The Almanac of American Politics* (National Journal 1996).

Campbell, James E., *The Presidential Pulse of Congressional Elections* (Univ. Press of Ky. 1993).

Fiorina, Morris P., *Congress: Keystone of the Washington Establishment*, 2d ed. (Yale Univ. Press 1989).

Kaptur, Marcy, *Women of Congress: A Twentieth-Century Odyssey* (Congressional Quarterly 1996).

Mayhew, David R., *Congress: The Electoral Connection* (Yale Univ. Press 1974).

Sinclair, Barbara, *Legislators, Leaders, and Lawmaking: The U.S. House of Representatives in the Postreform Era* (Johns Hopkins Univ. Press 1995).

Thurber, James A., and Roger Davidson, eds., *Remaking Congress: Change and Stability in the 1990s* (Congressional Quarterly 1995).

TOM M. LANSFORD

CONSERVATION AND CONSERVATION MOVEMENTS

Conservation is usually assumed to be synonymous with environmentalism. However, the intellectual movement to conserve natural resources spans nearly two hundred years, stemming from a unique combination of romantic views of nature and conservative efforts to reduce waste. Existing long before an environmental sensibility found expression and application, conservation is a part of environmentalism.

American environmental concern traces back to Jeffersonian ideas of a unique American connection to land and the romantic ethos of the nineteenth century. Open land, sometimes viewed as "wilderness," defined the New World for many European settlers. Thomas Jefferson argued that this open land could be transformed into an American strength as an agrarian republic. While much of the nation would pursue land use similar to Jefferson's ideal, some urban Americans remained intrigued by Jefferson's idea of a unique American connection to the natural environment, realized in such European forms as parks and gardens and in the intellectual tradition of Romanticism. By the end of the 1800s, wealthy urbanites pursued "wild" adventures in sites such as the Adirondack Mountain region of New York, initiated organizations to conserve animal species or limit pollution, and, finally, set aside areas of nature from development. While the first national parks, Yellowstone and Yosemite, proved to be watershed events in environmental history, they were not initially reserved to protect wilderness areas.

Much nineteenth-century environmentalism occurred without strict organization or philosophy, as the development of the first national parks exemplifies. Some scholars have chosen to view nineteenth-century environmentalism as a product of Gilded Age decadence rather than as an emerging new consciousness toward natural-resource use. For instance, Yellowstone, established in 1872, developed closely with railroad interests to attract tourists to the American West. Its oddities (geysers, waterfalls) proved more important to observers than its unspoiled wilderness, making its utility for settlement questionable and allowing its sponsors to dub the area "worthless for development." Such a designation made lawmakers more willing to sponsor setting it aside for altruistic reasons.

The Progressive period energized many Americans to identify social ills and use the government to correct them. The impulse to discontinue waste of resources and the pollution (physical and spiritual) in American communities rapidly became an expression for Americans' unique connection to the land. This impulse also helped define the term *conservation*, derived from the act of conserving. The leadership of President Theodore Roosevelt and his chief of forestry, Gifford Pinchot, galvanized upper-class interest in national policies. These policies deviated in two directions, preservation and conservation. Roosevelt greatly admired the national parks as places where "bits of the old wilderness scenery and the old wilderness life are to be kept unspoiled for the benefit of our children's children." With Roosevelt's spiritual and political support, preservationists linked protecting natural areas from development to such American icons as Jeffersonian ideals and Romanticism. Preservationist argu-

ments, though, were quite different from those of conservationists.

Conservationists, such as Pinchot, sought to qualify the preservationist impulse with a dose of utilitarian reality. The mark of an ascendant society, they argued, was the awareness of limits and the use of the government to manage resources in danger. Forest resources would be primary to Pinchot's concern. The first practicing American forester, Pinchot urged Americans to manage forests differently than had Europe. Under Pinchot's advice, President Roosevelt moved the few national forests created in 1891 out of the jurisdiction of the Department of Agriculture and into the care of an independent Forest Service. During his administration, Roosevelt added 150 million acres (61 million ha) of national forests. Under Pinchot's direction, the U.S. Forest Service became one of the most publicly recognized government agencies of the Roosevelt era. In addition to using a mailing list of over one hundred thousand, Pinchot's frequent public appearances and articles for popular magazines combined with his personal connections to make forests into a national cause célèbre. This public standing, created through forest conservation, further inflamed the approaching altercation that would define the early environmental movement.

While the difference between preservation and conservation may not have been clear to Americans at the beginning of the twentieth century, popular culture and the writing of muckraking journalists clearly reflected a time of changing sensibilities. After the 1906 San Francisco fire, the nation confronted its feelings in order to define national policy. San Francisco, in search of a dependable supply of water, requested that the Hetch Hetchy Valley, located within the boundaries of Yosemite National Park, be flooded in order to create a reservoir to protect against future fires. Preservationists, rallied by the popular magazine articles of naturalist John Muir, boisterously refused to compromise the authenticity of a national park's natural environment. Reviving romantic notions and even transcendental philosophies, Muir used this pulpit to urge, "Thousands of tired, nerve-shaken, over-civilized people are beginning to find out that going to the

John Muir (*right*) and President Theodore Roosevelt in California's Yosemite Valley.

mountains is going home; that wildness is a necessity; and that mountain parks and reservations are useful not only as fountains of timber and irrigating rivers, but as fountains of life." He called those wishing to develop the site "temple destroyers." In reaction, Pinchot defined the conservationist mantra by claiming that such a reservoir represented the "greatest good for the greatest number" of people and therefore should be the nation's priority. The dam and reservoir were approved in 1913, but the battle fueled the emergence of the modern environmental movement.

The conservation impulse by the end of the twentieth century had become a moderate environmental commitment appealing to many Americans. Earth Day and other events functioned to spur an environmental conscience in the mass public. Maybe the single best expression of this impulse, though, was the fashion in which many communities responded by organizing ongoing efforts to alter wasteful patterns. Recycling proved to be the most persistent of these grassroots efforts. This ethic of restraint, reinforced by over-used landfills and excessive litter, gave communities a new mandate in managing the population's waste. Reusing products or creating useful byproducts from waste of-

fered application of this new ethic while also providing new opportunities for economic profit and development.

[*See also* ENVIRONMENT AND ENVIRONMENTALISM, *article on* ENVIRONMENTAL STUDIES; NATURE, *article on* THE IDEA OF NATURE.]

BIBLIOGRAPHY

Fox, Stephen, *The American Conservation Movement: John Muir and His Legacy* (Univ. of Wis. Press 1981).

Nash, Roderick, *Wilderness and the American Mind*, 3d ed. (Yale Univ. Press 1982).

Opie, John, *Nature's Nation: An Environmental History of the United States* (Harcourt 1998).

Sale, Kirkpatrick, *The Green Revolution: The American Environmental Movement, 1962–1992* (Hill & Wang 1993).

Worster, Donald, *Nature's Economy: The Roots of Ecology* (Cambridge 1977).

BRIAN BLACK

CONSERVATISM

Historians have long recognized that American politics lacked the ideological orientations common to those of Europe. This condition has been noted in the analysis of the relative weakness of the American Left, but it applies equally to the Right—and specifically to conservatism, one of the main philosophies of the Right. The rise of self-identified conservatism can be traced directly to the publication of Russell Kirk's *The Conservative Mind: From Burke to Eliot* (1953) and to William F. Buckley's founding of *National Review* magazine in 1955. The rise of organizations such as the Intercollegiate Studies Institute and the Young Americans for Freedom played a vital role in the recruitment of youth. In the area of political activities, the Republican Party was eventually taken over as a principal conservative vehicle, although in some areas, such as New York State, this movement was aided by the activities of third parties such as the New York State Conservative Party and the Right-To-Life Party.

In 1964 the conservative political movement captured the national Republican Party and nominated Republican Senator Barry Goldwater from Arizona for president. Although Goldwater was defeated in the landslide election of President Lyndon B. Johnson, the very fact of the nomination and campaign of Goldwater represented the growing strength of the movement. In 1952 Dwight Eisenhower had received the Republican Party's nomination for president, having bested the choice of the conservatives, Ohio Senator Robert Taft. In 1968 conservatives accepted Richard Nixon, a moderate Republican, as the nominee, but by 1980 they were able to nominate and elect California Governor Ronald Reagan as president.

The evolution of an American conservative philosophy was neither a smooth nor a unitary process. Over the decades, racist and anti-Semitic figures and philosophies were purged from the conservative movement, and, beginning with Ayn Rand's "excommunication" by the *National Review,* an imprecise line was drawn between traditional conservatism and libertarian ideology.

One of the first tasks of conservative intellectuals was to trace their own somewhat obscured traditions. Quite naturally, conservatives looked to Edmund Burke and his monumental *Reflections on the Revolution in France* (1790) as the origin of modern, self-conscious conservatism, and they traced conservative ideas back into the central intellectual traditions of the West, from antiquity through the Middle Ages into the Renaissance.

Founding and Constitution. In tracing their ideology through American history, conservative intellectuals struggled to come to terms with two of the most important events of that history: the American Revolution and the adoption of the U.S. Constitution. Were the pro-British Tories the true conservatives and were the American rebels liberals and radicals? Conservative scholars such as Willmore Kendall, George Carey, Forrest MacDonald, and Harry V. Jaffa saw the War of Independence not as a left-wing revolution but rather as a conservative movement to defend the status-quo ante. The colonists, insisted conservative historians, had been contented subjects of the British Empire for almost two centuries. They had honored their monarchs, fought for the empire, and acknowledged the supremacy of Parliament in regulating the general re-

lations of the empire. George III and his Parliament were radical innovators who attempted to repress the traditional rights of colonial subjects and to turn the empire into a unitary state. In line with this interpretation, conservatives read the Declaration of Independence as a traditional, natural-law justification against tyrannical government, phrased in the natural-rights language of John Locke as modified by Thomas Jefferson.

American conservatives have emphasized the Constitution's role as the guiding political document of the United States, and they have protested its distortion and abuse by modern governmental practice and the misinterpretations of an activist judiciary. For conservatives, the Constitution's success came in part from the colonists' love of their traditions. A number of the Constitution's features reflected the traditional ways that colonists had been governed by the British Empire, since many of Britain's constitutional conventions were carried over into the new U.S. Constitution; conservatives rejected the view of the Constitution as a radical departure from prior practice.

The checks and balances of the constitutional system appealed to conservatives' fear of tyranny. Beginning with the New Deal and the wartime presidency of Franklin D. Roosevelt and increasing with the cold-war presidencies, conservatives objected to the idea of an "imperial presidency," in which they saw Congress surrendering many of its prerogatives to the executive branch. Federalism, often misidentified as "states' rights," enjoyed a central place in American conservative constitutional theory. Under the original design of the Union, shared sovereignty between the federal government and the states, each in its respective sphere, was heavily emphasized. Conservatives saw this federalism not only as an important bastion against tyranny but also a design to allow local laws to reflect the cultural and religious differences in the separate societies that comprised in the various states.

At the time of the rise of conservatism in America, the judicial branch entered an extremely activist phase, and it was often state authority that suffered at the hands of federal judges. Conservatives reacted against what they perceived as judicial usurpation. Conservatives have become champions of various interpretivist hermeneutics for Constitution exegesis, especially the philosophy of original intent; they have formed groups such as the Federalist Society and Judicial Watch to attack judicial activism both by political means and by scholarship.

Economic Order. Conservatives advocate the advantages of the free market, rejecting the rise of the welfare state and excessive governmental regulation as economically destructive and politically dangerous. They have never advocated an extreme libertarianism that would repudiate all governmental interventions, but they have argued for the natural-law-based Roman Catholic social teaching concerning the principle of subsidiarity; that is to say, that activities should be done on the lowest feasible level of society. Ideally individuals and families should care for themselves and contribute to the overall social good; then private charities and religious organizations should assist the disadvantaged; and only then should government become involved, in an ascending order: local, state, and federal.

Conservatives tend to endorse the views of such classical economists as Adam Smith, Jean-Bapiste Say, and others, and to embrace one of the modern liberty-oriented schools of economic thought, such as the Chicago school, exemplified by Milton Friedman, or the Austrian school, exemplified by Friedrick von Hayek and Ludwig von Mises. Beyond the economic devastation wrought by governmental interference, conservatives emphasize the danger to political liberty represented by massive infusions of government largess. The increasing dependence of voters on the bounty of government and the creation of classes of governmental clients who depend utterly on government handouts threaten the operation of democracy and the freedom of states within the federal union.

Defense and Communism. Although the collapse of the Soviet Union removed communism as a major issue in U.S. politics, the conservative movement began at the time that the United States was struggling to combat communism at home and to contain Soviet expansionism abroad. Conservatives led the way, in alliance with cold-war liberals, in recognizing the danger that expansionist totalitarianism presented to the West. Beyond the communist threat, conservatives emphasized the need for a strong defense posture, especially given the necessary U.S. role as the postwar guarantor of international order. During the Korean War, and later the confrontations with Fidel Castro's Cuba, and then the Vietnam War, conservatives condemned the no-win strategies that the United States and its allies had adopted.

To the conservative view, pacifism, world federalism, and the like are utopian delusions arising from historical ignorance, moral failures, and heterodox religious impulses. The failure of Western leaders and theoreticians to take proper account of the necessary use of force in the imperfect world of international politics was characterized as the "suicide of the West" by James Burnham in his 1964 book of the same name.

Morality and Religion. Conservatives have eschewed the relativism and subjectivism that they believed permeated modern ethics, and they have especially denounced the decline of religious practice and theological doctrine, a development they have seen as underlying the distortion of modern morals. An unusual combination of conservative Catholics, fundamentalist Christians, and Orthodox Jews has united in opposition to the rise of secular-humanist values and against the inner decay of religion, reflected in a "religion of humanitarianism" and a pseudo-ecumenism, which Catholic conservatives identified as the heresy of indifferentism that holds all beliefs to be equal.

The self-centeredness of modern humanity, exacerbated by an arrogance born of material prosperity and scientific triumphs, has made people unwilling to accept divine and ecclesiastic authority. Conservatism in religious belief and practice does not automatically equate to political conservatism, but the two seem to have often kept company with one another. In Catholicism, *Triumph* magazine was founded by William F. Buckley's brother-in-law L. Brent Bozell, who was active in Catholics United for the Faith, and *National Review* itself took a critical view of many of the changes in post–Vatican II Catholic liturgy, teaching, and moral practice. Eventually other Catholic groups were founded, including the Society of Catholic Social Scientists and the Hildebrand Institute, that were committed to the full magisterium of the Church. Similar movements arose in Protestantism; eventually the intellectual ferment and doctrinal controversies spilled over into political activism.

Two of the events that crystallized political activities by these groups (which had been stirred by the Supreme Court's decisions banning school prayer and similar judgments on church-state relations) were *Roe* v. *Wade* (1973), which legalized abortion-on-demand across the country, and the government's toleration and seeming promotion of homosexuality. Developments such as these provoked the rise of the Moral Majority, founded by the Reverend Jerry Falwell, and numerous other politically oriented religious groups.

Education. Conservatives see the "decline of Western civilization" as a result of the deterioration of education. The lack of academic rigor is by now well recognized in the United States and in many other Western nations, but even earlier conservatives had objected to the general direction education had taken under the guidance of the disciples of John Dewey. The death of classical language studies, of detailed knowledge of history, philosophy, and literature, and of familiarity with the Constitution and classical political theory all have been lamented.

Education, which is supposed to serve as a means to propagate and sustain civilization, has become, in the view of the conservatives, a source of radical attacks on that civilization. According to conservatives sex education was utilized to undermine religious morality and parental authority; history was now taught topically, allowing teachers to propagandize ahistorical ideologies; and political theory (now called civics) became a mindless veneration of concepts such as democracy and

equality, wrenched from their traditional meanings and historical contexts. Despite having won some major political and cultural victories, most conservative thinkers would assess their successes as representing only retardations of the ongoing decline of the nation and of American culture.

[See also LIBERALISM; LIBERTARIANISM; INDIVIDUALISM; POLITICAL PARTIES; POLITICAL CULTURE.*]*

BIBLIOGRAPHY

Buckley, William F., Jr., and Charles R. Kesler, eds., *Keeping the Tablets: Modern American Conservative Thought* (Perennial Lib. 1988).

Filler, Louis, *Dictionary of American Conservatism* (Philosophical Lib. 1987).

Kirk, Russell, *The Conservative Mind—From Burke to Eliot,* 7th rev. ed. (Regnery Pub. 1986).

Nash, George H., *The Conservative Intellectual Movement in America since 1945* (Basic Bks. 1976).

Weaver, Mary Joe, and R. Scott Appleby, eds., *Being Right: Conservative Catholics in America* (Ind. Univ. Press 1995).

PATRICK M. O'NEIL

CONSTITUTION

Under the Articles of Confederation, which were drafted in 1776, approved by Congress in 1777, and finally fully ratified in 1781, the U.S. national government was weak and inefficient, while relations between the states proved chaotic and often hostile. There was no real executive power provided, and a judicial branch was entirely absent.

Foreign powers treated the United States with contempt, while various states were driven close to war by border disputes and conflicting land claims in the West. States interfered with one another's commerce and discriminated against one another's citizens. States began to default on their debts; the "continental" currency had become valueless and the national government often could not pay its army.

States withheld their payments to the national treasury and freely ignored congressional statute as they pleased. In some areas hard-pressed farmers who faced foreclosure banded together in armed

The top half of the original first page of the Constitution of the United States of America (1787).

resistance to the officers of the law. In western Massachusetts the most famous of these revolts, Shays' Rebellion, occurred in 1786–1787.

In 1785 Congress, realizing the inadequacy of the Articles, went along with the Virginia legislature's call for a convention at Annapolis, Maryland, to propose amendments to the Articles—especially those dealing with the problems arising in commerce. The Annapolis Convention proposed no amendments, but delegates urged Congress and the states to convene a new convention to consider more extensive changes in the design of the government.

When delegates convened at Philadelphia in the summer of 1787, they promptly elected the well-respected George Washington to preside, and they concluded that a new organic law, not amendments to the old, was required. This decision raised two issues for the delegates to consider: how was the adoption of a new Constitution to be reconciled with the Articles of Confederation and how would this new Constitution provide for its own amendment in the future.

Under Article VII, the framers decided that the new Constitution should take effect in those states ratifying when nine had so ratified. This blatantly contradicted the Articles' requirement of unanimous consent of the states to any alterations. James Madison (Virginia) defended the arrangement with the argument that the Articles had never been a national constitution in any true sense because the states had retained full sovereignty under it. It was better understood as a treaty between sovereign states, Madison insisted, and as such it could be set aside, for international law recognizes that treaties may be set aside for a number of reasons. At least two of those reasons applied to the Articles: parties to the compact had broken its terms and it no longer served the purposes for which it was established.

The method of ratification for the Constitution designated in Article VII was a convention in each of the several states, which meant popularly elected conventions. This method is most significant because the ratification was not by state legislatures, as had been the ratification of the Articles, nor was it to be by Congress and the state legislatures, as was prescribed for amendments of the Articles. In one sense, it was a radical reversion to the ultimate source of political authority, the people themselves—who were held to have only delegated their authority to representatives. On the other hand, as a practical matter, the Constitution was reported back to Congress, which, on its own initiative, urged the various states to set up ratifying conventions. Ultimately, each state did set up such conventions through the action of its legislature.

With its final ratification by each state, the Constitution's ratification process truly could erase any shadow of illegitimacy, for, on the one hand, the ratification had appealed to the philosophically significant sovereignty of the people but, on the other hand, it had actually been ratified (de facto, at least) by every legal source of authority (Congress, the state legislatures, and the people). This truly was the import of the phrase "We the People of the United States . . . " with which the Preamble of the Constitution begins. The new constitutional order also avoided association with the deplorable weakness of the Articles by not presenting itself as an amendment to the Articles and by not carrying over congressional legislation passed under the Articles, in contrast to its retention of preexisting international treaties (Article VI, paragraph ii).

Public fears concerning the consequences of ratification were addressed by the specific pledge to honor the debts and contracts that the United States had entered into under the Articles even after the adoption of the Constitution (Article VI, section 1). A great flaw of the Articles, the violation by the states of their obligations to the Confederation, was addressed by the supremacy clause, which held the U.S. Constitution, the federal statutes, and treaties to be the "supreme Law of the Land" and bound state judges to that federal supremacy (Article VI, paragraph ii). In addition, the Constitution placed responsibility for state obedience to federal law on state officials by requiring all executive, legislative, and judicial officers of the state and federal governments to swear an oath to uphold the Constitution (Article VI, paragraph iii).

One of the great silences of the Constitution concerned the right of a state to leave the Union. Clearly, if a state requests such a separation and Congress approves, such a separation would unquestionably be constitutional. Beyond this, however, does a state possess an inherent right to secede without congressional approval? When the great national crisis arrived in 1860 in the wake of the election of Abraham Lincoln to the presidency, no one could demonstrate with irrefutable logic that secession was, or was not, constitutionally permissible. The bloodiest war in American history settled that question in the negative but only as a practical matter; the intent of the document remains a mystery. Many of the original ratifying states clearly thought they had the option of secession since that could be the only practical meaning of their "conditional ratification" of the Constitution, subject to the rapid adoption of a Bill of Rights.

Secession (in effect) was threatened by the New England states during the War of 1812 through the Hartford Convention and even before that during the Embargo period. Secession was bruited about again by prominent New England statesmen during the Mexican War and the subsequent territorial acquisitions. Firebrands in South Carolina threatened secession during the Tariff Crisis in the time of Andrew Jackson's presidency. When the great sectional crisis of 1860–1861 arose, the Southern states attempted by the ordinances of secession and their state secession conventions to imitate (in reverse) the original actions of the Constitution's ratification.

Delegates had to design a plan for amendment of the new Constitution that avoided the fatal flaws that plagued such procedures—too great an ease of amendment or too arduous conditions for change. The Articles' rule of unanimity had been a disaster, as had the law of the British Constitution that no act of Parliament signed by the monarch could be unconstitutional. Avoiding these extremes, the convention adopted Article V, with its requirements for supermajorities and its four alternative methods of amendment.

Amendments can be proposed by two-thirds of both houses of Congress or by a national convention (which Congress is obliged to call when petitioned by two-thirds of the states) and an amendment must be ratified by three-fourths of the states, either by the legislatures or by ratifying conventions, as Congress shall provide. By these alternative procedures neither Congress nor the state legislatures can act as an absolute bar to constitutional change, but neither can either one act alone without calling on the people.

Slavery had to be accommodated, for although many delegates had moral objections to the "peculiar institution," the Southern states would not ratify the Constitution if it lacked special protections for slavery. By the famous three-fifths clause (Article I, section 1, paragraph iii), slaves were to be counted as three-fifths of a person for the purposes of representation and direct taxation. Under the fugitive slave clause (Article IV, section 2, paragraph iii), slaveholders were to enjoy the right to reclaim slaves who had fled into another state, and the clause entrenching the slave trade prior to 1808 (Article I, section 9, paragraph i) was made immune to amendment prior to that date (Article V).

The great issue that most divided the states, however, was not slavery but congressional representation. The small states wished to continue the equality of representation they had under the Articles (the New Jersey plan), while the large states wished proportional, population-based representa-

tion (the Virginia plan). The great compromise that solved this problem and made the adoption of the Constitution possible involved the creation of a bicameral legislature, like the British Parliament, with a Senate preserving state equality (Article I, section 3, paragraph i) and with a House of Representatives based almost exclusively on proportional representation (Article I, section 2, paragraph iii).

Congress was granted a wide but delineated variety of powers (Article I, section 8) including a general taxation and borrowing power and the regulation of international and interstate commerce, of naturalization, and of bankruptcy. The Constitution also created a national currency and a standard of weights and measures, a postal system, and a federal judiciary. Congress was also granted power to make rules for the army, navy, and state militias (when they shall be called into the service of the Union), to regulate a federal capital district and its own facilities within the several states, to govern the territories (Article IV, section 3, paragraph ii), to admit new states to the Union (Article IV, section 3, paragraph i), and to regulate comity between the states (Article IV, section 1). In addition, Congress was given the specific right to make criminal statutes against counterfeiters, pirates, and offenders against the "Law of Nations" (Article I, section 8, paragraphs vi and x), as well as against treason (Article III, section 3, paragraph ii). With great foresight, the Constitution endowed Congress with wide legislative discretion by the "necessary and proper" clause, which Chief Justice John Marshall utilized in *McCulloch* v. *Maryland* (1819) to justify a loose construction of congressional legislative authority.

In supplying two of the great omissions of the Articles—an executive and a judiciary—the framers demonstrated the greatest care. The powers of the presidency were modeled on those of the British monarch at that time but with certain vital distinctions. The president was to be elected by a vote of the electoral college (Article II, section 1, paragraphs ii–iii) and was subject to impeachment by the House (Article I, section 2, paragraph v) and trial and removal by the Senate (Article I, section

3, paragraphs vi–vii) for "Treason, Bribery, or other high Crimes and Misdemeanors" (Article II, section 4).

Presidential power to convene Congress was restricted to "extraordinary Occasions" (Article II, section 3), with the Constitution providing the date for the required annual meeting, subject to revision by statute (Article I, section 4, paragraph ii), and presidential power to adjourn Congress restricted to times when the houses cannot agree (Article I, section 3). Furthermore, the presidential veto was subject to override by a two-thirds vote of both houses (Article I, section 7, paragraph ii).

Like the British monarch, the president possessed the power of pardon, command of the military (including the militias when called into service of the Union), and authority over the members of the executive branch (Article II, section 2, paragraph i). He also enjoyed the right, with the "Advise and Consent" of the Senate (by a two-thirds vote), to conclude treaties and with senatorial consent (by majority vote) to appoint judges and ministers of state (Article II, section 2, paragraph ii). Like the king of Britain, he took a specially prescribed oath upon assuming office (Article II, section 1, paragraph viii), and he was obliged to give Congress information on the "State of the Union" (Article II, section 3), like the royal "Speech from the Throne."

The structure of the federal judiciary was left in general to the discretion of Congress (Article III, section 1), but the Constitution provided for a Supreme Court whose original jurisdiction it prescribed but whose appellate jurisdiction it made subject to congressional limitations (Article III, section 1, and Article III, section 2, paragraph ii). The general grant of federal judicial power was given a wide scope, including matters of law and equity that might arise under the Constitution or under the treaties and laws of the United States.

The framers were concerned to eliminate the strife among the states that had characterized government under the Articles, and toward this end they imposed certain restrictions on the states. States were forbidden to issue "Letters of Marque and Reprisal" (which authorized privateers), enter into any treaty with foreign powers (Article I, section 10, paragraph i) or any compact with any other state, and they were not to keep troops or ships of war (Article I, section 10, paragraph iii). States were obliged to extend to the citizens of other states all "Privileges and Immunities of Citizens" (Article IV, section 2, paragraph i), to extradite escaped criminals and to make rendition of fugitive slaves (Article IV, section 2, paragraphs ii and iii), and to extend "full Faith and Credit" to the public acts of other states (comity) (Article IV, section 1).

Scholars have spoken of the system of checks and balances within the constitutional scheme of government, but certain myths, errors, and omissions have crept into popular understanding of that doctrine. Most presentations of the theory have emphasized the role of the three branches of the federal government in maintaining checks and balances but have ignored the role of states and of the electorate in that process. In addition, many theorists have overemphasized the equality and separateness of the branches, ignoring ultimate legislative supremacy and suggesting a system foredoomed to unrelieved stalemate in the governing processes.

In line with the political philosophy of John Locke and others, the framers made the legislative element the most powerful. Except for the president and vice president, all executive-branch members have had the offices created by congressional legislation, and all inferior tribunals of the federal judiciary are similarly created. Even the Supreme Court has the number of justices set by law and its appellate jurisdiction subject to congressional regulation. Nothing can become law without an enactment by Congress, and although the president enjoys the veto power it is subject to congressional override by a two-thirds vote of both houses (Article I, section 7, paragraph ii).

The congressional power of legislating, of the purse, and of impeachment, as well as its control over the structure, jurisdiction, and membership of the courts, give Congress the predominance of power within the national government, when it wills to use its powers. The framers thought this appropriate because the House was directly, popularly elected, thus creating a check to be exercised by the people. In addition, the Congress has its own internal checks in its bicameral structure and the multiplicity of its membership.

The independence of the branches can also be overemphasized, for most functions are carried on with concurrent activity by the other branches. The president participates in the legislative process by his veto power and by his right to advise Congress on necessary legislation, as well as by his sole right to propose treaties (Article II, section 2, paragraph ii), and the vice president actually presides over the Senate, voting to break a tie (Article I, section 3, paragraph iv). Congress affects both the executive and judicial branches by its role in approving presidential appointments, and the Congress and president jointly shape the judicial branch by the appointments made thereto.

An often ignored aspect of checks and balances, however, involves the federal nature of the system and the role of citizens. Under the Constitution, the states were given various protections from federal interference. Congress cannot form new states from the junction of existing states or by the division of an existing state without the consent of the states involved (Article IV, section 3, paragraph i). The states are guaranteed the right to appoint officers in the militia and to train the militia "according to the discipline prescribed by Congress" (Article I, section 8, paragraph xvi). The federal government was further forbidden to impose mercantilistic regulations favoring states and areas, as Great Britain had done in colonial times. Duties, imposts, and excises were required to be uniform throughout the Union (Article I, section 8, paragraph i); direct taxes could only be levied in proportion to population (Article I, section 9, paragraph iv); and no duties could be placed on exports and no preferences given by regulation to ports of any state (Article I, section 9, paragraphs v and vi). States retained full control of their electoral franchise, for the Constitution prescribed no requirement for voters—merely linking the requirement for voters for the members of the House with those required for voting for members of the most numerous branch of the state legislature (Article I, section 2, paragraph i).

The states were generally left to arrange their own political and constitutional order without federal interference, but the U.S. Constitution did set certain ultimate limits. State governments are protected from violent internal revolution and anarchy by the duty of the United States to aid them, on their request, with the suppression of domestic violence, but states are also obliged to retain a republican form by the guarantee clause (Article IV, section 4). In addition, the Constitution sets limits to potential state abuses by requiring states to recognize the public acts and judicial proceedings of other states by the full faith and credit clause (Article IV, section 1). States cannot deny to citizens of other states the privileges and immunities of their own citizens (Article IV, section 2, paragraph i), and states are mandated to provide the rendition of fugitive slaves (Article IV, section 2, paragraph iii) and the extradition of fleeing felons (Article IV, section 2, paragraph ii). State economic regulation is limited both by the interstate commerce clause (Article I, section 8, paragraph iii) and by specific prohibitions on coining money, emitting bills of credit, monetizing paper, or enacting laws impairing the obligation of contract (Article I, section 10, paragraph i), as well as by the ban on state imposts and duties on imports and exports (Article I, section 10, paragraph ii). The democratic character of the state is also supported by the proscription on a state's granting titles of nobility or passing bills of attainder or ex-post-facto laws (Article I, section 10, paragraph i). Later amendments to the Constitution have further democratized the proceedings and institutions of the states by abolishing slavery (Thirteenth Amendment), widening the franchise (Fifteenth, Nineteenth, Twenty-third, Twenty-fourth, and Twenty-sixth Amendments), and by guaranteeing equal protection of the law and civil rights to all citizens (Fourteenth Amendment).

In terms of formal alteration of the Constitution by the amendment process, it has been a relatively rare event. In the first year of the operation of the Constitution (1789), Congress proposed twelve amendments to the states for ratification. Ten of these were ratified, becoming the Bill of Rights (1792). The single greatest issue for amendments outside of the Bill of Rights has been expansion of the franchise. The Fifteenth Amendment (1870) enfranchised blacks, while the Nineteenth (1920) granted suffrage to women. The Twenty-third (1963) granted the vote in presidential elections to residents of the District of Columbia, while the Twenty-fourth (1964) forbade disenfranchisement of citizens for nonpayment of any poll tax, and the Twenty-sixth (1971) enfranchised those eighteen years of age and older.

A series of amendments expanded federal power to deal with problems or alleged problems in society. The Thirteenth Amendment (1865) ended slavery, while the Fourteenth (1868) created a national citizenship and guaranteed the rights of citizens against state actions. The Sixteenth (1913) constitutionalized the income tax, while the Eighteenth (1919) established national prohibition of alcoholic beverages, and the Twenty-first (1933) repealed the Eighteenth.

The remainder of the amendments tinkered with the mechanisms of government, with major and minor alterations alike. The Eleventh Amendment (1795) withdrew the federal judicial authority over private suits against states, restoring a limited sovereign immunity to states, while the Twelfth (1803) altered slightly the electoral college selection of president and vice president. The Seventeenth (1913) altered the election of senators from one by state legislatures to direct election by the people. The Twentieth (1933) changed the date of the commencement of the presidential term and slightly altered the rules for presidential succession. The Twenty-second (1951) limited presidents to election to two terms or service for a total of ten years, and the Twenty-fifth (1967) further refined presidential succession and provided also for filling vacancies in the vice presidency through nomination by the president and confirmation by the Congress, as well as setting up procedures to deal with presidential incapacity. Finally, the Twenty-seventh (1992) required that a congressional election intervene before any congressional pay raise can take effect.

Although there have been few formal amendments to the Constitution, many scholars insist that the Constitution as it operates at the beginning of the twenty-first century is significantly changed from the Constitution that the framers inaugurated at the close of the eighteenth. Supreme Court decisions have been a major agent of change both when they have drawn out the internal logic of the document to new applications and when they have read new doctrines and mandates into the organic law either in response to political necessity or to ideological fervor. Beyond court decisions, however, many of the details of the constitutional order have been filled in by governmental practice from the earliest days of the republic.

Executive privilege, presidential immunity, the right of presidents to dismiss from office the members of the executive branch, the right of presidents to abrogate treaties, the right of the chief magistrate to establish executive agreements with foreign powers without congressional approval, and much more besides were determined by ongoing practice more than a century before courts were called on to delineate and legitimate the scope of these unenumerated powers.

For Americans the Constitution has become more than simply the basic rules for the ordering of government, and it has taken on iconic status as the embodiment of the nation. From colonial times, there has been so much racial, ethnic, and cultural diversity (increasing with each succeeding decade) that there can be no self-image of the ideal American. There is no national religion, and such linguistic unity as there once was is now receding. The flag and the office of the presidency have totemic power, but nothing rivals the sheer emotional force of the U.S. Constitution as the living symbol of the nation.

Only the most radical fringes of the American polity reject the authority of the Constitution. Even most extremists, who do, in fact, reject the values implicit in that document, usually claim to be its true disciples, substituting their own idiosyncratic interpretations for the ordinary understanding of the provisions of the document. When the Southern states seceded, they claimed a constitutional right to do so, and when they set up their own Constitution of the Confederate States of America, they copied the Constitution with minimal alterations.

In the decades of the late twentieth century and early twenty-first century, a sustained ideological battle has engaged between those supporting a interpretivist reading of the Constitution and those committed to one of the noninterpretivist hermeneutics. Inaccurately but commonly styled "strict constructionism versus loose constructionism," this philosophical battle pitted those who believe in interpreting the Constitution in line with the intentions of the framers and those who favor judicial restraint against those who believe that the courts must construe the Constitution in light of the changing needs and nature of society. On the outcome of this struggle depends the future shape of the Constitution and, perhaps, of American society.

[See also BILL OF RIGHTS.*]*

BIBLIOGRAPHY

Buel, Richard, Jr., *Securing the Revolution: Ideology in American Politics 1789–1815* (Cornell Univ. Press 1972).

Corwin, Edward S., *The "Higher Law" Background of American Constitutional Law* (Cornell Univ. Press 1961).

Encyclopedia of the American Constitution, ed. by Leonard W. Levy, Kenneth L. Karst, and Dennis J. Mahoney (Macmillan 1986).

Ferrand, Max, ed., *Records of the Federal Convention of 1787* (Yale Univ. Press 1934).

Vile, M. J. C., *Constitutionalism and the Separation of Powers* (Oxford 1967).

Warren, Charles, *The Making of the Constitution* (Little, Brown 1937).

PATRICK M. O'NEIL

CONSUMERISM

Consumerism in American studies typically connotes a relationship between industrial or modern systems of marketing, on the one hand, and the consumption of goods and the rise of mass culture, on the other. Although *consumerism* may be used in the political sense to denote a social movement and the policy of monitoring products and services in the interest of buyers, it refers in American studies to the cultural web of shoppers, manufacturers, sellers, and advertisers, and the ways in which their social visions, material environments, and models of action enter into everyday life and expressive forms such as architecture, literature, and art. The term *consumer culture* is frequently used in American studies to address such concerns and to emphasize the influence of institutions and behaviors associated with mass consumption. Acknowledging a historic shift from a preindustrial producer society to a consumer society, cultural approaches interpret ways that craftlike skills are applied to shopping, display, and marketing viewed as learned experiences that form cultural traditions, rituals, and communities. In relation to this societal shift *consumership* can be used to suggest buyers' distinctive orientations. The implication of this focus on mass culture is that the wide economic system of consumption can be transnational while cultural forms of consumership can display national as well as regional characteristics. Further, the system of consumption is central to the material reproduction of social identities, relationships, and experiences. Several areas of concern are apparent in approaches to consumer culture within American studies: (1) history and material change; (2) control and the rhetoric of persuasion; and (3) meanings, expressions, and values.

History and Material Change. Consumer culture emerged out of the mercantile, colonial system of exploiting the Americas for raw material that was manufactured into finished goods in Europe. The argument proceeds that settlers therefore became reliant on consuming goods from abroad, and conflicts arose between colonizers and colonists for control of the production and flow of goods. A class structure emerged with the feature of a new American middle class of merchants brokering a consumer system that allowed growth of local markets. Pressures to expand manufactures and to build a transportation network of canals and roads came at least in part from the call for ready-made goods that would facilitate easy movement into the American frontier.

Although the extent of consumership during the colonial period and its influence on emerging na-

© CHRIS GARDNER/AP/WIDE WORLD PHOTOS

Shoppers carry bags full of toys purchased at a mall in Philadelphia on the day after Thanksgiving. Shoppers began their holiday gift buying at five A.M.

tional and regional societies has received attention from scholars, the emphasis in assessing consumer culture has been on the coincident rise of industrialism and mass culture during the latter part of the nineteenth century. During that time social and material environments changed in response to consumer demands caused by a shift from a producer to an industrial economy. Industrial wage earners relied on consumer goods and services for subsistence. From the secure but limited range of local markets and elite consumers, business imagined the growth and profits made possible by coast-to-coast distribution via mass transportation of ready-made, nonessential goods to the ordinary consumer in the hinterlands. These changes involved risks, for they demanded speculation on future orders, which meant possible overproduction and loss. Many Americans needed advice and reorientation—"object lessons," as they were called in the rhetoric of the day—in the new institutions of advertising, department stores, metropolitan newspapers, photography, installment plans, and mail-order catalogs. New figures also arose—"drummers" promoting special brands, "admen" specializing in rhetoric of persuasion, department store "moguls" exerting

public influence and developing name recognition, "counter girls" offering hospitable receptions for shoppers, and "designers" creating shop windows and interior displays.

Into the twentieth century consumer culture advanced. The social and material changes it inspired, some distinctive to the United States and others cutting across modern industrial nation-states, raised issues for exploration in American studies, such as the relationship of department stores to the expansion of urbanization, as well as the growth of fast-food establishments along the routes of first railroad and later highway travel. Other material changes that illustrate social and cultural shifts resulting from growing consumerism include: spaces in the family home to store and display accumulated goods; the desire for souvenirs and trinkets to savor the experience of travel and special events; the reorientation of public institutions such as galleries and museums toward "collectible" goods; the rise of "collecting" badges and pins in youth organizations such as the Boy Scouts; the evolution of mail-order and brand-name strategies in the age of the Internet; and construction of total consumer environments with connected communities in the forms of malls, centers, and expositions.

Control and the Rhetoric of Persuasion. An issue of debate is whether the spread of consumer culture was in the best interests of Americans. How were the masses convinced to embrace the system, especially during economically unstable periods of the 1890s and 1930s? A theory of cultural hegemony holds that elites used such popular venues as world's fairs, pageants, and museums to persuade an uneasy populace that the future of progress through industrial growth and ease of life in "laborsaving" consumer goods outweighed the loss of intimacy, security, and community. Advertising, packaging, and exhibiting of commodities, therefore, became essential to conveying a persuasive rhetoric of future abundance; luxuries appeared accessible to the masses, changing fashion became desirable for everyday life, and household goods became symbols of achievement. Although promising prosperity, critics argue that these features of consumer culture created more inequities of class, race, and ethnicity. They point to a "therapeutic" rhetoric in marketing that caused insecurities about individuals' status and worth in order to generate demand for products that could help them conform to popular standards of cleanliness, appearance, and behavior.

The rhetoric of persuasion could translate into a competitive system generating increased consumption in exchange for social status. At the end of the nineteenth century, Thorstein Veblen coined the term *conspicuous consumption* to identify the rise of a new, upwardly aspiring group he dubbed *the leisure class.* By this class's ability to display goods, particularly those that required excess labor to maintain, their leisure was conveyed to an envious public. The new fashion of a clean-shaven face, he mused, evidenced the ample time that a man could spare for the unnecessary chore, and his ability to afford the many accessories needed for the task. The model of conspicuous consumption created an ideal of fashion for others to follow. The model designated a hierarchy from the leisure class downward; those below would strive toward the position and display of wealth demonstrated by the leisure class, which because of its vested interests would profit further from expanding consumption.

Although cultural hegemony theory emphasizes the hidden exertion of influence by elites, buyers can also exert power to shape consumer culture and, occasionally, social structure. Boycotts during the civil rights movement and consumer protection movements utilized purchasing power to effect change. Daniel Boorstin in his popular histories of America extended this argument by citing consumer culture as a prime democratizing and nationalizing force in industrial America. In addition to creating national "brands" recognizable and accessible to all, consumerism encouraged the rise of what Boorstin called "consumption communities" outside of place, whose overlapping interests, connected by shared tastes and goods, clustered Americans into multiple overlapping social networks that diversified the American social landscape and therefore prevented the tyranny of large special interests. The rise of an elastic middle class, encourage-

ment of innovation and invention for a mass-consumer market, affordability of fashionable goods for the masses, and use of consumer power as entrance into the national arena by immigrants, women, and minorities were, for him, evidence of a distinctively American version of mass consumerism with the result of democratization. Such consumer institutions as credit cards, rural free delivery, and money-back guarantees that developed in the United States were facilitated by American conditions of rapid economic expansion and social mobility over a wide expanse of land. The expectation of a democratic ethos in consumer culture was implicit in the revelations and subsequent outcry during the 1990s over Asian "sweatshops" using child labor to create consumer goods for an American market, particularly when those goods were represented by the all-American figure of a television talk-show host.

Meanings, Expressions, and Values. Beyond the development of consumer institutions is the question of how consumer experiences are interpreted by and for the public in cultural expressions. In what ways do aesthetic and value systems related to consumerism become embedded in art, architecture, literature, and folklore? Children's humor, in the form of parodies of jingles and slogans, commonly refer to product advertising. Often the parodies critically comment on the control exerted by adults over children, or they use consumer symbols to mark their worldly awareness of popular culture as a stage beyond the expression of childhood fantasy in "innocent" rhymes and narratives. Among the verses entering American oral tradition, for example, was "McDonald's is your kind of place/Hamburgers in your face/French fries up your nose/Two pickles up your nose/Ketchup running down your back/I want my money back/Before I have a heart attack." In folklore as in literature, consumerism is often related to questions of the moral value or sentiment in acquisitiveness, the temptation of material appearances, and the depth of emotion possible through mere material things. Theodore Dreiser's central character in *Sister Carrie* (1900) finds the "lure of the material" as she wanders around a Chicago department store, and the prose used to describe it reflects the realistic attention to detail characteristic of an industrial, consumer age. The pivotal theme of Harold Frederic's *The Damnation of Theron Ware,* a best-seller of 1896, is the downfall of a Methodist minister who succumbs to various worldly temptations. The name *Theron Ware* is a clue to the theme of consumption in the novel (Theron is usually linked to an ancient tyrant; Ware suggests salable, often manufactured, goods). Imitating Washington Irving's "Rip Van Winkle," Bradford Peck's Percy Brantford, in the utopian novel *The World a Department Store* (1900), falls asleep and wakes up years later to encounter a world where all productive activities, even cooking, are ordered out. In a utopian landscape based on the layout of a department store, services are paid for and regulated by a credit system.

In addition to novels, comics, and films emphasizing the theme of the "lure of the material," cultural forms arise for interpretation that are geared toward a consumer model. It is possible to see the rise of the novel as the preferred literary form in America, replacing poetry, as evidence of consumer culture. Many books became available in collectible sets, including Horatio Alger stories and Nancy Drew mysteries, that repeated themes in prescribed formats. The formulaic "dime novels" of the nineteenth century, often featuring Western dramas, were popular, disposable sources of entertainment, as were the comic books of the twentieth century. With books becoming artifacts of consumption, consumer goods were expected to be predictable, reliable, and disposable.

In American holiday celebrations, consumer spending as a form of emotional exchange became predominant. While American consumer culture promised a perfection of design and taste to inspire all Americans, it was the rough-hewn spirit of preindustrial America, the "old-fashioned value," that still suggested human depth and sentimental meaning. The depth came from a feeling of rooted community and compassion associated with an older system of exchange. The surface quality of consumer goods expanded the form and variety of community, of belonging to a mass society, while at the same time flattering the self of the person who owned the goods.

Having read and interpreted various texts on consumerism, American studies scholars ultimately posed the question of whether the modern everyday role of "consumer" meant being an active participant or a passive spectator in the production of culture. Scholars explored the theme of American materialism in the global triumph of American consumerism; and American studies became an international concern, following the exportation of cultural products to other countries. In a variety of settings, they question the meanings of goods as values and structures in the ways in which they have been consumed and adapted.

[See also ADVERTISING.*]*

BIBLIOGRAPHY

Alfino, Mark, John S. Caputo, and Robin Wynyard, eds., *McDonaldization Revisited: Critical Essays on Consumer Culture* (Praeger 1998).

Benson, Susan Porter, *Counter Cultures: Saleswomen, Managers, and Customers in American Department Stores, 1890–1940* (Univ. of Ill. Press 1986).

Boorstin, Daniel, *The Americans: The Democratic Experience* (Random House 1973).

Bronner, Simon J., ed., *Consuming Visions: Accumulation and Display of Goods in America, 1880–1920* (W. W. Norton 1989).

Horowitz, Daniel, *The Morality of Spending: Attitudes toward the Consumer Society in America, 1875–1940* (Johns Hopkins Univ. Press 1985).

Ewen, Stuart, *Captains of Consciousness: Advertising and the Social Roots of the Consumer Culture* (McGraw-Hill 1976).

Fox, Richard Wightman, and T. J. Jackson Lears, eds., *The Culture of Consumption: Critical Essays in American History, 1880–1980* (Pantheon 1983).

Leach, William, *Land of Desire: Merchants, Power, and the Rise of a New American Culture* (Pantheon 1993).

Lears, T. J. Jackson, *Fables of Abundance: A Cultural History of Advertising in America* (Basic Bks. 1994).

Ohmann, Richard, *Selling Culture: Magazines, Markets, and Class at the Turn of the Century* (Verso 1996).

Twitchell, James B., *Lead Us into Temptation: The Triumph of American Materialism* (Columbia Univ. Press 1999).

Weems, Robert E., Jr., *Desegregating the Dollar: African American Consumerism in the Twentieth Century* (N.Y. Univ. Press 1998).

SIMON J. BRONNER

CORPORATIONS

The corporation is the predominant form of business organization in the United States today. While businesses in other forms (such as sole proprietorships and partnerships) are more numerous, corporations as a category generate more revenue and net income and have more employees and accumulated wealth than all other categories combined.

A corporation is a "person" in the eyes of the law, formed pursuant to the law of one of the states (although a few corporations are creatures of federal law), as an entity separate from its owners. In general, a corporation can have perpetual existence, and its owners are not responsible (beyond their investment in the corporation) for the corporation's debts. A corporation can issue stock, borrow money, own property, and sue and be sued. Today, one or more individuals or corporations can form a new corporation simply by filing the appropriate documents in a state office and paying a modest fee. In earlier times, the formation of a corporation was not so easy.

The origin of the modern corporation can be traced back to the merchant cities of medieval Italy and Germany, and English investors and adventurers copied these forms in the early fifteenth century. The Virginia Company, which financed the settlement of Jamestown, was a corporation chartered by King James I. Other corporations were chartered either by the king or by Parliament to settle many of the other American colonies or to conduct trade in the West Indies or Hudson Bay. Colonial legislatures granted a few corporate charters before the Revolution, and state legislatures continued this practice afterward.

The notion that a group of individuals should be able to unite for a commercial purpose began to gather momentum as the industrial age developed. A state's power to create a corporation had been based on the earlier English concept that a corporation should provide some public benefit in exchange for its charter. The earliest American corporations after the Revolution were chartered to develop canals; to operate banks; to build toll roads, bridges, and railroads; or, in a few cases, to build factories. In each case the promoter of the business had to demonstrate to the state legislature that a public purpose was being served, and the act of the legislature granting the charter usually noted that public purpose.

There was little differentiation between private enterprise and public-works efforts in the first half of the nineteenth century. Public funds and private capital were often invested side by side in the formation of these corporations. Even where there was no direct public investment, a favorable industrial policy helped the rise of these private corporations.

The real development of the modern business corporation started just before the Civil War and accelerated in the immediate postwar period. Several forces combined to give rise to this phenomenon. The country entered into a long period of economic prosperity, although there were several periods of sharp downturns. The Homestead Act (1862) promoted westward expansion and settlement. Several Supreme Court rulings in the 1870s and 1880s eliminated state-created barriers to corporations that were engaged in interstate commerce. The National Banking Act (1863) established the national banking system, which built investor confidence in capital markets; that confidence helped companies raise money for new or expanding enterprises.

Most states changed their method of creating corporations in the period from 1850 to 1875. The earlier view had been that a corporate form should not be allowed unless there was some specific public interest being served. The rapid business expansion led to changes in state laws, eliminating the need for special legislative acts for corporate charters. When promoters found it easier to acquire charters, pursuant to statutes of general applicability, with a simplified, administrative approach, the number of new corporations increased steadily. The increase in newly formed corporations did not change the recurrences of the usual business cycle, however. Periods of strong economic growth led to occasional times of overproduction, which often led to ruinous price drops and to periods of economic contraction.

Since there were no laws prohibiting combinations of corporations, some industrial leaders saw an opportunity to overcome this unfortunate aspect of the free market. Earlier cycles of competition between companies were replaced by an era of combinations—trusts, syndicates, mergers, and monopolies. By the beginning of the twentieth century, nearly every industry had some sort of combination protecting its members from competing with each other. The Standard Oil Trust controlled ninety percent of the oil refining industry; United States Steel was formed in 1901 by the consolidation of several of the then-largest steel companies, and it controlled two-thirds of the steel industry. DuPont Company, American Tobacco Company, and General Electric Company controlled eighty percent of their respective markets. The American Sugar Refining Company owned ninety-eight percent of the nation's sugar refining capacity.

While the original objective, in the cases of some of these industries, at least, was the avoidance of the extremes of boom and bust, the lack of competition led to unrestrained price increases, extreme profits, and a number of abuses. In the railroad business, for example, the long-haul short-haul abuse focused attention on the evils of an unregulated monopoly.

The relationship between government and business corporations changed in the last few years of the nineteenth century, in reaction to the growth of monopolies and the attendant abuses. A number of states passed laws regulating railroad and warehouse prices, and these statutes had varying degrees of success. At the federal level, the Interstate Commerce Act, passed in 1887, marked the real first step in this new direction. The Interstate Commerce Commission, created by that act, had the power to investigate complaints and to regulate prices. In 1890 Congress passed the Sherman Antitrust Act, which prohibited monopolies.

The Sherman Act was more a statement of public policy than an immediate governmental assault on monopolies. The Sherman Act did not supplement the budget or manpower of the Department of Justice, so the majority of early cases involved private plaintiffs. In addition, the Supreme Court did not interpret the new statute to say that all trusts were bad. For example, the Supreme Court ruled in 1895 that the American Sugar Refining Company, with its ninety-eight percent share of the market, was not an illegal trust. The Court did uphold the Sherman Act in 1911, in breaking up the Standard Oil and American Tobacco trusts, however.

Congressional impatience with the pace of antitrust efforts led to the passage of two important statutes in 1914. The Clayton Act expanded the definition of illegal trade practices to include discriminatory pricing, exclusive dealing requirements, and tie-in sales. The act also prohibits mergers that "may" lessen competition—a much broader concept than a monopoly. The Federal Trade Commission Act prohibits "unfair" trade practices and creates an enforcement agency. With the addition of these two statutes, the federal government attained the ability to regulate corporations in all aspects of their businesses.

The Clayton Act not only increased governmental regulation of business but also had an important provision in another direction. The Clayton Act specifically excluded from antitrust regulation all labor unions. For the preceding fifty years, businesses had used the common-law definitions of illegal conspiracies to fight labor's efforts to organize factory and railroad workers. The courts interpreted the Interstate Commerce Act and the Sherman Act to prohibit unions. The Clayton Act's exclusion of labor from the antitrust laws had only temporary effect; the Supreme Court invalidated it in 1921. In 1935, however, the National Labor Relations Act strengthened the ability of unions to organize labor.

At about the same time that the relationship between government and business corporations was changing, the relationship between owners and managers of corporations was changing as well. Earlier corporations were often mere extensions of the personality of the founder (an entrepreneur, an inventor, or a promoter). As ownership of corporations became more widespread, there developed a separation between ownership and management. With this separation came the growth of a class of professional managers who brought a sense of institutional permanency.

The other aspect of this separation of ownership from management was on the ownership side. A rapid growth of broader public ownership of industrial corporations started in the late 1890s, as more and more companies' shares were listed and traded on the stock markets. The public's enthusiasm for investing in the stock market grew steadily as industrial consolidations brought financial stability and opportunities for speculative trading. All of that changed with the stock market crash in 1929 and the ensuing Depression.

In the early 1930s, Congress determined that one of the causes of the crash was the unregulated nature of the capital markets. The result of this determination was another aspect of governmental regulation of corporations, the federal securities laws. The Securities Act of 1933 and the Securities Exchange Act of 1934 established a framework for regulating the capital markets and created the Securities and Exchange Commission (SEC). The SEC provides rules for the issuing and trading of corporate stocks and bonds and for some of the internal workings of corporations, such as the election of officers. The SEC also requires standardized accounting rules for the financial information that corporations must furnish the public.

Corporations today are the primary form of business enterprise. Corporations whose stock is publicly traded on a stock exchange or an "over-the-counter" market provide the most visible examples of the presence of corporations in our economy. The formation of new business ventures, which became especially newsworthy in the 1990s, also demonstrates the importance of the corporate form of business. Nearly every case of a start-up business success story involves one or more entrepreneurs beginning in an informal setting, as a sole proprietorship or a partnership. The pivotal moment is almost always when the business adopts a corporate form and seeks new capital.

[See also MILITARY-INDUSTRIAL COMPLEX; FREE ENTERPRISE.]

BIBLIOGRAPHY

Baskin, Jonathan Barron, and Paul J. Miranti, Jr., *A History of Corporate Finance* (Cambridge 1997).

Davis, Joseph S., *Essays in the Earlier History of American Corporations* (Harvard Univ. Press 1917).

Goodrich, Carter, *The Government and the Economy, 1783–1861* (Bobbs 1967).

Kaysen, Carl, ed., *The American Corporation Today* (Oxford 1996).

Nester, William R., *A Short History of American Industrial Policies* (St. Martin's 1998).

Sobel, Robert, *The Age of Giant Corporations: A Microeconomic History of American Business, 1914–1992,* 3d ed. (Greenwood Press 1993).

ELI BORTMAN

COTTON

Plantation agriculture was well suited to the semitropical climate of the American South. This form of production, of course, carried a severe social price in its employment of slaves. Additionally, plantations restricted the types of crops that could be grown. Plantation agriculture initially was based on tobacco, which could not be grown in Europe. By 1800, though, a new plantation crop called cotton was sweeping the South. Its expansion depended on some of the nation's earliest technological innovations.

In its raw form cotton does not immediately appear to be one of the world's most useful substances. Naturally beautiful, a field of cotton plants is a blend of many colors and textures. Squares or flower buds form on the cotton plants four to six weeks after the seedlings have emerged. Creamy to dark yellow blossoms that appear on the cotton plant three weeks after the buds form eventually turn pink and then dark red before falling off. After the bloom falls off, a tiny ovary left on the cotton plant ripens and enlarges into a pod called a cotton boll. Cotton bolls open fifty to seventy days after bloom, letting air in to dry the white, clean fiber and fluff it for harvest. After leaves are removed to minimize staining of the lint, the mature seed cotton is ready to be harvested. While the growth process has remained the same throughout the history of cotton's use by humans, the harvesting process has varied a great deal.

Harvesting cotton was a time-consuming, labor-intensive process throughout its history. The floss needed to be literally pried from the boll, leaving fingers torn or hardened with calluses. This floss still required attention, and workers spent long hours pulling tiny seeds from it. This portion of the process was ripe for innovation. The successful inventor was young Eli Whitney, who had worked in various trades before choosing to become a school teacher. After completing his education, Whitney traveled south to accept a teaching post in South Carolina. During a stopover at a friend's plantation, he was told of the need for a machine that could clean upland cotton of its seed. The silky, long-fiber cotton, which would grow on the long, sandy islands off the coast of Georgia, could easily be separated from its black seed; however, this type would not grow on the mainland and throughout the South. In these areas only upland cotton could succeed, and it had shorter fibers that clung tightly to the seed, which made it difficult to clean.

Within six months Whitney had a working model of a cotton gin that would clean the upland cotton. Eli Whitney applied for a patent on June 20, 1793. The new cotton gin would allow one worker to clean ten times more cotton than before and clean it much better. It seemed that the labor-saving device could make unnecessary legions of slaves; however, the innovation merely signaled the massive expansion of plantation agriculture, which meant more slave labor was needed. Cotton production grew from three million pounds (1.4 million kg) a year in 1792 to eleven million pounds (5 million kg) in 1797.

The original model of Eli Whitney's cotton gin.

The surplus production of cotton proved a great stimulus to other industrial development. After 1815 cotton was the most valuable export from the ports of New Orleans, Baltimore, and New York. Hundreds of mills used water power to create textiles from cotton. Samuel Slater pioneered the introduction of manufacturing technology to the United States in Pawtucket, Rhode Island, in 1789. With his *Report on Manufactures* of the 1790s, Alexander Hamilton spurred the development of Paterson, New Jersey, and introduced the idea of manufacturing centers as a federal concern. Francis Cabot Lowell then proceeded to make the Merrimack River the nation's textile hub beginning in the 1810s. Lowell, Massachusetts, his manufacturing town, would entirely reconstruct many ideas of American economic development.

The expansion of cotton growing created what many historians call "the Cotton Kingdom," stretching from South Carolina to Texas and Arkansas. The cotton industry thus firmly tied slavery into the Southern economy. It not only dominated the life of the South but also influenced the economy of the nation. Following the Civil War, the South's textile revolution brought the cotton mills to the cotton, and by 1915 it had overtaken New England as the nation's leading textile producer.

The natural inclinations of cotton have contributed to its history positively and negatively. For instance, cotton minimizes groundwater contamination, adapts to poor soils, and is an efficient user of fertilizer. While it quickly depletes the nutrients in soils, it can grow in fairly unfertile areas. However, cotton is susceptible to specific pests. The boll weevil is the primary insect enemy of cotton. This pest has plagued U.S. cotton producers since 1892. It can complete an entire life cycle in three weeks, lay two hundred eggs per female—each in a separate cotton square or boll, ensuring the destruction of each—and spread rapidly, covering 40 to 160 miles (64 to 257 km) per year.

Cotton's attachment to slavery made farming additionally difficult for former slaves after the Civil War. During Reconstruction ex-slaves wanted land, independence, and freedom from cotton or anything else that suggested the old system of slavery. On the other hand, ex-masters had every incentive to keep freedmen landless, dependent, and working in their cotton fields. For the old planting classes, the key to the profitable cultivation of cotton was cheap labor. The compromise became sharecropping. Ex-slaves did not own the land, but they were granted the right to work farms as individual families. They received a share of the crop, as did the landlord. Cotton was the only type of labor that many ex-slaves knew; through sharecropping, many African Americans remained virtual slaves in the cotton kingdom for a century longer.

[See also Plantation; South, The; Slavery; Tobacco.*]*

BIBLIOGRAPHY

Gross, Laurence F., *The Course of Industrial Decline* (Johns Hopkins Univ. Press 1993).

Olmsted, Frederick Law, *The Cotton Kingdom,* ed. by Arthur M. Schlesinger (Da Capo 1996).

McHugh, Cathy, *Mill Family: The Labor System in the Southern Cotton Textile Industry* (Oxford 1988).

Smith, Wayne C., *Cotton* (Wiley 1999).

Stewart, Mart, *"What Nature Suffers to Groe:" Life, Labor, and Landscape on the Georgia Coast, 1680–1920* (Univ. of Ga. Press 1996).

Brian Black

COUNTERCULTURE

The notion of the counterculture conjures up images from the late 1960s and early 1970s: hippies with love beads; flower children in rural communes or urban crash-pads practicing free love and voluntary poverty in a dreamy haze of pot smoke, acid trips, and psychedelic rock; and faded recollections of the musical *Hair.* Behind these dated stereotypes of misguided but sweet-tempered innocence lies a much broader phenomenon deeply rooted in American life.

The counterculture belonged to a strain of antinomianism that went back to the Protestant sources of American culture, including an aversion to hierarchy and tradition, a tendency to form small dissident sects, and a romantic faith in self-expression and personal morality as vehicles of salvation. In the hands of some of the greatest American writers of the nineteenth century, such as Ralph Waldo Emerson and Walt Whitman, this romantic Protestantism was secularized into an energetic individualism, a return to nature, a faith in fraternity and equality, and a vehement but heterodox spiritual intensity. Utopian social experiments such as Brook Farm pursued the communal side of this quest for heaven on earth.

Other antecedents of the counterculture can be seen in the "beloved community" of the Greenwich Village radicals during World War I and the rebellious youth culture of the Jazz Age, as evoked by such expatriate writers as F. Scott Fitzgerald and Ernest Hemingway. They saw American puritanism as small-minded hypocrisy, disdained the philistinism of small-town values, and mocked the work ethic of the Gilded Age as a cover for materialism, the worship of what William James called the "bitch goddess of success." These writers reflected major shifts in American values, stimulated by advertising and the mass media, which helped create a new culture of leisure and consumption.

All these developments were heightened after World War II. Unparalleled economic growth, a steady migration to the suburbs, and some amazing advances in technology (beginning with the automobile) brought utopia within reach of the middle-class family. At the same time new art movements, appealing directly to the young, put their stress on energy, spontaneity, improvisation, and personal authenticity. This wave of innovation embraced the bebop virtuosity of jazz musicians including Charlie Parker; the abstract expressionism of such painters as Jackson Pollock; lyrical novels and poems by J. D. Salinger, Jack Kerouac, Gary Snyder, and Allen Ginsberg; youth movies such as *Blackboard Jungle* and *Rebel without a Cause;* sensitive "method" acting by Marlon Brando and James Dean; and the erotically charged rock music of Chuck Berry, "Little Richard" Penniman, and Elvis Presley, which, like so much else in the counterculture, had crossed over from the black community. Meanwhile, liberal critics of conformity such as David Riesman and William H. Whyte gave way to Freudian radicals including Norman Mailer, Herbert Marcuse, Paul Goodman, and Norman O. Brown, who assailed cold-war America as politically and sexually repressive.

As the children of the postwar baby boom came of age, these bohemian adventures were taken up on a mass scale. In the climate of political revulsion that set in during the Vietnam War, especially on college campuses, sex, drugs, and rock music grew into messianic expressions of youthful alienation as well as strong generational bonds. With the introduction of the birth-control pill in 1962, sex became freer and far less inhibited. Marijuana (long a staple of the jazz world) and LSD (lysergic acid diethylamide) turned into widely used drugs, promising not just kicks but nirvana or salvation. With Bob Dylan, the Beatles, and the Rolling Stones—followed by psychedelic groups such as the Jefferson Airplane and the Grateful Dead—rock music became the oral poetry of the younger generation.

By the late 1960s the counterculture spawned spectacular "be-ins" and "love-ins" in large public parks and brought together masses of longhaired, near-naked kids who ended up stoned in the rain and mud at the 1969 Woodstock Festival. Such spectacles fascinated and horrified middle-class Americans and stirred enormous media attention. Under

the eyes of the camera, they turned into scenes of public theater directed against war, repression, hatred, acquisitiveness, machismo, ambition, and straightlaced morality. Members of the Youth International Party, the Yippies, led by Abbie Hoffman and Jerry Rubin, threw money onto the floor of the New York Stock Exchange to show their contempt for materialism. In the Haight-Ashbury section of San Francisco and the East Village of New York City, a core of anarchist activists, the Diggers, opened stores that simply gave things away. Other young people retreated to communes where conventional sex roles and economic roles broke down along with conventional ways of raising children.

Early commentators such as Theodore Roszak in *The Making of a Counter Culture* (1969) and Charles Reich in *The Greening of America* (1970) saw this as a momentous shift in human consciousness, an embrace of spirituality and sensuality in place of competitiveness, rationalism, and technology—in short, a break with the Faustian ambitions of Western man. But as the affluence of the 1960s gave way to the economic distress of the 1970s, such jaundiced observers as Daniel Bell, Christopher Lasch, and Tom Wolfe portrayed the counterculture as more narcissistic than spiritual. They saw its hedonism and promiscuity as a cover for inner emptiness and a spin-off of the consumption ethic of the postwar prosperity.

Within a few years there could be no question that American capitalism welcomed the counterculture as a way of marketing desire and stimulating sales. The middle class was changing, shaking off the old Protestant ethic of thrift and self-discipline. After the 1960s it became fashionable to be hip, stylish, a rebel, and a nonconformist. The Me Generation morphed into the Pepsi Generation. Like the economy, a media-saturated culture thrived on novelty. The critics of the counterculture understood very well how it could be embraced by the middle class, but its weaknesses were rooted in American individualism and anti-intellectualism, the cult of the primitive, not in any desire to turn a buck by marketing a new lifestyle.

Although they were media-savvy, the hippies and Yippies were genuine dissenters at the feast of American capitalism, adding a boisterous touch of comic irreverence to the protest culture of the age. They challenged authority not through argument but by mocking its pretensions and acting out their vision of the simple life. But this therapeutic faith in authenticity and self-fulfillment was in tune with some wider currents in American life. Their legacy can still be seen in the fluidity of today's sex roles and social styles, in the strength of the environmental movement, the growing attraction to Eastern religious practices, natural foods and fibers, and homeopathic medicine, and perhaps even in the fervent attachment to the virtual community of the Internet, which many have seen as the electronic version of the counterculture.

[See also BEAT WRITERS; FREE LOVE; WOODSTOCK.*]*

BIBLIOGRAPHY

Bell, Daniel, *The Cultural Contradictions of Capitalism* (Basic Bks. 1976).

Dickstein, Morris, *Gates of Eden: Americana Culture in the Sixties* (Harvard Univ. Press 1997).

Frank, Thomas, *The Conquest of Cool: Business Culture, Counterculture, and the Rise of Hip Consumerism* (Univ. of Chicago Press 1997).

Hoffman, Abbie, *Soon to be a Major Motion Picture* (Putnam 1980).

Lasch, Christopher, *The Culture of Narcissism: American Life in an Age of Diminishing Expectations* (Norton 1978).

MORRIS DICKSTEIN

COUNTRY MUSIC

Country music has roots in various strains of folk music, including African American blues and a wide range of traditional British music. It is also a commercial enterprise that has grown into a billion-dollar business. The tension between profit and authenticity has proven to be a key issue in analytical approaches to the form. Likewise, country music's identity is a subject of intense interest for scholars, musicians, and fans, all of whom debate the nature of the music's message and its audience. Is country music the singing voice of rustic farmhands or of the urban working class? Is it the "white man's blues," or is it, as the interstate highway markers going into Nashville, Tennessee, proclaim, "America's Music"? Perhaps the primary reason for this diversity of interpretation is the fact that country music is actually a broad rubric for several diverse styles of music that share family resemblances in varying combinations.

When country music first emerged in the radio and record business it was not called country and it was not headquartered in Nashville. Although the vast majority of country musicians have been white Southerners, many ethnic groups have participated in the form. In 1922 Fiddlin' John Carson (1868–1949) inaugurated country music performances on the airwaves in Atlanta, Georgia. The next year Ralph Peer, a talent scout for Okeh and Victor records, went to Atlanta to record local musicians. While he concentrated on blues musicians, he also recorded several numbers by Carson. The most legendary moment occurred four years later at Peer's recording sessions in Bristol, Tennessee, in the Appalachians near the Virginia border. Over the course of two weeks, Peer recorded numerous artists, most notably Jimmie Rodgers (1897–1933) and the Carter Family, a female duet consisting of sisters-in-law Sara and Maybelle Carter, with Sara's husband A. P. doing backup singing. (Members of the extended Carter family who also performed include June Carter Cash—married to well-known country singer Johnny Cash—and Carlene Carter.) At the same time that Peer was seeking local talent to bring to the national market, Vernon Dalhart (1883–1948), an operatically trained professional singer, enjoyed country music's first million-selling record in 1924–1925 with "The Wreck of the Old '97." These pioneers were sold under the category of "old time" or "hillbilly" music. In the meantime radio "barn dances" and "old time music hours" proliferated on stations throughout the country, including Nashville's WSM, home of the Grand Ole Opry since 1925 (called WSM Barn Dance during its first two years).

Because it has been a hybrid and diverse form since its origin, generalizations about country music are difficult to make. The acoustic guitar is inte-

The Grand Ole Opry in Nashville, Tennessee, country music's most famous venue.

gral to the music both as a symbol of the wandering troubadour, à la Jimmie Rodgers, and as an opportunity to display musical virtuosity, for example, Maybelle Carter's legendary picking technique. For the most part, however, country music showcases its lyrics, which while often ostensibly simple demonstrate a sophisticated range of figurative speech. Funny song titles such as Jerry Reed's "She Got the Goldmine (I Got the Shaft)" gain the most fame but many songs develop complex metaphors such as Merle Haggard's "Hungry Eyes," an image that condenses the plight of a woman whose discomfort in the gaze of better-off onlookers gave her a taste for luxury she couldn't afford. Country voices are typically untrained but remarkably eloquent, the better to showcase the narrative and sometimes witty qualities of a song. The Dobro, or more recently the steel guitar, can be a prominent and very expressive feature, but its keening sound is almost always used to reinforce the singer's lamentation.

Similarly, country music often exploits the fiddle's ability to mimic cheer or despair. In fact, the fiddle and steel guitar are so closely associated with country music that often both are used simply to certify that a song is a country song.

The Carter Family and Jimmie Rodgers introduced two of country music's enduring themes. The harmonious Carters focused on rural nostalgia, family values, life's inevitable losses, and the compensations offered by righteousness, while Rodgers's loner persona reveled in yodeling boasts about doing wrong. His "In the Jailhouse Now," for example, contrasts sharply with the determined optimism of the Carter Family's "Keep on the Sunny Side."

The Grand Ole Opry acquired its name when host George Hays made a point of contrasting the contents of his show with the classical music program that preceded it, and to this day the Opry consciously retains its down-home appeal. The show has always featured a broad spectrum of country music styles, from harmonica player Deford Bailey (1899–1982) to the rustic comedy of finishing-school graduate Minnie Pearl (Sarah Colley, 1912–1996) to the hottest new stars. It gained national exposure and became the most important of the radio barn dance shows in 1939 when the National Broadcasting Company (NBC) network began broadcasting a segment of the show on Saturday nights. For most artists, an invitation to join the Opry cast is an unmistakable sign that they have achieved stardom. On the other hand, ever since Hank Williams was fired from the show for absenteeism and drunkenness in 1952, artists who are not invited to join the show can also claim a certain badge of honor.

The late 1920s and 1930s added singing cowboys and cowgirls to the mix. Many performers eschewed overalls for the standard Western costume of fancy boots, shirt, and a tall hat. Beginning in 1935 Gene Autry brought this image and his music to enthusiastic movie audiences. Tex Ritter, Roy Rogers, and Dale Evans followed him on the screen shortly thereafter. Thanks to the popularity of the style, many musicians, whether they came from the West or the Mississippi Delta, called their music Western in place of the more pejorative "hillbilly" and the more nostalgic "old time." In fact, as the style evolved, the Westerners added amplifiers, electrified instruments, a danceable beat, and sometimes even reed and brass instruments. Western swing—best exemplified by Bob Wills (1905–1975) and his Texas Playboys—and honky-tonk music such as that of Ernest Tubb (1914–1984) developed out of musicians trying to be heard above barroom din. Both styles contrast sharply with the traditional themes of the era's most popular artist, Appalachian-born Roy Acuff. The difference is apparent in the teary sincerity and soaring Dobro of Acuff's graveyard-themed "Lonely Mound of Clay" in contrast to Ernest Tubb's "Walking the Floor over You," a stoic address to a fickle woman.

Although such early stars as Jimmie Rodgers achieved impressive record sales, most historians and analysts of country music credit World War II with bringing country music to a national audience. Troupes of performers roved the country performing in military hospitals and camps. In January 1944 *Billboard* magazine acknowledged the music's prominence by publishing a chart devoted to the "Most-Played Juke Box Folk Records"; for a few months in 1947 the chart was called "Most-Played Juke Box Hillbilly Records" before changing back to "Folk." In 1949 the qualifier "Country and Western" was added. (In late 1962 *Billboard* dropped the term *Western* in favor of *Country* alone.) As these categories proliferated, yet another form of country music was christened: bluegrass. Although Bill Monroe (1911–1996) and the Blue Grass Boys had been members of the Grand Ole Opry's cast since 1939, the word *bluegrass*—used to characterize the virtuosic acoustic sound and nostalgic themes favored by Monroe and the musicians influenced by him—did not appear regularly until the early 1950s.

Country music's most legendary star, Hank Williams (1923–1952), began recording right after the war, although he had to wait until 1949 for his breakthrough hit, a yodeling version of a Tin Pan Alley song, "The Lovesick Blues." Dressed in Western wear and borrowing the hard-driving rhythm and hard-living themes of Western honky-tonkers,

Williams also sang about romantic strife with Acuff's emotional intensity. His liquor-sodden death seemed to add compelling authenticity to country music's most forlorn songs, and his unprecedented success created a dramatic tension between the disorderly mental landscape of the honky-tonk and the gray-flannel ease of a supposedly more urbane America. In fact, in such songs as "Mind Your Own Business" and "Honky Tonk Blues," Williams dramatized the rift between the happy days of the postwar era and the losers in the rat race.

After Williams's death, the birth of rock and roll thrust country music into an identity crisis. While Ray Price and Lefty Frizzell (1928–1975) flourished in the honky-tonk tradition and crooning balladeers such as Eddy Arnold and Jim Reeves achieved great success, this rollicking newcomer managed to influence the sound and themes of country music for several years to come; rock and roll would also amplify the nagging sense of self-consciousness and defensive pride that Williams had articulated. At first, such seminal rock stars as Jerry Lee Lewis and Elvis Presley (who made early public appearances as "The Hillbilly Cat,") topped the country charts. Stylistic terms such as *rockabilly* and *hillbilly boogie* convey the hybrid sounds that listeners found so exciting. Nevertheless, several institutional forces helped to separate the musical styles. *Country Song Roundup,* the longest-running fan magazine, featured articles on readers' reactions to questions such as "Is He or Isn't He a Hillbilly?" in reference to Conway Twitty. Country's uniqueness was thematized in songs such as Simon Crum's "Country Music Is Here to Stay" in 1958. (Crum was the alter ego of Ferlin Husky.) The Maddox Brothers and Rose sent up rock's manic energy with "The Death of Rock and Roll" (1956). Disc jockeys founded the Country Music Association in 1958. At the same time Nashville producers, led by Chet Atkins, deliberately set out to create music with a wide popular appeal—known as the Nashville sound or countrypolitan. Patsy Cline (1932–1963), for example, was produced in a sophisticated style in spite of her preference for rougher hillbilly sounds. The change did, however, result in significant success on both the pop and country charts.

COLLECTION OF HAROLD MADAGAN

Country singer Patsy Cline (*right*) greeting fans in a parade in Winchester, Virginia, in 1956.

Although country music became more closely identified with Nashville in the postwar era, the wilder Western styles continued to flourish. Buck Owens and his Buckaroos enjoyed a string of number-one hits in the mid-1960s without ever bowing to the Nashville establishment. Owens lived and recorded in Bakersfield, California, and expressed no interest in joining the Grand Ole Opry. His distinctive sound blended lively electric guitars, crack fiddling, pedal steel, tenor harmony, and an irresistible beat. Owens was greatly flattered by the Beatles's version of his 1963 hit "Act Naturally," but in 1965 he also published a pledge to sing "no song that is not a country song."

In the late 1960s through the 1980s, Merle Haggard, another star from Bakersfield, brought together many of country music's key themes. His "Okie from Muskogee" and "Are the Good Times Really Over" contrasted the values of the silent majority with the rock-and-roll-oriented counterculture. In his "Workin' Man Blues" and "Hungry Eyes" Haggard articulated the pain of the poor in an age of abundance.

George Jones, another star of the 1960s and 1970s, carried on the tradition of heartaches and hangovers. He brought Hank Williams's scenes of

shame to suburbia where he presented himself as an abandoned husband presiding over a broken dream home: "A Good Year for the Roses," "The Grand Tour," and "If Drinking Don't Kill Me" all invite onlookers to scenes of shame.

With their emphasis on the outsider and their avoidance of pop-oriented sounds, Williams, Haggard, and Jones exemplify what came to be known as hard country music in the early 1970s. Similarly, Loretta Lynn, the major female star of the 1970s, portrayed herself as a coalminer's daughter and pointedly contrasted the life of the lower-middle-class housewife to that of Elizabeth "Liz" (Taylor) and Jacqueline "Jackie" Onassis in "One's on the Way." Her 1975 song celebrating the advent of the birth control pill was banned at some country stations, a controversy she ascribed to the fact that most program managers were men.

While hard country made musical drama out of social alienation, several outsiders made remarkable entrances into country music in the 1960s and 1970s. In 1962, Ray Charles, a rhythm-and-blues star, made a well-received album called *Modern Sounds in Country and Western Music*. Charley Pride, while not the first or only African American performer in country music, was the sixth-best-selling artist of the 1970s. Johnny Rodriguez, who often broke into Spanish while singing his country hits, was the first Chicano country star. The early 1960s folk revival brought new admirers to pioneers such as Maybelle Carter and Bill Monroe. New links to rock music were formed when artists such as the Byrds, Bob Dylan, and the Nitty Gritty Dirt Band recorded country-inspired albums; traditionalist Emmylou Harris made her recording debut on Gram Parsons's first solo album *GP* (1973).

Country-rock may have reached its zenith of popularity in the 1970s with the Eagles, a California-based band whose hits charted on the rock rather than the country top forty. Nevertheless, in the 1980s hard country allied itself with rock music in order to demonstrate its distinction from pop-oriented, or crossover, country artists such as John Denver, Olivia Newton-John, and Kenny Rogers. Like the Carter Family, these artists celebrated ro-

mance and rural idylls in such tunes as Denver's "Thank God I'm a Country Boy" and Newton-John's "I Honestly Love You." Hank Williams, Jr., and a loose coalition of musicians known collectively as The Outlaws (most notably Waylon Jennings and Wille Nelson) used thundering percussion and heavy bass guitars to amplify their lyrics. Their themes, though, continued to draw the line between both the urbane world of upward mobility and rural nostalgia by creating a metaphorical country inhabited by outlaws and snarling "country boys" such as Hank, Jr.

The mid-to-late 1980s also heard a hard country revival in the voices of new traditionalists such as Randy Travis, Ricky Skaggs, Reba McEntire, Alan Jackson, and Dwight Yoakam. But the biggest star of the period managed to be nearly all things to all people; Garth Brooks combined the flamboyance of a rock star, the reverence of an Opry star, and the rowdiness of a hard country singer to achieve unprecedented sales and fame. Such songs as "Friends in Low Places" revel in downward mobility, while Brooks's most famous song, "The Dance," movingly reinforces the widespread belief in achieving gain through pain. The music video, which Brooks introduces by explicitly rejecting the notion that "The Dance" is a song about failed romance, associates joining the dance with heroic Americanism. While Brooks sings the song, images of John F. Kennedy, John Wayne, Martin Luther King, Jr., rodeo star Lane Frost, and others flash across the screen.

While music videos allow artists to add another dimension of significance to a song, video has also been blamed for focusing the attention of fans on youthful good looks at the expense of the voices of experience such as Haggard, Jones, and Jennings. The radio format of the 1990s (Hot New Country) concentrated almost exclusively on such young and photogenic artists as the midriff-baring beauty Shania Twain and the muscle-bound heartthrob Billy Ray Cyrus. By the beginning of the twenty-first century, the Americana format, allowing for more traditional sounds, had not really caught on, and the alternative country movement, which hyperbolically embraces country's most morbid and antisocial themes, remained marginal.

[See also MUSIC; FOLK MUSICAL TRADITIONS; POPULAR SONG.]

BIBLIOGRAPHY

Bufwack, Mary A., and Robert K. Oermann, *Finding Her Voice: The Saga of Women in Country Music* (Crown 1993).

Cantwell, Robert, *Bluegrass Breakdown: The Making of the Old Southern Sound* (1984; Da Capo 1992).

Ellison, Curtis W., *Country Music Culture: From Hard Times to Heaven* (Univ. Press of Miss. 1995).

Malone, Bill, *Country Music USA* (Univ. of Tex. Press 1985).

Peterson, Richard A., *Creating Country Music: Fabricating Authenticity* (Univ. of Chicago Press 1997).

Tichi, Cecelia, *High Lonesome: The American Culture of Country Music* (Univ. of N.C. Press 1994).

Whitburn, Joel, *Joel Whitburn's Top Country Singles: 1944–1997; Chart Data Compiled from Billboard's Country Singles Charts, 1944–1997*, 4th ed. (Record Research 1998).

BARBARA CHING

COWBOYS

From Deadwood Dick to John Wayne to the Marlboro Man, the cowboy is an enduring icon of American life. Popular culture continues to refer to the image of cowboys to embody an independent, carefree, but sturdy and honorable existence. The image embodies strength and durability at a time when such attributes may be hard to find. The historical record, however, tells a different story.

While commercial farming was the basis for most western settlement, cattle ranching—one of the West's most romanticized industries—was also rapidly evolving. In some parts of the western United States, ranching was a much more prominent practice than farming. Early in the nineteenth century herds of cattle, introduced by the Spanish and expanded by Mexican ranchers, roamed southern Texas and bred with cattle brought by Anglo settlers. The resulting longhorn breed multiplied and became valuable by the 1860s. By 1870 thousands of Texas cattle were herded into "drives" to Kansas, Missouri, and Wyoming. At the northern

BUFFALO BILL HISTORICAL CENTER, CODY, WYOMING/GIFT OF MRS. MARGARET H. SKOGLUND

A cowboy rounds up a calf in this painting, *The Littlest Rebel* by Robert William Meyers.

terminus, cattle were sold to northern ranches or loaded onto trains bound for Chicago and St. Louis for slaughter and distribution. While the long drive added to the romantic image when depicted in films such as *Red River*, forcing cattle to trek almost sixteen hundred miles (2,574 km) was not very efficient, particularly because it made cattle meat sinewy and tough.

Between 1860 and 1880 the cattle population of Kansas, Nebraska, Colorado, Wyoming, Montana, and the Dakotas increased from 130 thousand to 4.5 million. Development of the ranching frontier sparked several kinds of contests over land. In Texas and New Mexico, Anglos had received grants of land previously unoccupied by Mexicans. Driven by a desire for more, they wrested control of additional parcels from Mexican Americans and Indians through taxation, fraud, and raw economic muscle. Eventually, the *Tejanos*, as Texas Mexicans were called, became wage laborers as *vaqueros* ("horse riders") or the first cowboys.

Cattle raisers needed vast pastures for grazing, and they wanted to incur as little expense as possible by using land not desirable for farming. Referred to as "open-range ranching," this method of raising cattle depended on field workers on horseback who became known as "cowboys." The original vaquero carried no gun and his main weapon and tool was the lariat, a strong rawhide rope. With it, a vaquero could bring a wild bull to the ground. These are the genuine roots of the actual cowboy, a lonely man in the middle of a barren land. The popular image of the cowboy is quite different.

Late-nineteenth-century Americans imagined the West as the premodern world that they had lost through technological development and urbanization. In the West of this mythic construction, life was primitive, simple, real, and basic. This was directly in contrast to the complexity and rapidity of life everywhere else in the United States after 1870. In this conception of the West, everything mattered and the fundamental decisions of everyday life supposedly involved clear moral choices. These ideas of the place merged in the mythologized form of the lonely cowhand. From roughly 1900 to 1959 a significant portion of America's adolescent male population spent most Saturdays at the movies watching such cowboy heroes as Roy Rogers, Tom Mix, Lash LaRue, Gene Autry, and Hopalong Cassidy. Feature films, radio shows, and television programs also helped to solidify the myth of the cowboy.

Many scholars point to Owen Wister's *The Virginian* as the precursor of the Western genre. Published in 1902 Wister's book depicted cowboys with wild and manly faces, who were passionate and spirited. Behind a stoic façade was hidden a true nobility; beneath a rough exterior, such characters normally possessed heroic stature. In the popular culture, this character was personified by actor John Wayne. The myth became far-reaching enough that it could, by extension, romanticize some of the West's most vile outlaws. Billy the Kid, one of the best examples of the heroic outlaw, actually was a relatively inconsequential gunman killed in 1881 at the age of twenty-one by Pat Garrett. By this time, however, he was also a national figure owing to reports of his crimes in the *National Police Gazette* and other Eastern newspapers.

THE STOCK MARKET

A rodeo in Bruneau, Idaho.

The first rendition of Billy the Kid's status after the shooting was as a villain. By the 1920s the mythic "Kid" resembled the social bandits who rode with the likes of Jesse James, never robbing poor people and only killing for revenge or in self-defense. Pat Garrett's shooting of Billy the Kid slowly took on the popular aura of a tragic moment, when the democratic freedom of the young West was metaphorically shot down in the 1930 feature film *Billy the Kid.* Such myths and stories changed the broader conceptions in all of American society, with different groups recasting the stories differently. The West became in this sense a national mirror. When Americans looked into the imagined West for images of themselves, their own situation often determined what was most attractive or enticing.

As the idea of the cowboy endures as a touchstone for strength and character, the mythic cowboy has often clouded out the reality of the vacqueros, as well as that of the numerous black cowboys. At the close of the twentieth century, the image of the Marlboro Man advertising cigarettes is much more familiar to Americans than real cowboys doing actual work. The myth and the reality are each important American stories; often, however, it seems as if the two have little in common.

THE GRANGER COLLECTION

A Native American depiction of the combatants in the Battle of Little Bighorn: General George Custer, Crazy Horse, and Sitting Bull. (Pictography by Amos Bad Heart Bull, an Oglala Sioux from the Pine Ridge Reservation.)

[See also WEST, THE.]

BIBLIOGRAPHY

Limerick, Patricia Nelson, *The Legacy of Conquest: The Unbroken Past of the American West* (Norton 1987).

Milner, Clyde A., II, et al., *The Oxford History of the American West* (Oxford 1994).

Stewart, Paul W., *Black Cowboys* (Phillips Pub. 1986).

Tompkins, Jane, *West of Everything: The Inner Life of Westerns* (Oxford 1992).

White, Richard, *"It's Your Misfortune and None of My Own": A History of the American West* (Univ. of Okla. Press 1991).

BRIAN BLACK

CRAZY HORSE

Celebrated for his ferocity in battle, Tashunca-Uitco, commonly known as Crazy Horse, was recognized among his own people as a visionary leader committed to preserving the traditions and values of the Lakota way of life. Born (1843?) near Bear Butte, in present-day South Dakota, Crazy Horse, even as a youth, was a legendary warrior. He stole horses from the Crow before he was thirteen and led his first war party before turning twenty. Crazy Horse fought in the 1865–1868 war led by the Oglala chief Red Cloud against American settlers in Wyoming and played a key role in destroying William J. Fetterman's brigade at Fort Phil Kearny in 1867.

Crazy Horse earned his reputation among the Lakota not only by his skill and daring in battle but also by his fierce determination to preserve his people's traditional way of life. He refused, for example, to allow any photographs to be taken of himself. And he fought to prevent American encroachment on Lakota lands following the Fort Laramie Treaty of 1868, helping to attack a surveying party sent into the Black Hills by General George Armstrong Custer in 1873.

When the War Department ordered all Lakota bands onto their reservations in 1876, Crazy Horse became a leader of the resistance. Closely allied to the Cheyenne through his first marriage to a Cheyenne woman, he gathered a force of twelve hundred Oglala and Cheyenne at his village. The combined army then proceeded to turn back General George Crook on June 17, 1876, as Crook tried to advance up Rosebud Creek toward Sitting Bull's encampment on the Little Bighorn. After this victory Crazy Horse joined forces with Sitting Bull and on June 25 led his band in the counterattack that destroyed Custer's Seventh Cavalry, flanking the Americans from the north and west as Hunkpapa warriors led by Chief Gall charged from the south and east.

Following the Sioux victory at the Little Bighorn, Sitting Bull and Gall retreated to Canada, but Crazy Horse remained to battle General Nelson Miles as he pursued the Lakota and their allies relentlessly throughout the winter of 1876–1877. This constant military harassment and the decline of the buffalo population eventually forced Crazy Horse to surrender on May 6, 1877; except for Gall and Sitting

Bull, he was the last important chief to yield. On September 5, 1877, while under U.S. Army protection, Crazy Horse was stabbed in the back by an American soldier at Fort Robinson, Nebraska.

Crazy Horse defended his people and their way of life in the only manner he knew once he saw the Fort Laramie Treaty broken. This treaty, signed by the president of the United States, said, "Paha Sapa, the Black Hills, will forever and ever be the sacred land of the Indians." Crazy Horse took to the warpath only after he saw his friend Conquering Bear killed, only after he saw the failure of government agents to bring required treaty guarantees such as meat, clothing, tents, and necessities for existence. In battle, the Lakota war leader would rally his warriors with the cry, "It is a good day to fight—it is a good day to die."

In the minds of many Native Americans, the life and death of Crazy Horse parallels their tragic history since the white settlers invaded their homes and lands. This has also been the impetus behind an effort to commemorate the leader. Since 1949 Korczak Ziolkowski and his family, who carved Mount Rushmore, have been transforming another South Dakota mountain into an image of Crazy Horse on horseback.

BIBLIOGRAPHY

Hardorff, Richard G., ed., *The Surrender and Death of Crazy Horse: A Source Book about a Tragic Episode in Lakota History* (Arthur H. Clarke Co. 1998).
Kadlecek, Edward, *To Kill an Eagle: Indian Views on the Death of Crazy Horse* (Johnson Bks. 1981).
McMurtry, Larry, *Crazy Horse* (Viking 1999).
Sajna, Mike, *Crazy Horse: The Life behind the Legend* (Wiley 2000).
White, Richard, *"It's Your Misfortune and None of My Own": A History of the American West* (Univ. of Okla. Press 1991).

BRIAN BLACK

CREDIT CARD

During the twentieth century the credit card evolved from a cardboard slip identifying the wealthy owner of a store charge account to a high-technology payments-and-credit mechanism, available to most Americans, and usable throughout the world. Its rapid growth in the second half of the century was made possible by the increasing wealth of an economy that provided more families with discretionary income that could be used to purchase nonessential items or committed to the repayment of debt.

Consumer credit has been in existence since biblical times, as evidenced by the prohibitions against usury in the Old Testament and in the Babylonian Code of Hammurabi (1750 B.C.). Ethical opposition to consumer credit continued to be prevalent in Europe through the nineteenth century because of the power that the lender had over a desperate borrower in times of bare subsistence. In contrast, consumer credit has been much more widely accepted in the United States from its inception, since the geographic expansion of the nation kept breaking up extended families and forcing settlers to depend on the extension of credit by nonfamily. This attitude enabled Americans to develop both the consumer credit industry and the credit card.

In 1914 a number of retailers began to issue cards to their higher-income customers to promote store loyalty as well as to generate the sale of higher-priced items that could be repaid over time using the stores' existing installment plans. In 1928 the paper cards turned into metal "charga-plates," which were adaptations of embossed address plates. During the next thirty years, innovations included minimum monthly payments, finance charges, and the thirty-day grace period before finance charges were assessed. In the early 1920s gasoline companies began issuing "courtesy" cards to their customers and in 1936 the airlines formed their own customer credit plan.

In 1949 Diners Club began the first so-called universal card, which could be used by the customer with all types of merchants. The universal card substituted the credit of a known third party, the credit card issuer, for the credit of individual customers who could not have accounts with every merchant. These cards were financed by merchant discounts subtracted from purchases. Diners Club began by charging a discount of seven percent. The success of Diners Club attracted competition from Carte Blanche and American Express, who entered the credit card business in 1958. During this period several banks introduced universal cards with the added feature of revolving credit, which opened up a second source of income for the card issuers.

The first national network of bank cards was formed by Bank of America in 1966 when it introduced BankAmericard, later known as Visa. A competing network of banks formed the rival Interbank Card Association, later known as MasterCard. In order to build economies of scale, the bank-card companies mailed millions of unsolicited cards in the late 1960s and willingly absorbed the losses from anticipated fraud and uncollectible accounts. Alarmed by the damaging effect on many consumers of unsolicited cards, Congress outlawed this practice in 1970.

Competition among the three "travel and entertainment" cards—Diners Club, Carte Blanche, and American Express—which charged no interest to customers and relied only on high merchant discounts and annual customer fees for income, led to consolidation. Citicorp (later Citigroup) purchased Carte Blanche in 1978 and Diners Club in 1980. Banks added annual fees as well when consumer credit limitations were imposed in 1979, but these were dropped during the 1980s when General Motors Corporation (GM) and other large companies entered the industry by distributing "free" credit cards. Rebates in the form of discounts on their products or cash helped promote cards offered by a number of nonbanks, including Sears, Roebuck & Company (Discover Card), American Telephone and Telegraph Company, and General Electric Company, as well as GM.

During the 1980s the maturity of the credit card industry brought general profitability to the industry for the first time. In fact, credit card operations became the most profitable line of business for many issuing banks. This quest for profits in an era when most Americans had as many cards as they wanted led to a period of intense marketing for customers, which continued into the twenty-first century. Billions of mailings (more than three billion in 1997) are made each year offering consumers additional credit or an opportunity to move their outstanding balances to a new company for lower rates of interest, some of which are "teaser" rates that last for only six months. Card companies buy existing accounts from each other in a secondary market and package credit card balances in the form of bonds, which are sold in the capital markets. As credit cards have become more sophisticated and more competitive, the industry has consolidated dramatically with the top ten issuers accounting for more than half of all outstanding balances.

The decrease in the cost of telecommunications, accompanied by an increase in computer technology, facilitated a second use for the plastic card. It could be used for debit or payment directly from the card-owner's bank account rather than by a third party. This began with the inception of automated teller machines (ATMs) in the late 1960s and later moved to point-of-sale debit machines at merchants such as grocery stores. However, a public conditioned to expect thirty days of "free" credit kept the debit card from displacing the credit card. By the end of the twentieth century, razor-thin merchant discounts encouraged many supermarkets to begin accepting credit cards from their customers.

The smart card was another promising technological innovation that failed to displace the credit card during the twentieth century. A chip on this card allowed consumers to download funds from their bank accounts to the card, which could be used as cash. Again, consumer reluctance to give up the free float on credit cards, as well as the difficulty of equipping all merchants with smart-card readers, has held up the acceptance of the smart card.

[See also ADVERTISING; CONSUMERISM.]

BIBLIOGRAPHY

Mandell, Lewis, *The Credit Card Industry, A History* (Twayne 1990).
Manning, Robert D., *Credit Card Nation* (Basic Bks. 2000).

Nocera, Joseph, *A Piece of the Action: How the Middle Class Joined the Money Class* (Simon & Schuster 1994).

LEWIS MANDELL

CRÈVECOEUR, JEAN DE

Michel-Guillaume-Jean de Crèvecoeur was born in 1735 to a family of minor nobility in Normandy, France. He was educated in England and came of age in America, first serving in the British colonial militia and then observing firsthand the American Revolution and the attendant national growing pains. Best known for his *Letters from an American Farmer* (1782), Crèvecoeur also wrote travel essays and a variety of sketches about his adopted homeland. His *Letters* are a minor classic of American literature, and they fed the eager European imagination about the wonders of the New World.

Crèvecoeur declared in a 1785 letter to a friend, "I am no author, but a plain scribbler." This modesty of tone, though an insistent feature of his work, is of course unrelated to Crèvecoeur's position and achievements: he was undoubtedly well educated, well bred, and well connected (that 1785 letter to a "friend," for instance, was to none other than La Rochefoucauld). During his residence in New York (1759–1768), when he farmed at his estate, Pine Hill, and began to compose the *Letters*, Crèvecoeur was sociable with the local Tories and also corresponded familiarly with the French *philosophes*, for whom the *Letters* were later to become a favorite. He also scaled down his formidable name to simply Hector St. John and began formulating the central idea of his major text—namely that in America the European underwent a "great metamorphosis," a sort of "resurrection." He became a "new man."

The *Letters* are written in the unassuming voice of the fictional James the Farmer, who is requested by an Englishman, "Mr. F. B.," to satisfy his curiosity about America. Crèvecoeur wrote in a tradition of eyewitness literature about the New World, a genre that enjoyed popularity in Europe; but he offered the insider observations of a resident, instead of the bland comments of a tourist. His *Letters* dictate terms to Europe, in their diffident way, about how America will repair the ills of the Old World. They also offer an American literary voice that European readers have always cherished and always misjudged: the American primitive, who is unexpectedly insightful and ironic, and wiser than his "civilized" counterparts.

Crèvecoeur divides the *Letters* into inquiries about three regions in America and their activities: the South and its slavery; New England and its whaling; and the Middle-Atlantic states and their farms. This last region, where Crèvecoeur himself resided, is clearly the most important in the recollections of the beauties and perfections of his adopted homeland. "Here . . . every thing is modern, peaceful, and benign," he declares, sketching for European readers the twin advantages of the New World. First, it was "modern"; it labored under no antique feuds (such as wars or rumors of wars) or ancient institutions (such as an established church or a monarchy) to spoil its novel political harmonies and rustic pleasures. Second, America could extend its perfections to all who migrated there: it restored the "natural man" and revived his innate goodness. Crèvecoeur lavishes attention in the early chapters on the pleasures of nature, such as beekeeping, farming, and American natural beauty. But the later chapters of the *Letters* are less cheerful: Crèvecoeur writes about the disruptions to his agrarian reverie, brought on by the incipient American Revolution, with clear distaste. Eventually, Crèvecoeur's experience of the American Revolution shook his faith in the revolutionaries and their ideals. He sought to avoid party lines, but he was suspected of espionage by both sides during the conflict and sailed back to Europe to sell his *Letters* to a publisher.

The *Letters* have not yet achieved the highest standing in the American canon, partly because readers have misread their unassuming tone—and their deep irony. Many have found them an artifact of Augustan quaintness rather than a radical decree against the dissolution and corruption of Europe, and for the ideals of America. Indeed, their best audience was in Paris, among the radicalized philosophes, who flattered Crèvecoeur with a diplomatic post in the 1780s, returning him to New York. His least enthusiastic audience was back in America. George Washington found the *Letters* amusing but a little "too flattering," and by the 1850s leading literary men of New York City patronized Crèvecoeur's work as "sentimental . . . in the French school . . . looking at homely American life through the Claude Lorraine [that is, arcadian] glass of fanciful enthusiasm."

In the twentieth century Crèvecoeur was rediscovered. He is regarded by some as the eighteenth-century Henry David Thoreau for his affinity to that Romantic's passion for the natural world. He is also likened to Alexis de Tocqueville, another French observer of American life, whose *Democracy in America* stirred queries similar to Crèvecoeur's own most trenchant and most enduring question—a question still quite vivid in American studies. It is the title of Crèvecoeur's best-known "Letter" and an apt description of his philosophical legacy: what, he asks, is an American?

BIBLIOGRAPHY

Lawrence, D. H., *Studies in Classic American Literature* (Doubleday 1953).

Mitchell, Julia P., *St. Jean de Crèvecoeur* (Columbia Univ. Press 1916).

Rice, Howard C., *Le Cultivateur Américain* (Champion 1933).

St. John de Crèvecoeur, J. Hector, *Letters from an American Farmer,* with intro. by W. B. Blake (Dent 1912).

Stone, Albert E., Jr., "Crèvecoeur's *Letters* and the Beginnings of an American Literature," *Emory Univ. Quarterly* 18 (1962):197–213.

KRIS FRESONKE

CRIME

While there is no single, clear definition of *crime* in the broadest sense, there is considerable agreement on which actions committed in the United States are most deserving of punishment. Crime is commonly defined as a violation of social rules of conduct, interpreted and expressed by a written code created by people holding social and political power. In the United States the rules must be codified or written down. Crimes are often categorized as either *mala in se* or *mala prohibita* crimes. *Mala in se* crimes are those acts that are almost universally considered wrong or evil, such as murder. *Mala prohibita* crimes are those acts that are prohibited by law, such as traffic violations.

Criminologists commonly refer to three different views on the social origins of crime and criminal law: the consensus view, the conflict view, and the pluralistic view. According to the consensus view, crimes are seen as behaviors that are essentially harmful to the well-being of citizens or society or both. Crimes are controlled or prohibited by existing criminal law. Criminal law is seen as having a social control function, restraining those who take advantage of the weaknesses of others. Criminal law is a set of rules that express the norms, goals, and values of the majority of society. The conflict view of crime, on the other hand, sees the true purpose of criminal law to protect the power of the upper classes to the detriment of the poorer classes. Society is seen as a collection of diverse groups that are in constant conflict for control of limited resources. The conflict view rejects the power and authority of the legal code to define crime. The definition of crime is not inherent in behavior but in political power. Criminal law is seen as being created by the ruling authorities. Finally, the pluralistic view, the most modern of the three, involves a blending of several viewpoints. It argues that criminal law is not created by one particular group but is shaped, rather, by multiple groups all seeking something different from a given legal issue. Each group may have a different motivation, one economic, one moral, another ideological. As each group gains power its views are reflected in the laws it creates. Criminal law, according to the pluralistic model, is seen as a flexible instrument that can change according to the whims of powerful individuals or groups.

Crime Trends. Official data frequently describe the changes in crime rates over time. In general most crime rates declined from 1880 until about 1930. The one exception during this period of decline was murder. More murders were committed in 1929 than in any year until 1991. Crime gradu-

ally increased from the 1930s until the 1960s. Then crime rose dramatically during the 1960s and 1970s. Overall crime peaked in 1981, then began a slight four-year decline. A gradual increase began in 1985 until the mid-1990s. By the beginning of the twenty-first century, the United States was experiencing another gradual decrease in many crimes.

A variety of techniques are available with which to study crime and its consequences. Some of the major methods used to gather crime data are surveys, official records, participant observation, and life histories. The best-known source of official record data on aggregate crime rates is the Uniform Crime Report (UCR), an annual publication of the Federal Bureau of Investigation (FBI). Over sixteen thousand police agencies participate in reporting data to the FBI. The UCR provides information on the number and characteristics of individuals arrested, the number of offenses by various geographic distinctions, and the number and location of assaults on police officers. The numbers of actual offenses known to the police are collected. Crimes are defined as Part I offenses, also known as index crimes, or Part II offenses, those offenses that are not index crimes and not traffic offenses. There are eight Part I offenses: criminal homicide, forcible rape, robbery, aggravated assault, burglary, larceny, motor-vehicle theft, and arson. Arrest information on race, sex, and age is reported for both Part I and Part II crimes. Information on the numbers of full-time sworn officers and assaults or murders of officers is provided. All crime data is expressed in raw numbers, percent changes between years, and in rate per one hundred thousand population. A major weakness of the data in the UCR is that it does not measure those crimes that go unreported to the police.

The Bureau of Justice Statistics sponsors the National Crime Survey (NCS), which is the most extensive victim survey in existence. The most recent surveys contain information from about forty-nine thousand households across the United States; this includes one hundred thousand individuals over the age of twelve in those households. Overall victimization trends can be traced from 1973, when the NCS began, to the present. A number of victim-

Nathan Leopold and Richard Loeb, wealthy teenagers, tried to commit a "perfect murder" in 1924.

ization patterns can be identified in the NCS data. Differential reporting depends on crime type—murder is the most likely to be reported, while petty theft is the least likely. The typical victim of a crime is young, African American, and male. One of the reasons for the racial difference is that African Americans are disproportionately victims of violent crime. The single biggest cause of death of young, urban black males is murder. Likely victimization sites include urban areas; likely times are evening hours for violent crimes, daylight for less serious crimes. The NCS also suffers from some perceived methodological flaws. This includes the over-reporting of some crimes, owing to a victim's misinterpretation of events. Also there is underreporting of other crimes, because it may be embarrassing to admit in front of interviewers or because the victim forgets.

Organized Crime. Organized crime occurs within a continuing structure designed, at least in part, for the purpose of conducting illegal activity. The structure can be as simple as a group of neighborhood youths who plan the sale and distribution of marijuana on their block, or as complex as hundreds of individuals organized into a large, eth-

nic crime syndicate such as the Italian Mafia or the Japanese Yakuza. The latter two groups are purported to control such illegal activities as the smuggling and national distribution of illegal drugs, gambling operations, loan-sharking, and the smuggling of illegal immigrants. What differentiates organized crime from other types of structured criminal activity is its enduring, transgenerational nature.

White Collar Crime. Edwin Sutherland first coined the term *white-collar crime* in 1949. He defined it as a crime committed by a person of respectability and high social status in the course of his occupation. Later criminologists have expanded that definition to include corporations engaged in illicit activities. White-collar crime can be as simple as taking supplies (paper and pens) home from the office to the complex negotiations of insider trading on stock, which cost companies millions of dollars. Nearly all estimates show that white-collar crime costs the U.S. economy considerably more money than do individual property crimes such as burglary. The actual amount is difficult to determine since white-collar crime frequently goes undetected or unreported because companies fear reprisals from their stockholders and damage to their corporate image. Quite often the offender is merely asked to leave the employment of the company, fearing no criminal prosecution. Even when white-collar criminals are apprehended, prosecuted, and convicted, the punishments meted out are often slight in comparison to the financial costs of their deeds. A good example is the savings and loan bailout of the late 1980s. That bailout cost the federal government many billions of dollars, yet some of the officials of the financial institutions who were convicted of misconduct completed their prison sentences in relatively brief amounts of time. With ever-increasing use of computers and other developing technologies, people are subject to new threats of theft and sabotage.

Drugs and Crime. Under the Reagan and Bush presidencies of the 1980s and early 1990s, the United States waged a War on Drugs. This policy war led to the lengthening of sentences for crimes involving the use, sale, and distribution of illegal drugs, as well as strict enforcement of drug laws and stiffer penalties for repeat offenders. Drug use can be linked to many crimes in the United States. Quite often crimes such as burglary or robbery, which are not typical drug crimes, are committed while the perpetrator is under the influence of a drug. When alcohol use is also considered, the numbers are staggering. By some estimates as many as two out of three crimes of all categories are committed while the offender is under the influence of some mind-altering substance. The War on Drugs during the 1980s and into the 1990s helped create a very large prison population.

Guns and Crime. The relationship between guns and crime is very strong. Roughly two-thirds of all murders in the United States are committed with some sort of firearm. Handguns alone are involved in over fifty percent of all murders. Firearms may escalate assaults into murders. For example, a barroom brawl can quickly escalate into homicide if a gun is available. Guns are also used in the commission of other crimes. They are involved in forty percent of all robberies and twenty-five percent of all aggravated assaults. Firearms can give offenders the opportunity to commit a crime that they might not have considered without a gun.

Victimless Crimes. Victimless crimes are those law violations in which there are no immediate or apparent injured parties, such as drug use and prostitution. There was a movement in the 1970s to legalize some of these "crimes." Indeed, possession of small amounts of marijuana went from a felony offense to a misdemeanor offense during this period. This legalization movement cooled in the 1980s and 1990s. However, the debate over how offenders of victimless crimes are treated in the United States continues. Some national political parties have called for the decriminalization of victimless crimes, referring to them as matters of personal freedom or matters of commerce between individuals.

Criminological Theories. Cesar Lombroso is often called the father of modern criminology because he encouraged scholars to think about crimi-

© DAVID YOUNG-WOLFF/PHOTOEDIT/PNI

Two uniformed police officers apprehend and handcuff three male suspects.

nality from the scientific perspective. In his day Lombroso was considered a reformer because he wanted to study crime in order to eradicate the problem. He assumed that there was a difference between people who committed criminal acts and those who did not; criminal behavior may be attributable to some physiological mechanism. One of Lombroso's revelations came from the study of a notorious mass-murderer's skull. In noticing that the skull had a unique shape, he assumed that criminals were atavists, or characteristic of less-evolved ancestors. Other researchers noticed that boys with certain body types were more prone to delinquent behavior. While these are not considered to be leading theories in criminology, parts of these theories are still alive, since humans are frequently judged by others based on their appearance. Also, as males mature they are somewhat less likely to commit crimes. Some criminologists have argued that part of the decrease in crime in the 1980s and 1990s may be explained by the general U.S. population's having a smaller proportion of young adult males than in the prior years. A common explanation for the rapid increase in crime during the 1960s and 1970s is the large number of young males of the baby boom generation reaching their years of active criminal activity.

Some theorists have argued that property crimes are often committed as acts of frustration, when individuals cannot achieve material success in more legitimate ways. Out of frustration, they act in a deviant manner by, for example, stealing or vandalism. One topic often studied by psychologists is the link between frustration and aggression. People act violently because they have learned that violence is an appropriate form of self-expression. Some theorists claim that aggressors who achieve some type of reward for their actions are likely to continue their violent behavior. Marvin Wolfgang and Franco Ferracuti in *The Subculture of Violence* (1967) suggested the existence of subcultures located in regions where violence was considered normal behavior under some circumstances. Some argue that the South and the West are more accepting of violence, as are certain metropolitan regions.

There are neighborhoods where some types of crimes occur more than others. Neighborhoods with high levels of graffiti and homes in disrepair may reflect an environment in which there are few controls for the residents in the area. Areas with large numbers of single-parent households are less capable of providing adequate supervision for the youth of the neighborhood. These areas record rising levels of crime.

While a disproportionate number of the poor population is arrested and convicted of property crimes, some studies claim that wealthier people are less likely to get caught and convicted of many of their crimes. William Chambliss's classic study, *Race, Sex, and Gangs: The Saints and the Roughnecks* (1973), focuses on how youths of differing social class who commit similar acts are treated differently by members of the criminal justice system. The "Saints" were a gang of youths who committed multiple violations of laws but were not arrested owing to their upper-middle-class status. The "Roughnecks," poor and lower class, were continuously arrested for committing similar violations.

Travis Hirschi claims that the quality of a youth's social bonds will encourage or deter delinquent behavior. Social bond theory has four elements: attachment, commitment, involvement, and belief. Individuals are expected to create affective ties. If they make a commitment to conformist behavior and are involved in positive activities for a substantial portion of their time, they will develop a belief that obeying society's rules is the proper prescription for their behavior. Modern police work frequently uses the term *community policing* to describe a philosophy that encourages law-enforcement officers to bond with members of a community in order to prevent crime. In addition to working in a community to address issues of simple disorder and crime prevention, staff are reaching out with programs such as Drug Abuse Resistance Education (DARE) to attempt to reduce substance abuse and violence. Educational programs and support services are frequently credited for declines in some crimes such as domestic violence and substance abuse.

Before routine activities theory was developed, most criminological theories focused on the factors that motivate or dispose individuals to engage in crime. In other words, they studied the motivations of the offenders. Routine activities theory takes motivation as a given for all criminals and instead focuses on the opportunities for crime. Lawrence Cohen and Marcus Felson claim that three conditions must be met for crimes to occur. First motivated offenders must exist. Second, suitable targets must be available. Finally, there must be a lack of capable guardians offering protection. The probability of being victimized varies with one's "routine activities," such as going to work, drinking at a bar, or staying at home. The targets of crime cannot be protected by what are referred to as capable guardians. Several studies have supported the idea that people who pursue activities outside of their homes are more likely to be victimized by robbery. Fear of crime serves a purpose because those individuals who are most afraid of victimization are often the least likely to be victimized. Females and the elderly are more likely to express higher levels of fear but they are substantially less likely to be victimized. Fear of crime leads many people to take precautionary measures to avoid being victimized.

Media and Crime. Some people argue that the media help fight crime. People learn moral stories when criminals are apprehended and punished, while "real life" television shows devoted to exploring police work and criminal activities encourage people to work with law enforcement agencies in catching criminals. Conversely, say critics, the media can encourage criminal behavior by glorifying the deviant or lawbreakers. Some have argued that widely publicizing shootings at schools in the 1990s encouraged other schoolchildren to become copycat murderers. In addition, video games with violent scenarios continue to grow as a popular source of entertainment and are frequently accused of stimulating aggressive or violent behavior.

The news media do not report all crime. Crimes are more likely to get media attention based on their severity and not their frequency. For example, homicide usually makes up less than one percent of a metropolitan area's index crimes, but studies consistently show that it is the most commonly reported crime in the news media. With the significant attention given by the media, the public may develop the false perception that homicide is the predominant concern of the justice system. Crime is of general interest to a large portion of the population, so it may be reported in the media when there are few other significant newsworthy actions occurring.

The History and Philosophy of Punishment. Imprisonment for breaking laws is actually a modern concept in punishment. Historically the most frequently used forms of punishment for breaking laws or rules of a social group were physical. Banishment, branding, whipping, amputation, crippling, and being locked in public cages or in the stocks were typical forms of punishment, but the most common was death. In general human life had little value in many past societies. In ancient Greek and Roman societies the most common form of punishment was banishment or exile from the community. Interpersonal violence was considered to be a private matter between the individuals involved. The Middle Ages saw little law or governmental control. Blood feuds (often carried on by an injured person's family) or fines (often entail-

THE GRANGER COLLECTION

The pillory enforced morality in Puritan New England.

ing the forfeiture of land or property to the aggrieved family, developed to minimize the bloodshed caused by these feuds) settled offenses. While the wealthy would pay money to the poor for any harm suffered, the poor still received physical punishment for their crimes.

In early colonial America most crimes were of a religious nature and the punishment administered was designed to purify the soul. The punishments administered, although not as cruel as those in Europe, were still physical and harsh. As other colonies were started in America, the nature of crimes and their punishments began to change. The Quakers of Pennsylvania did not create the same strict laws and harsh punishments as the Puritan society of Massachusetts. Crimes in the Southern colonies tended to focus on property and civil law. Religion, although a factor, did not play as large a role in the development of their laws. The Southern colonies eventually developed special laws to deal with the treatment and punishment of slaves, who suffered various forms of physical punishment. Slaves in general were treated as property and the killing of another person's slave would require monetary payment to the slave's owner. Throughout the American colonial period banishment was a common form of punishment. Commonly an offender would be told to leave town and never return. Living away from the community meant that a person was more vulnerable to attacks from outlaws and hostile Native American tribes. The death penalty was not used as frequently in the American colonies as it was in Europe during the same period. The colonies were always in need of human labor and colonial governments were reluctant to kill a potential worker.

Later forms of punishment varied from earlier forms, mostly in their severity. Fines, or monetary payments made to the court reflecting the cost to society of an offense, are still commonly used. Another monetary punishment is restitution, where the offender must make monetary payments to the injured party. Incarceration by confinement in a prison, jail, or treatment facility is widely used. Modern capital punishment, or the death penalty, has been reinstituted in almost every state in the United States. What has changed in the United States is the elimination of corporal punishment and the creation of such community sentences as probation, which involves supervision of offenders while they live in the community under certain rules imposed by the court.

Prisons. The concept of lengthy periods of incarceration in prison was not widely practiced as a correctional method until the nineteenth century. Several factors contributed to the development of prisons. The first were the philosophers of the Enlightenment movement, who sought to change the harsh punishments and torture that had been the norm. Another was the influence of religious groups with humanitarian ideals, such as the Quakers. There was also the potential of prison industry; prisoners were a source of cheap labor.

Correctional reform was first instituted in America. The modern American system of prisons can be traced to Pennsylvania. The Quakers were opposed to the physical forms of punishment that were common throughout Europe and America. They favored a system that would allow a convicted felon to reflect on his actions and do penance—hence, the origin of the penitentiary. They developed the Pennsylvania system of corrections and

built the Western Pennsylvania Penitentiary as their model prison. Built on a semicircular design, each cell was designed as a miniature prison. The Quakers considered it a place to do penance. The prisoners did piecework that could be passed through a hole in the door. This was done to minimize contact with prisoners, who essentially served their entire sentences in solitary confinement. This constant isolation from human contact eventually led many prisoners to mental illness and suicide.

The Auburn prison in New York was built in 1816. It was known as the tier system because cells were built vertically, one on top of another, on five floors of the structure. It was also known as the congregate system because the inmates ate and worked in groups while in total silence. They slept in single tiny cells. The philosophy of Auburn was based on the fears of punishment and silent confinement. Prisoners were beaten for any disobedience, which included talking. Prisoners used a sign language and the passing of notes to communicate without alerting the guards. Auburn prison had fewer instances of mental illness and suicide than the Western Pennsylvania Penitentiary.

The Auburn system prevailed as the American system of corrections. Congregate working conditions allowed manufacturing labor within the walls of the prison. This was very important at the beginning of the Industrial Revolution, when labor was scarce and demand for goods was high. Solitary confinement was used only as a form of punishment for the unruly. Military regimentation and discipline were used to control prisoners. Prisoners marched in lockstep to meals, to work, and back to their cells.

About 1870 another era of correctional reform began, headed by Zebulon Brockway, warden of Elmira Reformatory in New York. He advocated individual treatment of inmates and developed the idea of the indeterminate sentence, which created parole. Brockway and his followers called for the education of illiterates and vocational training but Brockway also called for military-like training to discipline inmates and organize the prison. His biggest contribution was the humanitarian treatment of prisoners.

Prison reformers of the twentieth century continued the theme of humanitarian treatment, seeking to abolish the corporal punishment of prisoners (whippings and floggings were common forms of discipline within American prisons well into the 1900s). There was also a movement to bring meaningful prison industry and vocational training inside the prison walls. The teaching of such skills as farming and ranching did not benefit those prisoners who came from, and would return to, an urban environment. One of the biggest reforms dealt with offering educational programs within prisons. Many offenders arrived at prison with little education; most lacked a high school diploma and many were functionally illiterate. Prison-constructed classrooms began to offer formal courses. Almost all prisons today provide classes and instruction for prisoners to obtain a Graduation Equivalency Diploma (GED) while incarcerated. Another movement sought to bring the "better elements" of society into the prison environment, including teachers and ministers to influence the prisoners toward a better life. This movement has grown to encompass many other professions and organizations, such as social workers and Alcoholics Anonymous.

Community corrections programs began in the 1960s with the goal of achieving reintegration of the offender back into society. Several correctional measures fall under this category. Currently halfway houses in the United States hold an estimated twelve thousand residents. The number of inmates in America's prisons and jails more than doubled in the 1990s to over 1.8 million. This growth in prison population can be attributed to public opinion, which has demanded a more punitive response to offenders. Mandatory and determinate sentences instituted during the crack cocaine epidemic of the 1980s increased the possibility of incarceration and limited the chance for early release.

[See also LAW; POLICE; FEDERAL BUREAU OF INVESTIGATION; SERIAL KILLERS.]

BIBLIOGRAPHY

Akers, Ronald L., *Deviant Behavior: A Social Learning Approach*, 3d ed. (Wadsworth Pub. 1985).

Black, Donald J., *The Behavior of Law* (Academic Press 1976).

Cohen, Lawrence E., and Marcus Felson, "Social Change and Crime Rate Trends: A Routine Activity Approach," *American Sociological Review* 43 (1979):162–176.

Glueck, Sheldon, and Eleanor Glueck, *Physique and Delinquency* (Harper & Brothers 1956).

Hirschi, Travis, *Causes of Delinquency* (Univ. of Calif. Press 1969).

Kleck, Gary, *Point Blank: Guns and Violence in America* (Aldine de Gruyter 1991).

Lombrosco, Cesar, *Criminal Man* (Putnam 1911).

Shover, Neal, *Aging Criminals* (Sage Pub. 1985).

Straus, Murray A., Richard J. Gelles, and Suzanne K. Steinmetz, *Behind Closed Doors: Violence in the American Family* (Anchor Bks. 1980).

Sutherland, Edwin, *White Collar Crime: The Uncut Version* (Yale Univ. Press 1983).

Vold, George B., and Thomas J. Bernard, *Theoretical Criminology*, 3d ed. (Oxford 1986).

Wolfgang, Marvin E., and Franco Ferracuti, *The Subculture of Violence: Towards an Integrated Theory in Criminology* (Tavistock Pub. 1967).

Wright, James D., Peter H. Rossi, and Kathleen Daly, *Under the Gun: Weapons, Crime, and Violence in America* (Aldine Pub. 1983).

JOHN C. KILBURN

CULTURAL PLURALISM

The term *cultural pluralism* refers to the diversity of groups making up a society. Groups such as ethnic and religious minorities, those sharing a political philosophy or ideology, and voluntary organizations such as the Boy Scouts and the American Legion have certain rights protected by law. The very existence of such groups is generally held to be beneficial to society as a whole.

In the United States this general acceptance of cultural pluralism has not always led to formal political representation for each and every group. It has, however, contributed to the rise of the "balanced ticket," in which different ethnic and religious groups may be taken into account in putting forth candidates for an election; and to gerrymandering, in which political districts are carved out to ensure appropriate representation of different interests. The belief in cultural pluralism has led, at various times, to equal opportunity and affirmative action programs, to civil rights movements, and to calls for tolerance. Occasionally the conflict between the rights of the individual and the rights of the group has come to the fore, such as in the case of university campus "hate speech" rules that ban the use of certain characterizations of members of a group while at the same time limiting free speech.

Cultural pluralism is generally not an issue that the American electorate feels comfortable pursuing. The American electorate prefers to gloss over the differences between individual freedom and group equality, tending to conflate them in order to minimize conflict. Late-twentieth-century reactions against affirmative action were based on the argument that advancing entire groups toward equality might impinge on the liberty of any given individual.

At the beginning of the twentieth century, however, the predominant notion in the United States was not that of cultural pluralism but of "Americanization." The influx of new immigrants, largely Roman Catholic and Jewish and hailing from southern and eastern Europe, frightened old-line Americans whose (largely Protestant) ancestors had come from northern Europe. Americanization efforts sought to teach the new immigrants English and other mainstays of the American way of life. World War I further entrenched these attitudes in the American psyche.

The end of the war and a severe restriction on immigration led to a reexamination of just what it meant to be an American. Arguments concerning the multicultural heritage of the United States, along with contributions made in many areas by the new immigrants, had an impact on American thinking. Greater tolerance of cultural differences emerged as a creative force, one that could enrich the melting pot of American life. There was a movement toward incorporating the best from different heritages into a greater America.

In place, then, of eliminating all alien ideas and behaviors arose a new idea of cultural pluralism. Many scholars argued that keeping a number of cultures alive would benefit the country. Others held that, left alone, pluralism would disappear of its own accord. These latter scholars maintained that the American cultural character was still in the process of formation. When formed, it would benefit from the incorporation of elements from the many different cultures present in America. Still other commentators, mostly political conservatives, argued that multiculturalism was detrimental to what they felt was a more "original" (generally white Anglo-Saxon Protestant) American identity.

Education is an area in which cultural pluralism played a major role. Over recent decades there has been a growing awareness that American education tended in the past to give predominant attention to western European, and mainly British, culture; contributions to American thought from other cultures and areas of the world were being neglected. Recognizing such shortcomings, American educators turned their attention to including in the curricula contributions from the country's many different ethnic, cultural, and religious groups. According to Geneva Gay, supporters of multicultural education agree that such education "should include ethnic identities, cultural pluralism, unequal distribution of resources and opportunities, and other sociopolitical problems stemming from long histories of oppression." Many conservatives continue to bristle at the suggestion.

Interestingly, an early proponent of the pluralistic viewpoint was Alain Locke, an African American humanist associated with the Harlem Renaissance. Locke argued that it is imperative to be sensitive to "the uniqueness of each personality" and that only a truly democratic ethos can guarantee such a cultural awareness. This awareness, in turn, will aid in the emergence of a philosophy that will discern values to guide human conduct and interrelationships. From that concern came such movements as multicultural education and respect for the traditions of new immigrants, as well as the various incorporative movements to end racial, ethnic, gender, and other forms of prejudice and discrimination.

[See also AMERICA; AMERICAN DREAM; AMERICANIZATION.]

BIBLIOGRAPHY

Gay, Geneva, *A Synthesis of Scholarship in Multicultural Education* (NCREL 1994) [NCREL's Urban Education Program as part of its Urban Education Monograph Series].

Naylor, Larry, ed., *Cultural Diversity in the United States* (Bergin & Garvey 1997).

Salamone, Frank A., "The Illusion of Ethnic Identity: An Introduction to Ethnicity and Its Uses," in *Cultural Diversity in the United States,* ed. by Larry Naylor (Bergin & Garvey 1997).

FRANK A. SALAMONE

CULTURE AND CULTURAL STUDIES

Culture is an elusive term that for decades has been at the heart of the American studies project. In his often-cited 1957 essay, "Can 'American Studies' Develop a Method?," Henry Nash Smith defined American studies as "the study of American culture, past and present, as a whole," and he defined culture as "the way in which subjective experience is organized." For Smith, organized subjective experience was not simply private or individual. Insofar as private individual experience was organized, it was cultural—the pattern of organization originated outside the individual, at a different analytical level. By "as a whole," Smith meant not that American studies should only produce systemic analyses of the entirety of life in the United States but that the attempt to make sense of any slice of American life required an approach that could interpret that slice as one section of a totality, that could consider anthropological as well as literary factors, historical as well as social contexts. According to Smith it was the effort to understand American culture as a whole that motivated the interdisciplinary impulse that has been the methodological hallmark of American studies. American studies became the interdisciplinary effort to understand all

the factors that organize present or have organized past subjective experience in the United States.

American studies has continued to rely on the concept of *culture* as a foundational term despite there being surprisingly little internal agreement about what the term precisely means. Perhaps its ability to elude constraining definition has been one of the sources of its effectiveness. As a pragmatic concept that resists efforts to specify its precise workings or demarcate its conceptual boundaries, culture suggests a way of thinking about human actions and beliefs that implies a certain systematic coherence (organized subjective experience) along with a kernel of the unexplainable that refuses the reduction of collective human behavior to mechanistic metaphors (organized subjective experience). Culture is produced by humans and is, therefore, a result of organized human activities and beliefs. But culture is also a cause. It is not only organized experience, it is one of the factors that organizes experience. To think about culture is to think about the ways in which experience becomes organized; to think culturally is to acknowledge that culture itself is a causal factor in culture.

Part of the difficulty with the use of culture in American studies is that several opposing and conflicting meanings were brought together in Smith's classic formulation. In one way of thinking, culture was akin to civilization—to be cultured was to be aware of "the best that had been thought and said," and it was characterized by the "love of perfection." This was the meaning of culture as it was articulated in Matthew Arnold's writings. An Englishman, Arnold had toured the United States as a popular lecturer, and his writings spread widely across the country during the late nineteenth century. This concept of culture was ethnocentric and hierarchical, but it was also critical. It promulgated the criticism of existing modes of thought with the goal of such criticism being the improvement of individuals within a society. In this framework, culture was not simply an effect of society, it was a means of perfecting society.

The second concept of culture also developed during this period as comparative ethnology became an established academic practice. Ethnologists attempted to describe as completely as possible the ways that different groups of people lived together. They documented kinship structures, belief systems, and technological developments, along with patterns of cultivation and exchange. Ethnology grew as a field of scholarly inquiry as European empires became increasingly aware of the many differences among the groups of people they were bringing under their political and economic control. The effective implementation of imperial policies of trade, resource exploitation, and political domination required knowledge of the people being subjugated. Comparative ethnology developed as a means of acquiring such knowledge but also as a means of legitimating empires. In this period of imperialism and social Darwinism, the concept of culture took on many of the characteristics of two neighboring terms, *nation* and *race*. Ethnology ranked cultures within a developmental, historically evolutionary scale. European cultures, which were understood to correspond to the different European nations, were believed to be the most highly developed in the world; colonial cultures were assigned lower places on the scale. Therefore the ethnological concept of culture was also ethnocentric and hierarchical, but its function was to enable the description of distinctly different ways of life as they were lived by distinctly different groups of people. Culture, then, became multiple cultures; the goal of studying cultures was not to criticize them but to place them in a ranked order of human development. Finally, the late nineteenth century also saw the revival of Johann Gottfried von Herder's theories, initially published almost a century before, arguing that a coherent German *Kultur* ("culture") could be found in the everyday practices of the German *Volk* ("people") and that this *Kultur* was the foundation on which a German nation must be built. According to Herder, the nation was a modern achievement, the authentic outgrowth of the culture that defined a distinct people.

During the first two decades of the twentieth century, a number of scholars who had been trained as ethnologists attempted to limit the hierarchical ranking of cultures, to distinguish the concept of culture from race, and to eradicate the sour taste of racism from their work. Foremost among them in the United States was Franz Boas. While Boas himself was not the first to publish a coherent and complete discussion of an antihierarchical relativist understanding of culture, his own work on Native American cultures demonstrated this vision, and his students, among them Edward Sapir, Ruth Benedict, and Margaret Mead, did go on to elaborate its principles. Boas and his students helped transform comparative ethnology into anthropology, and, in the process, they established a fundamental principle of cultural relativism—cultures should not be judged by standards external to themselves. Boas argued that different cultures were functionally equivalent; they were different solutions to the complex problems of living as human beings. Boas taught that no one culture should be considered superior to any other. The job of the anthropologist was not to rank or evaluate cultures but to describe them completely and accurately. In his eagerness to separate analytically the concepts of culture and race, however, Boas seemed to endorse the link between culture and nation. He argued that people of many different races could participate in the same culture, and he held up the United States and American culture as a primary example of this phenomenon.

When Smith and others in American studies took up the concept of culture, they adopted a term that was both descriptive and prescriptive; relativistic yet retaining hierarchical tinges; concerned with literature and art yet committed to understanding the complex wholes that encompassed collective human beliefs and behaviors. This version of culture could not be reduced to race, yet in its necessary attachment to human groups, it was still easily linked to nation. American studies scholars could agree that their task was to study American culture, but there was very little agreement on how to study it and what it actually did consist of. This absence at the heart of the American studies movement prompted considerable theoretical debate over the next several decades.

For what came to be known as the myth-and-symbol school of American studies, culture was best studied through the analysis of particular literary and cultural texts and artifacts, such as Henry David Thoreau's *Walden* or New York's Brooklyn Bridge. These texts and artifacts were made up of symbols, which were best understood within the contexts of larger myths. Culture itself was understood to consist of these larger myths. The majority of myth-and-symbol scholars were content to accept Smith's fuzzy categories, for they were not so interested in refining one specific methodology or with attaining the repeatable and disconfirmable status of social science for their works. In his "defense of an unscientific method," Leo Marx articulated a view of culture not as a thing but as a contextualizing process, "the intricate, never-ending, and imperfectly understood process that brings the subject matter of the humanities into existence." These were largely literary scholars, whose analyses were intended to be interpretive, not replicable. Culture, for these scholars, was made up "not of 'facts' or sense data alone, but of those mediating forms that organize, define and subdue the details of experience, bringing them into conformity with existing patterns." Attempting in 1984 to explain what myth-and-symbol scholars had accomplished in the preceding decades, Alan Trachtenberg wrote that, "Myths . . . function, then, as the indispensable forms whereby and in which a society constitutes its agreed-upon collective reality: not only a view of the world, of what it is and looks like, but also a view of individual behavior, of the determinants of behavior, and of relations between the self and collectivity." Culture was identified with myth, and myth was identified with ideology. The purpose of this American studies scholarship was not to produce complete descriptions of a whole way of life—social, economic, political—but to provide an effective critique of American ideology as this ideology was manifested in its cultural products.

In response (and in sometimes heated opposition) to the myth-and-symbol approach, scholars who had been trained at or were working in the American civilization department at the University of Pennsylvania (UPenn) elaborated a more coherent and operational understanding of culture. By the mid-1950s the anthropological definition of cul-

ture had become quite elaborate. Two anthropological theorists, Alfred Kroeber and Clyde Kluckhorn, struggled to explain the concept in one elongated sentence. "Culture consists of patterns, explicit and implicit, of and for behavior acquired and transmitted by symbols, constituting the distinctive achievement of human groups, including their embodiments in artifacts; the essential core of culture consists of traditional (historically derived and selected) ideas and especially their attached values; culture systems may, on the one hand, be considered as products of action, on the other as conditioning elements of further action." Although here again culture was transmitted by symbols, this definition emphasized the significance of patterns and products of action, shifting the focus from the criticism of ideology to the analysis of behavior. This was the most complete statement of the social-scientific culture concept as it was adopted at UPenn.

In a retrospective account first published in 1970, Murray Murphey stated that American civilization at UPenn had "moved from an interdisciplinary to a disciplinary approach, which defined its subject matter as American society and culture, past and present and its method as that of the social sciences, applied to both contemporary and historical data." Murphey went on to define the culture of America as "the learned repeated behavior characteristic of that society. . . . The culture is broadly conceived as including not only patterns of overt action, but the patterns of thought, emotion, belief and attitude which find expression largely through verbal behavior. . . . In every case [the] emphasis is upon the systematic character of culture—upon the patterned interaction of individuals as occupants of significant social positions." Bruce Kuklick asserted in 1972 that "the imputation of collective beliefs is an extraordinarily complex empirical procedure," arguing that myth-and-symbol's interpretive analysis of cultural products failed to capture the important aspects of past cultures. For Kuklick, the most appropriate means of studying culture was to define culture in terms of behavior and develop empirical ethnographic techniques for collecting disconfirmable data and producing replicable analyses of this behavior. Anthony F. C. Wallace, an anthropologist at UPenn who worked closely with the American civilization department, developed a method for uncovering the cognitive procedures that members of a culture used to solve problems and for generalizing from observed behavior to patterns in the culture. This version of culture was not concerned with the unique event or even with the uniquely articulate or revealing artifact. Instead, it saw culture as a set of patterns, and these patterns were the key to understanding society as a whole. The ethnographic theory of culture that was termed the *culture concept* was fundamentally materialist and behaviorist. For advocates of this approach, culture was a response to the set of problems thrown up by material conditions. Although advocates of the culture concept were interested in verbal behavior, they did not postulate a distinct realm of art, literature, or ideas that could then reflect back on, and hope to transform, material conditions. Culture was simply what one needed to know or believe in order to act like a member of a particular society.

By the mid-1970s, however, the discipline of anthropology had shifted its understanding of culture. No longer focusing strictly on operational techniques for gathering falsifiable data, anthropologists were beginning to interrogate their own writings, to emphasize the writing of ethnographies as acts of interpretation. In his widely anthologized essay, "Thick Description," Clifford Geertz advanced a semiotic concept of culture. "Believing . . . that man is an animal suspended in webs of significance he himself has spun," Geertz announced, "I take culture to be those webs, and the analysis of it to be therefore not an experimental science in search of law but an interpretive one in search of meaning." Geertz argued that culture was public—symbolic behavior—and that the proper question to ask of a cultural event was not what one needed to know to participate in the event but what the event meant to its participants. "Culture consists of socially established structures of meaning." Geertz's semiotic concept of culture quickly became orthodoxy in anthropology and was highly influential throughout American studies; external factors helped to spread

this view of culture as well. To think of culture as meaning, rather than as a set of rules for proper behavior, helped to make sense of the tremendous social transformations that swept through American society in the 1960s and early 1970s. After the civil rights movement, the anti–Vietnam War movement, and the beginnings of second-wave feminism, it was no longer possible to conceive of a singular American culture whose determining patterns could somehow be uncovered. The presence of multiple cultures inside the United States began to seem undeniable. The more literary-minded American studies scholars were no longer pursuing a singular "best that had been thought and said." Like their colleagues in the "new" social history, they had become more interested in documenting and interpreting the cultural traditions of multiple groups inside the United States. Of course, once culture was reconceived as meaning, once American culture was shown to be multiple, and once the ethnographer's job was seen as being interpretive, then the culture concept no longer seemed so distant from the contextualizing myths that engaged the myth-and-symbol scholars.

It was also during the mid-1970s that a group of researchers associated with England's Birmingham Centre for Contemporary Cultural Studies began to publish works that demonstrated the beneficent confluence of meaning-based theories of culture with ethnographic methods. Birmingham's method of cultural studies was based on Marxist understandings of the relationship between meaning (culture) and material conditions (society). The Centre itself produced collaborative ethnographic and archival research into working-class history, popular music, popular reading practices, television viewing, the role of education in the reproduction of the English working class, and other practices of everyday life. Initially these studies developed out of the culturalist wing of western Marxism. The works of Raymond Williams and E. P. Thompson in particular helped establish the basic framework within which culture appeared not simply as a whole way of life but a whole way of conflict. Cultures were not simply functional systems that produced consensual solutions to the problems of life; they were also arenas of arts, ideas, and lived experience where the basic struggles over resources, over the proper ways in which to organize daily life and, indeed, subjective experience was fought out. Raymond Williams rethought some of the basic terms of Marxist cultural analysis, in the process mitigating some of the more mechanical aspects of the theory. For Williams, the material base and the cultural superstructure were not connected through a linear causal model. Instead, social structures were saturated with and enabled by cultural relations, just as cultural forms and expressions were inextricably linked to social structures. Culture was neither completely separate from society, nor was it simply an effect of society. Cultural criticism could help transform consciousness, and consciousness could interact productively with material conditions. Williams's evocative concept, "structures of feeling," captures the interwoven complexity of material conditions and subjective experience insisted on by cultural Marxism.

Increasingly, however, a dissatisfaction developed with the model of subjectivity advocated by culturalist forms of Marxist analysis. If the working class and ethnic minorities in England were capable of acting in their own interest, why did they vote for Margaret Thatcher? (A similar question arose concerning the blue-collar support for President Ronald Reagan in the United States.) Under the leadership of Stuart Hall, the director of the Birmingham Centre from 1969 to 1979 and the director of Cultural Studies for the Open University throughout the 1980s, cultural studies researchers began looking toward the blend of structuralism, psychoanalysis, and Marxism exemplified by the theories of Louis Althusser to help answer such questions. Althusser's conceptualization of ideology as one's imagined relation to the real relations of production was combined with Antonio Gramsci's notions of cultural hegemony and organic intellectuals to produce a cultural theory and a research agenda with explicitly progressive political goals. Dick Hebdige's *Subculture: The Meaning of Style* brought together these theories of meaning and identity with an ethnographic investigation of youth musical practices and introduced the Bir-

mingham cultural studies approach to American studies scholars interested in popular music, media studies, the daily lives of young people, and in developing approaches to multiple (perhaps sub-) cultures struggling in the United States. One of the great appeals of the cultural studies method was its rather pragmatic approach to theories of subjectivity. In several programmatic articles Hall argued that theory was never a replacement for empirical research, and that once theories of culture, meaning, identity, and communication became rigid, stale, and predictable, their usefulness had disappeared.

In the United States the influence of cultural studies was first felt in university communications departments specializing in media studies and popular culture. By the mid-1980s American studies scholars who maintained an interest in these neighboring fields had begun to adopt some of their methods. Janice Radway's highly influential *Reading the Romance* blended feminist psychoanalysis with ethnographic techniques to find contradictory meanings in women's readings of popular romances. George Lipsitz's work on the popular cultures of America's working class and ethnic and racial minorities benefited from the more specialized and detailed understanding of cultural struggle advocated by cultural studies. Cultural and literary historians, such as T. J. Jackson Lears and Richard Brodhead, blended Gramscian hegemony with Michel Foucault's linkage of power and knowledge to produce influential interpretations of the ways in which past meanings helped shape present conditions.

Perhaps the most enduring influence of cultural studies' understanding of culture lies in its ability to grow, to continue to develop more detailed and specific means of conceptualizing the struggles engaged in by the many conflicting groups that inhabit the United States. American studies scholars investigating racial formation among Asian Americans and Latinos and Latinas have adopted the techniques of reading cultural texts as representative condensations of power struggles along with an ethnographic approach to capturing the structures of feeling that develop in the material conditions of border communities. Queer studies scholars are using theories of performance and performativity as developed by Judith Butler and Eve Sedgwick to expand and render even more complex the cultural studies approach to processes of identity formation and analyses of subjective experience. Students of commercial culture are exploring Pierre Bourdieu's specifications of fields of cultural production, habitus, and cultural capital. While some researchers have advocated abandoning the concept of culture for progressive humanistic scholarship, arguing that it continues to reproduce its problematic links to the concepts of race and nation, American studies scholars have continued to find the concept of culture not merely useful but necessary for the project of understanding the collective meanings and the fragmented lived experiences that characterize life in the United States.

[See also POPULAR CULTURE; AMERICAN STUDIES.*]*

BIBLIOGRAPHY

Arnold, Matthew, *Culture and Anarchy: An Essay in Political and Social Criticism,* ed. by Ian Gregor (1869; Bobbs-Merrill 1971).

Bourdieu, Pierre, *The Field of Cultural Production: Essays on Art and Literature* (Columbia Univ. Press 1993).

Butler, Judith, *The Psychic Life of Power: Theories in Subjection* (Stanford Univ. Press 1997).

Denning, Michael, "'The Special American Conditions': Marxism and American Studies," *American Quarterly* (1989):346–379.

Geertz, Clifford, "Thick Description: Toward an Interpretive Theory of Culture," *The Interpretation of Cultures: Selected Essays* (Basic Bks. 1973).

Hall, Stuart, "Signification, Representation, Ideology: Althusser and the Post-Structuralist Debates," in *Critical Studies in Mass Communication* (The Association 1985).

Hebdige, Dick, *Subculture: The Meaning of Style* (Routledge 1991).

Hegeman, Susan, *Patterns for America: Modernism and the Concept of Culture* (Princeton Univ. Press 1999).

Johnson, Richard, "What Is Cultural Studies, Anyway?," *Social Text* (Winter 1986/1987):38–80.

Kuklick, Bruce, "Myth and Symbol in American Studies," *American Quarterly* (October 1972):435–450.

Marx, Leo, "American Studies: Defense of an Unscientific Method," *New Literary History* (1969).

Murphey, Murray, "American Civilization at Pennsylvania," *American Quarterly* (1977):489–502.

Pfister, Joel, "The Americanization of Cultural Studies," *Yale Journal of Criticism* (1991):199–229.

Radway, Janice, *Reading the Romance: Women, Patriarchy, and Popular Literature* (Univ. of N.C. Press 1984).

Saldívar, José David, *Border Matters: Remapping American Cultural Studies* (Univ. of Calif. Press 1997).

Sapir, Edward, *Collected Writings in Language, Culture and Personality,* ed. by David Mandelbaum (Univ. of Calif. Press 1949).

Shank, Barry, "The Continuing Embarrassment of Culture: From the Culture Concept to Cultural Studies," *American Studies* (Summer 1997):95–116.

Smith, Henry Nash, "Can 'American Studies' Develop a Method?," *American Quarterly* 1957:197–208.

Trachtenberg, Alan, "Myth and Symbol," *Massachusetts Review* (1984):667–673.

Wallace, Anthony F. C., *Culture and Personality,* 2d ed. (Random House 1970).

Williams, Raymond, *Marxism and Literature* (Oxford 1977).

BARRY SHANK

CYBERCULTURE

Cyberculture, a neologism derived from the term *cybernetics* (the scientific study of methods of control and communication), describes various forms of human social interaction and aesthetic expression within the digital environment. Cyberculture remains eclectic and ever-changing, shaped by diverse legal, social, political, economic, and cultural forces that are redefined by each new generation to go online.

Digital media have been met with competing claims, some utopian, others apocalyptic, but all pointing toward computers as the catalyst for more far-reaching change in American and global culture. The familiar phrase "digital revolution" actually encapsulates a broad array of different ideas. For some, the digital revolution is understood primarily in technological terms—a profound shift in the information infrastructure that expands the speed and scope of human communication. For others, the digital revolution is understood as an economic transformation: e-commerce, the dramatic increase in small-scale companies, customized interactions, telecommuting. Others predict a transformation of education, expanding school resources and facilitating more learner-centered pedagogies. The digital revolution is also understood in political terms as enabling a more participatory democracy. Some understand the digital revolution in psychological terms, as a redefinition of what it means to be human, brought about by the ability to experiment with online identities. Finally, the digital revolution is understood in cultural terms as inspiring new forms of human expression and a more grassroots media culture.

The early development of the Internet was funded by the military to ensure a reliable and decentralized means of communication in the case of a nuclear attack; it was quickly embraced by industry and research institutions as a vehicle for long-distance collaboration. Ironically, key figures of the 1960s counterculture, such as drug guru Timothy Leary and Grateful Dead lyricist John Perry Barlow, were among the early adapters, reconceiving the Internet as an "electronic frontier," an untamed and unregulated space of innovation, exploration, and free expression. So-called hackers used their technical mastery to penetrate, illicitly, powerful government, military, and corporate institutions. The earliest hackers were governed by strict ethical principles (seeking to break and enter without doing damage) and motivated by a political critique of the unequal distribution of knowledge and power. Each of these groups sought to remake the cyberculture in their own terms and has had a lasting impact on the public's understanding of the online world.

Early discourse about digital media was shaped by two potentially contradictory political impulses: one toward libertarianism, with the decentralized qualities of the Internet seen as paving the way for defederalization; the other toward communitarianism, with the weblike structure of digital communications pointing toward the interconnectedness of human experience. A third important strand of thought within this early cyberculture emphasized the importance of maintaining personal privacy in the face of expanded surveillance and record-keeping powers.

Journalist Howard Rheingold coined the phrase *virtual community* to refer to the new forms of social interaction arising online. These interactions were defined through shared interests rather than a common geographic location. Some suggested that cyberspace constituted the new public sphere. Critics, on the other hand, wondered whether online sociality undermined face-to-face communities, fostering further alienation and loneliness.

The term *cyberspace* originated from William Gibson's influential science-fiction novel *Neuromancer* (1984), one of many significant science-fiction novels that broadened public awareness of the coming era of digital change. Inspired by the "digital revolution" and "electronic-frontier" rhetoric, these cyberpunk writers depicted the struggle between hacker "cowboys," who sought to exploit the grassroots and resistant potential of the Internet, and the multinational media conglomerates, who control the flow of information in order to gain their own economic advantage.

Companies such as America Online and CompuServe Interactive Services helped to market the Internet to a broader segment of the American public. Initially, there was a significant gender gap in terms of access to cyberspace. By the end of the twentieth century, thanks to concerted efforts by "cyberfeminists," women had more or less achieved parity with men online. The "digital divide," racial minorities' unequal access to digital resources, has only recently reached public consciousness. Many minority artists, activists, and entrepreneurs have sought to develop World Wide Web content more relevant to their communities.

From the outset, cyberculture aspired to be a global culture enabling the flow of ideas across national borders. Access to digital media has been uneven, dominated by countries in North America, western Europe, and along the Pacific rim. Some national governments sought to block or regulate the flow of information, fearing a further erosion of their national cultures and a threat to their politi-

A customer in a "cybercafé" surfs the Internet while sipping cappuccino.

cal authority. On the other hand, the Web has strengthened ties among migrant, immigrant, and exile communities and their mother countries.

Sociologists have employed such terms as *generation.com* or *screenagers* to describe the generation of young people who came of age with the personal computer in the home. Almost a quarter of the world's Internet users are under the age of fifteen. These youth are especially adept at navigating through digital environments, participating in online chat rooms, downloading digitized sound and image files, playing computer games, or creating new works using sound sampling or digital darkroom techniques. A succession of "moral panics" have surrounded youth access to digital media, focusing first on pornography and later on the fear that computer and video games were inspiring juvenile violence. A consensus regarding ways to address these issues remains elusive.

The Web has sparked a dramatic expansion of grassroots (or "do-it-yourself") cultural production. Many users have built their own home pages as vehicles for sharing personal experiences, expressing their cultural preferences, or displaying original artwork. Diverse groups began publishing webzines, or online publications. Fans flocked to the Web, circulating original fiction or grassroots program guides based on favorite films and television shows. In later years, the digital-cinema movement has provided a means for would-be filmmakers to get greater exposure, and young composers have used MP3 files to distribute their music to a wider audience.

As public access to cyberspace broadened, corporate interest in digital media significantly increased. In 1995 less than ten percent of Web sites were commercial. By 1999 more than eighty percent were related to e-commerce or were owned by corporate interests. The growth of e-commerce has proven to be a mixed blessing: online bookstores, for example, have expanded access to a diverse array of books and music but they have also further eroded the base of support for independent booksellers.

In the context of concentrated media ownership within transmedia and multinational conglomerates, there has been a growing incentive toward media convergence, the speedy flow of intellectual property across multiple media channels. Media convergence has increased the value of successful intellectual properties and thus encouraged media corporations to seek tighter control on their use. This new economic logic of media convergence thus runs counter to the more grassroots aspects of cyberculture, sparking growing numbers of legal battles as companies seek to shut down the online distribution of digitized music files or remove fan Web sites believed to be infringing studio copyright interests. The outcome of these struggles will help to determine the future shape of cyberculture.

[See also TECHNOLOGY, AN OVERVIEW; COMPUTERS.*]*

BIBLIOGRAPHY

Bolter, David Jay, and Richard Grusin, *Remediation: Understanding New Media* (MIT Press 1999).

Derry, Mark, ed., *Flame Wars: The Discourse of Cyberspace* (Duke Univ. Press 1994).

Jenkins, Henry, "The Work of Theory in the Age of Digital Transformation," *A Companion to Film Theory,* ed. by Toby Miller and Robert Stam (Blackwell 1999).

Johnson, Steven, *Interface Culture: How New Technology Transforms the Way We Create and Communicate* (Harper 1997).

Katz, Jon, *Media Rants: Postpolitics in the Digital Nation* (HardWired 1997).

Rheingold, Howard, *The Virtual Community: Homesteading on the Electronic Frontier* (Addison-Wesley 1993).

Stefik, Mark J., *Internet Dreams: Archetypes, Myths and Metaphors* (MIT Press 1997).

Turkle, Sherry, *Life on Screen: Identity in the Age of the Internet* (Simon & Schuster 1995).

HENRY JENKINS